AN APPALACHIAN REAWAKENING

WEST VIRGINIA AND APPALACHIA

A SERIES EDITED BY RONALD L. LEWIS,

KEN FONES-WOLF, and KEVIN BARKSDALE

VOLUME 12
Other books in the series:

An Appalachian New Deal: West Virginia in the Great Depression
By Jerry Bruce Thomas

Culture, Class, and Politics in Modern Appalachia
Edited by Jennifer Egolf, Ken Fones-Wolf, and Louis C. Martin

Governor William E. Glasscock
and Progressive Politics in West Virginia
By Gary Jackson Tucker

Matewan Before the Massacre
By Rebecca J. Bailey

Sectionalism in Virginia from 1776 to 1881, Second Edition
By Charles Ambler;
Introduction to the second edition by Barbara Rasmussen

Monongah: The Tragic Story
of the 1907 Monongah Mine Disaster
By Davitt McAteer

Bringing Down the Mountains
By Shirley Stewart Burns

Afflicting the Comfortable
By Thomas F. Stafford

Clash of Loyalties
By John Shaffer

The Blackwater Chronicle
By Philip Pendleton Kennedy; Edited by Timothy Sweet

AN APPALACHIAN REAWAKENING

West Virginia and the Perils of the
New Machine Age, 1945–1972

JERRY BRUCE THOMAS

WEST VIRGINIA UNIVERSITY PRESS
MORGANTOWN 2010

West Virginia University Press, Morgantown 26506
Copyright 2010 by West Virginia University Press

All rights reserved.

First edition published 2010
Printed in the United States of America

18 17 16 15 14 13 12 11 10   1 2 3 4 5 6 7 8 9

ISBN-13: 978-1-933202-58-7 (pbk. : alk. paper)
ISBN-10: 1-933202-58-0 (pbk. : alk. paper)
ISBN-13: 978-1-933202-59-4 (cloth : alk. paper)
ISBN-10: 1-933202-59-9 (cloth : alk. paper)

Library of Congress Cataloguing-in-Publication Data

Thomas, Jerry Bruce, 1941–
An Appalachian reawakening : West Virginia and the perils of the new machine age, 1945-1972 / by Jerry Bruce Thomas. — 1st ed.
  p.   cm. — (West Virginia and Appalachia ; v. 11)
Includes bibliographical references and index.
ISBN-13: 978-1-933202-58-7 (pbk. : alk. paper)
ISBN-10: 1-933202-58-0 (pbk. : alk. paper)
ISBN-13: 978-1-933202-59-4 (cloth : alk. paper)
ISBN-10: 1-933202-59-9 (cloth : alk. paper)
 1. West Virginia—History--20th century. 2. West Virginia—Social conditions—20th century. 3. West Virginia—Politics and government—20th century. 4. West Virginia—Economic conditions—20th century. 5. Social change—West Virginia—History—20th century. I. Title.

F245.T47 2010
975.4'043—dc22

Library of Congress Control Number: 2010015690

Cover design by Than Saffel
Cover image:
Robert L. Lepper (American 1906 - 1991)
Mural for The Mineral Industries Building
1941-1942; egg-oil emulsion on canvas; 12 x 46 1/2 feet
White Hall, West Virginia University
The Art Museum of West Virginia University Collection

To Vicky

This project is being presented
with financial assistance from the West Virginia Humanities Council, a
state affiliate of the National Endowment for the Humanities. Any views,
findings, conclusions or recommendations do not neccessarily represent
those of the West Virginia Humanities Council
or the National Endowment for the Humanities.

Contents

Acknowledgments ix

Introduction 1

1. A New Machine Age in the Hills 9

2. American Paradox, Appalachian Stereotype 40

3. Civil Rights in the New Machine Age 85

4. Good Intentions: The New Frontier and the War on Poverty 126

5. Raising Hell in the Hills and Hollows: AVs, VISTAs, and Community Action 170

6. From the Silver Bridge to Farmington and Rumblings at the Grassroots 216

7. The Black Lung Association, Miners for Democracy, and the New Feminism 258

8. The Strip Mining Dilemma and a Climactic Debate 286

9. Buffalo Creek: Appalachian Apotheosis 315

Epilogue: Another Reawakening? 336

Notes 344

Bibliography 422

Index 443

Acknowledgments

It is a pleasure to acknowledge those who have helped make this book possible. Grants from the West Virginia Humanities Council and the Shepherd University Professional Development Committee helped defray costs for summer research forays, and the Humanities Council is also providing a subsidy to support publication. Shepherd University helped with a sabbatical that released me from teaching duties for a semester. I am also grateful to my colleagues in the Shepherd history department who provided encouragement and a congenial atmosphere for scholarly pursuits. Director Carrie Mullen, the board of editors, and the staff of West Virginia University Press have played very critical roles in turning a rough manuscript into a book.

Many archivists and librarians have given crucial help, beginning with the excellent staff of professionals at the Ruth Scarborough Library, Shepherd University. I made repeated visits to the West Virginia and Regional History Collection at West Virginia University and always found the staff to be patient, helpful, and efficient. I also thank the staffs at the National Archives; West Virginia State Archives; Special Collections Division at the Morrow Library, Marshall University; Margaret I. King Library, University of Kentucky; Special Collections and Archives, Hutchins Library, Berea College; Archives, Drain-Jordan Library, West Virginia State University; and Archives of Appalachia, East Tennessee State University. Archivists especially helpful in tracking down suitable images for the book were Lori Hostuttler of the WVU West Virginia and Regional History collection, Debra Basham of the West Virginia State Archives, Ellen Hassig Ressmeyer of WV State University, and Ned L. Irwin of East Tennessee State University.

Appalachian scholars Ronald L. Lewis, Ken Fones-Wolf, Kevin Barksdale, Thomas Kiffmeyer, and an anonymous reader for West Virginia University Press read an early version of the complete manuscript and made many useful suggestions for changes. My good friend

Michael Austin critiqued chapter 1. Shepherd colleagues Robert Parkinson and Mark Stern helped me to see some things I missed in chapter 3. Marie Tyler-McGraw read chapters 4 and 5 and provided me with copies of some of her Appalachian materials. Jack Canfield, Governor Hulett C. Smith's former press aide, read the same chapters and shared some of his recollections, as did former Appalachian Volunteer Gibbs Kinderman. Kinderman circulated the chapter on the AVs to former AVs and associates resulting in thoughtful recollections, criticism, and commentary from Sue Ella Kobak, Joseph Mulloy, Thomas Rhodenbaugh, Douglas Yarrow, and David Walls. Professor Walls graciously provided me with a copy of a paper on the AVs and community organizing he presented at a recent Appalachian Studies Association meeting. To Douglas Yarrow I owe a special debt of gratitude for his generous sharing not only of his memories but also of his excellent photographs. Beth Spence, who worked as a volunteer and journalist at Buffalo Creek after the flood, read chapter 9 and gave me a deeper sense of the profound and enduring emotional impact that disaster had upon the people of the region. Gary Simmons shared with me audio discs of interviews he conducted for the West Virginia Documentary Consortium, and film maker Wayne Ewing provided me with a copy of his *If Elected*, a video documentary of the 1972 election in West Virginia. I cannot fail to acknowledge the Blue Moon Associates of Shepherdstown, friends who have given almost weekly advice, diversion, and good cheer throughout this project. I am deeply grateful to all.

My wife Vicky, to whom this book is dedicated, is the one to whom I owe the greatest acknowledgment. Without her support, this book could not have been written. She has tolerated my excessively long preoccupation with this project with unfailing enthusiasm, encouragement, and love. She also read the manuscript with a keen eye, catching errors and making many useful suggestions.

To the many on whose works I have relied, I hope that in all cases I have given proper credit and represented their views accurately. None of those who have given their help and advice so generously bear any responsibility for errors or inaccuracies that remain. For those, I alone am responsible.

Introduction

An Appalachian New Deal, my book about the Great Depression in West Virginia, drew part of its inspiration from curiosity about the difficult times my parents' generation had as they grew to maturity in the state during the 1930s.¹ In *An Appalachian Reawakening: West Virginia and the Perils of the New Machine Age*, I focus on the post–World War II era, especially the 1950s and 1960s, a time in which my own generation came of age in West Virginia. As in *An Appalachian New Deal*, I have tried to put the story in the broad context of American and Appalachian history but with a particular focus on West Virginia, the one state most thoroughly Appalachian.²

In writing or teaching history, time provides perspective and diminishes the influence of one's personal relationship to events, social milieu, and personalities of an era that might color one's judgment. It is, for example, much easier to discuss with scholarly equanimity the third-century BCE Chinese emperor, Qin Shi Huangdi, than, say, former President George W. Bush, as I have had occasion to do when teaching in the same semester classes on ancient civilization and recent American history. On the other hand, living in the time and place one writes about has advantages. Writing about Appalachians, I write about friends, neighbors, family, and ancestors going back to the eighteenth century. Most of my ancestors resided in West Virginia, but a few slipped over into eastern Kentucky for a time. Typically for residents of the area, they fought on both sides during the Civil War. Some of my lineal predecessors even claimed Native American princesses for the family tree. I also write about coal company towns as a native of the coalfields, having been delivered in a coal company house by a coal company doctor (at Tidewater, in McDowell County) and having experienced at a young age (in Glen Rogers, Wyoming County) things such as the omnipresence of the mine whistle in community life, marking time and the changing of the shifts, as well as sounding the alarm for emergencies (which occurred all too often);³ shopping at the company store (a 1940s version of a shopping mall);

or the social customs, strange to a youngster, which mandated that some people could sit only in the balcony at the movie theater and that black and white people must live in different parts of town, go to different schools, or even play pool on separate sides of the pool room (a facility to which, my sister recently told me, women were not admitted).[4] Preparing this book, I thought about the tragedies of Aberfan, Wales, and Buffalo Creek (and of the continuing threat of slag piles and black water impoundments throughout Appalachia), I remembered the huge smoking pile (it glowed in the dark) across the creek, up the hollow, and not far from the yellow brick elementary school and the playground where my first-grade class played.

In about 1949, in my family's version of the post-war move to suburbia, we moved to a newly constructed home just outside the small county seat town of Pineville. My classmates and I grew up there in the 1950s not only as children of Appalachia but also as the first American generation to fully experience the impact of television and the drive-in culture. Early in the decade my parents bought the first family television. It fell to me "to run the line" (removing tree limbs that might have fallen across the line while keeping a sharp eye for copperheads and rattlesnakes) on our equivalent of cable television, a shared line to a hilltop antenna that could capture television signals, a common mountaineer accommodation to the television age. Sometime in 1954, my father loaded us up in the Chevy and took us for our first ride on the new West Virginia Turnpike. Though it had only two lanes, they ran broad, relatively straight and with gentle grades, a marvel of the new age to those accustomed to the narrow, steep, serpentine, and often pot-holed two-lane roads of southern Appalachia that made paper sacks necessary gear for backseat passengers. As teenagers, even as the Appalachian economy ran counter to the national prosperity of the day, my classmates and I enjoyed the emerging drive-in culture at the Annette and Cow Shed in Pineville, the Sterling in Welch (with its special-recipe subs), and the Pineville Drive-in Theater. We were exposed to the same music, movies, and television as our peers in other parts of America during that time. Some of us listened to the radio (which had decent network and wire service news in those days), read newspapers and magazines, and had some notion of national and world events. We did not realize that we lived in a region "which centuries of isolation and economic privation had made as distant from the rest of the country in culture and politics as it was in miles," as one urban journalist later wrote about the Appalachian coalfields.[5]

With the emerging economic problems of the 1950s, friends and family also became a part of the Great Appalachian Migration. As coal mine employment declined, some of my classmates left with their families long before we graduated from high school. Many of those whose families remained until they could graduate found little option but to enter the armed forces or to migrate to Ohio, Michigan, and seaboard Virginia for industrial jobs or to Washington, D.C. for clerical work. Nevertheless, in 1959, even as unemployment grew and the local economy struggled, 44 percent of my eighty-three graduating classmates reported that they would attend college. A few found local employment and remained in the area, but many packed their bags and left soon after graduation.[6]

As its residents faced the difficult times of the 1950s and 1960s, West Virginia and the rest of Appalachia became the focus of national attention. The metropolitan press saw Appalachian poverty as a paradox, a disturbing contradiction of American prosperity. Noting the rising interest in Appalachia, Robert F. Munn wrote in *Mountain Life and Work* that in the past "scholars ignored us and journalists found us dull," but now "the *New York Times* and the *Wall Street Journal* publish 'think' pieces about us, and there is no end of non-think pieces."[7] I recall the impact of Roul Tunley's *Saturday Evening Post* article "The Strange Case of West Virginia" (a folded and creased copy of which I have kept since its publication in 1960), contrasting the beauty of the state with its "chronic, grinding poverty." Part of the reason for the journalistic focus on West Virginia at that time was the Democratic primary in West Virginia, seen as critical to the presidential prospects of Senator John F. Kennedy. Tunley's article outraged many West Virginians, though Tunley probably presented a more balanced report than other metropolitan reporters who tended to prefer stereotypes rather than facts and nuanced reporting.[8]

Even after the 1960 election, Appalachian poverty continued to draw the prying eyes and cameras of the urban reporters and television correspondents, because they believed it contradicted American expectations. Russell Baker, an Appalachian-born *New York Times* columnist, wrote after a trip through central West Virginia in 1963 that it appeared that the post-war American prosperity had leapfrogged the Appalachians.⁹ Baker and others asked why Appalachia was so poor in a land of plenty. Some social scientists of the time offered the culture of poverty theory to explain poverty generally and Appalachian poverty specifically. The culture of poverty concept influenced both the history of Appalachia (especially the history told by non-historian observers) and the government prescription for the treatment of poverty. The notion as applied to Appalachia had deep roots, going back to the late nineteenth-century metropolitan musings that had shaped the vision of Appalachia as a "strange land, inhabited by a peculiar people, a discrete region, in but not of America" as Henry Shapiro demonstrated in *Appalachia on Our Mind: The Southern Mountains and Mountaineers in the American Consciousness, 1870–1920.*¹⁰

Much in the same vein as the early writers discussed by Shapiro, Depression-era Quaker journalist Malcolm Harrison Ross (from whom I borrowed the subtitle "A New Machine Age in the Hills") wrote about the impact of mining machines in producing the unemployment after the Great Crash of 1929. Ross, though sympathetic, also wrote condescendingly and disparagingly of mountaineer culture and character, a common tendency of others of that time and later, including the English historian Arnold Toynbee, who (though he had never been to Appalachia) proclaimed "Appalachian 'mountain people' today are no better than barbarians."¹¹ Even the influential Kentucky lawyer, activist, and writer Harry Caudill, who, in his *Night Comes to the Cumberlands,* carefully outlined the dilemmas brought upon the people of eastern Kentucky by the coal industry, also described the people of the region in such a way as to suggest that they shared responsibility for the region's problems. Jack E. Weller, who came from New York to serve a Presbyterian parish in southern West Virginia from 1952 to 1965, provided probably the most influential statement of the culture of poverty concept as related to Appalachia in his book *Yesterday's People.* Weller wrote of his experience, assessing sensitively how extractive industries exploited the local people, but also extensively listing shortcomings in the character of the Appalachians and expressing a deep pessimism that, given the nature of the people, things could ever change for the better. Weller listed as his influences social classification ideas in Herbert Gans'

Urban Villagers (1962), Caudill's *Night Comes to the Cumberlands* (1963), and a few nineteenth- and early twentieth-century books about Appalachia that had contributed to the "strange land, peculiar people" idea. Brief and clearly written, *Yesterday's People* found a wide audience and impressed War on Poverty policy makers. Another sociologist, Kai Erikson, writing of the Buffalo Creek disaster in 1972, also discussed alleged characteristics of Appalachian culture and its fatalistic tendencies and had an enduring impact on sociology students' perceptions of Appalachia because textbook writers took the Yale professor's views as authoritative.[12]

The most sophisticated formulation of the culture of poverty incorporated modernization theory, then popular because of the interest in the former colonial nations, "the third world," or underdeveloped nations, many of whom suffered from severe poverty. What did such nations need to join the developed nations? Anthropologist Oscar Lewis, in his book *The Children of Sanchez* (1961), provided an answer in a compellingly written study of a Mexican-American family, which suggested that because of ingrained traits passed down from generation to generation, poor people lacked not only the skills but the habits and attitudes necessary to thrive in modern society. The lesson for those who would help the poor face the modern world was that they must change the poor, and this was the lesson underlined by Jack Weller in *Yesterday's People*.[13]

Appalachian scholars and activists of the late 1960s rather quickly came to see the culture of poverty concept as simply "blaming the victim," a way to try to help the poor without addressing the real problems, but for a time, those who looked for solutions to Appalachian poverty sincerely believed that certain attitudes ingrained in the Appalachian people would have to be changed. To influential southern sociologist Rupert Vance, the crux of the problem was clear. The mountains had created a fatalistic and fundamentalist people unable to improve, and as he wrote in an introductory note to *Yesterday's People*: "To change the mountains is to change the mountain personality."[14]

Some Appalachian scholars took this insight to heart. In 1967, a critical moment in the War on Poverty, several Appalachian social scientists held a conference at West Virginia University that sought to provide "professional field workers in programs of directed change," such as social workers, VISTA volunteers, and Extension agents with practical advice on how to promote modernizing change in "the once predominantly rural, relatively isolated Appalachian mountain region of America," which, like " Africa, once the Dark Continent, is experiencing a tremendous awakening as it gropes its way into the twentieth century." The culture of poverty theme permeated the presentations, which were later published together in the hopes that they would form something of a handbook for rural poverty warriors.[15]

Much of the work of Appalachian historical scholarship since the 1960s has been dedicated to replacing the culture of poverty thesis. The primary impulse in the 1970s sought to escape fatalism, familism, and all the aspects of the Appalachian image that essentially said the problem with Appalachia is the people. Much of the new scholarship turned to a model that focused on the exploitative nature of much of the economic activity of the region. They argued that activities carried out by non-resident corporations with little concern for the local impact of their operations accounted for many of Appalachia's enduring problems rather than any genetic or cultural shortcomings of the people. These studies basically saw Appalachia as an internal colony with its wealth being drained away to the metropolitan areas. A more recent modification of that interpretation uses the world systems concept of Immanuel Wallerstein, which in effect says that resource regions like Appalachia are on the periphery of the world system and inevitably suffer the consequences of the inequity of their relationship to the core areas.[16] Those who look to the world systems approach have moved Appalachian scholarship to a new stage.[17]

Another corrective theme in recent work is Appalachian diversity, and *An Appalachian Reawakening* reflects that impulse.[18] African Americans in West Virginia, devastated by the consequences of the new machines and under intense pressure to join the Great Migration, proved to be pioneers in pushing back against the complacency or quiescence of American and Appalachian society in the 1950s, providing early and effective (and insufficiently recognized) examples of the adaptation of the sit-in to civil rights demonstrations. Women, black and white, also played important roles in the various movements of the Appalachian reawakening and, by the end of the period, had become influential in state government and community activism and had begun to attack traditional gender restrictions in employment.

The opening chapters describe the conditions that by the end of the 1950s attracted the attention of journalists, social scientists, and others to West Virginia as the essence of Appalachia, a contradiction of American prosperity. These chapters trace the transformation in the coal industry and associated businesses and industries that led to fewer jobs, a rise in the dangers of mining, a more aggressive assault on the environment, the fade of mountain agriculture, and a broad-based economic decline. They also note the impact of common American themes of the day such as automobiles and television. Based on oral history collections and the rich historiography of migration, chapter 2 also examines the impact of the decline on the people of West Virginia, many of whom joined the Appalachian Great Migration. Along with the economic pressures and consonant with the general "politics of consensus" of the 1950s, a mood of quiescence (mistakenly take by some as evidence of fatalism) spread through the coalfields. But newspapers, civic organizations, and politicians continued to debate the state's problems. In addition to the economic problems, the state faced the challenges of education in the age of Sputnik and the challenge of obsolescent and often corrupt political institutions.

Chapters 4 and 5 deal with the New Frontier and the War on Poverty, liberal programs of the 1960s that focused especially on Appalachian poverty and the problems generated by the new machine age. More than thirty years ago, Allen J. Matusow, in *The Unraveling of America: A History of Liberalism in America in the 1960s*, made the point that, because of widely varying local circumstances, the real story of the Community Action Program (the key element in fulfilling the requirement of "maximum feasible participation" of the War on Poverty legislation) could not be fully understood "until an army of local historians recovers the program's lost fragments." He also noted that the confidential reports of the Office of Economic Opportunity's Office of Inspection provided the best single source on local community action agencies.[19] Based largely on these reports in the National Archives, the rich documentary and oral archives of the Appalachian Volunteers at Berea College, and the papers of

Governor Hulett C. Smith at the West Virginia and Regional History Collection at West Virginia University, chapters 4 and 5 put together some fragments of West Virginia's War on Poverty, evaluate these short-lived and ill-fated programs, the efforts in some counties to achieve "maximum feasible participation," the Red Scare-like atmosphere that arose in West Virginia and Appalachia in response, and the enduring influence of War on Poverty programs.

Chapters 6 through 9 recount the tragedies and troubles of 1968 and afterward, the waning of the War on Poverty, and the beginning of an Appalachian reawakening. Tragedies such as the Silver Bridge collapse, the Hominy Falls and Farmington mine disasters, and the Buffalo Creek Flood called forth a rank-and-file revolt in the United Mine Workers against a notoriously corrupt leadership and grassroots organizing among retired miners and their wives, inspiring the dream of a reformed and democratized union movement in the United States. From these efforts also came the Black Lung Association, one of the most powerful and successful movements for industrial health and safety in American history. The environmental consequences of strip mining stirred a serious grassroots and political movement throughout Appalachia to seriously restrict or ban the practice. In West Virginia these efforts resulted in the most serious effort of any state legislature to address the issue, leading to a climactic legislative debate and election. In Mingo County, another grassroots movement, the Fair Elections Committee, fought for electoral reform. Poverty warriors, including many community action veterans and former Appalachian Volunteers, and VISTA workers played important roles in these movements, which inspired enduring grassroots awareness throughout Appalachia.

1

A New Machine Age in the Hills

A machine age twilight has settled over the coal hills . . . There, . . . a region of small farmers was made momentarily prosperous by a sudden invasion of industry; then the wave passed, leaving them spoilt for the old way of life and helpless to face the new. Here, in miniature, is a cycle which technology seems to be working out in America at large.

          Malcolm Harrison Ross, *Machine Age in the Hills*, 1933

A lot of people in the rest of the country think that Appalachia has never caught up with the times, but this isn't true . . . The problems in Appalachia are largely the result of progress rather than stagnation—of a superbly advanced technology rather than a primitive technology.

          Daniel Patrick Moynihan, Appalachian Labor Conference, 1964

The nation generally prospered in the 1950s, a decade later described by historians with such superlatives as "amazing" and the "Biggest Boom Yet."[1] Lingering pent-up demand from the war period, technological advances, the development of many new industries, growth of great urban centers, and increasing exports combined to produce a rising prosperity. As the economy expanded with a steady growth rate of 4.7 percent, the standard of living improved remarkably, if unevenly. Despite three mild recessions, personal income rose to record levels by the end of the decade. Looking back over the 1950s from the perspective of 1963, economic historian Harold Vatter wrote that the remarkable capacity of the American economy represented "the crossing of a great divide in the history of humanity." Such productivity, Vatter suggested, offered the hope that "poverty can be eliminated in the near future."[2] Even the once benighted South of the Depression era existed only in memory, as "a modern economic infrastructure" made up of services, manufacturing, and trade dwarfed the old colonial economy of the region.³

In West Virginia and Appalachia, however, the forces that transformed the national economy had perverse impacts, undermining rather than uplifting, and the prospect of eliminating poverty receded rather than advancing. At the end of the decade, the Ford Foundation joined with colleges, universities, and churches in the region to investigate the matter, starting with the simple, understated premise that "over a period of time, the Appalachians have come to be recognized as a definite problem in the national economy."⁴ At about the same time, at the beginning of the 1960s, Harry Caudill, an eastern Kentucky lawyer and state legislator, gave eloquent voice to the predicament of Appalachia, "this paradox of medieval stagnation in the midst of twentieth century prosperity and progress," in his devastating and highly readable *Night Comes to the Cumberlands: A Biography of a Depressed Area*, marred only by an ungenerous portrait of the long-suffering residents of the area.⁵ Caudill focused on the Appalachian counties of eastern Kentucky, but the same kind of night came to West Virginia, the one state completely within Appalachia, and for much of the metropolitan press, the Mountain State, an "American paradox," epitomized the Appalachian contradiction to the national prosperity.⁶

During the post–World War II period, at nearly every turn, new technologies created dilemmas and dangers for workers and residents, and though Appalachia was in some ways on the cutting edge of the technological revolution, it failed to share in the general prosperity that swept the country, even as the region supplied much of the energy that fueled the Great Boom, and the "sweat, muscles, and backs" of Appalachian migrants provided much of the labor that helped to sustain it.⁷ The new machine age would also offer an irresistible siren lure to the leadership of the United Mine Workers of America, drawing the union away from its reformist and militant tendencies of the Depression era (which had offered some countervailing force to powerful corporate interests) and, through diminution of its membership, undermining its hard-earned political clout. John L. Lewis and the union leadership cynically ignored the dangers the new machines posed to workers' health as the price of a new arrangement with management and also as part of the price for saving the industry. The rank and file would retreat for a time into a judicious silence, quietly acquiescing to forces beyond their control.[8] Despite it all, West Virginians and Appalachians generally shared in the mass culture of the age, including the advance of automobiles and television, and enjoyed their own modifications to the general culture as well as things uniquely Appalachian.

Appalachian Contradiction

The Mountain State suffered the largest rate of decline in employment among the fifty states and the District of Columbia as manufacturing and mining employment tumbled, mountain agriculture faded, and a general economic malaise pervaded the state. The unemployment figures illustrate the depth of the problem: while the national employment rate increased 15.5 percent, employment in West Virginia declined by 14.3 percent.[9]

At the end of World War II, prospects seemed bright in West Virginia. Veterans returned with high hopes and soon found jobs. Construction boomed as West Virginians who had made money during the war and veterans who benefited from the GI Bill shared somewhat in the national trend to suburbanization, creating mountaintop suburbs around the larger towns and cities, like South Hills in Charleston and Marland Heights in Weirton ("One of the Largest Subdivisions in the State—Over 2100 Lots Fully Improved," proclaimed an ad in a state magazine). The chemical industry, stimulated by the war, successfully converted to peacetime as the center shifted from the Kanawha Valley to Ohio Valley cities Parkersburg and Moundsville. By 1948, the chemical industry employed 25,000 workers, and at the end of the 1950s, nearly fifty chemical plants operated in the state.[10] The steel industry, concentrated in the Northern Panhandle, enjoyed boom times from the war into the 1950s, employing 22,596 in 1950.[11] Manufacturing employed 127,354 in 1947, an increase of nearly 50,000 from 1939.[12]

In the coal industry, employment rose from 97,380 in 1945 to an all-time high of 125,669 by 1948. Then the bottom fell out of the post-war prosperity in West Virginia as the collapse of the coal industry led the way in a downward spiral. In the next two years, mining employment fell by some 6,000 and then plummeted throughout the 1950s, reaching 48,696 in 1960.[13]

A Revolution in Coal

During the post-war decade, the coal industry faced increasingly stiff competition from other energy sources like oil, gas, hydroelectricity, and atomic power. New technology made these sources cheaper and more attractive than coal for many uses. In what one writer called a "Brutus blow,"[14] railroads replaced coal-burning steam locomotives with diesel engines, so even the trains that hauled West Virginia coal stopped using coal. Because railroads also now required fewer workers to maintain and operate the less labor-intensive diesels, in the 1950s, 9,231 West Virginia railroad workers joined the miners made jobless by technological change. Railway towns like Bluefield, Williamson, Huntington, Grafton, and Hinton reeled from the loss. In Hinton, for example, the Chesapeake and Ohio Railway shops cut 800 jobs between 1953 and 1963, plunging the small Summers County town into despair. Other industrial energy users also dropped coal for heating and power generation in favor of oil or gas. New homeowners, even in West Virginia, used the new, cleaner oil and gas furnaces rather than coal furnaces, and often those with older homes converted to oil and gas or electricity, reducing to almost nothing the retail home-heating market, which had once been a mainstay of the coal industry. Ultimately offsetting the market losses, steel plants grew larger and consumed more coal, and electric-generating plants increased their consumption of coal fivefold in the two and a half decades from 1933 to 1956.[15]

In the early 1950s, when the market growth in other areas had not become clear, the coal industry and coal state politicians blamed imported oil, claiming that foreign oil refiners dumped residual oil on the market at prices calculated to drive coal out. Whatever the case, the disruption or disappearance of traditional coal markets led to falling coal production, narrower profit margins, and discharge notices for growing numbers of miners as coal operators mechanized to reduce labor costs. Beginning in 1948, with the introduction of Joy Manufacturing Company's 3JCM-2, continuous mining machines came on the market that revolutionized mining. For coal companies the revolution could not have arrived sooner, because coal production in 1949 fell to its lowest level since 1939, forcing companies to seek ways to compete more efficiently.[16]

A New Machine Age in the Hills

Miner operating a Joy Manufacturing Company continuous mining machine at a Consolidation Coal Company mine. West Virginia and Regional History Collection, West Virginia University Libraries.

Better mechanical loaders also became available, and with innovations in conveyance, soon it became possible for fewer miners to cut, load, and transport coal from deep mines to the surface in a continuous, coordinated process, epitomizing the much-discussed phenomenon of the day called "automation," which in 1960, Americans feared more than the Soviet Union, according to a Gallup poll, because it threatened to eliminate most of the best-paying blue-collar jobs.[17] Though costs ranging up to as much as $80,000 each for the new machines gave tight-fisted mining executives pause and indeed made the revolution affordable only by the highly capitalized operators, the compelling economics of mechanization spelled disaster for coal miners and for the region that had come to depend on the industry. As coal industry historian Curtis Seltzer has pointed out: "A continuous miner with 10 men could produce three times as much coal as 86 men in a hand loading section and half again as much coal as 30 men on a machine-loading section. . . . The total cost per ton was $5.28 for hand loading, $3.79 for machine loading, and $3.16 for continuous mining." The new technology nearly eliminated the need for hand loaders and opened the door for more productive and profitable mining with a much smaller labor force. Other innovations contributed to the changes, such as using steel roof bolts with large plates at the head instead of wooden timbers to reinforce the overhead (which eliminated the jobs of those who cut and shipped mine timbers) and eliminating rails inside the mines with the use of rubber-wheeled cars.[18] Because coal mining took place in many areas of the region and had long affected the economy, society, and politics, the revolution in mining techniques had profound consequences for the people of West Virginia and Appalachia.

The new system transformed underground coal mining, reducing some risks to the miner but creating many new ones in what would remain the most dangerous occupation in the country.[19] West Virginia's role as the leading bituminous coal producer had been achieved with what state mines chief Frank B. King in a 1954 survey called "a horrifying and needless great loss of life." In the fifty years from 1904 to 1954, 17,234 men had been killed in the state's coalmines. Mine explosions attracted the most attention because of the incidents involving multiple deaths, like the 1907 Monongah blast, which killed 361 miners, or the Eccles explosion of 1913, which killed 183. In most years, however, slate and coal falls had the deadliest impact, killing victims one and two at a time, and accounting for 8,801 deaths in King's grim survey. Next came haulage accidents, killing 3,805 and then explosions, which accounted for 2,050 of the fifty-year death total. The total death toll would be substantially higher if the statistics included deaths from job-related diseases, and it is likely that the official statistics underreported deaths.[20]

In some respects the trend toward mechanization made for a safer work environment by substituting machines for men in the most onerous and dangerous phases of mining. Injuries related to hand cutting and loading decreased. Stricter state and federal laws, although not carefully enforced, actually contributed to lowering the number of mine fatalities in West Virginia, which fell below 200 annually for the first time in 1945 and then to 113 in 1954.[21] Raw numbers, however, mislead, because although the number of deaths declined, the *rate* of injury and death increased, as the total number of miners fell. As J. Davitt McAteer pointed out in a 1969 study, a West Virginia miner's chances of being killed in the mine grew from one in 453 in 1948 to one in 273 in 1968, so the net effect of the new technology made mining more rather than less dangerous.[22]

The new machines created new hazards. They accelerated the pace of work and increased the noise level at the workplace, increasing the likelihood of a careless but critical mistake, making it difficult for miners to listen for dangerous situations (such as stresses in the roof), and creating hearing loss in machine operators. The machines increased the amount of dust in the air, increasing the dangers of lung diseases such as bronchitis, silicosis, and the closely related coal workers' pneumoconiosis—black lung disease, which in a little more than a decade became pandemic in the mining regions. The clouds of dust also reduced visibility, obscuring the working face for machine operators and other workers. The danger of catastrophic blasts continued, because even though the new machines eliminated the traditional undercutting of the coal and the use of explosives to blast it down, the pervasive fine dust created by continuous miners clawing at the seam with huge rotating discs had its own explosive qualities. If not carefully controlled through ventilation and the use of rock dust, a chemically inert neutralizing substance, coal dust could be highly explosive, and in combination with methane, a naturally occurring gas found in many mines, it could be especially deadly. The rotating drums of cutting bits might strike the solid rock of roof or floor and provide the spark needed for ignition.[23] The danger of explosion received grim reinforcement when on successive days in October 1958, mine explosions at Bishop, McDowell County, and at Burton Mine, near Richwood, killed thirty-six.[24] In March 1960, an explosion and fire in Island Creek Coal Company's no. 22 mine at Holden resulted in a futile eight-day effort to rescue eighteen miners trapped inside, the longest and one of the most expensive rescue operations in American mining history up to that time.[25]

In addition to the continuous miners, companies also turned to strip mining and auger mining to achieve economies, with devastating effects on employment as well as the environment (as further explored in chapter 8). Underground mining also had a substantial environmental impact. Disposal of the waste products from the mining process, slate, and other refuse posed a problem for mining engineers that they solved by simply dumping such material on the mining site, creating huge heaps of slag (also called gob piles or slate dumps). Through spontaneous combustion these dumps would burn for years, emitting noxious gases, primarily sulfur dioxide, and killing vegetation in the surrounding area. After having burned out, the residue from these dumps, called "red dog," could be used as a loose road-surfacing substitute for gravel in the coal towns. The slag heaps also contributed to water pollution as runoff from the piles entered the creeks, rivers, and ground water. Sometimes the dumps blocked streams, creating dangerous water impoundments of the kind that that would produce the Buffalo Creek disaster of 1972, one of the worst man-made disasters in American history (as further discussed in chapter 9). Drainage from the mines themselves also contributed to water pollution. Some areas also suffered from surface subsidence after many years of underground mining, particularly after longwall mining, a highly efficient form of retreat mining (which left behind no coal pillars or other supports for the roof), became the standard practice of well-capitalized mining operations.[26]

Many Appalachian coal operators first glimpsed the new machines that transformed the industry in the southern West Virginia town of Bluefield, a center for the distribution of mining equipment. There, mining machinery firms, in cooperation with the Pocahontas Coal Operators Association, sponsored the Southern Appalachian Industrial Exhibit, better known as the Bluefield Coal Show. The event began in 1935 and was held every two years thereafter with the exception of the war years. During the 1950s, Coal Show crowds of 35,000 to 50,000 witnessed the crowning of Queen Bituminous (usually the daughter of someone engaged in coal mining) and visited some 230 booths scattered about the Norfolk and Western's huge freight terminal. In 1952 visitors to the Coal Show saw an emphasis on improved coal-cleaning plants, coal-cutting machines, continuous miners, rubber-wheeled shuttle cars, and the new diesel mine locomotives. An outdoor exhibit featured displays of heavy machinery for strip mining, including huge bulldozers, power shovels and draglines, and oversized trucks.[27]

Paradoxically, the technology revolution operated in such a way as to not only create ever-larger operations but also to perpetuate small mines. While big operating companies sought economies by replacing labor with the new machines, small coal operators took another tack, which relied in most cases not on the economics of the new machine age but on distinctly old-fashioned methods. If the big companies represented the radicals in this revolution, the small operators stood at the barricades to repulse the change, desperately clinging to the old ways as their defense against the revolution that sought to eliminate them and their way of life. They lowered costs not through the economies offered by large scale but by staying small and operating on a non-union basis, thereby avoiding not only union pay scales but also payments to the union welfare funds and some safety costs associated with union oversight. The federal coalmine safety law of 1952 exempted small mines from some safety measures required of larger mines. Small non-union operators also often flew in the face of the technology revolution, buying used and outmoded equipment and using antiquated mining techniques. They avoided marketing and processing costs by selling their coal as it came from the mine to the larger producers or to cleaning plants, who would process and market it as their own. Some small mines also sold coal from their own trucks to local people who still heated with coal.[28]

In 1958, West Virginia State Mines Director Crawford Wilson reported that the department issued permits throughout the state for numerous small mines employing five to fifteen miners. These small mines, traditionally called "snowbirds" but more often termed "dog holes" or "punch mines" in the parlance of the era, revived methods of an earlier day. In these mines, miners often used mules, donkeys, or ponies for haulage, and in some mines they even pushed the cars by hand. Miners laid off by conventional mining companies snapped up the jobs available in these marginal operations, because, Wilson said, "they love mining and they can make a living." Wilson insisted that the department required the observation of modern safety procedures even if the mines used primitive methods.[29] George Titler, president of United Mine Workers of America (UMWA), district 29, doubted that the union could ever have much success organizing small mines, which he called "kinship mines," operations in which the few miners would all be related. In addition to underground mines, some of these small operations mined abandoned strip mines. During World War II, some strippers would strip twenty miles around a mountain, but when the overburden became too high, they would move out, leaving twenty miles of coal faced up, which offered anyone with a pick and shovel the opportunity to enter the mining business.[30] Not all small operators used old-fashioned equipment. It took little capital to purchase a small bulldozer and a truck and thus to carve out a road to an appropriate site to begin either a small stripping operation or even an underground mine. Some of the underground miners, often working in narrow seams, used miniaturized, battery-operated tractors less than thirty inches high to haul coal from inside the mine. Many small truck mines developed in Appalachia in the post-1950 era, especially in the thin-seamed drift mines in Virginia, eastern Kentucky, and West Virginia.[31] By 1962, 1,392 small mines (defined by the state department of mines as operations employing fourteen men or less) operated in the West Virginia compared to 438 large mines (those having fifteen or more employees).[32]

An example of a small kinship mining operation raises doubts about Crawford's safety assurances and demonstrates how little it took to enter the coal mining business. George "Nub" Moran, a mine mechanic at Stotesbury in Raleigh County, received notice on Valentine's Day, 1958, that the mine that employed him would close in two weeks. At the time he owed for a house and car and "a bunch of other debts" and had two children in school. He signed up for unemployment at $120 per month, which did not begin to cover the bills. So, Moran later recalled:

Me and my brother decided to open a little punch mine. That's what a lot of people did. We found a lease about twenty miles away for 35 cent per ton royalties. The company we leased from lent us some equipment which had been covered up at another mine when the highwall had fallen on it. We had to go and get the equipment, transport it to our mine, clean it up and keep it running. It cost 15 cents per ton to lease the equipment. We had to buy our own powder and pay ourselves something. We had a four wheel drag cable car, and we shot from the solid. Didn't have a cutting machine. Some times we shot a case of powder and didn't get a ton of coal. We had an old truck to drive up there. Sometimes we'd have a couple of flats a day. We were gone eighteen hours a day. During the summer we just about broke even, but the winter killed us. On them tore up roads, we couldn't get up to the mine a lot of times. Finally we just had to give it up.[33]

In his book *The Logan Coal Field of West Virginia,* coal operator Walter R. Thurmond credited the technological revolution of the 1950s with saving the coal industry from ruin, but he also noted that both miners and middle-sized operators paid a large price. While many miners lost their jobs, the larger firms in the industry tended to take over mid-sized companies that lacked the capital to purchase the new machines and to pursue a profitable scale of operations.[34] Reflecting on this period at a conference on mining history in 1979, John B. "Jack" Long, one of the pioneers in West Virginia mining equipment production, cast the issue in terms of global competition, arguing that the West Virginia mining firms and miners that survived in the late 1940s and early 1950s represented one of the most successful groups ever assembled in any industry. In a time of declining markets and prices, Long said, they increased production by almost 300 percent and out-produced West German and Japanese miners almost ten to one. Unlike Thurmond, Long had sympathy neither for the miners who lost their jobs nor for the firms that failed. He sympathized entirely with the hardy group of workers that survived—about 50,000—which he believed failed to receive adequate recognition for its heroic achievements, because the group that had lost their jobs—about 75,000—did not "just disappear." Immobilized by the welfare system, Long argued, they made welfare payments a business and became one of the most successful pressure groups in history, eventually getting "punitive legislation" passed that won black lung benefits from both the state and the federal government and even successfully promoting one of their number to the presidency of the UMWA. He expressed the hope that the second group would "phase out" and allow the "positive group" to receive its just historical recognition. His views probably exemplified those of most coal industry executives.[35]

In 1936, Long's father, Armistead Rosser Long, a retired mining engineer, had founded the Long-Airdox Company of Oak Hill, a firm pioneering in the machinery and steel fabricating industry within the coalfields. The firm began by manufacturing mine cars, but as the competition from cheaper energy sources threatened the coal industry in the post-war period, Rosser and Jack Long (who had an engineering degree from the University of North Carolina) invented many devices to complement the revolution taking place in the industry, subcontracting much of the fabrication work to small shops in the coalfields. By the 1950s they had changed their emphasis from mine cars and devised various other conveyance devices, including chain and belt conveyors, which helped move the coal at reduced costs. By 1958, the company could provide mining firms with continuous haulage systems to convey coal from multiple working faces to the surface. In 1960, Jack Long sold Long-Airdox to Chicago-based Marmon Harrington Company, and the firm subsequently left Oak Hill, but many small fabricating shops remained in the West Virginia coalfields.[36]

As Long's career demonstrated, the technological revolution that swept the Appalachian fields and eliminated many mining jobs also generated new types of manufacturing jobs in the coalfields linked to the new methods. Mechanical loading and continuous miners produced a dirtier coal, requiring new preparation techniques and safety procedures, and strip-mining operations sometimes required unique and site specific devices. Many small manufacturers arose in West Virginia to supply mining companies with customized coal handling and conveyance devices specifically designed for their particular circumstances. These small plants and shops gave opportunities to coalfield entrepreneurs and to skilled workers (some of them former miners) like draftsmen and welders trained by high school trade and vocational programs. The jobs produced by the small manufacturers, however, did not fully offset the jobs lost in coal mining as the industry replaced workers with machines.[37]

The UMWA Embraces the Revolution

The United Mine Workers of America embraced the coal industry's cost-cutting technology at a heavy price for miners and Appalachia. John L. Lewis's chief biographers generously say that Lewis could not have anticipated the heavy price that would be paid, but others say that Lewis understood well the consequences of continuous miners and other new machines for the respiratory health of his members.[38] During World War II and in the early post-war period, the union, led by Lewis, followed a confrontational approach with both industry and government. Though Lewis, along with other labor leaders, took a "no strike" pledge at the beginning of the war, he repeatedly shut down the industry. The federal government seized and operated the mines several times. When, in 1945, Lewis demanded a new health care plan financed through a ten cent per ton levy on production, the coal industry leaders refused. In 1946, the UMWA struck, leading to another government takeover. During this period of government operation, the government carried out a health and medical survey of the coalfields, called "the Boone Report" (for Rear Admiral Joel T. Boone, USN, who was in charge of the survey).[39] Despite the confrontational relationship of the Depression and wartime periods, in the post-war era Lewis began to find common ground with business and conservative forces who mobilized to resist any expansion of New Deal-type social policies. The anti-labor political climate of the day led to the passage of the Taft-Hartley Act in 1947, which placed various restraints on the power of unions. Like other labor leaders, Lewis condemned Taft-Hartley, but rather than seeking government programs to obtain adequate health and welfare for miners, he preferred to deal directly with management. The UMWA led the way for other unions in post-war bargaining for company-funded pensions and health plans.[40]

In a series of agreements between the UMWA and industry groups between 1946 and 1950, the union's welfare and retirement fund grew into a full-fledged program that replaced the old scheme of deducting from miners' wages to pay for a company doctor. Instead, companies would now pay a fixed amount per ton of coal mined, eventually set at forty cents. The 1950 contract with the operators represented a historic compromise in which the operators essentially agreed to union control of the fund in return for union support of extensive mechanization. Lewis had always accepted mechanization as inevitable and readily accepted the subsequent reductions in mining jobs and decline in working conditions in return for better wages and a health and pension fund.

After the 1950 agreement, Lewis led no further major strikes, and mechanization advanced rapidly.[41] Coal industry historian Curtis Seltzer calls the deal "a coal-blooded conspiracy against both the union's rank and file and small coal producers."[42] Because the agreement with the industry based payments into the fund on tonnage, the UMWA ceased to be an adversarial agent toward the coal companies and collaborated in a commitment to put production above all other considerations, including safety.[43] The UMWA's new arrangement with management reflected a more general "labor-capital accord" after World War II, brought about by a powerful remobilization of business and conservative forces, which rejected New Deal reformism and may well have prevented a more progressive approach to

Appalachian and American social problems related to unemployment, workplace health and safety, and environmental concerns.[44]

Consolidation Coal Company officials host UMWA leader John L. Lewis (seated to the right of the speaker) at Fairmont, West Virginia, 1948, during a time of growing cooperation between union and coal industry leaders. West Virginia and Regional History Collection, West Virginia University Libraries.

According to his chief biographers, Lewis "never truly grasped what modernization meant to the unemployed coal miner." The UMWA leader prided himself on being an economic realist. Like Jack Long and coal industry leaders, he saw modernization of the industry (by which he meant the application of labor-saving technology) as inevitable and necessary. The role of a union was to increase wages, and workers operating machines could command higher wages than manual coal diggers and loaders. The unemployed, he believed, would simply be reabsorbed into the economy. The shock of unemployment would be mitigated for older miners who would have social security and their UMWA pension checks. Despite the neoclassical neatness of the theory, Lewis's deal with the industry had devastating consequences for the miners, the union, and the region. A union with a shrinking work force had declining influence, both economically and politically, and with fewer workers and increasing numbers of retirees, pressure on the welfare and retirement fund became unsupportable over time. Moreover, the massive unemployment that resulted from the transformation of the coal industry contributed to the growing squalor of Appalachia, and neither the operators nor the union did anything to help the unemployed relocate or train for other work, nor did they seek government help for the workers abandoned by the industry. The economy did not reabsorb them all, as Lewis and Long had hoped and expected. Contrary to Jack Long's interpretation, most of the thousands of miners who lost their jobs did "just disappear," often reluctantly, as they left Appalachia in search of jobs, becoming part of the Great Migration. A remnant remained, however. Some discharged miners, lacking skills adaptable to other industries, stayed on in their worked out or closed down coal camps, working for much less than miners' wages if they could find work, joining with a few others in working "dog holes," or not working at all and living on meager welfare payments and food rations. For those who did continue to work, the industry did little to suppress the dust the new machines generated or to adequately dispose of the growing waste created by the new processes, making inevitable a contagion of black lung disease and creating conditions that would lead to disasters like Farmington and Buffalo Creek (as will be further discussed later).[45]

The new machine age in the hills revolutionized coalfield life as well as mining practices. During the 1950s, many large companies abandoned older, less efficient mines and closed down the old coal towns that the pioneer companies had built when they opened their mines in areas remote from commercial centers. Now, with a reduced and more mobile labor force, coal companies sold off or dismantled company housing and closed down company stores. The once booming Kaymoor in the New River Gorge exemplifies the trend. At its peak Kaymoor had over 150 company houses, but in

1954 the company began demolishing houses. By 1958 the population had moved away. Vandalism and fires destroyed the few remaining houses. Many coal towns disappeared like Kaymoor, often leaving in their wake abandoned slag piles, rotting and rusting remnants of old houses, company stores, rails, mine shops, and tipples.[46]

Abandoned and decaying site of a Mingo County coal town showing tipple in the background, company offices and store to the left, and grass growing over the rails, a typical scene in Appalachian coal country in the 1950s and 1960s. Photograph by Douglas Yarrow.

The Fade of the Mountain Farm

In addition to the collapse in mining, agricultural employment also continued to decline at a rate faster than the nationwide trend, falling from 120,000 to 75,000 over the decade. Advancing agricultural technology and improvements in transportation of agricultural products contributed to making the self-sustaining mountain agriculture of the past increasingly anachronistic.[47] Tractors and other farm machines of the new age could not operate on many rugged mountain tracts. In much of West Virginia and other parts of Appalachia, the average mountain farm contained less than fifty-five acres. In the southern mountain counties, where miners had engaged in some subsistence farming in the past, farming virtually disappeared.[48] A post-war report on agriculture by the state planning board had suggested that the end of the war might lead to some repopulation of rural areas as veterans and those who had left for urban employment during the war demobilized. Less optimistically, the board foresaw a difficult future for state agriculture as technology became more critical to commercial success. Mountain agriculture, of course, had been in trouble before the war. More than three-quarters of pre-war farms had not produced enough for an adequate living for a farm family. Driven to supplement the family income, almost half of all West Virginia farmers had turned to itinerancy, working an average of 164 days off the farm before the war. Many of the youngest farmers left their hillside tracts for the lure of a better life in cities outside the state, leaving behind an aging population less able to adapt to new ways of life. Erosion had taken 75 percent of the surface soil on 25 percent of the acreage, and the state's rugged topography limited the commercial potential of farming. The board, however, believed some things might be done to improve farm income. Farmers might switch to intensive cultivation of crops like strawberries, cauliflower, Christmas trees, and native nuts and fruits. Smaller farms should be consolidated, submarginal farms reforested, and agriculture and other industries should seek closer cooperation. The board also insisted that farmers needed better roads to succeed commercially.[49]

By the early 1960s, however, little had improved, and inadequate income among small farmers of Appalachia contributed mightily to the poverty of the region. Almost two-thirds of all Appalachian counties fell into the lowest one-fifth income category of all counties in the country. Mountain farms once barely adequate for subsistence agriculture fell below the size believed necessary for achieving adequate incomes as commercial operations. An agronomist of the West Virginia University Experiment Station concluded that "there is little prospect for small Appalachian farms to achieve satisfactory incomes, because small farms cannot be enlarged to commercial size."⁵⁰ Some thought sustainability rather than commercial viability should be the goal on mountain farms, but as gross farm income in West Virginia declined steadily, the value of self-produced products consumed by farm households, an important indicator of the health of subsistence farming, also fell by two-thirds between 1948 and 1964.⁵¹

An aerial view shows some of the best Appalachian farmland in Germany Valley, Pendleton County, circa 1940. West Virginia and Regional History Collection, West Virginia Libraries.

Hardy County exemplifies the plight of the Appalachian agricultural counties. Located in the South Branch Valley, one of West Virginia's richest farming areas with more large farms than typical in Appalachia and far from the mining regions, Hardy nonetheless fell into the poorest fifth of the nation's counties. The poverty of Hardy and similar Appalachian agricultural counties raises the question as to whether their problems have any common ties with the coal mining counties. If it is coal that causes the problems in the mining counties, what is at the root of poverty in the agricultural counties?

A look at its early twentieth-century history shows that although Hardy had no coal, it nevertheless had suffered in strikingly similar ways the same kind of heedless exploitation of natural resources that plagued the mining areas. Even before the belated arrival of the railroad in the early twentieth century, timbering, lumber mills, and tanneries had emerged in Hardy, replete with company towns, work camps, and dire environmental consequences. Tanneries used lime in their hide processing, creating a black ooze that flowed into local streams, threatening the water supply and aquatic life. Deforestation brought about by the lumber industry's "cut and run" practices of that era destroyed wildlife habitat and left large areas of the county a bleak, dreary wilderness of stumps and brush for many years. With the natural constraints on water flow removed, Hardy suffered an era of severe floods. Residents of Hardy, just as elsewhere in Appalachia, had ambivalent feelings toward the consequences of the "modern civilization" for which they had yearned. They welcomed the wages and businesses, but they worried about the destruction of the county's natural beauty, pollution, the dangers to the water supply, and the impact on traditional pursuits such as hunting, fishing, and the gathering of wild herbs. Census statistics show that the new economic system increased the number of very small farms operated by marginal farmers who depended for cash not on their farms but on itinerancy or "public work" such as stripping and hauling bark or supplying cordwood for tanneries. This way of life, common to many rural Appalachian counties, could not be sustained later in the century as opportunities for off-farm work faded.[52]

With a population of 9,308 in 1960, Hardy had lost 7 percent of its population during the 1950s, and like the coalfield counties, it too suffered the consequences of the new machine age. More than half of the families had incomes under the federal benchmark for poverty, $3,000 per year. Many descended from the self-sufficient family farmers who had drifted into poverty as the mechanization of agriculture made the old ways obsolete. The development of synthetic fibers in the post-war period had closed the last tannery in Moorefield, the county seat. In the timber industry, chain saws replaced axes and reduced the need for timber men. Poultry raising had boomed in the county during World War II, but in the 1950s competition from huge southern operations drove Hardy County's small producers from the markets of Washington, Baltimore, and Philadelphia. Other small agricultural counties suffered similar fates.[53]

The post-war planners thought forestry had the potential to provide income for owners of mountain tracts, but unwise cutting and poor management practices in the past had seriously depleted the value of the state's forestry crop and contributed to erosion and water quality problems.[54] With substantial reforestation of lands previously devoted to other crops, improved protection of forests by the state, selective cutting, and sound practices designed to produce a sustained yield, the board believed forestry could become a more profitable pursuit for farmers and landowners.[55] Despite efforts at conservation and reforestation, however, wood and wood products industries never realized the hopes of the post-war planners. Lumber production in the 1950s never exceeded one-fourth that of the pre–World War II era, and 3,284 jobs in lumber and wood products industries disappeared in the 1950s, although forestry remained one of the few industries in West Virginia in which the job creation rate exceeded the national average. Like coal and other extractive industries, timbering "left a legacy of depleted resources, scarred terrain, and fleeting prosperity."[56]

A General Economic Decline

The problems West Virginia faced affected many industries and most of the state, not just the coal and agricultural counties. The struggling bellwether industries such as coal and railroads had linkage effects that drew down others, like banking, construction, manufacturing, and retail sales. When mining employment fell, it impacted many other enterprises and most of the cities, creating ripple effects throughout the state economy. The two largest cities in the state, Charleston and Huntington, had many companies with financial, legal, real estate, and transportation ties with the coalfields as did the smaller cities of Morgantown, Fairmont, Wheeling, Bluefield, and Clarksburg. Other industries had their own problems, however, unrelated to coal or agriculture but they shared the dilemmas associated with adjusting to the post-war transformation in the national economy, especially the technological advance.[57] The 1950s marked a decline also in the Eastern Panhandle, where Martinsburg had been an important regional textile center, beginning with the closing of Berkeley Woolen Mill in 1949 and continuing with the closing of Dunn Woolen Mill in 1953. Employment in Martinsburg textile and garment factories declined from 3,254 in 1944 to 1,800 by 1963. The industry faded because of labor-management conflict (the International Ladies Garment Workers Union persisted over the years in efforts to organize the workers, and management adamantly resisted), the rise of synthetics, the forbidding costs of retooling aging plants to produce new products, and international competition. The problems of the textile industry account for rising unemployment in Berkeley County, which, though not as severe as in the coal regions, reached 10 percent by 1962.[58] In April 1958, Albert S. Caldwell, president of the Tri-County Central Labor Council of the Eastern Panhandle wrote from Martinsburg alerting Governor Underwood to the rising unemployment in the area, saying "steps must be taken promptly and decisively to mitigate suffering."[59] The glass industry, with centers in Grafton and Morgantown, faded for reasons similar to those that caused a decline in the textile industry.[60] The Northern Panhandle steel industry, lagging behind Europe and Japan in adopting new technology, weathered the 1950s but also began to fade by the early 1960s.[61] During the 1950s, the total number of manufacturing establishments in the state increased by only 8 percent.[62]

West Virginians and the Mass Culture of the Age

Some West Virginians, of course, shared the prosperity that the country generally enjoyed and resented criticisms, especially by media critics from outside the state. Even in smaller cities and towns, middle-class families lived lives not much different from the rest of the country and distinctly different from the lives of those who struggled on in worked-out mining towns or with small farms or in mountain hollows. Wherever they lived, most West Virginians shared in many of the national trends of the decade including the fascination with automobiles, the rise of television, popular movies, and the spreading availability of rock 'n' roll, rhythm and blues, as well as country, bluegrass, gospel and other popular music via radio, television, and widely retailed 45 and 33 rpm vinyl discs. Though these conclusions are impressionistic, the Ford Foundation survey of southern Appalachian households made in the summer of 1958 provides some statistical support for the impression. The data might understate the case for West Virginia, because it defined Appalachian West Virginia in such a way as to exclude all of the Northern Panhandle and some other northern counties. The survey found that 86.4 percent had electric or gas stoves, 78.2 percent had television sets, and 23.8 percent had deep freezes. The survey listed nearly half of the households as middle class and 11.8 as upper class. The survey's data also provided evidence that the people of Appalachia rejected "fatalism," a trait often ascribed to them in the past.[63]

In the 1950s (as further discussed in the next chapter), the state tried to improve its highway system, but most roads remained meandering, outmoded, and sometimes pot-holed, two-lane highways that often followed tortuous narrow cuts along steep mountainsides. Nevertheless, West Virginians took to the roads in great numbers. By 1957, 444,000 automobiles, 119,000 trucks, and 826 buses competed for space.[64] Automobile dealerships and service stations dotted the map, as did drive-in restaurants, drive-in movies, and motels. Alex Schoenbaum, a Charleston businessman, pioneered in the drive-in restaurant business, opening the Parkette in 1947, offering a fifteen-cent hamburger and curb service at a West Side Charleston location. By the early 1950s, he had opened two other drive-ins and helped create the Big Boy franchise. In about 1953, he changed the name of the Parkette to Shoney's and created a multi-state drive-in empire of the Shoney's chain, which later became a family-oriented restaurant. Most West Virginia towns had their local drive-ins that became automotive gathering spots.[65] West Virginians, also like other Americans, watched movies in their cars at drive-in theaters. In 1945 the Mount Zion Drive-In Theater opened in rural Calhoun County, and by the mid-1950s, West Virginians watched movies under the stars and in their cars in seventy-six different locations.[66]

West Virginians also welcomed television, an electronic manifestation of the new machine age, but the mountains made reception difficult in many areas of the state, inspiring innovative efforts by mountaineers to capture television signals. Governor Okey Patteson helped dedicate the first television station in West Virginia, WSAZ of Huntington, on November 15, 1949, and in fairly short order the television age brought to West Virginians in even remote locations the same fare as enjoyed by metropolitan viewers.[67] By 1957 nine television stations in the state transmitted programs that included largely national network programming and news.[68] In border areas, especially in the north and east, viewers received telecasts from urban centers like Pittsburgh and Washington. In the early days mountainous areas distant from transmitters experienced "snowy" reception, and rooftop antennas helped only slightly, particularly in towns built on valley floors and surrounded by signal-blocking mountains. To improve reception, residents of some neighborhoods and towns ran wires to an antenna located at the top of the highest hill, sharing the signal on a community line. Often this just involved a few neighbors cooperating to capture a better signal, but some, like Ira Homer Ferrell of Piedmont and Carl Gainer of Richwood (who served several terms as a state senator), saw the business possibilities and organized what were probably the first cable systems in the state. At first Ferrell and friends carried a television to the top of a mountain to watch television. Seeking something more satisfactory, he and his friends conducted many experiments seeking ways to bring the signal from the mountaintop into their homes. In 1951, they established the Upper Potomac Television Company to provide service to the Tri-Towns region of Piedmont and the Maryland towns of Westernport and Luke. At about the same time Gainer provided a community antenna service for Richwood residents.[69]

In his memoir of growing up in Mineral County, Henry Louis Gates, Jr., one of the preeminent scholars of African American studies, recalls the arrival of television in Piedmont. The development of the cable service there made it possible to view twelve channels, and the little Mineral County town, like many others in West Virginia, "was transformed from a radio culture to one with the fullest range of television, literally overnight." Gates and his family enjoyed their new window on the world but regretted the lack of African American fare in the early network shows.[70] West Virginia stations also developed their own programming, including news and entertainment. Several stations had daytime musical variety and interview programs. WSAZ, which went on the air as channel 5 but soon became channel 3, had an early daily variety show known as "Coffee Time," featuring Sue Chambers, Dean Sturm, and a live band, Brownie Benson's Combo. A "Charm School" segment of the show featured Chambers demonstrating exercises and discussing fashion and beauty issues.[71]

WSAZ began to telecast regional news soon after going on the air with Nick Basso as the first news director. By August 1954, WSAZ had facilities in Charleston where Bos Johnson served as co-anchor with Basso in a dual city newscast.[72]

In its early days, WSAZ—following in the footsteps of many West Virginia radio stations—filled some of its time with live country music programs, including Texas Slim and his Prairie Buckeroos, Richard Cox and the Harvesters, and briefly, bluegrass pioneers Ralph and Carter Stanley and the Clinch Mountain Boys. Several groups performed live on a *Saturday Night Jamboree* that flourished for more than a decade, ranking as the ninth most popular show in the region by 1956. Another country music show that thrived on WSAZ and other regional stations featured Lester Flatt and Earl Scruggs and the Foggy Mountain Boys. Sponsored by Martha White Mills, the group appeared live Monday through Thursday at 6:00 PM on an Appalachian circuit that included Chattanooga, Knoxville, Bluefield, and Huntington. On Friday they alternated among television stations in Wheeling, Parkersburg, and Clarksburg. On Saturday night the band played the "Grand Ole Opry" in Nashville. Buddy Starcher performed the most popular live country show in Charleston with a one- or two-hour morning slot on WCHS-TV in the early 1960s. Other television stations in the state also featured live country programs in the early days, but WHIS-TV in Bluefield had the longest running country show, featuring Cecil Surratt and Smitty Smith, from 1955 to 1969, and a wider variety of live programs than any other West Virginia station.[73]

WOAY, channel 4 in Oak Hill, programmed live country music after going on the air in December 1954, notably Rex and Eleanor Parker, who sang country gospel music.[74] WOAY also developed one of the unique and popular programs of the era in southern West Virginia, broadcasting live wrestling from Fayetteville. Viewers enjoyed the mayhem and blood, although most probably knew that much of it was staged, and that the red splatters involved more red dye or beet juice than real blood. Some wrestlers did use devices to produce shallow but bloody skin cuts. Shirley Love, who did the announcing and helped produce these contests (and also later became a state senator), recalls that they rigged his table at ringside to fly apart when struck by a gladiator tossed from the ring. Love himself occasionally became entangled with the wrestlers. Policemen (usually off-duty officers hired for the purpose) would sometimes have to be called in to escort overenthusiastic fans out of the building. WOAY also developed its own version of *American Bandstand*, inviting high school students to its studio for a televised Saturday dance party.[75]

Unfortunately, the amount of local live television programming would fade in the mid-1960s as competition from networks and syndicated programs made it difficult to compete. Except for news and sports programming, most locally produced programs faded from the airwaves. As country music historian Ivan Tribe has noted, technology and changing times sounded the death knell for this brief period of local television creativity in the 1950s and early 1960s, which went the way of "the village opera house, vaudeville, silent films, and live radio."[76]

How did television affect West Virginians? One is tempted to conclude that watching serials such as *I Love Lucy* or *Leave it to Beaver* or network news shows like John Cameron Swayze's the *Camel News Caravan* on NBC (or the *Huntley-Brinkley Report* after 1956) or *Douglas Edwards with the News* on CBS made West Virginians part of what Canadian critic Marshall McLuan called a global village, a common point of departure that, for better or worse, diminished provinciality and regional idiosyncrasies and helped to standardize tastes. Students of popular culture, however, have long debated the national impact of television with little consensus except to suggest that Americans in the 1950s and later strongly resisted the homogenized culture that television constantly set before them.[77] In *Yesterday's People*, Presbyterian minister Jack E. Weller (who strongly reinforced the culture of poverty idea) claimed that in the southern West Virginia area where he served, mountaineer families at first resisted television as an evil influence, but, he said, "now almost every home has in its central room the very symbol of the outside world, drumming its wares into every ear and flashing them before every eye." A coworker claimed that television did more "to change the ideas of the mountain people in ten years than the church has done in a generation."[78]

Two concrete points can be made about West Virginia and television. In 1956, a telegenic young man from Tyler County, Cecil Harland Underwood, found the medium useful in his effort to reverse the long domination of the Governor's Mansion by Democrats (as further discussed in the next chapter), and his success had a lasting impact on the practice of politics in West Virginia, making the old courthouse-based politics less important, weakening party machines, and—especially in statewide races—enhancing the chances of the well-financed candidate who could exploit television. Also, from time to time, the state's paradoxical image attracted the cameras of the networks just as it did print journalists, usually when bad things happened. Robert G. Sherrill of *The Nation* would maintain in the 1960s (in the aftermath of the Hominy Falls and Farmington mine disasters, as will be seen in chapter 7) that television helped transform the alleged fatalistic tendencies of West Virginia coal miners and turned them into rebels when they saw their issues reported and their leaders' true character revealed by the "drama-hunting cameras of national television." Though Sherrill overemphasized Appalachian fatalism and underemphasized the long incubation period of the miners' complaints, it seems likely that television helped stir the miners' revolt just as it would help build grassroots opposition to the Vietnam War by bringing the horrors of war into the living rooms of American viewers. Because it invited exploitation by those with the deepest pockets, television also provided a means for well-financed corporations and politicians to influence popular views on such things as surface mining, making it difficult for poorly funded public interest and grassroots organizations to compete in critical public issue debates.[79]

The Great Migration: Leaving "Those Hills, the Place I Call Home"

Despite evidence of middle-class West Virginians' adaptations to the new machine age, in the areas of greatest economic distress, many miners, farmers, factory workers, and others who saw no hope in staying resumed the exodus of the war period. This movement of West Virginians constituted part of what is known as the Great Migration, the period from 1940 to 1960 when more than 7 million people left Appalachia and only 3 million moved in, leaving a net loss in population of 4 million.[80] In the 1950s West Virginia experienced a net loss of 145,131 residents, 7.2 percent of the population, and the exodus continued into the 1960s. The Great Migration had its antecedents in the decline of the big logging boom of the early part of the century, and in the many farmers who wearied of trying to scratch a living out of mountain farms and left for better opportunities in farming elsewhere, became full-time coal miners, or found work in steel mills or other industries in other states. During the Great Depression, when it seemed cities and factories of other states offered no hope to those who sought a better life, many who had left in earlier migrations came back to the land, briefly reversing the trend. A substantial migration took place during World War II, though many of those who left during the war returned afterward, and the 1950 census showed some increase over 1940. As the exodus resumed in the 1950s, forty of the fifty-five counties lost population, and rural and coalfield counties lost the most. Rural Tucker lost almost 27 percent and Pocahontas 19 percent. McDowell led the coalfield counties, losing some 27,528, about 28 percent of its population. The Ohio River counties, the Kanawha Valley, the Northern Panhandle (except for Ohio County), and the Eastern Panhandle registered gains, but not enough to offset losses elsewhere.[81] These departures devastated the towns and counties losing population, draining the tax base and thereby further impoverishing those left behind. Single persons and young families—often better educated than those who stayed—made up the bulk of the migrants, but they often found they had less education and fewer skills than those they settled among in other states, making for difficult adjustments for some of those who left.[82]

Appalachian migrants tended to move to areas where they had contact with previous migrants, sometimes kinsmen. Kentucky people often went to the southwestern Ohio cities of Cincinnati, Hamilton, and Dayton. Western West Virginians more often headed to central and northeastern Ohio cities such as Columbus, Akron, and Cleveland. Those from eastern West Virginia favored Pittsburgh, Baltimore, or the District of Columbia. These migratory trends persisted, and by the end of the 1960s, Cleveland and Akron had become "West Virginia cities" and Hamilton and Cincinnati "Kentucky cities."[83]

The story of the Great Migration has as many chapters as the number of people who left, and all are rich in human interest. Bynum "Junior" Gilbert, a veteran of both the Depression-era Civilian Conservation Corps and the Navy of World War II, returned from the war to a hand-loading job in a Raleigh County coal mine. He later told an interviewer that hand loaders resented the cutting machine operators as the machines began to take over. He said the machine jobs usually went to "company sucks." Then bad times hit and many lost their jobs:

The coal business went bad here in 1952 or 1953. There wasn't much work anywhere. If you didn't want your family to starve, you had to take off for where the work was. That meant going to Cleveland or Chicago or Detroit. We packed the kids in the car and went to Cleveland since one of my buddies said that they were hiring at the Fisher body plant. Sure enough, I got a job there.

On a visit home in the summer of 1956, Gilbert got a job as a cutting machine operator at Helen and moved his family back from Cleveland. Gilbert paid a heavy price for his return to West Virginia. Eventually he suffered a severe leg injury in a roof fall and developed a breathing impairment. The doctor called it silicosis, but it was probably pneumoconiosis, black lung disease.[84] Many migrants shuttled back and forth between the Midwest and their mountain homes, sometimes on a seasonal basis. Historian Chad Berry tells of a West Virginian who went to Chicago in 1950 to look for work, hoping to save money and return home when things looked up. He continued to travel back and forth for a decade. In 1960, despairing of a permanent recovery in West Virginia, he finally moved his family to Chicago.[85]

Although the feelings of the migrants as expressed in interviews and memoirs are impressions measured by no science, leaving their homes in the hills and valleys and towns and coal camps of the Mountain State often proved a painful experience. Many who left hoped to return; and the friends and families they left behind expected to welcome them home someday. Few could ever again find adequate employment "back home" (as they universally spoke of it), so they tried to adjust to life and labor in different places, and many longed for the homes and the people they had left behind. Some of those who left fleeing the consequences of the new machine age in the hills would find reason to return when their adopted homes would suffer similar problems. Some who left the hard times in the mountains adjusted to life in other places and never wanted to return.[86] Berry cites the example of Ozzie Stroud who grew up in

Mingo County, realizing even as an adolescent that he would have to leave home when he finished school, a reality faced by many young people of Appalachia. Stroud's family struggled, because his father, a coal miner, had suffered a disabling injury and had trouble getting help from Social Security. Stroud later recalled that the only choices in Mingo were "you either worked in the coal mines, or you was a schoolteacher, school bus driver, or you was on welfare." Though he reluctantly left Mingo County as soon as he graduated, he adjusted well to life and work in Chicago and Columbus, telling an interviewer: "You know, life seemed to open up after you got out of the state of West Virginia."[87] Generally, according to historian Berry's account, the evidence from the peak years of the Great Migration, 1945–1960, shows that the white blue-collar migrants from the South to the Midwest adjusted well to the move as their economic status had become by the end of the period indistinguishable from their Midwestern blue-collar neighbors'. The early migrants had faced criticisms and negative stereotyping in the cities to which they moved, largely because of the difficulties brought about by the flood of southern migrants in World War II. Later, as they became the cheap labor that fueled the economic boom of the 1950s, hiring supervisors and journalists began to speak and write more positively of the migrants, revising the old stereotypes. The negative stereotypes persisted, but revisionist scholarship has made a solid case that Appalachian migrants did well economically by migrating.[88]

The rate of black migration, closely tied to the decline in mining employment (as further discussed in chapter 3) exceeded that of white migration. An African American miner of Raleigh County, Willie Collins, one of few (like Gilbert) to lose his mining job, leave, and return to mine again, received his cut-off slip in 1953. He left his wife and six children to go to Ohio to look for work. "The thing I could never figure out," Collins later recalled, "was how the rest of the country was making money hand over fist, things were booming, and down here everybody was out of work." In Ohio Collins found a job washing cars, but made just enough to live on. He hated the cold weather and finally "just picked up and come home" where he and his wife raised a garden, did odd jobs, and drew a small unemployment check until he went back to work in the mines in 1955.[89]

More often, those who left could return only for brief and often melancholy visits. Carl E. Feather recalls the end of a typical visit to his parents' Tucker County home in Sissaboo Hollow from Kingsville Township, Ohio, where he grew up but which his family never called home:

> The hollow faded quickly in the rearview mirror as we headed north on Route 219, our image of home blurred by the tears, our hearts aching from the fresh reopening of departing's scar. But there were no opportunities in this hollow, no Ford plants, natural gas company garages, or bustling railroad yards to feed the children, pay the mortgage, and heat the house with fuels conveniently delivered to concealed furnaces.

Feather's account suggests that the longing for the lost home extended to the second generation, those who grew up elsewhere.[90] Chad Berry also notes the persistence of "the divided heart," the yearning for a return to where their ancestors were buried. Some Appalachians who did well in exile returned to their homeland when they retired.[91]

Hazel Dickens, who became something of a songstress of the Appalachian diaspora, grew up the daughter of a Mercer County Primitive Baptist preacher who farmed a bit and used his truck to haul timbers for the mines (to be used in shoring up the overhead) and coal for the miners to heat their homes. In about 1951, at age 16, Hazel, one of eleven children, left home, and living with older siblings in Baltimore, supported herself waiting tables in restaurants, working as a retail clerk, and in textile mills, a tin can factory, and an electric iron plant. Better than any social scientist's statistics, she captured the lament of the exile when she wrote and recorded for Rounder Records "West Virginia, My Home" with the refrain:

> West Virginia, oh my home
> West Virginia, where I belong:
> In the dead of night
> In the still and the quiet
> I slip away like a bird in flight
> Back to those hills, the place that I call home.[92]

Conclusion

Throughout Appalachia and West Virginia (the one state most thoroughly Appalachian) the new machines of the post-World War II era brought economic and social disruption even as the nation enjoyed "the biggest boom yet" and "grand expectations." The revolution in the coal industry, replacing coal diggers with machine operators and tying health and retirement benefits to production, drove the changes, which imperiled the environment, the health, and the employment of the mountaineers. Whether coal miners, railroad workers, builders, textile workers, glass manufacturers, mountain farmers—indeed in almost all job categories in the state—unemployment came in startling numbers and made the area, in the catchphrase of the time, "a pocket of poverty." Whether in Chester or Canebrake, Martinsburg or Ceredo, economic and social issues multiplied, including for too many, joblessness and poverty. Far from being fatalistic, most West Virginians hoped for a better day, and increasing numbers, often the best, the brightest, and the youngest, usually reluctantly, sought it elsewhere—and many, overcoming negative stereotypes about hillbillies and mountaineers, found what they sought. Though logic would suggest that those who stayed might have been more apathetic and less hopeful, the 1958 survey sponsored by the Ford Foundation found that Appalachian residents who stayed behind had high aspirations for their children and believed that the status quo could be changed for the better.[93] Some, trapped by unemployment, poverty, debilitating injuries, ill health, and other consequences of the new machine age, did become dependent on welfare payments. Others, though, clearly rejected fatalism, and, as residents of the region did during the Great Depression, ultimately joined grassroots activist organizations to try to bring order and justice to their lives. In addition to the dominance of absentee-owned corporations, and the foreclosure of options by a pattern of absentee land ownership, the next chapter examines another, closely related obstacle to change in West Virginia—a state government with an outmoded constitution, a spoils-based bureaucracy, a well-earned reputation for corruption, and a tendency to represent best the most powerful economic interests of the new machine age, often at the expense of the general welfare.

2

American Paradox, Appalachian Stereotype

A veritable chain of weather-worn, moth-eaten towns from Chester to Canebrake have lost touch with progress.

Charleston Gazette, October 12, 1958

You must remember that we're going through a violent industrial revolution—with few of the things other states have to cushion the shock. It'll be all right eventually, but it sure is a hell of a rough ride along the way.

Unidentified West Virginian quoted by Roul Tunley,
Saturday Evening Post, February 6, 1960

The Appalachian reality ran counter to the ebullient national mood of the 1950s. A "politics of consensus" accompanied the growing national affluence. The Taft-Hartley Act, the Cold War, the Korean War, McCarthyism, and the politics of anticommunism further put a chill on the kind of reform and union activism that had marked the 1930s and the New Deal era. The prevailing mood discouraged reform or protests against racism, sexism, the persistent poverty of those who did not share in the affluence, the new industrial workplace dangers, and environmental adversities in Appalachia and elsewhere. The American people enjoyed the cars, television, movies, consumer appliances, and other benefits of a new prosperity even as they worried about communism, both domestic and foreign, and "automation."[1]

While the general culture basked in prosperity's glow, the American dream fell short of reality for many in the mountains of Appalachia. The survey of the Southern Appalachian region sponsored by the Ford Foundation at the close of the 1950s suggested that in rural Appalachia the persistence of "familism" in the face of the technological revolution retarded the development of complex organizational systems typical of the more industrialized parts of the United States. In matters of state and local government, education, health care, and "providing for the social and economic welfare of those who are inevitably socially dispossessed in an era of rapid change," the survey concluded, the region had failed to keep pace with national standards.[2] In truth, an exploitative system of absentee land and resource ownership, the impact of the new machine age, and the demands of the global economy had more to do with Appalachia's ills than familism or fatalism or other academic, journalistic, and political diagnoses of what ailed the region. By the end of the 1950s, in part because it was the one state most completely Appalachian and maybe also because urban journalists could more readily access it, West Virginia began to attract attention as an "American paradox," a state left behind by the nation's progress, exemplifying many of the shortcomings of Appalachian development as perceived by the broader culture and as defined by the Appalachian survey and metropolitan observers.[3]

The Alienation of the Land

One of the critical problems of Appalachia—the system of extensive absentee land ownership—had its roots in land speculation dating to colonial and revolutionary times. Much of the territory won through the exertions of Euro-American pioneers (and at the expense of Native Americans) fell into the hands of land companies and shrewd speculators, many of them prominent men of the late eighteenth century. George Washington, for example, took advantage of the French and Indian War to engross some 33,000 acres along the Ohio and Kanawha rivers by buying up military warrants issued to veterans of that conflict. Similarly in the Revolutionary era, the land won by the blood and treasure of many generally fell into the clutches of a few speculators, many of whom never saw the land they claimed. Virginia's post-revolutionary land policies tended to favor the speculators at the expense of pioneer settlers. The state made several vast land grants in the Trans-Allegheny region, and speculators, seized by a near mania, engrossed thousands of acres more. Prominent politicians and eastern merchants vied with one another in accumulating wilderness empires in what would become West Virginia and Kentucky.[4] Appalachian scholar Wilma A. Dunaway's analysis of county tax lists has revealed that by 1800 a few distant speculators had engrossed 93.3 percent of the acreage of West Virginia, leaving very little to actual settlers.[5]

The vagaries of Virginia land law and the post-Revolutionary speculative boom also resulted in extensive legal haggling over land titles, making it difficult for pioneer settlers and yeomen farmers to defend their holdings against the speculators. The insecurity in titles discouraged settlers and led many to go elsewhere, contributing to the paucity of population. A small population that owned few of the wealth-producing resources could not adequately address economic, political, and educational problems. The absentee owners had little interest in the problems faced by the few residents of the area and consequently resisted taxes and public improvements favored by residents. In his study of the period, West Virginia historian Otis Rice concluded that the early Virginia land system and its consequences laid the basis for an economic exploitation "such as few areas of the United States have experienced. Armed with laws which placed no restraint upon their greed, the speculators—the economic royalists of the post-Revolutionary generation—planted the seeds which in the mid-twentieth century bore bitter fruit in the form of Appalachia."[6]

A study financed by the Appalachian Regional Commission in 1978 and undertaken by the Appalachian Alliance (a federation of fifty regional organization created at a meeting in Williamson, West Virginia, in May 1977) demonstrated to no one's surprise that the pattern of absentee ownership established in the eighteenth century persisted into the twentieth. The modern-day descendants of the early land companies and speculators were large land and mining corporations that controlled most of the land and mineral resources in several Appalachian counties. Like their ancestors, twentieth-century absentees paid little in taxes and showed no interest in the social infrastructure of roads, schools, and other public facilities so important to the general well-being of a people. Absentee ownership meant a restricted tax base with the burden of taxation and the hopes of progress resting on the backs of local residents, who owned few of the wealth-producing resources.[7]

Horse-and-Buggy Vestiges

At mid-twentieth century, a time when the state needed thoughtful and innovative responses to the challenges of the new machine age, like others in Appalachia, it suffered not only from the problems of absentee ownership but it also carried the burden of obsolescent horse-and-buggy institutions that made it difficult to break from the status quo. In the rest of Appalachia, mountain counties found themselves minorities without influence, ignored by low-country state politicians except when their votes might be useful in an election. In West Virginia, all counties were Appalachian, so the state, having escaped the lowlander-highlander dichotomy in the Civil War, had the potential to fashion a policy that might benefit all, but the topography nevertheless created divisions among the Mountain State's highlanders.[8]

Unfortunately, like other states in the region, West Virginia relied on an outdated constitution that had been crafted by conservatives as something of a counterrevolutionary document in the era of Reconstruction. Equally eager to minimize the powers of state government, to promote railroads, and to exploit the rich natural resources of the state, the constitution they wrote provided for a dual executive branch with power divided between a weak governor and a board of control which had budget-preparation authority.[9] By the 1950s it had become a sprawling, jury-rigged government structure ill-equipped to marshal the state's limited resources to meet the problems of the new age. Lack of an effective central accounting authority contributed to the marked frequency of malfeasance, and the persistence of patronage politics hindered the development of a professional civil service. The state also had fifty-five mostly small counties, many with inadequate resources or the capacity to properly fulfill their constitutional duties.[10]

As the Appalachian survey pointed out, counties arose before the automobile age. In an era of slow and difficult travel, access to the county seat had to be determined primarily by how long it took to ride a horse there from the most distant reaches. By the 1950s, when neighboring county seats often were within less than two hours drive time, many Appalachian counties lacked adequate sources of income to carry out their functions and dissipated public funds in an unnecessary duplication of offices, which of course helped to perpetuate local political machines. The office of sheriff, steeped in politics, offered the chief reward to aspiring county politicians, whether compensated by fee or salary. In addition to responsibilities for keeping the peace and tax collection, sheriffs also had responsibility for the county jails. When the Federal Bureau of Prisons carried out a survey of West Virginia jails in 1946, it found them "anachronisms in our social order." "The majority of them are totally unfit for human habitation," the prison survey concluded.[11] The description still fit county jails in much of southern Appalachia at the beginning of the 1960s. Just as the state government had divided executive power, the counties had no real executive as the constitution assigned the chief powers of county government to an elected three- to five-person county court. The survey of Appalachia suggested that many of the functions of Appalachian counties could be more effectively carried out by regional bodies, but it held out little hope that consolidation of counties or even of jails could be achieved in West Virginia or elsewhere in Appalachia.[12]

In the 1950s, as unemployment grew, some families subsisted on government programs such as Aid to Families with Dependent Children. Coal miners or their widows also drew small pensions from the UMWA's Health and Retirement Funds, and some drew social security retirement checks. Families receiving an income of $130 or less became eligible for monthly rations of flour, cornmeal, rice, butter, and cheese to supplement their meager resources. County politicians came to control the distribution of the monthly welfare checks and commodities, enhancing their ability to influence local patronage, perpetuate their own power, and to maintain the status quo. Many local politicians also had long-standing ties with absentee landowners and corporations and worked to protect those interests. Under such a system, few residents actively participated in politics, and little incentive for change existed.[13]

The state's system of taxation reflected the long-standing influence of the major corporate interests, heirs of the speculative absentee owners of the revolutionary period. Despite the state's wealth in natural resources, little had redounded to the benefit of the citizens. West Virginia's government had struggled through most of its history with inadequate revenues to support needed public services such as schools, roads, and state institutions. A great deal of wealth left the state with the removal of natural resources by timber, railroad, and mining interests largely controlled by nonresident corporations. At the beginning of the twentieth century, the West Virginia Tax Commission, moved by the progressive trends of the day, had made a modest proposal for a severance tax as a way to modernize the state's financial and administrative structure. The rise of industry placed growing requirements on state government, and the tax commission sought a way to raise the revenue to support needed public services. Even the small tax sought by a commission dominated by the business elite aroused bitter opposition from the local representatives of non-resident corporate interests. The defeat of the severance tax proposals in the Progressive Era meant that the state's resources "would continue to be exploited, not developed, chiefly for benefit of nonresident corporations."[14]

In 1932, in the midst of the Great Depression, voters eager for "tax relief" approved a tax limitation amendment to the state constitution. The amendment, written by politicians eager for votes, transformed the system of taxation by placing limits on the various categories of property taxes. The measure had several enduring consequences. Because counties and cities had relied heavily on property taxes, it severely limited the tax base of local government and shifted primary responsibility for education, roads, and relief of the destitute from local governments to the government in Charleston. It also severely restricted the property tax altogether (a great boon to the nonresident property owners who controlled most of the state's riches in natural resources). Thereafter only Alabama among the Appalachian states relied less on the property tax than West Virginia. To finance its expanded responsibilities, the state imposed a complicated mix of largely indirect and regressive taxes, principally the consumer sales tax, which derived little from the principal wealth of the state. The new sources of revenue failed to make up for the lost revenue under the old system. Moreover the new system left the state and its subdivisions with chronically under-financed public services in meeting the problems of the post-war era.[15] One way to wring more revenue out of the property tax would have been to increase property assessment ratios, but a tax commission set up by Governor William C. Marland in 1954 found that 37 of the 55 counties had lower assessments in 1953 than in 1932. The commission concluded: "In West Virginia, property is valued erratically, taxed lightly, and distributed unevenly."[16]

Discussions of the tax burden in West Virginia would be incomplete without taking into account the impact of the notoriously corrupt political culture of the state, which could be construed as an informal hidden tax. The obsolescent structure of county government and the connection of many courthouse lawyers and local real estate agents with absentee landowners tended to encourage the development of local bosses, courthouse gangs, and patronage machines. On the state level, the Democratic majority, riven by factions and largely committed to the coal industry and other dominant economic forces, could neither formulate nor sustain a consistent program. The Republican opposition offered formulaic assertions of conservative bromides that largely reflected the wishes of business executives, many of whom communicated with their local allies from out of state headquarters. Both parties relied on funding from the state's major economic interests and resisted any policy that might threaten those interests, and too many of both parties looked to fatten their own wallets at the expense of public interests. West Virginia earned the reputation as a state where both Democrats and Republicans routinely bought votes. In 1946, editor Carey McWilliams of *The Nation* magazine wrote after a visit to the state: "It would be accurate to say that there are rotten boroughs in West Virginia, but it would be closer to the truth to say that the state itself is a rotten borough."[17]

Sixteen years later, in his classic account of the 1960 presidential election, journalist Theodore H. White included the state among those whose politics were "the most squalid, corrupt, and despicable."[18] Covering the 1960 Democratic primary in the state, *Look* magazine described "the tangy flavor of local election practices which can confound any out-of-state politician." *Life* quoted Logan County lawyer Dan Dahill: "With $5,000 you can elect a man to any office except sheriff. This costs $40,000." Successful candidates "contributed" certain fees to be listed on the "slate" of the machine. As Dahill further described the system, for $2.00 to $5.00 local voters disinclined to decide for themselves left the casting of their ballots to election commissioners, called "Lever Brothers" (in reference to a major soap company of the day), because they pulled the lever in the voting booth. Voters could also be persuaded with moonshine or half-pints, which, though illegal in West Virginia, campaigners could purchase across the border in Kentucky.[19]

Despite the prevailing political culture and the institutional obstacles, the governors of the 1950s, driven by the stark realities of collapse before them, sometimes offered innovative ideas to deal with critical issues of schools, roads, health care, and social welfare, but the weakness of the office, the predominance of a culture of graft, and the commitment of the state's major economic powers to the status quo made effective responses to the problems of the decade by the state and local institutions nearly impossible.

The Patteson Era

In 1948, as Harry S. Truman surprised the pundits by defeating Thomas E. Dewey in the presidential election, Okey Patteson, an automobile dealer from Mount Hope in Fayette County, defeated Republican Herbert S. Boreman for governor, extending the Democrats' domination of the state government that began in 1933. Climbing the typical rungs of the political ladder in the state, Patteson had served as president of the Fayette County Court during the Great Depression and as sheriff during the war. He headed the state Democratic campaign effort in 1944 and served as executive assistant to Governor Clarence Meadows from January 15, 1945, to January 1, 1948.[20] Patteson had lost his legs in a hunting accident as a young man, and his personal determination in dealing with his disability impressed voters and reminded them of Franklin D. Roosevelt's struggles with the crippling effects of polio.[21]

During the Patteson era, before the economic disaster of the 1950s struck, the state took promising steps toward addressing the problems in transportation, education, and medical care, but some critical decisions made at the time proved to be shortsighted. In the 1948 election the voters approved a badly needed $50 million bond issue to improve farm-to-market roads. Both primary and secondary roads had deteriorated badly during the war years, and severe winters and floods in the immediate post-war years contributed to further deterioration and rising maintenance needs. The state road commission warned that most primary roads needed to be rebuilt. During the next four years the state tried to make up for long neglect of its secondary roads, building almost 3,000 miles of new secondary roads and building or repairing more than 600 bridges.[22] The improvement of rural roads, though considered by the state road commission only "a drop in the bucket" compared to what needed to be done, also had unintended consequences. Short-run railroad passenger lines that had once provided the main mode of transportation for many rural West Virginians found they could no longer maintain operations as more people turned to automobiles.[23] As roads improved and more rural families owned cars, the young people tended to look away from farm life. Also small churches faded, as rural families drove to growing congregations in towns, and many small schools disappeared as, with motorized transportation, it made sense to consolidate schools.[24]

West Virginia also sought to build a superhighway to traverse the state and to link with other roads being planned in the post-war period to create a North-South highway from Virginia to the Great Lakes. In 1947 the legislature authorized the building of a turnpike "with multiple lanes in each direction" separated by a safety island. The road would link Charleston with southern counties and put West Virginia in the middle of the projected North-South road. Two years later Governor Patteson established the West Virginia Turnpike Commission, a state agency charged with building and operating the 88-mile toll road between Princeton, at the southern end of the state, and Charleston, the state capital, to the northwest. The road probably could not have been built except by the sale of bonds and the charging of tolls, but the means of financing gave investment bankers, not legislators, the last word on the kind of road to be built. Because of the difficult terrain and high cost per mile of building a four-lane road through West Virginia, financial advisers representing the major investment banks insisted that the commission trim the project to two lanes. To be able to sell the bonds, the Turnpike Commission felt it had to surrender to the bankers' wishes, but would design the turnpike for the possibility of later broadening. On the basis of the revised plan the Commission sold $96 million in bonds and awarded construction contracts. Governor Patteson, however, insisted that the legislation required that the highway be four lanes and ordered all work stopped. The Guaranty Trust Company of New York brought suit to compel the Turnpike Commission to proceed with construction. Federal district court judge Ben Moore upheld the Turnpike Commission's scaled-down construction plan and confirmed the victory of the investment bankers. Construction resumed, but even with the two-lane plan, the commission had to sell another $37 million in bonds, bringing the total cost to $133 million, almost tripling the amount the state had committed to spend on roads in the rest of the state.²⁵

Builders of the West Virginia Turnpike (completed in 1954) used innovative technology to traverse some of the most rugged topography in the United States, but as a two-lane road, it fell short of the conventional notion of a twentieth-century superhighway. This section, north of Long Branch, Fayette County, shows sandstone, one of the most difficult materials to drill and cut. West Virginia and Regional History Collection, West Virginia Libraries.

Trimming the plans for building the turnpike made it possible to get the support of investment bankers, but it assured that the road would be immediately outmoded and incompatible with the four-lane interstate highway system that began to develop later in the decade. Also West Virginia's turnpike would not match the standards of older state turnpikes such as the New Jersey or Pennsylvania. Nevertheless, the turnpike opened in 1954 to great acclaim for its cutting-edge technology. Called by builders "the toughest road job east of the Rockies," it used techniques never before used in the East. It featured seventy-six bridges, a tunnel, gentle grades and slight curves and a nearly straight passage through terrain where most roads "twist and turn like an enraged rattler," as an engineer of the Automotive Safety Foundation put it. It seemed an anomaly, a turnpike with only two lanes and no divider whose cost per mile nearly equaled the cost for four lanes in other states, a highly innovative road that fell short in some important particulars of what conventional wisdom mandated a modern superhighway should be. Its toll rates almost doubled those of the Pennsylvania Turnpike. Despite the rates, interstate truckers loved it. It saved twenty-two miles and two hours driving time between the Virginia border and Charleston, eliminating long hard pulls on narrow and serpentine mountain roads, making the toll well worth the cost for truckers. It did nothing, however, for travelers or shippers in other parts of the state, and southern West Virginians complained that the tolls they had to pay to travel the road to their state capital unfairly taxed them.[26]

Others, nevertheless, hoped that the north-south turnpike would soon be followed by an east-west line with an ambitious ultimate goal. Leading citizens of the small eastern mountain city of Elkins (the county seat of Randolph County) organized the Crozet Super Highway Commission in the hope that the next step would be the building of a turnpike from Harpers Ferry in the Eastern Panhandle across the state to Huntington via Wardensville, Moorefield, Elkins, Sutton, and Charleston. They named it Crozet in honor of Claudius Crozet, an early nineteenth-century Virginian road builder. In 1954 D. D. Brown of Elkins sent a proposal of the Crozet Commission to the President's Advisory Committee on a National Highway Program. It called for a national turnpike from Boston to San Diego that would pass through Elkins.[27] Though the Crozet Superhighway remained but an ambitious dream, it represented the yearning of West Virginians to fully join the age of the automobile and superhighways.

Within a decade of its completion, the West Virginia Turnpike's deficiencies became apparent. In 1965 the *Charleston Gazette* expressed a widespread sense that the turnpike had been an embarrassment almost from the beginning. Not only did it remain for many years only two lanes for most of its length, the rough surface of concrete slabs separated by expansion joints rattled travelers and their vehicles, promised improvements came slowly, and it became statistically the most dangerous turnpike in the country.[28]

The building of new secondary roads with the 1948 bond money and the opening of the turnpike on November 8, 1954, inspired hopes that the state might finally be on the way to solving its road problems. Neither the bond issue nor the turnpike, however, adequately compensated for the years of neglect. Much of the bond issue money went to pave, repair, and maintain previously built roads. Rising costs of materials, equipment, and manpower, expenditures to deal with snow removal during harsh winters, roads washed out by spring floods, and the corrosive effects of a rising volume of heavy truck traffic limited the effect of the $50 million bond issue, which turned out to be far less than was needed. In 1953, a lame duck Governor Patteson told the legislature that engineers estimated that it would take "at least six hundred million dollars to build sufficient all-weather roads in our state."[29]

Patteson's engineers' estimate missed the mark by at least half. The following year a legislative committee investigating the State Road Commission authorized a survey of West Virginia's road problems by the Automotive Safety Foundation. At a time when the race was on among the states to build ever-better roads, the ASF found West Virginia to be at a severe disadvantage because of unique conditions that made the average per mile cost higher than in any other state. The ASF listed the challenges that made the Mountain State a road builder's nightmare, especially noting the rugged terrain extending over most of the state. The ASF engineers described West Virginia's road-building problems as being more difficult than even in the Rocky Mountain states where road builders faced an easier task because of the straighter streams, valleys, and passes. "In West Virginia," one of the engineers complained, "you can't even find a straight valley to follow." The ASF study concluded that it would take at least a billion dollars to make needed upgrades in the state's road system.[30]

As many states with a less challenging topography upgraded roads, making them more attractive to various manufacturers who needed reliable roads to ship their goods, West Virginia struggled to build and maintain roads in the face of a much higher cost per mile. The number of miles upgraded, the level of maintenance, and the state of art of the roads built kept West Virginia behind other states in the improvement of its system during the 1950s, as automobiles and trucking became increasingly important to the prevailing economic development doctrine of that era.[31]

Few at the time questioned whether the turnpike and the interstates that would soon follow represented the best investment for the people of the state, nor did the state have a clear-cut plan for maximizing road expenditures; but clearly the new super roads favored some interests over others. Nationally, urban critics like Lewis Mumford (*The City in History*, 1961) and John Keats (*The Insolent Chariots*, 1958) indicted the focus on super roads and indeed on the automobile and believed the impact on cities harmful. In the 1950s especially, as historian Kenneth T. Jackson has observed, "expressways represented progress and modernity, and mayors and public officials stumbled over themselves in seeking federal largesse for more and wider roads."[32] If the roads hurt cities, as the critics maintained, they also hastened the demise of Appalachian agriculture as they made the costs of farm products produced in other states cheaper for the West Virginia consumer than many local products. Some in West Virginia advocated better roads linking agricultural and industrial regions within the state rather than the construction of expressways connecting with other states. As early as 1949 the Beckley Area Rural Development Program sought to make an eleven-county southern region of the state more interconnected and self-sufficient by advocating east-west roads that would connect the western coal mining counties and agricultural counties to the east of Beckley. Such a linkage, its advocates believed, would bolster regional agriculture and eliminate the flow of mining area payroll monies to distant foodstuff suppliers.[33]

More careful attention to the building and improvement of the statewide network of primary and secondary roads or even of putting more of the road-building money into education might have been better options than the focus on throughways that hastened traffic through the state, giving employment to motel, restaurant, and service station employees who worked along the roadways, but providing slight benefit to struggling and decaying communities just a few miles from the new roads.

In addition to its efforts in road-building and maintenance, the Patteson administration also presided over the largest school construction program in the history of the state up to that time, supported increases in teachers' salaries to try to address a growing teacher shortage, and increased state aid to public schools. State colleges, having substantially expanded enrollments as a consequence of the GI Bill, received appropriations for expansion programs.[34] Calling attention to the "distressing shortage of doctors, dentists, and nurses," Patteson also strongly urged the legislature to establish a school of medicine, dentistry, and nursing at West Virginia University. In West Virginia there was only one doctor for every 1,400 residents. New veterans' hospitals at Beckley and Clarksburg stood idle, because not enough doctors and nurses could be hired to staff them. Public health nursing fell short of need by some 75 percent.[35]

Patteson's leadership overcame the sectional wrangling over the location and legislative fears of the cost for a school of medicine that had prevented action in the past. Despite arguments that it would be unfair to children, the legislature finally agreed that a tax on soft drinks would help finance the new school. Help also came from the Hill-Burton Hospital Survey and Construction Act, enacted by Congress in 1946 to provide matching federal funds for construction of hospitals in rural states. After legislators haggled over the question of where the medical school should be located without resolution, the legislation establishing the school empowered the governor to decide on the location. Governor Patteson solicited a variety of opinions from sources both within and outside the state. Some experts advised that the school be located in one of the larger cities closer to the center of population such as Huntington or Charleston. Patteson rejected that advice and decided to locate the school in Morgantown, the university city near the border with Pennsylvania, even though this would place the medical school at a considerable distance from major state population centers. The Morgantown location could take advantage of the university's academic departments and administrative structure, providing some short-term advantages. At the time, even critics of Patteson's decision credited him with the leadership that made the medical school a reality.[36]

Despite a substantial shortage in state hospital facilities, the federal Hill-Burton hospital construction program made the situation better than it might have been. The act encouraged the building of hospitals and medical schools in rural states with underserved populations by providing half the cost of construction.[37] Between 1946 and 1958, more than $64 million dollars went into West Virginia hospitals and other medical facilities under the Act, almost $42 million coming from state and local contributions. The facilities built included, in addition to the medical school at West Virginia University, general hospitals, tuberculosis centers, institutions for the treatment of the chronically ill, rehabilitation facilities, public health centers, a state laboratory, and nurses' training schools. Even with this substantial building program, in 1958 the state met only 48 percent of its hospital and medical facility needs based on Hill-Burton formulas.[38]

The United Mine Workers of America's system of clinics and hospitals in the period 1957 to 1964 also contributed to basic health care. As early as 1951 the UMWA's Welfare and Retirement Fund carried out a detailed examination of hospital care in the coalfields and found not only a shortage of hospital beds but also a lack of acceptable care. Of five hospitals in the Beckley area, for example, the Fund study concluded that only two, and to a limited extent, a third, provided adequate services. Moreover the hospitals employed closed staff practices that discouraged other doctors from locating in the area. Because of the overall shortage and inadequacy of hospitals in the central Appalachian area, the Fund decided to build its own, creating a nonprofit corporation, the Miners Memorial Hospital Association, to own and operate ten hospitals, including three in West Virginia at Beckley, Man, and Williamson. Unlike other hospitals in the region, the miners' hospitals sponsored outpatient clinics that did minor surgery, therapy and testing as well as routine physician care.[39] The Ford Foundation survey of the southern Appalachians focused on the UMWA system of hospitals as both a regional and national success story, but the very success of the program threw into "bold relief the plight of thousands of low income mountain families who are not employed in coal mining."[40]

McCarthyism: The Second Red Scare

McCarthyism, one of the major political distractions of the 1950s that contributed to the unwillingness to deal with American social problems, first emerged in West Virginia. During the early 1950s, West Virginians, like other Americans, worried about growing Cold

War tensions and the Korean War. Some wondered why, after the great sacrifices of World War II, the world continued to be a dangerous place and why the United States, the greatest military power, could not resolve world problems. On February 9, 1950, as part of a "Lincoln's Birthday Tour," Wisconsin senator Joseph McCarthy, in an address to the Ohio County Republican Women's Club at Wheeling, offered a simple explanation, launching his charges of Communist infiltration of the State Department and setting off the phenomenon known as McCarthyism. What precisely McCarthy said that day became controversial. In prepared remarks that he distributed upon arrival (with the notation that the content was subject to change) he said that he had a list of 205 names of communists "known to the Secretary of State and who are still working and shaping the policy of the State Department." Several reporters and others who heard the address and officials of WWVA radio, which broadcast the speech, signed affidavits that he used the figure 205 in his comments. McCarthy himself insisted that he said fifty-seven. Later he used the number eighty and the term "loyalty risks" rather than "communists." Whatever the number, he never shared the list, although he did have a version of the speech printed in the *Congressional Record*. The argument over how many never really mattered much. McCarthy's Wheeling speech mattered because it immediately attracted to his side an entourage of reporters eager to report his charges, catapulting a previously obscure senator to the center of national attention, fanning the flames of fear about communism, and giving a name to the excesses emanating from that fear.[41]

Just four months after McCarthy's momentous visit to Wheeling, nearby Weirton also bore witness to the ways in which self-interested patriotism could be put to use during the Cold War. From the days of the early New Deal, through World War II and the early postwar years, the Weirton Steel Company had become notorious as the lone major holdout against unionism in the steel industry, fighting off repeated organizing efforts of the United Steelworkers Union of America. The company founder, Ernest Weir, had always insisted that his company would tolerate neither unions nor New Deal-inspired labor-management practices. He saw New Deal liberalism and the labor movement as the chief threats to American democracy. Weirton Steel came to employ more workers than any other single enterprise in the state, and Weir and his associates in the management of the firm successfully held out against unionism by paying attractive wages, engaging in company welfare activities, maintaining a company organization (the Weirton Independent Union), and using an authoritarian management style. In 1947, with a population of about 25,000, Weirton (which had grown up around a village called Holliday Cove) became an incorporated city, "the home of the mighty tin can," and Weir's ally and associate, Thomas Millsop, became the mayor. With advancing years Weir retreated to Weir Lodge, his home above the town, and Millsop and others took up more of the active management of the company.[42]

In the summer of 1950, Weirton Steel faced a challenge to its labor practices, unique in the steel industry, as a federal court found it in violation of the Wagner Act, which prohibited company interference with the operations of a union. While the company appealed the ruling, Millsop, as both mayor and company president, sought to inoculate the community against the potential threat of an organizing drive by calling on all residents to engage in a weeklong celebration dedicated to preserving the American way of life. Weirton's celebration of Americanism Week took place beginning on June 20, 1950, with a parade, patriotic speeches, a pageant on the evolution of the American flag, and a "Fight Socialism-Communism Day." Similar patriotic demonstrations took place in many communities across the country at the height of the Cold War as a way of affirming American values in the face of the international threat of Communism and also as way for organizations like the National Association of Manufacturers and Chambers of Commerce, fearful of the resumption of New Deal reformism, to throw up barriers against liberalism and the labor movement. Weirton's Americanism festival embraced these general concerns but also drew specific motivation from the impending court appeal.[43]

On July 28, 1950, the U.S. Court of Appeals upheld the finding that Weirton Independent Union was company-dominated and that Weirton Steel had engaged in unfair labor practices. The Court ordered WIU to disband. Weirton Steel now had to allow the United Steel Workers to carry out an organizing drive. After the WIU disbanded, the Weirton Defense Committee, a coalition of merchants and businessmen closely tied to the Chamber of Commerce, organized the Independent Steelworkers Union (ISU) to contest USWA for the loyalty of the Weirton steelworkers. In an election conducted by the National Labor Relations Board on October 27, 1950, ISU won. The Freedoms Foundation, a patriotic group founded in 1949, named Weirton "Freedom Town, USA," commending the town, the company, and its founder for their contributions to freedom in 1950. The USWA never successfully organized Weirton Steel.[44]

Another notoriously bitter fight over unionization that reflected some of the tensions of the early 1950s took place in the coal industry at the Elk River Coal and Lumber Company in Clay County. There, company president Joseph Gardner "J. G." Bradley, much like Ernest Weir, fought New Deal liberalism with "welfare capitalism," providing workers with attractive houses, schools, and recreational facilities in the company town of Widen. After two failed attempts to organize in the New Deal era, the UMWA engaged in a long, divisive, sometimes violent, and ultimately unsuccessful attempt in the early 1950s. Only after Bradley sold the mine to Clinchfield Coal Company in 1959 did the UMWA succeed. In 1963, the mine closed and Widen, Bradley's model town, became another Appalachian ghost town.[45]

During Joseph McCarthy's rise, West Virginia senators Harley M. Kilgore and Matthew M. Neely opposed him, and Kilgore led the fight against the McCarran Internal Security Act, which required communists and other subversive groups to register with the Attorney General. Individuals in such groups would suffer substantial limitations of their rights as citizens. President Harry S. Truman, calling it the greatest danger to freedom of press, speech, and assembly since the Sedition Act of 1798, vetoed the measure. In the emotional atmosphere of the day, with McCarthy's charges resonating with a large part of the public and with the advent of the Korean War, in September 1950, Congress overwhelmingly passed the McCarran Act over the president's veto.[46]

Historian Charles H. McCormick provided an excellent case study of an incident in West Virginia that typified the spirit of the times, which McCormick prefers to label as the Second Red Scare rather than the age of McCarthyism. His account tells of the firing of art professor Luella Raab Mundel at Fairmont State College in 1951 and of her efforts, ultimately unsuccessful, to win her job back and to defend her reputation and academic freedom. The State Board of

Education, which then supervised the state college system, chose to dismiss Mundel despite the college president's recommendation that she be retained. Mundel had spoken out against some of the excesses of anticommunist speakers in meetings held in Fairmont. The Board acted on the recommendation of the board member from Fairmont who had been named by Senator Neely when he was governor. When Mundel sued for libel, Neely, the erstwhile crusader for liberal causes, successfully defended Mundel's accusers.[47]

In 1952 Gen. Dwight D. Eisenhower, the popular former commander of Allied Forces in Europe, defeated the Democratic candidate Adlai Stevenson, leading the Republican Party's successful effort to capture the White House for the first time since Herbert Hoover left office in 1933. The long reign of the Democrats in West Virginia continued, however, in spite of Eisenhower's victory and in the face of continued disunity in the state Democratic Party. The statehouse Democratic machine, as in the days before Matthew M. Neely had defeated the statehouse stalwarts of the Depression era, began to cooperate more closely with the coal industry, straining the ties between the Democrats and the United Mine Workers of America, although the national UMWA leadership itself now often found common ground with industrial leaders.[48]

In the 1952 Democratic primary, the UMWA refused to support the statehouse machine's candidate for governor, William Casey Marland, the 33-year-old attorney general. State UMWA leaders claimed that Patteson and Marland sided with coal operators, citing Patteson's support of legislation favored by the coal operators and noting that Marland's father, Joseph Wesley Marland, was superintendent of the Raleigh-Wyoming Mining Company's coal operations in Glen Rogers, Wyoming County. Marland, however, carried a membership card of the Glen Rogers UMWA Local No. 6004. After working around the mines as a laborer and slate picker during the summers of his youth, he joined the union in 1937, staying out of college for a year to work as a weigh boss inside the mine. A star athlete and valedictorian at Glen Rogers High School, he earned a football scholarship to the University of Alabama. He later went to law school at West Virginia University, postponing his graduation there with a stint in the Navy during World War II. In 1949, when the elected attorney general resigned, Governor Patteson appointed Marland, only two years out of law school, to fill the vacancy. In 1950 he won the election to fill the last two years of the unexpired term. In 1952 with the support of both Patteson and United States Senator Matthew M. Neely in the gubernatorial primary, Marland prevailed in the race for governor over both the UMWA's choice, sixth district congressman E. H. Hedrick, and Cyrus Kump, son of the former governor Guy Kump. In the general election Marland defeated Republican Rush Dew Holt, former United States senator (dubbed "the Boy Senator" when elected in 1934 six months shy of his thirtieth birthday) and former Democrat, in a hard-fought campaign. Holt drew considerable blood by hammering on the themes of corruption and mismanagement as General Eisenhower and the national Republican Party coined the phrase *K1, C2* (Korea, Communism, and corruption) in their successful effort to win the White House for the first time since Franklin D. Roosevelt defeated Herbert Hoover in 1932. The *Charleston Gazette*, usually pro-Democrat, supported Holt over Marland, but John L. Lewis brought the UMWA into line for the Democratic nominees, including Marland and Senator Harley Kilgore, who faced a challenge from former Republican senator Chapman Revercomb. Embracing McCarthyism wholeheartedly, Revercomb brought McCarthy back to the state where he had launched his anticommunist crusade to endorse and campaign for him. In a radio address, Revercomb charged that "Communists have infiltrated the nerve centers of our governmental, educational, and economic institutions" and that Senator Kilgore "has . . . aided, appeased, and sympathized with the Communist cause in America." He further charged that Kilgore's Communist sympathies had contributed to the deaths of American soldiers in Korea. Votes from the coalfield counties proved crucial to Marland as he managed to win by only 27,000 votes over Holt. McCarthy's political influence in West Virginia appeared slight, however, as Kilgore survived Revercomb's attempt to paint him as a Communist sympathizer and became the first West Virginia Democrat to win a third consecutive term as senator.[49]

"Like a Bolt of Lightning": Marland's Severance Tax Proposal

Governor Marland demonstrated unprecedented originality in presenting proposals to smash the paradigm that kept the state constantly struggling to keep up. Unfortunately his political skills fell short of his boldness, and he bungled the effort badly. Perhaps underestimating the political power of coal and its allied industries, he failed to lay the groundwork and to build support before he sprang his unprecedented proposals on an unsuspecting legislature. When the defenders of the coal industry responded negatively, he reacted intemperately. Even many of his original supporters, including former governor Patteson, turned their backs on him, and after a stormy first session, Governor Marland constantly found himself at odds with the Democratic majority in the legislature.[50]

Just three days after his inauguration, Marland stunned the legislature (Cecil Underwood, Marland's successor, later described it as "like a bolt of lightning"[51]) as he spelled out a plan that he believed would generate $23,250,000 to attack the basic problems of roads and schools. A one-cent-per-gallon increase in the gasoline tax would generate four million dollars and would go directly to the road fund. An increase in the state tax on pari-mutuel betting at horse tracks would raise $1,500,000, which would be devoted to the program for free textbooks in elementary schools. Marland saved the bombshell for last: a severance tax on natural resources, chiefly coal, which at ten cents per ton would generate $18,000,000.[52]

Governor Marland's efforts to address the revenue problem with a severance tax ignited a contentious debate that raged for two months. The United Mine Workers, the West Virginia Federation of Labor, the West Virginia CIO, the West Virginia Education Association, and all but one member of the state's seven-member congressional delegation supported Marland's plan. Arrayed against the plan were the coal industry, the West Virginia Chamber of Commerce, the Republican Party, conservative Democrats and many state newspapers. The *Charleston Gazette* blasted the governor's plan the day after he presented it, calling it an irresponsible notion that would destroy the coal industry in the state. Because of the new competition the coal industry faced, the *Gazette* charged, it would be economic suicide for the state to burden its chief industry with a new tax. Marland responded to the *Gazette*'s attack by claiming that the editorial policy of the *Gazette* reflected the wishes of the coal industry and its apologists, pointing out that the editorial board of the *Gazette* included Carl Andrews, secretary of the West Virginia Coal Operators Association. Marland noted that the consumer sales tax paid by citizens of the state generated almost three times the amount the coal industry contributed to the cost of government. As for property taxes cited by the *Gazette*, Marland said the industry paid far below its fair share because of the undervaluation of assessments. He also maintained that severance taxes paid to the state would become deductions on the federal income tax of coal operators, reducing by half or more the real cost per ton of the tax. Other mining states, he observed, required companies to pay corporate income taxes, and some, like Louisiana, already had severance taxes. He pointed out that the UMWA, representing the miners, those most directly affected by the fate of the coal industry, strongly supported the measure. As for the destruction of the Democratic Party, which the *Gazette* predicted should Marland's proposal be enacted into law, Marland argued that the party's failure would be more likely if it did not find a way to address the problems of roads and schools in the state. The confrontation between the *Gazette* and the governor established the basic issues of the debate in legislative hearings and on editorial pages of state newspapers. In the end, Marland could not persuade the legislative leaders of his own party to support his proposal. The finance committees of both houses failed to report out the bill. The House of Delegates administered the final blow on March 6, voting to postpone further consideration indefinitely.[53]

Counseled to put the tax proposal aside and to focus on cleaning up the State Road Commission, which many viewed as a corrupt organization that misused the substantial funds given it during the Patteson administration, Marland instead made an impassioned plea for the support of his tax plan, saying prophetically "whether we like it or not, West Virginia's hills will be stripped, the bowels of the earth will be mined, and the refuse strewn across our valleys and our mountains in the form of burning slate dumps."[54] Veteran *Charleston Daily Mail* political reporter Bob Mellace later recalled: "From then on it was downhill—it became Marland versus everybody else. It was almost a conspiracy to tear Bill Marland down."[55]

The abortive effort to enact a severance tax left Marland's administration and the Democratic Party in disarray at a critical time. Despite a large Democratic majority, the legislature opposed all the governor's major initiatives throughout his administration. As the problems of the decade multiplied, the state government, paralyzed by the standoff between Marland and the legislature, proved incapable of responding. Unable to accomplish his legislative goals, Marland devoted himself to advocating tax reform and to promoting industrial development. In January 1954, he announced the creation by executive order of the Governor's Commission on State and Local Finance. The commission hired Dr. John F. Sly of Princeton University as research consultant.[56] Sly, who had been a professor of political science at West Virginia University in the early days of the Great Depression, had some experience with West Virginia's tax problems, having helped Governor Guy Kump draft legislation dealing with the Tax Limitation Amendment passed by voters in the 1932 election. Sly had later urged Kump to seek revision of the Tax Limitation Amendment, regarding it as a serious public policy mistake that benefited out-of-state interests at the expense of in-state taxpayers, who suffered from reduced services. Kump and most state politicians, however, regarded any criticism of the Tax Limitation Amendment as heretical and political suicide. The creators of this fiscal anomaly and their successors lacked the political nerve to admit their error, and powerful corporate interests with headquarters outside the state worked to retain their advantages under the system.[57]

Marland's Commission on State and Local Finance surveyed the sources of state revenue and compared them with other states. Based on the premise that excess government spending had caused the Depression, the legislature had the written the Tax Limitation Amendment with the goal of curtailing government spending by denying government of revenue sources upon which it had previously relied. One theory at the time held that lowered assessments of real property would actually bring about increased revenue. A 1953 study showed that in fact the assessed value usually reflected only 30 to 35 percent of real value. It suggested that more realistic assessments could double and triple tax revenues, which could then be applied to issues such as better schools and roads. The problem, of course, was that the chief property owners and their political allies blocked any reform of the system of taxation.[58]

Hard Times and the Search for Panaceas

By the time Marland became governor, economic disaster loomed, and conditions grew worse as the decade wore on, affecting not only mining communities and rural areas, but towns and cities throughout the state as well. Reports and constituent letters of the era preserved in Senator Harley Kilgore's files give some sense of the growing alarm. Kilgore received numerous petitions from union locals, civic clubs, American Legion posts, women's clubs, and local development organizations from all over the state, calling attention to their dire circumstances. Many also shared with the senator what they were trying to do to improve their situation. Most, perhaps remembering the work relief programs of the New Deal, called upon Kilgore to support some kind of federal work relief. [59]

Conditions in Mingo, bordering on Kentucky in the southwest, reflected the situation in many coalfield counties. During World War II, the coal industry in the county boomed, and the Norfolk and Western terminal at Williamson had flourished. Many local workers found attractive opportunities in war industries outside the area, and the region suffered a labor shortage during the war. During the post-war period, coal and railroad employment remained high. Some women who had worked in war plants returned to the area but withdrew from the labor market. Between 1950 and 1953, however, coal industry employment dropped 23 percent, and other employment fell 17 percent.[60]

In Raleigh County, officers of the Slab Fork District Forum urged upon Senator Kilgore the great need for job relief. "To keep our people here from destitution," they pleaded, "there must be other jobs outside of the coal mines." They urged that a "vast public works program" be started. They also called for an increase in the minimum wage to $1.25 and a reduction in the workday from eight hours to six.[61] The Upper Kanawha Valley Development Association sought to make a Cold War virtue of the area's rugged topography. They wanted the senator to help them confirm their theory that "our native hills do offer a maximum of security from anything other than a direct hit." They hoped to use this information "as a selling point in an approach to new and diversified industry." They sent along a copy of their brochure, which featured their slogan in large capital letters: "MORE WORKERS THAN WORK" and "PROTECTION IN CASE OF WAR."[62]

Beckley banker G. C. Hedrick sought to rekindle the "back to the country" movement of the Great Depression when he proposed to Kilgore that the government help miners get a few acres to farm and supply them with horses and mules. This way, he said, "they can likely exist with one or two days in the mine." In 1953, Hedrick wrote, "you could not give horses and mules away," but a year later, underemployed miners eager to do some farming to supplement their falling incomes had driven the price upward to $100. Kilgore, unimpressed with the back-to-the-land solutions, replied that the area needed new industries rather than continuing to rely on one that could give workers only two days a week.[63]

Writing to Senator Kilgore in the spring of 1955, Beckley newspaper publisher Charles Hodel characterized southern West Virginia as "probably the most depressed and distressed region in the United States." An 18 percent decline in coal production had produced overall payroll reductions of 40 percent in the region. He wanted federal help in road building. He also advocated the improvement of the Raleigh County Memorial Airport so it could accommodate a fighter-bomber squadron of the Air National Guard. Road construction and improvement would be crucial to a local plan that sought to make the 60 percent remaining payrolls in the region equivalent to 100 percent of previous payrolls. The plan, devised by the Beckley Area Rural Development Program and launched in 1949, sought to make the eleven-county southern region self-sufficient in agriculture, eliminating the flow of local payroll monies to distant foodstuff suppliers. Counties to the east of Beckley, Hodel maintained, had the potential to produce enough to feed the region, including the counties to the west that lacked much arable land. Beckley served as the distribution center. Like others who puzzled over West Virginia's dilemma, Hodel believed new road construction would open the door to a more balanced regional economy, but he looked more to improvement of intrastate connections rather than to the construction of expressways connecting with other states. If better roads could be built to connect the western coal mining counties and the eastern agricultural counties, both would be better off as less local money would be drained off to other states.[64]

West Virginia's cities suffered along with rural areas, coal camps, and small towns. In 1954, Elmer Prince, the city manager of Morgantown, provided Senator Kilgore with a summary of the collapse in the Morgantown area. Prince found that local employment in coal had dropped from over 5,000 in 1952 to 3,100 in 1954, a 26 percent reduction in employment and a 31 percent decline in payrolls. Falling coal industry payrolls had linkage effects on other industries such as construction, which fell 44 percent over the three-year period.[65]

By 1954, Huntington, the largest city in the state, also suffered growing unemployment, primarily because of cutbacks in manufacturing. As an industrial, financial, and transportation center closely tied to the coal economy and natural gas, Huntington suffered with the technological changes that transformed the regional economy. The city's largest employer, the Chesapeake and Ohio Railroad, dropped coal-powered locomotives for the less labor-intensive diesels, sharply reducing its number of workers, and the C&O cutbacks affected other employers in the city. Many wage earners left their families behind to seek work in Dayton, Detroit, Cleveland, Columbus, and Cincinnati. So many workers traveled back and forth that special buses ran between Huntington and Detroit. The closing of five large plants in 1956–57 (two electrical machinery plants, two furniture plants, and a cigar factory) erased 2,000 jobs. The local transportation utilities industry also cut back. Altogether, some 5,000 jobs disappeared by the end of the decade, and Huntington landed on the Labor Department's list of "areas of substantial and persistent unemployment." By 1958, Charleston had supplanted Huntington as the state's largest city.[66] The economic collapse inspired much discussion around the state about what could be done to diversify the state's economy and to find work for the unemployed.

After spending an afternoon meeting with state labor leaders on the problem on April 19, 1954, Governor Marland told newsmen, "I have been pacing the floor and conferring with everyone I can" to find a solution. If the funds could be raised, Marland thought a public works program such as a road building would be one way of addressing the problem in the short run.[67] In May, Congressman Robert C. Byrd organized a conference on economic development, bringing together various federal officials and state business, labor, and government leaders. Meeting at the Daniel Boone Hotel in Charleston, the federal officials emphasized that efforts to attract new industry had to begin with local communities, and Byrd, who moderated the program, summarized by saying, "We of West Virginia must help ourselves." In the question and answer period, however, some in attendance, including radio executive Henry Dieffenbach of Logan and United Mine Workers District 17 chief William Blizzard, insisted that West

Virginia's problems could not wait. Attracting industry took time and could not be done quickly enough to help jobless coal miners."[68]

Conventional wisdom had it that West Virginia needed to diversify, and many towns and cities sought a way out of their dependence on coal. Most found it a slow and difficult process, and some concluded that if coal was their curse, it probably also offered the only cure. The rugged terrain of many towns that depended on coal inhibited their ability to make sweeping changes, and though few local committees spoke of it, absentee ownership of much of the land by those committed to exploitation of coal, land, gas, and other natural resources often precluded alternate land uses. Unable to attract new businesses, many concluded that they "must stick with their present industry for better or worse."[69] With that notion in mind, in early 1957 the officers of the Crum Industrial Organization sought Senator Chapman Revercomb's help. Pointing out that with one exception "every coal mine that was in Wayne and Mingo counties west of Williamson . . . has been eliminated or gone out of business," they asked the senator to support flood control and canalization of the Tug Fork River in the hope that it might lead to reopening of the mines.[70]

Hinton, the county seat of Summers County, suffering from the loss of mining employment and the decline of the Chesapeake and Ohio Railway yard, tried with little success to attract industry. The local Chamber of Commerce raised $50,000 to entice a manufacturer that made components for the Navy Air Corps, but after reaching a peak employment of sixty people, the firm failed. Then Hinton got a window sash and shutters firm, but a little town in Indiana coaxed it away. It had twelve other nibbles, but nothing worked out. The labor force melted away as many joined the Great Migration. Summers County lost 18.5 percent of its population during the 1950s.[71]

Other towns, if they took the initiative themselves, might be successful in finding new businesses and industry, and a series by business editor Wallace Knight in the *Charleston Gazette* cited examples of local groups trying to find new industries, including the Milton Industrial Association, a Lincoln County Development Association, and the Upper Kanawha Valley Development Association.[72] Several cities prepared expensive brochures and booklets in the attempt to attract new industries. The Morgantown Chamber of Commerce sent out many brochures titled *I Like It Here, So Will You*. The Beckley area Chamber of Commerce hoped the turnpike would help the effort to diversify and sent out a thick booklet, *The Beckley Story*. In Fairmont, the Greater Fairmont Development Association had just begun its work. Wood County's Little Kanawha Regional Council, with headquarters in Parkersburg, began in 1946 and had enjoyed the greatest success, helping to attract such plants and firms as the American Cyanamid Company, DuPont, Linde Air Products, Spencer Manufacturing Company, and Timber Products Company.[73]

Like governors in other states at the time, especially in the South, Marland tried to lure outside investment to develop new industries. The West Virginia Industrial and Publicity Commission dated to post-war efforts to boost the state, and Marland reinvigorated the effort. Through the work of the commission, advertisement, and personal speaking tours, Marland tried to persuade industrialists to locate plants in the state. He also hired the Arthur D. Little firm of Cambridge, Massachusetts, to study West Virginia's economy and to make recommendations for appropriate industrial development for the state.[74] Released on August 6, 1955, the Little report reinforced the conventional wisdom that West Virginia's economy relied too much on coal and other natural resources and should attempt to diversify. It urged the state to seek more metalworking, chemical, apparel, and woodworking firms. The report focused on the state's need to improve its poor roads and below average schools, two major liabilities that managers and technical personnel of new industry would see in West Virginia as a potential site for new industry.[75]

Emphasizing the positives in the Little report, for the next sixteen months Marland traveled around the country urging industrialists to locate plants in West Virginia. His basic pitch boosted West Virginia as a good location for access to many markets, and for its labor supply, low taxes, and plentiful supply of raw materials and electricity.[76] On one of his typical tours, in early March, 1956, he invited representatives of several industries to luncheons at the Waldorf-Astoria hotel in New York City where he urged them to consider West Virginia for the location of branch plants or regional distribution facilities.[77] As in much of what he did, however, Marland's industrial promotion campaign aroused angry opposition. When he informed Governor Abraham Ribicoff of Connecticut that he would be visiting Hartford to talk with local industrialists, Ribicoff fired off a telegram telling him that his trip "would be a waste of time" and that there would be "wide and deep resentment of a trip intended to try and take away our industries." Governor Dennis J. Roberts of Rhode Island joined Ribicoff in protesting what he called a "raiding party" and told Marland that "the wisdom of involving the Governor of West Virginia in such a visit is questionable."[78] Former New Hampshire governor Hugh Gregg, who attended one of the Marland luncheons in Boston, defended Marland, saying he was no industrial pirate, but simply doing what many governors did to try to attract new industries to their states.[79]

Marland's industrial development program convinced some companies to build plants in West Virginia. Between 1954 and 1957, the Industrial and Publicity Commission listed seventy-five new industrial plants that had moved to West Virginia and claimed the state had been involved in recruiting thirty of them. Kaiser Aluminum's Ravenswood plant on the Ohio River in Jackson County, one of the most impressive of the new plants, projected an eventual need for one thousand workers. The recession of the early 1950s also moderated in 1955 and 1956 with lower rates of unemployment and lower rates of migration from the state.[80]

The positive blip in the statistics of the mid-1950s raised hopes briefly but turned out to be misleading. Another national recession soon dashed hopes that West Virginia's recovery had begun. The coal industry, however, found its way to more profitable operation. Mechanization of the industry through the adoption of advanced technology made coal more competitive, and in the late 1950s prospects further brightened as the expanding demand for electricity also created a growing market for coal. The recovery of the state's chief industry, however, offered no hope for reemployment of thousands of dismissed coal miners, whose jobs had disappeared forever. At an industrial development conference at West Virginia University on May 12, 1954, Governor Marland put his finger on the immediate dilemma when he said, "We find ourselves in the peculiar position of having an industry whose production prognosis is positive but whose future employment opportunities are very definitely on the negative side."[81]

Marland: Flawed Champion of Change

In 1956, the Democratic Party suffered its most severe defeat in West Virginia since 1928. Governor Marland's severance tax proposal had split the party badly, and rather than trying to mend fences, he made the situation worse in the 1954 election when he unsuccessfully tried to purge Democrats in the southern counties who had opposed him. In the next session of the legislature, state senators demonstrated their bitterness by rejecting nine of the governor's appointees. When Marland ran for the United States Senate in 1956 (seeking the seat made vacant by Harley Kilgore's death), Democratic primary opponents charged him with corruption. They claimed that the Marland administration required state employees to pay into a political slush fund (misleadingly called the "Flower Fund") as a condition of employment. Because roads remained a major issue and consumed much of the state budget, the State Road Commission also drew much fire as a notorious spoils organization for statehouse and county machine politicians. These practices predated Marland, and some of those who self-righteously attacked the governor had themselves benefited from the system, but they now seized upon "corruption" as an attack tool. Marland hurt his own cause with an arrogant personal style, creating additional enemies within the party by acting arbitrarily at times in personnel matters. He also saw to it that his father and brother received lucrative state contracts and employment, and he arranged to have a state road built past his farm in rural Kanawha County. By the end of his term Marland retained few supporters among party leaders. Popular former governor Okey Patteson said his support of Marland had been "a tragic mistake."[82]

Thomas F. Stafford, who knew Marland and (as editor of the *Raleigh Register*) had been one of few editors who supported the severance tax, said Marland "had one of the best minds of all the governors I have known, but he could be stubborn and foolish. . . . He had none of the hill-country charm and political savvy of his predecessor."[83] Milton J. Ferguson, who served as tax commissioner in the Marland administration, later described Marland as a brilliant young man who had led his law school class at West Virginia University but lamented that Homer Hanna, then the power behind the throne in the statehouse machine, had pushed him along too fast. Ferguson said Marland gave him free reign to make his own appointments and "never tried to pawn any political hacks on me" or interfered in the operation of the tax department in any way. Though Ferguson thought Marland a bit too pro-labor, he strongly supported the governor's severance tax proposal.⁸⁴ Marland's successor Cecil Underwood told an interviewer in 1998 that Marland's combative approach to issues made for his rocky relationship with the legislature. When asked why Patteson broke with his protégé, Underwood suggested that "Governor Marland's wholesale, ruthless firing of people who had been there a long time—many of them Governor Patteson's friends—probably ruptured their relationship."⁸⁵

Governor William Casey Marland in a non-controversial moment, crowning the homecoming queen at West Virginia University in 1955. West Virginia and Regional History Collection, West Virginia University Libraries.

Rumors that Marland had a drinking problem plagued his administration almost from the start. One story had it that the governor had been openly intoxicated during a conference at the Greenbrier in the spring of 1953. Another had him drunk while reviewing National Guard troops at Camp Pickett, Virginia. Contradicting such reports, reporter Mellace claimed in an interview in 1998 that though he covered Marland for four years, he never saw him drunk. According to Mellace and Herb Little, a retired Associated Press correspondent, Marland's opponents spread such nasty rumors to undermine him.[86] Similarly, a scholar who studied the Marland administration concluded that had he not taken on the coal industry and its minions and been vilified by them, his accomplishments in bringing new industry to the Ohio Valley would have qualified him as one of the state's best governors. His opponents, "home grown sharks" of the coal industry and absentee owners, however, "ripped him to shreds" by carrying out a vicious whispering campaign against him that fixed his image among the public as "a drunken, bumbling fool, running around over the United States partying and begging."[87]

Although Marland later twice sought election to the United States Senate, he never held political office after his term as governor. In some respects his political career ended two months into his administration as governor when he dared to challenge the chief economic interests of the state. The lesson for others who might question certain economic shibboleths of the state's power brokers seemed clear. It would be more than thirty years before the idea of a severance tax would be considered again. Eventually Marland's personal life suffered as well, as his alleged alcoholism became apparent. He lost several executive positions in business and ended up making his living as a cab driver in Chicago. Marland died in 1965, at age 47.[88]

The Emergence of Cecil Underwood

The Democrats' implosion of the Marland era, a fading coalfield vote as the number of miners declined, allegations of corruption, and an effective Republican campaign opened the door for a Republican resurgence in 1956. President Eisenhower carried the state in defeating the Democratic presidential nominee, Adlai Stevenson, for the second time. Republican Cecil Harland Underwood, only 34-years-old, exploited Democratic divisions and evidences of corruption such as the Flower Fund and engaged in innovative campaigning (television and canvassing by helicopter) to break the Democrats' long hold on the statehouse, defeating labor's choice, Robert H. Mollohan. Revelations that Mollohan, while superintendent of the Industrial School for Boys at Pruntytown, had allowed a coal company to strip coal on state land added to his and the party's woes.[89] Tutored by Lawrence H. "Bud" Rogers, a Huntington television executive, Underwood agreed to field questions from a panel of reporters moderated by Nick Basso, the channel 3 news director, who was hired by the campaign. Underwood's unrehearsed responses served his campaign well, so he repeated the format on other television stations. Underwood also leased a helicopter to fly around the state during the closing days of the campaign, making sixty-six stops in ten days, and closing with a rally in his hometown, Sistersville, in Tyler County. Weather problems and mechanical issues helped attract attention as Underwood conducted his whirlwind tour of the state. Contributions to the campaign at each stop paid for the helicopter lease.[90]

Chapman Revercomb, moderating his redbaiting of 1952, defeated Marland in the race for the United States Senate seat left vacant by the death of Harley Kilgore. Two Republicans, Will E. Neal and Arch Moore, defeated Democratic incumbents for seats in Congress, and Republican R. Virgil Rohrbaugh defeated William Woodson Trent, who had served as Superintendent of Schools since 1933. Republicans also gained seats in the legislature, but Democrats retained control of both houses, assuring that divided government would continue.[91]

The first Republican governor in twenty-four years, Underwood faced many of the same public policy dilemmas as governor that Marland had, and he offered a similar solution—raise taxes. Born in Tyler County in 1922, Underwood became the state's youngest governor, being a few months younger than Marland had been at the time of his inauguration. Underwood had served as a schoolteacher, college professor, and vice president in charge of public relations at Salem College, his alma mater. As a graduate student at West Virginia University, he had written a master's thesis, "The Legislative Process in West Virginia." He became a Tyler County representative to the House of Delegates at age 22, and during his twelve years as a member of the House (serving as minority floor leader from 1949 to 1957), Underwood consistently advocated cutting taxes and routinely voted against budgets with increased revenue. As governor, however, Underwood faced the stark reality of the long-term underfunding of education, roads, health, and other programs. In 1958 he proposed a budget that he would have never voted for during his House tenure: $52 million in new taxes, far more than even Marland had proposed. Underwood's plan, however, avoided taxing large business interests directly and instead sought increases in the consumers' sales tax, higher gross sales taxes, and racing and highway users' taxes. Citing the challenges to education posed by the recent launching of the Russian space vehicle Sputnik, he also called for an income tax to raise $15 million to be dedicated to education. Underwood said that West Virginians of past generations had vacillated too often and postponed needed improvements. Now, he said, "We must either progress or irreparably become a substandard state, one of hollow industrial shells, mutilated country sides, decrepit towns, barely traversable roads . . . populated by an arrested people who have lost hope, ambition and the will to create." He proposed a $500 million, ten-year program to build expressways that would link with the interstate highway system. Although the Democratic legislative majority refused to pass Underwood's major proposals, it cooperated more with Underwood than it had with Marland, agreeing in 1957 to Underwood's proposals to establish the Department of Finance and Administration and the Department of Mental Health.[92]

The Interstate Highways Act of 1956, the most significant domestic legislation of President Eisenhower's first term, provided substantial federal subsidies for highways throughout the country. Although many critics feared the impact of the program, it met with widespread approval of the general public, and it directly benefited the real estate, automobile, trucking, construction, and petroleum industries.[93] Announcement of West Virginia's original share in the interstate system provided a great lift to the Underwood administration, although it also put pressure on the state to find the 10 percent matching funds to complete the mileage assigned to the state. It also created an immediate dilemma, because the State Road Commission had neither engineering plans on the shelf nor adequate engineering expertise to quickly plan for the new roads. The state trailed others by almost two years in devising the necessary plans, and the road commission finally turned to the use of private engineering firms to speed up the planning process, a method that raised questions in the press. Underwood, however, endorsed the use of private consultants, insisting that "reports of a few isolated incidents of possible misdoing" should not be allowed to endanger the interstate program.[94]

In October 1958, Secretary of Commerce Sinclair Weeks came to West Virginia (in one of his last official acts after resigning from Eisenhower's cabinet) to attend groundbreaking ceremonies for Interstate 77, which would fulfill the dream of many to have a north-south road linking West Virginia and its southern neighbors to the Great Lakes. Soon thereafter Governor Underwood revealed plans to build forty-five miles of I-64 between Nitro and Huntington, part of an interstate that would cross the state from the Virginia border near White Sulphur Springs to the Kentucky border via Huntington. Underwood noted that planning had also begun on Interstate 70, which would cross the Northern Panhandle near Wheeling and Interstate 81 crossing the Eastern Panhandle in the Martinsburg area. When Secretary Weeks visited, he told newsmen that West Virginia would not likely receive more mileage as most of the 41,000 miles provided for in the Interstate Highway Act had been designated. This left many areas of the state displeased, especially those interested in upgrading U.S. 19 from Beckley to the Pennsylvania line via Sutton, Clarksburg, and Morgantown. Altogether, West Virginia obtained an allotment of 306 interstate miles by the end of Underwood's administration.[95]

The Challenges of Education in the Age of Sputnik

When Marland and Underwood proposed taxes to improve schools, they knew West Virginia badly needed to do better in education. With teachers' salaries trailing other states, the school system faced a brain drain as teachers found they could earn more elsewhere. Throughout the 1950s, the *West Virginia School Journal*, the organ of the West Virginia Education Association, lamented the exodus to other states as teachers joined blue-collar workers in seeking better opportunities elsewhere. In 1953, more than 300 left. Five years later, "the roof fell in," as the *School Journal* put it, and 1,339 teachers quit or left to teach in another state.[96] Many of the departing teachers headed to Florida, with its better salaries and sunny climate. A. L. Hardman, sports editor of the *Charleston Gazette*, visited Fort Lauderdale in 1954 and discovered sixteen former West Virginia teachers on the staff of Fort Lauderdale High School. All cited substantially higher pay, less demanding work assignments, and lower living costs as reasons that drew them to Florida. Hardman found that most Florida cities had former West Virginians on their school faculties and continued to receive applications from others.[97] In a typical example of how this exodus worked, in early June 1958 (the year the "roof fell in"), Jack Buford Christian, principal of Oceana High School in Wyoming County, and his wife Jeanine decided to vacation in Florida. While there they ran into former West Virginians employed by Florida schools. When offered a position with the Miami school system by a former graduate school classmate at the University of Florida, Jack accepted it on the spot. The Christians returned to Oceana, packed up and moved within two weeks. For years afterward, friends and relatives in Wyoming County asked them when they planned to return, not imagining that the move could be permanent. In time, Christian would help other West Virginia teachers and school administrators seeking to join the exodus.[98]

As the state struggled to keep teachers, a survey of the system in 1957 compounded the dilemma as it revealed serious shortcomings in the achievement levels of West Virginia schoolchildren. Compiled and written by Eston K. Feaster, dean of the college of education at West Virginia University, the Feaster Report concluded that West Virginia children trailed the national average in achievement by as much as two grades. The report attributed the low scores primarily to weaknesses in reading. Phares Reeder, the executive secretary of the West Virginia Education Association, called the report a tragedy, but blamed the schools' failures on the lack of funding, citing the state's forty-second ranking in financial support for education. "It takes a competitive salary to attract and to keep capable young teachers in the classrooms," Reeder wrote. "It takes money to provide the teaching tools, equipment, and classrooms."[99]

The Feaster Report had some shock value as it pointed out the poor condition of state schools without any sugar coating. J. Martin Taylor, a professor of education at Fairmont State College, said telling West Virginians the results of the survey compared to the "physician's task of informing his patient he has a malignancy." Others, including Reeder, compared the impact of the Feaster Report to the shock of Sputnik. The launching of the artificial space satellite by the Russians in October 1957 suggested that America's Cold War enemies had better scientists and led to immediate demands for improving science education. Science teachers questioned by the *West Virginia School Journal* believed that science instruction should be changed to introduce science at an earlier age, including installing laboratories in elementary schools and reducing extracurricular activities to give students more time for science instruction.[100]

Many West Virginians gazed up from their mountain valleys and hillsides to see Sputnik on that October night. Among those watching was Big Creek High School student Homer Hickam Jr. In *October Sky*, his memoir of growing up in southern West Virginia, Hickam tells the story of watching in his backyard "in Coalwood, McDowell County, U.S.A" and seeing "the bright little ball moving majestically across the narrow star field between the ridgelines." Hickam also recalls that as quickly as the fall semester of 1958, Sputnik inspired renewed vigor in the science curriculum at Big Creek High School as elsewhere across West Virginia and indeed across the United States. He says, "in the fall of 1958 it felt to the high school students of the United States as if the country was launching *us* in reply." Hickam and some of his classmates met the challenge by experimenting with rockets and entering science fair competitions. Later Hickam become an aerospace engineer and worked for the National Aeronautics and Space Administration.[101]

A Changing of the Guard

The 1958 election marked a striking changing of the political guard. The Democrats staged a comeback as new leadership emerged to replace Matthew Mansfield Neely, long-time leader of the federal wing of the Democrats, who died in January, 1956. Congressman Robert C. Byrd led the ticket in defeating Republican incumbent Chapman Revercomb for a full six-year senate term, launching a senate career that would extend into the twenty-first century. Former congressman Jennings Randolph, who defeated former governor Marland in the primary, won the other senate seat to complete Neely's unexpired term, defeating Republican John D. Hoblitzell, who had been appointed to the position by Underwood on Neely's death. Former Marshall College professor Ken Hechler (author of a popular World War II history, *The Bridge at Remagen*) defeated incumbent Republican Will Neal in the fourth congressional district. Republican Congressman Arch A. Moore survived the Democratic resurgence, winning a second term by 9,000 votes against former congressman Robert Mollohan, who had been the Democrats' nominee for governor in 1956. Byrd, Randolph, Hechler, and Moore, like Cecil Underwood, would all be around for a long time, and each would play an important role in West Virginia politics, but of them all only one, Congressman Hechler, would ultimately dare to consistently question the prevailing shibboleths and to point out the dangers of the new machine age such as black lung, strip mining, air and water pollution, gob piles, and the corruption of the UMWA.[102]

The changes did not make much difference, either, in the male-dominated nature of state politics. Though both parties always named women to their state and national committees, few women sought elective office. Occasionally in the first half of the twentieth century, women received appointments to serve out unexpired terms of deceased male relatives. Governor Underwood had appointed Helen Holt, widow of former United States Senator Rush Dew Holt (who had switched from Democrat to Republican after his election in 1934), as secretary of state on the death of the incumbent, but she failed in an effort to be the first woman to be elected to a statewide office. Elizabeth Kee, a Democrat, had become the first West Virginia woman to serve in Congress when she succeeded her husband John in the fifth congressional district upon his death in 1951. She had been elected in 1952, reelected in 1956, and ran unopposed in 1958.[103] Elizabeth Hallanan, a Kanawha County Republican, resigned a seat in the House of Delegates to run for the state senate, but lost. No women held seats in the state senate, but three were elected to the House of Delegates in 1958, including the most persistently successful woman politician in the state during the 1950s, Elizabeth Simpson Drewry, an African American Democrat from McDowell County, who, beginning in 1950, was elected to seven consecutive terms in the House. In 1955 Drewry submitted a resolution leading to a statewide vote on a constitutional amendment giving women the right to sit on juries. With ratification by voters in 1956, West

Virginia became the last state to grant women this right. On the county level, few women served as county commissioners or even on boards of education.[104]

A Deteriorating Economy and Agonizing Reappraisals

The deteriorating economy in West Virginia in 1958 and 1959 brought increased attention from the legislature, Congress, the national press, and television. In 1958 the rising unemployment required a special summer session of the legislature to extend unemployment benefits for an additional twelve weeks. At the end of the year, over 300,000 of the state's two million residents qualified for federal food commodities. By 1959 unemployment had reached an estimated 75,000.[105] When Congress passed an area redevelopment bill that would provide public works, job training, and increased welfare benefits, President Eisenhower vetoed it as too costly and inflationary.[106]

Meanwhile West Virginians engaged in agonizing reappraisals of the state's condition. An editorial in the *Charleston Gazette* found the roots of West Virginia's problems not so much in foreign competition in U.S. markets as in "an industrial revolution spreading like wildfire across America." As the country moved to a new plateau, West Virginia trailed along in the backwash because "we haven't taken the necessary steps to be a part of the groundswell." Reciting the collapse of coal, timber, agriculture, and even manufacturing, the *Gazette* laid part of the blame on a failure to keep up. Factories failed to adopt new technology, and farmers clung to "old time methods." Since World War II, thousands of young people, miners, and factory workers had joined the Great Migration from Appalachia. In a year when southern and border states led the nation in manufacturing growth, West Virginia opened only one factory of any consequence. In searching for the answer to the state's problem, the editorial cited the example of Grafton, where the last of four glass plants had recently closed, dismissing 485 employees. The plant closed in part because of the company's desire to be closer to markets, but also because "Grafton failed to keep its house in order." Grafton's ugly, down-at-the-heels look "bespeaks a general lack of community pride and an almost total lack of interest in self improvement," and no industry would want to locate in such a place. The *Gazette* held up

Grafton as typical, not unique: "A veritable chain of weather-worn, moth-eaten towns from Chester to Canebrake have lost touch with progress." To address these problems, West Virginia, the *Gazette* opined, needed a statewide campaign to abandon "old ways, old attitudes, and old procedures." The *Gazette* had it only half-right. A large part of the problem was not the failure to adopt new technology, but the impact on people when West Virginia industries like coal and railroads adopted cutting-edge technology that reduced the need for workers and devastated communities. The *Gazette* accurately described the difficulty of the state government, cities, towns, and counties in adjusting to the new machine age or to "be a part of the groundswell." The editorial, however, did not go into the economic and institutional problems that made it so difficult for the state to accommodate change.[107]

In March 1959, Huntington television executive and Underwood ally Lawrence H. Rogers, in an editorial on WSAZ, called for less talk and more action on the problem. In response to the television editorial, Governor Underwood received many letters urging a special session of the legislature to take action. A typical letter (from a Beckley writer) called for an "Operation Bootstrap."[108] Congressman John M. Slack toured the coalfields in his district, and Senator Jennings Randolph held hearings in southern West Virginia on the unemployment problem. Governor Underwood, however, who had spoken eloquently on the problem in addresses to the legislature throughout his term, criticized others for publicizing the state's poverty. In December, responding to growing criticism for lack of action, Underwood toured the coalfields and depressed areas of fifteen counties. On December 15, he reported on his trip with a television address, illustrated with photographs. Underwood concluded his presentation saying that West Virginia's problems would be resolved "not by words, but by action, not by partisan maneuvering but by political cooperation."[109]

Unfortunately the chasm between the legislative and executive branches and the factionalism within the majority party continued to paralyze state action in the face of the growing crisis. In March 1959, observing the condition of the state's economy, the divided nature of West Virginia politics and the contentious and ineffective state legislature as West Virginia approached the centenary of its birth, West

Virginia University historian Festus P. Summers, co-author of the West Virginia history textbook used in college classes and a member of the Centennial Commission, wrote to Charles Hodel, chairman of the commission: "I fear that if Lincoln should look down upon the state he helped create he would have to confess to being a party to a house divided after all."[110]

"An American Paradox": Imperfections in the Glare of National Attention

In the election year 1960, West Virginia's dilemma attracted attention from the national media; reporters came to the state to cover the Democratic primary fight between Senators Hubert H. Humphrey and John F. Kennedy for the presidential nomination, and discovered a state apparently out of step with the nation. On February 6, the *Saturday Evening Post* published "The Strange Case of West Virginia," a lengthy article by Roul Tunley, which called the state "an American paradox," noting the wealth in resources and natural beauty alongside "chronic, grinding poverty." Tunley cited the series by the *Charleston Gazette* that summarized the state's problems, setting off a debate that led to certain unpleasant conclusions. Despite its rich natural resource production, the state led the nation in unemployment with a rate three times the national average. Other inconvenient facts included a high rate of illiteracy, schools ranked among the lowest in the nation, the highest rate of white illegitimacy, lowest annual farm income, and the highest rate of population loss. Tunley contrasted these grim statistics with the bustling modernity of Charleston and the luxury of the Greenbrier resort at White Sulphur Springs.[111] Harrison Salisbury of the *New York Times* (who made a name for himself reporting about the Soviet Union) wrote similarly of the paradox of prosperity and poverty existing side by side. He noted that West Virginia had "the blue book names of American industry–Union Carbide and Carbon, du Pont, Owen-Illinois Glass, International Nickel, American Viscose, Monsanto, Interwoven Stocking, Sylvania Electric, and dozens of others." In contrast to the blue book list of corporations, Salisbury also reached for the stereotype as he pointed out "the West Virginia of Kelly's Creek where men who have not worked since the mine closed in 1952 sit on the porch, the stoop, or the loafer's bench and stare sad-faced and gentle-eyed at the scarred hillside."[112]

Less-balanced accounts than Tunley's and Salisbury's appeared in *Life, Newsweek, Time, New Republic,* and *U.S. News.*[113] Most focused on the state's poverty as well as allegations of religious bigotry and political corruption. The NBC television network also featured coalfield poverty on the Huntley-Brinkley news program. Governor Underwood, who had been persuaded to run for the U.S. Senate by Vice President Nixon, the Republican presidential nominee—with the promise of an appointment as secretary of the interior should his candidacy fail—denounced the reports as "rigged" and "distorted" and declared the visit of David Brinkley, one of the NBC anchormen, "obnoxious to all decent citizens."[114]

After the *Saturday Evening Post* article, Senator Byrd took to the senate floor for a two-hour speech attacking Tunley and other writers for focusing on "the exception rather than the rule, the extreme rather than the normal." Byrd particularly noted a quotation from the article, allegedly from a Midwestern newspaper, that called West Virginians "shoeless, shiftless, beer-swilling clods who wouldn't go to a church that didn't use rattlesnakes in the service." Byrd argued that "it is not a question of laziness, but one of finding employment during our state's industrial revolution." He defended the character of his fellow mountaineers, saying, "They are a kindly people, even if they are without work and living in a shanty in an abandoned coal town."[115]

When journalist Theodore H. White wrote his Pulitzer-winning *The Making of the President, 1960,* he recounted his visit to the state during the presidential primary campaign. He focused on the state's poverty and corruption, but he tried to balance his unflattering account of the state with condescending compliments, calling West Virginians "handsome people and, beyond doubt, the best-mannered and most courteous in the nation." He also proclaimed the relations of white West Virginians with "their Negroes" the best of any state in the country.[116]

Many West Virginians agreed with Senator Byrd and Governor Underwood that reports in the national media unfairly skewered the state, giving too much attention to the negatives and too little to the positives. Those who lived in circumstances comparable to any other place in America resented the constant reporting of West Virginia's problems,[117] but the reports, though in some cases sensationalized, reflected real problems. West Virginians who sought to minimize the grim picture presented by the decline of employment in coal and agriculture ignored the reality of a broad-based decline. These two industries had so many linkages to other economic activities that their falls pulled others downward. The decline of mining employment hurt most retail lines in the coalfields and construction suffered. Most areas of employment experienced declines in the 1950s.[118] Even in growth areas of the state and in depressed urban centers such as Morgantown and Huntington that had affluence alongside poverty, better-off residents could not help but be affected by the conditions that surrounded them. At the end of the decade, the average per capita income in the state was $1,686, about 25 percent below the national average, and only three small counties—Hancock, Ohio, and Jackson—exceeded the national average.[119]

Planning for Regional Action

At the end of the 1950s, Bert Combs, the governor of Kentucky (whose Appalachian eastern region shared West Virginia's problems) promoted the notion of a regional organization of governors to coordinate a joint attack on the common problems of the Appalachian states. When an organizational meeting took place in Annapolis, Maryland, on May 20, 1960, Cecil Underwood, one of the eleven governors invited, represented West Virginia. The journalistic focus on the West Virginia primary election battle between Kennedy and Humphrey had helped call attention to the region's poverty. An extensive report commissioned by the Maryland Department of Economic Development detailed the problems unique to Appalachia and formed the basis for discussion at the Annapolis meeting. One area of debate at the conference was whether areas of Pennsylvania and New York should be considered as part of Appalachia, a term somewhat nebulous in definition. The majority agreed that all should be included. They also agreed with Underwood that the region's common areas of concern included unemployment and chronic poverty. He said if West Virginia had acted after World War II when it became clear that major changes in the coal industry would produce massive unemployment, it might have avoided the problems. The governors debated the role the federal government should play in addressing regional issues. Underwood defended President Eisenhower's recent veto of the Area Redevelopment Act, saying it would have just created another federal agency state governments would have to deal with. He argued that the help the Appalachian states needed required no new federal agency. Other governors expressed disappointment at Eisenhower's veto, and Combs insisted that coordination of local, federal, and regional efforts required a federal agency. Underwood and the representative of Governor Nelson Rockefeller of New York also opposed the creation of a new interstate organization, favoring instead an *ad hoc*, temporary committee. The participants agreed to establish an interim committee composed of representatives appointed by the governors of each participating state. This committee would lay the groundwork for another meeting of the governors, which would lead eventually to the creation of the Appalachian Regional Commission.[120]

Affection in Adversity

During the difficult times of the 1950s, West Virginians generally continued to have a strong affection for their state, despite its blemishes, and defended it against its critics even as they themselves complained and even when circumstances compelled them reluctantly to leave, or as mining supply manufacturer Jack Long bluntly put it, to "just fade away" (as noted in chapter 1). Even in hard times, they took pride in their local communities (though they might appear "weather worn and moth eaten" to visitors), and large crowds turned out to cheer on high school athletic teams and marching bands, even as many students knew that after graduation they would have to leave the state. Having no metropolis with major professional sports teams to serve as a focus of state pride, and because the state often suffered much criticism in the national media, West Virginians also tended to look to the successes of collegiate sports teams such as West Virginia University's Sugar Bowl football team of 1954 (which lost to Georgia Tech) and the Mountaineer basketball teams of the 1950s (led by the high-scoring Rodney "Hot Rod" Hundley of Charleston), which achieved high national ranking. The 1959 team, led by Jerry West of Cabin Creek (a typically depressed mining community), played in the national championship game, losing to California by a single point.

Even West Virginians who had not attended the university or other state institutions took vicarious pleasure in West Virginia teams that achieved national attention.[121]

Conclusion

The social pathologies cited by White, Tunley, and other journalistic critics and studied by the Ford Foundation survey (which was not published until 1962) grew out of long-term economic problems that had been obscured by the relative prosperity of the 1940s. In the 1950s, West Virginia and Appalachia indeed became paradoxical exceptions to the national trend. West Virginia's woes derived from dependence on a resource-based economy highly sensitive to the whims of the national and global markets, the overweening power of out-of-state economic interests and their local agents (whose influence inhibited the state's capacity to diversify and change), a technological revolution that left too many of its citizens unemployed and poor and degraded the environment, and a rugged topography that drove up transportation costs and limited conventional agricultural and industrial possibilities. In the face of these difficulties, the state's antiquated governmental structure and corrupt political culture produced leaders too often caught up in embarrassing scandals and unwilling or unable to effectively challenge the constraining orthodoxies of the past or to address inadequate investment in critical social infrastructure such as schools, roads, and social services. In chapter 3, we will see that despite the devastating impact of the new machine age on the African American community and in the face of prevailing constraints on reform and the general mood of quiescence in Appalachia as elsewhere, civil rights reformers would work to address the issues of segregation and inequality. In doing so, they would blaze the trail to an Appalachian reawakening.

3

Civil Rights in the New Machine Age

As quick as they could, the company was moving in loaders, roof bolting machines, cutting machines, and new motors, and they mined as much coal with 100 men as they had with 300 or 400 before. And just about everyone on them machines was white.

           Willie Collins, Raleigh County coal miner

No matter where you are, it's all South: New York is up South; West Virginia, middle South; and Mississippi, down South.

        Billy Scott, research chemist, Carbide Technical Center

During the 1950s, "the politics of consensus" prevailed, and groups that did not share in the bounty, including the residents of Appalachia, generally suffered in silence. The civil rights movement, however, challenged the consensus and provided one of the great dynamics of American society. From the 1950s and on into the 1960s, it was the era of *Brown v Board of Education,* "massive resistance," Rosa Parks and the Montgomery bus boycott, Martin Luther King's ringing oratory, NAACP, CORE, SNCC, lunch counter sit-ins, street demonstrations, the Civil Rights Act, voting rights struggles, and Birmingham fire hoses and burned-out Freedom Rider buses. As the focus shifted from the South to urban ghettoes of the North in the 1960s, black youths turned from the peaceful methods of the early movement to the confrontation and rebellion of Black Power.[1]

  West Virginia's story of this time reflects the national one but has its own unique features. The issues of race and civil rights cannot be separated from the broader themes of West Virginia and Appalachian history, including the impact of technological change in the post–World War II era. As machines manufactured by companies with names like Jeffrey and Joy transformed coal mining and coal miners lost their jobs, African Americans got the pink slips first. As the state's population declined, the rate of black decline tripled the rate of white decline, and substantial numbers of African Americans joined the Appalachian Great Migration.[2] Just as the civil rights movement nationally would develop methods used by others seeking social justice, African Americans who stayed behind developed grassroots leadership that showed the way for others in the Appalachian reawakening of the 1960s.

African Americans in West Virginia: Balancing Two Segregationist Parties

Because it needed to bring in immigrant and African American workers as its coalfields and other industries developed, West Virginia grew more ethnically diverse than the rest of the Appalachian region as pockets of foreign-born populations and African Americans resided in some of the industrial areas of the state.[3] The African American population never exceeded seven percent of the state's total, but because it tended to be concentrated in a few coal-mining counties, it developed a substantial sense of community. In the late nineteenth century and early twentieth century, as historian Joe William Trotter has shown, many black workers came from agricultural areas of the South to work in the burgeoning coalfields of West Virginia. They concentrated in the southern mining counties where a lively black culture developed. Jefferson, an Eastern Panhandle agricultural county, already had a substantial black population that descended from antebellum slavery. Though West Virginia (like sixteen other states) segregated its schools by law, race did not have the same profound impact and domineering hold on the psyche of West Virginians as it did on Southerners of the former Confederacy. In the years before the Great Depression, blacks in Republican-controlled West Virginia endured racial discrimination and segregation, but not the disfranchisement typical of southern states controlled by the Democratic Party. Blacks in West Virginia continued to have the right to vote and often gave the Republican Party the margin it needed to retain control of the state through the first three decades of the twentieth century. Because black votes could determine the political balance

Civil Rights in the New Machine Age   87

of power between Democrats and Republicans, the leadership of the small black minority in West Virginia received patronage and wielded some political influence. Their white allies, mostly Republican, saw to the expansion of state-supported black institutions, the curbing of lynching, and increased legal protections for blacks.[4]

TABLE 1: AFRICAN AMERICAN AND TOTAL POPULATION OF WEST VIRGINIA, 1880–1970[5]

Year	Black Population	Percent Increase (Decrease)	Total Population	Percent Increase (Decrease)	Blacks as Percent of Total
1880	25,886	……	618,347	…	4.2
1890	32,690	26.3	762,794	23.3	4.3
1900	43,449	32.9	958,800	25.7	4.5
1910	64,173	47.7	1,221,119	27.4	5.3
1920	86,345	34.6	1,463,701	19.9	5.9
1930	114,893	33.1	1,729,205	18.1	6.6
1940	117,754	2.5	1,901,974	10.0	6.2
1950	114,867	(2.5)	2,005,552	5.4	5.7
1960	89, 838	(22.2)	1,860,421	(7.2)	4.8
1970	73,931	(18.4)	1,774,237	(6.2)	4.2

When the Depression came, it presented a difficult political dilemma for African Americans in West Virginia, who had fared better under Republican control than blacks in the Democrat-controlled states to the south. West Virginia Democrats, who rose to power with the collapse of the Republican regime in the 1932 election, understood the important role the black vote had played in the past and cultivated black support by using patronage. The Democrats established a separate black board of education, mandated a black assistant superintendent in the five counties with significant black population, and provided for a black assistant director of public assistance in any county with 10 percent black population. Although this paternalistic tokenism did not address the deeper issues of racism and discrimination, the Democratic response reassured black leaders, who had to choose between two segregationist parties, that Democrats could provide the same benefits that Republicans had. More important, New Deal programs to help the unemployed, especially the Works Progress Administration, provided jobs and new facilities for black communities. By 1936 blacks had abandoned the party of Lincoln for the party of Roosevelt.[6] The war years provided opportunities for blacks in the armed forces and in industry beyond the borders of the state, and the African American population of the state declined slightly during the 1940s, a prelude to much higher losses in the 1950s and 1960s that would come with the severe reverses in mining employment.

Jim Crow and the Impact of the Revolution in Coal

Before the new machines transformed the coal industry and before the 1954 Supreme Court decision requiring the end of segregated schools, de jure segregation—that is, segregation required by state law—existed in West Virginia only regarding education and marriage. The state had never followed the example of former states of the Confederacy in disenfranchising black voters or in enacting extensive Jim Crow laws. De facto segregation, however, prevailed in places of public accommodations, employment, and housing whether in the cities, small towns, or coal towns. In his memoir of growing up in Piedmont, Mineral County, Henry Louis Gates Jr. (chairman of Afro-American Studies at Harvard University), recalls the segregation of that small West Virginia town, where most of the black men worked as dock loaders at the paper mill: "For most of my childhood we couldn't eat in restaurants or sleep in hotels, we couldn't use certain bathhouses or try on clothes in stores."[7] Ruth Jarret, wife of Coach Jim Jarret of Charleston's Garnet High School, recalled in a 1983 interview that when black high school teams traveled in the days of segregation, few hotels or restaurants would serve them, so they would eat in the school cafeterias and stay overnight with the players and coaches of the other team. Because segregation compelled them to share facilities, strong relationships developed among the state's black communities.[8]

Many black West Virginians lived in company-owned coal towns, and the coal industry largely determined the nature of race relations and the fate of black families in the state. Though the Urban League commended the United Mine Workers of America for its progressive racial stance, the UMWA did nothing to break down a racial job hierarchy in the mines, nor did it address the segregated society outside the mines. Segregation prevailed in company housing, schools, churches, and most other aspects of life. Governor William C. Marland's Wyoming County hometown, Glen Rogers (where his father was mine superintendent), epitomized coal town racial relations, even as it sought to represent the cutting edge of modernity. At Glen Rogers, the Chicago-based Old Ben Coal Corporation maintained segregated facilities in a new masonry construction recreation center built after a New Year's Eve fire destroyed the old wooden center in 1945. The theater restricted blacks to the balcony (as was common practice in West Virginia at the time), and the large new pool hall separated black and white patrons with two counters running across the middle. Clerks of both races served food and drinks and collected table fees across both counters. Players on opposite sides of the room played at similar tables. Whites and blacks shouted amicably and familiarly to each other across the divide, but they remained on their respective sides of the pool room, in an Appalachian coal town version of "separate but equal" as mandated by a northern corporation.[9]

As early as 1947, West Virginia State College, a state-supported black school at Institute, near Charleston, anticipated the change in mining technology and the impact that it could have on black miners and the black community by trying to train miners through extension programs in the coalfields. Noting that John L. Lewis had predicted that 98,000 miners would be displaced, the extension division's 1947 annual report warned: "How many of these displaced miners will be Negroes depends on how many of them are now weaning themselves from the pick and shovel and eyeing the controls and mechanisms of modern mining machinery." The success of the training program depended on acceptance by the coal operators, many of whom, the report noted, still had a discriminatory attitude. In some places, operators would not allow black miners to participate in the kind of training available to whites. To try to reach African Americans denied training in conventional ways, the West Virginia State College extension program held an annual miners' encampment at Camp Washington Carver at Clifftop, Fayette County.[10]

Group portrait of coal miners in rescue gear at the Mine Rescue Training Station, Kilsyth West Virginia, about 1947. West Virginia and Regional History Collection, West Virginia University Libraries.

Despite West Virginia State's efforts to prepare them, the coal industry's technological advances of the 1950s had a devastating effect on African Americans. The new machines indiscriminately took the jobs of both black and white miners, but mining companies dismissed black miners sooner and at a higher rate, in part because they did the work—digging and loading—that machines took over. Employed primarily as unskilled loaders, blacks had little opportunity to learn the skilled positions or to obtain skilled jobs if they did. Management either believed that black miners could not learn to operate the new machines or that they were too unreliable. Seniority gave no leverage, as companies laid miners off according to job classification, not time spent on the job. The UMWA's image as a racially integrated union suffered, because the union did little to protect black workers or to help them upgrade their skills. Black miners believed that the machines also broke down a certain level of integration that had existed in the mines as coal companies assigned whites to machine operated sections and blacks to the manual loading sections, which of course received the first discharge notices. The machines transformed the miner's work, creating new jobs in areas like electricity and machine maintenance, and making unskilled work like digging and loading obsolescent. In effect, as far as both management and the union were concerned, the machines made black miners obsolescent as well. The numbers of black West Virginia miners fell from 22,089 in 1930 to 15,423 in 1950 to 1,685 in 1970, a decline from 23 percent to about 4 percent of the total mine work force.[11]

Willie Collins, an African American coal miner who grew up on Cabin Creek during the mine wars of the post World War I era, told an interviewer in 1973 of his experiences, which give some idea of what black miners faced in the era. A World War II veteran, he had spent most of his enlistment building roads in India and Burma. When he came back to West Virginia in 1946, he hoped to get similar work outside around the mines at Tams in Raleigh County's Winding Gulf coalfield. The "office girl" at Tams told him the company hired blacks only for jobs in the mines, so he took a mining job and worked until one day in 1953 when he received his cutoff notice as he walked out of the mine at the end of his shift. As noted in chapter 1, he left his family and went to Ohio where he washed cars, but he just scraped by and could not get used to the cold weather. Finally he went back to Tams. Since the coal company now had many empty houses, they charged low rent. He and his wife gardened, and he did odd jobs and collected unemployment to support his family of eight. Finally in 1955 he got another mining job, but two things immediately impressed him: "how many machines there were and how few colored there were. As quick as they could, the company was moving in loaders, roof bolting machines, cutting machines, and new motors, and they mined as much coal with 100 men as they had with 300 or 400 before. And just about everyone on them machines was white."[12]

In addition to losing mining jobs, African Americans in West Virginia also now faced competition from unemployed white miners for jobs traditionally considered black jobs, such as ditch digging and hod carrying, further complicating the efforts of blacks to remain in the state. Some of the unemployed men moved with their families from the coal camps to towns and cities in West Virginia, but most of them left the state as the African American population of the state plummeted.[13]

Desegregating the Schools: The Impact of *Brown*

Historians have generally given West Virginia high marks for its desegregation efforts, particularly in regard to education,[14] but the record reveals that the West Virginia counties with significant African American populations did little better than the states of the former Confederacy. When the Supreme Court ordered school desegregation in *Brown v. Board of Education of Topeka, Kansas* on May 17, 1954, most of the governors in states with segregated school systems proclaimed their opposition. In neighboring Virginia, Governor Thomas Stanley pledged to "use every means at my command to continue segregated schools in Virginia," and he went so far as to suggest repeal of the state constitutional requirement for public schools. By the spring of 1956, the Virginia legislature had passed a resolution supporting the concept of interposition (that is, interposing state law over federal law), Senator Harry Flood Byrd had issued a call for massive resistance, and the mainstream of Virginian politicians became committed to the all-out defense of white supremacy. Most of the other legislatures in the former Confederacy also passed resolutions supporting the doctrine of interposition (maintaining that state law could contravene federal law), and members of southern congressional delegations endorsed a Southern Manifesto, which declared *Brown* "contrary to the Constitution."[15]

West Virginia's immediate response to *Brown* resembled that of Kentucky and other border states. Historian Steven Channing calls Kentucky Governor Lawrence Wetherby's response to *Brown* (calling for cooperation with federal law) "courageous," given the highly charged reaction of many whites at the time to the idea of school desegregation. Governor Marland of West Virginia just as courageously quickly proclaimed his determination to carry out the requirements of the law. State officials, including School Superintendent William Woodson Trent, also moved quickly to acknowledge *Brown* as the law of the land and to predict that desegregation would proceed quietly and smoothly in West Virginia. No West Virginia congressmen signed the Southern Manifesto, a statement of southern congressmen calling for resistance to *Brown*, although Senator Robert C. Byrd would later be among the leaders in the fight against the Civil Rights Act of 1964.[16]

Some rather vocal opposition to Marland's stand arose, and he received dozens of virulently racist letters condemning his action.[17] Because Marland had already committed political suicide by alarming the economic and political powers of the state with his coal taxation proposal, his stand on *Brown* had no effect on his political career. West Virginia politicians and legislators generally felt no need to resist *Brown* at all costs or to engage in the politics of race baiting, to which some politicians in the former Confederate states turned during the uncertainties and upheaval of the civil rights era. Such appeals had no resonance in West Virginia where the electorate worried more about charges of political corruption and economic issues as the new machine age further undermined the state economy.[18]

Despite Marland's forthrightness and the speed with which official West Virginia acknowledged the Supreme Court ruling as the law of the land, the state's record overall gives slight cause for celebration. It is likely that economic circumstances in West Virginia would have eventually led to school integration in most of the state even if the Supreme Court had not required it, although Henry Louis Gates says that without *Brown* and the quick response to it by the Mineral County school board, schools in his hometown, Piedmont, might not have integrated for another hundred years.[19] The revolutionary impact of mechanization on black coal miners certainly conditioned West Virginia's response to *Brown*. The state's small African American population, concentrated primarily in a few coal-mining counties, was being rapidly "modernized" right out of the state, reducing the need for black schools, at almost exactly the same time that the Supreme Court handed down its momentous decision. In 1953 the 26,133 African Americans enrolled in West Virginia schools accounted for slightly less than 6 percent of the state's public school population of 446,710. The system employed about a thousand African American teachers and slightly more that fifteen thousand white teachers.[20] State law required county school boards to provide a school for black students if as many as ten black students resided in a county. Counties might avoid building a school for a small population by providing transportation and tuition for students to attend a school in another county. At the beginning of the 1950s thirty-three black high schools operated in the state, most of them with small enrollments, and several counties transported their few black students to schools in other counties.[21]

For a poor state like West Virginia that underfunded education on all levels, it made compelling financial sense to abandon the dual system and to close black schools with low enrollments, inadequate academic programs, and decaying facilities. Even in the absence of legal compulsion, it is likely that economic realities eventually would have persuaded most West Virginia counties to move away from the dual system if they could overcome the state constitution's mandated school segregation. After *Brown*, and the acknowledgment by state authorities that the federal law superseded the state constitution, most boards in counties with few blacks—like Gates's Mineral County—welcomed the opportunity to close schools that had once served a larger population but now weighed upon the school boards like albatrosses.[22]

Further evidence of the trend in West Virginia is that, even before *Brown*, members of the black West Virginia State Teachers Association (WVSTA) and the white West Virginia Education Association (WVEA) had formed joint committees to discuss integrating the groups. The WVSTA had been founded in 1893 after WVEA refused to admit blacks to membership. With the rise in black population connected with the growth of the southern coalfields, the WVSTA became an influential lobbying organization, persuading the legislature to give equal pay to black teachers and to require that any county that did not provide a black high school pay tuition and an allowance to enable black students to attend high school outside the county. WVSTA also successfully lobbied for the requirement that the state board of education have at least one black member. By the 1950s, however, the decline in black population undermined the membership and influence of the WVSTA, making it increasingly difficult to maintain as a viable organization. For some time the two organizations had a somewhat symbiotic relationship. As WVEA chapters in some counties began to admit black members, a few black teachers held memberships in both associations. The black association often met at the same time and in the same town as WVEA in order to economize by using the same speakers. In October 1953, members of WVSTA voted to support a merger with WVEA. In May 1954, in the wake of *Brown*, WVEA followed suit. In October 1954, the WVSTA and WVEA held their last separate conventions at the same time in Charleston, coming together for a joint closing session, which marked the end of segregation in the state teachers' organizations and the end of WVSTA, as the black teachers organization ceased to exist.[23]

In West Virginia school desegregation proceeded rapidly in counties that had little black population, and West Virginia legislators and educators generally ignored calls from southern states to resist *Brown* at all costs. In the few counties that retained significant numbers of African Americans, however, the school systems delayed fully integrating until a decade or more after the Supreme Court decision and then only under the pressure of federal agencies and NAACP lawsuits. The state board never devised a statewide plan and placed little pressure on the counties that did not move quickly. From the time of the *Brown* decision, both Governor Marland and Superintendent Trent proclaimed the state's acceptance of *Brown*'s mandate but insisted that the method and pace of meeting the Supreme Court's mandate would be determined by the school boards in each county. Overall, despite the early positive response of the state, its record was decidedly mixed.[24]

A Rehearsal for Desegregation

Amid optimistic early statements about school integration in West Virginia and the nearly universal expressions of support by political and educational leaders of both races, some counties pressed forward with desegregation plans in the fall of 1954, but this effort, which in retrospect might be seen as a rehearsal for desegregation, brought some surprises and unwelcome national attention as white parents and students resisted with demonstrations, forcing some school boards to postpone desegregation. These incidents raised national concerns that even in West Virginia, the northernmost of the seventeen states with segregated schools, desegregation of the schools would be difficult. Most of the county school systems with substantial black population delayed movement toward integration while awaiting further guidance from the Supreme Court, but some counties moved ahead with either full or partial integration.

In Greenbrier County the board opted for a plan that allowed students to choose whether to change schools, but when black students attempted to attend a combined white elementary and high school in Rupert and a high school in White Sulphur Springs, white parents and students organized protest demonstrations and boycotted the schools. At Rupert, where twelve black students had enrolled, a caravan of some twenty cars arrived with white parents, 80 percent of them concerned mothers, who set up picket lines and told children to go home. At White Sulphur Springs, 300 white high school students, about three-fourths of the total, went on strike to protest the enrollment of twenty-five black students from Bolling High School, the county's black high school located in Lewisburg, nine mines away. The white students paraded through the town's streets carrying placards proclaiming "No Negroes Wanted in Our Schools." Some 700 white parents and townsmen gathered at the high school athletic field and voted to physically remove any students who attended classes until the school board abandoned the integration plan. African Americans made up about 600 of the town's population of 2,643, and a group of 175 black residents met at the Baptist Church. When they decided to withhold their children from the schools until the board provided equal facilities, Willard A. Brown, legal advisor of the state NAACP, persuaded them to await the Supreme Court's amplification of the *Brown* decision. In the face of the white resistance, the Greenbrier County Board of Education, after a stormy all-day session that went from 9 a.m. to 10:30 p.m., decided to call off its integration plans for 1954. County superintendent Delvin D. Harrah accordingly ordered the black students to return to their former schools. In Barbour County, parents demonstrated to prevent the integration of an elementary school, but Philippi High School integrated without incident.[25] The Boone County board ignored protests and student strikes, and eventually the protests there faded.[26]

Some school boards took the path of token integration in 1954. Huntington's Citizens Commission on Human Relations commended the Cabell County School Board and citizens of the county for the peaceful manner in which school desegregation began, in contrast to other areas of the state, although it resulted in only fourteen black students transferring to white schools. Huntington, the state's largest city, had allowed students entering elementary school or junior high school the choice of changing schools.[27] Parkersburg (Wood County) carried out a similar plan. Wayne County ended its practice of paying tuition for black students to attend black schools in Cabell and enrolled four black students. Monongalia, with a black student population of 210 in one high school and three elementary schools, integrated completely in 1954, but retained only eight of the county's fourteen black teachers. In Randolph County the black Riverside School (which included all twelve grades) closed, and the fifty students enrolled in white schools. Only one Riverside teacher received assignment to the county high school in Elkins. Pocahontas and Monroe counties, eastern counties bordering on Virginia, integrated high schools but not elementary schools. For Pocahontas this meant the end of $6,000 in expenses to send students to black high schools in four surrounding counties. In some counties that had not provided for a desegregation plan, including Kanawha, schools turned away black students who sought to enroll in the fall of 1954.[28]

Although its school board chose to delay until 1955, Kanawha County carried out the most effective early desegregation. One of the largest systems, Kanawha (including the city of Charleston), had about 55,000 students including some 3,200 blacks. In 1955, about 800 black students in the first, second, and seventh grades moved to white schools without incident. Superintendent Virgil Flinn warned against any interference by parents or others, saying he would do everything in his power to see to the success of the plan. In 1956, the Kanawha board closed all black schools in the county, including Garnet High School, thus integrating completely within three years.[29] Marion moved even more quickly, integrating schools within one year after the *Brown* ruling. The county closed Fairmont's black Dunbar High School in 1955, and the students moved to traditionally white West Fairmont High School or other white schools in the county.[30] Raleigh County attempted to desegregate in 1955, but white protests and demonstrations at several schools led the county school board to back away. It would be another decade before Raleigh fully integrated its schools.[31]

When the Greenbrier County board failed to renew the attempt to integrate in 1955, the West Virginia branch of the NAACP went to federal district court seeking an injunction to force immediate and complete integration. After a three day hearing, Judge Ben Moore proposed a plan for voluntary integration, to begin at the start of the second semester, and both the board and the NAACP accepted the plan. The NAACP meanwhile pressed the fight for integration by sending letters to other counties not moving forward with integration plans.[32]

Persistent Segregation

The *Charleston Gazette* hailed the peaceful steps toward integration of West Virginia schools in 1955 as evidence that the "stormy period" some had expected would not take place. The demonstrations of the previous year, the *Gazette* suggested, represented the last gasp of "the most bitter opponents." They had their day but found themselves in a small minority as most West Virginians desired to "abide by the law."[33] The *Gazette*'s celebratory tone proved premature. Though incidents of violence remained minimal, and some counties moved with dispatch to end segregation, it would be more than a decade before the dual system would end in the counties with the greatest number of black students. Moreover, the *Gazette* gave no attention to the impact on black students who, with little or no preparation on the part of school authorities, had to leave their old schools and to undergo the daunting challenge of entering white schools as a distinct minority. Several West Virginia counties, primarily in the southern coalfields, resisted school desegregation for years, finally agreeing to the complete elimination of their dual systems only because of pressure from the NAACP, prodding of the West Virginia Human Rights Commission, and, after the Civil Rights Act of 1964, threats that they would lose federal funds if they did not comply.

Although the 1956 election brought something of a political revolution to the state as a Republican governor and a Republican school superintendent were elected for the first time since 1928, most state officials continued to support school integration. In 1957, Governor Cecil Underwood provided the only dissenting vote when the Southern Governors' Conference condemned President Eisenhower's use of troops to protect black students integrating Little Rock Central High School, Arkansas. The NAACP awarded Underwood honorary membership for taking this stand.[34]

By 1958, of the fifty-five counties, twenty-four county school systems had completely integrated, eleven had no black students, and twenty had partially desegregated. Many of the southern counties, where most of the black students resided, continued to resist desegregation almost as determinedly as the last ditch Jim Crow counties in the Deep South resisted. Despite the state's official embrace of *Brown* as the law of the land, only about 40 percent of black students attended integrated schools by 1958.[35]

Nevertheless, when the opening of schools in 1958 brought continued strong resistance to integration in Virginia, Arkansas, and other southern states, some West Virginians, focusing on the successes in Kanawha County, suggested that others could learn from West Virginia's example.[36] In 1959 the West Virginia Advisory Committee to the U.S. Civil Rights Commission reported with muted enthusiasm that school integration "is progressing at perhaps a little better than average rate."[37]

By 1963, the process of school desegregation remained incomplete and in many ways unsatisfactory. Blacks complained that many all-black schools continued; faculties remained largely segregated; black principals remained only in black schools; with one notable exception, no black coaches became head coaches in integrated schools; and school boards no longer hired new black teachers. The numbers of black teachers fell sharply. The West Virginia Human Rights Commission condemned the continuation of all-black schools, suggesting that county boards kept the small black schools operating primarily to avoid the integration of teachers, citing the cases of Conley High School in Wyoming County with fifty-seven students and five teachers and Bolling School in Lewisburg with ninety-eight students and eight teachers. The commission also noted the "almost complete absence of any positive program for human relations in the schools."[38]

The only things being done came from the initiative of individual teachers. No county undertook a program to promote mutual understanding. The WVHRC claimed that "the education community has by and large remained silent as to the significance of the social revolution that is taking place."[39] It is striking that the organ of the WVEA, the *West Virginia School Journal*, gave little attention to integration or to issues of student adjustment.[40]

Many aspects of the process of school integration caused bitter feelings among African Americans. In the first news conference after *Brown*, State Superintendent Trent noted that a higher percentage of black teachers than white teachers held appropriate degrees. Many qualified white teachers had moved to states with higher pay, compelling counties to rely on white teachers with emergency certifications.[41] Black teachers came to feel that school boards made them take a back seat to these white teachers with inferior qualifications. The case of basketball coach James R. Jarret, a graduate of Howard University, typifies the kind of thing that happened to black teachers with desegregation, though, because of his reputation and special skills, Jarret fared better than most. Jarret had a successful fifteen-year career in Kanawha County's black school system, coaching at Boyd Junior High from 1935 to 1942 and at Garnet, Charleston's black high school, from 1948 to 1955. At Garnet he coached both football and basketball, and his basketball teams compiled a remarkable record of 170 victories, including three state championships, and only 40 losses.[42] During his days at Garnet, to make ends meet on his small teaching salary, Jarret also worked as a busboy at a local hotel and carried mail for the post office in the summer. With desegregation and the closure of Garnet, Jarret lost his head coaching positions, going to Charleston High School as an assistant football coach and social studies teacher. When the basketball head coach position came open in 1958, the school board and the principal floated two names of much less qualified whites as the likely new coach, but according to the *Charleston Gazette*, "public sentiment dictated against the mistreatment of a veteran like Jarret." After an embarrassing delay and much temporizing, Charleston High School announced Jarret's appointment as head coach, the first of a black coach to head a major sport at an integrated high school in the state.[43]

Black administrators, teachers, and coaches with less compelling records than Jarret's often had difficulty keeping their jobs. Not until ten years after *Brown* was an African American ever assigned as a principal in Kanawha County. In 1967 the WVHRC noted the drastic decline in black teachers since 1955 and the difficulty black teachers, regardless of qualifications, had in gaining employment. Most black principals and coaches lost their positions and accepted assistant roles or demotion to classroom teaching. In McDowell County, for example, from 1964 to 1966 the number of black principals dwindled from over twenty to six. No black high school principal was retained as principal of an integrated high school. Crews cleaning out the former black high schools to make way for new functions discarded records, trophies, and most of the collections of black history and literature. Worst of all, black students became less active in organizations like honors, bands, and school clubs. Majorette, drum major, and cheerleading positions appeared to be closed to black students in most schools. Only in athletics were blacks well represented. School boards even dropped the names of the old schools, names of local and national black heroes like Douglass, Garnet, Dunbar, Carter G. Woodson, and Stratton.[44]

In 1964, fully a decade after *Brown*, the Human Rights Commission cited seven county systems (Fayette, Jefferson, Mercer, Raleigh, Mingo, Wyoming, and McDowell)—all southern coal counties except Jefferson—that continued to operate segregated schools. The State Board of Education, while affirming its commitment to integration, took no action to compel the segregationist counties to comply.[45] The passage of the 1964 Civil Rights Act put federal pressure on those counties that tried to hang on to segregated schools, because failure to comply with the law could result in the loss of federal aid in such areas as the hot lunch program, counseling services, and vocational and adult education programs.[46] In a speech in Charleston on September 7, 1965, Howard McKinney, executive director of the state human rights commission, demanded that members of the State Board of Education "quit playing footsy with the segregationists" and start providing leadership. He declared that more than a decade after the *Brown* decision, "there is not a single all-Negro high school in the state which can be justified on an educational basis. All of them are monuments to a bigoted society, and are preserved for the one purpose of keeping the Negro teacher out of the integrated classroom." Even in counties with a better record in desegregating schools, only a half-dozen blacks across the state served as principals of integrated schools.[47]

McDowell, one of the southern coal-producing counties, and Jefferson, an agricultural county in the Eastern Panhandle, provide contrasting examples of the counties that resisted full integration. Until the 1880s, McDowell County had been very sparsely populated, but with the arrival of the Norfolk and Western Railroad, coal mining boomed and coal operators had to recruit a labor force from outside the area. As a result, McDowell came to rely heavily on African Americans and immigrants to mine coal. At the time of *Brown*, 24 percent of the population was African American. The county's segregated public school system enrolled over 24,000 students in the early 1950s, and included four black high schools. In contrast to the black and white schools of southern states of the former Confederacy, the separate systems in McDowell paid black and white teachers according to the same pay scales, and all schools had similar student-teacher ratios. Nevertheless, substantial inequalities existed in equipment and buildings.[48]

In 1955 the McDowell County Board of Education, while acknowledging the *Brown* decision, took the position that "we find but little interest among parents, Negro and white, in changing schools." The board asserted that it could best serve students and parents by making as few changes as possible. The McDowell County chapter of the NAACP selected a committee to meet with the Board of Education to insist that blacks wanted integration. The committee urged that the board take immediate steps that would lead to "early elimination of segregation in the public schools." The board responded by establishing advisory committees with black and white members in each of the county's five magisterial districts.[49]

Under pressure from the advisory boards and the threat of legal action from the state NAACP, the McDowell school board in February 1956 modified its policy to make clear that parents might choose to move their children to new schools in the fall of 1956, establishing a freedom of choice plan, which some other counties had already employed as a device to minimize integration and to maintain separate black and white faculties. As late as 1963, McDowell still operated twenty-three all-black elementary schools, one junior high school, and four high schools, about one-third of the total all-black schools remaining in the state.[50] This kind of limited, token integration remained the rule in McDowell until Title IV of the 1964 Civil Rights Act compelled more rapid movement toward the end of dual systems, but not until March 1966 did the McDowell County Board of Education finally approve a plan to close its remaining all-black schools.[51]

In the agricultural Eastern Panhandle, Jefferson County had a black population of 15.9 percent in 1954. Unlike the African American miners of the southern coal mining counties like McDowell, who had emigrated to the area from the South in the late nineteenth and early twentieth centuries, Jefferson county African American families traced their roots to antebellum slavery in the area. A survey of the Jefferson school system in 1954 included the three black elementary schools and Page-Jackson, the black high school, and maintained that these schools "will continue to serve well for a considerable time." The survey recommended that the three white high schools (Charles Town, Harpers Ferry, and Shepherdstown) be consolidated "sometime in the future." As it did not mention Page-Jackson as part of the recommended consolidation, the 1954 report, prepared before the Supreme Court handed down the *Brown* decision in May, seems to have anticipated continued segregation.[52]

After *Brown*, Jefferson operated a freedom of choice plan that maintained a dual system with token integration. As in the case of McDowell County, only the threat of withholding federal funds in the Civil Rights Act of 1964 brought full compliance with integration. In July 1965, county superintendent T. A. Lowery told the Jefferson school board that the federal government would no longer accept the freedom of choice plan. The board, unwilling to lose federal aid, then quickly planned for the integration of the three black elementary schools and the closing of Page-Jackson High School in the fall of 1966. By then Page-Jackson had only 113 students.[53]

The southern mining counties Mingo, Wyoming, Fayette, and Mercer also resisted full school integration, and in 1965 they too faced the loss of federal funds for noncompliance with the *Brown* decision.[54] Eventually legal action by the West Virginia NAACP and pressure from the federal government ended the last vestiges of West Virginia's dual system in education. The NAACP resorted to legal action in some dozen cases involving school integration, eventually prevailing in all of them.[55] Mercer County resisted pressures until the school board became the target of an investigation by the civil rights division of the U.S. Department of Justice. In 1968, the board finally agreed to close the five remaining all-black schools in the county, including the last all-black high school in the state, Bluefield Park Central, which closed in 1969, as did Genoa Junior High in Bluefield. The last all-black school to close was Piney Oaks Elementary in Raleigh County in 1971.[56]

School desegregation produced bittersweet fruits for the African American community in West Virginia, which had always had close ties with the black public schools. In the segregated black system, not only did the schools educate the children but the teachers also provided community leadership and school buildings served as community centers, often bearing names of respected figures in local and national black history. It is also no small matter that teaching provided the best jobs available for educated black women. Integration changed the nature of the relationship between African Americans and the schools, and the anticipated benefits of integration came disappointingly slowly, if at all. Nevertheless, African Americans welcomed school integration, says historian Ancella Bickley, and though "the elation faded after the closing of the black schools, few wanted to go back."[57] Nancy Smith Robinson, a 1946 graduate of Douglass High School in Huntington (which closed in 1966) expressed a similar view to an interviewer in 1993: "When Douglass closed we lost that closeness. It's not that we were against desegregation. We just hoped integration could come with the same closeness."[58] Henry Louis Gates Jr., in *Colored People*, recalls the fondness that Piedmont African Americans had for Howard High School: "They liked the teachers, they liked the principal, they liked the building and basketball team. They liked its dignity and pride." But he also recalls, "They did not like its worn-down textbooks, the ones sent up by the board of education when the white schools got tired of them or when they were outdated." Gates, excited and scared, entered the first grade in 1956, one year after Mineral County schools had been integrated. He says that the older African American kids of Piedmont, who had grown up in a rigidly segregated society and had gone to segregated schools, had a more difficult transition.[59]

As one who experienced the transformation as a teenager in Charleston, Kojo Jones remembered it as a traumatic time that fell far short of the ideal of integration held out by black and white leaders. Black students received no counseling or help to face the substantial cultural and psychological shock of moving from black schools to schools where they became a distinct racial minority. Jones thinks his generation of black students would have been better off if the battle had been waged for better funding of black institutions rather than for integration.[60] The reality in West Virginia, however, was that segregation probably could not have been sustained much longer as black enrollments declined precipitously in the coalfield counties with the exodus of African American miners.

Integrating Higher Education

Like the states of the former Confederacy and most border states, West Virginia had also segregated higher education by law. The first effort to provide some measure of higher education for blacks came when the state awarded a subsidy to Storer College, a private institution in Harpers Ferry established by northern philanthropists in the post-Civil War era.[61] In the 1890s the legislature established the West Virginia Colored Institute as a land grant institution in Kanawha County and Bluefield Colored Institute in Mercer County. During the Depression years the legislature changed the names of these institutions to West Virginia State College and Bluefield State College. West Virginia State gained a national reputation and drew its student body from many different states. It also attracted an excellent faculty. The Strayer report of 1945 cited the college as "one of the two or three leading institutions" among land grant colleges for blacks. Bluefield State struggled with inadequate facilities and low appropriations, finally achieving accreditation as a teaching college in 1947. These institutions trained teachers for the state's black schools and gave vocational courses for black students whose local school districts did not provide separate black facilities.[62]

The first break in the system of segregation in higher education came in 1938, when the Supreme Court in *Missouri ex rel. Gaines* held that the state of Missouri could not deny a black applicant admission to the university law school, even if it offered to pay the student's tuition to attend an integrated school in another state.[63] West Virginia had routinely followed the very practice that the court found unconstitutional in the *Gaines* case. According to historian Charles Henry Ambler, in 1939 West Virginia University quietly opened its graduate programs to black students, but "in keeping with understandings among leaders of both races," the university did not publicize the new policy. Not surprisingly, given the lack of publicity, few black students enrolled.[64]

After a ruling by the state attorney general in 1948, some of the private church-related colleges in West Virginia, including Alderson-Broaddus, Bethany, West Virginia Wesleyan, and Davis and Elkins, began to accept African American students,[65] but all of the state colleges and the undergraduate divisions of West Virginia University remained segregated until the *Brown* decision in 1954. Soon after the Supreme Court's decision in 1954, Attorney General John G. Fox held that the segregation requirement in the state constitution no longer had effect. The state board of education declared that "any qualified student may be admitted to any state college" under the board's jurisdiction.[66] In 1955, West Virginia University enrolled some fifty black students; Marshall College, sixty; and Shepherd College, twenty-four. A few blacks enrolled at other colleges in the state that had previously been segregated.[67]

Hal Greer, among the black enrollees at Marshall in 1955, became the first African American athlete at Marshall and, through his exploits on the basketball court, helped to open the door for others. Soon after the Supreme Court handed down the *Brown* decision, Marshall University basketball coach Cam Henderson visited Greer at Huntington's Douglass High School and offered him a scholarship to attend his hometown college. Greer accepted and went on to have a very successful career at Marshall that led to a long tenure with the Syracuse Nationals and Philadelphia 76ers of the National Basketball Association. In 1997, the NBA named him one of the top fifty players in its history. But Greer faced difficult times during his Marshall years as restaurant and hotel operators in places like Charleston; Johnson City, Tennessee; and Morehead, Kentucky, sometimes refused to accommodate the team because of him. Huntington itself, his hometown, remained segregated through his undergraduate years.[68]

The desegregation of higher education in West Virginia profoundly affected black institutions. The one private black institution, Storer College in Harpers Ferry, closed its doors in 1955 after the loss of its small state subsidy.[69] West Virginia State quickly lost its identity as a black college with a student body drawn from many states as white students from the Charleston area quickly took advantage of the low tuition and convenient location of the college. In the first year of integration, 399 white students enrolled. The college attracted national attention as an example of what a *New York Times* article called "integration in reverse." At the end of a decade, black students made up only 20 percent of the student body. The college also lost its land grant status.[70]

Although many in the black community and alumni deeply regretted the transformation of West Virginia State, President William

J. L. Wallace hailed *Brown* as the salvation of the college, which found itself in a struggle for survival in the post-war period. After a brief increase in enrollment with the return of veterans, the school began a precipitous decline in 1948, which continued apace as the black population of the state dropped with the transformation of the coal industry in the early 1950s. As coal employment declined, Wallace later noted, some whites in the Charleston area found employment in the growing local chemical industry, but that industry remained largely closed to blacks. During the same time that in-state enrollment fell, out-of-state enrollment (which at times had made up as much as 60 percent of the total) also dropped as Southern states—wary of integrationist trends—began to put more money into black state colleges. Wallace watched in despair as the student base for West Virginia State withered. Then, *Brown* came and "the magic years began." In 1955 and 1956 the college experienced growth rates of 35 and 38 percent. Wallace recalled that some critics of the transformation "seemed to think I should have stood in the door like Wallace of Alabama did and say, 'No, no, no! You can't come in here!' but integrating the college made West Virginia State a dynamic growing college rather than a dying one."[71]

Bluefield State College, located in the center of the southern mining region, eventually experienced a similar fate, being transformed from a residential black institution to a primarily white commuter school. As the black mining population declined in the 1950s, student enrollments plummeted, but the college adjusted by offering courses of a more vocational and technological bent. Bluefield drew fewer white students than West Virginia State at first because Concord College, just a few miles away in Mercer County, served the needs of white students in the area, but in time white students became the primary source of enrollment growth as the historic African American population base in the area declined. As a consequence of the change, Bluefield State developed a somewhat schizophrenic character, as the college's dormitories continued to house almost exclusively African American students, and white students commuted to the school. As early as 1958 white students made up 38 percent of the enrollment, and by 1965 African Americans slipped into the minority. In that year the state board also hired a white president for Bluefield State, Wendell Hardway. For the next few years (as discussed further in chapter 6) the college went through a much more contentious transition than West Virginia State. As historian William P. Jackameit has pointed out, the transformation of West Virginia State and Bluefield State from predominantly black to predominantly white was unique. In the decade after the *Brown* decision, the traditionally black colleges in the rest of the country remained black.[72]

Integrating the Broader Society: A Grassroots Awakening

At the end of the 1950s the West Virginia Advisory Committee to the United States Civil Rights Commission reported that "the process of integrating has developed as smoothly in West Virginia as in any comparable state." The committee found discrimination in voting "practically non-existent." But serious issues remained. Substandard housing plagued all groups, compounding the problem of housing discrimination, which real estate brokers, sellers of property, and subdivision developers almost universally practiced. The committee also noted widespread discrimination in the fields of public accommodations and employment.[73] Henry Louis Gates Jr. recalls that the dawn of the civil rights era had little direct impact on Piedmont. Tongue in cheek, he says blacks and whites got along pretty well "as long as colored people didn't try to sit down in the Cut-Rate or at the Rendezvous Bar; or eat pizza at Eddie's or buy property; or move into the white neighborhoods or dance with, date, or dilate upon white people. Not to mention try to get a job in the craft unions at the paper mill. Or have a drink at the white VFW, or join the white American Legion, or get loans at the bank, or just generally get out of line. Other than that, colored and white got on pretty well."[74]

Racial tensions flared in West Virginia as elsewhere from time to time, and to break down the barriers that remained, grassroots efforts played a role as important as laws or institutions. Although it is a story largely untold, West Virginia had its share of civil rights demonstrations, evidence of a commitment by West Virginia African Americans and sympathetic whites to seek a full realization of constitutional guarantees and social justice. West Virginia's demonstrations occurred sporadically and few turned violent. Cities like Charleston, Huntington, and Bluefield experienced racial tensions, and in the Eastern Panhandle race relations probably more closely approximated those of the former Confederacy. Though far from ideal, race relations in West Virginia exhibited little of the violent bigotry exhibited in some of the racial clashes elsewhere. According to reports of the West Virginia Human Rights Commission, the most violent evidences of racial strife came from clashes between black and white teenagers.[75]

One writer characterizing the tone of race relations for the United States Civil Rights Commission in 1964 noted the steady and unemotional acceptance of the transition from segregation to integration in West Virginia. Most white people, he believed, had an attitude of "plebian goodwill" toward African Americans, although some viewed blacks as alien and inferior, and few had any personal contact with blacks. Most blacks, who continued to be victims of job discrimination and exploitation by the white community, harbored "an appreciable hatred toward whites."[76] In 1960 the median income for white families in West Virginia was $4,650, but for black families, it was only $2,874. With the loss of mining jobs for men and declining numbers of teaching jobs for women, and with competition from unemployed white workers for other work, many African Americans found themselves relegated to the traditional "Negro jobs," such as janitor, bellhop, maid, and shoeshine boy.[77]

A National Urban League survey of Charleston gives some sense of the situation for urban blacks in West Virginia after World War II. In 1946, blacks made up about 11 percent of the city's population. The majority worked as unskilled labor or as domestic servants and suffered from chronic unemployment. Some women worked in clerical work or in retail eating and drinking establishments. Municipal fire and police departments provided the most remunerative work, but the police employed only six blacks on a seventy-two man force. About 10 percent of federal postal employees were black.

The wartime influx of blacks into Charleston had worsened an already serious housing problem. Black citizens generally lived in dilapidated frame structures, and few could qualify for Federal Housing Administration loans. Another serious problem was a high rate of black juvenile delinquency. Blacks suffered from what the Urban League called "racial subordination," and neither local government nor civic organizations did anything to improve race relations. Black schools fell far short of white schools in resources. African American churches provided the center of black social life and the most important agency of community experience. Churches sponsored lectures, public meetings, concerts, and community programs. Charleston blacks also belonged to numerous social, civic, and fraternal organizations. The Urban League report (coming before machines became a further instrument of racial division in the mines) commended the United Mine Workers of America for its progress toward racial integration. The report concluded by calling for organize efforts in Charleston to improve black welfare in the city through more equitable employment and better housing. Other West Virginia cities, Huntington and Wheeling, presented similar circumstances.[78] On August 11, 1958, a hot Sunday summer afternoon, a small group of Charleston African Americans sat talking after services at Simpson Memorial Methodist Church about what might be done to improve what they regarded as the sad state of race relations in the city. One of the group, Cynthia H. Burks, said, "As we sit here talking, no Negro can get a cup of coffee, attend a movie, buy a decent house, sell over the counter, or stay in a hotel. In fact I can name more things we cannot do than I can name things we can do." She proposed "clearly, firmly, and without fear," as her friend Elizabeth Gilmore later recalled, that the group organized a local chapter of the Congress of Racial Equality (CORE). The others agreed, and the Charleston chapter of CORE was born.[79]

CORE, founded in 1942, pioneered the kinds of tactics that civil rights demonstrators would use in the 1960s, organizing sit-in demonstrations against segregated restaurants, theaters, and buses during World War II and afterwards. Eschewing the traditionally more legalistic approach of the National Association for the Advancement of Colored People, CORE played a major role in many 1960s civil rights demonstrations, such as the famous sit-in at Woolworth's in Greensboro, North Carolina, initiated on February 1, 1960, by four North Carolina A&T freshmen, and the Freedom Rides of May 1961 to integrate bus station facilities in the South.[80]

In August 1958, the national CORE organization had only two field agents and operated a skeletal organization out of a run-down walk-up at 39 Park Row in New York. It had little but advice to offer the fledgling Charleston chapter, but the local chapter that had its origins on that August Sunday in 1958 became the most active group organizing civil rights demonstrations in Charleston and claimed to be the only local organization to use sit-ins and public demonstrations to fight discrimination. During these months, however, the national CORE organization geared up to become one of the most effective organizations in the fight for civil rights.[81]

Before launching its activities, Charleston's CORE chapter announced that it planned to attack discrimination with Christian persuasion combined with nonviolent techniques made popular by Gandhi in India, including sit-ins and standing lines. Charleston CORE would first try to persuade local firms to stop discriminating against blacks and other minorities. If negotiations failed, then CORE would launch nonviolent demonstrations. Elizabeth Gilmore, the secretary of Charleston's CORE chapter, emphasized that "we don't advocate breaking any laws; we do not advocate fighting hate with hate, which only engenders hate." The *Charleston Gazette*, which of course relied on the advertisements of many of the establishments likely to be targeted, responded to the CORE announcement with the editorial advice that change took "an exasperatingly long time" in matters of race and that "we think it would be a mistake for CORE or any other group to lose patience to the extent of resorting to sit-in demonstrations."[82]

Gilmore, a fourth-generation black Charlestonian and the first woman licensed as a funeral director in West Virginia, operated Harden and Harden, a Charleston mortuary, with her husband and served as executive secretary of the CORE group, which included only about a dozen regular members. Long-time Sunday school superintendent of the Simpson Memorial Methodist Church, Gilmore received advice on organization and tactics from the national headquarters of CORE and published reports in the organization newsletter, *CORE-LATOR*. Though small in numbers, Charleston's CORE chapter could draw support from others for its demonstrations and claimed 300 associated members. In spite of the *Gazette*'s condescending advice, which represented the concern of the business community, in September 1958—some eighteen months before the famous Greensboro lunch counter sit-ins at Woolworth's—the Charleston CORE carried out a three-week demonstration and succeeded in persuading Woolworth's, Kresge's, and Newberry's to desegregate their lunch counters. Also beginning in September 1958, and continuing until April 1960, CORE and WE (World Equality), a student group from West Virginia State, picketed and held a lunch counter sit-in at the Diamond, Charleston's largest department store. The management threatened to arrest the demonstrators for trespassing on private property. Policemen arrived and walked about carrying guns, and passersby threatened the demonstrators with switchblade knives, but police arrested neither demonstrators nor those who threatened them. Sometimes white patrons at the Diamond lunch counter expressed sympathy and offered to share coffee or food with the sitters. Finally in May 1960, after almost two years of boycotts, sit-ins, and picketing, the Diamond integrated its coffee shop and cafeteria.[83] CORE and other groups negotiated to integrate other restaurants and dairy stores, the YMCA, YWCA, and the Capitol, Kearse, and Virginian theaters.[84]

An incident that drew embarrassing national attention to the continued segregation in Charleston and became something of a turning point in city racial relations came on January 16, 1959, when a leading Charleston hotel, the Daniel Boone, refused rooms to Elgin Baylor and other black members of the Minneapolis Lakers who came to town for a game with the Cincinnati Royals. The *New York Times* reported the story on page one the next day. Baylor told the *Times*: "They told us we couldn't even get in a halfway decent restaurant, and we had to buy some things at a grocery store and make sandwiches for dinner." The entire Minneapolis team found lodging in another hotel, but Baylor attended the game in street clothes, refusing to play in protest of the racial snub. The local businessmen's group that sponsored the game protested Baylor's action to the National Basketball Association. Because Baylor was becoming one of the leading stars of the NBA (he would win Rookie of the Year honors), the incident in Charleston created ripples across the league. The Lakers had experienced similar treatment in Houston and Charlotte, and team officials had promised Baylor they would play in no other cities with segregated facilities. Maurice Podoloff, the president of the National Basketball Association told the *Times* that "somebody slipped at Charleston," because the league had been assured that black players would suffer no such indignities in West Virginia. After the incident Podoloff brought the issue of accommodations for black players before an NBA owners' meeting. He urged that cities like Houston, Charlotte, and Charleston that discriminated against black players be prohibited from receiving NBA franchises. Robert Short, the Minneapolis owner, insisted that although Baylor's refusal to play cost his team the game, neither he nor the league would punish a player under the circumstances, which had created great emotional strain for the black players.[85]

Soon after the Baylor incident, a similar but even more poignant episode at the Daniel Boone received no media notice at the time but further reveals the depth of the mindless segregation to which some still clung. In this case, the hotel refused to provide accommodations to the first black student to win a Golden Horseshoe award, given annually to eighth-grade students who excel in West Virginia history. Because the hotel would not house the black student, his school principal in Mineral County told him he could not go to Charleston because a misspelled word had cost him the award. The student was Rocky Gates, the older brother of Henry Louis Gates Jr. The younger Gates won a Golden Horseshoe six years later and suffered no such slight.[86]

The CORE demonstrations and incidents like the Baylor matter aroused renewed interest in some communities in interracial cooperation. The West Virginia state government generally took a rhetorically positive position toward the advancement of civil rights, although its actions did not always match the rhetoric. The demonstrations in Charleston in 1958 led to the creation of the biracial Kanawha Valley Council on Human Relations in 1959. After the Elgin Baylor incident, Charleston Mayor John Copenhaver set up a human rights commission with a full-time director to help blacks find employment. The Mercer County Council on Human Relations emerged in 1960 in response to the first demonstrations against segregation in Bluefield.[87] In 1961, the state legislature established the West Virginia Human Rights Commission, charging it with promoting "mutual understanding among all social, religious, and ethnic groups" and eliminating any kind of discrimination based on race, creed, or religion.[88]

Although few opposed the legislation, some legislators claimed to fear "a morality witch hunt," so they saw to it that the commission would have limited funds and few powers. The commission could investigate and try to persuade, but it had no subpoena power and its findings could be used only to call attention to problems.[89] Nevertheless, the commission, wielding only the power of moral suasion, played an important role in efforts to move forward on civil rights in the 1960s. Thomas W. Gavett, a professor of industrial relations at West Virginia University, was the first chair of the commission, and Howard W. McKinney, who had been involved in similar work in Erie, Pennsylvania, carried on the day-to-day work of the commission as executive director.[90]

In its early years the commission encouraged desegregation of schools, keeping pressure on the State Board of Education. It also pushed for desegregation of public accomodations, particularly in regard to restaurants, hotels, motels, and swimming pools. The segregation of medical facilities also drew the commission's attention, as did discrimination in employment, both by public and private employers. In January 1962, at the commission's urging, Governor Barron issued an executive order prohibiting discrimination on the basis of race or religion in state hiring, although private discrimination in employment persisted.[91]

Though the efforts of the Human Rights Commission helped, the organized protests and demonstrations of the African American community played the more important role in dramatizing and pushing forward the cause of civil rights. In addition to the successful lunch counter sit-ins, between 1958 and 1964 the Charleston CORE chapter (coached in their tactics by the CORE national office) used the threat of demonstrations to persuade the Union Carbide and Chemical cafeteria and Charleston General Hospital to integrate their facilities. In cooperation with other organizations, CORE also negotiated for the integration of other restaurants and stores and carried out successful negotiations to persuade department stores and other large local employers to hire African Americans.[92]

CORE also organized the two largest demonstrations of the early 1960s in Charleston. The first, on April 3, 1964, came at the conclusion of an address by James Forman, the National Executive Secretary of the Student Nonviolent Coordinating Committee (SNCC), at a convocation at West Virginia State College. Several hundred persons, mostly black and white students from the college, marched through Charleston to demonstrate their support for passage of the Civil Rights Bill. Forman and Elizabeth Gilmore led the parade and spoke to the crowd from the steps of the state capitol. A week later Gilmore's CORE chapter and a group of West Virginia State students organized a picket line at the Daniel Boone Hotel to protest Senator Robert C. Byrd's appearance at a Democratic Women's luncheon.

Marching students sang freedom songs and carried signs reading, "We Are Against Byrd's Herd," "Out With Byrd," and "Byrd is for the Byrds."[93] In July, Byrd—who twenty-two years before had organized a klavern of the Ku Klux Klan in Raleigh County—led an unsuccessful last-ditch filibuster effort to stop the Civil Rights Bill. He held the floor for fourteen hours and thirteen minutes, the longest speech in the longest filibuster in Senate history.[94]

The second-largest demonstration occurred on March 16, 1965, when some 700 African Americans and several dozen whites marched, prayed, and sang through the streets of Charleston one day after President Johnson, reacting to events in Selma, Alabama, had gone before Congress to call for a strong new voting rights law. The Charleston chapters of NAACP, CORE, and a student group at West Virginia State College organized the demonstration to support the drive for voting rights and in memory of Unitarian minister James Reeb, who had been clubbed to death by a white mob during a demonstration in Selma. The marchers, many of them college students and led by black and white ministers walking arm-in-arm, heard a memorial service for Reeb on the steps of the Old Post Office on Capitol Street and then walked to a meeting with Governor Hulett C. Smith on the Statehouse steps. Smith expressed his strong support for President Johnson's voting rights bill.[95]

Huntington also had a number of demonstrations, and as in the case of Charleston, the demonstrators in Huntington included a group of black and white college students and some local people. In the early 1960s, Huntington, with a black population of about six percent, had substantial segregation of public facilities such as restaurants and theaters, as well as residential segregation and job discrimination. The prevailing system relied on informal or tacit understandings rather than any laws or ordinances. In comparison with the former states of the Confederacy, Huntington's racial climate displayed less overt hostility and racial defamation. A color line existed nonetheless, though whites tended to deny its existence. Blacks hesitated to challenge it for fear of economic retaliation, a matter of no small concern given the "substantial and persistent unemployment" that Huntington had experienced during the past decade.[96]

In the spring of 1963 students at Marshall University organized the Civic Interest Progressives (CIP) and brought the civil rights movement to the university and to the city of Huntington. Made up of twelve to fifteen black and white student activists, most of whom were not Huntington residents, and loosely connected to the Student Non-Violent Coordinating Committee (SNCC), they focused on Huntington issues and cooperated with student groups in Charleston and elsewhere in support of the broader movement. Led by basketball player Phil Carter (who after his student days returned to Marshall as a social work professor), CIP used innovative techniques and determination in its fight to bring down the barriers of segregation in Huntington. Although some local black leaders doubted the wisdom of demonstrations, Marian T. "Bunche" Gay and her sister Antoinette Lease strongly supported the students, opening their home for CIP meetings. The Huntington chapter of NAACP, led by Gus Cleckley, attorneys Charles Gipson and Herbert Henderson, Rev. Charles Smith of the First Baptist Church, and longtime local black activist Memphis Tennessee Garrison all supported CIP in various ways.[97]

West Virginia State College students march through the streets of Charleston to the capitol in support of the 1965 federal voting rights bill. West Virginia State University Archives.

Under the urging of the West Virginia Human Rights Commission, Huntington established a Human Rights Commission (HHRC) in 1963, but HHRC had no power to act. It appeased some blacks and their liberal white allies by providing a sounding board, but it accomplished little on its own. Similarly, some white ministers expressed support, but a majority of the Huntington Ministerial Association opposed changing the tacit arrangements governing relationships between blacks and whites. Marshall University president Stewart H. Smith expressed sympathy with the civil rights movement and pressured local establishments to provide facilities for visiting black athletes of the Mid-American Conference, but he did little else to aid the cause.[98]

Even before they organized CIP, the students had tasted success in the spring of 1962, persuading the Palace Theater to end its discriminatory policies after less than two weeks of picketing. About a year later, after formally organizing, CIP carried out demonstrations at Bailey's Cafeteria, an establishment that catered to the city's white middle-class professionals. After the manager refused to serve blacks, saying if he did he would lose all his white customers, CIP staged a "share-in." On April 25, 1963, five white students entered Bailey's and ordered, and then five blacks came in and shared. The manager responded by taking pictures of the participants. Five days later, the manager stopped the five whites at the door. CIP then began picketing the restaurant. The restaurant sought an injunction to stop the picketing, but circuit court judge John W. Hereford refused to grant it, and the West Virginia Human Rights Commission endorsed the CIP demonstration. Now the city fathers fell in line behind CIP as well. The Huntington City Council passed a resolution calling for all public or semi-private facilities to be open "without regard to race, color, or creed." The ministerial association deplored the restaurant's refusal to serve blacks and supported CIP's right to picket. Finally the Huntington Human Rights Commission brokered a deal between CIP and Bailey's to bring about a phased integration of the restaurant.[99]

A more difficult struggle took place between CIP and its supporters and the White Pantry restaurant and its owner Roba Quesenberry, who became something of a champion of segregationists in Huntington and West Virginia. Through the summer and fall of 1963 and winter of 1964, Quesenberry resisted sit-in demonstrators, pickets, and entreaties from city council, WVHRC, and HHRC. He sprayed insecticides, closed his business when demonstrators appeared, and unsuccessfully sought injunctions. Even after the passage of the Civil Rights Act of 1964 he persisted in resisting serving blacks. Finally, with the approval of the Act by the Supreme Court in December 1964, Quesenberry agreed to surrender, with one exception. He insisted on his right to refuse service to CIP leader Phil Carter. Carter said he had never wanted to eat there anyway.[100]

Demonstrations and sit-ins also played an important role in Bluefield, the southern city called by some the "Confederacy" of West Virginia. In the heyday of the southern West Virginia coal industry, a black middle class emerged in Bluefield which operated businesses catering to the needs of the substantial black working class in the coalfields. The African American community of Bluefield at its peak supported two black hotels, two hospitals, two drug stores, doctors, lawyers, dentists, several restaurants and grocery stores, a theater, an undertaker, barbers, and several churches. In 1930 more than three-fourths of the state's black population lived within 100 miles of Bluefield. Passenger trains from McDowell County brought many coalfield blacks to the city for business and recreation. As a coalfield commercial center and mining machinery distribution center, Bluefield suffered along with the coal towns it served as the coal industry struggled in the 1950s and 1960s.[101]

By the 1960s, with black population declining in the area because of the decline of coal mining employment, Bluefield began to attract notice as a part of the state particularly out of step with changes brought about by the civil rights movement. When the state Board of Health elected an African American doctor from Bluefield, P. R. Higginbotham, as chairman in 1962, it came as a shock to some that he had been denied membership in the Mercer County Medical Society. In 1963 the state American Legion switched its convention from Bluefield to Huntington, because the Bluefield hotels would not accept black Legionnaires. The NAACP launched boycotts in the summer of 1963 against supermarkets that would not hire blacks and against the *Bluefield Daily Telegraph*, which would not print any news or notices of the NAACP.[102] When the West Virginia Human Rights Commission held a hearing in Bluefield in the summer of 1963, it found little progress on racial matters, noting the poor communications between blacks and whites, continued segregation of restaurants, motels, and schools, and discrimination in hospitals.[103]

As in Charleston and Huntington, Bluefield's system of segregation grudgingly gave way to the pressures of demonstrators, the efforts of the Human Rights Commission, and the Civil Rights Act of 1964. Black churches, the local NAACP chapter, and Bluefield State College students organized demonstrations and protests. As early as March 1960, some 200 sit-in demonstrators targeted the Granada Theater. Other activities included a twelve-mile march to Princeton to protest conditions in the Mercer County school system.[104] The Bluefield Human Rights Commission held its first meeting in April 1962. Members agreed that they would not support demonstrations but would work through community leaders "to remove racial barriers and eliminate discriminatory practices." In 1963, the commission reported some progress in persuading downtown businesses such as bowling alleys and movie theaters to end segregation.[105]

As in Charleston, the lunch counter at Kresge's Department Store began to serve black customers after demonstrations carried out by young African Americans in spite of the prejudice of some of their elders against demonstrations. The persistence of segregation after the passage of the Civil Rights Act in public facilities like the city pool, Matz Hotel, and the YMCA-YWCA led to more demonstrations and a growing focus on Bluefield. On October 2, 1964, 150 Bluefield State and Concord College students organized by student chapters of the NAACP staged a sit-in in the Hotel Matz lobby after the manager refused to serve black members of the group in the dining room. When demonstrators appeared a second night, the manager closed the dining room.[106]

On November 21, students demonstrated outside the Young Mens' Christian Association protesting the segregationist policies of the Bluefield YMCA and YWCA. They carried signs reading: "The 'C' stands for Christian" and "Young Mens' Christian Association?" In December, police arrested three pickets at the YMCA and charged them with assault when they tried to prevent trustees from entering the building. A circuit court judge then issued an injunction to prevent demonstrators from blocking the entrances to the YMCA. After the injunction, students picketed the offices of the *Bluefield*

Daily Telegraph, protesting its editorial policy, and some also demonstrated outside city police headquarters.

A municipal judge convicted the three students arrested at the YMCA of assault. Trustee John Shott, a local radio and television executive, testified that the demonstrators had "malicious intent" as they pinned him and trustee J. H. Lazenby at the entrance of the Y building while singing "We got the board of trustees in our hands" (to the tune of "We've Got the Whole World in Our Hands"). The judge levied fines against the convicted students.[107]

The demonstrations in Bluefield began to attract sympathetic attention from around the region, and interest grew for "a march on Bluefield." John Nettles, a pre-ministerial student at Bluefield State and state youth president of the NAACP, organized the Bluefield demonstrations. In late January, he announced that NAACP chapters from Bluefield State and Concord and a group from Marshall University would take part in a civil rights march in Bluefield on February 13. Nettles said the purpose would be primarily to end segregation at the YMCA but also to call attention to "the general racial intolerance of the whole city," which he characterized as "Bluefield, Mississippi."[108] The Southern Conference Educational Fund later announced that 400 SCEF members from West Virginia, Virginia, Kentucky, Tennessee, and Maryland would also join the march.[109]

As the appointed day approached for the "March on Bluefield," local and state authorities anticipated it with growing anxiety. Nettles said some 1,000 demonstrators would march through the streets in "an attempt to reach the conscience of all people of this region."[110] City Manager Randolph G. Whittle Jr. agreed to issue a parade permit, and state officials planned to place thirty additional state troopers in the city for the event. Some local businessmen promised they would display typical Bluefield hospitality and have coffee and doughnuts for the marchers. The most important reaction, however, came when the YMCA board of trustees held a special meeting, elected two new trustees, and let it be known that it would reverse the segregation policy.[111] The continued pressure of student groups, concern about a mass rally, and fear that the publicity could cause *Look* magazine to drop Bluefield from contention as an All-American city had persuaded the trustees to give up the fight. To the disappointment of youthful march organizers, the NAACP leaders accordingly called off the march.[112]

The battle over the YMCA turned out to be a turning point in Bluefield. Gradually thereafter, other important barriers fell as the city hired black policemen and firemen, and a black police chief. Also during the 1960s, the city would elect black city council members and a black vice mayor. But some changes still came slowly. As late as 1964, Bluefield State College officials complained to the West Virginia Human Rights Commission that Mercer County refused to place black student teachers in predominantly white schools. Racial tensions at Bluefield State and a bombing incident led to an extremely charged atmosphere on campus in 1967–68 and an ugly crisis that divided the West Virginia Human Relations Commission and the state Board of Education (as noted in chapter 6). The Mercer County school board also held out on school integration longer than any other county in the state. The last all-black high school, Park Central of Bluefield, finally closed in 1969.[113]

Although the much-anticipated "March on Bluefield" never took place, students from four state colleges met after the cancellation and formed a nucleus for a state student movement which they hoped would provide help to civil rights demonstrators across the state. Concerned about the fate of a Concord student suspended for demonstrating, the group also sought the immediate dismissal of "all college administrators who stand in the way of academic freedom and are opposed to freedom of expression." The new organization was to be called SNAP, Students Now for Action and Progress. Student organizations from Bluefield State, West Virginia State, Concord, and Marshall agreed to cooperate in programs dealing with civil rights, education, poverty, and peace.[114]

As demonstrations against segregation chipped away at the vestiges of a de facto Jim Crow system in West Virginia's towns and cities, the Civil Rights Act of 1964 had a substantial impact. The West Virginia Human Rights Commission reported that remaining practices of discrimination in public accommodations "in all the better restaurants and hotel–motel accommodations throughout the state" virtually ceased to exist with passage of the Act. In many small towns and rural areas and in the less-than-first-class facilities black leaders told the WVHRC that discrimination continued and victims of discrimination feared economic retaliation if they complained. In cities like Huntington, Charleston, and Bluefield, open resistance to integration of public facilities faded, sometimes quickly, sometimes more slowly, and often grudgingly. Segregation in employment remained a serious problem, however, as the commission received a rising number of complaints, but some progress was being made in urban communities. In rural areas and small towns, however, the commission noted that African Americans could obtain employment only in national chains.[115]

Churches and Civil Rights

Black churches played a major role in many of the civil rights efforts in West Virginia. As noted above, a group from Simpson Memorial Methodist Church led by longtime Sunday school superintendent Elizabeth Gilmore organized the Charleston chapter of CORE. Methodist minister and post office employee Homer Davis headed UNION (United Neighborhood Interest Organization Network), a coalition of some 28 primarily African American organizations in the Kanawha Valley oriented toward Martin Luther King's Southern Christian Leadership Conference (SCLC). Rev. Moses Newsome of First Baptist in Charleston invited Martin Luther King to Charleston in 1960 in what turned out to be his only visit to West Virginia. In Huntington, Rev. Charles Smith of First Baptist Church strongly supported civil rights activism. Rev. C. Anderson Davis of Bluefield served as state president of the NAACP.[116]

The rise of new leadership in the black community provided another important dynamic of the civil rights movement in the 1960s in West Virginia (as elsewhere). The younger generation had less patience than their elders with the kind of racial compromises that had been made in the past. UNION, like King's SCLC, sought a different relationship not only with the white "establishment" but also within the black leadership. This new generation, a varied group of ministers, white-collar and blue-collar workers, chemists, post-office employees, and housewives rose from the grassroots. Younger and more militant, they tended to be critical of the old order of "self-appointed" black leaders "fostered by the white power structure," whom they believed had made too many compromises with injustice. They sought the support of the generation that had fought World War II and the Korean War, people, as Rev. Homer Davis said, "who have fought for freedom." Among this new generation, Marvin Robinson, a UNION organizer, bore scars from civil rights demonstrations in the Deep South. Robinson said the younger generation "want to see the fruit of the past civil rights drive in their own hands and want to have their own say in the making of the Great Society."[117]

By the time of the Civil Rights Act of 1964, white churches in West Virginia were beginning to assess their role in civil rights. West Virginia newspaper editors sometimes sharply criticized churches for focusing much energy and attention on such questions as drinking or Sunday shopping while ignoring issues of social and racial justice. Others saw the white churches as part of the problem. Elizabeth Gilmore, the executive secretary of the Charleston chapter of CORE, said of the white churches: "We don't look to them for support, because they've never given us any." Only one white minister joined CORE's demonstrations, "and he was promptly called on the carpet by his bishop," Gilmore said. At one public meeting, upon being asked to list the organizations most dedicated to segregation, she responded, "the Ku Klux Klan, the White Citizens Councils and the white Christian church."[118]

In the Charleston area, white ministers, often more liberal than their congregations, sometimes feared what their congregations or their church hierarchy might do if they tried to play an active role. Some of the ministers who had served churches in states of the former Confederacy had been forced to leave their former congregations because of their moderate views. Some West Virginia congregations and bishops also at times rebuked their pastors for participating in civil rights activities.[119] By the mid-1960s, nevertheless, some local white ministerial associations and the West Virginia Council of Churches began to join forces with UNION and other civil rights groups in working to desegregate swimming pools and to find ways to break down the pattern of segregated housing in the Kanawha Valley.[120]

Conclusion

As the Charleston chapter of the NAACP contemplated the future in meetings at the end of 1964, they focused on some of the same concerns similar chapters faced in other parts of the country: continued discrimination and even segregation in public school systems and persistent problems with housing and employment. But black leaders in West Virginia faced another dismaying issue—the continuing out-migration of the state's black population, driven largely by the revolution in the coal industry. Willard Brown, president of the Charleston chapter of the NAACP, called the trend "appalling and frightening." He lamented that 22.2 percent of the black population left during the 1950s, and similar figures might mark the 1960s as well. The problem now before them, he insisted, was to figure out how to make Charleston and West Virginia a better place for African Americans to live. The NAACP also faced a dilemma in maintaining interest in its programs. In the December meeting only twenty members attended as they engaged in a candid session of self-criticism, and generational differences emerged. One of the younger members, Rev. Homer Davis, president of the Kanawha Valley Council on Human Relations, argued that the NAACP had lost its revolutionary zeal. President Brown defended the record of the Charleston NAACP, arguing that it had played a role in every major advance in human relations in West Virginia since the chapter formed in 1919. Dr. Virgil Mathews, a chemist employed by Union Carbide, argued that with the 1954 *Brown* decision and the civil rights acts of 1957 and 1964 "half the fight has been won." Now the task was to gain full admittance to the economic sphere by pushing for job opportunities and housing. Mathews found the apathy of some blacks particularly disturbing given the relatively positive atmosphere in Charleston.[121]

The ultimate tragedy of the civil rights movement in West Virginia was that as it achieved historic goals and seemed in a position to advance the cause even further, the African American exodus brought about by technological change made the victories somewhat hollow and reduced the political clout of African Americans in the state. Some, like Kojo Jones, saw emptiness in the promises of integration and pain and tragedy in the loss of black community. The impact of the industrial revolution that swept West Virginia in the 1950s and 1960s—with its attendant diminution of the black population—probably made such losses inevitable, but no less poignant. Historian Joe W. Trotter has shown how African Americans in West Virginia tried to retain some vestiges of the past as they held on to their churches, fraternal orders, social clubs, civil rights organizations, and the black press, particularly the *Beacon Journal*, which in the 1950s replaced the *McDowell Times* as the main organ of black public opinion in the state.[122]

In the latter half of the 1960s and beyond, however, black West Virginians would not only work to expand civil rights and to improve conditions for African Americans, but they would also apply lessons learned in the civil rights movement to play important roles in the Appalachian reawakening including work in the war on poverty and in the fight against political corruption. They would fight against plans to destroy black neighborhoods like Triangle in Charleston (where some former mining families sought refuge) in the name of urban renewal, for black lung legislation, and for United Mine Workers' policies to protect pensions of widows and miners. Although black miners also supported the reform movement in the miners' union, they would be denied leadership roles in the Miners for Democracy. Bluefield would again be in the news as a divisive battle would be fought in 1968 over the fate of Bluefield State College.[123]

4

Good Intentions:
The New Frontier and the War on Poverty

In places like Clarksburg and Grafton and Jane Lew, the American from Megalopolis has the uneasy sensation of being displaced in time. They stir old memories of depression towns in the 1930s. It nags at the mind, and the mountain air is heavy with a sense of fundamental American failure.
Russell Baker, *New York Times*, August 22, 1963

There's nothing wrong with hillbillies—a description which Mountain people loathe—that a strong dose of equal opportunity wouldn't cure. Applying every yardstick of social well-being, their Appalachian homeland emerges a sordid blemish on the balance sheet of the wealthiest nation in the world.
Harry W. Ernst and Charles W. Drake, *The Nation*, May 30, 1959

By the end of the 1950s, West Virginia and Appalachia increasingly attracted attention as a region in need of help. Clearly the new machine age, whether because of "fundamental American failure" or as a "result of progress rather than stagnation," had resulted in massive unemployment, a great migration, and growing poverty. What, if anything, was to be done to address the Appalachian crisis? President Eisenhower twice vetoed area redevelopment acts in the late 1950s designed to address Appalachian issues, citing inflationary concerns, but journalists, scholars, and some government officials continued to examine the problems of the region.

The presidential election of 1960 focused the national media and the federal government on West Virginia and Appalachian issues and put in the White House a president sympathetic to Appalachia. As noted in chapter 2, the 1960 primary election in West Virginia also helped John F. Kennedy address the conventional wisdom of the day that a Catholic could not be elected president. By defeating Hubert Humphrey in overwhelmingly Protestant West Virginia, Kennedy demonstrated that Protestant voters could set aside their religious preferences to vote for a Catholic. In *The Making of the President, 1960*, journalist Theodore White suggested that although Kennedy's background of wealth and privilege provided him with little understanding of poverty and the struggles of less affluent Americans, his time in West Virginia had awakened in him sympathy for the unemployed coal miners and rural poor of Appalachia.[1] During the fall campaign against the Republican nominee Richard Nixon, Kennedy promised West Virginians that after his election he would send to Congress "a complete program to restore and revive the economy of West Virginia—to bring new industry and new jobs to your state, and all other neglected areas of our country."[2]

Structural Unemployment, Automation, and the Culture of Poverty

Kennedy and his advisors drew upon a substantial body of economic ideas that had developed in the 1950s as the economy, despite its general prosperity, had developed pockets of persistent poverty and unemployment. Some economists, social activists, and reform politicians saw the Appalachian problem as part of a greater national problem. They offered "structural unemployment" as an explanation for continued poverty in some areas and persistent unemployment rates of 7 percent or more even as most of the nation prospered. Structural unemployment explained the problems of the coal industry, and it explained why unemployed individuals did not easily move to different jobs, as John L. Lewis and Jack Long and other coal industry leaders, as noted earlier, expected they would do. Other industries such as automobiles, railroads, and radio production now could produce more with fewer workers. The skills of the unemployed did not fit the needs of the economy. Two studies by the Bureau of Labor Statistics in 1962 projected that the problem would grow in the decade ahead as fewer jobs would be available for the unskilled. Many workers would have to be "retrained for different jobs."[3]

A critical part of the structural unemployment issue—called "automation"—underlined the perils of the new technology of the post-war period. Just as had been the case since the beginning of the industrial revolution, new machines took the place of labor. In England's eighteenth-century transformation, textile machines, for example, made human weavers obsolete. Generally, however, society accommodated to new machines and new processes, but in the post-World War II era, with electronic and computer-driven mechanisms and continuous flow operations (as was happening in the coal industry), the fear arose that technological innovations would outrun the capacity of society to absorb them, and unemployment like that suffered by the coalfields would spread throughout the country. At a press conference in February 1962, President Kennedy held that the greatest domestic challenge of the decade was "to maintain full employment at a time when automation is replacing men."[4] Representative James Roosevelt, comparing the plight of unemployed industrial workers to the agricultural victims of the Great Depression, told the House of Representatives that the unemployed industrial worker "is the victim of the industrial dust bowls created by automation and technological advances."[5]

Because of the concerns about automation, an obvious need seemed to be to train workers with obsolescent skills so they could adapt to the demands of a new age, but some social and behavioral scientists believed many poor people did not simply lack the requisite skills—they also suffered from a "culture of poverty," a condition that passed from generation to generation in a self-perpetuating cycle of despair and incapacity. Anthropologist Oscar Lewis popularized the concept in a highly readable account of a Mexican family, *The Children of Sanchez* (1961). This book and his later *La Vida* (1965), about a poor Puerto Rican family, planted the notion that poor people bore much of the responsibility for their own fate. Though Lewis had written about Hispanics, he and others readily applied the conclusions to poor southern blacks who had moved to northern cities and to poor Appalachians. Some of the New Frontier–War on Poverty policy architects became convinced by the culture of poverty literature that in addition to skills training, poor people needed to learn new habits and to develop better values, and they believed government could become the necessary agent of acculturation. Later the culture of poverty concept would come under attack as middle-class condescension that projected the values of metropolitan intellectuals and "attacked the victims."[6]

The culture of poverty model also had special appeal to the poverty fighters in regard to Appalachia. In 1962, North Carolina sociologist Rupert Vance urged that the government intervene to raise the "goals and aspirations of the people," because Appalachia's distinct culture approached "a permanent culture of poverty." As noted previously, Presbyterian minister Jack Weller who came from New York to preside over a Presbyterian project in southern West Virginia also ascribed to culture of poverty ideas in his *Yesterday's People* (1965), a book widely distributed among Appalachian poverty workers. Whether applied to Appalachia or northern urban ghettoes, the culture of poverty concept offered a way to attack poverty without advocating massive income redistribution or reforms of the economic and political systems, approaches that would present impossible political problems.[7]

Kennedy's New Frontier promised both relief and recovery for poverty-stricken areas. Relief programs included an increase in the distribution of surplus food, the introduction of an experimental food stamp program, and welfare benefits for unemployed fathers. West Virginia, one of the states most negatively affected by the new machine age, provided a testing ground for some of these initiatives as McDowell, Logan, and Mingo became the first counties in the country to experiment with food stamps, and the state's program to provide work for unemployed fathers provided a precedent for changes in the welfare laws and the manpower training programs of the federal government.[8]

Keeping his campaign promise, Kennedy set up a task force after his election to make recommendations for legislation to assist people in economically depressed areas, and he weighted it heavily with West Virginians. Called informally the West Virginia task force, it first met in Charleston on December 9, 1960.[9] Based partly on the task force's recommendations, Kennedy sent to Congress an area redevelopment bill soon after becoming president, and by May 1961, the Area Redevelopment Administration (ARA) began to organize. Just six weeks later, more than a thousand people gathered in Beckley to launch area redevelopment in West Virginia. Governor William Wallace Barron, U.S. Secretary of Commerce Luther Hodges, Senator Jennings Randolph, and representatives of ten federal agencies and departments attended the ceremonial occasion, raising hopes that something might be done. Throughout the state, groups organized in the hope they could bring redevelopment dollars to their communities.[10] Similar gatherings had taken place in 1954, when the Eisenhower administration had offered a slightly different version of community development which had promised federal help to communities that organized to address development needs.[11]

The Area Redevelopment Act (ARA), a 1960s version of the "trickle down" ideas of the early depression era, promised new jobs and development by making low interest loans available to businessmen and local governments. As in the earlier case, the amount appropriated fell far short of need, and businesses rather than public entities received the greatest benefit. Also, to get the legislation passed, Congress included more areas and thus blunted the impact of the appropriation by spreading it over 1,061 counties rather than by focusing on the neediest, as had been the original intent. The ARA also loaned money to many enterprises that failed to generate much employment. Another problem with ARA was that the neediest counties sometimes failed to receive funding, because they lacked the resources or personnel to devise the overall economic development plans or to provide the matching funds required by the legislation. Nevertheless, West Virginia counties received over half of the Appalachian funds. ARA tended to fund mostly "bricks and mortar" items, so two-thirds of the West Virginia grants or loans went to tourism projects like Hawks Nest State Park and Pipestem State Park. Though these grants excited the communities involved, some questioned whether they did much to address the basic problems.[12]

Apart from the tourism projects, another of the first ARA efforts inspired much hope but ended up as a fiasco that generated bitter recriminations and raised questions in the national press as to whether Appalachia could be changed. Eager to demonstrate the Kennedy administration's commitment, in early summer 1961, the ARA quickly approved a proposal from business and community interests in Mingo County to establish a woodworking plant. James H. "Buck" Harless, a Gilbert lumber company owner, headed the local proponents, who believed they could take advantage of the vast hardwood supplies of southern West Virginia with a woodworking plant to shape wood parts for shipment to furniture assembly plants in North Carolina and the northeast. Harless's group hoped that in time furniture makers attracted by the supply of shaped wood would move into the area and help to diversify the southern West Virginia economy, which had for so long depended on coal. In the meantime, the plant would provide a market for local hardwoods and give work to timber workers as well as to unemployed coal miners, most of whom who had little hope of returning to the mines. The former miners would have to be retrained, and thus the project offered a model for how unemployed miners might be rescued and restored to the work force. The plan seemed an ideal marriage of local need, local resources, local initiative, and the government's commitment to help. The ARA and the Small Business Administration provided most of the capital, working through local banks to provide long-term low-interest loans and mortgages, and the U.S. Department of Labor provided a training grant. The newly created West Virginia Department of Commerce also contributed a grant.[13]

The fate of the Mingo woodworking plant is quickly told. In September 1962, National Seating and Dimension, Incorporated (NSD), opened its plant in Varney, Mingo County. On March 5, 1963, a delegation of federal officials, including ARA administrator William L. Batt, toured the Varney plant, proudly hailing it as a model for area redevelopment. Because of all the attention Appalachia had drawn in the 1960 election and because of President Kennedy's strong commitment to address Appalachia's problems, the ARA eagerly sought an opportunity to tout its accomplishments. In November 1964, however, just two years after opening, the company closed its Varney plant and ceased operations. The *New York Times* reported the story on page one, citing the Mingo failure as evidence that the federal government had fumbled in its first major effort to attack poverty in Appalachia. Other newspapers called the NSD failure "an excellent example of bureaucratic bumbling" and "a lesson in the futility of trying to retrain coal miners." The *Wall Street Journal* story carried the headline "Labor Troubles to End Retraining Experiment in West Virginia Town. Strikes and Expense of Training Former Coal Miners Blamed for Closing of Woodworking Firm." The newspaper accounts depicted Harless and his associates as "gullible, honest businessmen who were ground up between Big Government and Big Union."[14]

Charleston Gazette business editor George Lawless offered a different explanation of what he called "a noble failure." Trying to piece together the reasons for NSD's collapse, he doubted management's self-serving explanation that the difficulty of retraining coal miners and troubles with the United Mine Workers (who had represented the workers in the plant) had doomed the enterprise. Lawless feared that the labor climate explanation would reinforce those who argued that Appalachia "either cannot or will not help itself" and hinder other efforts to fund Appalachian programs. The people of West Virginia would have to "take a bum rap" for bad management and inadequate government oversight, the real culprits in the failure of NSD, Lawless believed—not labor problems nor the difficulty of retraining miners.[15]

In a long response published in the *Gazette*, Buck Harless vehemently rejected Lawless's report, absolved management of most of the fault and reiterated that blame should be placed primarily on labor strife and the cost of retraining workers. He also noted the difficulty of hiring skilled supervisory personnel and persuading them to remain in Mingo County, which had few of the amenities well-trained personnel could expect elsewhere.[16] The woodworking plant's demise disappointed those who believed that retraining and economic diversification offered the best approach for addressing the critical issues of West Virginia and Appalachia, and it epitomized the disappointing results of ARA.[17]

The View from Megalopolis

Meanwhile, poverty in Appalachia continued to receive much attention in the national media. *Washington Post* reporter Julius Duscha traveled through southern West Virginia and eastern Kentucky soon after the West Virginia primary of 1960, concluding that southern Appalachia was "this country's most blighted area." He believed the region needed massive aid of the kind being given to the underdeveloped countries of the world.[18] In 1962, Michael Harrington published *The Other America*, noting various kinds of poverty and pointing out that in the land that prided itself on promise and prosperity, 25 percent of all Americans lived in poverty. Of Appalachia, Harrington said: "It seems likely that the Appalachians will continue going down, that its lovely mountains and hills will house a culture of poverty and despair, and that it will become a reservation for the old, apathetic, and the misfits."[19] President Kennedy read an extensive and laudatory review of Harrington's book by Dwight MacDonald in *The New Yorker* in January, 1963.[20] Appalachian poverty also received a good bit of attention in part because of the publication in 1962 and 1963 of two critical books focusing on the region. The prosaically but persuasively written *The Southern Appalachian Region: A Survey*, the culmination of a four-year project financed by the Ford Foundation, churches, and universities, laid much of the blame for the region's problems on mountain culture. Harry Caudill's compellingly written *Night Comes to the Cumberlands: A Biography of A Depressed Area*, described by Appalachian historian Ronald D Eller as "probably the most widely-read book ever written about Appalachia," blamed both corporate abuse and the cultural degeneracy of the people.[21]

The metropolitan press also continued to be captivated by Appalachian poverty, an embarrassing contradiction of American post-war triumphalism (a word coined to describe the mood) and Cold War prosperity. Russell Baker of the *New York Times* (a native of Appalachian Maryland) traveled through the central counties of West Virginia and towns like Clarksburg, Jane Lew, and Grafton in August 1963, and expressed the shock of a traveler from the great American megalopolis seeing out-of-date towns and buildings and people wearing out-of-date clothes, giving one the sensation, Baker said, of "being displaced in time." Baker found no evidence of the great American boom—"no new housing subdivisions in the towns, no new glass facades, no new schools, none of the monstrous new farming machines, no glittering glass motels." "It becomes apparent," he wrote, that "the future has leapfrogged the Appalachians."[22]

On October 20, 1963, Homer Bigart, another *Times* reporter, filed a particularly moving report describing the difficult circumstances of the families of unemployed coal miners and subsistence farmers of eastern Kentucky. Nine days later, Bigart also reported on the woebegone condition of West Virginia towns like Hinton and Ansted, suffering from the collapse of coal and the decline of railroad employment. President Kennedy, moved by Harrington's exposé, the *New York Times* articles, memories of his own experiences campaigning in West Virginia, and other reports of the continuing plight of Appalachia, began to mobilize his cabinet and other high officials for a broader-gauged program to attack poverty in Appalachia and elsewhere, planning that Lyndon B. Johnson would inherit after Kennedy's assassination just a month later. Johnson would call it the War on Poverty. Kennedy had also already set up the President's Appalachian Regional Commission (a forerunner to the commission established by Congress in 1965) to suggest solutions for Appalachia's problems and had asked his cabinet to focus on alleviating the plight of the Appalachian poor during the winter of 1963–64.[23]

A "Robber Barron" of the New Frontier

Generally Appalachian counties in other states faced the problem of being minority counties, hoping for the kindness and charity of the non-Appalachian and sometimes metropolitan low-country majority. In West Virginia, however, all the counties are Appalachian, or depending on how Appalachian is defined, at least the majority. The counties that attracted the most attention as being representative of the worst of Appalachia often had substantial political power in West Virginia. This would seem to be an advantage, making it possible to address Appalachian issues as a state rather than as a minority region within a state. Unfortunately, the good intentions of the New Frontier would be administered in West Virginia by probably the most corrupt statehouse regime in the state's history. William Wallace "Wally" Barron defeated Republican Harold E. Neely in the 1960 state gubernatorial election, restoring Democratic control of the executive branch, and ending a long period, stretching back to William C. Marland's earliest days as governor, when the legislature and governor had found little common ground. A native of Elkins, Barron earned a law degree from West Virginia University and worked his way up the political ladder by serving as mayor of Elkins and later two terms in the House of Delegates. Governor Marland appointed him chairman of the State Liquor Control Commission, but fired him in 1955, because, according to Barron, "We couldn't agree on what was good government." Despite having been fired from an appointive position, in 1956 Barron successfully ran for attorney general. His record, however, failed to convince the strongly pro-Democratic *Charleston Gazette* that he deserved endorsement in his campaign for governor against Neely. The newspaper endorsed neither.[24]

Although his administration became known as the most corrupt in a long tradition of corruption, when Barron left office at the end of his term, the full extent of the malfeasance remained unknown to the public, and journalists accorded Barron surprisingly good marks as governor. He won election by campaigning for a statewide cleanup of rivers, roadways, and public sites, and as governor he voiced strong support for civil rights, the New Frontier, the beginnings of the War on Poverty, and the Appalachian governors' push for an Appalachian regional commission (serving for a time as chair of the Council of Appalachian Governors). Because West Virginia epitomized Appalachian poverty, and also because John F. Kennedy took a special interest in the state that had been so important in his winning the Democratic nomination, it became a testing ground or laboratory for some early experiments in addressing poverty and economic stagnation. Also, in part because of a rising national economy, West Virginia in the Barron years began to show movement away from the dilemmas of the 1950s. Unemployment dropped from 106,000 to 40,000 and although population loss continued, the pace slowed. Unlike his two predecessors, Marland and Underwood, who had faced divided government and recalcitrant legislators, Barron broke the legislative deadlock that had resulted from the constant dueling between governor and legislature, particularly in the areas of taxation and finance. Barron showed negotiating skills, bringing opposing sides together around a conference table to work out compromises. In one session, Barron persuaded the legislature to adopt a state income tax that would produce $17.5 million annually, an increase in the consumer sales tax by one cent, and establishment of a Department of Commerce. The new revenue enabled the state to provide more support for schools and roads and to establish a work relief program. Even before he took office, Barron had asked the legislature to create an emergency jobs program that would provide state employment for 5,000 workers. A one-cent increase in the sales tax (raising it to three cents on the dollar) financed what people in the state called "the crash program." Similar to a Kentucky make work scheme called Happy Pappies, it later became part of a new federal program, Aid to Dependent Children of the Unemployed (ADCU). Barron also supported civil rights initiatives, including the establishment of the West Virginia Human Rights Commission, and he presided over the state's centennial celebration. In his last address to the legislature, Barron claimed that his administration had brought about the longest peacetime economic expansion in the state's history.²⁵

Probably part of the Centennial celebration, Governor William Wallace Barron (second from left) hosts breakfast attended by former governors Homer Holt (1941–1945), Cecil Underwood (1957–1961), and Okey Patteson (1949–1953). Photograph by Emil Varney, circa 1963. West Virginia State Archives.

Despite legislative successes and improvements in the state's economy, Barron's administration earned a reputation for sleaziness, even before the legal troubles that emerged after his term ended. During the 1960 Democratic primary, one of his Democratic opponents, state treasurer Orel Skeen, produced a tape recording that purported to document Barron offering a bribe to Skeen to stay out of the race for governor. Barron sued for slander, but after the election he settled the matter privately. During his administration, rumors abounded of indiscretions. In 1963 the chambers of commerce of Huntington and Charleston issued a joint statement condemning the "moral tone" of the state government. At the end of his term he told a newspaper interviewer that the appearance of wrongdoing had arisen because some of his most trusted officials had padded expense accounts and had used public funds to buy luxury cars and furniture for their personal use. He insisted that his record would withstand the test of time and history.[26] A *Gazette* editorial at the end of his term praised the Barron administration for its accomplishments and farsightedness but condemned the corrupt image and the unwillingness of the governor to fire those who disgraced his administration "through incompetence, or stupidity or obvious self-service."[27]

Barron's confidence about the durability of his record proved ill-founded, as federal prosecutions eventually revealed that the corruption consisted of far more than the padding of expense accounts and extended beyond the governor's associates to Barron himself. The former governor's eventual conviction (further discussed in chapter 6) marked the climax of one of the most dismal eras of corruption in the state's history. The achievements credited to the Barron administration came at a cost not listed in the financial records of the era but one that must be seen as a corruption tax, an enervating levy that West Virginians and other Appalachian residents pay all too often.

The Centennial: Accentuating the Positive

The full story of the Barron era corruption had not yet emerged at the time of the celebrations commemorating the state's birth in 1863. At a time when the national media had made the state a symbol for all that was perceived to be wrong with Appalachia, the centennial celebrations offered the opportunity to focus on the positive and to discuss state and regional problems in a creative way. As a practical matter it also provided venues and occasions for President Kennedy and Vice President Johnson to announce important federal initiatives to help the state fight its economic dilemmas. Preparations for the centennial had started in 1956 when Governor Marland appointed a commission headed by Arthur Burke Koontz, a Charleston attorney and banker. The celebrations began on West Virginia Day, June 20, 1962, with the appearance of former president Harry S. Truman at the state capitol. During the period from May to September 1963, a centennial exhibits train, using rolling stock donated by state railroads, traveled through the state stopping in fifty-eight towns. The *Rhododendron*, a centennial showboat with a theater seating 264, performed the Civil War era melodrama *East Lynne* and other shows as it traveled the state's waterways and stopped in twenty-one towns. Vice President Johnson spoke at a Forum of the Future at the Charleston Civic Center in April, and President Kennedy spoke outside at the capitol in a keynote speech abbreviated by heavy rain on West Virginia Day, June 20, 1963. Driven inside by the downpour, Kennedy announced to a small group of state officials who gathered in the governor's office that a federal grant would help build or improve four state parks, news that sparked hope in some that finally something would be done to diversify the state's economy and to generate new sources of employment.[28]

An incident during the centennial celebration that revealed the growing sensitivity of some West Virginians to being constantly portrayed as the prime exhibit for persistent American poverty resulted from the art contest sponsored by the Centennial Commission. The commission offered a $1,963 prize for the work by a West Virginia artist that best expressed the spirit of the state. Joe Moss, a young art instructor at West Virginia University, won for *West Virginia Moon*, an impressionistic piece featuring six rough boards, a part of a screen door frame, and a bit of paint suggesting a moon and a man. Furious state critics likened the piece to an outhouse, an inappropriate symbol for a state aspiring to project industrial leadership and prosperity and eager to escape the negative images of the metropolitan media. The *Huntington Herald-Advertiser* called it "a body blow to tourism." The *Chicago Tribune* reviewer thought it looked like the tailgate of an old truck. Contest judge James Johnson Sweeney, director of Houston's Museum of Fine Arts (and later director of the Guggenheim Museum in New York), told *Time* magazine that he picked *West Virginia Moon* simply because he liked it best. Governor Barron, infuriated at the commission's choice, privately told Moss that he had done the state a disservice by reinforcing views like those of Roul Tunley of the *Saturday Evening Post* and other journalists who focused on the negatives about the state. Moss told

Time Magazine: "It isn't intended to be uncomplimentary. It looks complimentary, maybe."[29] *West Virginia Moon* hit a nerve among middle-class West Virginians tired of criticism of the state and the negative stereotypes of hillbillies and mountaineers. It certainly represented a stronger dose of realism than Governor Barron and others committed to boosterism rather than a realistic assessment of the state's predicament thought proper.

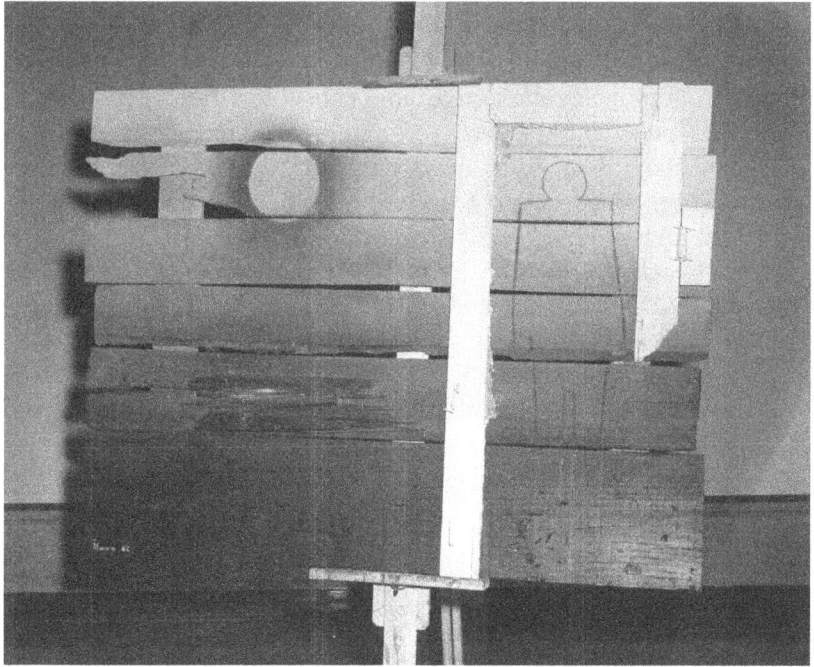

West Virginia Moon, by Joe Moss of Morgantown, first prize winner in West Virginia painting competition sponsored by the West Virginia Centennial Commission. The piece scandalized boosters who feared it might hurt efforts to promote a new image of West Virginia. West Virginia and Regional History Collection, West Virginia University Libaries.

LBJ and the War on Poverty

After President Kennedy's assassination in November 1963, some of the president's advisors worried that the plans to fight poverty might fall by the wayside, but Lyndon B. Johnson put his own stamp on poverty programs that had been in the planning stage and rushed them forward. On January 8, 1964, in his State of the Union address, Johnson asked Congress to declare an "unconditional war on poverty."[30] Johnson had mixed motivations for embracing the notion of fighting poverty. He admired Franklin D. Roosevelt's New Deal and wanted to complete what Roosevelt had started. He also believed that the United States had the resources to fight poverty and should enter the battle. As the quintessential politician he also wanted to shape Kennedy's ideas into a program of legislation that would provide the basis for his election to the presidency in 1964.[31]

Though much of the journalistic exposition of poverty had featured rural areas and Appalachia, congressional hearings on Johnson's poverty legislation and planning within the administration focused primarily on urban poverty, giving a striking lack of attention to Appalachian issues and to the structural foundations of Appalachian poverty. Senator Robert C. Byrd, listed as a cosponsor of the bill, did not speak in its favor. Senator Jennings Randolph, the only Appalachian member of the senate select committee holding hearings on the bill, attended only one day out of four.[32] Nevertheless, on April 24–25, 1964, Johnson helped to dramatize the need for the War on Poverty with a trip to eastern Kentucky and West Virginia, ending at the Huntington Tri-State Airport. By August, the president had signed the Economic Opportunity Act. The administration launched a broad range of programs under the Office of Economic Opportunity (OEO), headed by R. Sargent Shriver, Kennedy's brother-in-law and director of the Peace Corps.[33]

Johnson, eager to make civil rights and anti-poverty programs the themes of his administration—and with an election rapidly approaching—pushed his advisers to devise plans quickly for a war on poverty. Rather than addressing structural bases of poverty or trying to put money into hands of those who lacked it, approaches that would be expensive and politically divisive, the early battles of the War on Poverty sought to attack the culture of poverty. They would equip the poor to do better and encourage passive communities of poor people to seek a voice. Among the programs of OEO, Job Corps offered opportunities for unemployed youth to learn marketable skills, and the Volunteers in Service to America (VISTA) called upon volunteers (who came mostly from middle-class youth) to help fight domestic poverty as the Peace Corps did abroad. Head Start sought to prepare poor preschool youngsters for the classroom.[34]

Hulett C. Smith's Sin of Omission

State politics continued to play a big role in the way anti-poverty and development policies were actually carried out in West Virginia. In the 1964 election, President Johnson easily prevailed over Republican Barry Goldwater, and Democrat Hulett C. Smith, a Beckley insurance man and son of former congressman Joe L. Smith, frustrated Cecil Underwood's second effort to return to the Governor's Mansion. Smith, who had been state party chairman during the failed gubernatorial campaign of Robert Mollohan in 1956, served in the Barron administration as the first commissioner of the new Department of Commerce but avoided being tarred by the brush of corruption that tainted many of that administration. Despite advice to the contrary from friends, Smith retained many of the Barron appointees including road commissioner Burl Sawyers, commissioner of finance and administration Truman Gore, liquor commissioner Clarence Elmore (who ran Smith's campaign), welfare commissioner W. Bernard Smith (who would resign in 1961 to run for the state senate), and motor vehicles commissioner Jack Nuckols. All of these ended up under indictments before the end of the Smith administration, and some of the charges covered activities extending beyond the time of the Barron administration into Smith's. Some thought this made a mockery of Smith's inaugural pledge to create "an administration of excellence" and of Johnson's Great Society. Though Smith was never charged, many of the department heads he retained from the Barron administration ended up in prison. Thomas Stafford, the *Charleston Gazette* political reporter who did much to reveal the graft and corruption of the Barron and Smith associates, had begun his journalistic career in Beckley, Smith's hometown. He knew Smith well and had even helped in his election campaign. In his memoir, Stafford claimed that he strongly advised the governor to clean house at the beginning of his administration. Key members of Smith's staff also urged him to start the new administration with a clean slate. Smith, said Stafford, committed "the sin of omission, of neglecting to clean house by dismissing the members of the Barron crowd at the beginning of his own term."[35] Jefferson Monroe, whom Smith appointed to head the state OEO agency in 1966, later recalled urging Smith to "get rid of the crooks," telling him that they would drag down everything they were trying to do. But Smith, said Monroe, "wasn't ornery enough to get rid of the crooked politicians who helped him get elected."[36]

Whether Smith's rejection of the advice of friends sprung from a misguided sense of loyalty or from other motives is unclear, but what is certain is that the striking record of corruption of these men tainted and stood in the way of the many good intentions Smith expressed as governor and that the War on Poverty expressed for Appalachia. From the time of his unsuccessful first run for governor in the 1960 Democratic primary until his farewell speech to the legislature in 1968, Smith advocated a constitutional convention to modernize the state's 1872 constitution, which he believed too antiquated to be adequately repaired through amendment. He appointed a commission that held meetings and produced suggestions, but the state legislature and the state supreme court of appeals could never agree on a proper statement to put before a referendum to authorize a constitutional convention. He suffered another bitter disappointment in 1966 when voters rejected a constitutional amendment that would have allowed a governor to succeed himself. Smith had hoped to run for a second term in 1968, but the failure of the succession amendment foreclosed that possibility, leaving him a lame duck for the final two years of his term. The Valentine's Day indictments of 1968 (further discussed in chapter 6) also left his administration demoralized. Two of the most important achievements of the Smith administration came in the form of constitutional amendments ratified by voters in the same 1968 election that chose his successor: the Modern Budget Amendment (which made the governor rather than the board of public works primarily responsible for the preparation of the state budget) and a $350 million Road Bond Amendment, which would enable the state to meet matching requirements for Appalachian highway funds. Governor Smith strongly supported increased spending for education and roads and established a Governor's Task Force on Strip Mining to push for a law imposing some limitations on strip mining, a topic further explored in chapter 8.[37]

Challenges of "Creative Federalism"

Though they welcomed the attention and concern and especially the federal dollars, the programs of the New Frontier and the War on Poverty presented difficult challenges for West Virginia's public agencies and politicians, as was the case throughout Appalachia. Much like the conflicts between the state and the federal government during the New Deal years, state and federal notions of how the War on Poverty should be carried out in the 1960s profoundly differed. State and local governments often misunderstood the federal mandates or lacked the personnel, skills, or the will to carry them out. Federal agents, who generally had little knowledge of Appalachia or West Virginia, often assumed a condescending and adversarial tone to state counterparts. On the state level confusion over the chain of command and jealousies and rivalries among agencies and administrators, inadequate staff or expertise, and preoccupation with conventional responsibilities made execution of policies difficult. Moreover, ongoing prosecutions for political corruption, the threat felt by entrenched Democratic machines in some counties, and even philosophical opposition to the goals of the program frustrated the War on Poverty in West Virginia. The Democratic political establishment, torn between its commitment to the status quo (which came under attack in many of the War on Poverty programs) and its eagerness for federal dollars, grew disenchanted. All of these conflicting currents played out against a background of Appalachian victimization by the economic transformations of the time and the social divisions based on the Vietnam War, race, class, gender, and generation, although race appears to have been less of a factor in the community action imbroglios in West Virginia than in the South and in big cities across the country.[38]

Disappointments of the Crash Program

What West Virginians called "the crash program" (and Kentuckians called "Happy Pappies") provides a prime example of good intentions gone awry, in part because of the incapacity of state government to follow through on the federal government's efforts to help the state with one of its promising innovative efforts and also because local governments tended to revert to pattern, bending the new initiative to fit the needs of the county patronage machines. An initiative of the Barron administration, the program began in 1961 as a pioneering effort under the new West Virginia Department of Commerce (administered by commissioner Hulett C. Smith) to provide a work-relief and job-training program for unemployed fathers. Here, some thought, was a way out of the Appalachian wilderness that could blaze the path for others. Financed by a sales tax, the program paid welfare fathers one dollar an hour to work for the state road commission and other state agencies. The head of the program, Frederick Ehle, later told an OEO investigator that "under Commerce, it got to be a lot of patronage, and we had people stumbling all over each other."[39] Then congress amended the Social Security Act to provide maintenance support for children of unemployed parents on a matching 70–30 basis under Aid to Dependent Children of the Unemployed (ADCU), and supervision shifted from Social Security to the Department of Welfare. The program provided work relief for about 13,000 unemployed fathers at its peak, but the job training component of ADCU never fulfilled the hope that it might prepare the unemployed for new jobs.[40]

On June 5, 1965, Anthony J. Celebrezze, Secretary of Health, Education, and Welfare, came to Charleston to address the Jefferson-Jackson Day dinner and to announce a federal anti-poverty grant of $11,848,400 to "fill in the gaps" in the West Virginia work-training program, the largest single grant to the state during the first year of the War on Poverty and the largest in the country to that point under Title V, work experience.[41] Ambitious and idealistic, the grant promised a program that would help 12,000 parents, including 2,000 women, in all fifty-five counties of the state to escape the relief rolls. It sought to demonstrate that "hardcore" unemployed workers could be helped back into productive lives. According to the plan, the ADCU workers would receive basic adult education, leading in some cases to high-school equivalency. It also would include better job training, medical screening, and intensified social services for families of the unemployed to not only improve the employability of the participants, but to raise the general health and welfare standards of their families as well.[42] Although the grant required no matching funds from the state, it expected West Virginia to employ additional qualified social workers and adult education teachers. Harry

Hoffmann wrote in his *Gazette* column, *Politics*, that it appeared that after much experimentation, the country had found a solution to the unemployment problem, and "West Virginia, by its willingness to pioneer in finding a way out of the wilderness of despair, appears to have played an important role."[43]

The West Virginia Work and Training program, however, fell far short of the heady expectations. Almost ten months after the starting date, only forty of the fifty-five counties had initiated activities under the program, and only 8,230 workers (including less than 100 women) had been enrolled instead of the promised 12,000. The enrollees received no vocational training, only rudimentary social services, and thirty-one counties had either no adult education classes or had just begun classes. The 160 counselor-supervisors provided for in the grant had never been hired. Pre-employment physicals required in the grant had not been done. Most of the enrollees worked for the State Road Commission cutting brush, as they had done under the original crash program. Others dug graves, collected trash, made repairs on private properties, moved furniture, built walls, and painted bridges. A few operated heavy equipment. Clearly, the program fell far short of the goal of imparting useful new skills to help the unemployed move toward more productive lives.[44]

OEO evaluators found an abysmal lack of cooperation and coordination among state agencies in the planning and administration of the work-training grant. The commissioner of the Welfare Department, Lontz L. Vincent, had long experience in welfare work, going back to the early days of the New Deal. Appointed commissioner in July 1965, after the resignation of Barron appointee W. Bernard Smith,[45] Vincent must have seemed the ideal administrator for the program, but Charles Munson and Larrie Bailey, hired to directly oversee the work-experience program under Title V of the Economic Opportunity Act, complained bitterly that Commissioner Vincent and district welfare administrators blocked their efforts at every turn. Only the cooperation of some county school superintendents enabled them to finally launch some adult education.[46] In April, OEO administrators estimated that more than half the grant would be unexpended when the grant period came to an end in June.[47]

The new program overwhelmed the already understaffed state Welfare Department. One of the ironies of welfare is that the need for it is greatest in the states least able to provide for it. The federal

Department of Health, Education and Welfare had already put the West Virginia Department of Welfare on notice that it must increase its social work staff to meet federal standards in order to continue to qualify for federal dollars. The department responded with an innovative plan to recruit and train 450 new workers, including 190 social workers, leading to a tripling in size in four years and consequent growing pains. Even so, in 1967 Governor Smith testified before a congressional subcommittee on intergovernmental relations that the department had 600 vacancies. Faced with the necessity of administering another large program when it lacked funding and staff to carry out its customary tasks, the department's administrators felt overwhelmed, and they resented the need to answer to OEO as well as to HEW and the Labor Department, even as they struggled to carry out their assigned tasks under West Virginia law.[48] When OEO Director Shriver read a confidential report about West Virginia's Work Training fiasco, he scribbled on the memo, "This is a disgrace."[49]

OEO evaluators also noted that "there are political overtones almost anywhere you turn in West Virginia."[50] Huey Perry, the community action director in Mingo County, told the federal evaluators that politics determined "what counties and what towns get what projects and who is hired to run them." A "highly-placed" political figure told an OEO investigator that political self-aggrandizement drove efforts to seek federal money and that state politicians "will do anything to get Federal money, including damn near perjuring themselves." The same person said that virtually all state jobs were political jobs, so when administrations changed in Charleston, 25,000 jobs did too.[51] The highly personal spoils system that prevailed in West Virginia, much like what had been common in southern states in the pre-war years, nourished politics but did little to provide professional staffing, rationalized procedures, or sensitivity to citizen needs. West Virginia lagged behind other states in establishing a viable merit system. By the end of 1967, the state civil service program counted only about 7,500 employees.[52] A few hours before leaving office in 1969, Hulett C. Smith placed almost 2,000 additional state employees under the Civil Service System, grandfathering in some Democratic appointees.[53]

The ADCU program continued to vex those who believed the lack of real training and useful social services frustrated and disappointed enrollees whose hopes had been raised only to be dashed with placement in dead-end make-work jobs that gave them no prospects of continuing employment. Few enrollees realized the crash program promise of good jobs. In Mingo County ADCU participants told an interviewer that the notorious local political machine used the ADCU jobs as patronage to stay in power, subjecting recipients to intimidation and humiliation. One positive feature of the program was that it kept the father at home, unlike Aid to Families with Dependent Children (AFDC) which had unintentionally encouraged fathers to leave home so the family could be certified for assistance.[54] In 1968 Congress sought to reform welfare with a Work Incentive Program (WIN). At the same time, it became clear that the funding from the OEO grant that had supported the ADCU training program would soon expire and not be renewed. In the waning days of the Smith administration, the governor called a special session of the legislature to coordinate state law with the new federal welfare legislation. The WIN program sought to cut costs, reorganize the remnant of the crash program, and to provide employment training for a smaller group of potentially employable welfare clients. The revised program put worker training under the state department of employment security.[55]

From Head Start to VISTA

Some aspects of West Virginia's response to the War on Poverty struck a more positive chord than the ADCU program, especially those dealing with young people. Governor Smith took pride in the state's success in obtaining federal funds for OEO programs, especially Head Start, Job Corps, Neighborhood Youth Corps, and a state mental health program that used VISTA volunteers. Indeed, by the end of 1965, OEO director Shriver congratulated Smith that West Virginia was the only state in the country with a Head Start program in every county. At the same time, West Virginia, with $28,630,515 ranked eleventh among the states in the amount of money received in the War on Poverty.[56]

Head Start derived much of its inspiration from the culture of poverty idea. It was designed to help poor children, presumably at a disadvantage because of their culture of poverty background, to prepare for the first grade, and it won broad support from the beginning and also generated high expectations. Like other programs, OEO launched Head Start with a sense of urgency and little planning. On March 8, 1965, OEO director Shriver announced the program in a speech to the West Virginia legislature. Three weeks later Governor Smith addressed a hastily organized group of educators from around the state who met to put together a statewide plan for a summer program. Smith told those attending that Head Start would determine the kind of people who would be living in West Virginia in twenty years.[57] Headed by Mrs. Smith with the administrative assistance of Elizabeth DePaulo, the program operated in all fifty-five counties in the summer of 1965, enrolling more than 18,000 children. The children took field trips to the state capital, state parks, museums, and police and fire stations. Teachers exposed them to music, pictures, and books during classroom activities. The children (about half of whom had never been examined by a doctor) also received physical examinations. The examinations revealed that a large percentage had eye defects of varying seriousness, about 90 percent needed dental treatment, and a few had more serious diseases such as tuberculosis and heart defects. The program provided treatment for emergency cases and referred others to appropriate agencies. Teachers, school officials, and parents praised the program, and speaking at the National Governor's Conference at Minneapolis, OEO director Sargent Shriver singled out the West Virginia Head Start project for special praise. Smith told Shriver Head Start was "the most worthwhile and beneficial undertaking in the War on Poverty in our state."[58] The public enthusiasm of this first summer helped to make Head Start one of the programs that would survive the end of the War on Poverty.[59]

West Virginia also participated actively in Job Corps, a program that sought to provide some rudimentary training in preparation for the job market and also in those personal characteristics that might contribute to success. OEO at first saw Job Corps as a male-only organization similar to the Depression-era Civilian Conservation Corps. In hearings on the original OEO legislation, Congresswoman Edith Green of Oregon, a former schoolteacher and sharp-minded feminist, insisted that women be included.[60] Her persistence led the administration to include women, and West Virginia received early authorization to establish women's residential centers in Charleston and Huntington. OEO also established Job Corps conservation camps for young men at Sam Michaels Farm in Jefferson County and at Neola in Greenbrier County. The conservation camps each had a capacity of 100 to 150, and the residential centers each could accommodate 300 young women. In 1965, West Virginia ranked first among the states on a per capita basis in the number of applicants to the program with some 10,000 applicants and of the 13,000 already enrolled at centers around the country, almost 1,000 were West Virginians.[61]

In some parts of the country, Job Corps aroused bitter public reactions when the young enrollees, many with criminal records, inevitably became involved in questionable activities, and these difficulties caused much early reaction against OEO.[62] In West Virginia, residents of Harpers Ferry and Charles Town opposed early plans to locate a center at Bolivar Heights, near Harpers Ferry High School, based in part on concerns that young black men would be part of the Job Corps contingent. Sam Michaels, a local landowner, however, agreed to give the Job Corps seventy-seven acres between Charles Town and Harpers Ferry, assuring that the Eastern Panhandle would get a Job Corps center. Charleston residents and city authorities welcomed the women's Job Corps Center, established in a six-story downtown hotel. There enrollees studied to become beauticians, secretaries, business machine operators, cashiers, practical nurses, and assemblers of electronic equipment. Charleston police treated incidents involving the residents discreetly. Mayor John Shanklin admitted that some had been apprehensive that the women might be involved in troubles. He insisted to a *New York Times* reporter that difficulties had been negligible. The reporter thought the mayor and others swept Job Corps problems under the rug, because they dared not jeopardize the flow of federal dollars.[63] Like Head Start, Jobs Corps would be more enduring than other aspects of the War on Poverty, because the public perceived them as having a very practical purpose.

The Neighborhood Youth Corps (NYC) and College Work-Study, much like similar New Deal-era organizations, provided other training and work opportunities for young people. The NYC, administered by the Labor Department, put poor local youths to work in their own neighborhoods working for county school systems, the State Road Commission, Department of Natural Resources, and in a few cases, for community action councils. Although the statute charged NYC with the promotion of job skills, it served primarily as a way to put some money in the pockets of poor adolescents and to keep them occupied. College work-study grants went to West Virginia University and to the state colleges to provide part-time employment for college students.[64]

Volunteers in Service to America (VISTA) began in West Virginia with a heavy concentration of volunteers working for the West Virginia Department of Mental Health in hospitals and mental health institutions. In October 1965, of 220 VISTAs in West Virginia, 168 worked for mental health. More than 300 West Virginians had volunteered for service in VISTA.[65] Dr. Mildred Bateman, director of the State Mental Health Department, credited the work of the VISTA volunteers in mental health aftercare and prevention with enabling the state to reduce the average daily population in the five state mental hospitals from 5,250 to 4,650, even in a time of rising admissions.[66] After the early push for mental health volunteers, more VISTAs accepted assignments to work for county community action agencies, and, as further discussed in the next chapter, some of these became highly controversial when they turned to organizing poor communities to assert their rights.[67]

Charleston as Prototype: Community Action and "Maximum Feasible Participation"

The most controversial part of the War on Poverty, the Community Action Program (CAP), funded local anti-poverty agencies (CAAs) that would presumably lead the fight to counteract the most problematic effects of the new machine age in Appalachia. The Economic Opportunity Act charged these agencies to seek "maximum feasible participation" of poor people. This concept had evolved from sociological theories about juvenile delinquency in urban slums by scholars of the Chicago school of sociology, notably Lloyd Ohlin and Richard Cloward. Opportunity theory suggested that the solution to juvenile delinquency lay in the reorganization of slum communities and opening up new opportunities for children of the poor. The President's Committee on Juvenile Delinquency, established by President Kennedy in May 1961, and chaired by Attorney General Robert F. Kennedy, first applied the opportunity theory in the establishment of experimental programs in sixteen cities, including

Charleston. After President Kennedy's assassination, President Johnson demanded a bold new approach to poverty, and the planners seized upon the juvenile delinquency program as a model for community action. The presidential urgency caused the planners to minimize the disappointing results of the experimental programs, which, in city after city, had simply fallen back upon traditional welfare concepts.[68] As presented to Johnson by his advisors around a small kitchen table at Johnson's Pedernales ranch in late 1963, the concept of community action by the poor, despite sounding "brand new and even faintly radical," as Johnson's memoir, *Vantage Point*, later put it, "was based on one of the oldest ideas of our democracy, as old as the New England town meeting—self-determination at the local level."[69]

Daniel Patrick Moynihan, who, as an assistant secretary of labor in the Kennedy and Johnson administrations, participated in early planning for the War on Poverty, later wrote that the phrase "maximum feasible participation," which became critical and controversial in the execution of community action programs, never received careful analysis in the hurried preparation of the legislation. He believed that it became more central to the operations of the community action program than the planners had intended. Indeed, David Hackett, who had worked with Ohlin and others in shaping the experimental juvenile delinquency programs and had actually composed the phrase, would later maintain that he and others who had used the phrase had not intended to promote confrontation.[70] Strongly committed to the concept and most influential in getting the phrase into the legislation, Richard Boone had worked for the Ford Foundation and with Hackett in the juvenile delinquency program before becoming one of those who helped to shape the OEO program. Strongly influenced by Chicago Depression-era organizer Saul Alinsky, Boone insisted on maximum feasible participation as a way to afford people at the grassroots political power to improve their ability to challenge the "establishment" in the fight against poverty.[71]

As previously noted, many of those who shaped and administered the War on Poverty relied not on the confrontational theories of Alinsky and Boone but rather on the notion of a culture of poverty. Allen J. Matusow, in his history of the War on Poverty, suggests that Johnson himself tended to think of community action as just a way to deliver an expanded flow of traditional services to Democratic neighborhoods in big cities and never realized that it might result in political and social conflict.[72] Johnson, however, insisted in his memoir that he received early warnings that community action carried political risks, but he said, "I thought local governments had to be challenged to be awakened."[73]

In most of the country and especially in Appalachia, local governments desperate for funds to meet escalating welfare costs and politicians grateful for patronage eagerly sought the windfall offered by the War on Poverty, but they felt no compelling need for a grassroots awakening, which would offer them unwanted competition. They expected that the funds would be expended in the conventional manner, through local appointed or elected officials, and would provide patronage for local political machines. Many did not grasp at first the unprecedented nature of the legislation, which, as carried out by OEO agents, sought to create informal grassroots organizations as the primary agents to plan the programs and to dispense the funds. Even more unconventional, historian Irwin Unger writes, "was the attempt to overcome the political apathy of the urban and rural poor and cut them in on a portion of the political and financial pie."[74] Darrell McGraw, an aide to Governor Smith at the time, later reflected on the striking notion that the "federal government was sufficiently secure to subsidize discontent."[75] In Appalachia such efforts flew in the face of conventional practice and aroused bitter opposition from entrenched political machines.

As one of the sixteen cities chosen for experimental programs under the President's Committee for Juvenile Delinquency, Charleston received start-up money in 1962. On February 5, 1964, even before the passage of War on Poverty legislation, Charleston received the first major grant in Appalachia, announced by Robert Kennedy and described by the *New York Times* as "a three year $12 million effort to expand opportunities for the youth of Kanawha County." Kennedy stressed that the Kanawha County project (clearly intended to be based on the "opportunity theory" of the Chicago sociologists) would serve as a prototype of President Johnson's forthcoming program against domestic poverty. The local agency administering the Charleston program took the name, Action for Appalachian Youth.[76]

To qualify for OEO grants, the War on Poverty legislation required county governments to establish local economic opportunity commissions, which were in turn charged with organizing local poor people to address their problems. In several West Virginia counties, as in big cities in other parts of America, the original community action agencies (CAAs) established by the local county courts found themselves challenged by organized groups of people who conventionally wielded no power. A few CAA organizations arose that truly generated grassroots action by poor people. Typically, the local politicians complained that these groups undermined the elected local officials. Further complicating matters, in some West Virginia counties (as further discussed in the next chapter) idealistic young VISTA Volunteers and Appalachian Volunteers, mostly from out of state, often long-haired, unkempt, and unconventional in their political views, played an active role in organizing poor people to take control of community action agencies.[77]

Hardy and McDowell: Appalachian Models for the War on Poverty

Because some West Virginia counties had already begun to organize community action and redevelopment plans under the Area Redevelopment Act, they could move quickly to seek funds under the War on Poverty legislation. Hard pressed for models for a rural war on poverty and pressured by the White House to quickly distribute appropriated funds, OEO seized upon Hardy, a typical Appalachian agricultural county in eastern West Virginia and McDowell, an example of a hard-hit Appalachian coalfield county in southern West Virginia, to receive early grants.[78]

In 1962, the Extension Service of West Virginia University's Appalachian Center helped Hardy and other rural West Virginia counties to work up community action plans as required to obtain federal funding under the Area Redevelopment Act. Ralph Fisher, editor of the *Moorefield Examiner* and a local stalwart of the Democratic Party, chaired the Hardy County Rural Area Development Committee, which included representatives from all parts of the county. Neighboring Mineral County incorporated its committee at the same time. As OEO scrambled to launch the War on Poverty after the passage of the Economic Opportunity Act of 1964, Director Sargent Shriver felt pressure from the White House to start spending the anti-poverty dollars. When these committees from the heart of

Appalachia walked in and presented them with proposals that appeared to meet the purposes of OEO, Shriver and his staff welcomed them. To cut administrative costs, the two counties joined forces as the Mineral-Hardy Rural Area Development Committee and hired an administrator, Wallace J. Lynch. The county governments designated the committee as their Community Action Agency. OEO quickly funded several of Mineral-Hardy's projects to the tune of $163,706, and suddenly Mineral-Hardy RAD, the first rural community action program (CAP) in the country funded by OEO, became the model for rural community action nationwide. Metropolitan news reporters descended on the area, and rural CAPs around the country requested copies of the Mineral-Hardy community action program.[79]

The Mineral-Hardy War on Poverty focused on poor children, providing programs that sought to help them escape poverty through health and education. This first action in the War on Poverty provided dental care and medical examinations, a summer camp for handicapped children, enrichment trips to Baltimore and Washington for fifth graders, and a preschool program that anticipated Head Start. All of these programs met important needs, but some local critics, though pleased that the county had received federal funds, understood that the programs addressed the results of poverty, not the causes. They also believed that most of the preschool and other service programs should be part of the regular school program, but the county already relied on state funds for 80 percent of its funding and could afford no frills. Based on local interviews, *Charleston Gazette* Washington correspondent Harry Ernst suggested that a real war against poverty in Hardy would require an attack on the poverty of the school system, improvements in local housing (34 percent of which had no indoor water or toilets), medical assistance for large, low-income families not on welfare, assistance in upgrading roads and community facilities, and most of all, employment. Fisher and others thought that tourism offered the best hope for bringing more jobs and dollars to the county, but Ernst suggested that heavier artillery than used in this first skirmish would be needed to achieve victory in the War on Poverty.[80]

The McDowell County CAP—like Mineral-Hardy—had also received special early attention and support from OEO. Because it symbolized so well the problems of Appalachian coal counties, and because it also had the help of the Council of the Southern Mountains, a private regional agency with long experience in dealing with government agencies, McDowell began as the favored program of the OEO in the coalfield region, receiving the greatest amount of funding and publicity. Ed Thomas, a Methodist minister from Keystone and Jefferson Monroe, a Presbyterian minister from Welch, organized the McDowell program by calling together county leaders and asking them what the county needed to do to fight poverty. Taking the ideas generated in that meeting, the two ministers drew up a program and went to Washington to seek approval. Responding to criticisms of their first draft, they hired Kelley girls to type rewrites and stayed until OEO approved their program, like Mineral-Hardy, one of the first rural programs to be approved nationwide. Monroe later recalled that they suddenly became heroes and experts, as others sought their advice on how to set up a community action program. They urged the Council of the Southern Mountains to move quickly to expand the McDowell County model through Appalachia, but CSM, a traditional missionary and philanthropic organization, began to be paralyzed by internal debates about the proper philosophy it should follow. Ed Thomas served as the early director of the McDowell CAP and gave energetic leadership in getting the McDowell program moving; but in late 1965, Thomas suffered a heart attack and was unable to return to work. Because of its early and substantial funding, the Council of the Southern Mountains' McDowell program had moved quickly forward to put into effect a "top-down" plan based on the establishment of community centers planned largely by county seat politicians. McDowell also operated a pilot food stamp program and in May 1965, received the first contingent of VISTA workers in West Virginia. Thomas assigned them to assist with the establishment and operation of community centers in Vivian and Warriormine.[81]

As time went on, Jefferson Monroe began to realize that the highly touted McDowell plan that he and Thomas and some of the leading citizens of the county had devised had serious flaws. It had been established by local authorities without consulting the poor people who would supposedly be the beneficiaries. Because of the early positive national attention it received, Governor Smith and his wife Mary Alice became very interested in the McDowell program, but Monroe himself became increasingly disenchanted with the program he had helped create.[82]

Meanwhile, in OEO itself, the Mid-Atlantic regional office debated a new strategy for fighting poverty in Appalachia. After a visit to eastern Kentucky in June 1965, OEO evaluator Frank Prial concluded that the poverty program in the region faced certain failure, because in Appalachia "none of the standard rules of democracy apply." He described an area where the coal companies controlled local government and resisted any change "unless the power structure can turn it to a profit." Moreover, Prial reported, no middle class existed to offset the overweening power of the economic interests. The United Mine Workers and most middle-class types such as doctors, lawyers, and the better teachers had vanished, leaving behind the old, young, sick, and "those who prey upon them." Local administrators of OEO programs, he said, had no understanding of what Congress intended in the OEO legislation. Prial condemned virtually all elected officials and the Council of the Southern Mountains, which had contracted with OEO to administer several programs, including the Appalachian Volunteers and the McDowell County program. Prial concluded that "someone is going to have to strong arm the power structures in the poor coal counties if anything is to be accomplished in the war on poverty."[83]

Jack Ciaccio, the head of the OEO Mid-Atlantic Office, thought Prial's sweeping generalizations went too far and in fact reflected the ideas of some of the local middle-class opposition in Kentucky, particularly Harry Caudill and *Whitesburg Mountain Eagle* editor Tom Gish. Ciaccio nevertheless agreed that community action boards in the region reflected the power structure and that services for the poor could be improved only "if the poor are organized, and protest—long and loud—about the lousy job that is being done."[84] Ciaccio believed OEO could diffuse power in Appalachia through several policies. He believed they should continue to fund the Council of the Southern Mountains, push for the formation of multi-county CAPs (thereby undermining the power of single-county fiefdoms), and insist that poor people be included on CAP boards as a requirement for federal funding. These policies, he believed, would help to insure a necessary ingredient for change, an organized opposition.[85]

Reaction in West Virginia

With these policies in place for Appalachian counties, the Mineral-Hardy and McDowell programs' days as the poster children of OEO rural programs soon ended. Relations deteriorated between the local committees and OEO regional agents who reflected the more militant policies OEO had determined to apply in Appalachia. In November 1965, Ralph Fisher shared his frustrations in an editorial that raised alarms in Charleston and Washington. Everything had been going fine, Fisher said, as OEO personnel praised the Mineral-Hardy program, and OEO staff and the local committee had worked together cooperatively. Gradually, however, the atmosphere changed. OEO demanded that six more counties (Hampshire, Grant, Pendleton, Morgan, Berkeley, and Jefferson) be brought into the Mineral-Hardy organization. Fisher's committee agreed to add three (Pendleton, Grant, and Hampshire, all of the South Branch Valley), forming the Eastern West Virginia Planning and Development Association, Inc. When they met with a new area coordinator of OEO, Yale graduate and former State Department employee Ray Collins, the early cooperative atmosphere disappeared. Collins, Fisher said, had no understanding of local conditions. Collins pounded on the table, demanded that they have more representatives of the poor, that they seek $500,000 instead of $200,000 for their preschool program, and that they extensively revise their plans. There followed long delays in Washington and then more revisions of the plans and changing of rules. Then instead of the $500,000 for the preschool program in five counties that Collins had insisted they apply for, OEO funded the grant for only $134,000, barely enough for one county. School administrators who had been encouraged by OEO to plan for full funding felt betrayed. Fisher complained that OEO, which had been so helpful and receptive at the beginning, had turned into an inept bureaucracy. At a meeting in Washington of all Appalachian CAP administrators, OEO officials said they did not have enough stenographers to put messages in writing, so they tried to conduct all business by telephone. Now no one would say yes or no, and, Fisher wrote, "Everyone is a chief in the outfit and there are no Indians to do the work."[86]

Ralph Fisher's public outburst against OEO brought to a head growing tensions between the state and regional OEO authorities. Some of the tension grew from the bureaucratic awkwardness of the Economic Opportunity Act, which put the states in the position of organizing and providing technical assistance to local CAPS but gave OEO regional coordinators administrative oversight after the programs had been approved by Washington. Accordingly, West Virginia had organized its own Economic Opportunity Agency and received a grant to fund the agency, but OEO regional agents rather than the state agency oversaw the local programs. The arrangement contributed to the great personal animosity that grew between personnel in the state agency and the regional agents. Although West Virginia cooperated with most of the OEO programs, community action became a source of great tension between the state and federal agents of OEO. At the beginning of his term, Governor Smith appointed Paul Crabtree, who formerly had an office in Washington to handle federal programs for Governor Barron, to administer the state economic opportunity agency. Crabtree, young, ambitious, and energetic, did a good job organizing the programs that the state could control, but he resisted the community action program and especially resented the attitude of federal officials. He agreed with Ralph Fisher that OEO representatives demanded much but issued conflicting rules and guidelines, acted too slowly on grant applications, and assumed an overbearing attitude. In memos to Governor Smith, he also claimed federal OEO agents used revolutionary rhetoric in urging that the West Virginia OEO encourage community action organizations to overthrow local authorities.[87]

Just two days before Fisher's editorial appeared, West Virginia–Kentucky Area OEO coordinator Ray Collins (the same agent who had pounded the table in Moorefield) sent an unflattering assessment of the West Virginia Economic Opportunity Agency to Theodore Berry, the OEO director of community action. Collins reported that the four assistant coordinators on Crabtree's staff offered "politically inhibited" advice and lacked the technical competence to be of much help to the local community action agencies. The West Virginia OEO, he claimed, tried to control the anti-poverty program and to take undue credit for successes. Crabtree himself, Collins reported, tended to see the state OEO as more of a public relations agency rather than one that could provide the technical and planning help that local community action agencies needed. Collins's report credited Crabtree with success in obtaining substantial sums of money for Head Start, work programs, the National Youth Corps, and Job Corps but suggested that the success also came about because Washington recognized the need in the state and gave West Virginia high priority.[88]

Even as the regional OEO coordinator criticized the state economic opportunity agency, the OEO general counsel suspected that the West Virginia Economic Opportunity Agency might be involved in political activity in violation of the Hatch Act, which precludes partisan activity by government officials receiving federal funds. The suspicion no doubt arose because Governor Smith appointed members of his own staff to be the state OEO officials, and the agency office was just steps away from the governor's office. As noted earlier, the state had little merit-based civil service for administrators at the time. Though an investigation found no Hatch Act violations that could be proved, it demonstrated a close connection between the agency and the governor's office. A confidential memo to Sargent Shriver attached to the report warned: "This kiss me cousin relationship may have charm for the parties involved, but offers little romance for the War on Poverty and for its opponents who could use this case in a 'political influence' argument."[89] The same investigator also concluded from a brief visit with Governor Smith and his wife, Mary Alice, who headed the summer program of Head Start, that they both had reservations about representation of the poor. Smith urged that OEO "go slowly and be flexible" about involving the poor and called for an understanding of "the mountain intellect," a view expanded upon by the first lady. The Smiths, Presbyterians, perhaps had been influenced by reading the views of Presbyterian minister Jack Weller, who had operated a church program in Boone County for years and had recently published his observations on Appalachian culture in *Yesterday's People*.[90]

In November, Governor Smith grew alarmed about the community action program. Ralph Fisher's editorial appeared on November 10, and on November 16, an OEO team from Washington met with Governor Smith and his aides to address Smith's concerns.[91] After the visit, Paul Crabtree, his chief aide, flew into a rage. He told Smith that the OEO team had insulted the dignity of the governor and the state. He felt the OEO agents knew nothing of the state's background and history and talked to them as though West Virginia were a southern state. He told the governor that "this entire program is futile, politically dangerous," and he added, the OEO regional officials *"never will work with us."* He presented the governor a draft statement announcing that West Virginia would abolish its Economic Opportunity Agency as of January 15, 1966. The statement summarized complaints about OEO, quoted alleged statements made by OEO agents about "overthrowing constituted authorities," and went on to say that OEO encouraged "activities within our state which are not in keeping with the highest aspirations of a democratic society."[92]

To announce that West Virginia would close down its economic opportunity agency, as Crabtree advised, or to suggest that OEO agents encouraged anti-democratic activity, would have been political bombshells, especially since West Virginia had received favored treatment in many of the War on Poverty programs. Smith chose not to follow the course Crabtree recommended, but on November 20, apparently after having contacted other officials in Washington, he forwarded a letter to Vice President Humphrey with copies to Senator Byrd and Senator Randolph. The letter included Crabtree's complaints as well as Ralph Fisher's editorial from the *Moorefield Examiner*. Smith suggested that "if what is happening in West Virginia is happening throughout the Nation" the vice president might want to investigate further, implying that some sort of national conspiracy might be afoot.[93] Meanwhile, he publicly questioned the usefulness of the community action programs. In one of a series of "Government to the People" meetings, he told questioners at a meeting at Scott High School in Boone County that the War on Poverty community action plans disappointed him. He called them "paper tigers, plans on paper, but nothing really is being done."[94]

Governor Smith's protest joined a growing chorus of complaints from disenchanted Democratic leaders across the country. All through the spring, summer, and early fall of 1965, troubles grew between mayors of large cities and groups that organized against the original community action boards designated by mayors. In some cases militant groups who took over urban CAPs turned them into new-style patronage machines. In May, the mayors of Los Angeles and San Francisco introduced a resolution at the National Conference of Mayors in St. Louis condemning OEO for "failure to recognize the legal and moral responsibility of local officials who are accountable to the taxpayers for expenditures of local funds."[95] Because a majority of the mayors had no wish to embarrass the president, the conference did not pass the resolution. Instead, Vice President Humphrey, in St. Louis to address the conference, agreed to carry the mayors' grievances to the White House. In the summer and fall of 1965 the dissatisfaction of governors and mayors grew, angering President Johnson, who felt the OEO community action program caused him too many problems, especially at a time when Vietnam increasingly absorbed his attention.[96]

Guns Over Butter: OEO in Retreat

In mid-November 1965, around the time that Governor Smith had contacted Senators Byrd and Randolph and Vice President Humphrey, Johnson asked his assistant, Joseph Califano, to quietly look into the dismantling of OEO. Johnson never followed through, probably because the political cost would have been too great, but clearly by the end of 1965, although he still championed the War on Poverty, Johnson's patience with OEO, especially community action, had reached an end. Thereafter complaining mayors and governors received reassurances, and faced with the rising demands of the Vietnam War, Johnson felt less regret that funding waned for the War on Poverty.[97]

In December 1965, the rising costs of the Vietnam War burst the bubble of high expectations at OEO. The classic dilemma of guns or butter forced hard thinking about domestic programs. Sargent Shriver had just approved a long-range plan for ending poverty generated by the agency's Office of Plans, Progress, and Evaluations. The new plan had set aside the sociologist's "opportunity" theories in favor of an economist-dominated plan for massive job creation, more social services for the poor, and a negative income tax to assist unemployables. The plan called for $10 billion in the first year, including $4 billion for OEO. When the costs of Vietnam became clear, however, the OEO's long-range plan died, and the poverty warriors had to face their war with paltry resources, less than 20 percent of what the plan had called for in the first year. With this realization "a pall descended on the agency that never lifted."[98]

Meanwhile, Governor Smith, who disliked conflict, wanted to try to ease the split between the state OEO office and regional OEO agents. Because Jefferson Monroe and Ed Thomas had some standing with OEO as authors of the McDowell County plan, Smith called them to Charleston and urged them to go to Washington to find out what could be done to heal the breach between the state OEO office and the regional OEO officials. Flown to Washington in a state plane, Monroe and Thomas discussed the federal-state rift with one of the

Mid-Atlantic OEO agents. Upon their return they urged Smith to offer to remove Paul Crabtree as head of the state OEO if offending federal agents could also be removed from the regional office. According to Monroe's account, Smith followed their advice and called OEO director Sargent Shriver to arrange a deal.[99]

Reorganizing the State OEO

For a time thereafter, criticism of community action waned. In West Virginia, Governor Smith backed away from public criticism of the community action programs and OEO regional officers in the early months of 1966. A Smith aide told OEO regional agents that the governor had come to realize that Crabtree bore some responsibility for the difficulties between the state and regional OEO officials and that his attitude caused much potential damage. West Virginia was, after all, a major beneficiary of OEO funding. Although Smith retained Crabtree as his chief of staff, to repair the damaged relationship between the regional officers and the state agency, Smith reorganized the state Economic Opportunity Agency, naming Eugene Thoenen, Crabtree's deputy, as administrator of the agency. About six months later, Smith called Jefferson Monroe and asked him to come to Charleston to head the agency. Monroe explained to Smith that he no longer believed in the top-down philosophy of the McDowell plan and that Smith therefore might not want him in the job. Smith insisted, however, and Monroe, whose congregation had not fully embraced his efforts in the poverty war, resigned his pastorate in Welch to go to Charleston. Ironically, as federal funding for community action waned, with Monroe as the director, the tone of the state agency became briefly much more positive toward the more daring community action programs.[100] Constantly walking a tightrope as he defended the poverty warriors against the complaints Smith received from politicians, Monroe brought about a broader and more positive view toward poor people's groups, CAP agencies, AVs, VISTAs, OEO agents, and others involved in the War on Poverty. Smith and Monroe had many long discussions, and despite a growing reaction against community action, the governor kept Monroe in the job, and Monroe felt that Smith and especially Mrs. Smith supported his efforts until political pressures in 1968 caused the governor to turn away from community action.[101]

The new arrangement did not resolve all the problems. As OEO in Appalachia turned increasingly toward a model encouraging broader participation of the poor, the Eastern West Virginia Community Action Program continued to have problems with Washington. In June 1967, as it investigated the Eastern West Virginia CAP for audit irregularities, OEO withdrew support of the program, and the Eastern West Virginia CAP board simply dropped out of the program. OEO publicly announced funding had been withdrawn because of inadequate representation of the poor. As Governor Smith prepared to visit Moorefield, an aide warned him that the real reason that the Eastern West Virginia CAP board dropped out of "the War on Poverty" was that the board members had learned of the organization's financial mess and simply abandoned their support.[102]

"Rethinking OEO's Approach": Assessing McDowell and Kanawha

McDowell County's program also fell from favor in Washington. Nothing better illustrates the different perspectives of OEO and the state Economic Opportunity Agency (before Jefferson Monroe took over) than their different assessments of the McDowell County program. In early 1966, a report of the state Economic Opportunity Agency pronounced the McDowell program in a class by itself, with nine community centers up and running and "encompassing the entirety of the desirable features of a CAA." The report said "quality as well as competence" characterized the McDowell CAA, and it suggested that every CAA director in the state would benefit from visiting McDowell "to see an operative program and its relation to the community which it serves."[103]

Less than a year after the glowing assessment by Smith's staff, an OEO team from Washington visited McDowell County. Not just a routine administrative visit, the OEO sent the team to McDowell to devise a national assessment model for OEO rural programs.[104] What better place to begin than with one of the most highly touted rural programs in the country? After a two-day visit that included meetings with the board of directors and the staff and visits to McDowell's eight community centers, the evaluation team gloomily concluded that "community action is not practiced nor understood by this CAA." They found that the program had been drawn up without broad consultation with the communities or with the "targeted population" of the area. The team recommended that the McDowell board be restructured by adding a representative of the poor from each of the eight community centers as well as representatives of public and private agencies. The team also insisted that the community centers be made more representative of the people in the communities rather than just places where activities organized by the central office of the CAA took place.[105]

Some members of the OEO evaluation team blamed the "failure" of the McDowell program on OEO itself. One said, "OEO failed McDowell as much as the McDowell CAA is failing" the poor people of the county and called for "a real rethinking of OEO's approach vis-à-vis 'the rural problem,'" The same writer suggested that "the most realistic approach may be preparation of the younger generations for ultimate relocation."[106] The acting director of the OEO's rural task force and the chairman of the evaluation team, Richard Wenner, wrote that because OEO funded McDowell in 1964 "as one of the first rural CAAs in the nation, much of the blame for where it is today must lie with OEO." He condescendingly pointed out that "no one has given adequate guidance, technical assistance or training to a group of isolated mountain people who had no reason to really understand the lofty concepts of community action, involvement of the poor, participatory democracy, etc." Wenner thought the local shortage of expertise could be overcome only by "a sophisticated, intensive program of training and technical assistance." As technical assistance fell under the responsibility of the state, this also served as veiled criticism of the governor's agency.[107]

The Kanawha County community action program, despite its favored early attention as a pilot program and substantial federal funding, also never measured up to the OEO's community action standards. In addition to its funding from the President's Committee on Juvenile Delinquency, the Kanawha program also received grants from the Labor Department under the Manpower Development and Training Act to provide training for disadvantaged youths.[108] When OEO entered the picture in 1965, the county court designated the existing program, Action for Appalachian Youth—Community Development (AAY—CD) as Kanawha County's CAA. Under pressure from the regional OEO, the board expanded in December 1965 to include more neighborhood people. The board president, Kanawha County circuit judge William J. Thompson, dominated the board from its beginning. Despite having received substantial funding in its first three years, the program had little to show for its efforts. Staff salaries and expensive headquarters offices soaked up much of the money as the director made more than the mayor of Charleston, and five deputy directors matched the salaries of the mayor and superintendent of schools. Its youth job training project placed a small number of youth in jobs, and the community development program established seventeen community centers scattered over 975 mountainous square miles. After an injudicious and failed effort to convert an old school in the predominantly black Triangle neighborhood in the heart of Charleston into a dormitory for rural white youth receiving job training, AAY, after long delays, finally turned the building into a community center. The Triangle Improvement Association, a black community organization, blamed racism for the delays, but OEO investigators reported that administrative incompetence had more to do with it than racism. Named the John F. Kennedy Center, the community center's program reflected more of a settlement house approach than the kind of action agency favored by OEO. The other neighborhood groups, organized by paid neighborhood workers, met in generally dilapidated quarters and typically ran recreational programs for youth. A few addressed community issues like roads. John D. Rockefeller, IV, the twenty-seven-year-old neighborhood worker in Emmons who would soon launch a political career in the state by running for the House of Delegates, proved something of a curiosity to the press and federal evaluators. OEO evaluators found the Kanawha AAY-CD lacking in leadership and imagination, despite its high administrative salaries, but held out the hope that the community centers might provide the basis for the development of a real CAA program, that is to say, one that embraced "maximum feasible participation of the poor."[109]

The ARC: A Lost Opportunity?

Although not part of the official war on poverty, the Appalachian Regional Commission, established by Congress in 1965, provided funding for public works projects in impoverished areas with the primary goal of stimulating economic growth. Economic growth, like the social science theories that inspired much of the War on Poverty, offered a way of lifting regions out of poverty without dealing with troublesome structural problems. A critical concept behind the bill featured directing resources toward growth centers rather than to dying mining camps and fading rural hollows. The prevailing theory held that development funds could have more impact if invested in urban centers where jobs would grow, offering opportunities to those living in poor rural areas. Good roads would help the poor in the hinterlands to come to the urban centers for work.[110] Some Appalachian critics called attention to the growth center concept in the Appalachian Regional Development bill before Congress passed it. The *Charleston Gazette* wondered if the people of Appalachia had been led to expect too much, believing as they did that the bill "will strike a hard blow at the stark misery found in so many of the counties comprising Appalachia." The bill, however, required concentration in the areas where there is "the greatest potential for future growth, and where the expected return on public dollars will be greatest." The *Gazette* argued that the poorest areas that suffered most and offered the least opportunity for substantial return on the taxpayer's dollar "should demand the lion's share of concern." The *Gazette* also noted that the bulk of the ARC's funds would go to roads, not necessarily the areas requiring the greatest attention.[111]

Governor Smith, in testifying before Congress, strongly supported passage of the legislation, but he also urged that money be included to help the states control mine refuse heaps or gob piles as they were commonly called, a desperate need that would go largely unattended by either the state or federal governments, leaving many residents of the coalfields living in dangerous conditions that would be revealed all too clearly by the Buffalo Creek tragedy of 1972 (as will be noted in chapter 9). He also sought the addition of funds for water systems, sewer lines, street paving, parking facilities, and conservation projects, noting the difficulty small municipalities in Appalachia had in raising funds for such facilities.[112]

Harry Caudill attacked the Appalachian Regional Development Act almost immediately in an article in *The Atlantic*. He recalled that poverty in West Virginia had left John F. Kennedy shaken and depressed and committed to help and that Lyndon Johnson had come to share that feeling. But these good intentions alone would not suffice. Neither the task force under the chairmanship of Franklin D. Roosevelt Jr. that drafted the act, nor Kennedy nor Johnson nor the

Congress fully understood the needs, Caudill argued. They failed to put into the measure anything to attack the real problems such as absentee ownership of resources, a tax structure rigged for the benefit of the out of state investors rather than for the citizens of the state, poor rural schools, strip mining and the need for reclamation and reforestation, and inadequate hospital care for indigent people. Like the *Gazette*, Caudill also criticized the emphasis on road improvement, arguing that roads would not get at the major problems of the region.[113] Although the regional governors managed to persuade the ARC to modify the growth center concept to allow more attention to smaller cities and county seats, the ultimate goal remained to move Appalachia toward urbanization. Executive Director Ralph Widner, an urban planner from Pennsylvania, told *Harper's* that little dying towns in Appalachia should "die faster" and millions of rural dwellers and former coal miners should move to metropolitan areas or to medium-sized cities in the region. His conclusion coincided with the OEO evaluator of rural programs who had concluded that the best thing to do for the youth of McDowell County was to prepare them to leave.[114]

In the first five years of West Virginia's participation in the Appalachian program, the primary emphasis would be on development highways and access roads. The state received some $123,000,000 of ARC funds from 1965 to 1970, and about $93,000,000 went into roads. Some funding also went into health and hospitals, libraries, vocational and higher education, and airports.[115] As was often the case with other federal agencies, ARC tended to be critical of the state's efforts. In June 1968, the ARC staffers found West Virginia's ARC planning inadequate. Executive Director Ralph Widner told Angus Peyton, Commissioner of Commerce, and the state's chief ARC administrator, that the state had invested most not in the areas of greatest potential for future economic development (as the legislation called for) nor in the southern coalfield areas suffering the most severe economic and social problems but in the area along the eastern boundary of the state in the Appalachian highlands with the least population and the fewest problems. Widner also said the state had done little to find solutions to its many problems. The goal, Widner said, was to move away from the haphazard system of grants-in-aid applications and to devise a development strategy to guide federal assistance. "It appears," he wrote, "that we have some distance to travel in bringing about such a strategy in West Virginia." Widner urged that the emphasis had to be on developing staff at the state and district levels "capable of understanding how to effectively utilize public funds to promote economic development."[116] From the ARC's perspective, a change of leadership in Charleston made no difference. When Arch Moore became governor in January 1969, he removed ARC matters from the Department of Commerce to a newly created Office of Federal-State Relations under the supervision of Billy L. Coffindaffer and directly responsible to the governor. ARC remained harshly critical of West Virginia's planning, finding it fundamentally inadequate. The 1970 plan confused the goal of increasing public revenues with the goal of "providing the foundations for a self-sustaining, growing economy having a standard of living . . . comparable to the average for the U.S."[117]

Conclusion

The election of John F. Kennedy as president in 1960 put Appalachian concerns high on the agenda of the federal government, and West Virginia received favored treatment in the early days of the New Frontier and the War on Poverty. Early attention from the Area Redevelopment Administration, Charleston's selection as one of the cities in the experimental program on juvenile delinquency, experiments in turning welfare into manpower development through state-federal cooperation, and trials of food stamps marked the New Frontier efforts in West Virginia. The War on Poverty also focused on the state, sending some of its earliest VISTA volunteers to southern counties and making two of its earliest grants in rural America to Hardy and McDowell, counties that quickly presented plans to OEO officials eager to move forward in Appalachia. The well-intended experiments of the early 1960s in "creative federalism" fell short of expectations as federal and state agencies came to the table with different expectations and frequently clashed. Though the state embraced programs directed toward helping the poor help themselves such as Head Start and Job Corp, as a small state with a bureaucracy based more on politics than technical skills, it sometimes lacked the capacity or the will to carry out objectives set forth in federal legislation. Even though the state's unemployment rate fell, the persistent poverty of some areas led some federal officials to conclude that the best solution for some rural people was to encourage movement to an urban area. As the Vietnam War escalated and the Johnson administration scaled back plans for the War on Poverty, OEO's plans for Appalachia banked more on the promises of "maximum feasible participation" as a way for the people of the region to improve their circumstances.

5
Raising Hell in the Hills and Hollows:
AVs, VISTAs, and Community Action

> We should abandon the State Economic Opportunity Agency, because its plan for this year neatly balances boondoggle and bureaucracy and seems more designed to raise hell than the standard of living.
> Paul Crabtree to Governor Hulett C. Smith, July 18, 1968

> We've given the rest of America a pretty bad impression of us. West Virginians are supposed to be hospitable, open people—yet we clobbered the hell out of these young people who came to try to help us. It's a shame, really.
> Jefferson Monroe, West Virginia EOA Director, October 1, 1968

The Mineral-Hardy community action program, the Council of the Southern Mountains' program in McDowell County (reminiscent of the settlement house approach of an earlier day), and the ambitious but underachieving Kanawha County program drew much attention in the early months of the War on Poverty, but all fell short of the ideal of "maximum feasible participation" as envisioned by the federal Office of Economic Opportunity. From 1965 to 1968, however, several community action programs, largely through the efforts of Appalachian and VISTA volunteers, worked hard to stimulate grassroots community action. Their efforts alarmed local and state government officials and segments of the press, leading to something of a Red Scare in West Virginia. Leading politicians called for ending or severely restricting their activities, and the atmosphere had a chilling effect on the reform impulse, but it also contributed to the growth of private grassroots organizations that would continue to work for change, reform, and an Appalachian reawakening after the War on Poverty faded.

Huey Perry and the Mingo Model for "Maximum Feasible Participation"

Nowhere in West Virginia and perhaps nowhere in rural America did a rural agency focus from its beginning more completely on "maximum feasible participation of the poor" than the Mingo County Equal Opportunity Commission. In late 1964, the Mingo County Court established the commission, made up of local businessmen, to seek grants from OEO. The county court also named Gerald Chafin, a funeral director from Delbarton, as chairman of the commission. In June 1965, Chafin hired a local high school history teacher, Huey Perry, as executive director. Chafin told Perry he did not know much about the job or OEO, but he emphasized that it could mean bringing some federal dollars into the county. The commission members resented that neighboring McDowell already had received special attention from OEO. They pushed Perry to act quickly in filing grant applications that would start the federal dollars flowing into Mingo.[1]

An enclave of 423 square miles located in the rugged southwestern corner of West Virginia bordering Kentucky, Mingo County, like McDowell, typified the problems of the new machine age in Appalachia. Known earlier in the century as "Bloody Mingo" because of the violent coal mine wars, in 1960 Mingo had a population just short of 40,000 made up largely of native-born whites. The county suffered from the collapse of employment in coal mining, losing 16 percent of its population between 1950 and 1960 and another 18 percent in the 1960s, as the unemployed left for cities like Columbus and Detroit. In 1960, 46 percent of the county's families fell below the $3,000 per year poverty line. The census rated only 40 percent of houses "sound and with all plumbing facilities." Just 20 percent of the adult population had finished high school. Few job opportunities existed outside the coal mining industry. Public services such as schools, medical facilities, and roads suffered from lack of funds.[2] The unemployment rate hovered at 14 percent, and 30 percent of the population collected welfare checks. The elderly poor struggled to survive on Social Security or miners' welfare benefit checks.[3] The collapse of the Area Redevelopment Administration's showpiece bootstrap effort to encourage economic diversification and to retrain miners for woodworking in 1964[4] had left local leaders hopeful for another perhaps more effective infusion of federal money.

In *They'll Cut Off Your Project*, his account of community action in Mingo, Huey Perry says little about what influenced him to bring to Mingo County the kind of approach more typical of some urban areas, or what, in the words of condescending OEO analysts, had enabled a native inhabitant of Appalachia to grasp the "lofty concept" of community action. No long-haired outsider, Perry, a native resident of Mingo County, ordered the first VISTA volunteers who arrived in the county to get haircuts. Until he applied for the job of director of the Mingo County Community Action Agency at age 30, he had taught high school and sold used cars in the summer to make ends meet. He read in the local paper about President Johnson's trip on April 24–25, 1964, to nearby Inez, Kentucky, and noted that Johnson's plane had landed at Huntington's Tri-State Airport. Soon after his employment as director, OEO sent Perry to Virginia Tech for a two-week training session, which he says provided little direction as to what he should do.[5]

After his trip to Virginia Tech, Perry told his board that he would organize community action groups first to see what the poor people wanted, "unlike the welfare department or any other old-line agency that imposes ideas on the people."[6] When he went out to the hollows, the conditions he observed stunned him, even though he had lived in Appalachia all his life, and he later gave voice to his epiphany: "The visible effects of poverty were everywhere—the shacks, the filth, the pale, pot-bellied babies, the men with silicosis, coughing and gasping for breath, the outhouses, the dirt roads, and the one-room schools. Up and down the hollows, the front yards were strewn with junked cars, and the seats from the abandoned automobiles were used for beds and sofas."[7]

Perry also says he believed the language of the Economic Opportunity Act of 1964 meant "the poor must be organized into groups within their communities." In this way each would have a chance "to determine what his needs were and to participate in decisions that that would affect him and his community." He told his assistant Jimmy Wofford (who had campaigned across the state as a traveling troubadour with Hubert Humphrey in the 1960 Democratic primary) that if the poor were ever going to escape poverty, "they must develop the guts and courage to speak out against its causes." Perry believed his job with the Mingo County war on poverty was not to treat the symptoms of poverty, but to destroy the causes, and, he said, "I believe the political and economic system is one of the chief causes." If they could change Mingo County, perhaps all of West Virginia could be changed. Indeed, Perry believed that Mingo could be a model for the transformation of all of Appalachia.[8]

For more than three years, Perry worked to fulfill his dream of being an agent of change in Appalachia, and in the process he challenged the local political machine and drew much outside attention to the small Appalachian county. Perry's agency, avoiding the community center approach of most other West Virginia community action programs, organized twenty-eight community action groups representing the poor people of the county. These groups challenged the old order in various ways. Road Branch community action group, the first organized, won an early victory by demanding attention to the needs of their school, even threatening a pupil strike. Other community groups called attention to their schools and roads, set up year-round community-operated Head Start programs (using untrained welfare mothers as teachers), and challenged the school board's efforts to control Head Start staffing. They further alarmed the school board (and Governor Hulett C. Smith's administration) by carrying out a successful pupil strike to obtain free hot lunches for poor students. The community action groups operated the Neighborhood Youth Corps (which gave work to about 400 youth in repairing housing and doing community clean up work) and a home-improvement program. Mingo community action also obtained OEO funding for legal assistance for the poor.[9]

The Mingo County community action activities set politicians' teeth on edge. Organizations not controlled by the political machine challenged the conventional ways of doing things. The local machine thought the state or national Democratic Party should do something about the upstart poverty warriors. After the Road Branch group drew headlines by threatening a pupil strike if the school board did not repair the local school, Perry received an irate call from Paul Crabtree, Governor Smith's administrative assistant and the head of the state agency assigned to provide technical assistance to the county OEO operations. In a trembling voice, Crabtree warned Perry he could be arrested for fomenting a school strike. Perry angrily retorted that the community action group called the strike and that it was justified in doing so. When the school board responded to the Road Branch group by quickly sending out a repair crew, the story became an example of the power of group action for every group in Mingo County.[10] In May 1966, state senator Noah Floyd and two members of the local Chamber of Commerce, Howard Coleman and Sidney Copley, went to Washington to complain to Senator Robert C. Byrd. They charged that the Mingo war on poverty program sought to create a political movement, and they demanded an investigation.[11] Byrd passed the complaints on to OEO, and OEO sent an investigator to the county. The investigator reported that members of community action groups had publicly criticized the board of education and other county and state agencies. None of those who complained to Senator Byrd or others, however, could provide evidence of direct political activity by officials of the Mingo County community action agency.[12]

In December 1966, the Gilbert Creek community action group attracted much attention and raised howls of protest from grocers, other businessmen, and local politicians by setting up a community cooperative grocery store. *New York Times* news service reporter Marjorie Hunter quoted one local businessman as saying, "It's all a communist plot." Huey Perry told Hunter she could call it "poor power."[13] Hunter's report brought a media invasion and even led to a five- minute report about Mingo County and the rural war on poverty on CBS Evening News. Perry says the cooperative store project became the most publicized OEO project in the nation before it had ever opened its doors. Complaints rolled in from political officials, and Senator Byrd again demanded an investigation. He refused to believe Shriver's assurances that the cooperative had used no federal dollars. Byrd (who had once operated a grocery store himself) said small businesses "have enough problems without additional competition resulting from efforts on the part of anti-poverty workers." Fifth District Congressman James Kee also joined the chorus of complaints. In the face of the political storm, OEO stood by the cooperative store. Shriver reassured the critics that no OEO money financed it and that the Mingo County store "is one of the best examples of community action in the war against poverty."[14]

Ultimately, the most explosive activities of the Mingo County community action groups involved efforts to expose and to destroy the corrupt political regime in the county. Perry, like leaders of several of the more activist West Virginia CAAs, came to see political reform as the most critical goal of community action. Although tales of political corruption in Mingo and many of the coal counties of southern West Virginia had become legendary, state senator Noah Floyd represented for Perry the personification of the problem. All sixteen members of the Mingo County Democratic Executive Committee worked for either the county or the state. Because Floyd controlled these patronage jobs, he controlled the party. He catered to big business and local merchants to maintain his hold on local political power. The United Mine Workers of America once had provided some countervailing force, but the UMWA's power had waned as mining employment faded. Absentee landowners and other economic interests wielded substantial power, and Perry notes in his memoir, some observers thought Floyd's machine did the bidding of powerful interests such as United States Steel Corporation (which owned one-third of the county), the Norfolk and Western, and utilities.[15]

In the third year of the Mingo war on poverty, Perry says, the Mingo County EOC directed the energies of the poor away from any programs that treated only symptoms of poverty "toward the building of a political base from which the poor could attack poverty itself."[16] The third year also marked a peak in federal funding for the Mingo County program, as OEO responded positively to an effort devoted to the maximum feasible participation philosophy of the Equal Opportunity Act. Even as funding for anti-poverty programs fell sharply in 1967, the Mingo County Equal Opportunity Commission received grants from OEO and the Department of Labor of about a million dollars, double the amount for 1966. In addition to the other programs operated through OEO funding, several communities generated their own programs apart from any grants, including the Gilbert Creek cooperative store, refurbishment of an old company swimming pool in the Cinderella community, a locally funded community center building in Dingess, and a community park in Big Branch. At its peak, the Mingo EOC employed about 800 people, making it a serious rival to the county government's patronage machine in the job-starved community.[17]

In Charleston with a Mingo County community action group intent on putting poor people's views before the legislature, Ethel Wren observes action on the floor from the Senate gallery. Photograph by Douglas Yarrow.

The Rise of the Appalachian Volunteers

In Mingo and a few other West Virginia counties, the Appalachian Volunteers and VISTAs trained by AVs played a key role in stimulating grassroots activities by poor people. Distinct from the VISTA Volunteers, the Appalachian Volunteers originated late in 1963 as the Kennedy administration responded to the grim reports from eastern

Kentucky and West Virginia by putting together pilot programs in Appalachia that might lead to a general program. Richard Boone of the Ford Foundation and a member of the President's Committee on Juvenile Delinquency had helped design a plan for a National Service Corps in 1962, but it failed to pass Congress. As efforts to put an Appalachian program together proceeded in late 1963, Boone worked with Milton Ogle, a staff member of the Council of the Southern Mountains (CSM), to devise a plan for Appalachian Volunteers, and Ogle became the organization's director. Based on the premise that the Appalachian program should be neither a charity nor handout program but should address what local people perceived as their needs, Boone and Ogle decided to rely on a volunteer program using college students from Appalachia to spend weekends and vacations renovating eastern Kentucky schools, many of which had only one room, lacked insulation, and relied on pot-bellied stoves to keep children warm in the cold Appalachian winter. A long-time sponsor of regional programs of Christian uplift and missionary spirit, the CSM, headquartered at Berea College, depended on the goodwill of local governments and contributions from business interests in the region, so it favored cooperating with the dominant socioeconomic forces. To launch its first Appalachian Volunteer program in January 1964, CSM relied largely on materials donated from manufacturers and local businesses. Working on weekends, volunteers from area colleges and universities renovated and winterized some forty-four schools. In March the program received a $50,000 grant from the Area Redevelopment Administration and $33,000 from the Ford Foundation.[18]

In 1965, the War on Poverty in Appalachia expanded rapidly. As grant money from OEO flowed in, the Appalachian Volunteers departed from the original commitment to use volunteers indigenous to the mountains and began to hire staffers from outside the region. Harry Caudill's *Night Comes to the Cumberlands* (1962) and late 1964 television exposés such as CBS's "Christmas in Appalachia" and "Depression Area USA" with Charles Kuralt inspired idealistic college students from across the country to come to Appalachia as Appalachian or VISTA volunteers.[19]

Reform and idealism were in the air, inspired in part by John F. Kennedy, who in his inaugural address had famously said, "Ask not what your country can do for you. Ask what you can do for your country." Also spurred by the civil rights movement and reacting to what many saw as an unjust war in Vietnam, during the early to mid-1960s, many young people in the country began to question the mainstream culture and to confront racism and other social injustices. Gibbs Kinderman, a Harvard graduate of 1964, typified the kind of young people who responded to this time of questioning by answering the call to service in organizations like Peace Corps, VISTA, and Appalachian Volunteers. He later recalled that he and his friends read Jack Kerouac's *On the Road* during their senior year and talked about getting a Volkswagen bus and going on a road trip after graduation. Then a black acquaintance who had been in school with them came for a visit and told them about the civil rights efforts of the Student Nonviolent Coordinating Committee (SNCC) in Mississippi. Kinderman decided his road trip would be to go work with SNCC. After spending some time in Mississippi (living in the black community and being treated "like a nigger" by white Mississippians), he heard about the reform efforts in Appalachia and moved to Berea, Kentucky, to become the fourth staff member of the Appalachian Volunteers, telling himself he would stay only until Christmas.[20] Many of the AVs and VISTAs interviewed later expressed similar ideas about how they wanted to be a part of the idealism of the time and to try to do something that might make things better for Americans who did not share fully in the American dream.[21]

Historian Thomas J. Kiffmeyer maintains that the transformation of the Appalachian Volunteers from an indigenous group to one that drew from the whole country led to the radicalization of the organization. It is certainly the case that the Appalachian Volunteers who came from beyond Appalachia and the VISTA volunteers whom they sometimes trained and worked with had little patience with conditions they encountered. Just as the civil rights movement sometimes faced divisions over the best way to fight racism, those who wanted to confront the injustices they encountered in Appalachia tended to develop different strategies. A large faction soon questioned what they regarded as the old-fashioned and ineffective approach of the Council of the Southern Mountains, the AVs sponsoring organization. Those who worked in community action quickly became convinced that CSM's effort to work through local authorities and institutions meant giving in or "selling out to the establishment."

Mountaineer resentment of outsiders who came with a missionary attitude of "helping the poor" also became more of a dilemma when non-Appalachian volunteers became predominant. Many of the AVs came to feel that their early efforts treated only the symptoms, not the causes of poverty.[22] As David Whisnant put it in *Modernizing the Mountaineer*: "Idealistic students sent to paint schoolhouses soon discovered that fathers were unemployed, health care was all but unattainable, schoolteachers lost their jobs if they challenged the Board of Education, road repairs were correlated closely with voting patterns, and coal operators controlled county politics."[23] As noted in the previous chapter, OEO itself, in pursuit of "maximum feasible participation," pushed more activist programs and encouraged the AVs to organize local people to become involved in identifying and addressing local problems. For all these reasons, the organization gradually turned from the CSM's cooperative approach in favor of confronting the county governments and local school officials.[24]

By mid-1965, the Appalachian Volunteers staff, made up by then of a diverse group of largely non-Appalachian males, grew increasingly disenchanted with what they saw as the conservative orientation of the CSM and the administrative style of Perley F. Ayer, the executive director. Ayer, a transplanted New Englander, criticized AV staff members on the grounds of both personal morality and reform philosophy. Stories of AV "drunken sex parties" in Lexington and drinking parties that staff engaged in with trainees in Berea led Ayer to warn a staff member on April 9, 1965, that unless the staff could agree on a plan to put into effect "a high standard of moral purpose, . . . I shall feel it necessary to discontinue sponsorship of the whole program." At the same time of the recriminations over moral conduct, Ayer received a lengthy list of grievances from two former Berea students who trained as VISTA Volunteers under the tutelage of the AV staff. These two charged the AVs with advocating revolution, graft, and moral turpitude. Finally, suspecting them of seeking to organize "a general staff rebellion," on May 2, 1966, Ayer fired Milton Ogle and Daniel Fox, another staff member. The rest of the staff resigned in protest, and the AVs proceeded to break away from CSM and to reorganize as a separate nonprofit corporation with its headquarters in Bristol, Tennessee. The OEO reassigned its grants for AV programs to the new organization.[25]

Milton Ogle had come to believe the split between CSM and the AVs inevitable because the differences in philosophy had become too great. CSM continued to emphasize programs, but AV now saw itself as an action agency. Harry Caudill encouraged Ogle, writing him to say that the Volunteers, "with good fortune, could set in motion a revolutionary change of thought." Part of the "revolutionary change of thought" involved expansion into West Virginia with a focus on the coalfield counties, beginning in the summer of 1966 with short-term AV activities in Boone, Clay, McDowell, Mercer, Mingo, Raleigh, and Wyoming.[26]

AVs in West Virginia: "Outsiders and Trouble Makers" or "the Best Hope for Change"?

The Appalachian Volunteers in West Virginia developed their own ways of doing things and fairly quickly began to distance themselves from AV headquarters in Bristol. AVs shared a general consensus on their goals, but they debated organizational theories and constantly struggled to find a successful model. Former Kentucky AV staffer Thomas Rhodenbaugh suggests that West Virginia AV leaders used a more confrontational style inspired by Chicago organizer Saul Alinksy, departing from the incremental approach emphasizing empowerment of local people advocated by Milton Ogle and the Kentucky staff. Both groups improvised and experimented. Beginning in the summer of 1966, some of the AVs began to move away from the services model of the early AVs toward an issues orientation.[27]

That summer AV and VISTA volunteers in West Virginia carried out what OEO saw as some of its greatest community action successes. The Raleigh County Community Action Program attracted favorable attention from OEO headquarters in Washington by focusing on grassroots organizing, but like the Mingo program, it alarmed some state and local authorities and raised some questions about the appropriate limits for OEO employees and contractors in the public arena. Some OEO staff worried that organizing poor people with the goal to put pressure on local government could raise questions about violations of the Hatch Act (which prohibits political activity by public employees). Already sensitized to such issues by Mingo County OEO activities, the Raleigh County activities of AVs and

VISTAs further underlined for OEO that Volunteers walked a thin line between proper and improper activities in organizing community groups for political action.[28]

A southern coal mining county of about 610 square miles seventy miles southeast of Charleston, Raleigh's population dropped from 96,000 to 70,000 from 1950 to 1965. In 1965, despite an improvement in West Virginia's economic statistics, Raleigh's unemployment rate remained at about 14 percent. The downtown area of Beckley, the county seat, bustled with commercial activities and betrayed to casual visitors little hint that it was the center of a chronically depressed area.[29]

Political questions also loomed large in Raleigh, because it played a dominant role in state politics. Both Governor Smith (whose cousin John Smith was mayor of Beckley) and Senator Byrd had grown up in Raleigh County, though in somewhat different circumstances. Born in Beckley on October 21, 1918, Smith grew up there but attended schools in Washington, D.C., as well as in Beckley. His father, Joe L. Smith, served eight consecutive terms as congressman from 1928 to 1944 and wielded considerable influence in state politics. Governor Smith had received an undergraduate economics degree from the University of Pennsylvania's Wharton School of Finance and Administration. He returned to Beckley and operated the family-owned radio station, WJLS, before World War II. During the war, Smith served in the U.S. Navy in the Bureau of Ordnance, rising to the rank of lieutenant by the end of the war. Back in Beckley after the war he became involved in insurance and banking.[30]

Byrd, on the other hand, was born in North Wilkesboro, North Carolina, on November 20, 1917, as Cornelius Calvin Sale Jr. His mother died a year later (on Armistice Eve), victim of the influenza epidemic of 1918. The child's paternal aunt and her husband, Titus Dalton Byrd, adopted him when he was two years old, renaming him Robert Carlyle Byrd. The Byrds lived in Mercer County, West Virginia, for a time and later moved to Stotesbury, Raleigh County, where Byrd's adoptive father worked as a miner. During World War II, Byrd, by then married and the father of two daughters, worked as a welder in the shipyards of Baltimore and Tampa. After the war, he returned to Raleigh County, where he worked as a meat cutter and grocery store manager and (as noted in chapter 3) organized a local klavern of the Ku Klux Klan. In 1946, he launched his political career in a successful run for the House of Delegates, drawing attention to his campaign by fiddling on the stump.[31]

After a conventional and lackluster beginning under the guidance of the county court, during which few people outside of Beckley knew Raleigh County had a community action program, the Raleigh County CAP became for a brief season another model of the poor-oriented grassroots activism favored by OEO. The transformation of the Raleigh CAP came after the arrival of some forty Appalachian and VISTA volunteers in the summer of 1966, part of a contingent of some 500 summer volunteers who fanned out across Appalachia, some of them in preparation for Peace Corps assignments. The 500 boarded a train in Washington and traveled together to Bristol, Tennessee, something of a troop train of the War on Poverty. According to an OEO report, the Raleigh AV-VISTAs achieved more in a shorter period "than other equally dedicated and equally intelligent volunteers in other parts of Appalachia."[32]

Circumstances in Raleigh, such as a less monolithic political structure and bigger, less isolated, and more heavily populated hollows, favored community action work. In eastern Kentucky, ten or twenty families might live in a hollow, but in Raleigh County, hollows might contain 200 families. The larger numbers meant larger and more effective community organizations and the greater likelihood of natural local leadership. Also, southern West Virginia had a stronger tradition of the United Mine Workers, providing something of a counterbalance to local elites. Although the union's influence had declined as the number of miners fell during the 1950s, many former miners and their wives had the experience of having been part of an organization willing to take action to advance members' rights.[33]

Economic conditions in southern West Virginia were somewhat better than in eastern Kentucky, making control of CAAs less critical in matters of political control and patronage.[34] Naomi Weintraub Cohen later recalled that the VISTA training at East Tennessee State University (including reading Harry Caudill's *Night Comes to the Cumberlands*) had led the volunteers to expect that conditions in West Virginia would be as bad as in eastern Kentucky. She said, "I really expected to find only people living in shacks and nobody with bathrooms or cars or anything like that." She discovered, instead, a wide variety of circumstances and living conditions in Pine Knob, the Raleigh County community to which she was assigned and where she focused on local concerns about strip mining.³⁵

In the summer of 1966, Gibbs Kinderman (having stayed with the AVs well beyond his original intentions) organized a takeover of the Raleigh County CAP program by representatives of the hollow communities. With the help of Steve Kramer, 23, a native of Queens, New York, who left graduate school in philosophy at New York University to become an AV field man in Southern West Virginia, Kinderman coordinated VISTA volunteers and forty summer Appalachian Volunteers (called VISTA Associates) in organizing community groups in predominantly black East Beckley and in the coal communities in the mountain hollows outside Beckley.³⁶ According to the agreement with OEO, the AVs would train the summer volunteers and administer the program, which would take place during nine weeks of the summer of 1966. Local community councils organized with the assistance of the AVs and AV field staff developed the projects, which generally revolved around local rural schools, as had been the case with earlier AV programs. The agreement with OEO, however, gave no strict guidelines as to projects and was written so broadly as to allow the AVs substantial discretion in the shaping of the summer activities.³⁷

To establish ties with the communities, the AV-VISTAs first organized baseball leagues, softball leagues, and other young people's activities, including a Camp Cornflake. These provided contacts that enabled them to tell people in the rural communities about the Raleigh County CAP Program, which few people outside of Beckley knew about and which had done little in its first year. Then they organized community meetings, encouraging local people to speak out and to organize into community associations.³⁸ Historian and former Kennedy White House aide Arthur Schlesinger Jr. happened to be on hand in Beckley on July 21 at a rousing meeting of the associations the Volunteers had organized. His daughter Kathy, a VISTA volunteer in Mercer County, had invited him to come to West Virginia to meet Kinderman, her fiancé, and to attend a meeting of the Raleigh County associations. Fascinated by what he observed, Schlesinger wrote a personal letter to Sargent Shriver (mailed to his Rockville address) describing the situation in Beckley in glowing terms. The OEO regional coordinator for the area had told the Raleigh County CAP that its funding would be cut off if they did not replace the director of the county CAP, an ineffective former assistant superintendent of schools. About 150 people, many from the outlying communities and about one-third African Americans, attended the meeting. Many urged the director to resign, but, Schlesinger reported, "He responded by an outburst of really terrible demagoguery, saying that the federal government could not come into Raleigh County and tell the taxpayers who should run their anti-poverty program." The demonstration of grassroots and multiracial enthusiasm at the meeting "impressed and encouraged" Schlesinger; however, he feared that, because Beckley was the hometown of Governor Smith and Senator Byrd, the unpopular director would remain, "betraying the poor people of Raleigh County," who he said would feel "disenchanted and frustrated." Shriver immediately forwarded Schlesinger's account to OEO's investigations division with the notation to "get on to this one for me fast if possible."[39]

Within a month Shriver assured Schlesinger that a thorough inspection of the Raleigh County Community Action Program showed that "real movement" had taken place. Shriver reported that the local CAP director about whom Schlesinger had expressed concern had resigned because of "the positive actions of the men and women from the hollows and creeks, the people whom the program is designed to help."[40] The community associations organized by the Volunteers took advantage of CAP bylaws that made attendance at two consecutive monthly meetings the only requirement to become a voting board member. The organizers saw to it that representatives of the poor became the majority on the Raleigh County CAP board, making it possible for them to elect the officers. They elected Chester Workman, a firebrand middle-aged miner from Richmond district, as president and Hettie Trent, the elderly black leader of the East Beckley group, as secretary. Workman and the new board made it clear they no longer needed the services of the incumbent director, and he resigned. Remarkably, after two other candidates turned down the job, Kinderman resigned as an AV supervisor to become the CAP director. The new CAP regime in Raleigh encouraged hollow communities to demand better roads, lights, sewers, and water supply. AVs Naomi Weintraub and David Biesemeyer helped organize a citizen's task force, which testified before a legislative committee in support of Governor Smith's bill to regulate strip mining; organized a tutoring program; arranged for a delegation of poor people to go to Washington in August to meet with OEO and other officials; and set up a mimeographed community newspaper, *Raleigh Peoples' Press*.[41]

The activities of the AVs and VISTAs in Raleigh County aroused local opposition, especially from the politicians. Senator Jennings Randolph forwarded to OEO a complaint from a resident of Glen Daniels who asked for a congressional committee to investigate the VISTA workers. The writer claimed that the volunteers brought about "class division, strife, and malice." "Now that funds are available," the writer continued, "please give us a chance to work out our own problems and not send an avalanche of 'young beatniks' to do it for us."[42] Sheriff Okey Mills sent letters to all members of the West Virginia Democratic congressional delegation also asking that the VISTA program in Raleigh County be investigated. He said the only person that might be pleased with the program was Communist Party leader Gus Hall. Mills threatened to expose all of this to Drew Pearson, a nationally syndicated muckraking columnist of the day, if Democratic Party leaders did not do something.[43]

It annoyed the Beckley police chief that a white VISTA woman lived in predominantly black East Beckley with a black female Volunteer. The police chief and Sheriff Mills, who saw these young "outsiders" as suspicious characters, saw to it that law enforcement officers frequently stopped volunteers for license checks. Beckley Mayor John Smith (the governor's cousin) resented the role the volunteers played in organizing black East Beckley citizens to demand action on sewer extensions. Senator Byrd came down from Washington, and after hearing complaints from people in the school system reportedly made ten speeches in four days denouncing the volunteers as "outsiders and troublemakers." On the other hand, the Hodel brothers, John and Emil, publishers of Beckley's morning and afternoon newspapers, publicized the volunteers' activities and defended them from criticism. Charles Holland, administrator of the Appalachian Regional Hospital in Beckley, told a meeting of the Chamber of Commerce that the volunteers represented "the best hope for change and improvement that had come into the county in a long time."[44]

In Charleston, Governor Smith took some heat from associates in his home county during the summer and fall of 1966; however, despite his threats to withhold approval of additional VISTAs for Raleigh County, he did nothing immediately to undermine the volunteers and in some cases he supported them. When Saxon-Posey community people organized by the volunteers notified the local newspapers and the *Charleston Gazette* that they would boycott schools and take children to sit-ins at the State Road Commission to demand road improvements, the governor dispatched a special assistant, Darrell McGraw, to deal with the situation. McGraw (described by an OEO investigator as a "hollow boy") had grown up in neighboring Wyoming County, and understood local conditions. He helped to defuse the boycott by inviting community representatives to visit him in Charleston and by seeing to it that state road workers improved the road and an old wooden bridge in the community. McGraw and Jefferson Monroe, the director of the state Economic Opportunity Agency, told an OEO investigator that they applauded the Volunteers' efforts. McGraw noted, however, that the volunteers should be aware of the state's limited resources. Monroe (who had helped draw up the McDowell County community action plan) thought the AVs and VISTAs tended to immediately label every official an enemy, sometimes turning potential friends into foes, but he credited the Volunteers with changing his mind about how community action should work. "It took the AV's and VISTAs to show me that the only way to work for poor people is to work with them," he told the OEO investigator.[45]

The summer programs of 1966 brought fundamental change to the AV focus. Because the flooding of Appalachia with some 500 summer volunteers had been much less successful elsewhere than in Raleigh County, the AVs decided that they would no longer recruit large numbers of volunteers for summer programs like the school painting and renovations that had been the main thrust of the original Volunteers. Also, the AVs moved away from the original emphasis on recruiting residents of Appalachia. Now they focused on year-round activities carried out by VISTA volunteers assigned by OEO and trained and supervised by the small AV staff of paid professionals.[46] They also narrowed the geographical focus to coalfield counties and to emphasize organizing communities in the way Kinderman and the Raleigh County AV-VISTAs had done, having poor people take control of the community action agencies. Emblematic of the new orientation was the Appalachian Community Meeting held in Washington on August 22–23, 1966. Promoters billed the meeting as a coming together of Appalachian people who shared a heritage of poverty and "economic and political exploitation" in an effort to establish a dialogue "with those who control the resources of this country." Gibbs Kinderman emphasized that it would not be "a march on Washington." "That has a demanding tone to it," he said. "Our trip will be a cooperative thing—intended to create a dialogue between the people and government."[47] Much of the program in Washington, however, attacked community action as carried out by county CAPs in the southern Appalachians and called for greater participation of the poor in shaping programs.[48]

For Joseph Mulloy and others who were there, the Appalachian Community Meeting in Washington became a significant turning point. Mulloy's AV experience began in 1965 when he served as a University of Kentucky student weekend volunteer. He later worked in the central office in Berea and Bristol before becoming a field man in southwest Virginia in June 1966. In 1967 he moved on to Pike County, Kentucky. As Mulloy recalls, "much of the early AV work was good but had a heavy emphasis on what we later termed as a band aid approach to treating the symptoms of poverty. But at this meeting, one after another, local community leaders stood up on our last night at the Hawthorne School (where we were all staying) and spoke eloquently of what needed to be done." The speakers told the AVs they appreciated their work but said, "if you really want to help us," they should get involved in broader issues like "roads, water systems, corrupt elections, unresponsiveness of the CAPs to the needs of the poor, and especially in Kentucky at that time, strip mining." Mulloy says the AV's positive response to this cry from the grassroots sparked a backlash from government officials in Appalachia and Washington.[49]

By the end of 1966 Senator Byrd had become an outspoken opponent of the War on Poverty, calling for cutting the OEO budget by one-half or two-thirds. He doubted whether the OEO programs had helped either West Virginia or the country. He told an interviewer that OEO had been poorly managed, wasteful, and of little help to poor people. He advocated eliminating Job Corps, VISTA, and some community action programs. He proposed to keep Head Start and the Neighborhood Youth Corps, programs that enjoyed general support. He especially criticized VISTA, saying, "I don't believe these characters shipped in from other areas of the country are competent to advise our people in West Virginia on how to solve their local problems." Similarly, he said in some areas community action programs "have constituted a haven for individuals who want to stir up strife and dissention."⁵⁰

West Virginia Senator Robert C. Byrd, a critic of the civil rights and anti-poverty legislation of the 1960s, discusses issues with President Lyndon B. Johnson, circa 1965. West Virginia and Regional History Collection, West Virginia University Libraries.

The West Virginia AVs hoped to follow up on their successes of 1966 with a continuation of community action and organization based on critical issues. On January 28, 1967, some 500 low-income people, AVs, and VISTAs met in a conference at Marshall University in Huntington (billed as "Appalachia Speaks") to assess the effectiveness of the War on Poverty. OEO regional director Leveo Sanchez attended the meeting, and Chester Workman, president of the Raleigh County Community Action Association, presided. Harry Caudill, the Whitesburg, Kentucky, lawyer and author of *Night Comes to the Cumberlands* gave the keynote address, saying that the resources of Appalachia had been plundered, leaving the people little to show for it. He urged that communities "take immediate and positive steps to regain the land which 'belongs to out-of-state-businesses who don't care what happens to the land.'" Caudill also blamed Appalachian farmers themselves for poor and outdated farming techniques, which left the land unable to support the population. In the general session, OEO regional director Sanchez listened as people from eastern Kentucky and West Virginia discussed problems such as control of OEO programs by local politicians, graft and corruption on the county level in some of the poverty programs, the slowness of OEO to fund proposals, and the failure of OEO officials from Washington to talk to poor people. For the most part, poor people attending the program praised the work of the AVs and VISTAs. They also passed resolutions on a variety of issues, including endorsement of Governor Hulett C. Smith's task force on surface mining and a bill pending before the legislature to put restrictions on strip mining. Other resolutions called for better funding of legal services for the poor, the addition of courses in Appalachian history and culture in the schools, the relaxation of qualifications for Head Start aides (to enable Head Start to employ more low-income mothers), financial aid for the unemployed who wished to relocate, restoration of drastic cuts in the ADCU program, inclusion of more poor people on CAP boards, larger corporate income taxes and severance taxes on natural resources, more support for civic-owned industries and more cooperatives for poor people.[51]

Rising Militancy in Appalachia

On a six-day swing through Central Appalachia in late March 1967, *New York Times* reporter Ben Franklin interviewed people in West Virginia, Kentucky, Virginia, and Tennessee who suggested that a mood of anger and militancy grew apace, replacing what Franklin characterized as the widespread fatalism that some Appalachian writers and public health officials had labeled as a form of regional mental illness. They attributed the new mood to reactions against the failures of some government programs and to the unexpected successes of some government anti-poverty fighters, especially the Appalachian

Volunteers and VISTA workers. Franklin cited a push for public ownership of natural resources as one bit of evidence for the new mood. On a March Saturday in the depressed southern West Virginia railroad town of Hinton, in a restaurant dining room, members of a group called the Congress for Appalachian Development approved a plan modeled on the Tennessee Valley Authority to promote the public takeover of much of the coal reserves in Central Appalachia. The idea, advocated by Harry Caudill, envisioned persuading legislatures to authorize some of the poorest counties in the country to own their coal reserves and to use the mineral wealth to fuel new publicly owned mine mouth power stations. These stations would sell cheap power to expanding eastern and midwestern markets. The public utility districts (PUDs) would mine coal only through underground mines, ending strip mining. Revenue from power sales would fund the capital outlay to acquire the mines and to build the power stations and would also fund the building of a system of new towns. Lewis G. Smith, a retired land planner who had worked for the United States Bureau of Reclamation, had mapped out large areas of mountaintop land suitable for the new settlements. His plan included a system of dams and lakes for the area stretching from Charleston to Chattanooga, which could be developed by the PUDS for recreation and conservation purposes. Caudill served as chairman of CAD and Milton Ogle, the director of the AVs, served as secretary-treasurer. Asserting that the "poor are ready to rise," Caudill told Franklin "I believe we are finally under way toward raising a considerable dissent against the fact that these mountain counties are just . . . hollow shells with no revenue and no jobs." Though Caudill presented CAD as evidence of grassroots revolt, it probably represented instead the revolt of a few regional middle-class intellectuals. Closer to evidence of a grassroots rebellion, Franklin reported the story of the United Appalachian Communities, an unusual grassroots movement led by twenty-five year old Franklin Sims of Corbin, Kentucky, which organized against the Cumberland Valley Economic Opportunity Council. Similar to the Raleigh County revolt, the poor people's organization persuaded OEO to cut off funding with a public condemnation of the "ruling faction" of businessmen who had controlled the council.[52]

Meanwhile, in West Virginia, the AVs began 1967 flushed with victory in Raleigh County and hopeful that the Raleigh model could be copied in other coalfield counties and that the CAP boards could be seized by representatives of poor communities organized by VISTAs trained and supervised by the AVs. Many of the AV staffers also had come to believe that the OEO programs themselves offered no real hope for the poor. Rather than trying to put into effect the programs handed down from Washington, the AVs increasingly focused on issues such as tax reform, opposition to strip mining, election reform, welfare reform, local road improvements, and education reform. Staff meetings, however, involved much debate over whether it made sense to reform the present system at all. AV assistant director for West Virginia, Eric Metzner, reported that "there is some worry about introducing poor people to a 'how to get it done under present systems' philosophy' if the present system does not work." Cooperating with liberal politicians also seemed of little use. "Should we be tying poor people to such a system," Metzner asked, "or working with people to devise something new and satisfactory?" As for Metzner, whose views represented a minority, he hoped the AVs would choose radicalism, although he did not spell out just what that meant.[53]

A new AV initiative in Logan County in the fall of 1967 led by field man Bob Tanner began with the premise that OEO programs and CAP were irrelevant. The county anti-poverty agency, Pride Inc., had accomplished little in the way of community organizing and typified the CAP controlled by local politicians. The director, Irwin Queen, represented Logan in the House of Delegates. Queen strongly opposed the introduction of AVs into Logan, calling it a "guerrilla warfare type operation" and feared AVs would attempt to do in Logan what they did in Raleigh. Meanwhile AV field man Steve Kramer, a veteran of Raleigh County's organizing successes of 1966, helped the Mercer County Equal Opportunity Commission defeat a local school bond in November, in part because the commission and its supporters believed that the proposal would reinforce continuing segregation in Mercer County schools. In Wyoming County, field supervisors Richard Glass and Pat Wilson organized a "people's group," Wyoming County United Communities, which, in Raleigh County fashion, overthrew the county CAP in November 1967 by turning out large crowds of people who in the past had had little contact with the county court. In the face of a gathering of some 250 crowding the courtroom in Pineville, the CAP chairman threw down his papers and walked out. After the CAP chair walked out, the group elected Hershel Shrewsberry, the chair of United Communities, as the new CAP chair and then a new board hired him as director of the program. Among other things, the Wyoming group started Head Start, worked on housing improvements, promoted community health projects, and organized a sit-in on the steps of the county board of education that persuaded the board to include in their budget free school lunches for indigent children. In retrospect these developments appear as the last gasps of AV-inspired efforts to transform local community action programs, as the political terrain faced by AVs soon became as rugged as the mountains in which they worked.[54]

AVs Under Attack

Events of 1967 largely outside West Virginia proved disastrous for the Appalachian Volunteers and for the community action programs with which they had become closely identified. In keeping with a widespread notion among the AVs that they should focus more on critical issues, on April 1, 1967, the AVs hired Alan McSurely, a professional organizer who had worked in anti-poverty programs in Washington, D.C. McSurely spelled out and distributed to AVs a radical program that would include setting up a national central committee with the goal of bringing about a revolution. As David Whisnant has noted, another recently hired AV staffer, Gary Bickel, described McSurely's tract as Marxist-Leninist and argued that McSurely himself was unacceptable to the AVs. Harvard psychologist and AV consultant Robert Coles, an important link to foundation funding, also protested. AV director Milton Ogle agreed and, with only one dissenting vote of the full AV staff, fired McSurely.[55]

Now convinced that painting schoolhouses represented little more than treating the symptoms of poverty rather than the causes, in the spring of 1967, AV field man Joe Mulloy moved into Pike County, Kentucky, one of the most notorious coal-operator dominated counties in Appalachia. Concerned especially with the growing destructiveness of strip mining, Mulloy contacted Steve Daugherty, the AV field man in Harlan County. Daugherty brought members of the Appalachian Group to Save the Land and People (AGSLP) to Island Creek. The residents and AGSLP devised a legal strategy and tactics for a demonstration. On June 29, 1967, Mulloy and his wife stood in front of coal company bulldozers with Island Creek farmer Jink Ray, who for forty-six years had farmed the land the company planned to strip. Some two dozen neighbors stood with Ray and the Mulloys. Ray and his supporters ignored a court order and persisted in their protest until Governor Edward Breathitt revoked the coal company's permit on August 1. The success of the protest at Jink Ray's farm heartened opponents of strip mining, but it turned out to be a Pyrrhic victory. On August 11 and 12, Pike County authorities arrested Alan and Margaret McSurely (who were working in Pike County), Joseph Mulloy, and others on charges of sedition under a 1920 Kentucky statute. Robert Holcomb, the president of the Pike County Chamber of Commerce, declared that they were communists who intended "to take over the county." A grand jury quickly returned indictments on the sedition charges, but on September 14, 1967, a three-judge federal panel declared the Kentucky law unconstitutional and dismissed the charges.[56] Mulloy's troubles continued. Just one day after the ruling on the Kentucky sedition law, his Kentucky draft board revoked his deferment and issued an induction order. After the board refused to grant him conscientious objector status, he decided to refuse induction. Unwilling to force the AV organization to take an unpopular position on the war and the draft, particularly given the AVs' already precarious position, AV director Milton Ogle asked Mulloy to resign. When he refused, the AV staff voted 20–19 to recommend his dismissal, and in early December, Ogle fired him.[57]

Although a federal court had dismissed the Pike County sedition charges, the incident inflamed public opinion and gave ammunition to those who opposed the AVs and the War on Poverty generally and tended to amplify the kinds of complaints that had been more easily dismissed before. In West Virginia, Governor Smith had approved the 1967 AV program in the state in spite of substantial complaints about the AVs in the summer of 1966. Some complained about the philosophy and activities of the Volunteers, but more often the complaints protested, as Smith noted, "alleged immorality, uncleanliness, unconventionality, and personal obnoxiousness" on the part of some of the AVs in West Virginia. In approving the 1967 program, Smith felt that the good done by the AVs outweighed the "flaws and peccadilloes" of a few.[58]

By August 1967, Smith began to have second thoughts about the AVs and VISTAs. He wrote a "Dear Sarge" letter to OEO director

Shriver to say that the reassurances he had received from VISTA and Milton Ogle of the AVs had not been honored. He cited recent incidents that caused him to question his judgment in approving the AVs' 1967 contract. One involved "a riotous all-night party" at Babcock State Park on July 22 after which the park superintendent charged that AVs and VISTAs destroyed park property, interfered with other park guests, tampered with automobiles, and generally disturbed the peace. Reports from Wyoming County alleged that immoral conduct involving promiscuity "across racial lines" had "seriously weakened" confidence in the AV-VISTA program there. On August 6, AV-VISTA workers from Raleigh County drove a clearly marked U.S government car to Charleston to attend a demonstration protesting American involvement in the Vietnam War. State Senator Carl Gainer protested to the governor that AV-VISTA workers in Nicholas County had "called for the mass dismissal of a number of the county's elected officials and school personnel." In his letter to Shriver, Smith affirmed the validity of social protest but claimed, "the absence of constructive alternatives to the problems of the community has led to a general feeling that the VISTA-AV group is composed of 'trouble-makers' who offer only negative solutions to community problems." Some in the community charged the AV-VISTAs with teaching "ideas that are Communistic." Smith also noted that West Virginia news media reports of AV-VISTA workers' arrests in Kentucky on sedition charges and "their alleged possession of Communist literature and paraphernalia" had further undermined confidence in the AV-VISTA program.[59]

Within four days a large OEO delegation arrived in Charleston to throw water on the latest fire. Smith held a press conference to introduce the visitors who came, he said, "to help us unravel the problems that might have been created through a misunderstanding of my letter to Shriver." Smith wanted it understood that he intended no "blanket indictment" of either VISTA or the Appalachian Volunteers. He distributed to the press the letter he had sent to Shriver, answered questions, and said any final conclusions awaited an investigation to be conducted by OEO.[60]

The Appalachian Volunteers conducted their own investigation of the Babcock incident and concluded that reports of what happened there had been overblown. Milton Ogle, the AV director, reported his findings to Jefferson Monroe, Governor Smith's coordinator of OEO matters. Some eighty-four people attended the affair, which had been planned as a training session. They had planned to stay in tents, but a rainstorm led most of the group to leave the park. Some who remained sought shelter in two cabins that had been rented. A gathering in one of the cabins interrupted the natural quietness of a summer night in the park with loud singing and laughter. Ogle admitted that alcohol had been present, but "no one was drunk." He regretted that the noise of the AV group disturbed and alarmed families in the neighboring cabins, but he suggested that much of the animus toward the Volunteers came from "deep felt, unspoken feelings" generated by "the fact that black and white were together having a social, if somewhat loud, gathering." Ogle thought the incident served one good purpose by bringing to the attention of the Volunteers and staff "that we are very much in the public light and must take *exceptional* precautions to avoid unfortunate occurrences such as this."[61]

The OEO investigation also discounted the most serious charges regarding the Babcock incident and the other matters mentioned by Governor Smith. It found that the Volunteers did disturb neighboring cabins at Babcock on July 22, but that they had not destroyed property or tampered with vehicles. Twenty-one interviews in Wyoming County uncovered no concrete evidence of AV-VISTA immorality, but the investigating team feared that the rumors might continue. The investigation further found that a VISTA volunteer did violate regulations by driving a government vehicle to Charleston for social purposes, and the vehicle had been transferred from her use. The investigators also concluded that activities of the AV-VISTA group in Nicholas County fell well within the bounds required by OEO. As for the "sedition" incident in eastern Kentucky, the report noted that all charges in the case had been dismissed.[62]

The OEO report left critics unconvinced. Speaking on the floor of the Senate on October 3, Senator Byrd read into the record Governor Smith's letter to Shriver and charged that OEO's defense of the AVs in the sedition case indicated how little control the agency had over its programs on the local level. He asserted that anti-poverty workers in Kentucky and West Virginia were "revolutionaries bent on destroying the present order of society instead of trying to improve conditions within the framework that exists." He further charged that OEO whitewashed Governor Smith's complaints about its programs, including charges that "Appalachian Volunteers engaged in immoral and illegal activities." He complained that the response to Governor Smith conformed to a pattern of ignoring charges of misconduct on the part of poverty workers. He conceded that some VISTA workers in the state did useful work, particularly those in mental health, but others, he said, "look worse than even the poorest of our people," and some "foment unrest, dissatisfaction, and trouble." Byrd also attacked the basic premise of the poverty program, saying, "It's all fine in theory to involve the poor, but where the poor have had little experience and practice, they all too often can be misled by persons who have their own, not the poor's, interests and welfare in mind." Byrd called for a comprehensive reappraisal of the poverty programs, which he believed had been "shockingly mismanaged."[63]

Byrd's speech contributed to the congressional attack on the OEO budget for fiscal 1967–68. Republicans and conservative Democrats like Byrd railed at the excesses of the War on Poverty, and friends feared OEO might not survive. Byrd went on to co-sponsor with Republican Senator John Sherman Cooper of Kentucky an amendment to the Economic Opportunity Act. Generally know as the Byrd Amendment, it required that VISTA workers document their integrity as well as their qualifications to perform their assignments.[64] In the House, Edith Green of Oregon sought to appease urban mayors and Southern Democrats who, like Byrd, saw local community action groups as waging guerrilla war against the establishment. The Green Amendment (called the "bossism and boll weevil amendment" by opponents) provided local governments with the option of taking over community action agencies, making it possible for mayors and county governments to seize control of community action agencies. As Allen J. Matusow points out, Green never made clear if her chief motivation was to kill community action (which she hated) or to save the administration's bill. Shriver (who had been prepared to resign to save OEO) quietly appreciated the help. Another thing that helped save OEO was that, unlike in West Virginia, relations between governing bodies and their CAAs in much of the country had improved over the days in 1965 when the big city mayors had urged Vice President Humphrey to rein in OEO. Even some Republican mayors found OEO programs useful in curbing black discontent. So, for a variety of reasons, OEO survived the attacks of 1967 and received funding for the next fiscal year, but the atmosphere clearly had changed.[65]

In 1968 complaints against OEO programs in West Virginia, however, continued unabated, with Senator Byrd leading the attack. The stresses of a particularly contentious election year added fuel to the fire. On March 15, 1968, Senator Byrd presented Sargent Shriver a litany of complaints about VISTA workers throughout West Virginia. Byrd said he had often referred constituent complaints to OEO about "the activities and appearance of VISTA workers" from other states "and I have just as often received reports back from your agency which seem to attempt to justify the VISTA workers and place the blame upon the complaining citizens." He said that in Boone County VISTA workers "have urged on and have led citizens to invade the schools, demanding as their right free lunches for their children, heedless of the school's resources for sustaining this program." He also charged that they refused to cooperate with established community agencies and "appear intent upon sowing the seeds of rebellion." He reminded Shriver of the Byrd Amendment (requiring documentation of Volunteer integrity and qualifications), saying its purpose had been to avoid the kind of situation that now prevailed in Boone. He asked that "the outsiders in Boone County, known as VISTA workers, may be given a one-way ticket back to their homes, which lie beyond the boundaries of West Virginia."[66] At the end of the year he continued to attack, telling an audience of 500 teachers and students at Gassaway High School that he opposed both VISTA and Job Corps. In both instances he expressed concerns about "too much mixing of outsiders who didn't want to come in here, and had no intention of staying here, and have proven it by leaving."[67]

Congressman John Slack and Governor Smith also received complaints about VISTA workers in Boone County. Slack published the charges in his newsletter of early March. Richard Cartwright Austin, a Presbyterian minister and the director of the West Virginia Mountain Project of the United Presbyterian Church, the VISTA's sponsoring agency in Boone County, sent Slack a telegram expressing his shock that the congressman would give credence to "rash and misleading charges." He demanded an apology and cooperation in an investigation to set the record straight.[68]

On March 27, a delegation from Boone County presented Governor Smith a petition with about 2,000 signatures (gathered by ADCU workers) asking for the removal of VISTA volunteers from the

Sherman and Peytona districts of the county. Writing for this group, Manuel Arvon, principal of Sherman High School in Seth, charged that the "VISTA workers are subversive in that they are against the best interests of our country and our way of life. Their stated purpose is that they wish to help the poor people, but their actions, we feel, will lead to rebellion and revolt—their ultimate goal." Arvon insisted that investigations by OEO ignored the facts.[69]

An OEO report in April reviewed the charges against the Boone County volunteers. In addition to the usual claim that the volunteers dressed badly and bathed infrequently, school authorities cited their investigations of fairness in the distribution of free school lunches, and merchants protested their collection of price comparisons showing that local stores charged higher prices than stores in adjoining counties. Complaints also focused on a meeting called by VISTAs to discuss how a community might get a bridge built over a creek. At the meeting mothers brought up charges that a local grade school principal used obscene language and circulated pornographic books. According to the OEO report, the VISTAs had nothing to do with these charges, which appeared to be without foundation. OEO concluded that the volunteers in Boone County involved themselves in issues important to poor people such as hot lunches for the children of welfare recipients and consumer education, issues that were valid areas of VISTA work.[70]

Jefferson Monroe, director of the state economic opportunity agency, told Governor Smith that that the attack on the VISTAs and the Presbyterian's West Virginia Mountain Project "used John Birch tactics," referring to a right-wing extremist organization of the day. He felt it would be politically unwise to align the administration with such execrable methods. Monroe (a Presbyterian minister) told Smith (a Presbyterian elder) that the Mountain Project stood out as one of the places where the Presbyterian Church actually tried to put the gospel into action. On April 2, Monroe noted, representatives of all the nine churches in the Mountain Project heard testimony from both sides and voted 30 to 1 to continue its sponsorship of the VISTAs. He told the governor that "for us to dignify the charges and maliciousness" of the group complaining about the Mountain Project, "would be a travesty of all that is just and right."[71]

Jack Weller (author of *Yesterday's People*) directed the Mountain Project from 1957 to 1965, but his successors had very different views from Weller, who felt the Appalachian traits of his parishioners inhibited their adjustment to the modern world. After Weller left, the project became a lightning rod for controversy because of the community organizing commitment of Austin, who assumed the directorship in 1966, and the project's "minister of community development," James Somerville, who arrived in March 1967. Both strongly advocated working with rather than for poor people. Somerville told an interviewer he learned his activist methods from the Appalachian Volunteers. Son of a Presbyterian minister, Somerville grew up in South Carolina and attended the conservative Columbia Theological Seminary in Atlanta. After seminary he served four small churches around Haynesville, Alabama, until his liberal views on civil rights made him unwelcome. He then served five years at a small pastorate in Wise County, Virginia, until he resigned to become director of the local anti-poverty program. Although his program won praise among anti-poverty circles in Washington, Somerville, much like Jefferson Monroe, became convinced by the AVs he worked with that the social services approach of his agency should be replaced with a grassroots organizing philosophy. The board of his agency disagreed, and Somerville left Virginia for Boone County and the Mountain Project. The local newspaper, the weekly *Coal Valley News*, greeted his arrival with an editorial "Quit Preachin' and Gone to Meddlin,'" which complained that churches had no business organizing poor people. Later, the same weekly proclaimed: "Truth is, we have been invaded by a bunch of socialistic preacher-punks and their VISTA communal-life perverts in a program that is TOTALLY LAWLESS AND UNCONSTITUTIONAL."[72]

In the end Governor Smith, eager to limit political damage in a difficult election year, decided to quietly and gradually call a halt to VISTA operations in Boone. He wrote to Arvon that "reports indicate that limited action on my part is warranted at this time." The Boone County Mountain Project sponsored by the Presbyterian Church would expire on August 31. Smith requested VISTAs assigned to the project, whose one-year assignment would not end until November 10, be transferred from Boone by August 31.[73] He also directed Dr. Mildred Bateman of the Department of Mental Health not to assign any VISTAs to Boone County. He explained to Bateman that "I am simply trying to let this situation become passive and dormant, and feel that the interests of the State, your program, and the VISTA concept itself, would be better served if we declared a moratorium on VISTA work in Boone County altogether."[74] Only after he had made these decisions did he agree to meet with representatives of the poor people's organization, Boone County Association for the Needy (B-CAN), on August 12, 1968. The group's president, Chester Wiseman, told the governor that the VISTAs had been the backbone of the poor people's organization in trying to do something about school lunches for needy children, an effort that had led B-CAN first to raise money to feed poor children and then to talk to PTAs, school boards, principals, and state education officials, and even to a subcommittee of the United States Senate. When the school administrators ignored them, Wiseman told the governor, B-CAN finally obtained a grant from OEO to supplement the county's school lunch budget. B-CAN now hoped to sponsor a new VISTA community organization project. There is no record of the governor's response to the B-CAN delegation, but he had already decided to place a moratorium on additional volunteers to Boone, and the decision as to what the future might hold for Boone and B-CAN's hopes would rest with the next governor.[75]

Community action in Webster County became another stormy battle between a disenchanted and conservative local CAP board (the Webster County Program Development Council), OEO representatives who demanded more representation of the poor, and a CAA director, Millard Mott, who, in the summer of 1967, with the encouragement of OEO officials and perhaps with the idea of copying the Raleigh model, cancelled the community center approach of the local board and focused on mobilizing poor people to "demand their rights." In disgust, the original board members prepared a history to document what they believed to be the hijacking of the original community action group by the CAP director, aided and abetted by OEO regional agents and state agency director Jefferson Monroe. The Webster Country Program Development Council had begun in 1959 without any financial assistance, but when OEO money became available, the council had repeatedly submitted proposals until OEO finally approved their program. Clearly their idea was to improve the poor people, not the system. They had worked, they said, "to break down the anti-social attitude of many poor people, to get them to change their way of life and to instill into them an ambition to do better." The Webster CAA had employed a home economist to give instruction in homemaking, provided free clothes distribution centers, and in several community centers provided recreation, arts and crafts, and a workshop program. All of this changed in May 1967, when the Webster group hired Mott, a former OEO program analyst, as program director. Mott began to distribute literature around the county "calculated . . . to stir up trouble, incite the poor people to perform acts such as marching, picketing, [and] writing letters for publication." The board also condemned the state agency that was supposed to provide technical assistance to the program. The board eventually managed to fire Mott, but OEO threatened to cut off funding for the Program Development Council. In June 1968, the Webster County group asked Governor Smith to investigate and also to dismiss state director Monroe.[76]

In the Red Scare-like alarm about community action, AVs, and VISTAs, the Appalachian South Folklife Center in Pipestem also came under attack. Don West, a former union organizer, civil rights pioneer, preacher, college professor, journalist, and poet, and co-founder of the Highlander Folk Center in Tennessee, established the Pipestem Center in 1965 on a 350-acre tract in Summers County. The Center's literature described it as "a universal Christian Center in the Judeo-Christian tradition dedicated to a mountain heritage of freedom, self-respect, and independence with human dignity." Mrs. Wilbur Cohen, wife of the U.S. Secretary of Health, Education, and Welfare, helped secure two private philanthropic grants to fund the Center, and West invested his life savings in it. Among other activities, the Center conducted summer camps for low-income children and training sessions for AVs and VISTAs. In August 1968, the center held an Appalachian Folklife Festival, which West hoped would become an annual event. Like the AVs, however, the Folklife Center came under severe criticism. Two weekly newspapers, the *Kanawha Valley News Leader* and the *Princeton Times* worried that, as the *Times* said, the Folklife Center "can only be a most devastating influence to Southern West Virginia and the entire nation." The newspapers hinted broadly of a "Communist Conspiracy." West told a journalist visiting his camp that he had been called a communist by Southern politicians and segregationists, but he said "there is no way I could be a communist." He worried that in the prevailing atmosphere the Center could be burned by "hate-stirred vigilantes."[77]

Meanwhile, across the country the Green Amendment loomed over community action agencies that challenged local government as a sword of Damocles, but the sword did not fall immediately in West Virginia or in most of the country. OEO had sufficiently reined in the urban community action programs so that big city mayors no longer saw them as threats. In 1968, only nineteen local governments in the whole country exercised the prerogative to take over the community action agencies.[78] The amendment, however, symbolized Congress's commitment to move away from "maximum feasible participation" in the War on Poverty, and it had a chilling effect on community action programs that in any way threatened the local brokers of political power. In Mingo, Raleigh, and Webster counties, the county courts sought to take over the CAAs, but Governor Smith continued to support independent community action agencies for almost another year after the enactment of the Green Amendment. The changed atmosphere with dwindling funds and growing public hostility perhaps made it seem unnecessary to follow through with Green. Smith also received conflicting advice about community action among his own advisors and perhaps had mixed feelings himself. Jefferson Monroe, the director of the state economic opportunity agency, strongly supported community action and independent CAAs and worked with the AVs, VISTAs, and poor people's groups. Paul Crabtree, Smith's chief administrative aide, continued to be extremely hostile to OEO and especially to community action, VISTAs and AVs. In mid-1968, Crabtree again urged that the state Economic Opportunity Agency be discontinued, telling the governor that Monroe's plan for the agency "neatly balances boondoggle and bureaucracy, and seems more designed to raise hell than the standard of living."[79] Whether he agreed altogether with Crabtree or not, with the deterioration of the political outlook for Democrats in 1968, Smith appears to have concluded that community action and the AVs had become expendable.

Governor Smith Closes Ranks with the Critics

As late as April 1968, Smith still resisted the idea that county courts should take over the community action groups. At a news conference he characterized the protests of community action groups in Mingo County as citizen participation, and said, "that's what we've been asking them to do."[80] By August 1968, however, Smith, weary of the confrontational turn of the AVs and concerned about the election, closed ranks with Crabtree, Senator Byrd, and county court Democrats. In addition to the Boone County imbroglio, the Webster County confrontation, continued static from other counties such as Raleigh, Wyoming, Nicholas, Mercer, and Mingo, poor people organized by AVs joined the poor people's march on Washington in May. Some 100 of them (called "riffraff" by Senator Byrd) held a rally surrounding Byrd's house in Arlington. At about the same time, a poor people's meeting in Charleston in late May and early June (encouraged by AV "issues organizing") irritated Smith. Calling themselves the Ad Hoc Committee for the Poor, Unemployed, and Disadvantaged Citizens of West Virginia, the demonstrators camped on the State House lawn and held a meeting at John Adams Junior High School demanding a special session of the legislature to provide jobs and relief for the unemployed. VISTAs and AVs had organized the demonstration. The *Charleston Daily Mail* reported that these activities had raised great concern in the governor's office. In what might be seen as something of a valedictory for the War on Poverty in West Virginia, Jeff Monroe, perhaps imagining the Biblical handwriting on the wall, defended the actions of his office, community action, and the AVs in a long memo to Smith. Monroe said it had been necessary in carrying out the War on Poverty and promoting the purposes of the governor's administration to work with OEO, community action programs, AVs, VISTAs, and groups of poor people. At times, some of these groups and organizations did inappropriate things, Monroe admitted, but by retaining close ties with them, the agency had been able to avert problems. He insisted that he had tried to stop the demonstration on the State House lawn, even spending about two hours with the demonstrators and AVs, advising them that the demonstration would not help their cause. Monroe said he and several of his staff attended the meeting at John Adams and defended the governor's position. He also took issue with the tendency to label the support AVs and VISTAs gave to poor people's groups "as something akin to outside agitation." He called "just and proper" the work of the volunteers in helping the state to confront its "serious and critical problems."[81]

Politicians, perhaps sensing blood in the water, continued to pressure the governor. On July 18, State Senator Noah Floyd brought a delegation of "reputable and responsible citizens" from Mingo County to confer with the governor on the VISTAs and AVs and to discuss their desire that—in the spirit of the Green Amendment—the county court be allowed to assume control of the Mingo EOC. In the governor's absence, his aide, Paul Crabtree, met with the group and offered sympathy. Floyd and others in the delegation repeated the familiar litany about the volunteers' lack of cleanliness and low level of morality, citing interracial social activities as evidence of moral degeneracy. They chiefly complained, however, that the volunteers had developed a political organization, even going so far as to present a slate of candidates in the primary election. They asserted that the volunteers disrupted community life by creating confusion and dissension "among those who are ill-educated or ill-equipped to understand their motives." The group recommended that both the VISTA and AV programs be terminated as soon as possible, and they noted that the county court had unanimously concurred with the recommendation.[82]

Back home, the Mingo group organized a letter-writing campaign to Governor Smith. One writer described the Mingo Equal Opportunity Commission (the local CAA) as "a monster, devouring and destroying as it goes" and an organization that catered to "illiterate people who cannot think for themselves, who can be led as a sheep to the slaughter."[83] Finally in a special session of the legislature in September, Smith asked for changes in West Virginia law to reflect federal law, enabling county courts, with concurrence of the governor, to assume control of community action agencies. State Senator Floyd and Delegate T. I. Varney, both from Mingo County, eagerly sponsored the legislation. Smith then recognized decisions of the county courts of Webster, Raleigh, and Mingo to designate themselves to replace the existing CAAs in their counties. He made the announcement in Mingo County at a triumphant political rally of the local Democratic organization.[84]

Feeling that the governor's action spelled the death of the poverty program, Huey Perry and the Mingo County EOC fought back, successfully appealing to Republican gubernatorial candidate Arch Moore to denounce Smith's action. Moore, unlikely to win many votes in Mingo, had nothing to lose, and welcomed the opportunity to cause distress in the opposition camp. He pledged that if elected he would not authorize the county courts to take over. Unless the Democratic candidate James Sprouse also pledged to support the EOC, Perry's organization planned to drive to Charleston to protest, using a black hearse with a sign reading "Death of the Poverty Program." On the appointed day, 200 cars and about 800 people rallied at EOC headquarters in Cinderella Hollow, but at the last moment Sprouse headquarters announced that, if elected, Sprouse would also continue recognition of the Mingo EOC. The assembled mourners called off the drive to Charleston. They changed the sign on the hearse to read "Death of the County Court," and turned the occasion into a victory parade through the county.[85]

Despite Huey Perry's tactical victory, the Republican victory in the 1968 election would bring about great change in the War on Poverty and community action. OEO continued to exist through Nixon's first term, total spending for poverty-related programs actually increased, and Moore kept his promise not to turn control of CAAs over to county courts, but the push for maximum feasible participation of the poor came to an end as did the threat to traditional local political powers.[86]

Torn by crises within the organization and growing attacks on it from outside (including McCarthy-era-type hearings in Pike County, Kentucky by the Kentucky Un-American Activities Committee), the Appalachian Volunteers faded quickly in 1968. Frightened politicians dropped support for them, refusing to approve their budget requests. West Virginia AVs had become increasingly alienated and isolated from the organization headquarters in Bristol, Tennessee (and later Prestonsburg, Kentucky) and the operations in eastern Kentucky, feeling that the problems in Kentucky differed from those in West Virginia and that West Virginia AVs had a different style. West Virginia AV staff meetings involved much discussion of "the system" and some AV field men despaired of reform. The Vietnam War and a sense that even the best accomplishments of the AVs did little to improve the situation for poor people in West Virginia drove much of the rising radicalism in the organization. The firing of Joe Mulloy met with the general disapproval of West Virginia AV staffers, but they also rejected assistant director Eric Metzner's proposal to make this issue the occasion for a total split with the organization. At the end of 1967, Metzner, writing from West Virginia AV headquarters in Pineville, expressed the growing pessimism: "The most important problems await us. We have no surefire organizing technique, no firm philosophy which we can all support, and hundreds of hollows with thousands of people in them who are poor."[87] West Virginia AV David Biesemeyer reported a great deal of "demoralization and disorganization" among AVs and expected the demise of the West Virginia AVs by the end of the summer. The West Virginia AV application for funding after October 1 had been rejected, and by then nearly all the staff had found jobs with other organizations.[88]

The atmosphere disheartened many AVs and VISTAs who had volunteered their efforts over the past three years. For all their efforts, many middle-class West Virginians condemned them as "carpetbaggers, traitors, hippies, Communists, and moral degenerates." Peter Steven Ellis of Boston, nearing the end of his year of service, told a *Charleston Gazette* interviewer that the hostility of middle-class West Virginians to their activities "was amazing." Ellis had been driven out of Lincoln County and had ended up working in Charleston helping to operate a community youth center and working with youth in the Triangle District cleaning up vacant lots. Jefferson Monroe commented that "We've given the rest of America a pretty bad impression of us. West Virginians are supposed to be hospitable, open people—yet we clobbered hell out of these young people who came to try to help us. It's a shame, really."[89]

At about this time, songwriter Michael Kline and his associate John Martin put out a record album, privately distributed from Kline's Capon Bridge, West Virginia, home, featuring songs about AVs, VISTAs, and the poverty war. The title song, "The Poverty War Is Dead" (sung to the tune of "Go Tell Aunt Rhody"), captured something of the spirit of the time among the disheartened AVs and VISTAs:

Go tell Sargent Shriver, go tell Robert McNamara, go tell Lyndon Johnson,
The poverty war is dead.
The one that they been a savin' on, the one we been a slavin' on, the one they been
economizin' on, for to feather their pretty heads.

Died in the Congress, died in the Congress, died in the Congress,
Because it was painted red.[90]

A year later, *Washington Post* columnist William Grieder reported that the AVs, "one of the bold experiments in social change," had been abandoned by OEO after the Republican governor of Kentucky,

Louie Nunn, vetoed the AVs' grant application. Sources at OEO said that no one expected a former Republican congressman (OEO director Donald Rumsfeld) to override a governor's veto. Grieder wrote that in both West Virginia and Kentucky "dozens of grassroots organizations sprang up under AV tutelage and began challenging entrenched school boards and county officials on a long list of issues from hunger to new housing." AV director David Walls (Milton Ogle resigned in September 1968), a twenty-seven-year-old economics graduate from the University of California, told Grieder that his discussions with OEO convinced him to abandon hope that government funding would be revived. Disappointed that the experiment had ended, Walls said, "It's only at those moments when a great wave of indignation sweeps through the country that the federal government is moved to do very much . . . at the local level. This wave didn't last long."[91]

Assessing AVs and VISTAs

It is easy to understand why many of the young people in VISTA and the Appalachian Volunteers assigned to community action rather quickly came to the realization that they had been sent into a situation that offered small victories at best unless some major changes took place. They presumed a great deal and in matters of dress and deportment, like the typical college students of the day, made no compromises with local sensitivities. Bright, well-educated, generally articulate and insightful, they had little at risk and some felt compelled to confront "the system," whether it was the local school board or county court or the government in Washington. They projected to many an image of youthful irresponsibility and carelessness, and, quite apart from the overwrought charges of communism or sedition leveled against them, some occasionally did foolish things that undermined their effectiveness. On one occasion a Clay County VISTA somehow got past all the secretaries in the state capitol and walked into Governor Smith's office, "beard, sandals, tight unwashed jeans and all, [and] started telling the Governor about the dangers of the 'power structure.'"[92] Another story, perhaps apocryphal, has it that after an AV-sponsored delegation met with Governor Nunn of Kentucky, the governor's staff discovered that someone had left a deposit of human excrement on the carpet.[93]

In 1982, David Biesemeyer, one of the AV field men who had worked in Raleigh County, told an interviewer that in retrospect he felt that the "youthful irresponsibility" image had some justification. He admitted that he and his fellow AVs and VISTAs, young and inexperienced, could be careless with the lives of other people. "At any point at which things became too heavy, I could've left, and I knew that." He also said many daydreamed about a real revolution, but as for himself, Biesemeyer believed that the main thing was to make a difference in the lives of the people and make a difference in the country. Biesemeyer conceded that their critics might have been right about some aspects of their behavior, but the critics underestimated the local people the AVs worked with, portraying them as victims who "had no ability to defend themselves or to judge the motives of the VISTAS who were coming in." The critics—public officials, news media, and others—were wrong about that, Biesemeyer insisted. The people the volunteers worked with "recognized that we were just kids and that we could be careless with their lives," but they also understood that because of their education the volunteers could be very useful in helping local people to address and to articulate community concerns. Biesemeyer felt that the AVs and VISTAs and community action programs accomplished some useful things. He cited as an example the opportunities that developed for the wife of a disabled coal miner who became an aide in the Head Start program sponsored by the VISTA workers and eventually received a degree from Marshall University and became an accredited teacher. He also cited the long-term impact on the people who became involved in the community programs organized by the AVs and VISTAs. They learned to participate in the political process, which enabled them to gain more attention to their community needs, and even though the county commission (successor of the county court) later came to control community action, Biesemeyer felt the commission kept the door open to the new elements brought into the political process.[94]

Ronnie Sue Jaffe (a 1966 graduate of the University of Vermont), one of the 500 who came to Appalachia in 1966, worked in Buffalo Lick, Kanawha County; Pine Knob, Raleigh County; and later in Wyoming County. Looking back on the experience in 1987, she also admitted that the volunteers had been "too self-assured, too cocky, too young" and that they had known too little about local relations and community history. Nevertheless, she said, their youth and naiveté enabled them to tackle issues that others might not.[95]

Hershel Shrewsberry (a local typesetter who became the director of community action in Wyoming County) first learned of the AVs when a couple of them knocked on his door in Wyoming County looking for a place to stay. He thought that they looked strange with their long hair and knapsacks (in which "some people thought they carried hand grenades"), but he liked them, his family boarded one, and the AVs convinced him to become involved in community affairs.[96] Robert Coles' interviews with Appalachian residents who worked with AV and VISTA volunteers also suggest that the residents had rather clear-eyed assessments of these young "outsiders," seeing them with a mixture of skepticism, admiration, gratitude, and realism.[97]

The most trenchant criticisms of volunteers came from business executives and machine politicians in southern counties who saw the AVs as "outsiders" who stirred up local opposition and created rival patronage groups. Because the business interests funded politicians and these southern machines could deliver votes on election day, many elective officials felt compelled to respond to them. Some criticisms came from those who shared AV goals. Don West, the old mountain radical who co-founded the Highlander Center in Tennessee and later founded the Appalachian South Folklife Center in Mercer County, West Virginia, worked with the AVs, running training programs for them. In retrospect, however, he compared the AVs and VISTAs and poverty fighters of the 1960s to missionaries of the post-Civil War era and Northern radicals from the 1930s. West thought that, unlike those who came in the 1930s without salaries and faced thugs and violence, the latter day poverty fighters had it relatively easy, collecting good salaries from government programs and playing at being radicals without understanding the history of struggle that befell the mountain people nor trusting them to act for themselves. He also criticized those who set themselves up as experts and consultants after the poverty warrior jobs faded. In West's view, the 1960s taught native mountaineers that they must "organize and save [them]selves."[98] Historians Thomas Kiffmeyer and David E. Whisnant have also compared the AVs to earlier groups such as missionaries and reformers who came with good intentions and condescending attitudes. Kiffmeyer says the AVs and their predecessors "who came to save the mountaineers viewed their subjects as quaint, yet helpless and ignorant at best, and violent and resistant to improvement at worst." He says those who came as outsiders saw the mountain residents as outsiders "because they did not represent what the outside world considered normative." They thought the residents suffered from a culture of poverty.[99] Similarly, in his assessment of the AVs, historian David E. Whisnant asserted that they shared many of the paternalistic attitudes earlier missionary groups had brought to Appalachia in their efforts to bring change to the region, paying no attention to blacks and promoting "a *macho* spirit of competition" among field men that "not only was abusive to women but also prevented the AVs from seriously encouraging indigenous leadership."[100]

Both Kiffmeyer and Whisnant present well-researched and carefully nuanced views, some of these judgments seem too harsh regarding the AVs and VISTAs in West Virginia. Though their training probably predisposed them to arrive with the culture of poverty thesis, most seem to have quickly abandoned it. It is true that white males dominated as AV field men. Naomi Weintraub Cohen later recalled that while the "field men" ran around in cars "doing their thing," she, in the more traditionally appropriate role of "administrative assistant," did all the administrative work in the Raleigh County office to keep the organization running.[101] Also, twenty-three-year-olds assuming supervisory roles toward middle-aged local people appears presumptuous, to say the least. However, the AVs and VISTAs and the community action agencies through which they worked in West Virginia appear to have been committed to a broad participatory approach. They organized or encouraged existing organizations in black communities in East Beckley, Winding Gulf, Bluefield, Williamson (Vinson Street), Charleston, Huntington, and elsewhere, and when critics raised the "immorality" charges against the AVs and VISTAs, racial fraternization almost always formed a component of that charge. Even the more traditionally oriented community action agencies, like those in Kanawha and McDowell counties, operated with greater racial sensitivity than had been the norm with social service agencies in the past, taking care to establish community centers in black neighborhoods and to encourage local leadership. The groups organized by the AVs and VISTAs had both men and women and blacks and whites as officers, and the activist community action agencies provided employment as well as leadership development opportunities for local men and women.[102]

Though the community organizing models with which the AVs and VISTAs experimented offer no settled technique useful for community organizing today, their emphasis on working at the grassroots had enduring influence beyond the relatively brief period of the War on Poverty.[103] Despite the assumptions of metropolitan journalists and some social scientists about fatalism among mountaineers, the United Mine Workers had already provided a model for activism during the Great Depression. While the impact of the new machine age in the 1950s would curtail the promise of the union as a vehicle for social justice, grassroots organizing held appeal for many, including those who remembered the effectiveness of the union in its militant days. As Margaret Ripley Wolfe has noted, in eastern Kentucky the heritage of unionism inspired "a commitment to social justice and a sense of community that sustained activism"; and of course, the union experience had been even more powerful in West Virginia than in Kentucky.[104]

When the War on Poverty came along, it found a constituency at the grassroots that understood the legitimacy of protest and believed that government had a responsibility to help the poor and the disabled and those who had been victimized by their employers and by the union that had abandoned them. Many people of the area who had long protested the conditions they faced welcomed allies to their cause. Though most of the AVs and VISTAs came as the "outsiders" against whom Byrd, Floyd, Arvon, and others railed from the right, and West scorned from the left, they brought useful skills learned in the civil rights and anti-war movements, and several remained in the state after 1968, continuing to make useful contributions to the robust protest and reform crusades of the Appalachian reawakening like the Black Lung Movement, Miners for Democracy, environmental groups, and the new feminism.[105]

West Virginia's War on Poverty in Retrospect

What are we to make of West Virginia's War on Poverty in the end? First, it has to be said that the soldiers in this brief war marched with quixotic strategies under the command of impatient and distracted generals, with shifting and contradictory tactics and strategies, inadequate firepower, and dwindling support and mixed signals from public officials. It tried to do much with limited resources, and though it certainly did not end poverty or even make much of a dent in it, it had some beneficial consequences, and important parts of it survived the more conservative decades that followed. The most enduring parts delivered services or, like Head Start and Job Corps, sought to help individuals to improve themselves. Head Start, designed on the culture of poverty premise, survived because, even though some studies raised questions about whether it helped much, it was politically popular to try to help poor children prepare for school. Job Corps, inspired by the automation panic, also remained popular as an agency offering opportunity to those ill-prepared for the work of the new age. VISTA also survived as an agency more oriented to providing services rather than community action. More broadly, Medicare and Medicaid survived to provide basic medical insurance for the poor and elderly. Federal aid to education did not seem to have the hoped for effect as various national measurements of achievement showed declines beginning in the mid-1960s. Similarly, studies of the impact of Title I of the Elementary and Secondary Education Act of 1965, which was designed to provide increased funding for school districts with a high percentage of poor people, could demonstrate little positive impact on student achievement.[106]

The lack of funding after 1965 made community action the best hope for fighting poverty on the cheap. That citizens should participate in their government and have the right to petition for redress of grievances represented basic premises of American democracy, but only pure hubris could drive the notion that community action alone could win the War on Poverty. Some poverty warriors believed that poverty could be addressed only by the redistribution of wealth. Historian Allan J. Matusow says Johnson never considered redistribution, and even when local groups led by what Johnson called "kooks and sociologists" tried merely to redistribute local power rather than income, Johnson believed they exceeded the limit of permissible change in American political culture and turned his back on community action. Matusow said the epitaph of the War on Poverty should be "Declared, but never fought."[107]

In most of the country the push for maximum feasible participation came early, but difficulties in the big cities and President Johnson's discomfiture caused Shriver to back away from it by December of 1965.[108] In Appalachia, however, a region that largely inspired the War on Poverty, the regional officials of OEO pushed harder for maximum feasible participation as time went on, perhaps feeling that the poverty of the region justified more determined tactics and political risk-taking to achieve the goals of the Economic Opportunity Act. In West Virginia, OEO clearly favored the "bottom-up" examples of Mingo and Raleigh over the more moderate "top-down" approaches of eastern West Virginia (Mineral-Hardy), McDowell, and Kanawha counties and also encouraged the state to approve the AV- and VISTA-inspired community action efforts in the state. As noted in the preceding chapter, OEO regional officials also tried to use multi-county organizations to dilute the power of local elites (although, ironically, conservatives found multi-county organizations also could be used effectively to undercut the "bottom-up" county organizations), and helped community action militants to reorganize CAP boards with majorities of poor in order to achieve control. OEO pushed for multi-county organizations in eastern, northern, and central West Virginia. One of the most unusual was TRI-CAP, which combined Putnam, Kanawha, and Boone counties into a single CAP. Of course the few CAPs that achieved "maximum feasible participation of the poor" received the most attention, and not much appears in the records about the majority of the West Virginia counties. As leading West Virginia poverty warriors like Huey Perry and Jeff Monroe noted in retrospect, the number of programs in West Virginia and throughout the country that actually embraced the "maximum feasible participation of the poor" concept constituted a miniscule minority.[109]

In the Mountain State as in the rest of the country, a great variety of community action groups sprang up, most of them operated by the local political organizations. Some had trouble getting projects approved by OEO because of inadequate representation of the poor or simply because of unimaginative plans. Small counties had no planners or grant writers and so, even if local officials wanted to participate, most had limited institutional capacity to plan and to administer suitable programs. Some counties could not or did not devise plans acceptable to OEO, but most of the state came under the OEO umbrella in one way or another. The state had a statutory obligation to help local CAPs in planning, but even on the state level, West Virginia, with little professional bureaucracy, had but slight capacity to support the kind of planning and technical assistance expected by those who framed the legislation, as the state's execution and planning of the Work Training Program under Title V of the Economic Opportunity Act dismally demonstrated, and as the staff of ARC concluded about West Virginia's development planning (as noted in chapter 4). Some of the shortcomings of the state agencies reported by federal agencies might be seen as the result of metropolitan condescension; others came from unrealistic expectations of a small state's capacity by the legislative framers.

Another problem with the War on Poverty in Appalachia was that Lyndon Johnson's push for quick legislation and early implementation resulted in a hasty embrace of promising but untested ideas. It did little to take into account the problems of rural America generally or of Appalachia particularly. Congress had created a "one size fits all plan" that grew out of sociological theories designed more for an urban than a rural setting and based on middle class predilections and assumptions. Such a plan, David E. Whisnant argues persuasively in *Modernizing the Mountaineer*, "foreclosed the possibility of dealing constructively with the structural and systemic . . . poverty in Appalachia."[110] Barbara Ellen Smith makes the same point, noting that "structural economic issues like chronic unemployment, occupational segregation, and corporate control of regional resources not only were ignored but worse were screened from view by the Johnson administration's appealing but deceptive rhetoric about a 'Great Society' and an 'unconditional war on poverty.'"[111]

Don Marsh, reporter and editor of the *Charleston Gazette*, told an interviewer in 1987 that the War on Poverty created a lot of excitement and hope, but citizens' groups could not stay focused, and the moneyed interests and entrenched politicians prevailed in the end. Other than some good memories, better highways, Head Start, and some individual success stories, the War on Poverty failed, Marsh believed, and the effort simply created "vanity and vexation in pursuit of the wind."[112] To Marsh's brief list might be added other important programs of the 1960s that survived the succeeding conservative era such as Medicare, Medicaid, and federal education programs that provided funding to poor school districts. The educational and medical programs, however inadequate they proved to be in promoting improved education or health, had their origins in the good intentions of upper middle class Americans and policy makers of the 1960s to make a greater society for all.[113] Also important to note is the continuing influence of veteran poverty warriors as the War on Poverty faded and a new phase of reform from the grassroots began.

6

From the Silver Bridge to Farmington and Rumblings at the Grassroots

> From Monongah to Mannington, the same script is grimly familiar. The national searchlight is focused on a disaster. The company officials promise that everything possible is being done. The surviving coal miners and their sons say that, of course, they will go back in the mines. Soon everybody goes back to the status quo until the next disaster.
>
> Congressman Ken Hechler, 1968

> A new generation of coal miners had got some education, got smarter, done their service, maybe fought over there in Vietnam. They came back and they seen their daddies dying. . . they knew something was wrong. They figured they weren't going to be as dumb as people made miners out to be.
>
> Bynum "Junior" Gilbert, Raleigh County coal miner

The collapse of the Silver Bridge across the Ohio River between Point Pleasant, West Virginia, and Gallipolis, Ohio, on December 16, 1967, one of the worst bridge disasters in American history, proved to be but a prelude to 1968, an *annus horribilis* that unfolded with a long succession of disquieting events. The Vietcong Tet Offensive in Vietnam in January convinced many already skeptical Americans that the Johnson administration's optimistic assessments of the war had been misleading and escalated an already divisive debate about the war. The assassinations of the Reverend Martin Luther King Jr. (April 4) and Senator Robert F. Kennedy (June 5) took two figures from the American scene who many thought had offered the best hope for change. The year also saw urban riots, campus rebellions, a contentious and bloody Democratic convention in Chicago in late August, and a convulsive presidential election.[1]

West Virginia suffered through these travails with the rest of the country but also endured a remarkable series of its own, including the painful aftermath of the Silver Bridge collapse, political scandals and reversals of fortunes that further revealed the corrupt nature of state politics, campus tensions and a bombing, the worst airplane crash in the state's history, a near disastrous chemical fire and gas release, racial conflict, two mine disasters, rumblings at the grassroots as the poverty war faded, and a miners' revolt. In the face of all this, many reporters and editorialists found the "collapsing structure" imagery compelling.[2]

Prelude: The Silver Bridge

As the new machine age advanced rapidly in the post-World War II era, with its growing automobile traffic and ever larger trucks and heavier loads for aging highways and bridges, perils lurked in unanticipated places. In the waning light of late afternoon on December 15, 1967, cars and trucks hurried both ways in bumper-to-bumper traffic carrying holiday shoppers and commuters across the Ohio River on the Silver Bridge connecting Gallipolis and Point Pleasant. Suddenly, the 1,750-foot bridge collapsed, shearing away on the West Virginia side and spilling some seventy cars and trucks with their passengers and cargoes into the river and onto the Ohio shore under the bridge, resulting in the deaths of forty-six people. Rescue units rushed to the scene, but the descending dark of a cold December night hampered rescue operations. Governor Smith and Governor James A. Rhodes of Ohio also hurried to the scene with their staffs as did newspaper and television reporters from the regional and national media.[3]

Swollen by autumn rains to depths two feet over its normal level, the river current flowed at six miles per hour, making it impossible for divers in deep-sea gear to stand on the river bottom. Conditions delayed recovery efforts until the Army Corps of Engineers closed floodcontrol gates at twenty-three dams upriver between Point Pleasant and Pittsburgh and downriver at Gallipolis Roller Dam to cut the flow rate in half, enabling divers to return to around-the-clock operations. Nevertheless, many weeks passed before recovery efforts ended.[4]

The American Bridge Company had opened the Silver Bridge (so-called because of its aluminum-based paint) in 1928 as a privately operated toll bridge. The state of West Virginia later purchased and operated the bridge without tolls. One of the few examples of its type (a bridge built in Florianopolis, Brazil, in 1924 had used the same principle as did a nearby West Virginia bridge across the Ohio at St. Marys), the Silver Bridge hung from carbon steel chains suspended from towers, unlike other suspended bridges such as the Golden Gate Bridge in San Francisco or the Verrazano-Narrows Bridge in New York, which relied on massive spun cables. Two sets of 106-foot-high towers supported the chains, which extended from anchors on opposite shores of the river. The collapse began when one of the chains snapped just outside the Ohio side tower. The bridge had been engineered without any concern for redundancy, so when the structure failed at one point, the whole structure disintegrated. According to a report by the National Transportation and Safety Board (NTSB), an eyebar in the chain fractured because of "the joint action of stress corrosion and corrosion fatigue." At the time the builders designed the bridge in 1927, they failed to anticipate the long-term impact of corrosion. Neither did they anticipate the heavier loads nor rising traffic of the post-World War II era, designing the bridge to carry two-axle trucks with a capacity of fifteen tons rather than the three-axle tractor-trailers of thirty-six tons that regularly crossed the span by 1967. The NTSB report said the bridge had not been thoroughly inspected for sixteen years, but that the flaw that caused the eyebar to fracture could not have been detected in any case by conventional inspection methods.[5]

The collapse of the Silver Bridge raised concerns throughout the country about the decaying bridges of the automobile age and marked a turning point both in bridge engineering and in the way bridges would be inspected and maintained, bringing about greater federal attention to bridge construction, maintenance, and inspection. Some 550,000 bridges across the country, like the Silver Bridge, had received little or no attention after their construction, and many had been built early in the highway age. Four days after the collapse, Senator Jennings Randolph announced hearings of the Senate Public Works Committee that eventually led to the first federal bridge inspection requirements.[6]

Ohio River rushes by pier and wreckage of collapsed Silver Bridge between Point Pleasant, West Virginia, and Gallipolis, Ohio, December 1967. Maurice Hamill Collection, West Virginia State Archives.

Shortly after the Silver Bridge collapse, the State Road Commission closed the Ohio River Bridge at St. Marys, of similar design and vintage, and never reopened it. Because of the importance of the St. Marys bridge and the Silver Bridge to interstate transportation in the area, the federal government, with the Appalachian Regional Commission taking a leading role, helped expedite the building of a new bridge. The ARC staff demonstrated an ability to get things done by quickly bringing together the relevant agencies in the two states and pressuring the Army Corps of Engineers, making it possible to move toward the beginning of construction of a new bridge within three weeks.[7]

Remarkably, within two years after the collapse, the Silver Memorial Bridge opened just south of Point Pleasant to reconnect Mason County, West Virginia, and Gallia County, Ohio. Lawsuits against the firms involved in building the Silver Bridge, U.S. Steel and the J.E. Greiner Company, resulted in their agreement in 1972 to pay $950,000 to be divided among the estates of the forty-six killed in the collapse, a paltry amount considering the number of victims involved and compared to sizes of awards in comparable cases of more recent times.[8]

A Shaken Political Structure

Reverberations of the bridge disaster commanded the attention of Governor Hulett C. Smith's administration for months during its difficult final year. In much the same way that hidden corrosion brought the Silver Bridge down, concealed political corruption dating from the Barron years emerged to shake the Smith administration. In the fall of 1967, former Governor Barron had appeared to be preparing to run again for governor, as supporters distributed "Wally by Golly" campaign buttons. In early December 1967, however, a federal grand jury indicted liquor commissioner Clarence Elmore (a Barron administration holdover who had managed Smith's campaign for governor) on tax evasion charges. Smith immediately suspended him, but the Elmore indictment portended disaster for Barron and his associates as well as for the Smith administration and the hopes of the state Democratic Party in the 1968 election. Just two days after the Silver Bridge fell, the *New York Times* reported that "West Virginia's political structure was shaken this week" by reports that former governor Barron had received fees from coal companies to support passage of a law giving them authority to condemn private property and use it as right-of-way for a coal slurry pipeline and that the Justice Department had completed an investigation of the matter. Barron immediately called the reported payoff "an asinine lie" and reports of a Justice Department investigation "a vicious rumor." Coal slurry pipelines, a much discussed panacea for the industry's troubles in the early 1960s, had never been built; however, the West Virginia legislature passed a law in 1962 granting coal companies the right of eminent domain for building pipelines, making it the only state that had done so by 1964.[9]

The *Charleston Gazette*'s Thomas Stafford had already begun to publish investigative pieces on the schemes of Barron's henchmen before Barron left office in 1965. Less publicly, the FBI and federal prosecutors, led by former state tax commissioner Milton Ferguson, also focused on the former governor and his friends. On February 14, 1968, in what the state press labeled "the St. Valentine's Day Massacre," a grand jury in Huntington returned an indictment against Barron and five associates, including state road commissioner Burl Sawyers and his deputy Vincent J. Johnkoski, finance commissioner Truman Gore, Elkins lawyer Bonn Brown, and Clarksburg automobile dealer Alfred Shroath. After the Valentine's Day indictments, Governor Smith suspended Sawyers, Johnkoski, and Gore, the three additional Barron holdovers in his administration who had been indicted. The indictments fell as a heavy blow upon the Smith administration, causing discouragement and depression among state employees during its final year.[10]

When the original indictments came, they did not deal with coal slurry pipeline payoffs that had been alleged by the *New York Times*, but rather, with corruption in purchasing. According to prosecutor Ferguson, Barron and the others had entered into a conspiracy to bilk payments from state contractors. The scheme required that certain contractors with the state send payments to corporations that had been established for the purpose in Ohio and Florida. Other indictments followed. In trials that went on for years afterward dealing with the scheme and other cases of malfeasance, some eighteen men who had been high officials in the Barron and Smith administrations or their friends, relatives, and business associates pled guilty or were convicted on a variety of charges including conspiracy, extortion, tax evasion, falsification of records, and bribery. In August 1968, a jury acquitted Barron, but in 1970 he faced another indictment on charges of rigging purchasing contracts. He again escaped conviction as the Supreme Court of Appeals nullified the law on which the indictment had been based. In February 1971, the former governor and his wife faced indictments on charges of bribery in the original trial in which he had been acquitted. On March 29, 1971, he pled guilty to the bribery charges. Mrs. Barron had delivered the money—$25,000 in a brown paper bag—to the wife of the jury foreman. The federal judge dropped the charges against Mrs. Barron but sentenced the former governor to twenty-five years, and he served about four. When John G. Morgan interviewed Barron later for the book *West Virginia Governors*, Barron insisted that he had been innocent of the original charges but fear of conviction had led him to direct his wife to deliver a bribe to the jury foreman's wife. In 1983, prosecutor Milton Ferguson told an interviewer that only the bribed juror kept Barron from the conviction he deserved in the original trial.[11]

The Fair Elections Movement

The original indictments of Barron and his fellow conspirators only scratched the surface of political corruption, both at the state level and in the counties. The legislators and Governor Smith knew that political damage control required quick action in an election year. In a special session in September, a resolution authorized the establishment of the Purchasing Practices and Procedures Commission. Headed by John P. Duiguid, a member of a Washington law firm who had served in the Rackets Division of the Justice Department, the commission began to collect information on the extent of the corruption. The 1968 trials and the early commission investigations revealed that corrupt practices—rake-offs, kickbacks, influence peddling, rigged bidding, and undercover deals—had become the accepted method of doing business with the state.[12]

Those who fought for reform in the state faced an uphill battle. Don Marsh, a long-time political reporter and editor for the *Charleston Gazette*, later observed that in the 1960s many legislators, particularly those from the southern counties, consistently voted overwhelmingly against the interests of their constituents. When groups like the Methodist Church, Council of the Southern Mountains, Appalachian Volunteers, and VISTAs championed reform causes like fair elections or stronger strip mining laws, legislators, seeing them as enemies of the established order, responded with "contempt and loathing."[13]

Although the southern legislators often reflected the interests of the coal industry, a 1969 survey found that only three legislators had direct ties to the coal industry and five who were attorneys had coal industry clients. But the survey also concluded that because the state depended so heavily on coal, coal operators had no difficulty in persuading the legislature to do the industry's bidding. The general attitude of legislators was that coal must not be regulated in any way that might make it difficult for the industry. One legislator commented in the survey: "During the past twenty years emphasis has been placed on production, wages, hours, and profits, and not so much on health and safety in the mining industry." Laws reflected the industry's influence, requiring, for example, that coal company representatives be on the board responsible for hiring mine inspectors and that the burden of proof fell on the inspector to show a mine unsafe rather than on the operator to prove the mine safe. Should an operator willfully violate an inspector's orders, the only penalties that could be imposed were fines between $10 and $100. Although the governor officially appointed the director of the state Department of Mines, an informal committee of the major coal companies in the state actually selected the appointee.[14]

In many counties and most notoriously in the southern coalfields, courthouse machines allied with the predominant economic interests carefully controlled elections and sent to Charleston those who would defend those interests. In the face of this hoary tradition, a grassroots movement arose in Mingo County to confront one of the most corrupt county regimes in the state. On a Sunday in November 1967, at about the time former governor Barron and his associates began to face formidable legal problems, anti-poverty workers and low-income people from southern West Virginia counties attended a "Poor Peoples Congress" at Concord College in Athens, which led to the grassroots fair elections movement. Sponsored by anti-poverty agencies in southern West Virginia and the Appalachian Volunteers, the conference included a session on political corruption. John Callebs, a Marshall University professor who would soon become the Republican candidate for secretary of state, talked about the extent of voting fraud in the state's southern counties. He pointed out that in eight counties, voting registration lists exceeded the actual voting age population by more than 25,000. In Mingo County, based on the 1960 census, the number registered to vote (30,331) exceeded the voting age population by almost 10,000 and fell only slightly below the total population of the county.[15]

The Mingo County delegation left the Concord conference determined to learn more about state election laws and the situation in Mingo County. Led by former miners James Washington, a fifty-one-year-old African American, and Okey Ray Spence, a white forty-year-old from Delbarton, both disabled and supporting their families on welfare checks, a small but growing group of hollow dwellers spent the winter studying state election laws. Out of their discussions, the Mingo County Fair Elections Committee (FEC) emerged in early 1968. Aided by the Mingo County Equal Opportunity Commission (EOC), VISTAs, and Appalachian Volunteers, the FEC grew to several hundred people.[16]

Mingo County Fair Elections Committee and community action activists demonstrate against the Green Amendment ouside the courthouse in Williamson on March 30, 1968. Sign insists that "Community Action is the People, not the County Court." Photograph by Douglas Yarrow.

On March 30, 1968, some 700 demonstrators gathered outside the Mingo County courthouse in Williamson to protest the ongoing effort of the county court to take over the county community action program. The commissioners wanted control so they could quash the Fair Elections Committee and obtain the patronage that would come with control of the EOC budget. *Charleston Gazette* reporter K.W. Lee, who witnessed the demonstration, described the local political machine as "the most persuasive east of Mayor Richard Daley's Chicago" and noted that it "has reigned comfortably for decades through well-oiled machine politics and crooked election practices." In 1964, Lee noted, "registered voters outnumbered eligible voters in 29 of the state's 55 counties, and four years later the strange disproportion spread to 33 counties." Even more remarkable, the people of the state had accepted the long-standing corruption of state politics as a given and rarely challenged it. The Mingo County revolt, an unprecedented grassroots challenge to the corrupt county machine, gave hope to those who sought more democratic politics in West Virginia.[17]

On that March day in 1968, the Mingo County commissioners remained inside the courthouse, refusing to acknowledge the demonstrators outside who carried signs saying "Down with the Machine" and "We Want Honest Elections." The crowd cheered speakers like Nimrod Workman, a disabled coal miner who "sounded more like a hellfire and damnation Baptist preacher than a poverty crusader." After an hour, the demonstrators departed, avowing their determination to return to their hollow communities to fight for clean elections. The Mingo machine, aided by allies in Charleston and Washington, responded with harsh tactics, including physical intimidation, threats, and even arrests on charges such as maliciously challenging voters' rights to vote. In the face of intimidation by constables and deputy sheriffs, a small bipartisan group of women who knew their districts well (including Alma Jean Justice, Lerly Murphy, and Judy Trent) challenged the bloated registration lists in the county, finding evidence of people being recorded as voting long after their deaths or long after they had moved from the county. Even though state law gave no jurisdiction to magistrate courts in election law violations, the charges against the arrested women were tried in justice of the peace courts, which, in cavalier fashion, found those charged guilty, although none actually served the ninety-day terms as the local CAP paid their bonds. Some outsiders came into the county to show sympathy for the accused, including John Callebs and Charleston attorney and Republican House of Delegates member

Cleo Jones, who represented the Fair Elections Committee members without charge. Former Republican governor Cecil Underwood and liberal Democrat candidate for governor Paul Kaufman both spoke admiringly of the FEC and its political arm, the Political Action League. John D. ("Jay") Rockefeller IV, the Democratic candidate for secretary of state, also listened sympathetically to the FEC complaints and promised to work for election reforms.[18]

Mingo County Fair Elections Committee co-chair James Washington, a disabled former coal miner. Photograph by Douglas Yarrow.

More often, state and federal officials turned a deaf ear to the FEC. A trip to Washington by a large group of the FEC stalwarts organized by Appalachian Volunteer Claudia Schecter brought little encouragement from the state congressional delegation. Six FEC members walked out of the meeting with Senator Byrd, disgusted with his unresponsiveness to their plight. Meetings at the Justice Department, however, brought encouragement. The Federal Bureau of Investigation agreed to undertake a preliminary investigation, and the group also received sympathetic hearings with the election fraud, criminal, and civil rights divisions. In early April, the FBI informed the FEC that a formal investigation had begun and encouraged the FEC to present evidence of voting fraud and civil rights violations. Meanwhile, fearful because of threats of violence against their volunteer poll watchers on primary election day, the FEC's appeals to Governor Smith, the Justice Department, and White House failed to produce poll watchers as did mailed requests to civic groups around the state. A few outside observers appeared on primary election day, May 14, including a dozen AVs and VISTAs from throughout the state, but the FEC itself turned out scores of poll watchers as did some of the presidential primary campaign staffs. Even with all the poll watchers and all the FEC had done to try to assure a clean election, Mingo County Community Action Director Huey Perry later wrote, "The election was as corrupt as always."[19]

The FEC continued to work for a fair election in the fall, but its leaders insisted that voting fraud persisted during the November general election, with election officials escorting many voters to the machines to "assist" them. Well before the election many voters came to the courthouse to vote absentee ballots, 90 percent of them seeking the assistance of election clerks in marking their ballots. Fair Election members charged that the county machine used this means to buy votes. The persistent corruption after all their efforts discouraged FEC members. James Washington told Lee: "The machine people here know how they can get away with anything, and nobody at county, state, and national level wants to help us—nobody gives a damn for what we have been doing."[20] More discouragement came later when indictments of alleged vote buyers brought no convictions.

Some, however, found hope in what the Mingo County Fair Electioneers had achieved. People at the grassroots—housewives, ex-coal miners, and others victimized by the state's economy and dysfunctional social and political system—had at least managed to compel the county clerk's office to purge its registration rolls. The number registered to vote fell below the number eligible to vote for the first time in the county's history. They had also brought state and national attention to the corrupt system in Mingo, putting pressure on miscreants in Mingo and elsewhere in the state to adhere to election laws. Jay Rockefeller, elected secretary of state in the 1968 election (losing only in Mingo County), held hearings in the county soon after taking office in preparation for proposing several election law reforms to the legislature. Despite all that had happened, however, legislators resisted electoral reform. In what could only be seen as an insult to the fair election movement, Senate President Lloyd Jackson named Noah Floyd, the Mingo political boss, as chair of the senate committee on elections. Under the circumstances, it came as no surprise that the legislators also failed to enact Rockefeller's proposed reforms.[21]

Hope emerged again among the election reformers when, on August 5, 1970, U.S. Attorney General John Mitchell (who would later have his own legal problems in connection with the Watergate scandal and would end up going to prison) announced that a federal grand jury had returned indictments against key figures of the Mingo County machine, including Noah Floyd, T. I. Varney, Harry Artis, and Arnold Starr. The indictments charged that the four had conspired to influence the outcome of the general election in 1968. In the trial that followed, several witnesses testified that they had accepted money from the defendants for the purpose of buying votes. The defense questioned the reliability of the prosecution witnesses (some of them erstwhile associates of the defendants), calling them "thugs, thieves and hoodlums." The jury, apparently unable to distinguish between the defendants and the witnesses, found the defendants not guilty.[22] Federal prosecutors had more success prosecuting political miscreants from neighboring Logan County, as the federal district court would find former executive assistant to Governor Barron and state senator Curtis B. Trent, Sheriff Earl Ray Tomblin, and three other Democrats guilty of voting fraud and send them to brief prison terms.[23]

Despite the concerns raised by the Fair Elections Committee and ongoing investigations of state politicians, the 1968 election for governor continued to exemplify the sleazy side of West Virginia politics. Not only did the increasingly unpopular Vietnam War (in which some 700 West Virginians died) loom over the election, in West

Virginia the Democrats carried the burden of the St. Valentine's Day indictments, and the efforts of the Fair Election Movement in Mingo County raised questions about electoral practices in other southern counties critical to Democratic control of the state. Remarkably, some of the indicted stalwarts of the party worked against the election of the party's nominee. Governor Smith, though not one of the indicted officials, nevertheless could not escape taint by association with the "statehouse gang." A strong supporter of President Johnson and the Vietnam War, Smith felt undercut by Johnson's surprise announcement on March 31 that, in addition to calling a bombing halt and seeking negotiations in Vietnam, he would not seek another term as president. Smith had promised that he would—as West Virginia governors traditionally attempted—"anoint" a successor, but after Johnson's withdrawal, he changed his mind and announced at a press conference that he refused to designate any of the three candidates as the administration candidate.[24] With the indictments of many of the leaders of his administration, Smith's support might have had little value to potential candidates in any case. Some at the time thought the announcement disingenuous, suggesting that the word went out surreptitiously to party lieutenants that they should support Attorney General C. Donald Robertson (who later went to prison for tax evasion).[25] Smith's press secretary, Jack Canfield, says the governor's announcement shocked his closest advisors, who themselves supported different candidates but had expected Smith to name his choice.[26]

The King and Kennedy Assassinations

Just four days after Lyndon Johnson had shocked the country with his announcement that he would not run for reelection, on April 4, 1968, the ugly mood in the nation exploded into violence when an assassin, apparently James Earl Ray, gunned down civil rights leader Martin Luther King as he stood on the balcony of a motel in Memphis. Rioting and arson broke out in many cities across the country, including Washington, Chicago, and Detroit.[27]

West Virginia had a few outbursts of violence in the immediate aftermath of King's murder. Wheeling had two nights of arson, rock throwing, and minor vandalism, but police brought the situation under control without arrests. Black students at Wheeling High School walked out after staging a sit-down demonstration in a school hallway. Chesapeake, near Charleston, had an outbreak of vandalism, and in Dunbar, a white gunman wounded two black youths in a gun battle that raised alarms on the nearby campus of West Virginia State College. Despite the outbursts, calm generally prevailed in the state. War on Poverty community organizations helped maintain calm in Huntington. State Police Superintendent T. A. Welty reported that most people throughout the state had reacted with "good judgment" to the tragedy of King's assassination. State Human Rights Commission executive director Carl W. Glatt commended the lack of rioting and violence and noted the widespread spontaneous memorial services attended by both blacks and whites. State NAACP president Herbert H. Henderson vowed that the "NAACP shall continue to seek the equality of all West Virginians" in a peaceful manner.[28] Rev. Moses Newsome, pastor of the First Baptist Church in Charleston, recalled that King's only visit to West Virginia had been at his church in 1960. Newsome, who attended King's funeral in Atlanta, said, "Dr. King's impression of West Virginia then was that our state was considerably ahead of other so-called southern states in civil rights."[29]

Just two months after King's assassination, yet another murder shook the nation. On June 5, after winning the California Democratic primary, Senator Robert F. Kennedy of New York was assassinated by Sirhan Sirhan, a Palestinian Arab who resented Kennedy's pro-Israeli stance. Kennedy had toured southern West Virginia soon after announcing his candidacy, promising to help the state if elected president. His presence evoked the memory of his brother, and large crowds turned out in Princeton, Welch, Logan, and Charleston, as well as in towns throughout Mercer, Wyoming, Logan, Boone, and McDowell counties. Although his announcement had come too late to place his name on the West Virginia primary ballot, he hoped to win delegate commitments to support him in the Democratic convention, to be held in Chicago. Robert P. McDonough, who helped organize John F. Kennedy's 1960 primary victory in West Virginia, tried to pull the old organization together. The strategy was to support state party chairman James M. Sprouse for the gubernatorial nomination, hoping that Sprouse in turn would persuade uncommitted delegates to support Kennedy at the convention.[30]

A Long Hot Summer

During the summer of 1968, in the midst of a disturbing election year, West Virginia also experienced a series of tragic and near-tragic events that gave reason to be concerned about the future even as national and international events seemed to spin out of control. The state's major industry, coal, had long been seen as one of the country's most dangerous, and events of 1968 substantially reinforced that notion. On July 23, however, another major industry of the state long recognized as a major polluter of air and water demonstrated another of the perils of the new age when a major chlorine gas leak occurred at FMC Corporation's South Charleston chemical plant as a result of a warehouse fire. The gas caused extreme irritation to eyes and throats, which was in a sense a blessing because other more lethal gases might give no warning. Kanawha County police, fire department, and auxiliary units using gas masks mobilized during the night to evacuate some 1,500 residents of the city to higher ground. About thirty persons required hospitalization, and the FMC Corporation reported receipt of several hundred claims for injuries and property damage.[31] In the aftermath, Kanawha Valley Industrial Emergency Planning Council President Charles Jardin warned members of the Charleston Lions Club, meeting in the Daniel Boone Hotel, "There is probably as great a potential for a public disaster within five miles of where you are sitting as there is anywhere in the United States." When asked what might have happened had the gas been more lethal and less irritating, he said that it had been fortunate that there not more injuries or fatalities in the incident and pointed out that some of the plants in the Kanawha Valley used hydrogen cyanide, one of the deadliest gases in existence. He warned that no plans had been made to deal with a general public emergency that would result from a hydrogen cyanide leak. Charleston and Kanawha County had avoided a major disaster but the danger persisted.[32]

In addition to the tensions following the King assassination and unrest on traditionally black campuses at West Virginia State and Bluefield State, some urban areas of the state experienced racial disturbances in the summer and fall of 1968, raising concerns that West Virginia could face the kind of riots that had roiled many urban areas of the United States in 1967, the worst of which were in Detroit and

Newark.[33] The West Virginia Human Rights Commission reported that many of the problems in race relations in the state derived from local customs or traditions that violated both and state and federal civil rights laws. Many had to do with young people and summer recreational programs. Some communities held dances open to blacks and whites, but prohibited interracial dancing. Some public dances barred blacks altogether. Other communities allowed private groups to run publicly owned park, recreation, and swimming pool facilities on a white-only basis, raising protests among young blacks.[34] The commission urged that government officials move quickly to eliminate "all discriminatory practices in both the public and private sectors."[35]

In Charleston, the largest city in the state (having supplanted Huntington in 1958), protest demonstrations arose among black youths and residents in the Triangle area, where many renters faced eviction orders as the state razed the ramshackle buildings of the district to make way for a new water plant and interstate highway 64. By the summer of 1968, about half the buildings had been torn down, and ninety-nine additional families faced eviction notices. Because the housing being eliminated generally provided the lowest rents in the city, residents had difficulty finding alternative affordable housing, and this dilemma and other long-held grievances broke into the open during a series of demonstrations in early August. Part of the problem had to do with buck-passing among the State Road Commission, the city government of Charleston, and the federal Department of Housing and Urban Development as to which agency had responsibility for relocation assistance for Triangle families facing displacement. Many of the elderly black residents of the area had lived there all their lives and feared leaving the friends they could count on in times of need. Single mothers with children found it nearly impossible to find suitable affordable housing. Residents of the area suffered both unemployment and underemployment. In late July, the State Road Commission assured residents that none would be required to leave before the end of the year as long as they continued to pay rent to the SRC, which had purchased buildings in the path of the interstate.[36]

Continued unhappiness about the evictions and demolitions, the passage by city council of a housing code some residents said benefited only rats and roaches, high black unemployment, and the rising temperatures of early August led to two nights of demonstrations by some 500 residents of the area. On the second night several squads of policemen armed with riot gear surrounded the area but stayed well back of the Donnally Street playground in the heart of the Triangle, where the demonstrators gathered. Sometimes it seemed like a party, as they danced around a bonfire to the rhythm pounded out on an overturned garbage can. Police chief Dallas Bias listened to the shouted complaints and allowed the roiling discord to continue until 12:45 a.m.when he ordered the mostly teenage crowd to disperse. When they did not, the riot police moved into the playground area and herded them out amidst a shower of rocks, bottles, and cans. Gradually the protesters moved away, gathering in smaller groups on porches and steps, but the rest of the night passed in an uneasy truce between protestors and police.[37]

The next day, a Wednesday, Mayor Elmer Dodson and Police Chief Bias met with a delegation of young leaders under a tall tree at the Donnally Street playground. Twenty-six-year-old Jerry Harris, who had emerged as a spokesman for the Triangle residents, presented to the mayor a list of grievances, which had to do with long-standing issues including underemployment, relocation problems, unresponsive landlords, recreation facilities, and relations with police. The mayor ordered the Donnally Street pool to be kept open extra hours during the heat wave and the installation of bleachers on the playground where neighborhood youth played basketball games each evening. He also said his office would work with the local community action agency, AAY-Community Development, and the state Employment Security Office to address underemployment issues of Triangle residents. Harris agreed to cancel a protest rally scheduled for Wednesday night and thanked Bias and Dodson for meeting with his group and showing concern for the Triangle's problems. When a thunderstorm deluged Charleston on Wednesday night, bringing temperatures down, calm returned to the Triangle. The *Charleston Gazette*, which had been warning of the possibilities of problems in the city's slum areas for several years, praised the police and local leadership for averting serious riots, but called for calm, compassion, and understanding in dealing with the Triangle relocations and other more enduring issues in race relations, saying, "It is dangerous nonsense to believe the old ways can stand in Newark, Detroit, or Charleston."[38]

Just ten days after the chlorine gas leak and three days after the Triangle rumblings ended, Charleston and the state received another jolt on Saturday, August 10, when a twin engine Piedmont Airlines plane attempting a landing in foggy conditions crashed just short of the runway at Charleston's mountaintop airport, killing thirty-two. Three others died shortly thereafter, making the toll thirty-five and marking it as the worst air disaster in West Virginia history.[39] The crash at the Charleston airport, as shocking as the collapse of the Silver Bridge, added to the sense of unraveling that seemed to pervade the affairs of both the nation and West Virginia in 1968.

"The Lord Voted for Us": The 1968 Election

In late August, the 1968 Democratic National Convention, one of the most turbulent in the history of American politics, took place in Chicago. With Robert F. Kennedy dead, some of his supporters threw their backing to Senator George McGovern, but neither McGovern nor Eugene McCarthy had enough delegates to prevent Vice President Hubert Humphrey from winning the nomination on the first ballot. Events outside the hall, however, received more attention than the convention. Mayor Richard Daley, anticipating thousands of young antiwar and counterculture demonstrators, prepared by mobilizing almost 12,000 police and holding 7,500 national guardsmen in readiness. Because he denied demonstrators the right to march or hold peace rallies, confrontations occurred between policemen and demonstrators in the parks and in the area surrounding the convention. On the night of Humphrey's nomination, Daley's police attacked peaceful demonstrators seeking to march to the convention. The bloody scene in the streets in which steel-helmeted police attacked indiscriminately became the image of a convention that gave Humphrey the nomination but left the party divided and crippled facing the election.[40]

Jack Canfield, Governor Smith's press secretary, later recalled attending the convention with Smith and the West Virginia delegation: "It was the only time in my life I ever rode on a bus surrounded by policemen with rifles, or stayed at a hotel in which stink bombs were thrown by antiwar protestors." The West Virginia delegation's location at the front of the hall, just in front of Mayor Daley, gave them a good seat to hear Mayor Daley's unprintable epithets hurled at Senator Abraham Ribicoff, who in nominating George McGovern said that with McGovern, the "Gestapo tactics in the streets of Chicago" would not be tolerated.[41]

The divisions that troubled the national Democratic Party in Chicago also contributed to the disunity in the state party. State Democratic Chairman James M. Sprouse (who had supported Robert F. Kennedy for the presidential nomination) won the primary, defeating Robertson, whom many had perceived as the statehouse candidate. State Senator Paul Kaufman, a thoughtful advocate of structural change and the last best hope of the poverty warriors and grassroots reformers in the coalfields, came in third, in spite of an endorsement by the *Charleston Gazette*. The party faced the burden of the February indictments as ill-will continued between those who had supported Kennedy or McCarthy in the primary and those, like Governor Smith and leaders of the state AFL-CIO, who had supported Humphrey. Sprouse tried to avoid being linked to the "Statehouse Gang," so he had never shifted his support to Humphrey after Kennedy's murder. Some of the old machine Democrats even supported Arch Moore, the Republican nominee. When former governor Barron, after the indictments, found he could neither be the candidate nor the kingmaker in the Democratic Party, he threw the balance of his diminishing influence behind the Republican nominee. Moore had defeated Cecil Underwood in an extremely bitter fight in the Republican primary in which the candidates had exchanged charges of dishonesty and corruption. Barron, Clarence Elmore, and Burl Sawyers not only surreptitiously pulled strings for Moore, they also allegedly offered a bribe to Underwood to endorse Moore after the primary, and planted false stories about Sprouse in the *Charleston Daily Mail*. Underwood later claimed he rejected the offer of a high-paying executive position with Consolidation Coal Company as well as an appeal from Nixon's campaign manager John Mitchell, both arranged by former Democratic governor Barron, and instead remained silent in the general election. Presumably, Barron and his allies believed they might fare better with their legal problems with Moore rather than Sprouse as governor, though it is not clear why they might have thought that, since a victorious Moore would likely have little reason to help discredited and powerless Democrats. On the other hand, a victorious

Sprouse would have had a strong motivation to divorce himself from the discredited former leadership of the Democratic Party, and candidate Sprouse made that clear.[42]

Arch Moore artfully took advantage of the division and scandals that befell the Democrats, campaigning hard on the issue of corruption. His well-funded campaign also effectively used radio and television spots crafted by the Robert Goodman agency of Baltimore. Years later people would still recall the catchy campaign jingle popularly called "the Arch March."[43] Two days before the election, a helicopter carrying Moore attempted to land on the football field at Hamlin but hit the flagpole and crashed. Moore survived with some fractured ribs and was able to tell reporters the next day: "I'm convinced the Lord voted for us yesterday." Despite the impact of the February indictments, Byzantine intrigue in the Democratic Party, Moore's alleged support in Heavenly precincts, and the loss of Democratic presidential candidate Humphrey to Republican Richard Nixon (although Humphrey carried West Virginia), Moore defeated Sprouse by only 12,758 votes. Sprouse later won a lawsuit against the *Daily Mail*, and the Supreme Court of Appeals upheld an award of $250,000, ruling that the newspaper had knowingly characterized legitimate business transactions as fraudulent to lead the public to false conclusions about Sprouse's character. Carey McWilliams' 1946 characterization of the state as a rotten borough seemed to still be accurate.[44]

Campus Activism

In the spring of 1968, student uprisings affected many countries throughout the industrialized world. In France, student radicals contributed to bringing down the government of Charles DeGaulle. In Czechoslovakia, Soviet tanks rolled in during August ending student protests of Communist rule. Police battled militant students in West Germany, Japan, Italy, and Mexico. In the United States, some 400,000 students and faculty members joined antiwar protests on college and university campuses across the country.[45] Activism emerged at some West Virginia campuses, stimulated by the civil rights movement, opposition to the Vietnam War, and broader social and cultural issues (including those deriving from the distressing impact of the new machine age in West Virginia), but demonstrations and protests remained at a minimum at most state colleges and universities, perhaps because students at West Virginia schools came from a more rural and less affluent background than students at prestigious urban universities where the antiwar and other activist movements thrived. At West Virginia University, a small chapter of Students for a Democratic Society (SDS) struggled to survive in the early 1960s (fighting a losing battle in the name of antimilitarism to keep the mast of the USS *West Virginia* from being located on campus), but it rarely attracted more than ten to fifteen members. Joseph Gluck, the Dean of Students, later surmised that numbers remained low, because "many of our students were first generation, out of the hills and hollows, and couldn't afford to get caught up in the demonstrations."[46] Moreover, many WVU students had fathers, brothers, and cousins fighting in Vietnam.[47]

SDS at WVU faded in 1968, but in the spring of 1969 a party seeking to effect campus change, the Mountaineer Freedom Party, emerged. The Free University at WVU pushed for new curricular focuses, independently offering eight courses in the spring of 1969 including "Readings in Black Power," "Contemporary Philosophy," "The New Left in the Multiversity," "The Rape of Our Environment," and "How to Win Public Office and Influence a Society."[48] A free university at Marshall struggled to attract student support, but a debate over recognition of SDS in the spring of 1969 and the scheduled appearance of Marxist historian Herbert Aptheker escalated into something of a Red Scare in Huntington. A new president, Dr. Roland H. Nelson, had to face an aroused off-campus group headed by Mrs. E. Wyatt Payne, a civic leader and former member of the House of Delegates who had for years been Huntington's most outspoken anticommunist. Several local fundamentalist ministers also jumped into the fray, and their followers flooded Nelson's office with hundreds of letters denouncing SDS, Aptheker, and the Communist menace at Marshall. In spite of the community uproar and with the support of the faculty, Nelson recognized SDS (which disappeared in the early 1970s) and refused to interfere with the scheduled appearance by Aptheker. The next year Nelson left Marshall for a faculty position at the University of North Carolina at Greensboro.[49]

The most turbulent campus outbursts occurred at the traditionally black colleges, West Virginia State and Bluefield State, both of which by 1968 had white majorities. At West Virginia State, according to the recollection of William J. L. Wallace, who presided over great changes during his presidency (1953–1973), "the spirit of revolt" affected some black students who became frustrated as the transformation of the college failed to fulfill the promises of the civil rights era. He said that after hearing of the assassination of Martin Luther King on April 4, 1968, leaders of the state Human Rights Commission, fearing that black students on campus might be endangered by white students (perhaps because of the shooting in Dunbar, the predominantly white town near campus), sought to take over administration of the campus. Wallace claimed that state had no white students who wanted to attack black students. Instead, they had a group of black students "who wanted to make war on Dunbar." He recalled gathering with the angry group of black students in the student union and talking with them until their violent intentions subsided and cooler heads prevailed.[50]

Bluefield State, the other former all-black state college integrated as a consequence of *Brown v. Board of Education*, had a more turbulent transition than West Virginia State, though integration also led to enrollment growth at the Bluefield institution, from 310 students in 1955 to 1,145 in 1968, a year that became a decisive turning point in the college's history. As noted in chapter 3, largely because of the revolutionary changes in the coal industry, African Americans were leaving the southern West Virginia mining counties at a higher rate than whites, shrinking the enrollment base of what had been a black residential college. As the college grew in the years after *Brown*, white students who lived at home and commuted to the school accounted for most of the growth, becoming 62 percent of the enrollment by 1967. Similarly, the administration and faculty became predominantly white as the staff expanded. President Leroy Allen, an alumnus of the college, supported the civil rights activism of the students during the early 1960s and refused the business community's insistence that students be disciplined for participating in demonstrations. Apparently moved by complaints from Bluefield businessmen, the state board of education refused to approve a raise for Allen and then refused to renew his contract. Allen departed to become president of Cheyney State in Pennsylvania. Wendell Hardway, a white president, took over from an interim administrator in 1965. In the next three years, Hardway hired twenty-three new professors, all white, and many of them former associates of Hardway's at Glenville State College, who came to be called the "Glenville Gang." Hard feelings existed between the older mostly black faculty and the new white faculty.[51]

Over the years from 1954 to 1968, racial relations at the college grew increasingly difficult as black students resided in campus dormitories (and thus came more completely under the rules of the college administration) and white students commuted to classes. During the fall of 1967, students organized protests on campus. College authorities believed a fire in a campus building to have been set by student agitators, and disturbances broke out between blacks and whites at football games. Black students protested Concord College students' use of Confederate flags to celebrate touchdowns. On October 14 during the Bluefield State-Livingstone homecoming game, a student demonstration calling for Hardway's resignation forced the president and his family to move from one side of the field to the other under police escort. Agitation continued even as the president left at the end of the game under the protection of fifteen police officers. Pushing, shoving, rock throwing, and a general melee ensued. The college administration responded the following Monday by suspending ten students. Ten days after the melee, the State Board of Education held a closed hearing on campus as several hundred students demonstrated outside. The next day, students burned an effigy of President Hardway. As conditions at Bluefield State deteriorated, Governor Smith asked the West Virginia Human Rights Commission to investigate the situation. After six days of public hearings on campus, the commission reported to the governor that the incidents revealed "patterns of racial prejudice and racial discrimination" at the college, which it called "the 'step-child' institution of higher learning in West Virginia." The commission recommended integrating the dormitories, fairness in faculty and staff compensation, procedural guarantees for students in disciplinary hearings, and other changes at Bluefield State, but Governor Smith refused to endorse the recommendations or even to release the commission's full report to the public. He later defended his refusal by saying that the commission reached conclusions unjustified by the testimony in its hearings. On March 6, 1968, after a five-hour meeting involving Governor Smith, representatives of the NAACP, the Bluefield State College administration, and student leaders, the State Board of Education also refused to implement the commission's recommendations.

One week after Martin Luther King's assassination on April 4, the Human Rights Commission urged the governor to release its Bluefield report to the public to eliminate the misconceptions, speculations, and conjectures over what the press and others termed the "suppression" of the report. Smith, however, continued to refuse to make the report available to the public. On November 21, after college officials had curtailed campus activities and increased security upon receipt of an anonymous tip, a bomb exploded in the college's gymnasium, just as city and state police approached to conduct a search. No one was injured in the explosion. Police arrested and charged five persons, but no one was ever convicted. On December 9, 1968, just short of a year after he had received it, Governor Smith finally released the Human Rights Commission's Bluefield report in conjunction with a State Board of Education report that blamed the school's problems on "a militant cordon of students, faculty members, and outside interventionists." The Board of Education's report said the college's troubles came about because of the transition from an all-black to an integrated institution and especially in the resentment by some faculty at the changeover from a black to white administration. These faculty, abetted by a former administrator and outsiders "reportedly from the Black Power group" (as the Board of Education report said), encouraged the students to turn to demonstrations and violence. Clearly, the two agencies who had studied the situation at Bluefield State came away with different conclusions as to the origins of the difficulties and with different recommendations for the future of the institution. Unlike what HRC recommended, the future of Bluefield State would be as a predominantly white commuter college, not a residential college, as the dormitories on the campus closed their doors forever. The college administration replaced the men's dormitory with a parking lot. The women's dormitory, Mahood Hall, became the business department.[52]

After the release of the two reports, the State Board of Education came under fire from the *Charleston Gazette* and others. Recurring to the bridge analogy, the *Gazette* compared the situation at Bluefield State in the fall of 1967 to that of a bridge on the verge of collapse. The *Gazette* suggested that the Human Rights Commission had done a reasonably good job of recommending ways to fix the points of danger before a collapse, but that the governor and the State Board of Education had instead kept the report hidden for a year, refusing to implement its recommendations.[53] The state president of the NAACP, Herbert Henderson, called the State Board of Education's report "pure whitewash" and charged that it sought to cover up an effort to drive southern West Virginia blacks from the campus. He called for the firing of President Hardway and six others on his staff.[54]

On December 3, 1968, Bluefield State reopened for the first time since the November 21 bombing, but the dormitories remained closed, and armed guards of the Pinkerton Detective Agency checked the identity of anyone on campus after 4:30 p.m. The college arranged off-campus housing for the students with dormitory contracts. The State Board of Education described the campus as calm. Human Rights Commission chairman Rabbi Samuel Cooper described it as, "quiet as Czechoslovakia" (the eastern European country that had recently been brought under Russian military control).[55]

One of the most critical responses from the African American community to the Bluefield situation and to the general state of race relations in the state at the end of 1968 came from Rev. Charles Smith, pastor of the First Baptist Church of Huntington. Speaking to a gathering of black professionals and businessmen in Charleston, Smith, long active in anti-poverty and housing efforts in Huntington, attacked both black leaders in the state and the notion of racial toleration in West Virginia. As ugly as the Bluefield State situation was, he said, it stood as a symbol of the state's transition from segregation to integration in which the African American came out as the "real loser." Black students, he maintained, were amalgamated, not integrated, and shut out of most aspects of school life. Inhibited by the hostile white atmosphere, blacks took part in few activities. He cited the example of high school choirs in Huntington. Only six out of 189 black high school students participated in the choirs. The only integration in any aspect of school life, he said, occurred in athletics.[56]

The historians of Bluefield State College conclude that the decision to close the dormitories "had a catastrophic effect on the school's traditional mission and heritage. Without on-campus housing, Bluefield State could not attract the students who had historically filled its classrooms."[57] For better or worse, however, the changing demographics of southern West Virginia brought about by the new machine age (which meant falling black enrollments as black miners left the region in large numbers) combined with the impact of *Brown* made Bluefield State's traditional role as a segregated black residential college anachronistic. The example of West Virginia State College suggests that it would have been possible for the college to integrate and to retain its dormitories even as it moved to a predominantly commuter basis, a path recommended by the Human Rights Commission. The State Board of Education and Governor Smith, however, closed the dormitories, because they and the college administration wanted to quash any hint of black militancy.

John L.'s Broken Dream

The bright hopes for progressivism and social justice that the UMWA had earlier inspired among miners and Appalachian communities had faded in the 1950s as John L. Lewis, still revered by the miners, ran the union like a fiefdom. The humanitarian possibilities raised by the creation of the Welfare and Retirement Fund did not fit with the UMWA's drive in the 1950s and 1960s to create an economically efficient new structure in the coalfields. Throughout the 1950s (as noted in chapter 1), an aging Lewis cooperated with an industry determined to survive through mechanization. As mining jobs faded, Lewis compounded the damage by failing to devise programs to help miners find new livelihoods. He also played fast and loose with members' dues and welfare and retirement funds monies, engaging in ill-advised financial transactions that resulted in millions of dollars of losses.[58] Faced with recurrent fiscal crises, the fund managers from time to time cut programs that served the unemployed, the disabled, and the widowed, those whom the plan originally had intended to help.[59]

The depressed state of the industry in the 1950s and early 1960s combined with the rising number of pensioners led the fund to expend more than it received in royalties. Lewis ordered cuts in expenditures rather than demanding higher royalty payments to cover the rising deficits.[60] Along with periodic additional benefit cuts, in 1962 the trustees also ended the UMWA's brief and noble experiment in providing medical care through its own hospitals, as they put the ten Southern Appalachian hospitals of the fund up for sale, including the central hospitals at Beckley and Williamson and a satellite hospital at Man. They also lowered the qualifying age to fifty-five to encourage aging miners to retire rather than to take jobs at nonunion mines. The trustees further required that a miner's last year at work be at a union mine in order to qualify for a pension, a slap at long-time union miners who found themselves compelled to take nonunion work in a shrinking job market at the end of their working years.[61]

Lewis stepped aside as president in 1960, but he continued to dictate the policies of the welfare and retirement funds. In 1963 William Anthony "Tony" Boyle, who had been Lewis's chief assistant since 1947, became the new UMWA president. The Boyle regime continued the abuses that had grown up in Lewis's era and added some. Coal companies exploited the weakened leadership of the union by ignoring or undermining health and safety requirements, grievance procedures, and contract provisions, sometimes with Boyle's approval. Boyle had learned the job at Lewis's elbow and tried to run the union as his mentor had, but Boyle lacked Lewis's charismatic personality and presence, and unlike Lewis, who manipulated conventions to provide a rigged legitimacy, Boyle, lacking subtlety, bothered with no pretenses.[62]

Several distinct groups emerged in the 1960s that presaged the black lung rebellion and the movement to reform the UMWA. In northern West Virginia, miners joined others in eastern Ohio and southwestern Pennsylvania to become the center of swelling rank and file discontent in the union. In southern West Virginia, disabled miners and widows periodically tried to call attention to the human consequences of the union's changes in eligibility requirements for pensions and medical coverage. The canceling of hospital cards in July 1960 led to organizations of disabled miners and wildcat protest strikes in southern West Virginia.[63]

Though these early protests over the loss of medical coverage faded quickly, they clearly previewed the kind of passion that Appalachian miners could bring to bear on an issue of critical importance to them.[64] During the 1950s with layoffs advancing like a cancer through the mining regions, miners had dared not protest the conditions they faced. They knew they could easily be replaced if they complained, and most had been inculcated with an unquestioning attitude of union solidarity and faith in John L. Lewis during the struggles of the 1930s and 1940s. By the early 1960s, miners became less committed to blind faith in the union leadership and more ready to speak out because they had less respect for Boyle than they had for Lewis, who remained an iconic figure among the rank and file. Also, in 1964, employment began to level off and then increase slightly. By the late 1960s, ironically, companies began to complain of a shortage of miners. The supply of laid-off miners had been depleted by retirements or emigration from the coalfields, and the labor needs of mining companies had changed.[65]

As miners who had entered the work force in the Depression era or in the 1940s had aged during the 1950s, few younger workers had been hired as the older cohort of diggers and loaders had been replaced by machines. By the mid-1960s, with the average age of miners rising and technology becoming increasingly sophisticated, the industry faced a shortage of skilled workers. Personnel officers had difficulty hiring needed college graduates and mining engineers.[66] A generational dynamic also affected the nature of the labor force by the late 1960s as Vietnam veterans began to replace the World War II generation. Some of these new miners had long hair and beards and wore head bands. Bynum "Junior" Gilbert, a retired Raleigh County miner, told an interviewer in 1973 that the new generation "had got some education, got smarter, done their service, maybe fought over there in Vietnam. They came back and they seen their daddies dying. They knew something was wrong. They figured they weren't going to be as dumb as people made miners out to be." Gilbert also said Boyle "went around saying that hippies were interfering with the union. That shows how long it's been since he's been near a mine. We got hippies at Stotesbury with beards and sandals and the rest. They work as hard as anyone."[67]

With discontent toward Boyle's leadership rising among the miners, Boyle continued to conduct contract negotiations as Lewis had, arriving at agreements with an operators' representative without any consultation with representatives of the rank and file. Miners, however, signaled a new attitude in the 1960s with thousands walking out from time to time to protest contracts that failed to deal with health and safety issues or to oppose what they saw as unfair treatment by management. These events show a cumulatively rising discontent in the rank and file of the UMWA, a union that had long marched obediently to the drumbeat of John L. Lewis and his chorus of yes men. Over the decade the climate in the coalfields transformed from acquiescence and resignation to discontent and rebellion and helped shape the attitudes and tactics of the black lung movement.⁶⁸

Events in the coalfields attracted much attention and comment by newspapers, magazines, television documentaries, sociological reports, and books, and by the mid-1960s many songwriters sought to capture and to put in more broadly accessible and popular terms the growing despair of the coalminers. Warner Records recordings by Jean Ritchie, a Kentucky singer and writer who had moved to New York, voiced the laments of coal country people. Liner notes on the album *A Time for Singing* credited two mining songs, *The L&N Doesn't Stop Here Anymore* and *The Blue Diamond Mines*, to "Than Hall, an old-time resident of the Hazard, Kentucky coalfield," but Ritchie herself actually wrote the songs, using the pseudonym to protect her mother and other family members who still lived in Kentucky.⁶⁹ Though set in Kentucky, both songs could just as easily apply to many West Virginia communities or other mining areas of Appalachia. *Blue Diamond Mines* bewails the closing of the mine and the failure of the union:

John L. had a dream, but it's broken it seems;
now our union's a-lettin' us down.
Last week they took away my hospital card,
said 'Why don't you leave this old town?'

Billy Edd Wheeler, who grew up at Highcoal, Boone County, and attended Warren Wilson and Berea colleges and the Yale School of Drama, wrote *Coal Tattoo*, a song of protest against the machines, the company, and the union. The title refers to the bluish marks miners get from flying bits of coal in coal mine blasts.⁷⁰ Songs like those of Ritchie and Wheeler received wide circulation as others recorded them or sang them at miners' rallies.⁷¹

"78–4": Hominy Falls and Farmington

The outrage caused by the Hominy Falls and Farmington mining disasters of 1968 added to the already simmering coalfield discontents of the 1960s and resulted in a widespread and emotional grassroots rebellion and protest movement. The first incident occurred on May 6,

1968, at the Saxsewell No. 8 mine of Gauley Coal and Coke Company near Hominy Falls in Nicholas County, when a continuous miner crew cut into a water-filled abandoned mine and a wall of water rushed through the workings, trapping twenty-five men underground. After five agonizing days of extensive pumping to remove water from the mine, rescuers brought fifteen men to the surface. No contact had been made with the other trapped miners, and most newsmen and rescue experts doubted that others could be saved. In what the press labeled miraculous at the time, after another five days of continued pumping, rescuers brought six more men out. They then found the bodies of four men who had died in the initial rush of water into the mine. The official finding of an inquiry by the state Department of Mines held "engineering errors" to be the cause of the accident. The tragedy underlined the dangers of blundering into the flooded and abandoned mines of long-forgotten previous operations and the need to retain maps of former mines.[72] The Hominy Falls incident, like the collapse of the Silver Bridge, received wide coverage including national news services, radio, and television, and the media dubbed the outcome "the miracle of Hominy Falls." Just as television helped to shape opposition to the war in Vietnam, it also aroused coal miners. During the extensive media coverage of the incident, some of the miners and their families also objected to the insensitivity of the press and television crews, who focused on family members outside the mine in their excruciating wait for some shred of good news of their loved ones inside. In their frustration, at one point some miners awaiting news of their fellow workers at Hominy Falls threw rocks at reporters and film crews.[73]

The Farmington disaster on November 20, 1968, provided the ultimate flash point for rising rank-and-file discontent. A little town six miles west of Fairmont in northern West Virginia, Farmington (also near Mannington) was the site of Consolidation Coal Company's Number 9 mine. On that November day, the mine exploded, killing seventy-four men. The mine operated in a coal bed known to contain high amounts of methane gas. It also used the most advanced mining equipment, huge continuous miners that tore the coal from its bed using giant rotary bits, a method that eliminated the need to use explosives, but produced vast quantities of highly combustible coal dust. The combination of methane and coal dust if ignited could produce a deadly explosion.

The Federal Mine Safety Act of 1952 required rock dusting, a procedure that reduces the flammability of coal dust by diluting it with chemically inert rock dust. In all sixteen inspections of Consol Number 9 in the five years before November 20, 1968, the Bureau of Mines had cited the mine for insufficient rock dusting.[74]

Smoke rises from the Llewellyn Portal of Consolidation Coal Company's Number 9 Mine at Farmington, after the explosion on November 20, 1968. Department of Mines Collection, West Virginia State Archives.

In the aftermath of the explosion, various government, business, and union officials traveled to Farmington, and many made (in time-honored tradition) disingenuous statements to the assembled families and media. Governor Smith arrived the afternoon of the blast and told those assembled in the company store: "We must remember that this is a hazardous business, and what has occurred here is one of the hazards of mining."[75] The next day, unlike his mentor, John L. Lewis, who had always expressed outrage in the face of mine disasters, UMWA President Tony Boyle told the crowd, in a statement seen and heard on national television: "I share the grief. I've lost relatives in a mine explosion. But as long as we mine coal, there is always this inherent danger of explosion." He went on to praise Consolidation Coal Company as "one of the best companies to work with as far as cooperation and safety are concerned." Representing the Department of the Interior, assistant secretary J. Cordell Moore also praised the company, saying it had done all it could "to make this a safe mine. We don't understand why these things happen, but they do happen." John Roberts, the director of public relations for Consolidated Coal Company, told the assembled at a press conference, "This is something we have to live with."[76] All of these officials of the state, union, company, and federal government covered up, ignored, or did not bother to check into the record of mine inspection citations, which showed that the company had been lax in carrying out the rock dusting necessary to maintain minimal safety in a gassy mine. Consolidation's record in these matters reflected a general cavalier attitude toward safety requirements from the industry and the U.S. Bureau of Mines as repeated citations for violations went unheeded and inspired no sense of urgency.[77]

The widely broadcast and televised comments at Farmington outraged miners. Though accustomed to hearing company spokesmen and even government officials make ritualistic excuses in the aftermath of mine disasters, it infuriated them that their own spokesman now mouthed the same phrases. That Boyle would defend Consolidation Coal Company's safety record while seventy-eight UMWA brothers had died and remained buried in the mine convinced many rank-and-file miners that the union leadership no longer spoke for or defended the miners' interests.[78] As in the Hominy Falls disaster, television, now widely present in miners' homes, served to amplify and to make more immediate the horror in a way that newspapers and radios had not in the past. *The Nation* reporter Robert Sherrill suggested that the extensive attention on national television helped miners to begin to see themselves differently as "the drama-hunting cameras of national television" took advantage of the season (with Thanksgiving just a few days away and Christmas not far behind) to focus on the tragedy in West Virginia. As the argument continued over whether to seal the mine and thereby put an end to any hope for the trapped men, Sherrill wrote, "Day after day . . . . miners saw themselves and their occupation assume new dimensions of importance in the nation's eyes."[79] In the end, there would be no miracle at Farmington as there had been at Hominy Falls. In early December, company officials, with the concurrence of the U.S. Bureau of Mines, the State Department of Mines, and the UMWA, decided to call off recovery operations and to seal the mine to stop the possibility of further explosions, entombing the miners inside the mine.[80]

Not all officials responded to Farmington with fatalistic acceptance. When the fate of the trapped miners became clear, Congressman Ken Hechler, who had introduced the Johnson administration mine safety bill two months before, responded with outrage, attacking federal and state mining laws and the appearance of collusion between inspectors and coal companies. "Coal miners don't have to die," he wrote. "From Monongah to Mannington the same script is grimly familiar. The national spotlight is focused on a disaster. The company officials promise that everything possible is being done. The surviving coal miners and their sons say that, of course, they will go back to the status quo until the next disaster strikes in the coal mines." Hechler insisted that "coal miners have a right to live, to breathe, and to be protected by twentieth century safety standards."[81]

One federal official, lame-duck Secretary of the Interior Stuart Udall, whose department had ultimate responsibility for mine safety inspections, spoke with surprising candor at a mine safety conference in Washington several weeks after the Farmington explosion. Blaming all responsible parties, the individual miners, government at all levels, the industry, and the UMWA, Udall said, "We have accepted, even condoned, an attitude of fatalism that belongs to an age darker than the deepest recesses of any coal mine." To say simply "coal mining is an inherently dangerous business" or "as long as coal is mined, men will inevitably die underground," Udall insisted, could no longer be accepted.[82]

Black Lung: "The Road to a Dusty Death"

The outrage over Farmington further energized emerging coalfield concerns about health, safety, and welfare. In addition to the constant threats to life and limb from explosions, roof falls, and electrical and mechanical mishaps of various kinds, miners also faced a more insidious danger in the very air they breathed. Coal miners in America had long suffered from lung disorders, and researchers in the Bureau of Mines and the Public Health Service had carried out studies as early as the mid-1920s pointing to a serious disease caused by coal dust. These findings failed to persuade those in the coal industry and medical profession who clung to the "sheep-like notion" that coal mining provided a healthy work environment.[83] As early as the 1930s, doctors in England recognized coal worker's pneumoconiosis (CWP) as a disease, and British law recognized it by 1943. In America, however, much of the medical community refused to accept CWP as a serious disease and insisted that coal dust actually benefited miners, helping them to ward off silicosis, a disease that came from sustained inhalation of free silica dioxide or sand.[84]

In West Virginia during the Depression, the state responded to the Hawks Nest tragedy (in which hundreds of workers died of silicosis after working to blast a three-mile long tunnel to supply water to a Union Carbide and Chemical Corporation metallurgical complex) by establishing a compensation fund for death or disability from silicosis, but the 1935 law made it almost impossible to make a successful claim.[85] Over the years, the legislation had not been changed to accommodate the growth of information about lung diseases other than silicosis. A new medical perspective began to emerge after the establishment of the UMWA Miners Welfare and Retirement Fund. Administrators of the fund and some practicing physicians affiliated with fund-supported clinics conducted research, held conferences, and published articles in professional journals to promote recognition of coal workers' pneumoconiosis by the medical profession. The conventional belief held that silica alone caused serious lung disease in miners, but support gradually grew for the idea that coal dust itself caused a disease. In 1954, Dr. Joseph E. Martin, a physician in Elkins, West Virginia, in an article in the *American Journal of Public Health* used data from British medical research and his own clinical observations of 400 bituminous coal miners to advance the argument that exposure to coal dust caused a progressive, disabling, and ultimately fatal disease. Dr. Loren E. Kerr, Director of Occupational Health for the United Mine Workers and the staff of the Welfare and Retirement Fund promoted conferences on pneumoconiosis, and the fund sponsored speaking tours by British doctors who had studied the disease. A 1959 study by the Pennsylvania Department of Health (relying on cooperation of the medical staff at clinics affiliated with the fund) and a later medical survey by the U.S. Public Health Service found persuasive evidence of the disease with rising incidence related to age, years of employment, and coal dust exposure based on the job most frequently performed. Because the new machines in underground mining produced vast amounts of coal dust, the likelihood of contracting the disease grew with the mechanization of the mines.[86]

The disease, incurable and progressive, breaks down the ability of lungs to transfer oxygen to the bloodstream. The victim becomes increasingly short of breath and may suffer from bronchitis, emphysema, and heart failure. Working in a dust-free atmosphere will not reverse the progression of the disease. The state compensation board, however, routinely turned down miners who sought compensation for silicosis, because their X-rays provided no persuasive evidence. In most cases, those who were turned down had CWP, but they had no choice but to go back to work with impaired lungs.[87]

Despite the British studies as well as the Pennsylvania Department of Health study and the U.S. Public Health Service survey, the efforts of the UMWA Welfare and Retirement Fund and the doctors associated with it, the medical profession resisted accepting the notion of coal workers' pneumoconiosis (CWP) or what came to be called "black lung disease." The UMWA itself, committed to maximizing coal production in cooperation with industrial ownership, seemed to be pulled in two directions on the issue. While Dr. Kerr made the case for CWP, the union leadership did little to promote mine health and safety after the passage of the 1952 law. Black lung historian Alan Derickson says John L. Lewis understood the relationship between black lung and the very mechanization that the union embraced, but cynically did nothing about it. Richard P. Mulcahy, in his history of the UMWA Fund, recognizes that "while the Fund was advancing and fighting for the good of the miner, the union was gradually retreating from the field" but he says—perhaps too generously—that it was Lewis's pragmatism rather than cynicism that left the UMWA immobilized. Lewis the pragmatist believed he could always reconcile conflicting positions, but, Mulcahy says, "unfortunately the contradiction of mechanization versus black lung was so fundamental" that the two could not be easily reconciled.[88]

By 1968, Tony Boyle knew that miners wanted action on black lung, and belatedly he threw union support behind efforts to do something, but it turned out to be the classic case of too little, too late. Through most of its nine days, the UMWA convention at Denver in 1968 focused on sycophantic praise of Tony Boyle. Nevertheless, Dr. Lorin Kerr of the Welfare and Retirement Fund, whose efforts to promote black lung awareness had been circumscribed by the leadership's more immediate goal of cooperating with the industry, appeared on the program at Denver. In effect unleashed for the occasion, Kerr brought the delegates to their feet with a speech "Coal Workers Pneumoconiosis: The Road to a Dusty Death." He described the disease, called for a program to lower dust levels, and advocated efforts to get black lung disease accepted as a compensable condition.[89]

In the end it took a powerful grassroots movement among the coal miners and their wives and widows themselves, the efforts of three West Virginia rebel doctors, the help of VISTA volunteers and poverty workers, and the support of a renegade congressman, Ken Hechler, to compel the medical establishment as well as the state and federal governments to recognize the disease.[90] The three doctors, Isadore Erwin Buff, Donald Rasmussen and Hawey "Sonny" Wells Jr., faced not only the resistance of the coal industry but also skepticism from the medical profession. For many years Buff, a Charleston cardiologist, had railed against the coal industry and the medical establishment with a "take-no-prisoners" approach. Disorganized as a speaker, he nevertheless conveyed passionate conviction, dramatized the issue, and stirred coal miner audiences. For most of his career he concentrated on a lucrative Charleston cardiology practice. He began speaking out on air and water pollution problems as early as 1963. Appointed to the state Air Pollution Control Commission by Governor Smith in 1967, he accused the governor of covering up evidence of water pollution in the Charleston area. He became a black lung activist in his early sixties, an age when most doctors begin to retire. In mid-1968 he began to speak out, he said, because of patients he observed in his cardiology practice. Coal company doctors referred miners to him who had collapsed on the job, apparent victims of heart attacks. He insisted that the company doctors misdiagnosed the problem. Most of these patients had lung disease, not heart disease. State workers' compensation covered lung disease but not heart attacks, so if the company doctor recorded the diagnosis as a heart attack, the miner could neither receive compensation nor would he likely be able to continue working. Unable to get anywhere in his effort to gain official recognition of black lung as an occupational disease, Buff began to drive out to the coal mining communities of southern West Virginia to talk to miners in meeting halls and schoolrooms. Rather than using the clinical term pneumoconiosis, Buff told miners that they all had black lung disease. "Tell me brother," he would say, "how much longer do you think you're going to live? You've got the black lung. You can't walk ten steps without resting. You can't breathe. You spit up black juice. But the company says you have compensationitis." Though he would dramatically announce that they would all die of black lung, the miners cheered him, because they knew that what they were finally hearing from a doctor confirmed their own experiences.[91]

Dr. Donald Rasmussen of the Appalachian Regional Hospital in Beckley (one of the hospitals formerly operated by the UMWA) and his colleagues (including pathologist Hawey "Sonny" Wells) examined thousands of coal miners. Rasmussen observed that many coal miners displayed extreme shortness of breath even when chest X-rays and pulmonary function tests proved negative. After testing breathless miners' abilities to transfer oxygen into the blood through blood gas analyses, he found that miners with breathlessness had abnormalities in their abilities to oxygenate blood. He concluded that this abnormality had to be occupation related.[92] Like Buff, Rasmussen had certified men as disabled by pneumoconiosis only to have the state compensation commission board rule them ineligible for compensation using the rationale that pneumoconiosis was a benign disease.[93]

For a brief period in 1964 and 1965, the U.S. Public Health Service supported the research at Beckley. Working on a government salary and with enhanced laboratory facilities, Rasmussen and his associates began to focus more on their pneumoconiosis research. In 1966, however, Senator Byrd arranged to have the research project moved to the state medical center at West Virginia University. Called the Appalachian Laboratory for Occupational Respiratory Diseases, the doctors at Morgantown, headed by an Englishman, Dr. Keith Morgan, worked with much less urgency. They examined relatively few miners, and they disagreed with the Beckley group on its fundamental conclusion. The Morgantown group agreed that many coal miners had CWP, but they contended that the disease was benign in its early or simple phase. Only when the disease reached a "complicated" phase did it become problematic, and at that point, it could be detected by X-ray. Rasmussen and the Beckley group argued that black lung disabled miners even in the simple phase when X-ray evidence might not be conclusive. To accurately diagnose the disease, they argued that breathing and exercise tests should be used in conjunction with X-rays. More than just a debate among laboratory researchers about an esoteric topic, the fate of thousands of miners who sought compensation payments for their disease depended on the outcome. A great deal of coal industry and taxpayer money also was at stake.[94]

Organizing the Black Lung Coalition

While Buff began to stir the miners of the Kanawha Valley and Rasmussen and his associates sought to make the clinical case for a broader understanding of black lung disease, VISTA volunteers Craig Robinson, a twenty-five-year-old from Buffalo, New York, and Richard Bank, a recent graduate of the University of Pennsylvania law school, had been talking to miners in the area around Beckley. Robinson read everything he could about pneumoconiosis, talked to Rasmussen in Beckley, and gave short talks to miners. He and Bank also began to draft legislation to make necessary changes in the compensation law. Other VISTA and anti-poverty workers, including Molly Marshall in McDowell County and Bruce McKee in Logan, brought miners to hear Robinson's presentations. Robinson said the early meetings generated intense excitement among the black lung organizers, characterized by reporter K. W. Lee as "a curious collection of union miners, disabled miners, VISTA workers, and anti-poverty workers and miners' widows."[95]

Meanwhile, in mid-September, two months before the Farmington explosion, stories began to appear of miners organizing to seek compensation for black lung. Joe Malay, a veteran miner from Clifftop, Fayette County, organized a group of miners to visit with the UMWA's District 29 representative in Beckley, James Leeber. After a three-hour meeting, Leeber refused to help. A similar delegation from Twilight, Boone County, led by miner Ivan White went to Charleston to meet with George Burnette, the union's compensation lawyer at District 17 headquarters. Burnette also refused to help. For UMWA members to seek help beyond the union or through independent action went against union lore, which looking to the distant past of competing unions, warned against the threat of "dual unionism."[96]

In November, Robinson and Bank went to Montgomery, a mining and state college town south of Charleston, and heard Buff for the first time. They were amazed to hear him say what VISTAs had been saying for years. "We were ecstatic," Robinson said. Robinson played an important role promoting awareness about black lung as something of an intermediary between the doctors and the miners, distributing information and arranging meetings.[97]

Late in November, after the Farmington explosion, Joe Malay invited both Dr. Buff and Dr. Rasmussen to attend a meeting of miners at the Clifftop community center to speak on black lung. Buff provided the drama and Rasmussen provided the expert science. They had not known each other before the Clifftop meeting, but they quickly became a team promoting greater understanding of black lung among the miners and the general public. A week later Buff and Rasmussen met again in Washington on the eve of a mine safety conference at the Interior Department. Joining them at the Hay-Adams House was Dr. Hawey A. "Sonny" Wells, a pathologist who had worked with Rasmussen in Beckley in the mid-1960s. He had left Beckley in 1966 to head the chest laboratory at a Johnstown, Pennsylvania, hospital. He also taught at the West Virginia University Medical School. The three doctors agreed to organize a letterhead organization called Physicians for Miners' Health and Safety. Dr. Buff would be chair, Dr. Rasmussen, secretary, and Dr. Wells, coordinator. Jeanne Rasmussen, the doctor's wife and activist/coalfield journalist, agreed to be press secretary. In the weeks that followed, the doctors traveled together to many towns throughout the state to speak to coal miner groups about black lung.[98]

At first they appeared before small groups—25 or 30 people would be a good crowd—but in late December the movement began to take off. Coal miner Woodrow Mullins, a black lung victim, helped organize a meeting in Marmet, a little town on the Kanawha River near

Charleston. Mullins's daughter wrote letters to state senators and delegates and sent posters to union locals to invite them to Marmet. Over 300 people attended on a Sunday, three days before Christmas 1968, mostly coal miners representing all the UMWA locals in the Kanawha Valley. After hearing Buff and Rasmussen, the gathering voted unanimously to organize a statewide drive to approach the legislature en masse to seek a change in state compensation laws to recognize black lung.[99]

Conclusion

Given the cultural and political turmoil in 1968, the shock of Tet in Vietnam and the murders of King and Kennedy profoundly disheartened many and contributed to a growing sense of a society unraveling. These events also marked the waning of the era of resurgent liberalism that had begun with John F. Kennedy's election and hastened a turn to the right, in both the country and in West Virginia, where the Democratic statehouse regime that had controlled the state almost continuously since 1933 gave way to Republican Arch Moore.[100] The Silver Bridge disaster led to federal legislation requiring national bridge inspections. The state legislature established the Purchasing Practices and Procedures Commission and enacted legislation seeking to change the way the state did business, but the state Supreme Court of Appeals found the legislation unconstitutional, and political corruption continued.[101] The Fair Elections movement fell disappointingly short of its goals, but it did shine some light on corrupt procedures, bring about a cleanup of voter registration rolls, and call the attention of the U.S. Justice Department to political corruption in southern West Virginia. Campus turmoil in the state did not reach the levels of revolt as in more urban areas (though in the spring of 1970, Governer Moore would dispatch troopers to the West Virginia University campus to quell antiwar demonstrations there),[102] but events at Bluefield State College confirmed a basic transformation of the institution's traditional mission as a black residential college.

As the horrible year 1968 drew to a close, something new stirred in the Appalachian Mountains. The reaction to the disasters at Hominy Falls and Farmington brought to an end a long period in which coal miners had felt helpless in their quest to reverse the decline in employment and the increase in workplace and other dangers brought about by their union's deal with management, which had led to the new machine age. In the 1950s, they suffered in silence, joined the Great Migration, or in some cases, went on relief or accepted welfare. In the 1960s, discontent with their leadership grew. In the turbulent setting after Farmington, one of the most effective grassroots labor movements in the history of the state and of the country emerged in the coalfields.

7

An Appalachian Reawakening:
The Black Lung Association, Miners for Democracy, and the New Feminism

> Black lungs, full of coal dust
> Coal miners must breathe it or bust.
> Black lungs, gasping for breath
> With black lungs we are choking to death.
>
> — Song written by West Virginia coal miner James E. Wyatt

> For years miners had been beaten down. People thought we couldn't organize, that we were scared and dumb. But we showed them. And we showed that SOB Tony Boyle, who praised the company after Farmington.
>
> — Retired coal miner Lewis "Pops" Coleman, of Disabled Miners and Widows of West Virginia

The election of Richard Milhaus Nixon as president and Arch Alfred Moore Jr. as governor in 1968 signaled a turn to the right and away from the liberal programs of the 1960s, but the period of the late 1960s and early 1970s nevertheless brought about a rare expression of grassroots political and social activism in Appalachia and unusual successes for those who resisted the conventional wisdom and traditional elites and sought to address some of the problems of era. Though the War on Poverty continued for a time in a modified fashion, much of the reform impulse of 1968 and afterward sprang from the grassroots: active and retired coal miners, their wives, disgruntled small property owners, and others. The experiences gained by indigenous community leaders during the community action programs of the 1960s helped to maintain the energy behind some of the movements. VISTA also continued to be active, and former VISTA members and Appalachian Volunteers remained in the state, lending their experience, commitment, and passion to public interest organizations and to help grassroots movements.

West Virginia reformers continued to derive their greatest motivation from the dire consequences of the coal industry's technological revolution. Beyond West Virginia's unique Appalachian circumstances, West Virginians also reacted to the issues of race, gender, and the Vietnam War that stirred the nation. Just as the Mingo County Fair Elections Committee had sought, with mixed results, to tamper with entrenched political corruption but found the old order remarkably resilient, so other reformers foundered on the rocks of reaction. Doors began to open for women to play a larger role in politics and other matters. Taken together, the movements of this period represent a moment in West Virginia and Appalachian history when popular forces challenged the dominant economic and political powers with some striking successes. In the end, though the reformers fell short of achieving all that they sought, they had demonstrated the power of organization and the myth of Appalachian fatalism.[1]

"How Not to Do It": The Waning of the Poverty War

Though some of the impetus for grassroots action from War on Poverty programs survived the election of 1968, poverty warriors understood that funding community action programs now would be even more difficult, and they would have to seek a lower profile and to cultivate private sources of revenue. Huey Perry continued for a time after the election as director of the Mingo County Economic Opportunity Commission, but he knew the future looked unpromising. He later wrote: "There seemed good reason to fear for the survival of the Mingo County EOC, which had become the rural model for liberals in the Democratic Administration, and now with the Nixon Administration would probably be regarded as the prime example of 'how not to do it.'"[2] Even with the revelations of political corruption in Mingo and the election of a Republican governor, Perry's nemesis, Mingo Democrat boss Noah Floyd, still wielded enough power to be named chairman of the state senate elections committee and to see to it that the state Department of Employment Security named his brother, George Floyd, to head the Work Incentive program in Mingo.³

Perry's premonition that the Mingo model for community action would no longer be in favor in Washington turned out, of course, to be right. With Republicans in control in Washington, OEO, administered by former Republican congressman and future secretary of defense Donald Rumsfeld (and with the assistance of future vice president Richard Cheney), now criticized poverty agencies that had most successfully met the mandate of "maximum feasible participation of the poor." Such activities, the agency now claimed, only split communities and undermined well-established local institutions. Under the guidance of the new regime, the agency emphasized effective management, reducing the former emphasis on participation of the poor. Moreover, the agency warned that demonstrations against elected officials would result in the withdrawal of federal funds.⁴ TRI-CAP, which combined the community action programs of Kanawha, Boone, and Putnam counties, took the free hot lunch program from the Boone County Association of the Needy (B-CAN) and gave it to the newly organized Boone County Community Association. In the crowning irony, TRI-CAP designated Manual Arvon, Seth High School principal and outspoken critic of VISTA, B-CAN, and the free lunch program, as Boone County's "representative of the poor" on the TRI-CAP board.⁵

In a more promising trend of the new era, community action agencies encouraged the development of small cooperatives in agriculture and arts and crafts to generate supplementary income for low-income people. A farmers' cooperative in Wayne County specializing in tomatoes, beans, corn, and strawberries operated its own packing plant and shipped to several large West Virginia grocery chains. A similar cooperative in the Elk River area of Kanawha County marketed its products in the Charleston farmers' market. The Southern Regional Cooperative Business Development Corporation (SRCC), an OEO-funded organization, had its headquarters in Beckley and helped cooperatives in Raleigh, Summers, Mercer, McDowell, Wyoming, Mingo, Wayne, and Lincoln counties. SRCC sent an outreach staff throughout the region to educate cooperative members in bookkeeping and cooperative management. It helped groups to run small enterprises including a quilting bee in Lincoln County (made up of six elderly ladies), a beekeepers' cooperative in Raleigh, a wood bench cooperative in Wayne, a fiberglass plant in Mingo, and a sewing cooperative in Wyoming (which boasted of contracts with Bloomingdale's in New York).[6]

Though the Appalachian Volunteers disappeared in 1969, VISTA remained in operation and, to some extent, stepped into the vacuum left by the departure of the AVs. James Thibault, for example, a VISTA from Massachusetts, came to Cabin Creek in 1969 with the assignment to do something about the local water system but ended up focusing on an entirely different project that became a VISTA success story. Arriving in the bleak, grey season of late winter, he noticed that many of the homes he visited had beautiful many-colored quilts that stood out in stark contrast to the surrounding environment. He persuaded some of the quilters to take their quilts to Cape Cod where he had contacts he believed would be interested in buying the items. Former first lady Jackie Onassis bought some of the quilts, and the quilters ended up appearing on a Boston television program and getting orders from Filene's Department Store. Thus Cabin Creek Quilts was born, an enterprise that thrived for several years, providing a substantial income supplement to the quilters and their families. Thibault, who grew up in the Cape Cod area, remained in West Virginia after his VISTA service.[7]

West Virginians eager to continue a student volunteer effort similar to the AVs established the West Virginia Service Corps. The Corps recruited West Virginia college students for summer programs ranging from tutoring to community action, in the spirit of the original AVs. Secretary of State John D. Rockefeller IV's staff helped organize the effort. Rockefeller offered the organization space in his private office, but, sensitive to the fate of the AVs, the Service Corps requested that Rockefeller sever his connection as it wished to be politically independent. The group recruited 120 college students, all but seventeen West Virginia residents, and OEO funded the program for $64,000. Governor Moore, however, refused to approve the grant unless the students affiliated with his office.[8] In the end the Service Corps managed to put only sixty volunteers in the field for an anemic summer program that ran from June 6 to August 17, 1969.[9]

In the fall of 1968, in another effort to find funding for continuing poverty war projects, some of the people who had been connected with the various community action programs worked toward the establishment of a West Virginia Fund to promote improvements in education, economic opportunities, living environment, and the general welfare of West Virginians. They looked to the example of the North Carolina Fund, an influential private foundation established in the mid-1960s. A bipartisan effort that included Charleston newspaper publisher Ned Chilton, former Republican governor Cecil Underwood, Fair Elections leader James Washington, Secretary of State Jay Rockefeller, outgoing state OEO director Jefferson Monroe, and others from both parties, the West Virginia Fund failed to get off the ground when the new OEO regime in Washington, encouraged by the new administration in Charleston, failed to approve a planning grant application.[10]

Yet another organization that grew out of the community action spirit of the War on Poverty was Designs for Rural Action, organized in 1968 by Gibbs Kinderman and a few other former Appalachian Volunteers who set out to focus on "poor people's issues" such as welfare rights, much as they had done as AVs. They soon shifted their attention to other issues, especially black lung, and what became for them the most important cause, the reform of the United Mine Workers of America.[11] After his failed bid for the Democratic nomination for governor in 1968, former state senator Paul J. Kaufman organized the Appalachian Research and Defense Fund (Appalred) to address poor people's legal issues in eastern Kentucky and West Virginia, staffed by lawyers and activists with backgrounds in the poverty war. Kaufman thought a just society required lawyers prepared to challenge systemic ills such as "a discriminatory tax structure, primitive public school systems, inadequate medical facilities, natural resource exploitation, rigged elections and the like."[12] Appalred became especially active as an advocacy group for miners and widows making black lung claims after the passage of the state and federal black lung compensation laws in 1969.[13]

"A Divine Right to Breathe": The Miners' Revolt of 1969

The Marmet meeting of December 23, 1968 (noted in the previous chapter), encouraged disabled miner Woodrow Mullins and others in the Kanawha Valley that miners would join in an organized effort to do something about obtaining black lung compensation benefits. Taking Dr. Buff's advice to hire a lawyer who could put their concerns into specific legislative proposals, Mullins and a group of miners from the Kanawha Valley met with Paul J. Kaufman in early January. A natural ally of the mineworkers, Kaufman had long spoken out against out-of-state corporations and their local political allies who controlled the state. He agreed to draft black lung reform legislation and to serve as a paid lobbyist for the bill. The next night a larger group met at the Montgomery city hall to discuss how to raise money to finance lobbying efforts. Unknown to them, another group in Raleigh County, with the help of VISTA workers Rick Bank (a lawyer) and Craig Robinson, had already begun to draft a bill that they hoped would ease the way for workers to obtain compensation for occupational lung disease. The Montgomery meeting proved contentious and raised troubling questions. In addition to the difficulties of raising money, some worried that their activities might be seen by the UMWA as "dual unionism," a violation of the union constitution punishable by loss of membership, which would mean loss of employment as well as health and retirement benefits. Some expressed reluctance to risk their jobs by defying the union.[14]

After the meeting broke up without agreeing on a course of action, Mullins and a few others held a street corner caucus outside and decided that despite the issues raised in the larger meeting they would do whatever it took to keep the effort going and to raise the necessary funds. Ernest Riddle, a miner at nearby Longacre, suggested that if they formed an "association" dedicated to a single purpose, it could not be considered a dual union. The rump group quickly agreed to form the West Virginia Black Lung Association (BLA) and named Riddle treasurer. They chose Kanawha miner Charles Brooks, an African American who headed the UMWA local at Winifrede, as president. Brooks had gone to the union convention in Denver and had returned determined to fight for a black lung law but had been disappointed with the lack of support from the District 17 headquarters. Later, Brooks contacted Arnold Ray Miller, president of the local at the Bethlehem Steel Company's mine at Kayford, and Miller helped as the group successfully raised the necessary legal fees though contributions of locals throughout the Kanawha Valley. Meanwhile, the movement spread through southern West Virginia. On the first weekend in January, 450 miners rallied at Vivian. Others gathered on the same day in Delbarton and Logan, and then on successive weekends 200 rallied at Chelyan, 450 at Madison, and 750 at Pineville. Each rally featured the presentations of the three black lung doctors: Isadore Erwin Buff, Donald Rasmussen, and Hawey "Sonny" Wells.[15]

On January 26, a crowd variously estimated from 2,500 to 5,000 miners and their supporters rallied in the Charleston Civic Center to demand black lung legislation and better provisions for mine safety. Many wore black armbands with the words "Stop Murder" written against a background of skull and crossbones. They chanted "78–4, how many more," recalling the number who had died at Farmington and Hominy Falls. The rally opened with a song "Black Lungs," written and sung by sixty-year-old James E. Wyatt, who after forty years in the mines could only gasp the lines:

A young miner's lungs may be hearty and hale
When he enters the mines with his dinner pail
But coal dust and grime
In a few years time
Fills up his lungs, and they begin to fail.
Black lungs, full of coal dust
Coal miners must breathe it or bust.
Black lungs, gasping for breath
With black lungs we are choking to death.[16]

Speakers at the rally included physicians and legislators supporting the miners' cause. To the cheers and laughter of the assembled, Congressman Ken Hechler answered coal operators who denied that coal dust harmed lungs by holding up a twelve-pound stick of bologna. The miners also applauded when Hechler read a letter from safety and consumer advocate Ralph Nader that attacked Tony Boyle and the UMWA for having failed to protect mine workers and urged miners to seek new leadership. Dr. Buff of the Physicians Committee for Miners' Health and Safety probably did the most to fire up the miners with his usual depiction of lungs destroyed by coal dust and his attacks on the coal operators and doctors who opposed the miners' fight for compensation. One stooped man proclaimed afterward: "That's the best speech I've ever heard for miners—and I've heard John L. Lewis." Paul Kaufman spoke for the West Virginia Black Lung Association, House of Delegates member Warren McGraw talked about the legislation, and Drs. Rasmussen and Wells also spoke for the Physicians Committee for Miners Health and Safety.[17] Ben Franklin of the *New York Times* wrote: "It was the first time in memory of most living West Virginia miners that in an industry noted for fatalism and rural isolation, its men had banded together in such an organization."[18]

Of course, Franklin reflected common metropolitan misconceptions about coal miners, West Virginia, and Appalachia. The tradition of the UMWA did not embrace rural isolation. The older generation of miners surely remembered or knew about the militant labor organizations of the Great Depression, including the UMWA, when they had fought for the right to organize, and the younger generation, some of whom had fought in Vietnam, certainly did not fit the preconceptions of Franklin and others.[19]

The current leadership of the UMWA sought to squelch the incipient movement. On January 29, just three days after the Civic Center rally, UMWA District 17 President R. R. Humphreys sent a letter to every local in the district raising the specter of dual unionism. He ordered that the locals refuse to donate to the Black Lung Association (BLA) and to support the bill the union had prepared. In another time the charge of dual unionism might have silenced the independent black lung movement, but by now too many rank-and-file miners had committed themselves to support the BLA. Humphrey's letter now just provided more evidence that their union leaders marched to the beat of a different drummer.[20]

Substantial opposition to the views of Dr. Buff and the Physicians Committee for Miners Health and Safety arose in the West Virginia medical community. Dr. Keith Morgan, who headed the pneumoconiosis research at West Virginia University, said of Dr. Buff: "I don't really think he knows what black lung is." Dr. Rowland Burns, chief of staff at St. Mary's Hospital in Huntington and a spokesman for coal companies in compensation cases, accused Buff and the others of spreading alarmist publicity, making exaggerated claims, and trying to "incite miners."[21] Burns persuaded the Cabell County Medical Society to pass a resolution reprimanding physicians who had "unduly alarmed" coal miners. The resolution stated, "A disastrous disabling disease occurring in epidemic form affecting a great majority of coal miners does not exist." The Kanawha, Mercer, and Logan county physician groups passed similar resolutions.[22]

Buoyed by the physicians' resolutions, the West Virginia Coal Association called for an impartial evaluation of the medical facts before legislators attempted to write a black lung law. A spokesman claimed, "While these doctors have frightened coal miners' wives by telling them their husbands were dying of black lung, the vast majority of physicians had another story to tell: they have tried to present scientific, medical facts."[23] The Republican weekly *Kanawha Valley Leader* ridiculed the ideas of the black lung crusaders and no doubt represented the views of at least a part of coal industry management. The *Leader* held that miners should just accept the problems that go along with inhaling coal dust, the possibilities of explosions, slate falls, and other accidents as occupational hazards of the industry for which miners received substantial pay, not unlike what soldiers received for combat pay. The *Leader* warned that the problem should be given serious thought and attention and not be done "for the amusement of the buffs, buffoons, and bologna peddlers."[24]

It turned out that the state medical community and the coal industry spokesmen who sought a debate on the scientific and medical facts found that such a discussion did not serve their purposes. On February 11, as coal miners filled the House galleries as well as the corridors and grounds at the Capitol, the judiciary committees of the state Senate and House of Delegates held a joint hearing in the House chamber. The director of the UMWA's clinic in Fairmont, Dr. Murray Hunter, had assembled a panel of experts that cooperated with the Physicians for Miners' Health and Safety in presenting testimony that supported the BLA's cause. Drs. Buff and Rasmussen both testified. Buff gave his customary firebrand speech, insisting on the use of the term *black lung* rather than scientific terminology. Buff's presentation played well to the galleries but failed to impress the legislators, many of whom thought him an egocentric publicity hound. Dr. Rasmussen presented persuasive statistics on the prevalence of disabling lung disease among coal miners and introduced two veteran miners, both of whom could no longer work because of breathing problems but had been turned down for any compensation by the state Silicosis Board. Nationally and internationally known expert witnesses included Dr. Eugene Pendergass, a leading authority on radiology, Dr. Leon Cander, head of the University of Texas at San Antonio's Department of Physiology and Internal Medicine, and Dr. Jethro Gough, a Welshman flown in from Cardiff who was considered the world's leading authority on lung diseases affecting coal miners.[25]

The reformers hoped testimony in support of broadening the compensation law would make three important points. They wanted to show that silicosis did not exhaust the work-related lung disorders that affected miners and that coal miners' pneumoconiosis (CWP) did not require an X-ray for diagnosis. The reformers also wanted to establish a presumption of lung disease in miners who displayed symptoms after a period of time in the mines. Although the witnesses offered highly technical and recondite testimony, it supported the reformers' positions and impressed legislators. Gough helped make two of the key points. He traced the development of the definition of CWP in Britain, and he agreed with the West Virginia black lung doctors that simple CWP, though not necessarily fatal, could be disabling. Pendergass noted that American biomedical science had long resisted the broader British definition of CWP but now agreed with it. Pendergass also testified that in the case of simple CWP, the chest X-ray provided no "reliable evidence." Dr. Cander of the University of Texas, who had previously examined scores of miners in Pennsylvania, testified that almost no correlation existed between disability caused by the inhalation of dust and X-ray changes. Cander emphasized "the terribly important fact that it is exposure to coal dust that is the important thing," rather than what appears on the X-ray. This testimony supported the notion of "presumption."[26]

In the face of the highly persuasive scientific and medical testimony in support of reform, the coal industry's call for more scientific study seemed merely a tactic to delay or to stop consideration of new legislation. Those who testified against the reforms presented no convincing scientific arguments. Under grilling by Delegate McGraw, Dr. Rowland Burns, who had coordinated the denunciation of the black lung doctors by county medical societies, admitted that he was being paid by the coal operators association to testify. Dr. Keith Morgan, representing the Public Health Service team from Morgantown, made a poor showing, appearing arrogant and more bent on discrediting Dr. Buff and the Beckley group headed by Donald Rasmussen than on addressing the scientific and medical issues.[27]

Miners and their wives, of course, took a great interest in the legislation, and though most were unfamiliar with the workings of the legislature, some made it their business to lobby the legislators both before and after the hearings. Lewis "Pops" Coleman of Raleigh County, for example, had retired because of lung disease. He had joined a group of disabled miners and widows to press for reforms in the compensation law. Angry that the union gave them no help, for fourteen days Coleman, his wife, and another couple, members of Disabled Miners and Widows of Southern West Virginia, drove to Charleston and back every day. They set up a table in the Capitol to lobby the legislators. Other miners and retirees hung around the Capitol.[28]

Despite what reformers perceived as a victory in the hearings, the legislation remained in the House Judiciary Committee, chaired by Delegate J. E. "Ned" Watson (the great grandson of the founder of Consolidation Coal Company), for another week. Just three days after the hearing, a small group of miners held a demonstration at the Capitol warning of a national strike if the legislature failed to pass the miners' black lung compensation bill. Finally, after a week with no news of a bill reported out of committee, on Tuesday, February 18, a local dispute in Raleigh County led to a walkout that quickly and spontaneously turned into a protest of the legislature's failure to act. Within three days some 10,000 miners in southern West Virginia had joined the strike, and roving pickets began to persuade miners in the northern part of the state to join the movement.[29]

Some friends of the movement, including Congressman Hechler and chief lobbyist Paul Kaufman, as well as some of the leaders of the BLA, believed the wildcat strike premature, thinking it would have been better to wait and see what the legislature produced. Opponents seized upon the strike to resume the public attack on the reformers. House Judiciary Chairman Watson argued that VISTA workers were behind it: "The same kind of rabble rousers who have been causing all the other problems of which we are all aware for a great number of years."[30] The *Welch Daily News* commented editorially, "It smells like some rabble rousers are having a field day," but that "both state and federal compensation laws are more than adequate to repay miners for illnesses."[31]

On a snowy Sunday, February 23, a large and enthusiastic crowd of miners converged on a small union hall in Affinity, Raleigh County, to hear the black lung doctors, friendly legislators, and officers of the BLA. Some 500 jammed the hall, and 700 stood in the cold outside.

An Appalachian Reawakening

Despite a rather chaotic meeting with no agenda, a general agreement arose that miners and their supporters would continue to pressure the legislature by expanding the strike and by holding a mass meeting Wednesday in Charleston at the Civic Center, followed by a march on the Capitol.[32]

Defying the UMWA leadership, wildcat strikers march along the Kanawha Boulevard through Charleston to the Capitol to demand black lung legislation, February 1969. Photograph by Douglas Yarrow.

Meanwhile, Congressman Hechler and political allies in Washington pushed for federal health and safety legislation for coal mines. Hechler arranged for five widows of the Farmington disaster to go to Washington to pressure the Nixon administration to support the legislation and to retain the pro-reform John F. O'Leary (a career government man) as head of the Bureau of Mines. O'Leary, who assumed his position after Farmington, had pushed for stronger enforcement of existing laws, including an increase in spot inspections. Sara Lee Kaznoski of Barrackville led the delegation, which included Nora Snuffer and Mary Kay Rogers of Mannington, Laura Martin of Fairmont, and Frances Ferris of Shinnston. Other coal miners' wives of the area accompanied the widows. Hechler met them at the airport, and among others, they visited the Secretary of the Interior, Walter J. Hickel. Widow Kaznoski told Hickel that a country with the science that could send men to the moon—as it seemed would soon occur—ought to be able to give attention to problems on earth. Hickel agreed with the women that mine safety had been neglected too long. Kaznoski appeared on television, before committees of the

U.S. Senate and spoke to newspaper reporters to make the case for reform of the mine safety laws. The administration also later agreed to retain O'Leary after its appointee withdrew.[33]

On the eve of the mass meeting in Charleston, 30,000 men, nearly 75 percent of the state's miners, had joined the strike, which now reached into northern West Virginia. Caravans of men, women, and children made their way to Charleston for the rally, which began at 2 p.m.[34] The UMWA tried to stop the wildcat strike, but at the rally it became clear that the union had lost control of the miners. They jeered Tony Boyle's name whenever speakers mentioned him and cheered Hechler, whom the UMWA had savagely attacked as antiunion. The miners and their supporters, including many family members, marched through downtown Charleston and along Kanawha Boulevard to the Capitol, carrying signs that said "no law, no work," and wearing "78–4" buttons. When they passed the union headquarters along the march route they shook their fists and jeered, as union leaders remained inside behind closed blinds. Recently inaugurated governor Arch Moore addressed the marchers from the Capitol steps, promising them that if the legislature did not pass a black lung bill in the regular session, which would end in one week, he would introduce a bill of his own in a special summer session. The marchers booed Moore, shouting, "No, no, we want it now."[35]

The miners returned home determined to stay out until the legislature passed and the governor signed an acceptable bill. Mine owners meanwhile unsuccessfully sought an injunction to stop the strike. By the next weekend, 40,000 miners had suspended work, closing virtually all mines in West Virginia and inspiring sympathy walkouts in neighboring states as well. As black lung historian Alan Derickson notes, the black lung strike had become the largest work stoppage caused primarily by an occupational health issue and the biggest political strike in the nation's history.[36]

As the strike continued, the legislature struggled to come up with a bill before the end of the session. The very day of the march on the Capitol, the House Judiciary Committee reported out a bill, but BLA officers, advised by their lawyer, Paul Kaufman, rejected it as fatally flawed either by "mistake, mischief, or malice." Determined to oppose any reform, the president of the state coal association, Quinn Morton, denounced the same bill as "galloping socialism," the passage of which would "go down in infamy as one of the blackest days in the industrial history of West Virginia."[37]

Finally, in the waning hours of the session, the legislature agreed upon a compromise bill, and on March 11, Governor Moore signed it. Though the law failed to give the BLA and its supporters all they sought, it achieved far more than earlier had seemed possible, given the power of the coal industry and other economic interests over the legislature. The law met one of the reformers' goals by providing a broader definition of compensable disorders including "coal worker's pneumoconiosis, commonly known as black lung or miner's asthma."[38] Another provision complicated the definition by addressing coal operators' concerns and excluding "any ordinary disease of life to which the general public is exposed." On the key issue of the use of X-rays in diagnosis, the law opened the door to the kind of clinical and physiological data that Dr. Rasmussen and his Beckley group had advocated. It specified, "X-ray evidence shall not necessarily be held conclusive." As for the issue of presumption, another of the reformers' goals, the legislation provided that occupational causation would be presumed if the claimant had worked ten of the last fifteen years in a job involving dust exposure, a tougher standard than the five-year requirement the reformers had sought. Also, all claims remained contestable; no claimant could expect automatic entitlement. Another area of disappointment for the BLA and its allies was that the old Silicosis Medical Board (although renamed the Occupational Pneumoconiosis Board) administered the new law. Some of the reformers and especially miners had wanted to make it possible for miners to sue their employer, but legislative support for that was slight. The point of workers compensation was to persuade employers to pay into a common fund to establish general liability so they would not be individually liable. Moreover, because the law applied only to miners working at the time of its passage, it excluded the thousands of retired miners who probably most needed help. Neither did it address the need to work toward prevention. On the whole, however, the West Virginia legislature, notoriously dedicated to the notion that what was good for the coal industry was good for West Virginia, had produced a remarkable piece of legislation, the most liberal of its kind in the country, and one that gave coal miners a better chance to qualify for compensation.[39]

The passage of the West Virginia black lung legislation infused new life into the effort to reform federal coal mine safety laws. Federal legislation in 1941 provided for federal inspection of mines; but in practice, it proved weak and ineffective. The federal Coal Mine Safety Act that President Truman had signed in 1952 also provided for federal inspection of mines, but inspections occurred sporadically and the Bureau of Mines scarcely enforced the existing laws.[40] After several explosions in the early 1960s, President Kennedy had set up a task force to suggest improvements in the 1952 law, but the UMWA and the Bituminous Coal Operators Association (BCOA), allied in their commitment to promoting production at the expense of coal miners' health and safety, stood in the way of any effective reform bill. Congressman Hechler and others had been working on a new mine safety bill when the Farmington disaster occurred, and the black lung rebellion in West Virginia lent renewed urgency to the effort. Even some mining executives, generally no friends of federal programs, now foresaw that new federal legislation might help bring about some uniformity of regulations in the industry and forestall efforts to make the industry liable for federal black lung compensation.[41]

The resulting Federal Coal Mine Health and Safety Act of 1969, passed by Congress on December 18, 1969, and reluctantly signed by President Nixon on December 30, addressed both prevention and compensation. The act sought to radically reduce the incidence of pneumoconiosis by requiring that within three years mines adhere to a standard of two milligrams of coal dust per cubic meter of air. To reach the standard, coal operators had to make substantial investments in new equipment, modifications of machinery, and new personnel. The law required operators to check the mine atmosphere periodically and to submit samples to a federal facility. Compliance depended primarily on the goodwill of the operators. Another feature of prevention required periodic X-ray examinations of miners by the Department of Health, Education, and Welfare. Those found to have incipient pneumoconiosis had the right to request transfer to the least dusty location in the mine.[42]

Another path-breaking component of the act established a compensation program for black lung victims to be administered by the Social Security Administration. Even under new state laws that had more liberal definitions of eligibility, many former miners fell outside the limits. Because the definitions of eligibility and of black lung itself raised many questions, the federal act led to much debate and gave work to claimant advocates. No one had imagined the cost of the black lung benefit or the potential number of applicants, but SSA processed 586,400 claims in three and a half years, and more than 487,000 miners, widows, or dependents received benefits in 1974.[43]

The willingness of coal miners to put aside individual stoicism and sheep-like loyalty to a corrupt union and to engage in collective political protest gave the reform movement its unique impetus, but important economic and political changes of the era removed some obstacles that had stood in the way of change in the past. The black lung movement took place at a time of significant structural change in the coal industry and amidst an atmosphere of expanding federal activism. The disruptive technological and competitive transformation in the 1950s had led to something of an industrial shakeout. By the 1960s oil and other corporate money brought new management and new ways of thinking to the industry as Continental Oil bought Consolidation Coal Company's assets in 1965, and in 1968, Occidental Petroleum acquired Island Creek Coal Company, and Standard Oil of Ohio took controlling interest in the Enos and Old Ben mines.[44] The new management in coal, eager to bring order to the industry, and the expansive federalism of the 1960s contributed to a convergence of forces that made possible a national agreement that sought to minimize coal industry health and working conditions as competitive issues.[45]

In the end, the miners' revolt of 1969 stands out as a remarkable moment in the history of West Virginia, Appalachia, and the nation. Tens of thousands of workers, often dismissed as fatalistic or naive, rose up not only against the industrialists but also against their own union leadership to insist on justice. VISTA workers and veteran war on poverty organizers like Rick Bank and Craig Robinson and the black lung doctors Buff, Rasmussen, and Wells played important supportive roles, but as black lung historian Alan Derickson concludes, the ultimate dynamic spirit of the movement derived from "the determination of rank-and-file miners and their families to shut off the nation's principal source of energy if their demands were not met." Though the legislation did not eradicate dust disease, the incidence would decline sharply over the next quarter century.[46]

"I Want You All to Keep the Fight Up": Murder and Reform in the UMWA

The rank-and-file miners and their families showed a vigorous grassroots spirit, but their union did not. On May 29, 1969, while Congress still struggled to put together a federal mine safety law, Joseph A. "Jock" Yablonski declared his candidacy for president of the UMWA, challenging long-time leader William Anthony "Tony" Boyle. John L. Lewis had run the union as a fiefdom for some forty years. Boyle, his handpicked successor, had tried to continue in his mentor's footsteps, but he lacked Lewis's skill and commanding presence. His performance after the Farmington explosion and during the fight for black lung legislation enraged rank-and-file union members, and many reformers, including Ralph Nader, looked for someone to challenge Boyle. Yablonski, no neophyte outsider, had been a part of the union leadership for many years, serving on the Executive Board since 1942 and as president of District 5 from 1958 to 1965. He had not been in the mines for more than twenty-five years, but he pledged to restore democracy to the union, end nepotism and corruption, and to support health and safety reforms. He hoped the eighty-nine-year-old patriarch Lewis—who reportedly came to feel that his support of Boyle had been a mistake—would endorse him, but Lewis died thirteen days after Yablonski's announcement, with no word of support.[47]

Yablonski's campaign brought together the various reform elements including the black lung militants, disabled miners and widows, and those who wanted stronger union support for safety in the mines. Washington lawyer Joseph Rauh, introduced to Yablonski by Nader, attempted to compel Labor Department intervention in the campaign by citing various illegalities committed by the union during the election, but the department refused to act. On December 9, 1969, the union declared Tony Boyle the victor by a vote of 80,751 to 45,736. Just twenty days after the election, on New Years Eve 1969, gunmen entered Yablonski's home in Clarksville, Pennsylvania, and murdered Yablonski, his wife Margaret, and daughter, Charlotte. When the bodies were discovered five days later, the FBI immediately launched an investigation of the murders, and on January 8, the Labor Department ordered an investigation of the election.[48] On May 1, 1972, the Labor Department overturned the results of the

1969 UMWA election, and after two trials over several years, nine individuals, including Tony Boyle, eventually were convicted of the Yablonski murders. Boyle, who had conspired with others to hire the gunmen, received a life sentence.[49]

Yablonski's murder shocked, frightened, and demoralized the reformers for a time, but continued rank-and-file activity stimulated renewed efforts to reform the union. In addition to the Black Lung Association, other grassroots movements with similar names arose from time to time among West Virginia disabled miners and their wives who felt that the UMWA Retirement Fund Board administered the fund in a capricious and unjust manner. One of the most effective, known as the Association of Disabled Miners and Widows, formed in Beckley in late 1966 or early 1967. The organization found useful allies in Congressman Hechler and consumer crusader Ralph Nader who encouraged members to travel to Washington to tell their stories to those who might be helpful. In February 1968, with the help of Harry Huge, an attorney with the influential Washington law firm Porter and Arnold, the association brought suit against the fund, UMWA, BCOA, the UMWA-owned National Bank of Washington, and individuals associated with these organizations. The class action suit, *Blankenship v. Boyle*, brought to light substantial and long-term mishandling of fund monies, including holding large amounts in non-interest-bearing funds, and withholding medical treatment from miners whose employers had not paid royalties. As a consequence of these and other acts, in April 1971 federal district judge Gerhard Gesell found that a conspiracy had existed among certain trustees, the bank, and the union. The court ordered the severance of ties linking the fund, the UMWA, and the National Bank of Washington, relationships that had been illegal since the Taft-Hartley Act of 1948.[50]

A more radical organization representing the poorest of retired miners and their families was the Disabled Miners and Widows of Southern West Virginia, organized by Robert Payne, a black miner whose twenty-seven years in the mines ended in 1967 when an accident left him disabled. Payne later recalled that Yablonski had told him the election would be stolen, but had also said, "I want you all to keep the fight up." After Yablonski's murder, Payne decided to organize a group to try to do something about hospitalization and pensions for the disabled miners. When a committee went to the UMWA District 29 office asking for a meeting with Boyle about pensions and hospital cards, Payne felt that the district president, Jim Leeber, gave it the brush off. He told Leeber that if they had heard nothing within five days, "there will be a big coal strike in West Virginia."[51]

Payne thought Leeber did not take him or his committee seriously, but in June 1970 the promised strike began. The Disabled Miners and Widows of Southern West Virginia sought a pension and hospitalization plan for any miner who might become disabled and a guarantee that until she remarried the widow would keep the pension and hospitalization card. Payne told an interviewer in 1973 that the 1970 strike, starting in southern West Virginia just like the black lung strike, had spread to northern West Virginia, western Pennsylvania, and eastern Ohio, ultimately involving 40,000 miners. Though the union took a hard line and successfully suppressed the strike, Payne thought that the strike succeeded because "we showed the coal operators and the politicians that we're not going to be pushed and shoved around no longer." He also felt that the strike created more pressure for overturning Boyle's 1969 victory.[52]

The most important organization to emerge after the Yablonski murder was the Miners for Democracy (MFD), formed by miners and reformers (some from Designs for Rural Action) who had worked with Yablonski in his campaign and remained committed to the effort to overthrow the Boyle regime and to reform the UMWA. MFD gained strength as rank-and-file reform elements, including the BLA and the Disabled Miners and Widows, threw their support to the MFD. When the Labor Department voided the results of the 1969 election on May 1, 1972, MFD began planning for the new election. On May 27, MFD held a nominating convention in Wheeling. Some 500 miners attended the convention, which nominated 50-year-old BLA president Arnold Ray Miller. A veteran who had been wounded at Normandy, Miller worked in the mines for some twenty-two years before being forced to retire because of black lung and arthritis in 1970. Miller had little experience in union politics but succeeded in rallying the BLA elements around him to defeat Mike Trbovich, who had led in the organizing of MFD after Yablonski's death. Trbovich agreed to run as the MFD vice presidential nominee, and Harry Patrick as secretary-treasurer.[53]

The election, carried out under federal supervision by the Department of Labor, took place in early December. By the time of the election Boyle and his cronies faced mounting legal problems. The outcome of the *Blankenship* suit, conviction on illegal use of union funds for the 1969 campaign, and widespread coalfield belief that he would be convicted of directing the Yablonski murders made Boyle a vulnerable opponent for Miller and the MFD. The Labor Department certified Miller's victory on December 20, 1972. The *New York Times* called it a unique moment in history—"Nothing like it had ever happened in the American labor movement before." The MFD now faced the challenge of taking over and operating one of the most influential—and corrupt—unions in the country.[54]

West Virginia Women and the New Feminism

In an era that saw the rising of a new feminist consciousness across the nation, women began to play increasingly important activist roles in West Virginia, a state where in the 1950s women had struggled with little success to break through barriers in politics and other areas traditionally dominated by men (as noted in chapter 2). Because of the resource-based nature of the Appalachian economy, women had few job options, and the traditional gender-based restrictions continued until the late 1970s. The social movements and organizations of the 1950s, the 1960s civil rights movement, and the War on Poverty, however, attracted a high level of participation by women, although within these organizations women still faced barriers; for example, in the Appalachian Volunteers, men held most of the supervisory jobs. Regardless of obstacles, many women went on to play important roles in the reform movements of the era. Leah Curry, a native of Mingo County, headed that county's full time Head Start program, which was one of only two in the state and considered a model by the Office of Economic Opportunity. The Mingo County Community Action Program, not the school board, sponsored it, and Curry, in a unique approach, mobilized welfare women to teach.[55] Mingo residents Alma Jean Justice, Lerly Murphy, and Judy Trent (as noted in chapter 5) also played central roles in the Fair Elections movement, doing the research in the county clerk's office that revealed problems with voter registration and facing prosecution in county magistrate courts for their trouble.

Elizabeth Harden Gilmore (as noted in chapter 3) played a major role in the civil rights movement in Charleston, organizing a chapter of the Congress of Racial Equality. She also belonged to the League of Women Voters and the Kanawha County Council on Human Relations. In 1969 Governor Moore appointed her to the West Virginia Board of Regents, and she became the chair of the board.[56]

Several of the organizations in the fight against black lung and strip mining and for the reform of the UMWA included women in prominent and influential roles. Jeanne Rasmussen, who married Dr. Donald Rasmussen and moved to Beckley in the early 1960s, divided her time between being a mother of two children and a career as a freelance photojournalist. Fascinated by the coalfields, she spent a lot of time in the area around Beckley photographing mine sites and coal towns, primarily in the period from 1968 to 1973. She covered the Farmington explosion for the West Virginia *Hillbilly* and also had articles in *Mountain Life and Work*, the organ of the Council on the Southern Mountains; the *Charleston Gazette*; and Beckley newspapers. Brit Hume, in West Virginia at that time researching his book on the UMWA, credited her with being a helpful intermediary between writers and television crews who came into the state and the miners and local people they sought to interview.[57] She served as publicist for the Physicians' Committee for Miners' Health and Safety and also as the treasurer of Jock Yablonski's campaign to unseat Tony Boyle as president of the UMWA in 1969. In the tense period after Yablonski's murder, the Rasmussens received threats because of their activities, and UMWA members guarded their home.[58]

Many wives and widows of coal miners also became deeply involved in protest activities, participating in meetings, marches, and rallies and sometimes playing leading roles in the fight for reform. Nora Noonkester, of Midway, Raleigh County, served as the secretary of the Association of Disabled Miners and Widows and, in cooperation with Congressman Ken Hechler, worked hard lobbying Congress for black lung compensation. She told of black lung widows in her neighborhood and the hardships of former miners, their wives, and families as the men wasted away from pneumoconiosis. She and her organization also participated in the suit against the UMWA fund, *Blankenship v. Boyle*. Nora and her husband Eugene (a retired miner who suffered from black lung) traveled to Washington on August 4,

1969, to participate in the filing, an event that attracted front page coverage in the *Washington Post*, *New York Times*, and a mention in Mary McGrory's column in the *Washington Star*.[59] Margaret Workman, wife of Raleigh County CAP president Chester Workman, is another example of one who shared her husband's activism and became a community action stalwart in Richmond District, Raleigh County, during the 1960s and afterwards. She and her husband both supported early anti-strip mining efforts through the Richmond District Citizens Club to Abolish Strip Mining.[60]

As noted earlier, Sara Kaznoski of Barrackville, whose husband died in the Farmington explosion, became an outspoken activist in the aftermath of the disaster, fighting for black lung legislation and other causes to help miners and their families. She also campaigned for Jock Yablonski and for Democratic presidential nominee George McGovern in 1972. With other Farmington widows she appeared in the award-winning documentary, *Harlan County, USA*. After the disaster, Koznoski and Mary Rogers, another Farmington widow, organized the Farmington No. 9 Widows' Mine Disaster Committee. They worked to provide moral and spiritual support to widows and children victimized by coal industry disasters and also fought for state and federal mine legislation. Koznoski went to Washington on several occasions to lobby Congress as well as Nixon administration appointees and played a big role in getting health and safety legislation passed.[61]

Elective office remained limited for West Virginia women through most of the period. The most influential woman in the legislature was Democrat Jackie Withrow, who in 1960 became the first woman from Raleigh County to be elected to the legislature. Withrow, a county native, had been involved in numerous civic organizations. As a member of the General Federation of Women's Clubs she worked as a volunteer with mental patients, and she became a member of the Raleigh County Association for Mental Health. In visits to Huntington State Hospital, she noted the understaffing and the lack of any rehabilitative programs. She went with a group of women to the legislature and discovered that no one spoke for the mental patients. She decided to run for the House of Delegates so she could fill that need, and for a tenure of eighteen years she became the leading voice in the legislature for mental health issues, chairing the Health and Welfare Committee, a hard-working committee that visited every mental health facility and every juvenile correctional center in the state every summer and pushed legislation to improve the state's mental health care facilities. Withrow also cosponsored the black lung bill and defied the powerful strip mining interests in her own county to support abolitionist efforts. Carrying on a crusade started years earlier by Elizabeth Drewry, in 1969 she successfully led the fight for legislation to protect the black bear, West Virginia's state animal.[62]

Sara Kaznoski, whose husband died in the Farmington explosion, became an active and effective campaigner for widow's rights, mine safety, and black lung legislation. Here she lays a wreath at the opening of a memorial near the explosion site, 1974. Jeanne Rasmussen Collection, Archives of Appalachia, East Tennessee State University.

Elizabeth V. Hallanan, a Republican of Kanawha County, had a varied public career unusual for women in the period. During the 1950s, she served as a member of the State Board of Education and briefly as a member of the House of Delegates. In 1957 Governor Underwood appointed her as assistant commissioner of public institutions. In 1959 she became the first woman judge of a court of record in the state as judge of the first full-time juvenile court in Kanawha County. She served as member of the Public Service Commission from 1961 to 1975 and chaired the commission for several years. In 1983, President Ronald Reagan would appoint her a federal judge.[63] Governor Underwood appointed Mildred Mitchell-Bateman, an African American, as supervisor of professional services in the state Department of Mental Health in 1960. In 1962, on the death of the department director, Governor Barron appointed her to the post, which she held for fifteen years. She subsequently served as a chair of the Department of Psychiatry at the Marshall University Medical School and later as clinical director of Huntington State Hospital. The state hospital was renamed in her honor in 1999.[64]

By the 1970s, the women's movement began to have some effect on West Virginia elective politics and opening up non-traditional employment opportunities, eventually expanding dramatically the number of women in the legislature and opening the door to job opportunities long seen as closed to women. After the election of 1972, however, only one woman, Louise Leonard, a Republican of Jefferson County, served in the state senate and ten women in the House of Delegates. Among the twelve press and news media correspondents assigned to the legislature, the one woman, Fanny Seiler, represented the *Charleston Gazette*.[65] At the same time, only seventeen women served on county school boards (out of a total of 275 board positions in the state). Only one of the seventeen, Mrs. Guy H. Michael of Tucker County (as her name was listed in the *Blue Book*), presided. Of 171 county commissioners in the state, only five were women (in Lincoln, Marion, Pleasants, Roane, and Wayne).[66] As one of the few women on county school boards, Alice Moore, elected to the Kanawha board in 1970 (after having moved to West Virginia from Mississippi in 1967, stunned other board members with her assertive and uncompromising manner. Feminist scholar Carol Mason argues persuasively that Moore, who instigated the 1974 Kanawha County textbook controversy, was an important figure in the rise of the New Right in the culture wars of the 1970s.[67] In the late 1970s, some West Virginia women began to insist that the 1964 Civil Rights Act guaranteeing non-discrimination in employment meant that they had the right to seek employment in the kinds of jobs men had taken for granted for generations, including coal mining and the building trades.[68]

Charleston Gazette cartoonist James Dent often depicted Governor Moore as "King Arch." Here he shows King Arch telling Marshall University faculty and administrators that they are getting a medical school whether they want it or not, February 18, 1972. James Dent Collection, West Virginia State Archives.

Arch Moore: "An Egocentric Style of Government"

Although Governor Arch Moore fought bitterly with the Democratic-controlled legislature and the *Charleston Gazette,* his first administration (1969–73) produced important results. Articulate, hardworking, and abrasive, Moore seemed determined to broaden the limits of gubernatorial power, and, indeed, he found himself in a stronger position than any of his predecessors in the history of the state. In 1968, as they elected Moore, voters also approved a $350 million road bond referendum as well as the Modern Budget Amendment. The road bond money enabled Moore to fulfill West Virginia's matching commitments under the interstate and Appalachian highway development initiatives, eventually making him the governor who presided over the most road building in the state's history. The Modern Budget Amendment enhanced the governor's budgetary powers as it shifted the control of budget-making from the Board of Public Works to the governor. Moore also benefited from an uptick in the state's economy. In 1969 Moore signed the historic black lung legislation as well as the law creating the West Virginia Board of Regents, an agency to oversee state colleges and universities, and authorizations for public kindergartens and mental health centers. With the broadened powers of the office, Moore played hardball with the Democratic-controlled legislature, using what gubernatorial chronicler John G. Morgan called "an egocentric style of government."[69]

Though he signed the state black lung legislation and urged President Nixon to sign the federal 1969 Coal Mine Health and Safety Act, Moore generally supported the traditional prerogatives of the coal industry and other economic powers of the state and offered no sympathy or encouragement to those who sought stronger legislation to regulate or abolish strip mining. He used the veto power more frequently than any previous governor and took issues with the legislature to the Supreme Court of Appeals. He unsuccessfully challenged in court his predecessor's placing of 2,000 employees under civil service. When 2,627 state highway workers went on strike seeking the right of union representation, Moore fired them. He directed the highway commissioner to hire replacements for those who did not return to work. In 1970, voters ratified additional constitutional amendments including the Governor's Succession Amendment, which enabled the governor to serve two successive four-year terms. In 1971, coal operators and union leaders gave him much of the credit for settling a long strike. Far from the pinch-penny fiscal conservative of Republican tradition, Moore often proposed politically attractive but costly projects and defied the legislature to reject funding for them. Such projects in his first term included legislation authorizing the governor to issue revenue bonds for the construction of a science and culture center and authorization of a medical school at Marshall University (despite opposition from the faculty and administration who urged that the resources be used to improve existing programs) and a school of osteopathy at Lewisburg. Although the Moore administration reduced the numbers on welfare in the state, welfare payments actually increased. The state also faced two major disasters in Moore's first term: the November 14, 1970, crash near Huntington's Tri-State Airport of an airplane carrying Marshall University football players, coaches, and supporters, resulting in seventy-five deaths, the worst aviation disaster in state history; and the Buffalo Creek tragedy of 1972 (discussed in chapter 9).[70]

Moore campaigned in 1968 as the antidote to Democratic corruption, but both his Republican opponent during the primary, former Governor Cecil Underwood, and James M. Sprouse, his Democratic opponent in the general election, raised various questions about Moore's legal practice, land dealings, and tax filings. Moore denied all allegations and released a statement showing his earnings and taxes over a ten-year period. He refused, however, to release actual tax returns. After he was elected, stories appeared from time to time in the press alleging that the Justice Department sought prosecution of the governor on income tax violations. Moore denied all charges and called Jack Anderson, a syndicated columnist reporting one of the stories, "a muckraking liar."[71] In his memoir of reporting West Virginia politics, Thomas Stafford wrote of Moore's own "propensity for mendacity."[72] Similarly, biographer John Morgan wrote, "there sometimes existed an overstatement and credibility gap between the governor and the press."[73]

Conclusion

The period from 1969 to 1972 marked an Appalachian reawakening even as the War on Poverty faded. Coal miners and their wives supported by middle-class reformers (many of them former Appalachian or VISTA volunteers or current VISTAs) belied notions of mountaineer fatalism and carried out the biggest political strike in the history of the United States, compelling the state legislature and Congress to enact landmark legislation dealing with coal mine health and safety and winning compensation for victims of an occupational disease, pneumoconiosis. The reformers also succeeded in overturning the corrupt leadership of the United Mine Workers union and winning a significant case, *Blankenship v. Boyle*, leading to reform in the administration of the union's welfare and retirement funds. Women, in a West Virginia version of the new feminism, played an important role in the reform movements, and prospects grew for success in the political arena. Governor Moore, pragmatic and unpredictable, benefited from constitutional changes that enhanced the office of governor. He tested the limits of the amendments and promoted politically canny legislation, even as allegations of corruption continued to raise questions about the office and the man who held it.

The Appalachian reawakening of 1969 to 1972 failed to achieve all that it sought. As the next chapter will show, in 1971 and 1972 West Virginia reformers tried to abolish or severely restrict strip mining, but after a bitter and divisive debate in the legislature and in election of 1972, the effort failed, leaving bleak prospects for success on either the state or federal level.

8

The Strip Mining Dilemma and a Climactic Debate

> The removal of the steep slopes will bring a 100 percent improvement, and the ridge runners who have lived on these mountaintops will have a much better chance to develop corn patches into fields of 'still' raw materials, grazing crops, and farm homes instead of mountain shacks.
> W. E. E. Koepler, secretary, Pocahontas Operators Association, ca. 1930

> My valley and hundreds like it throughout Appalachia and the nation are dying today from the cancer of strip mining for coal.
> Richard Cartwright Austin, Congressional committee testimony, 1971

The development of surface mining or what is commonly called strip mining (as briefly noted in chapter 1) posed one of the transcendent dilemmas in West Virginia and Appalachia brought about by the new machine age in the hills. The fight against strip mining formed an important part of the Appalachian reawakening in the late 1960s and early 1970s as substantial resistance emerged throughout central Appalachia, although in the end, facing insuperable odds, it failed to achieve its goal. The opposition to strip mining did not end, however, and continued as a major cause uniting regional grassroots organizations. The fight for a ban in West Virginia in 1971–72 shows some similarities and differences to the black lung and mine safety fights. Ultimately the threat of the proposed strip ban to the unity of underground and surface miners proved crucial. Some mineworker leaders understood that the advance of strip mining threatened the livelihood of underground miners and flirted with an alliance with the reformers. In this case, however, the leaders of the reformed UMWA came to feel that they could not afford to antagonize their fellow miners and abandoned the environmentalists. Without the miners' support, so important in the black lung and mine safety fights, success proved elusive.[1]

Early Strip Mining

Some strip mining had been carried out early in the twentieth century in northern and central West Virginia. In view of later developments, it is striking to discover that in the early years of Appalachian strip mining, large land companies in southern West Virginia, accustomed to doing business with timber and underground mining companies, opposed stripping and refused to grant leases to strip mining companies, citing concerns (not unlike those of environmentalists of more recent times) about the defacing of the earth's surface, the loss of timber supplies, and the ruining of watersheds. In about 1930, W. E. E. Koepler, secretary of the Pocahontas Operators Association, told a Bluefield businessmen's group that the resistance of land companies ended when strippers agreed to "timber loss clauses," guaranteeing to recover all usable timber and to make it available for mine timbers to be used in underground mining. Koepler (sounding very much like surface mining defenders of more recent times) admitted that some resistance came from those who complained of the ugly consequences of stripping, but he dismissed the "scenic argument" against stripping by noting that few mining operations or coal towns were things of beauty. He acknowledged the horrible consequences strip mining had on agriculture, but he pointed out that England had laws requiring the restoration of surface-mined land for agricultural purposes. He suggested that the United States would do the same "in time," and bluegrass could grow over reclaimed land. In the meantime, Koepler offered a glowing vision of the near-utopian future that surface mining might bring. It would improve coal country by leveling land and removing mountaintops for recreational purposes such as baseball fields. Aviation enthusiasts could build local airfields to connect with transcontinental passenger flights at Charleston and Roanoke. More land would be made available for the building of adequate industrial sites, and "the ridge runners who have lived on these mountain tops," he declared, "will have a much better chance to develop corn patches into fields of 'still' raw materials, grazing crops, and farm homes instead of mountain shacks." Moreover, he pointed out, the jobs in stripping would be more highly skilled than the typical mining jobs and would pay much higher wages. He did not note that fewer workers would be needed.[2]

Thereafter, some surface mining began in southern West Virginia, but during World War II, as strip mining doubled in the state, it remained mostly in central and northern counties.[3] Shortages of miners during World War II led the federal Solid Fuels Administration to urge increased strip mining (which basically borrowed much of the equipment and engineering skills of the building and road construction industries), but wartime scarcities of needed equipment made it difficult for mining companies to switch to surface operations.[4]

Strip Mining's Economic Advantages and Environmental Challenges

In strip mining as carried out after World War II, coal companies discovered substantial advantages in moving from underground to surface mining. The new method required no placing of timbers or concerns about the overhead, and the absence of gases made it unnecessary to guard against mine fires and explosions. Surface mines could begin producing relatively quickly, and equipment could be transferred to other properties more easily than in the case of underground mining, where companies sometimes simply abandoned large machines when mining operations shifted to new sites. Surface operators could also dispense with much of the labor costs of underground mining by using huge power shovels, draglines, and bulldozers to remove the overburden (the earth and rocks between the surface and the coal seam). With the overburden removed, the operators used explosives to break up the coal and then, using power shovels, loaded it into large trucks. In hilly terrain as found in much of Appalachia, strip miners followed the contour of the land, pushing away the overburden to expose the coal. Contour mining produced a flat area on the downhill side (the bench) and on the uphill side a highwall that could become too high to mine further by conventional stripping. Then the strippers could remove additional coal by using augers of varying diameters that could penetrate the coal bed 300 feet or more. As the operator removed the auger, conveyor belts caught the coal and carried it directly into trucks, some of which carried 100 tons. Removing coal at rates in excess of twenty-five tons per minute, augers achieved substantial production economies. Some of the equipment used in surface mining, among the largest machines in the world, ultimately cost millions of dollars. Huge power shovels towered as much as 200 feet high and covered an area as large as a city block. In addition to contributing to the reduction in the mine labor force, these methods balanced substantial social and environmental costs against the economic advantages of surface mining. Operators pushed the "spoil" created by stripping over the bench and down the hill, creating a spoil bank, and sometimes filling streams and creating hazards for residents of the area as boulders tumbled down steep slopes and into roads and sometimes even buildings. Blasting used by operators often created "fly rock," stones of various sizes that could fly well beyond the operating site, endangering residents and their properties. Rains caused a heavily acidic and sulphurous runoff that polluted streams, ruined wells, killed plant life, and sometimes covered gardens with sludge. With the removal of mountain flora that helped absorb rains, water running down the hillsides also caused mudslides and quickly filled creeks and rivers, contributing to flash flooding.[5] Sometimes even municipalities could be affected. In September 1957, Governor Cecil Underwood received telegrams from concerned citizens of Matewan asking for help because a strip-mining operation just one mile outside the town limits endangered the town. State Department of Mines chief Crawford Wilson dispatched inspectors to the site who determined that the company's activities broke no laws. The company voluntarily agreed to remove some boulders that had rolled onto surrounding properties. Private property owners like those in Matewan apparently had little legal recourse when strip miners' activities endangered their properties and their lives.[6]

State Regulatory Efforts

As strip mining developed, the state took some legislative notice, but enforcement of the laws proved daunting, challenging the capacity and at times the will of state and local government officials to enforce laws against strippers who generated needed jobs, even though the new jobs might ultimately mean replacing traditional mining jobs. In 1939 the West Virginia legislature became one of the first to attempt to regulate surface mining, passing legislation that required grading and drainage of the spoil area. Governor Matthew Mansfield Neely (1941–45), in his last address to the legislature, called for more rigid control of strip mining, noting that it threatened soil and water conservation, and in 1945, the legislature responded with a law adding the requirement that vegetation be restored. In 1959, the legislature further required proof that vegetation growth had been established. In 1963, as adverse public feeling grew, the industry itself, as something of a public relations ploy, suggested that operators be required to pay $30 per acre to create a special fund for reclamation and repair of damage from old strip mines. A law passed at that time incorporated the industry's suggestion and further required (in the face of industry opposition) that all disturbed land be repaired rather than just the mined portion, which accounted for only about 20 percent of the damaged land in surface mining operations.

Despite the reputation of the West Virginia law of 1963 as being among the most progressive, concerns continued to grow as strip and auger mining expanded, accounting for 10 percent of the state's total coal output by 1964. In the winter of 1965, a committee of the House of Delegates made a series of visits to surface mining sites and found disturbing conditions. Delegate J. Paul England of Wyoming County, one of the prime movers in the passage of the 1963 law, told a reporter that the committee he headed believed the law should be strengthened by giving the surface mining inspectors enforcement power, raising the penalties for violations, clarifying responsibilities between the Department of Natural Resources and the Department of Mines, and ending political influence and favoritism in enforcement.[7] Some practical conservationists and advocates of reclamation also argued that West Virginia should follow the example of Pennsylvania and set aside some counties—particularly the mountainous southern counties—as areas inappropriate for surface mining.[8]

In January 1965, at the beginning of the Hulett C. Smith administration, the *Charleston Gazette* pointed out that strip-mining companies in Illinois, Indiana, Ohio, and Pennsylvania had been successfully experimenting with ways to restore strip-mined land, but West Virginia strippers had shown no similar concern. The newspaper called on the new governor to get tough with West Virginia strippers. "Let there be no nonsense," the *Gazette* said, "no alibis, no listening to patently phony statistics and figures of employment and of the money generated from this sinful enterprise in wages and in taxes. Compared with the inordinate harm done to the state's natural beauty—the ugly scar on hillsides, the leveling off of mountaintops, the pollution of water supplies after the stripper has left the scene of his plunders—profits to the state and its citizens are nonexistent." [9]

Concerned about the threats to scenic sites such as Grandview State Park near his hometown of Beckley, Governor Smith made surface-mining regulation a priority item in his legislative program. He named a Task Force on Strip Mining and cultivated the support of numerous conservation organizations around the state including the West Virginia Wildlife Federation, West Virginia Garden Clubs, the Isaak Walton League, and the West Virginia Sportsman's Association.[10] In addition to these traditional conservationist groups, substantial grassroots resistance to surface mining also became evident. Local community groups organized by VISTA and Appalachian Volunteers also supported the task force's bill, and on January 28, 1967, the poor people's conference meeting in Huntington endorsed the proposed legislation.[11] Ellis Bailey, a Raleigh county homeowner whose house, well, and garden had been severely damaged by strip miners, joined with other residents of Fayette, Wyoming, Raleigh, and Boone Counties to form the Citizens' Task Force on Surface Mining (CTFSM), which called for even stronger regulatory measures than Smith's proposed bill.[12] The group lobbied the legislature to call further attention to the issue and to insist that it involved a great deal more than preserving scenery. In support of his initiative, Governor Smith even enlisted artist Joe Moss—who had scandalized some with his centennial prize-winning *West Virginia Moon*—to produce another piece of art in support of the administration's bill. At the unveiling of the new piece, it appeared that Moss had simply produced a traditional landscape painting of beautiful West Virginia hills, the kind of art that might have satisfied former governor Barron and others who preferred a romantic rather than realistic view of the state. A minute after the unveiling, however, the painting exploded, and when the smoke cleared, the once beautiful landscape had become a strip-mined and polluted nightmare scene.[13]

The legislature finally passed a strip-mining law in 1967 that incorporated most of the recommendations of the governor's task force and suggestions of the England Committee, including placing surface-mine inspectors and enforcement of the law under the Department of Natural Resources rather than the Department of Mines. The law drew broad support, and some hailed it as historic at the time, but, the Department of Natural Resources soon found itself outmatched by the industry and perhaps overwhelmed by the enormity of the task as surface mining continued to grow and reclamation failed. As surface mining historian Chad Montrie notes: "Despite provisions making West Virginia's control law one of the toughest in the Appalachian region, regulatory agencies once again faltered in their enforcement duties, and the amount of unreclaimed land actually increased in the following years."[14]

The Battle to Abolish Strip Mining

Probably the most militant grassroots efforts to stop strip mining in any of the states came in eastern Kentucky during the period from the mid-1960s to 1972. Some residents there sought a ban as early as the late 1950s, and in the mid-1960s, a growing grassroots mobilization of farmers, miners, and the unemployed led to the organization of the Appalachian Group to Save the Land and the People (AGSLP). Appalachian Volunteers and VISTA workers strongly supported the efforts of AGSLP (as noted in chapter 5). The passage of regulatory laws had little impact as Kentucky's governors and regulatory agencies failed to enforce the laws. In 1967 and 1968, protestors in Kentucky blew up over $2 million worth of mining equipment. In 1971, abolitionists formed Save Our Kentucky to press for a legislation to phase out strip mining, but in the 1972 legislative session a bill to end stripping failed to move beyond committee. During the same period of the mid-1960s to 1972, these groups also engaged in numerous demonstrations at strip-mining sites.[15]

As early as the mid-1960s, some West Virginians, like Kentuckians and other residents of Appalachia, began to call for abolition rather than regulation and hoped and urged that the federal government might ban the practice.[16] On August 24, 1965, an editorial in the *Charleston Gazette* epitomized a growing sense of outrage among opponents of strip mining: "A whole region—Appalachia—lies stark, sad testimony to the ruthless, insane, spoliations conscienceless strip mining operators have been allowed to consummate over too many years in the absence of legislation or effective regulation. This industry has been a law unto itself . . . unrelenting in its dedication to doing permanent damage to nature, and resistant to any proposal shifting the burden of cleaning up their obscenities from society in general to the strip miner in particular." The *Gazette* argued that the taxes paid and job opportunities offered by the industry did not begin to pay for its excesses, which gave sufficient cause for the federal government "to legislate this unholy enterprise into extinction."[17] In a letter to the *Gazette* in February 1967, Nicholas County resident F. H. Stewart anticipated many of the arguments that strip-mine abolitionists would make in the 1970s and later. He pointed out that most of the workers in the industry came from out of state, had easily transferable skills, and could easily move on should stripping be halted. Moreover, ending strip mining would create more underground jobs. He argued that nothing justified strip mining. Only the strip-mine operator and "his well paid lobbyist" benefited, "at the expense of all other citizens."[18] Of course those who worked in the industry argued that they and the state benefited from an enterprise that represented substantial investment, jobs, and customers for local retailers.

In West Virginia, the battle over strip mining abolition reached a climactic turning point in 1971 when the state legislature, moved by grassroots forces allied with middle-class reformers, seriously debated abolition or geographic restrictions. Like the imbroglio over the severance tax in the Marland era, the outcome of the strip-mining debate had profound implications for the future of the state and its people. The West Virginia battle also involved several grassroots organizations composed largely of citizens of the coalfields who suffered the consequences of living where stripping took place. In February 1971, a poll cited by the *Gazette* showed Charleston residents supported a ban three to two. The *Montgomery Herald* in Fayette County conducted a poll that showed overwhelming support for ending strip mining.[19] The legislative effort in West Virginia came closer to succeeding than the one in Kentucky, but money and the imperatives of the new machine age trumped ideals, the environment, and concerns of small property owners and residents of strip-mining areas.

In the end the West Virginia legislature would effectively concede to the surface-mining industry license to reengineer the landscape and environment of much of the state, largely in the name of economic necessity—the nation's need for coal and the state's need for jobs—although surface mining tended increasingly to reduce the number of underground jobs and the number of miners.

Southern West Virginia strip mining site, early 1970s. Photograph by Douglas Yarrow.

Most of the strip mining took place in Barbour, Preston, and Harrison counties in the north and Boone, Fayette, Kanawha, McDowell, Nicholas, Raleigh, and Wyoming counties in the south, but some took place in twenty-seven of the fifty-five counties in the state.[20] By 1971, surface mining in the state had disturbed 250,000 acres, creating some 6,593 linear miles of highwalls, benches, and banks. Up to 100,000 additional acres adjacent to stripped areas had also been affected. Reclamation efforts under the 1963 and 1967 laws had fallen considerably short of expectations, causing doubt as to whether reclamation could ever succeed.[21] Indeed the fundamental notion that damages to the land, trees, water resources, animal life, and surrounding property could be undone, redeemed, rescued, made right, or made better, must be seen as a euphemism—a pleasant expression for an impossible idea. What had been done by the forces of nature over eons of time could not be replicated or improved upon by the best motivated engineers, earth-moving machines, heavily compacted raw earth, and a thin layer of organic material. In the best of circumstances, a small part of the disturbed land might be made useful for some purpose, but most ended up as rather raw land upon which the likely recovery of flora, fauna, and water resources remained remote.

As it became clear that the regulatory efforts of the 1960s had accomplished little, public demands grew for abolishing strip mining, and some politicians risked their political futures to put these demands before the legislature. In 1970, a Charleston music store-owner, Simon Hersh Galperin Jr., won election to the state senate in Kanawha, one of the leading strip-mining counties, as an advocate of banning stripping. Soon thereafter he attended the annual meeting of the West Virginia Surface Mining Association (WVSMA) and told the members that the 1967 law had failed to solve problems resulting from surface mining such as slope instability, erosion, and the threat to life and property in areas adjoining and downstream of stripping operations. Galperin cited the many people who had written, called, and visited him to relate their personal experiences and fears that when they went to sleep at night "their houses will not be there in the morning." Countering Galperin, WVSMA Director O. V. Linde dismissed his concerns and insisted that a balance could be struck between "use and conservation of natural resources."[22] Emblematic of the symbiotic relationship that frequently existed between would-be regulators and the regulated in the state, Linde had formerly served as the chief of the reclamation division of the Department of Natural Resources during the Barron administration.[23] Now he joined forces with those whom he had been previously positioned to regulate.

Secretary of State Rockefeller, who had attended the WVSMA meeting with Galperin, made a carefully calculated decision to support the fight for a ban against stripping in his campaign for governor in 1972, effectively opening the door for the people of the state to vote their opinions on this key issue. Rockefeller came to the decision after intensive study and long discussions with his staff. Politically ambitious, he regretted that he had not been in the fight for black lung compensation, and he thought taking a leadership role in fighting strip mining would be a politically sound move. Pete Thaw, his deputy, advised him to support abolition, and his staff strongly supported the decision.[24]

Rockefeller persuaded Richard Cartwright Austin, Galperin's legislative aide and a Presbyterian minister who had directed the church's West Virginia Mountain Project in Boone and Raleigh counties from 1965 to 1970, to head a new anti-strip mining organization, Citizens to Abolish Strip Mining (CASM).[25] Austin (on leave from his regular church assignment) not only founded and coordinated CASM, he also became secretary of the Appalachian Strip Mining Information Service, sending to subscribers a variety of books and pamphlets from his Seth address in Boone County. He wrote with Richard Borrelli *The Strip Mining of America* (August 1971) for the Sierra Club.[26]

Rockefeller declared his support for a ban soon after the establishment of CASM. He insisted that a ban would have a minimal impact on jobs, because the industry employed only 3,650 workers, less than one percent of the state's workforce. Most of the workers had easily transferable skills and should not face extended unemployment. Several labor leaders, including the president of the West Virginia Federation of Labor (AFL-CIO) president Miles Stanley, disagreed that the impact would be so slight, especially given the current 6.6 percent unemployment rate in the state. Stanley agreed that strip-mine reclamation fell short of what should be required, but he thought legislative remedies had not been exhausted. The AFL-CIO board of directors did not rule out a ban if the problem could not be solved through regulatory legislation. O. V. Linde argued that the 1967 legislation would meet most objections if properly enforced.[27]

Because the abolition movement tended to be a disparate coalition of small environmental and citizen groups with few financial resources, it needed the support of a large and influential organization like the UMWA, but the issue threatened to divide the union. Many rank-and-file underground miners understood that stripping represented the ultimate threat to mining jobs. Strippers were not miners in the traditional sense of the word. They operated earth-moving machines. They did not share the dangers and the sense of brotherhood of the underground miners. Although UMWA District 31 President L. J. Pnakovich opposed the proposed ban, leaders of the Black Lung Association including Arnold Miller and Ivan White (a retired miner who was also a member of the House of Delegates from Boone, a heavily stripped county) spoke out in favor of a ban. Residents of several southern counties who had organized the Citizens' Task Force on Surface Mining to lobby the legislature in 1967 resurrected the organization in 1971 to support Galperin's bill, and a number of similar organizations made public statements supporting abolition, including the Izaak Walton League and Citizens for Environmental Protection.[28] An organization called Concerned Citizens of West Virginia, Inc., which had supported the 1967 Surface Mining Act in the belief that it would curtail the damages of the strip mining industry, decided in 1971 that West Virginia's efforts to regulate the industry had demonstrated the impossibility of enforcement. "The industry and its suppliers and financial and political backers are just too powerful for any state officials to challenge," argued the organization in a public statement.[29]

Though stronger measures against strip mining had growing popular support, the coal industry's lobby knew how to keep legislators in line. A "coal suite" in the Daniel Boone Hotel in Charleston offered the lawmakers food, hard drinks, a place to play cards and lounge—and when key votes came up, the coal suite denizens knew how to vote.[30] *Charleston Daily Mail* correspondent Richard Grimes later wrote that the legislative fight for abolition never had a chance, because "most members either owned interest in a coal mine or had strong backers who did. Most senators weren't about to abolish stripping."[31]

Surface mining historian Chad Montrie also explains the failure to pass a ban on the basis of a breakdown in the democratic process caused by the dominance of the coal industry in West Virginia politics. He concluded that "protests, petitions, and widespread sentiment were not sufficient to affect legislators, many of whom were beholden to the coal industry and were always overwhelmingly against a total ban."[32]

Supporters of the surface-mining industry also rallied support to oppose the ban proposal. On January 20, 1971, the Surface Miners

Auxiliary of West Virginia, organized by wives of strip-mine employees led by Mrs. William Strange, rallied several thousand supporters in Charleston; and in February, WVSMA began a well-funded television campaign with commercials touting the industry's support for enforceable reclamation laws and featuring working people decrying the economic impact of a stripping ban.[33]

By February 15, several surface-mining bills had been introduced into the legislature including Galperin's abolition bill in the Senate and a similar bill in the House of Delegates proposed by Robert Steptoe of Berkeley County and Warren McGraw of Wyoming. On that day, some 1,000 demonstrators on both sides descended on the capitol. Scuffling broke out among abolition supporters and strip miners. Rockefeller led a parade of sixteen groups favoring abolition.[34] *Daily Mail* correspondent Grimes, unsympathetic to the abolition cause, later described the abolitionist demonstrators who crowded the hallways and galleries of the capitol as "mostly young adults who came in casual wear, long hair, beards and brought with them runny-nosed children."[35]

As the debate proceeded in West Virginia, one of the most persuasive arguments for abolition came from within the agency charged with administering the 1967 law. In late February 1971, in what might be seen as something of a West Virginia profile in courage, Norman Williams, assistant to the director of the Department of Natural Resources (DNR), broke with the Moore administration to speak out in favor of a strip-mine ban as he testified in hearings before the House Judiciary Committee. Williams, son of Methodist missionaries from Buckhannon who worked with Mohandas Gandhi in his campaign to eliminate untouchability, grew up in India. He and his wife eventually settled in Charleston, where they became leaders of the Unitarian-Universalist congregation and, like Williams's missionary parents, remained committed to human rights and social reform. This background influenced his decision to speak out. He asked the *Charleston Gazette* to cover his comments, knowing they would mean his dismissal. When the newspaper reported his apostasy, Governor Arch Moore fired him.[36]

Williams had helped draft the rules and regulations for the Surface Mine Reclamation Act of 1967 and led in a revision of the rules in the fall of 1970. He told the committee that because of discussions within the department, travels into the affected areas, and letters from people suffering from the effects of strip mining, he had reversed his previous opinion that the 1967 law could be effective. He agreed with strip-mining advocates that the law as written covered the major issues. He had come to believe it unenforceable, however, because "the Department of Natural Resources is completely outclassed by the industry." The environmental costs to the public that the law had been designed to prevent continued daily to be passed on to the community by the industry—things like massive siltation of streams, acid mine drainage, landslides, and scenic degradation. The law could not be enforced, Williams reasoned, because if DNR through its Land Reclamation Division enforced the law to its full extent, "the operator could be put out of business." So, Williams testified, those in charge of enforcement in effect quietly rewrote the law "to serve the profit-making interests of the strip mine operator at the expense of the small landowner living downstream and at incalculable expense to the environmental quality of West Virginia." A bias favoring the operator over the public interest, carefully cultivated by the surface mining industry, had existed in both the Smith and Moore administrations, Williams said, and it permeated the whole process of administering the law. Williams testified that Governor Moore had held up revised rules and regulations requiring his approval for months, preventing the Reclamation Division from discharging its statutory duty. To those who argued that the 1967 law could be fixed by writing more rules or providing more inspectors, Williams asked: "If the Governor . . . is afraid to speak out or to release the new rules and regulations on strip mining, what are we to expect of the reclamation inspector who earns $500–$600 per month, and whose decisions every day affect millions of dollars worth of coal?"[37]

The director of the Department of Natural Resources, Ira S. Latimer Jr., testifying before the same committee, defended strip mining, arguing that it could be adequately regulated.[38] The *Charleston Gazette* commented editorially on the debate in the legislature and in the Department of Natural Resources, maintaining that no one spoke for the people who lived in the vicinity of stripping operations "who wait in dread of the spring rains that surely will bring a new deluge of rock and siltation and debris upon them." The legislature and regulators paid too much concern to the profits of the strip operators and not enough to the environmental and physical impact on the state. Williams, the *Gazette* editorial concluded, "is a voice crying in the wilderness—and unless something is done, his voice will be echoing across a desolate land."[39]

During the debate the *Gazette* also published an article by Robert Daoust, a forester who had been employed by the West Virginia Forestry Division from 1961 to 1968 and later by the U.S. Army Corps of Engineers in the in the southeastern region of the United States. Daoust argued that the reclamation of strip-mined land in the mountains of West Virginia was "a virtual impossibility." Having crossed many miles of the stripped land by jeep and by foot in the normal course of his professional activities, Daoust found little effective reclamation. "The impoverished people who continue to reside in the midst of this desolation," he maintained, "are gambling with their lives. A heavy downpour and resultant flash flood can and will bury them under an avalanche of rock and mud." Foreseeing the possibility that state legislators could do something transcendently important, he predicted that the abolition of strip mining could be "the juncture in state history which future generations will gratefully . . . recall."[40]

One member of the House of Delegates, Ken Auvil of Barbour County, surveyed the 110 supervisors of soil conservation districts in the state regarding their attitudes toward surface mining. Of the forty-one who answered, nineteen supported abolition, and most of the rest favored stronger regulation and enforcement. Many of the respondents, who daily worked at the task of overseeing conservation and reclamation efforts, noted the difficulty of coaxing vegetation to grow on stripped lands.[41]

Speaking before the Wheeling chapter of CASM on the eve of the legislative debate, Galperin argued that abolition, not regulation, provided the only solution to the problems of surface mining, because, he charged, "there is no economic way to strip mine coal without destruction." Although West Virginia's 1967 Surface Mining Law was the toughest in the nation, the state Department of Natural Resources "has become the willing tool of the strip-mining industry—invariably acquiescing to every whim and demand of the coal barons." The surface-mining industry and its defenders countered abolitionist attacks by insisting that the industry provided needed jobs in a state with chronically high levels of unemployment. Galperin, however, argued that the 4,000 strip miners took the jobs of 6,800 underground miners and threatened the jobs of the 19,000 employees in the state recreation and tourism industry. "Either we will have a state of beauty which West Virginians and Americans continue to enjoy at great profit to ourselves," he concluded, "or we will have a stripped state enjoyed by none, at great profit to a few giant, absentee coal corporations."[42]

Chester Workman, a community action leader in Raleigh County, leads supporters and state officials in a walk-though inspection of a strip mining site, early 1970s. Photograph by Douglas Yarrow.

Governor Moore said little during most of the legislative debate over strip mining. Some environmental groups released a joint letter to Moore and the Department of Natural Resources deploring their "abdication of responsibility" in the enforcement of environmental laws and their "thundering silence" on strip mining and other environmental issues including protection of the Cheat River and Canaan Valley from the depredations of industrial developers.[43] When a reporter asked Moore in a press conference his views on the legislative debate on strip mining, he responded with an attack on "outsiders" and "troublemakers." They had disrupted the legislature and kept it from addressing serious state problems, he said, implying that he did not consider the environmental issues raised by surface mining as serious enough to require the legislature's attention.[44] Moore biographer Brad Crouser, reflecting the attitude of the administration, marvels that the state media took the movement for a strip-mine ban seriously. Crouser suggests that Rockefeller and the abolitionists drew support only from "college students, professors, and other environmental-friendly types," but that the "real" people, "those who knew they depended on coal to feed their families" outnumbered those who took the strip mine ban effort seriously.[45]

In the end, as the *Beckley Post-Herald and Register* put it, "The coal barons won again."[46] Galperin's original bill never made it out of committee. When the Senate debated a less daring bill, it rejected by a vote of 27–6 his proposed amendment to phase out the industry in two years, putting strip-mining abolition "over the spoilbank," as the *Gazette* reported. Surprisingly, senators from major strip-mining counties provided the votes for the Galperin amendment, voting the interests of their constituents who felt threatened by the conditions created by the industry rather than the interests of the coal companies.[47] William T. Brotherton, the senate majority leader of Kanawha County, later told Richard Grimes that after the vote, Secretary of State Rockefeller stopped him in the hallway outside the chamber and urged him to introduce a compromise amendment prepared by the secretary's staff. Reluctantly, Brotherton agreed to introduce it as his own.[48] The so-called Brotherton amendment would have imposed a moratorium on new surface-mining permits for one year in thirty-six counties during which the effects of the industry would be studied. In the other eighteen counties, accounting for the bulk of all surface mining in the state, new permits could not exceed more than 25 percent of 1970 permit acreage. The Brotherton amendment passed the Senate, but the House of Delegates rejected it. Later the House engaged in its longest debate on record, just under four hours, as it sought to pass some kind of compromise bill.[49]

As the legislature worked against the clock to end the session, a conference committee agreed on a watered-down compromise bill that imposed a two-year moratorium in the twenty-two counties where no strip mining had yet occurred but imposed no limitations on the counties with active strip-mining operations. It increased performance bonds to $560 per acre and imposed the requirement that drainage systems be in place and approved before operations could begin. The president of the West Virginia Surface Mine Association, Gil Frederick, praised the bill, calling it "fair and equitable." He told reporters that the measure would "result in significant improvements to the state environmental and economic outlook."[50] Abolitionists contended that the bill actually weakened many provisions of the existing law as it allowed multiseam mining in all strip operations and ended some rule-making by the Department of Natural Resources, leaving it up to strippers to police themselves in some operations previously under DNR rules. Galperin said the bill did "as little as possible for the people of West Virginia and as much as possible for the strip mine operators."[51] The *Beckley Post-Herald and Register*, in the heart of the southern coalfields, summed up the legislature's action in an editorial titled "How the People Were Betrayed."[52]

Ironically, the 1971 law, supposedly a "fair and equitable" compromise that would partially satisfy those who sought abolition of strip mining, ended up clearing the way for mountaintop removal mining as a preferred practice by DNR, the state regulatory agency. In a typical administrative delay involving the implementation of surface mining laws, it took DNR fifteen months to write and schedule for implementation rules to put the 1971 legislation into effect. When the legislature met in 1972, legislators could get no answers from DNR as to why legislation passed a year before still languished in the agency offices. Governor Moore's head of DNR, Ira S. Latimer Jr., later told an interviewer that DNR interpreted the 1971 law as requiring the dumping of the spoil in a designated area, not over the wall. Latimer said this led to "the mountaintop removal method, where the refuse is disposed of in a designated area," a process that, in his view, "worked out for the good." Those who had advocated a ban never imagined that the result would be a more radical form of surface mining.[53]

The Fight for a Federal Ban

While Galperin, McGraw, and Steptoe introduced the abolition legislation in the West Virginia legislature, on February 18, 1971, Ken

Hechler introduced a strip-mine ban bill in Congress, and in less than a day signed up twenty-nine cosponsors. Hechler recognized the potential economic and social impact of his bill but insisted that the "ruthless rape of the environment" must be stopped. "The damages are getting worse each time the gouging machines get bigger and deadlier," Hechler told Ward Sinclair, reporter for the *Louisville Courier-Journal*.[54] In a letter to colleagues seeking cosponsors, he warned them that they would hear "a lot of propaganda that 'strip mining is good for the land, because the strippers reclaim the land and wind up with fishing lakes and recreation areas.'" In most cases, he said, reclamation had not worked.[55] Richard Cartwright Austin (who served for a time as a member of Hechler's staff), testifying before a subcommittee on Mines and Mining of the U.S. House of Representatives on November 29, 1971, in support of Congressman Hechler's strip mining bill, related his observations of stripping in Boone County. He told the committee, "My valley and hundreds like it in Appalachia and throughout this nation are dying today from the cancer of strip mining for coal."[56]

The Stanford Report: Environmental Devastation or Economic Disaster

At the beginning of 1972, the movement for a state ban on stripping appeared to still be in play. As the legislature reconvened, Senator Galperin again proposed an abolition bill as well as a bill to provide job placement help for displaced strip miners. The legislature also debated but rejected proposals for a statewide referendum on strip mining. CASM's mailing list had grown to 5,000, and in early February the organization prepared television spots to counter the well-financed television campaign being run by the surface-mining interests. CASM, unable to match the television spending of the strippers, relied on the Federal Communications Commission "fairness doctrine" to persuade some stations to air the CASM spots. The organization also had abolition rallies scheduled at Camp Caesar in Webster Springs, the Parkersburg YMCA, Marshall University, and West Virginia University.[57] When the Stanford Report finally appeared, however, though it claimed to take no sides or to make no recommendations, most saw it as supporting the legislators who had refused to go along with abolition, and it took the wind out of the sails of the state abolition movement. "Subsequently," as historian Montrie notes, "Galperin's proposals died in committee and CASM dissolved for good."[58]

Part of the Brotherton moratorium proposal had included a provision that an independent study would be carried out to determine the impact of stripping on the state, and a senate resolution salvaged that part of his proposal. When it became clear that the legislature would not abolish surface mining in the 1971 session, the *Gazette* supported the idea of a study by independent experts and suggested the Conservation Foundation as an organization that had carried out similar studies in a dispassionate manner.[59] The Senate Government and Finance Committee, however, subsequently hired the Stanford Research Institute (SRI) to carry out the study. Hardly an objective scientific body, SRI board members had many connections to the energy industry including Continental Oil, which owned Consolidation Coal Company, one of the major producers of strip-mined coal in the state. In maybe its most telling detail, the Stanford Report described the rising profitability of surface mining, which had gone from $4.77 per ton in 1969 to $8.00 in 1971. In a bland and non-proscriptive style, the SRI report evoked the twin specters of economic devastation and environmental disaster, but, given the immediacy of abolition's economic impact, the report seemed stacked against it. Abolition, the report maintained, would cause severe economic difficulties for both the displaced strip-mine employees, the eight southern counties where most of the strip mining took place, and the state. West Virginia would lose between $162 million and $216 million annually, and 8,000 employees in surface mining and supportive industries would face at least temporary unemployment. The report also cast doubts on the capacity of underground mining in West Virginia to offset production losses that would result from an end to surface mining, although other states, especially in the west, could supply any deficit to the national supply that would be caused by a cessation of West Virginia surface mining. Moreover, the report pointed out, even with abolition, the impact of the stripping that had already taken place would remain. Any expanded deep mining that might take the place of surface mining would increase gob piles and their environmental impact. If, on the other hand, surface mining continued at its current pace with current reclamation practices, the amount of land left with inadequate vegetative cover would have serious environmental consequences, including rising sedimentation in waterways and the subjection of large areas to landslides. The report expressed concern particularly about the impact of stripping in the Coal River basin where up to two-thirds of the area had already been disturbed, and though the general tone of the report sought bland objectivity, it pointedly questioned why DNR granted permits that would allow such massive environmental impact. The report claimed that because of the terrain, "the amount of disturbance in linear miles of bench and high wall to produce 10 million tons of coal is roughly five times as great in Southern West Virginia as in other parts of the state." Also 10 percent of the land mined in the south would likely produce slides. Sediment increase, a major concern of the report, reduced the volume capacity of streams and led to flooding. Also, the report noted, "sediment interferes with normal physical and biological processes and can result in serious adverse effects on water treatment and on fish and wildlife."[60] Taken at face value, the Stanford Report presented two equally unattractive options, but the devastating economic scenario posed the most immediate threat, making the prediction of eventual environmental devastation appear less catastrophic. In any case the report armed the strip miners, giving them powerful ammunition for the debate.

The Election of 1972: A Strip-Mining Referendum?

In 1972, Governor Arch Moore hoped to become the first West Virginia governor to be elected to a second term in the past 100 years. The odds appeared good, although his relations with the legislature and with parts of the press, especially the *Charleston Gazette*, had been confrontational, and Democratic registration exceeded Republican in 1972 by almost 330,000 out of a total 1,046,000. Moore had cultivated an image as an activist governor and had clearly benefited from the constitutional amendment that had enhanced the powers of the state's chief executive. He also had succeeded in getting voters to support the Governors Succession Amendment in 1970, making it possible for him to run for a second term. The state also seemed to have emerged somewhat from the economic doldrums that had plagued the state for almost two decades, although the coal industry had fallen off since 1968, and at election time the unemployment rate was again on the rise. Moore also benefited from the legal difficulties Democratic leaders in the state had faced.[61]

The national context of the election had a profound effect. Taking advantage of reforms that reduced the power of party bosses and union officials and benefiting from missteps by potentially stronger nominees such as Edmund Muskie of Maine and Edward Kennedy of Massachusetts, a candidate perceived to be of the Democratic left, Senator George McGovern of South Dakota, won the Democratic nomination on the first ballot at the 1972 convention at Miami Beach. McGovern had a PhD in American history, had won the Distinguished Flying Cross as a bomber pilot in World War II, and had studied for the Methodist ministry. Though he had conventional views on many of the social and cultural issues of the day, he had been one of early critics of the Vietnam war, and many saw him as the candidate of the counterculture. He had indeed won the nomination by appealing to the Democratic left, but he proved a weak candidate, enabling Richard Nixon to seize the center and the election. Democratic complaints about "dirty tricks" and reports on the burglary of their national headquarters at the Watergate apartment complex in Washington attracted little attention before the election. Nixon won a landslide victory, the greatest of any Republican presidential candidate.[62]

The weakness of the Democratic presidential candidate made the task of West Virginia Democrats all the more difficult. However, John D. Rockefeller IV, thirty-five-year-old secretary of state, decided to challenge Moore well before McGovern had been selected. (Given the circumstances, it is an irony worth noting that McGovern the history student had written a dissertation highly critical of John D. Rockefeller's involvement in the Colorado coal industry in the early twentieth century.) According to Pete Thaw, Rockefeller's chief aide at the time, his staff knew Rockefeller needed a winning issue. After they had studied the strip-mining issue carefully, they met one Saturday morning and almost unanimously endorsed Jay's decision to embrace the abolition cause. Tom Winner of Raleigh County, who had just joined the staff (and who would be the unsuccessful Democratic nominee to succeed Rockefeller as secretary of state), tried to tell them that an abolitionist position could be politically costly, but Thaw later recalled that Rockefeller had thought about it carefully and sincerely believed he should support abolition. Thaw believed that the abolitionist stance led to Rockefeller's defeat and that it had cost him his job with Rockefeller.[63] In retrospect, however, it is unclear if Rockefeller lost because of his abolitionist stand or for other reasons.

It is clear that the Moore re-election campaign saw Rockefeller's commitment to the anti-strip-mining cause as a gift. As Rockefeller biographer Grimes put it, if the Moore forces had no big issue before, they had one now. The party line would be: "Jay Rockefeller was anti-coal, anti-West Virginia, and was ready to make the coal industry fold so Standard Oil could sell more of its products and Rockefellers would increase their profits." Now West Virginians, always a bit suspicious of Rockefeller, would have their suspicions reinforced by a vigorous Moore campaign that just repeated this mantra. At its crudest, as he barnstormed Logan and Mingo counties late in the campaign, Moore (taking his theme from a story that appeared in the *Huntington Herald-Dispatch*) evoked the Rockefeller threat by charging that Jay had been sent by his family to destroy the coal industry so that the Rockefellers, who allegedly controlled atomic energy, could dominate energy production.[64] Moreover, if the Moore campaign had worried about facing Rockefeller's deep pockets, that concern ended with Jay's openly abolitionist stance, because now the strip miners opened their checkbooks (or their cash boxes) and the money flowed into the Moore campaign for expensive ad campaigns and for participating in the old West Virginia tradition of buying onto slates.[65] In Mingo County this meant an alliance between Moore and Democratic machine boss Noah Floyd, who in spite of losing his senate seat in 1970 continued to control appointments in Mingo. Mingo County Fair Elections Committee chairman James Washington claimed that Floyd had picked all precinct workers, and they all supported Moore.[66]

As he cranked up for the political campaign, Rockefeller accepted the advice of Miles Stanley, head of the West Virginia Labor Federation, to hire Robert P. McDonough, a political operative who had helped organize John F. Kennedy's victory in the 1960 West Virginia presidential primary. He also hired other experienced campaigners, including James "Tiger" Morton and Jack Canfield, who had been press secretary to former Governor Hulett C. Smith.[67]

The Watergate investigations charged the Nixon administration with a veritable Pandora's box of illegal activities, among them "dirty tricks." The term would hold significance in the Rockefeller campaign as it faced activities of a similar nature or worse. Some of these tricks emanated directly from Moore campaign workers, but the most egregious seemed to come from defenders of strip mining. Moore operatives would go into Rockefeller headquarters, pretend to be supporters to obtain boxes of campaign materials, and then dump them in the Kanawha River after dark.[68] When Rockefeller went to Martinsburg in the first of several announcement conferences around the state, Moore organizers had put out advertisements announcing Rockefeller's appearance at the wrong hotel. When he went to Boone and Lincoln counties, Rockefeller faced a hostile situation and much harsher "tricks." Strip-mine employers gave their workers the day off to concentrate on intimidating both the Rockefeller campaigners and potential voters. In Whitesville and Danville they ordered merchants to lock their doors to keep Rockefeller and his entourage from entering. They warned people on the streets that if they talked to Rockefeller they would be beaten. A group of hostile strip miners and their wives followed Rockefeller about taunting him and drowning him out when he tried to speak. When a young girl in Danville spoke up in support of Rockefeller, a man knocked her to the ground. Some miners poured beer in the gas tank of Jay's car. Throughout the state but especially in the southern mining counties, these kinds of incidents as well as assassination and bombing threats and rifle-toting demonstrators plagued the campaign. Richard Grimes, who traveled with the campaign as a reporter, felt that local police and even the state police showed inadequate concern when they were called. He also noted the aplomb of the candidate in the face of the intimidation efforts of the demonstrators.[69]

Both Moore and Rockefeller easily won their primaries against marginal candidates and moved on to the general election. Though Rockefeller had made the abolition of strip mining a main tenet of his campaign, some of the strongest supporters of the ban felt that his support hurt the cause. As early as April 1971, after the failure of the effort in the West Virginia legislature, *Mountain Life and Work*, the publication of the Council of the Southern Mountains in Berea, Kentucky, charged that Rockefeller's entrance into the abolitionist fight had prevented success in West Virginia, because the fight ended up being more about Rockefeller than about the environment. Richard Austin, chairman of the board of CASM, wrote to the magazine to defend Rockefeller, but later, Gerald Sizemore resigned as president of CASM, charging that Rockefeller waffled on abolition. Senator Si Galperin of Kanawha County, a former close ally of Rockefeller in the legislative fight also felt that Rockefeller began to back away from the cause and to "sell out" for political expediency.[70] If Rockefeller tried to trim his sails on the surface-mining issue, he also stayed away from Buffalo Creek (which is discussed in the next chapter) as a political issue in the 1972 campaign, probably because of the sensitivity of the subject matter, though he did talk about mine safety issues.[71]

A sign on a taxi in Beckley, in the heart of Appalachian strip mining country, expresses the views of many local residents living in the vicinity of strip mines, circa 1971. Photograph by Douglas Yarrow.

Another critical campaign decision for Rockefeller was what to do about McGovern, whose national campaign developed no traction and who polled poorly in West Virginia, threatening to drag down other Democrats. Rockefeller staffer Tiger Morton told Grimes that Rockefeller's decision to stick with McGovern cost the campaign a lot of votes. He said he told Rockefeller that if McGovern polled less that 40 percent of the vote, Rockefeller would lose. As it turned out, McGovern carried only one West Virginia county (Logan) and got only 33 percent of the vote.[72] Rockefeller lost by the most substantial margin of any previous Democratic candidate for governor, with 350,462 votes compared to Moore's 423,817. Jennings Randolph retained his senate seat and the four Democratic congressmen were reelected.[73]

Strip mining stood out as the most clear-cut issue as Rockefeller based his campaign on ending strip mining, and Moore unequivocally opposed a ban on strip mining. In some respects, therefore, the election appeared to be the referendum on strip mining that the legislature had refused to authorize. If the strip-mining ban had been the only issue, the results would suggest that West Virginia voters overwhelmingly favored strip mining. The election, however, involved other questions, including Moore's substantial record during his first term and his skill as a campaigner, the success of the Republican campaign in attacking Rockefeller as a rich outsider who perhaps represented malevolent financial forces, the importance of the coal industry funding for the Moore campaign, and the lack of appeal of George McGovern to West Virginia voters.

After the election Rockefeller visited supporters around the state, and in a typical gathering at the Smokehouse Restaurant in Logan, he listed his stand on strip mining and the depressing effect of presidential nominee McGovern as the major factors in his defeat.[74] Some evidence in the returns, however, brings into question the notion that Moore's win meant voters overwhelmingly supported strip mining. One could make the case that a majority of the voters in southern West Virginia, where the most controversial strip mining took place, actually voted against the strippers. Of the fifty-three candidates endorsed by CASM, the pro-abolition group, twenty-five won. Congressman Ken Hechler, the outstanding advocate in Congress of a federal strip-mine ban, faced no problem winning reelection in his southern West Virginia district in which he had to run against James Kee in the primary, who was backed by both the coal industry and Tony Boyle's UMWA. Boone County black lung campaigner, UMWA reformer, and strip-mine opponent Ivan White defeated a strip-mine equipment seller for a seat in the House of Delegates. Four out of seven of CASM's State Senate and nineteen House of Delegates endorsements won, most from counties with substantial strip mining, including Jackie Withrow of Raleigh County. Rockefeller himself actually did best in coal counties, including the leading strip-mining counties. Despite the hostile atmosphere that he had faced from pro-strip-mining forces in Boone and Lincoln counties, for example, he carried Boone by about 1,500 votes and Lincoln by a very narrow margin. He also carried McDowell, Fayette, and Logan, all counties with substantial strip mining.[75] He did not carry two other important coal counties, Raleigh and Wyoming, but other factors in those counties (which together comprised a state senatorial district) raise questions about whether his losses in those counties represented a victory for strip mining. One of the most clear-cut contests on the abolition issue in the state took place in the state senatorial contest in that district. Tracy W. Hylton, a Raleigh County strip-mining operator and a state senator who sat on the natural resources committee, lost in the Democratic primary to Delegate Warren McGraw of Wyoming County, who as a member of the House of Delegates had introduced a strip-mining abolition bill and had campaigned strongly against Hylton on the strip-mining issue. After losing in the Democratic primary, Hylton converted to the Republican Party and fought McGraw again in the general election as the Republican candidate. McGraw's campaign signs read "Stop Surface Mining," and he openly denounced Hylton's failure to reclaim more than 10 percent of the land he had stripped. In his typical stump speech, McGraw asserted that the surface-mining industry was "devouring our state and flushing it down the river to New Orleans." Despite Hylton's well-financed campaign and McGraw's outspoken abolitionism in the heart of strip-mining country, McGraw won. Because he ran an unabashedly abolitionist campaign against a leading strip miner and prevailed, McGraw's campaign attracted national attention. Filmmaker Wayne Ewing captured some of the spirit of the times and the nature of canvassing in an Appalachian election as he followed

McGraw throughout the campaign, filming him at home, on the road, campaigning at mine sites as miners emerged from deep mines in mantrips, debating campaign strategy with his brother Darrell (former aide to Governor Smith) and watching the votes come in at the Wyoming and Raleigh county courthouses. Parts of Ewing's film appeared on the nationally televised program *Bill Moyer's Journal*.[76]

Hylton later told an interviewer that he switched parties to help defeat Rockefeller. Reflecting some of the emotion and the hard edge that accompanied anti-Rockefeller feeling in 1972, Hylton said, "I'm real proud the people of West Virginia had enough sense to reject that stupid fool, Rockefeller. . . . Who the hell is he to come in here with a degree in oriental languages and try to get elected governor? Government is business, the biggest there is, and it's getting bigger every day. You gotta have experience running something before you can run a state government."[77] Rockefeller's success in the coal-mining counties and the victories of Hechler, Withrow, White, McGraw, and other abolitionist candidates in the strip mining counties suggest that the cause attracted more than just students, professors, and young adults with long hair, beards, and runny-nosed children (as Crouser and Grimes had suggested), and also showed the likelihood that the majority of voters in Southern West Virginia, experiencing the devastation it caused, voted against strip mining.

Conclusion

The flurry of enthusiasm in late 1971 and early 1972, a critical part of the Appalachian reawakening, proved to be the high tide of support for the abolition of strip mining. The Stanford Report dealt a deadly blow to the movement in West Virginia and, consequently, in the nation as well. Enthusiasm for federal action faded when state legislatures in the mining states, especially Kentucky and West Virginia, failed to act favorably. Larger coal companies, eager to avoid the controversy, began to see limited federal regulation as a useful foil to the threat of abolition, although they insisted that uniform federal laws governing surface mining would be unworkable because of the diversity of conditions in the states. Representatives of various national conservation groups also hedged their bets, publicly favoring a ban but also entering into the discussion of what federal regulation might entail.

Fading support from the UMWA also hurt the cause. When Miners for Democracy chose Arnold Miller as its candidate to challenge Tony Boyle in May 1972, it appeared that the organization had picked an opponent of surface mining. MFD certainly contained reformers who had worked against stripping, but Miller, sensing the mood in the union, turned his back on abolition. The MFD endorsed stronger reclamation laws instead, and though Miller won the presidency of the UMWA in 1972, he narrowly prevailed in the Appalachian districts, making it more difficult for him to insist on strong federal legislation on strip mining.[78] Rockefeller, the most prominent supporter of abolition in the 1971 fight in West Virginia, also abandoned that position after the election of 1972 and became a supporter of strip mining. In the end, Miller, the underground miners, and Rockefeller all proved to be merely expedient environmentalists.[79] With the loss of these supporters, the fight to stop surface mining in the state would face bleak prospects even though citizen groups continued their opposition and even organized efforts on a broader geographical scale, bringing together efforts of groups in the various Appalachian states. In the fall of 1971, representatives from Save Our Kentucky, West Virginia's Citizens to Abolish Strip Mining, Stop Ohio Stripping, and the Wise County Environmental Council met in Huntington and formed the Appalachian Coalition, a regional organization to work for a federal ban.[80] The future, however, was with the strippers, and in retrospect, it appears that the fight in West Virginia in 1971–72 played a critical role in determining the outcome. If the Appalachian states would not abolish strip mining, the federal government would not either, especially as the energy crisis became a central national issue. Despite the heroic efforts of Congressman Hechler and the various Appalachian groups, Congress took five years to pass the Surface Mining Control and Reclamation Act, a measure that President Jimmy Carter acknowledged was "watered down" but necessary to enhance coal production in a time of growing energy concern.[81]

In 1972 the tragedy at Buffalo Creek, like the Farmington disaster, would reaffirm the dangers and realities of the new machine age in Appalachia and inspire enduring grassroots skepticism of the political and industrial leadership of the region.

9

Buffalo Creek:
Appalachian Apotheosis

The Pittston Company, through its officials, has shown flagrant disregard for the safety of residents of Buffalo Creek and other persons who live near coal refuse impoundments. This attitude appears to be prevalent throughout much of the coal industry.

                Governor's Ad Hoc Commission of Inquiry, *Final Report*

Officials of the Buffalo Mining–Pittston Company are guilty of murdering at least 124 men, women, and children living in Buffalo Creek Hollow.

                Citizens' Commission, *Disaster on Buffalo Creek*

The tragedy at Buffalo Creek—the worst flood in West Virginia history[1] and another of those horrible moments like Monongah, Hawks Nest, Hominy Falls, and Farmington that periodically call national attention to the dangers of life and labor in Appalachia—occurred as a direct consequence of the transformation worked in the Appalachian Mountains by the new machine age. In many ways it became the ultimate symbol of the predicament of Appalachia and its people, whose safety and well-being had become secondary to the demands of the national and global economies. Just as the state legislature and the federal government ultimately acquiesced in the reengineering of the mountains and the degradation of the state's environment and ecology by the surface-mining industry, despite the available knowledge regarding the environmental impact, neither governments nor corporations gave adequate attention to the health, safety, and welfare of the people of Buffalo Creek and other communities that lay in the path of potential man-made floods of coal slag dams. Already victims of a corporation focused only on production and the bottom line and careless of the lives of the people of the region, the people of Buffalo Creek also were victimized by feckless government agencies who just "passed the buck" to ignore their responsibilities (or went out of their way to favor coal companies) and even, albeit unintentionally, by a scholar who relied on the old stereotypes to suggest flaws in the people themselves as well as in the dams of Buffalo Creek. This surely represented the Appalachian apotheosis, the ultimate example of what ailed Appalachia.

Gob Piles and the Environment

West Virginians who fought against strip mining knew that even if strip mining could be eliminated the Appalachians still would face the environmental consequences of underground mining, but they had been willing to accept that reality. By 1972, underground mining had left a mark that would take a long time to repair. In the old days of pick mining and hand loading, miners separated coal from rock and slate inside the mine, and mine cars carried comparatively little waste to the surface. The revolution in coal mining that brought about more highly mechanized processes and strip mining also increased waste disposal problems for mining companies, transforming the volume and nature of the insults to the environment. By 1972, for every four tons of coal that came from underground on belts or mine cars or from surface mines on large trucks, roughly a ton of waste came along too, a mixture of rock dust, shale, clay, and other waste matter. Before loading the coal for shipment to market, this waste material (variously called gob, slag, or slate) had to be separated from the coal at a tipple or processing plant and disposed of in some manner. Coal companies in Appalachia generally dumped the waste material in hollows, creating noxious, burning slate piles as bits of coal in the waste ignited by spontaneous combustion and wafted dark sulfurous plumes of smoke over the surrounding landscape. Rain washing over these piles also created drainage of acidic silt. When Governor Hulett C. Smith testified in hearings on the Appalachian Regional Commission bill in 1965, he asked that the bill include funds to help West Virginia control its 218 gob piles "which pollute the atmosphere and mar the beauty of our countryside." He said "some have been burning for more than fifty years, and all of them smell like Hades." The dumps could also block or obliterate streams and result in unwanted and dangerous impoundments of water as well as polluting the runoff into streams. More than 900 such dumps existed in Appalachia in 1972.[2]

Growing environmental concerns in the New Frontier–Great Society years had led to the federal Clean Air Act in 1963 and a Clean Water Act in 1965.[3] Just as it attempted with little success to regulate strip mining, the West Virginia legislature also from time to time looked to air and water pollution, seeking to regulate chemical company emissions and to stop coal companies from dumping unfiltered coal waste water from the tipples into streams. It enacted additional legislation in 1964 and 1967 to create a State Water Board and to try to clean up the state's waterways.[4] The federal Mine Health and Safety Act of 1969, coming in the wake of the Farmington disaster, contained two safety standards relevant to water impoundments. One said "refuse piles shall not be used to impede drainage or impound water." Another required that all retaining dams be of "substantial construction" and be inspected at least once a week.[5]

With the development of state and federal laws regulating water pollution, coal companies experimented with methods to clarify the waste water used in their processing plants, removing the sludge and acids, so the water could be recycled in the cleaning process or released into the streams as clear water. They created settling ponds where, theoretically, the black water from the cleaning plant could be dumped, and the heavy solids would settle to the bottom, leaving clear water at the top to be reused or to be released. What to do with the sludge that settled to the bottom remained an issue, because eventually the sludge would fill the ponds. At a northern West Virginia mine in the mid 1960s, professors of the West Virginia University School of Mines experimented with pumping the sludge into abandoned mines. They understood that this solution might create other problems, such as adding to the acid drainage from old mines that threatened both streams and ground water. The WVU study also noted that settling ponds worked best in flat areas, a type of terrain in exceedingly scarce supply in much of Appalachia. In the mountains of West Virginia, most coal companies simply used the old slag piles and mine waste to make water impoundments in mountain hollows, where they would "clarify" and reuse water from their cleaning process or allow the water to seep through the impoundments to enter creeks and rivers, presumably being filtered in the process. Since they had to dump the slag somewhere, using it to create settling ponds gave coal companies a use for a useless product of their operations and a cheap way to address statutory requirements. Thus, in a land where few natural lakes occurred, hundreds of haphazardly constructed and inadequately inspected artificial black lakes and ponds full of sludge and acidic water proliferated in mountain hollows, endangering the water supply, flora, aquatic life, animal life, as well as the lives and property of residents.[6]

The Dams of Buffalo Creek Hollow

Buffalo Creek flows through a typical Appalachian hollow in the rugged terrain of Logan County. Three small streams (Main Fork, Middle Fork, and Lee Fork) meet at the head of the hollow near the conjunction of the county lines of Boone, Wyoming, and Logan to form Buffalo Creek. The creek flows westerly some seventeen miles, falling from an elevation of 1,793 feet to 710 feet through the narrow hollow in the mountains toward a junction with the Guyandotte River at the town of Man. The hollow provides a narrow bottom land of some sixty yards wide at the top, to as much as 200 in some spots along the creek's course. Here, squeezed in among rail lines, power lines, a road, commercial buildings, and bridges, coal companies had built houses during the early twentieth century. After World War II, as workers became more mobile, coal companies got out of the housing rental business, selling the houses to residents, who refurbished and improved them.[7]

Logan County had suffered like most of Appalachia after World War II, as coal companies replaced men with the new machines. In the 1950s and 1960s, the population of Logan County fell from 77,391 to 46,269, and unemployment remained high in 1972, including many young people and hundreds of Vietnam veterans.[8] Nevertheless, in 1971, according to a report of the West Virginia Coal Association, coal accounted for 49.5 percent of employment and 62.4 percent of wages in the county.[9] Some 5,000 people lived in Buffalo Hollow in the winter of 1972 in sixteen little villages strung out in a nearly continuous line of settlement from Saunders (or Three Forks) at the top to Kistler at the bottom. The livelihoods of virtually all the residents of the hollow depended either directly or indirectly on the coal industry, and miners (most of whom worked underground) could earn up to fifty dollars a shift. Having survived the shakeout that had come with mechanization, the employed miners considered themselves to be reasonably satisfied. In addition to the improvement and expansion of older houses, many miners had purchased new trailers, and some families had two cars.[10]

In the period after Farmington as miners marched and demonstrated for black lung laws and safety laws and for reform of their union and other reformers pushed for strip-mining abolition, coal industry spokesmen sometimes felt under siege in a way that they never had before. They decried the regulatory atmosphere of the post-Farmington era and issued dire warnings that labor and environmental issues disrupted production and increased costs. Despite the 1968 election of Richard Nixon (who had no interest in environmental issues), a rising national concern about the environment led to additional legislation including a Clean Air Act in 1970, creation of the Occupational Health and Safety Administration (OSHA) in 1970, the Environmental Protection Agency in 1970, and a Water Pollution Control Act in 1972. A contract dispute in 1971 idled the industry for forty-five days, and in 1972 the state's production fell to its lowest level since 1962 (excluding 1971).[11] When the Southern Virginias Coal Association met in its annual meeting on March 22, 1971, President Tom Waddington described how the association had tried to deal with the challenges of an era in which "the public image of coal in West Virginia compares . . . with that of the illegitimate child at a family reunion." The organization had worked to get a bill passed that would abolish inspections, but "the bill died aborning." He also outlined his public relations offensive throughout southern West Virginia that involved joining civic organizations, frequent speaking engagements, and joining the advisory boards of Concord and Bluefield State colleges.[12]

The West Virginia Coal Association also regretted the new legislation, especially the Clean Air Act. Because it restricted sulfur oxide emissions and particulates, the Clean Air Act forced many northeastern electrical utilities to switch from high sulfur coal to oil or lower sulfur coal, causing the closing of mines in northern West Virginia. An unintended consequence of the act increased the value of southern West Virginia low sulfur coal (and incidentally provided greater incentive for strip mining).[13]

Despite the post-Farmington state and federal reforms, the reasonably high standard of living achieved by the Buffalo Creek miners still came with substantial risk. Coal remained the most dangerous industry, and black lung disease had not been vanquished. In addition the workers and residents of Buffalo Hollow, like residents in many other Appalachian communities, lived in fear of the huge slate pile and water impoundments at the head of the hollow. Since 1945, when the Lorado Coal Mining Company opened the first mine in the area and soon thereafter completed a washing plant, a slag pile of the plant's refuse grew near the company's tipple on Middle Fork, near Saunders. Over the years, Lorado and its successor, Buffalo Mining Company, opened additional mines. In 1970 (as part of a shakeout in the industry which saw large corporations absorbing smaller, undercapitalized firms), the fourth largest coal-mining corporation in the country, the Pittston Coal Company, purchased the Buffalo Mining Company, which became a division of Pittston.[14] In the aftermath of the disaster, Pittston President Nicholas Camicia testified before one of the investigating bodies that Pittston had been able to acquire the Buffalo Mining Company after the Coal Mine Health and Safety Act of 1969 because, he suggested, the smaller firm lacked the expertise or the wherewithal to deal with the new federal requirements.[15] As the largest independent coal producer by 1972, selling to customers in the United States, Europe, and Japan, Pittston had the resources, but its wealth and capacity had done nothing to make the miners and residents of Buffalo Creek safer. Pittston ranked second in the country in the number of fatal and non-fatal accidents. Pittston eyed the world market, and it sought to minimize all production expenses in order to compete. Though coal from Buffalo Creek helped to make Toyotas and Renaults, better dams, safer practices, and concerns of local residents were not part of the equation.[16]

By 1972, the Buffalo Mining division of Pittston operated five underground mines, a strip mine, and two auger mines in the area. Also by then, the original slate dump had grown to over 200 feet high, 2,000 feet long and 400 feet wide, extending right to the edge of Middle Fork Creek, and it continued to smolder because of the continuing spontaneous combustion of coal waste. In 1960 Lorado

Mining Company had built a slate dam (called Dam No. 1, as it was the first of three water impoundments) on the floor of Middle Fork to provide a settling pond for the black water waste from the tipple. Trucks simply dumped slate and other mine refuse across the hollow extending the upper end of the existing slate pile, until it blocked the stream. The company recycled the clarified water to the cleaning plant. Dam No. 1 rose six to eight feet high and stretched some 100 feet across the hollow. After a time, however, sludge built up and lessened the water capacity of the impoundment. Soon thereafter, in 1967, Buffalo Creek Mining Company, having succeeded Lorado, began another impoundment upstream of Dam No. 1, called Dam No. 2, again simply using trucks to dump refuse across the hollow until it impounded the water. Dam No. 2 stretched 450 feet across Middle Fork Hollow and rose twenty feet above the floor. In 1968, the company began dumping slate across Middle Fork hollow for a third impoundment even further upstream. By 1970, the year Pittston bought out Buffalo Creek Mining Company, Dam No. 3 reached the other side of the hollow. By the time of the collapse in 1972, the dam had grown to a height of fifty feet high (substantially exceeding the fifteen feet limit set by state law), and stretched 450 to 600 feet across, and 400 to 500 feet broad. Behind this massive slate dam, water extended about a half mile and reached a depth of some thirty feet. None of the three dams met the federal requirement that such dams be "of substantial construction." None of the structures contained anything but mine waste dumped by trucks and compacted by bulldozers, nor did the company or any agency regularly inspect them. Investigations of the dams in the aftermath of the disaster by three different agencies agreed that the dams failed to meet minimal engineering and construction standards.[17]

Several incidents with the Three Forks dams and a tragic gob pile collapse in Wales raised concerns in the community over the years between 1966 and 1972. In 1966, after the Aberfan, Wales, incident led to the deaths of 144 people, including 116 children, Secretary of the Interior Stuart Udall ordered the U.S. Geological Survey and the Bureau of Mines to undertake a joint study of slate dumps in the United States. William E. Davies, a geologist with the Geological Survey, examined thirty-eight sites in West Virginia. He found thirty of them unstable and four critically dangerous. The Buffalo Creek slate dump he listed among the unstable, offering the opinion (in response to questions on a mimeographed questionnaire) that, after hurricane-like precipitation, the dump would be subject to a washout "from overflow of lake" with the result: "Large wash would fill valley." Udall prepared a summary of Davies' findings in West Virginia, noted the potential danger to people living below these dumps, and sent the information to both West Virginia senators, the governor, and the five congressmen. Only Congressman Hechler reacted. He visited the site and called for action to avoid the kind of catastrophe that had hit Aberfan.[18]

In early 1967, Dam No. 2 cracked, sending terrified local residents fleeing for higher ground in the middle of the night as flood waters destroyed part of the highway, a section of railroad track, and damaged some homes. About a year later, in February 1968, Pearl Woodrum, an elderly widow who lived near the slag pile and dams at Three Forks, wrote to Governor Hulett C. Smith about the dams: "Every time it rains it scares everyone to death. We are all afraid we will be washed away and drowned. They just keep dumping slate and slush in the water and making it more dangerous every day." Smith assured her the dam would be inspected.[19]

After Mrs. Woodrum's letter, Harold Snyder, Director of the Engineering Division of the Public Service Commission and DNR inspector Joseph C. Holly went to Middle Fork and met with Steve Dasovich, the vice president of the Buffalo Mining Company.[20] The date was February 26, precisely four years before the disaster. The company had already received warnings from Holly that Dam No.1 failed because it lacked emergency spillways. Holly had recommended to his agency that strong action be taken against the company, but nothing happened. Like DNR's state inspectors of strip mining who (as Norman Williams had testified) "were completely outclassed by the industry" and like the federal inspectors who had issued feckless citations to Consolidated Coal Company at Farmington's No. 8 mine, Joseph Holly and other state inspectors had no power to enforce, and frequently companies simply ignored citations of state agencies. In the aftermath of the disaster, state agencies passed the buck as to which had enforcement authority—the Public Service Commission, the Department of Natural Resources' Water Resources Division or Reclamation Division, or the local prosecuting attorney.[21] At least part of the problem in enforcement came from political officials putting pressure on state agencies to go easy on coal companies.[22]

Buffalo Mining eventually rigged a spillway for Dam No. 1, but proceeded to build Dam No. 2 without emergency spillways. As a result of the meeting with state agents, Dasovich, who had an engineering degree, sketched on a piece of scrap paper a plan for a huge new dam, No. 3, which, remarkably, also failed to contain emergency spillways.[23] After the 1968 meeting of Dasovich and the state agents, other incidents continued to raise questions about the safety of the dams, including a collapse of the face of Dam No. 3 in February 1971. In that incident, Dam No. 2 managed to contain the black water and sludge that poured out of Dam No. 3. Afterward, West Virginia inspectors cited Pittston for failing to provide an emergency overflow system for the large pond behind Dam No. 3, but by the time of the 1972 catastrophe, Pittston still had built no emergency spillways. Ignoring citations or challenging them seemed to be corporate policy. In 1971, Pittston operations challenged 5,000 federal citations and paid only $275 of the $1.3 million in fines levied against them.[24] In a civil proceeding deposition after the disaster, Dasovich admitted that he had not followed Department of Natural Resources guidelines for impoundments, nor had he made any engineering calculations at all in designing Dam No. 3. He had also ignored the warnings from DNR that the dam needed an emergency spillway. He explained that to make space for a spillway would have required closure of an access road to a mine and temporarily laying off ninety miners and reducing production. It seemed more important to him (and to his superiors at Pittston) to keep the miners working than to take the time to make safety improvements to the dam. He also admitted that they had continued to dump mine refuse on Dam No. 3 even after the Federal Coal Mine Health and Safety Standards Act of 1969 prohibited the practice. Dasovich explained, "We had no other place to dump it."[25]

The Dam Break

Even in the days before the dam break, others warned about potential problems along Buffalo Creek. Rufus Brooks, an anti-strip-mining activist and disabled miner who had lived on Buffalo Creek at Braeholm for forty-one years wrote to the Readers Forum of the

Charleston Gazette to say that eighteen families in Braeholm and a neighboring community had been hit by mud and water over seven months before, but the mining company had done nothing to compensate them for their losses. At the same time, Gerald Sizemore, president of the Citizens to Abolish Strip Mining, announced that the organization had petitioned the director of the Department of Natural Resources on behalf of forty-one individuals in Amherstdale complaining that strip mines in the area deposited sediment in Buffalo Creek, causing floods, landslides, and property damages. Sizemore warned of an "illegal, improper, and dangerous siltation dam" located behind the Amherstdale grade school. "This is a very dangerous situation and should be eliminated before someone is killed," Sizemore told reporters, just two weeks before the disaster.[26]

During the last week in February 1972, rain and snow led to rising water in creeks and rivers of southern West Virginia, a not unusual seasonal occurrence. The Tug and Guyandotte rivers both overflowed their banks. Governor Moore ordered the National Guard to help as the Black Bottom and Stollings sections of Logan County flooded on Thursday, February 24, and U.S. 119 was closed in several Logan communities.[27] At 9 p.m. on Friday, the U.S. Weather Bureau in Huntington issued an additional flood watch, creating some concern along Buffalo Creek among company officials and residents living in the upper half of the hollow. During the night of February 25, company officials checked the rising level in the dams, especially No. 3, and toward dawn of Saturday, February 26, they ordered a spillway cut across the barrier to allow water to drain off and to relieve some of the pressure. Steve Dasovich, however, (who later denied ordering the spillway cut) reassured deputy sheriffs who had been called to the scene that no evacuation would be necessary.[28] Years later, deputy sheriff Otto Mutters recalled that he received a call from the jail at 5 a.m. alerting him to the possible need to evacuate people. He jumped into his patrol car and sped up the hollow, trailing Dasovich. After Dasovich had visited the top of the dam, however, he returned to say the dam looked good. They had ditched around it and had taken care of the problem. But, as Mutters later recalled, he still feared the dam and went hastily door-to-door spreading the alarm. Because so many alarms had been raised over the years, however, some scoffed at his concern and declined to leave.[29]

The West Virginia Department of Highways reconstructed this striking aerial view of the three dams of the Buffalo Creek taken on February 27, 1972, after they had collapsed. West Virginia State Archives.

At 7:59 a.m. Dam No. 3 collapsed, and 132 million gallons of black water, sludge, mud, and assorted refuse roared out of Middle Fork into Buffalo Creek Hollow. As the wall of water hit the smoldering slag pile along the creek, it set off explosions. Within moments the roiling mass smashed through the town of Saunders, carrying everything with it including houses, cars, trailers, and a church. Starting as a twenty-foot-high wall at Saunders, it broadened and took on a somewhat lower profile as it advanced seventeen miles down the hollow toward the Guyandotte River, moving at about ten miles per hour and tossing houses and cars about as if they were toys. At about 10 a.m., the leading edge reached Man, where Buffalo Creek meets the Guyandotte. When the orgy of destruction finally ended, 125 people had died. Many, especially in the upper part of the hollow, had been swept up into the maelstrom in their homes with little warning. The devastation left some 4,000 of Buffalo Creek's 5,000 residents homeless, wandering about in a scene of utter destruction. The flood destroyed five towns and damaged eleven more, obliterating thirty businesses and 600 automobiles. It totally destroyed 507 homes, damaged 936 others, and demolished 30 mobile homes. Piles of debris littered the landscape. Black sludge covered everything.[30]

By Sunday afternoon, the National Guard moved in to close off the area as medical units from area hospitals arrived to assess the medical condition of survivors. Civil Defense helicopters evacuated the worst cases among the 1,100 injured. The Red Cross and Salvation Army began to provide food and temporary shelter in area schools. The Army Corps of Engineers soon undertook the task of clearing away the debris, and the Office of Emergency Preparedness set up an office to dispense $20,000,000 in relief. With many residents of the area left homeless, the Department of Housing and Urban Development took up the task of moving in temporary housing, eventually housing 2500 in thirteen trailer camps.

The Aftermath: A Familiar Script

As in the aftermath of the Farmington explosion, industry and government officials issued insensitive and ill-advised statements. A Pittston spokesman in New York, too eager to disclaim responsibility, told the *Charleston Gazette* that the Buffalo Creek flood was an "act of God." The company's dam simply was "incapable of holding the water that God poured into it."[31] A Buffalo Mining official, Ben Tudor, blamed West Virginia's environmental regulations for the disaster, telling a Kentucky newspaper the state DNR was "too concerned about trout downstream" and "had denied Buffalo Mining permission to drain off its massive impoundment." The state cared more for the fish than for the people, Tudor said, "and now both are gone."[32] Governor Arch Moore, enraged at press reports like the Tudor story, briefly imposed press censorship, ordering state police and national guardsmen to keep "irresponsible" news people out of the valley. In commenting on the news coverage, he told the *New York Times*: "The only really sad part about it is that the state of West Virginia took a terrible beating, which far overshadowed the beating which the individuals that lost their lives took, and I consider this an even greater tragedy than the accident itself."[33]

Buffalo Creek 327

A helicopter searches for survivors in the aftermath of the Buffalo Creek flood. Jeanne Rasmussen Collection, Archives of Appalachia, East Tennessee State University.

The business community feared that the impact of Buffalo Creek, echoing the Farmington explosion, would lead to demands for even stricter regulation of the coal industry and higher operating costs. *Business Week*, citing "cries for controls" reported that new laws and regulations would probably require major alterations in mining company dams and cleaning plants in Appalachia. Properly built dams would cost $100,000 to $250,000 each, and more sophisticated water recycling systems could cost much more. The stricter safety requirements of the Coal Mine Health and Safety Act, the business journal reported, had resulted in the disappearance of about 20 percent of all coal companies, usually the small and underfinanced. Tougher regulation of dams would likely lead to another round of small company failures.[34] But the troubles of small companies that *Business Week* worried about also opened opportunities for large corporations—like Pittston—to acquire the smaller firms during this period.

An Act of God?

Within a week of the dam collapse, Governor Moore appointed a nine member ad hoc commission to study the disaster. He named Jay Hilary Kelley, Dean of the West Virginia School of Mines, to chair the commission.[35] Critics pointed out that the commission included primarily representatives of state and federal agencies who had failed in their oversight responsibilities, others who tended to defend coal industry interests, and no community representatives or coal miners. Suspecting that Moore's group would simply whitewash the incident, a small group of critics organized a citizens' commission made up of members of the community, representatives of disabled miners, environmental groups, ministers, labor, and other public interest groups. Admittedly self-appointed, the Citizens' Commission claimed to represent no particular group but hoped to express "the frustrations and the fears of a citizenry that has been exploited too callously and too often." The Citizens' Commission held hearings in Accoville, and more than 200 survivors crowded into Buffalo Grade School to hear eyewitness accounts. One testified to the cheers of the crowd that God didn't drive the trucks that dumped the slag or run the bulldozers that compressed it to make the water impoundments.[36]

The Governor's Ad Hoc Commission held hearings at Man High School and in Charleston, meeting twenty-six times, interviewing ninety-one witnesses, and accumulating nine volumes of testimony. The commission gathered much information but had no subpoena or prosecutorial powers. Under no legal compulsion, Pittston officials refused to provide requested information, fearing that such information could be damaging in forthcoming lawsuits or criminal prosecutions. Given the makeup of the body and the way it had been appointed, the Ad Hoc Commission used unexpectedly frank language in condemning the Pittston Company and the coal industry generally. Early in its report, it pointedly disassociated itself from the theory of causation issued by the Pittston company spokesman when it said it found "no evidence of an act of God" in bringing about the tragedy. It noted the widespread popular blame placed on Pittston but suggested that others should share the blame, including ineffective government agencies and, in a remarkable effort to apportion some blame to the dead victims, "those who did not heed warnings" on the day of the disaster. But in the end, the commission placed the onus on Pittston, noting that "the Pittston Company has indicated indifference to the victims of the Buffalo Creek flood." It went on to say that the company "has shown flagrant disregard for the residents of Buffalo Creek and other persons who live near coal refuse impoundments." Going even further, the commission concluded: "This attitude appears to be prevalent throughout much of the coal industry." The commission called for the convening of a special grand jury in Logan County to determine whether criminal indictments should be brought.[37] Even more blunt, the Citizen's Commission report, which reached similar conclusions, called for the prosecution of company officials for murder.[38]

Despite the strong language of the Ad Hoc Commission, its lack of prosecutorial powers as well as the unwillingness of any state agency to either enforce regulatory laws or prosecute those who violated them left the matter of criminal proceedings in the hands of the Logan County government, a notoriously corrupt body by long tradition closely attuned to the coal industry. Several of its officials including a state senator, the sheriff, deputy sheriff, circuit clerk, and county clerk—the Logan County Five—were convicted of fraud in the 1970 election, a conviction upheld by the United States Supreme Court in 1974.[39] Because Logan County prosecutors already had become involved in civil suits on behalf of plaintiffs suing the coal company, the Logan County circuit judge Harvey Oaklund appointed Huntington lawyer Lafe Chafin and West Virginia University law school dean Willard Lorenson as special prosecutors to prepare the case for the special grand jury. When the special grand jury met after the 1972 election, however, it declined to issue any criminal indictments.[40]

Though no criminal indictments resulted from the Buffalo Creek disaster, the Buffalo Mining Company faced numerous liability claims and lawsuits. Its liability insurance company moved to settle claims by the fall of 1972, granting the appallingly small $10,000 West Virginia statutory limit for "wrongful death," and negotiating property claims to a small fraction of their value.[41] Although many of the survivors accepted the insurance company's offers, others sought legal representation. The Washington, D.C., law firm of Arnold and Porter persuaded some 600 claimants to hold out in the hopes of making Pittston pay. Using an unusual approach, claiming that the survivors suffered "psychic impairment," the firm sued Pittston for $50 million. In the end, the suit was settled for $13.5 million. According to Gerald Stern, the lead Arnold and Porter attorney in the case, the amount gave the plaintiffs full replacement values for their possessions and more than $10,000 for "wrongful death" claims. The biggest part of the settlement covered some $8 million for "psychic impairment." Expenses and Arnold and Porter's $3 million legal fee reduced the net amount of the awards.[42] Assistant State Attorney General Phillip Gaujot resigned and represented some 1,200 claimants in a suit against Pittston, which was settled in 1978 for $4.8 million.[43]

Another lawsuit against Pittston came from the state, and the manner of its resolution created an enduring controversy. In 1972 the legislature ordered Attorney General Chauncey Browning to sue Pittston for damages to the state's roads, bridges, and other facilities. Charleston attorney Stanley Preiser undertook the suit for the state, seeking $100 million, but in 1977, just before the end of his second term, Governor Moore accepted $1 million from Pittston in settlement of the suit, absolving the company of any further liability. At the same time, the Moore administration also refused to pay a Buffalo Creek cleanup bill from the Army Corps of Engineers for $3.7 million. Ten years later the U.S. Supreme Court ordered the state to pay the $3.7 million bill plus about $10 million interest. In 1989, the state finally paid $9.5 million to settle the debt to the Corps of Engineers. James A. Haught, who covered the Buffalo Creek disaster as an investigative reporter for the *Charleston Gazette*, says that no satisfactory answer has ever been given for why Governor Moore settled with Pittston without first requiring the firm to pay the pending Corps of Engineers bill. Former Moore staffer and biographer Brad Crouser defends Moore, maintaining that the governor had little to do with either the Army Corps of Engineers bill or the lawsuit against Pittston. Crouser says Kanawha circuit judge Thomas McHugh ruled many of the costs "unrecoverable," gutting the claim against Pittston. Citing an unnamed lawyer close to the settlement process, he says suggestions that Moore had taken a bribe to settle with Pittston had no merit. Also despite the U.S. Supreme Court's ruling to the contrary, Crouser insists that the Corps of Engineers had no legitimate claim against the state.[44]

In the 1972 election, Governor Moore proposed ten redevelopment projects to help the survivors of the Buffalo Creek disaster to recover, but after the immediate relief efforts, further recovery came slowly and few of the projects were completed. As time passed, residents felt that the state and federal government broke promises made at the time of the disaster. Three years later residents still awaited the promised new water and sewer systems as well as a new road from Man through Buffalo Creek to Raleigh County and connections to the West Virginia Turnpike. Many still waited in the HUD trailers for 750 promised new houses. Similarly, promises of a solid waste disposal system, a community center, recreation facilities, and a health clinic remained unfulfilled.[45] Eventually ninety apartments and seventeen of the promised homes were built on the site of an old gob pile in Robinette and two other locations. In pursuit of the road project, the state department of highways actually condemned and purchased hundreds of parcels of land from survivors, but instead of a projected four-lane super road, the state built a two-lane road which failed to establish the promised link to Raleigh County, and in many instances the state refused to sell the land back to the original owners.[46]

Kai Erikson and the Persisting Stereotype

Even in the telling of the story, the old stereotypes persisted. Kai Erikson's *Everything in Its Path: Destruction of Community in the Buffalo Creek Flood* not only became the most influential book about the disaster, it also helped define Appalachia for social scientists. Erikson, a social psychologist at Yale University, had no notion of writing a book about Buffalo Creek when the Arnold and Porter firm approached him to suggest a sociologist who might help with its lawsuit against Pittston Coal. After a visit to the area, Erikson, "awed and depressed" by what he had seen, volunteered his own services to the law firm, though he admitted that he "knew very little about Appalachia, very little about coal mining, and very little about the character of human disasters."[47] He nevertheless went on to write the book based on his research for Arnold and Porter, and perhaps because he was a Yale professor with an established reputation in the field of sociology, the book received much positive attention, won the prestigious Sorokin award, became a classic in the field—and reinforced negative stereotypes about Appalachian culture. At the beginning of the twenty-first century, sociology textbooks continued to cite it as authoritative. Marshall University scholars Lynda Ann Ewen and Julia A. Lewis have suggested that "Erikson's conclusions about the people of Appalachia and 'Appalachian culture' have, along with studies of snake handlers, come to define what students who study sociology know about West Virginia and more generally about Appalachia."[48] Though Erikson expressed great compassion for the residents of Buffalo Creek, wrote a clear narrative of what happened on February 26, 1972, and quoted extensively (but without attribution) the compelling words of the flood survivors, he also made many unwarranted assumptions about mountain culture based on archaic and unscientific sources, concluding that the culture of Appalachia had drifted from "individual freedom to enforced conformity, from self assertion to passivity, from ability to disability, from tidiness to an almost sullen kind of slovenliness, and from independence to an ever-growing dependency."[49] Erikson acknowledged the exploitation of the people by business and political forces, but he nevertheless focused on the people and their culture as problematic, not unlike other well-intentioned writers such as Jack E. Weller in *Yesterday's People* and Brit Hume in *Death and the Mines*.[50] Another problem with Erikson's work was that he and his co-workers made a quick trip into Buffalo Creek, conducted interviews opening up all the anguished feelings of the flood survivors, and then left the survivors in the hands of overwhelmed local mental health officials who knew little about how to deal with post-traumatic stress and the double loss of family and community.[51]

Preventing Another Buffalo Creek?

Much like the Farmington disaster inspired health and safety legislation, the enormity of the Buffalo Creek flood aroused widespread resolve among citizens and government officials to prevent future similar disasters and led to reforms in state and federal laws concerning coal slag dams. Soon after the dam collapse, Governor Moore ordered the draining of 100 settling ponds in the state.[52] In 1973, the West Virginia Legislature passed the Dam Control Act, requiring stricter standards for all dams in the state. It also passed a Coal

Refuse Act, placing some restrictions on slag piles. Later, the federal Surface Mining Control and Reclamation Act of 1977 outlawed the kind of sketch Steve Dasovich used for Dam No. 3, requiring that coal operators obtain state and federal approval for plans before building dams. The new rules required that all dams be built on solid ground, not on top of old coal waste impoundments, have spillways or drainage pipes to keep water in the impoundments at a safe level, and be regularly inspected.[53]

Jack Spadaro, a young instructor at the West Virginia School of Mines in 1972, became the staff engineer of the Governor's Ad Hoc Commission and later ran the state programs to regulate and improve coal dam safety. Jointly, the Army Corps of Engineers, the Soil Conservation Service, Bureau of Mines, and the state DNR carried out an aerial survey that ranked dams, establishing 150 dams as high risk. The new legislation required companies to either drain or repair existing dams and gave agencies sufficient clout to require coal companies to cooperate. The failure to cooperate could result in closure of a mining operation's cleaning plant, which would mean the stopping of production.[54]

With the reforms, concern about the coal waste impoundments, slag piles, and slurry would fade quickly from public view, but in the nearly four decades since the disaster, numerous slurry spills and impoundment accidents have occurred throughout Appalachia.[55] In a twenty-five-year retrospective series on Buffalo Creek in 1997, *Charleston Gazette* journalist Ken Ward Jr. brought the issue to public attention again when he noted that the potential for disaster still loomed over many West Virginia communities. In 1997, over 1,000 coal waste dams existed, 232 in West Virginia, and most were much larger than the Buffalo Creek dam. Should one of the larger dams break, the potential for destruction would be even greater than in the Buffalo Creek disaster. Inspectors of the Mine Health and Safety Administration and of the West Virginia Division of Environmental Protection insisted that because of more effective laws and closer regulation, none of the new era dams could become another Buffalo Creek. Ward, using a Freedom of Information Act inquiry, found that in the twenty-year period between 1977 and 1997, five coal waste dams had experienced serious failures. Ward also questioned why statutes and regulations continued to allow coal companies to use coal-processing refuse to build dams. Given the criticisms of the Buffalo Creek investigations that almost uniformly blamed the dam failure on the use of gob or slag as a construction material, it would seem that the reforms ignored one of the major lessons of the Buffalo Creek disaster. A Division of Environmental Protection safety engineer in Logan, Jim Pierce, told Ward (unconsciously repeating a rationale offered by Steve Dasovich twenty-five years before): "There's no other efficient way to get rid of the sludge. If we want a coal industry in this area, this is a necessary evil we have to live with. But at least now we have greatly diminished the risk involved."[56]

As an alternative to sludge impoundments, some companies turned to injecting slurry into abandoned mines, often with the deleterious results suggested by the WVU professors in 1967: the slurry contaminates drinking water in surrounding communities. In 2008, at Prenter, in Boone County, tests found that the water contained arsenic, barium, lead, and manganese in unhealthy levels. Investigations by the West Virginia Department of Environmental Protection have been inconclusive. No state or federal agency has yet confirmed a link between coal slurry injection and drinking water contamination, at least in part because of the difficulty of tracing material injected deep underground. It is likely that the problem comes from the leaching of the slurry into aquifers. In some cases the slurry has blown out the sides of mountains, spilling into streams and onto the surface. Coalfield residents with black or orange water streaming from their taps think the link is obvious.[57]

The most dangerous spill incident since Buffalo Creek, described as one of the worst environmental disasters that has ever occurred in the southeastern United States, took place in Martin County, Kentucky, in October 2001. The sludge in an impoundment similar to those at Buffalo Creek broke through the floor into an abandoned mine, sending a massive stream of sludge out into tributaries of the Big Sandy and Tug Fork rivers and contaminating water, land, and residential properties over a distance of eighty miles. Incredibly, no one died. An official of the Massey Energy subsidiary operating the impoundment used the same rationale as the Pittston official after Buffalo Creek, insisting that the collapse was an "act of God."[58]

In 2009, West Virginia had 560 dams including about 100 coal slurry impoundments. The U.S. Army Corps of Engineers National

Inventory of dams listed 382 as high-hazard, including 30 that needed repairs.[59] Most of the coal slurry impoundments of the twenty-first century are significantly larger than the Buffalo Creek dams of 1972, so the potential for another, even greater disaster exists.

Epilogue:
Another Reawakening?

In the fall of 1971, John Denver's recording "Take Me Home, Country Roads" hit the airwaves and became not only a hit in West Virginia but throughout the country. Being the object of so much negative attention for so long, West Virginians welcomed Denver's song although Denver and his co-writers knew little about the state. The song mentions the Shenandoah River and Blue Ridge Mountains, which only pass through a few miles of the Eastern Panhandle. The key line was "Almost Heaven, West Virginia." On the charts for several months into 1972, the song became something of an unofficial state anthem. Governor Arch Moore and his commerce commissioner Lysander Dudley recognized the benefits of the tune in an election year and arranged to have "Almost Heaven" stamped on license plates and tourist advertising.[1] Politics and reality aside, most West Virginians happily embraced Denver's ditty with its simple lyrics and catchy tune, even during the grim aftermath of the Buffalo Creek disaster.

Despite the War on Poverty and all that has intervened in the four decades since, and despite the efficient and impressive technology of the coal industry a decade into the new century, much of the poverty and insecurity of the new machine age persists for many in central Appalachia. The eventful era from Farmington in 1968 to Buffalo Creek in 1972 inspired an Appalachian reawakening and successful grassroots-driven battles to improve coal mine health and safety and to reform the United Mine Workers of America. The civil rights movement, building on earlier achievements, continued to advance, and the women's movement emerged. Efforts to ban or to judiciously restrict strip mining and to reform state politics proved less successful. After 1972, both Jay Rockefeller (who after his defeat in 1972 would serve as president of West Virginia Wesleyan College until resigning in 1975 to run successfully for governor in 1976) and Arnold Miller, the new president of the UMWA put in office by the reformers, abandoned the fight over strip mining, leaving the grassroots citizen's groups without powerful allies.

By 1972, the War on Poverty had ended. Some aspects of it, notably Head Start, Job Corps, and VISTA, continued for many decades thereafter and into the new century. Another monument of the era, the Appalachian Regional Commission, also continued (despite efforts to eliminate it in the 1980s) and was largely responsible for nearly 2,300 miles of roads built in the region by the beginning of the new century and improvements in water plants and sewer facilities. Some regional centers reaped the benefits. Raleigh County, for example, after suffering severe population losses in the 1950s and 1960s, resumed growth after ARC funds helped make Beckley a regional transportation and tourism hub. Beckley grew from the tenth to the third largest city in the state.[2]

Forty years after the launching of the War on Poverty, some areas in the thirteen-state Appalachian region had improved markedly, and the regional poverty rate had fallen from 31 percent in 1960 to 13.6 percent in 2000.[3] But much poverty remained, especially in the rural counties of central Appalachia, where per capita payments for income maintenance programs more than doubled similar payments in other parts of Appalachia. Though Raleigh County reversed its population losses and seemed in some ways to exemplify the success of the ARC's regional growth center concept, in 1998 26.6 percent of the population still relied on government transfer payments for income.[4] McDowell, one of the early target counties of the War on Poverty, continued to languish with 38 percent of the population below the poverty line and median household income at less than half the national average. The poverty of McDowell, the other southern West Virginia coal mining counties, and other rural areas of Appalachia persisted even as the coal industry flourished and continued to find ways to produce more coal with fewer workers. In 2003, coal trains hauled more than 4 million tons of coal out of McDowell, but the industry employed only 700 coal miners.[5] In 1948 it took 126,000 miners to produce 169 million tons of coal in the state.[6] By 2002, the rising efficiency of the industry made it possible to produce 164 million tons of coal with just 15,377 miners.[7] As Appalachian historian Ronald D Eller notes in *Uneven Ground*, like the rest of America, Appalachia moved away from an industrial-based to a service-oriented economy. Now fewer workers can hope to be coal miners, one of the few well-paying jobs for workers in the region. The lower-skilled and undereducated have to compete for retail jobs as sales clerks, waiters, receptionists, stockroom workers, and other entry-level jobs.[8] As early as 1997, Walmart became the largest private sector employer in West Virginia, and by 2009 the firm employed nearly as many workers in the state as the entire coal industry.[9] By 2010, coal represented about 6 percent of West Virginia's gross domestic product, less than the percentages for retail and manufacturing, but the industry continued to be critical to the state's economy. An estimate put the industry's total job impact across the state at 37,000, accounting for up to 40 percent of the labor force in some counties. The industry also generates severance tax revenues of hundreds of millions of dollars.[10]

The UMWA, once something of a countervailing force to coal industry management in the state, has declined in influence as its numbers have dwindled. Some of the largest mountaintop removal operations are non-union, and ironically, a fierce anti-union sentiment has developed among many in southern West Virginia, the scene of the historic UMWA demonstrations and strikes of the 1960s and 1970s.[11] Emblematic of the new era, on Labor Day 2009, far more people attended a celebration sponsored by Massey Energy on a reclaimed mining site at Holden in Logan County than the traditional UMWA Labor Day rally at Spencer.[12]

Just as poverty persists, so do the perils of life and labor in Appalachia. The enormity of the tragedies at Farmington and Buffalo Creek created powerful forces for change, and the consequent reforms made mining immeasurably safer, but mine disasters still happen, black lung is resurgent, and flooding grows more severe. At Sago, Upshur County, on January 2, 2006, twelve miners died in a mine explosion, and on April 5, 2010, another explosion killed twenty-nine at Massey Energy's Upper Big Branch mine at Montcoal, Raleigh County. From 1969 to 1995 black lung disease decreased by 90 percent and seemed on the road to eradication, but in the last ten years coal miners' pneumoconiosis has been listed as the cause of death for more than 10,000 miners, and the prevalence has more than doubled with severe cases being observed in underground miners as young as 39. The hot spots for the re-emerging disease are in central Appalachia: southern West Virginia, eastern Kentucky, and parts of Virginia. Death rates are highest in West Virginia. The technology exists to prevent the disease, but whether because of inadequate enforcement of dust standards by government agencies, the flouting of them by workers or employers, or other reasons, prevention no longer works as well as it did, and too many coal miners die unnecessarily.[13]

Beyond the impact on coal miners, a recent sobering study by Michael Hendryx, a professor of public health at West Virginia University and Melissa Ahern of Washington State University strongly suggests that living near underground and mountaintop removal mines and coal processing facilities in West Virginia leads to higher overall mortality rates, especially for chronic lung, heart, and kidney disease as well as lung and digestive-system cancers. They found mortality rates higher in Appalachian counties with high levels of mining than in counties with lower levels or none at all. The counties with the highest rate of mining also had the poorest socioeconomic conditions. They conclude that "the human cost of Appalachian coal mining outweighs its economic benefits." Although the authors admit that their study cannot conclusively prove that mining pollution causes the elevated mortality rates, since they cannot know what the rates would be in the absence of mining, the statistics suggest a strong correlation.[14] In early 2010, the journal *Science* published a study by researchers from several universities that found mountaintop removal mining harmful to human health as well as destructive to the ecosystem. The lead author, Margaret Palmer of the University of Maryland Center for Environmental Science, said: "The science is so overwhelming that the only conclusion that one can reach is that mountaintop mining needs to be stopped." Chris Hamilton of the West Virginia Coal Association rejected the study saying, "It's just flat-out wrong."[15]

After the failure of the attempts to restrict or to abolish strip mining in 1971–72, a new era in mining technology began in the Appalachians with multiple seam and mountain top removal mining. In the 1970s and 1980s, operators imported to the Appalachian hills the methods and yet another generation of larger machines from the open-pit mines of the West. Now instead of hundreds of acres, sites grew to thousands with draglines as high as twenty-story apartment buildings. The rocks and soil removed from the mountains filled the valleys and streams below, burying hundreds of miles of streams such as Little Coal, Guyandotte, Tug Fork, Big Coal, Twelve Pole, and Mud in southern West Virginia.[16]

In the face of a growing public outcry against mountaintop removal mining in Appalachia, defenders continue to argue that flattened land provides opportunities for development that never before existed, but a relatively small percentage of surface-mined land is ever used for such purposes. As Pocahontas Coal executive W. E. E. Koepler had imagined back in the days of the Great Depression, some of the flattened mountains have become airports or recreational sites (notably the Twisted Gun Golf Course on a remote former mountaintop in Mingo County). In eastern Kentucky around the town of Hazard reclaimed mine lands have provided building sites for subdivisions, retail stores, restaurants and hotels, an industrial park, airport, National Guard armory, and even a nursing home for veterans. But these kinds of uses of reclaimed mine lands are the rare exception. Over the past thirty years, applications for surface mining typically commit to reclaim the site after mining as grasslands or fish and wildlife habitat. Between 1999 and 2009, fewer than 3 percent of applications in Kentucky proposed any other kind of reclamation. A study of southern West Virginia in 2002 similarly concluded that only about 3 percent of surface-mined land would ever be developed.[17]

Compliant coal companies who followed the early rules of the Surface Mining Control and Reclamation Act of 1977 generally reclaimed the land by burying the rocks, compacting the surface, and planting fast-growing grasses, a method that made the return of typical Appalachian flora unlikely. As companies collected their bond money and moved on, such lands usually reverted to low-quality shrub and forest cover with little or no commercial value. Hoping to find at least some common ground between those who oppose and those who support MTR, the Office of Surface Mining (OSM) now encourages reclamation through loose grading rather than compaction, establishing a soil base friendlier to reforestation, and offering the hope of the eventual return of valuable hardwood forests and some semblance of the former Appalachian ecology. Even if this effort succeeds, millions of acres have already been reclaimed as grasslands. Moreover, some 500,000 to 1,000,000 acres of unreclaimed land still exist, much of it dating from the early days of strip mining, posing various environmental problems that endanger the public. As neither the states nor the federal government budget funds for such activities, OSM encourages volunteer efforts to roughen and loosen the compacted soils of past reclamation efforts.[18]

As part of a court settlement in a 1998 case, the federal government agreed to assign scientists in various agencies the task of studying the environmental impact of mountaintop removal mining in Appalachia to find ways to limit the environmental damage, especially to streams. They found that between 1985 and 2001, MTR buried or polluted 1,200 miles of streams in the region and cut down 7 percent of the Appalachian forest. The interagency scientific analysis concluded that, unabated, MTR would result in a loss of more that 1.4 million acres by the end of the decade, severely affecting fish, wildlife, and bird species as well as neighboring communities. The Bush administration, to the shock of the scientists, required that their environmental impact statement eliminate suggestions for less destructive methods and "focus on centralizing and streamlining coal permitting."[19]

In the period after Farmington and Buffalo Creek, Appalachian grassroots forces accomplished a great deal, though they failed to stop or to moderate strip mining. Lacking support from the UMWA after the early 1970s, the loosely organized groups could call attention to critical issues, but given the reality of the powerful forces they faced, they could not win. Efforts to organize on a regional basis also had little success although groups like the Council of the Southern Mountains or Appalachian Alliance (which arose after a disastrous flood of the Tug River in 1977 and brought together some 75 organizations with up to 1,000 members) had occasional successes.[20] One of the most enduring regional organizations has been the Appalachian Studies Association, an alliance of scholars, activists, and community people. The ASA helped the Appalachian Alliance carry out the Appalachian Land Ownership Study, and scholar-activist cooperation also helped Appalshop, a grassroots-based multimedia production collective in Whitesburg, Kentucky.[21]

Could there be another Appalachian reawakening, another time when the conjunction of events, social forces, personalities, organizations, and commitment is such that some of the continuing dilemmas of the region could be successfully addressed as in the period after Farmington and Buffalo Creek? In 2008, summarizing some of the sad facts of the state's history in an essay "Night Comes to the Appalachians" in the *New York Review of Books*, Michael Tomasky, a native of Morgantown, reluctantly concluded that "West Virginia is a place of the past." Now, he wrote, "There is only the grinding present, centered on the huge coal industry, the men who own it, the politicians, and the judges and bureaucrats they appoint; and there is a commonly held fear that even the little hope that exists now could evaporate."[22] Others see evidence of a "Coalfield Uprising," a new grassroots movement to fight mountaintop removal and to advocate for other Appalachian issues. Increasing numbers of Appalachians lobby Congress and demand change. Activist groups coordinate efforts, exchange ideas, and some engage in demonstrations. Among the many regional groups are the Ohio Valley Environmental Coalition, West Virginia Highlands Conservancy, West Virginia Environmental Coalition, United Mountain Defense, Coal River Mountain Watch, Mountain Justice, Alliance for Appalachia, Kentuckians for the Commonwealth, Save Our Cumberland Mountains, Appalachian Center for the Economy and Environment, Appalachian Voices, and Keeper of the Mountains Foundation. A major journalistic watchdog of the coal industry is Ken Ward Jr., of the *Charleston Gazette*, whose blog "Coal Tattoo" is one of the best day-to-day sources for environmental and coal industry developments.[23] Jack Spadaro, who helped coordinate the state's response to Buffalo Creek, said in a 2008 interview: "I'm seeing people now from the whole region joining together to fight mountaintop removal. I'm very optimistic that we will ultimately prevail; it's too precious to let go."[24] In the summer of 2009, Republican Senator Lamar Alexander of Tennessee and Democratic Senator Benjamin L. Cardin of Maryland introduced the Appalachian Restoration Act, a bill to ban mountaintop removal.[25]

State and regional politicians in Kentucky and West Virginia align themselves with the rich and powerful coal industry and dare not question the conventional wisdom. In November 2009, Governor Joe Manchin of West Virginia called together the state's major political and economic power brokers, including executives of the major coal producers to forge a united front against federal regulators, accused by coal officials and their allies of sending mixed signals. Among those at the meeting, Senator Rockefeller, who fought strip mining early in his career, praised the flattened land left by mountaintop removal mining as an aid to economic development.[26]

In an unusual break with this united front, just three weeks later, Senator Robert C. Byrd, one of the industry's staunchest allies for more than half a century, issued an opinion piece calling upon the coal industry to "embrace the future." Byrd outlined a future that would include fewer mining jobs and rising production costs as operating companies pursued waning deposits and thinner seams. He pointed out that a majority in Congress opposed mountaintop removal mining and that it made no sense to deny the mounting science of climate change, because some form of climate legislation would likely become public policy. Byrd urged that it made much more sense to accept the realities and work toward some kind of prudent middle ground rather than engaging in "fearmongering, grandstanding, and outrage" as a strategy.[27]

A majority probably believes (as the industry's allies and effective public relations tell them) that no sustainable economic alternatives to the status quo exist and that the state and the region must follow the will of King Coal, no matter how costly to the environment, the health of coalfield residents, and the future prospects of the region. A weakened UMWA no longer offers a countervailing force, and the miners, a dwindling component of the labor force, passionately resist any change that threatens their well-paying jobs. After several emotional demonstrations over the summer and fall of 2009 and in early 2010, on January 25, Governor Manchin issued a warning that intimidation and violence would not be tolerated.[28] The challenge of the new Appalachian reawakening will be to revisit some of the same mining health and safety issues as well as to persuade the people of Appalachia that there can be mining without mountaintop removal and that there can be a future without coal, a future that will come in any case and for which preparations should be accelerated.

Notes

Introduction

1. Jerry Bruce Thomas, *An Appalachian New Deal: West Virginia in the Great Depression* (Lexington: University Press of Kentucky, 1998).
2. The definition of Appalachia and even a precise delineation of its boundaries vary. One notable effort to explain the notion or "invention" of Appalachia from the perspective of intellectual history is: Henry Shapiro, *Appalachia on Our Mind: The Southern Mountains and Mountaineers in the American Consciousness, 1870–1920* (Chapel Hill: University of North Carolina Press, 1978). One attempt to delineate its boundaries excluded West Virginia's Northern Panhandle and much of the Ohio River Valley: Thomas R. Ford, ed., *The Southern Appalachian Region: A Survey* (Lexington: University of Kentucky Press, 1962), 48–49. The official government delineation of boundaries set forth by Congress in establishing the Appalachian Regional Commission includes all of West Virginia. John Alexander Williams offers good answers to the what and where of Appalachia in *Appalachia: A History* (Chapel Hill: University of North Carolina Press, 2002), 1–18. See also Richard B. Drake, *A History of Appalachia* (Lexington: University Press of Kentucky, 2001), vii–ix. Some of the best of recent scholarship on Appalachia can be found in three useful anthologies: Dwight B. Billings, Gurney Norman, and Katherine Ledford, eds., *Backtalk from Appalachia: Confronting Stereotypes* (Lexington: University Press of Kentucky, 1999); Richard A. Straw and H. Tyler Blethen, *High Mountains Rising: Appalachia in Time and Place* (Urbana: University of Illinois Press, 2004); Stephen L. Fisher, ed., *Fighting Back in Appalachia: Traditions of Resistance and Change* (Philadelphia: Temple University Press, 1993). When this book neared completion of a first draft, I received two important books that cover some of the same "uneven ground" that I traverse. Both have enriched my understanding and enhanced this book. Ronald D Eller's *Uneven Ground: Appalachia since 1945* (Lexington: University Press of Kentucky, 2008) is magisterial and sweeping, synthesizing much of the research on Appalachia in an account that covers from 1945 to the present. My focus is less comprehensive, focusing on

West Virginia and taking the story only to 1972. Thomas Kiffmyer's *Reformers to Radicals: The Appalachian Volunteers and the War on Poverty* (Lexington: University of Kentucky Press, 2008) focuses primarily on Kentucky, though he also touches upon West Virginia. Kiffmyer and I see the AVs somewhat differently, possibly because of different circumstances in the two states. At the end of the 1960s, David S. Walls and John B. Stephenson edited an anthology recounting some of the issues and events of the decade in Appalachia. Several of the articles therein as well as the title have influenced this book. *Appalachia in the Sixties: Decade of Reawakening* (Lexington: The University Press of Kentucky, 1972).

3. Over the years of its operation, 1921–1960, 160 workers died in mining accidents at Glen Rogers: Bud Perry and Karl C. Lilly, *Reopening Glen Rogers* (n.d., n.p., Chapman Printing), 43.

4. See chap. 3 for a further discussion of Glen Rogers as an example of modernized segregation.

5. Brit Hume, *Death and the Mines: Rebellion and Murder in the UMW* (New York: Grossman, 1971), 94. For an excellent collection of articles about Appalachian stereotypes, see Billings, Norman, and Ledford, eds., *Back Talk from Appalachia*. See especially in regard to West Virginians confronting stereotypes, Denise Giardina, "Appalachian Images: A Personal History," 161–173 and Stephen L. Fisher, "Appalachian Stepchild," 187–190.

6. *The Pinevillian*, May 22, 1959. See chap. 1 for an account of the Great Migration.

7. Robert F. Munn, "The Latest Rediscovery of Appalachia," in *Appalachia in the Sixties*, eds. Walls and Stephenson, 25–30. Munn was the Director of Libraries at West Virginia University.

8. Roul Tunley, "The Strange Case of West Virginia," *Saturday Evening Post* (Feb. 6, 1969): 19–20, 64–66. See chap. 2 for more on the Tunley article and similar literature.

9. Russell Baker, *New York Times*, August 22, 1963.

10. Shapiro, *Appalachia on Our Mind*, xiv.

11. Malcolm Harrison Ross, *Machine Age in the Hills* (New York: MacMillan, 1933); Harry Caudill quotes Toynbee in the foreword to Jack E. Weller, *Yesterday's People: Life in Contemporary Appalachia* (Lexington: University of Kentucky Press, 1965), xii.

12. Weller, *Yesterday's People*; Kai Erikson, *Everything in Its Path: Destruction of Community in the Buffalo Creek Flood* (New York:

Simon and Schuster, 1976); "The Mountain Ethos," 79–93. For critiques of Erikson's book and of the culture of poverty thesis see review by Dwight Billings and Sally Maggard in *Social Forces*, 57, no. 2 (Dec. 1978): 722–23 and Lynda Ann Ewing and Julia A. Lewis, "Buffalo Creek Revisited: Deconstructing Kai Erikson's Stereotypes," *Appalachian Journal: A Regional Studies Review*, 27, no. 1 (Fall, 1999): 22–45. The Buffalo Creek disaster is discussed in chap. 9.

13. I read *The Children of Sanchez* in 1963 as part of training for Peace Corps community action work in Latin America, and strange to say, shortly thereafter young college graduates from other parts of the country would be reading it to prepare for War on Poverty programs in Appalachia. Just as many VISTA and Appalachian workers would find it irrelevant in Appalachia, I also found that even in a Latin culture it missed the point. The problems were institutional. For critiques of Lewis's *The Children of Sanchez* and the culture of poverty thesis, see Ronald D Eller, *Uneven Ground: Appalachia since 1945* (Lexington: University Press of Kentucky), 100, 137 and Irwin Unger, *The Best of Intentions: The Triumph and Failure of the Great Society under Kennedy, Johnson, and Nixon* (New York: Doubleday, 1996), 28–30.

14. Rupert B. Vance, in "An Introductory Note," to Weller, *Yesterday's People*, ix.

15. John D. Photiadis and Harry K. Schwarzweller, eds., *Change in Rural Appalachia: Implications for Rural Programs* (Philadelphia: University of Pennsylvania Press, 1967), vii; Jennifer Egolf, Ken Fones-Wolf, and Louis C. Martin, eds., *Culture, Class, and Politics in Modern Appalachia: Essays in Honor of Ronald L. Lewis* (Morgantown: West Virginia University Press, 2009); Dwight B. Billings, "Introduction: Writing Appalachia: Old Ways, New Ways, and WVU Ways," 1–28.

16. A summary of recent Appalachian scholarship focusing on the work of West Virginia University history professor Ronald L. Lewis and his students is Billings, "Writing Appalachia," in Egolf, Fones-Wolf, and Martin, *Culture, Class, and Politics*, 1–28.

17. Ibid. The world systems approach has led to some remarkably stimulating and deeply researched additions to Appalachian Studies. Among them are Wilma A. Dunaway, *The First American Frontier: Transition to Capitalism in Southern Appalachia, 1700–1860* (Chapel Hill: University of North Carolina Press, 1996); Dwight B. Billings, Kathleen M. Blee, *The Road to Poverty: The Making of Wealth and Hardship in Appalachia* (Cambridge: Cambridge University Press, 2000); Ronald L. Lewis, *Transforming the Appalachian Countryside:*

Railroads, Deforestation, and Social Change in West Virginia, 1880–1920 (Chapel Hill: University of North Carolina Press,1998). Among Wallerstein's works are: *The Capitalist World Economy* (Cambridge: Cambridge University Press, 1979) and *Historical Capitalism* (London: Verson ed., 1983).

18. A summary of recent Appalachian scholarship focusing on the work of West Virginia University professor Ronald L. Lewis and his students is Billings, "Writing Appalachia," in *Culture, Class, and Politics in Modern Appalachia*, 1–28.

19. Allan J. Matusow, *The Unraveling of America: A History of Liberalism in the 1960s* (New York: Harper and Row, 1984), 254–55, 442.

1. A New Machine Age in the Hills

1. James T. Patterson, *Grand Expectations: The United States, 1945–1974* (New York: Oxford University Press, 1997), 61.

2. Harold Vatter, *The U.S Economy in the 1950s* (New York: W. W. Norton, 1963), 1. Like Vatter, many historians of the period stress its affluence. Among them are John Patrick Diggins, *The Proud Decades: America in War and Peace, 1941–1960* (New York: W. W. Norton and Company, 1988), 178–180; James T. Patterson, *Grand Expectations: The United States, 1945–1974* (New York: Oxford University Press, 1997), whose chapter on the economy of the 1950s is titled "The Biggest Boom Yet"; David Halberstam, *The Fifties* (New York: Villard Books, 1993); William H. Chafe, *The Unfinished Journey: America Since World War II*, 5th ed (New York: Oxford University Press, 2003), 107.

3. Numan V. Bartley, *The New South, 1945–1980: The Story of the South's Modernization* (A History of the South, v. 11 (Baton Rouge: Louisiana State University Press, 1995), 107.

4. Thomas R. Ford, ed., *The Appalachian Region: A Survey* (Lexington: University of Kentucky Press), 3.

5. Harry M. Caudill, *Night Comes to the Cumberlands: A Biography of a Depressed Area* (Boston: Little, Brown and Company, 1962), xii.

6. The term "American paradox" appears in Roul Tunley, "The Strange Case of West Virginia," *Saturday Evening Post* (Feb. 6, 1960): 19–20; 64–66. Tunley's article and similar treatments by the metropolitan press are further discussed in chapters 2 and 4.

7. Chad Berry, *Southern Migrants, Northern Exiles* (Urbana: University of Illinois Press, 2000), 104–05; Bartley, *The New South*, 146.

8. Alan Derickson, *Black Lung: Anatomy of a Public Health Disaster* (Ithaca, NY: Cornell University Press, 1998), 112–140; Curtis Seltzer, *Fire in the Hole* (Lexington: University Press of Kentucky, 1985), 71–84, 88; Ronald D Eller, *Uneven Ground: Appalachia Since 1945* (Lexington: University Press of Kentucky, 2008), 18–19; John Gaventa, *Power and Powerlessness: Quiescence and Rebellion in an Appalachian Valley* (Urbana: University of Illinois Press, 1980).

9. Based on report by Lowell D. Ashby in U.S. Commerce Department, "Survey of Current Business Conditions," cited in Harry Ernst, "50s Depression Seen Blessing in Disguise," in *Charleston Gazette*, November 13, 1964.

10. Quote from *West Virginia State Magazine* 3, no. 4 (Feb. 1952), end paper; John Alexander Williams, *West Virginia, A Bicentennial History* (New York: W. W. Norton and Company, 1976), 172–77.

11. Lou Martin, "Steel Industry," in *West Virginia Encyclopedia*, ed. Ken Sullivan (Charleston: West Virginia Humanities Council, 2006): 681–82.

12. U.S. Department of Commerce, Bureau of the Census, *Historical Statistics of the United States: Colonial Times to 1790*, Bicentennial Edition, Pt. I, (Washington, 1975), "General Statistics for Manufacturing by State," 73.

13. Howard W. Carson, ed., *West Virginia Blue Book, 1973* (Charleston: West Virginia State Senate, 1973), 1042.

14. C. L. Christenson, *Economic Redevelopment in Bituminous Coal: The Special Case of Technological Advance in United States Coal Mines, 1930–1960* (Cambridge: Harvard University Press, 1962), 252.

15. Christenson, *Economic Redevelopment in Bituminous Coal*, 73–85; Melvyn Dubofsky and Warren Van Tine, *John L. Lewis, A Biography* (Urbana: University of Illinois Press, 1986), 344; Ernst, "50s Depression"; John B. Long, "Personal Observations Relating to Development of a Mining Machine Industry in W.Va. and to the W.Va. Coal Mining Industry Itself, 1945–1970," paper given at Bluefield, September 14, 1979, at conference on coal history, in John B. Long Manuscript, West Virginia State Archives; Homer Bigart, "Depression Hit Town is Buoyant," *New York Times*, Oct. 29, 1963, 21. Curtis Seltzer makes the case that the conventional notion of coal being subject to boom and bust cycles is erroneous. He says that except for a few years of erratic, transient surges, the industry stagnated from 1920 to 1970: Seltzer, *Fire in the Hole*, 34–36. See also Caudill's pioneering account, *Night Comes to the Cumberlands*, especially 305–64.

16. "Continuous Coal Mining," *Fortune* (June, 1950): 110–14; Dubofsky and Van Tine, *John L. Lewis*, 350.
17. Irwin Unger, *The Best of Intentions: The Triumph and Failure of the Great Society Under Kennedy, Johnson, and Nixon* (New York: Doubleday, 1996), 28.
18. Christenson, *Economic Redevelopment in Bituminous Coal*, 134–35; quote from Seltzer, *Fire in the Hole*, 65; Paul H. Rakes, "West Virginia Coal Mine Fatalities: The Subculture of Danger and a Statistical Overview of the Pre-enforcement Era," *West Virginia History*, New Series, vol. 2, no. 1 (Spring 2008): 1–26; Derickson, *Black Lung*; Barbara Ellen Smith, *Digging Our Own Graves: Coal Miners and the Struggle Over Black Lung Disease* (Philadelphia: Temple University Press, 1987), 47; Jack Temple Kirby, *Rural Worlds Lost: The American South, 1920–1960* (Baton Rogue: Louisiana State University Press, 1987), 108–09.
19. A 1950 census report listed death rates for coal miners at nearly twice the rates of all working men, even excluding deaths due to accident. From 1960 to 1965 injury frequency rates *increased* in the industry as coal mining remained the most dangerous industry in the country with injury rates considerably higher than the next most dangerous industry, lumbering. James D. McAteer, *Coal Mine Health and Safety: The Case of West Virginia* (New York: Praeger, 1973), 104–06.
20. Neil Boggs, "Mine Safety Program Lowers Fatality Rate," *Charleston Gazette*, April 22, 1954. A recent account of the Monongah disaster says company officials undercounted the death toll and that it likely exceeded 550: Davitt McAteer, *Monongah: The Tragic Story of the 1907 Monongah Mine Disaster, the Worst Industrial Accident in U.S. History* (Morgantown: West Virginia University Press, 2007), 238.
21. Boggs, "Mine Safety Program."
22. McAteer, *Coal Mine Health and Safety*, x.
23. For authoritative accounts of the medical issues and the coal miners' struggle to obtain recognition of black lung disease see Derickson, *Black Lung*; Smith, *Digging Our Own Graves*; Ivana Krajcinovic, *From Company Doctors to Managed Care: The United Mine Workers' Noble Experiment* (Ithaca: Cornell University Press, 1997); Richard P. Mulcahy, *A Social Contract for the Coal Fields: The Rise and Fall of the United Mine Workers of America Welfare and Retirement Fund* (Knoxville: University of Tennessee Press, 2000). See also chapter six below for further discussion of the black lung movement. On the impact of the continuous miner on mining dangers, see McAteer, *Coal*

Mine Health and Safety, 16–17; Rakes, "West Virginia Coal Mine Fatalities," 13.

24. George Lawless, "West Virginia's Top Ten Stories in 1958," *Sunday Gazette-Mail*, Dec. 28, 1958.
25. "Disaster Mine 'No. 22' Closes," *Charleston Gazette*, March 5, 1965, 1.
26. Barlow, *Coal and Coal Mining*, 43–46; Hume, *Death and the Mines*, 99.
27. A. S. Barksdale, "Bluefield Coal Show, Gala Event," *West Virginia State Magazine* 3, no. 7 (May, 1954): 17–18, 21, 24.
28. Walter R. Thurmond, *The Logan Coalfield of West Virginia: A Brief History* (Morgantown: West Virginia University Library, 1964), 72–73.
29. "Mine Mechanization is Causing Return to Methods of Old," *Charleston Gazette*, December 23, 1958.
30. "Union to Base Drive on Pensions," *Charleston Gazette*, March 5, 1965, 19.
31. Christenson, *Economic Redevelopment in Bituminous Coal*, 162–64.
32. J. Howard Myers, ed., *West Virginia Blue Book, 1963*, "Comparative Data, Mine Statistics," 916–17.
33. In "Faces of Coal," Transcript of interviews done by William Mares in 1972–73, in Raleigh County Coal Miners Collection, West Virginia State Archives, Charleston, West Virginia.
34. Thurmond, *Logan Coal Field*, 71–72.
35. Long, "Mining Machine Industry," 9. Chapters 6 and 7 below examine the movements to obtain black lung legislation and the Miners for Democracy, which managed to replace W. A. "Tony" Boyle with Arnold Miller as UMWA president.
36. Ibid.; "Long Airdox Company," http://www.marmon.com/Publications/Interchange/95Febp2.htm. See also "Long Super Mine Car Co. is Nationally Known Firm," *West Virginia State Magazine* 2, no. 8 (June 1951): 19; "Piggyback Nationally-Known in Industry," ibid., 4, no. 1 (November, 1952): 19, 42.
37. Long, "Mining Machinery Industry," 2–5.
38. Melvyn Dubofsky and Warren Van Tine, *John L. Lewis: A Biography* (Urbana: University of Illinois Press), 355–59. Derickson, *Black Lung*, 138, says Lewis understood the dangers to the membership but tacitly accepted a decline in working conditions as the price of the fund and as part of the price for the survival of the industry.
39. U.S. Department of the Interior, *A Medical Survey of the Bituminous Coal Industry: Report of the Coal Mines Administration* (Washington:

Government Printing Office, 1947); Dubofsky and Van Tine, *John L. Lewis*, 302–47.

40. Nelson Lichtenstein, "From Corporatism to Collective Bargaining: Organized Labor and the Eclipse of Social Democracy in the Post War Era," ed. Steve Frazier and Gary Gerstle, *The Rise and Fall of the New Deal Order, 1930–1980* (Princeton: Princeton University Press, 1989), 122–43.

41. Two book-length studies of the UMWA's welfare and medical funds experiment are Krajcinovic, *From Company Doctors to Managed Care* and Mulcahy, *A Social Contract for the Coal Fields*. Mulcahy tends to be somewhat more sympathetic to problems faced by the union leadership and fund managers. See also George S. Goldstein, "The Rise and Decline of the UMWA Health and Retirement Funds Program, 1946–1995," ed. John M. Laslett, *The United Mineworkers of America: A Model of Industrial Solidarity?* (University Park: The Pennsylvania State University Press, 1996), 239–50 and Dubofsky and Van Tine, *John L. Lewis*, 336–48.

42. Seltzer, *Fire in the Hole*, 71.

43. McAteer, *Coal Mine Health and Safety*, 100–03.

44. Lichtenstein, "From Corporatism to Collective Bargaining," 122–23.

45. Dubofsky and Van Tine, *John L. Lewis*, 356–57; Long, "Mining Machine Industry," 9. See also Crandall A. Shifflett, *Coal Towns: Life, Work, and Culture in Company Towns of Southern Appalachia, 1880–1960* (Knoxville: University of Tennessee Press, 1991), 210; Ronald L. Lewis, *Black Coal Miners in America: Race, Class, and Community Conflict* (Lexington: University Press of Kentucky, 1987), 178–79; Seltzer, *Fire in the Hole*, 36–37; Derickson, *Black Lung*, 139–42.

46. Shifflett, *Coal Towns*, 211.

47. *An Economic Atlas for West Virginia* (Charleston: West Virginia Department of Commerce, Planning and Research Division, n.d.), 2.

48. Eller, *Uneven Ground*, 29.

49. West Virginia State Planning Board, *Report of the Coordinating Committee in the Field of Agriculture and Rural Life, July 1, 1946* (Charleston, 1946), 13–17, 30.

50. Anthony L. Pavlick, *Towards Solving the Low Income Problem of Small Farmers in the Appalachian Area* (West Virginian University Experiment Station, Bulletin 499T, June 1964), 5. See also Roy E. Proctor and T. Kelley White, "Agriculture: A Reassessment," ed. Ford, *Southern Appalachian Region*, 87–101.

51. *West Virginia Blue Book, 1965*, 874.
52. Jerry Bruce Thomas, "Some Common Appalachian Themes in Hardy County, 1890–1940," Keynote Address, Symposium on "Good Times and Hard Times, 1890–1940," August 5, 2006, Lost River State Park, Mathias, West Virginia; Richard K. MacMaster, *History of Hardy County, 1786–1986* (Moorefield: Hardy County Centennial Commission and Hardy County Public Library Commission, 1986), 185–310. Somewhat similar accounts of other non-mining Appalachian counties can be found in Barbara Rasmussen, *Absentee Landowning and Exploitation in West Virginia, 1760–1920* (Lexington: University Press of Kentucky, 1994). A striking study of one county that puts the origins of Appalachian poverty in the context of global capitalism is Dwight B. Billings and Kathleen M. Blee, *The Road to Poverty: The Making of Wealth and Hardship in Appalachia* (Cambridge: Cambridge University Press, 2000). See also in chapter 2 below, "The Alienation of the Land."
53. Harry Ernst, "No Magic: Much Work Remains Ahead for Poor of Hardy County," *Charleston Gazette*, April 24, 1965.
54. An excellent account of the impact of the lumber industry in its heyday is Ronald L. Lewis, *Transforming the Appalachian Countryside: Railroads, Deforestation, and Social Change in West Virginia, 1880–1920* (Chapel Hill: University of North Carolina Press, 1998); see also Roy B. Clarkson, *Tumult on the Mountains: Lumbering in West Virginia, 1770–1920* (Parsons, WV: McClain, 1964).
55. State Planning Board, *Agriculture and Rural Life*, 24–30.
56. *Charleston Gazette*, Nov. 13, 1964; quotation from Otis K. Rice and Stephen W. Brown, *West Virginia: A History*, 2 ed. (Lexington: University Press of Kentucky, 1993), 198.
57. A study by the U.S. Department of Commerce in 1964 listed the following job losses in various state industries over the decade: mining: 75,217; agriculture: 37,952; contract construction: 2,875; textile mill products: 1,686; lumber and wood products: 3,234; railroads: 9,231; food and dairy product stores: 3,053; wholesale trade: 447; eating and drinking establishments: 1,346; hotels and other personal services: 2,682; business and repair services: 1,538; entertainment and recreation: 441; other transportation: 757. These West Virginia industries exceeded the national rate in producing jobs: forestry and fisheries, food and kindred product manufacturers, apparel manufacturers, printing and publishing, manufacturers of motor vehicles and equipment, trucking and warehousing, and communications. Cited in Harry Ernst, "50s Depression a Blessing in Disguise," *Charleston Gazette*, Nov. 13, 1964.

58. Jerra Jenrette, "'There's No Damn Reason for It—It's Just Our Policy': Labor–Management Conflict in Martinsburg, West Virginia's Textile and Garment Industries" (PhD diss., West Virginia University, 1996), 324–25, 355–62.
59. Albert S. Caldwell to Underwood, April 9, 1958, b. 61, f. 315, Governors' Papers, WVRHC.
60. *Charleston Gazette*, Oct. 12, 1958.
61. Martin, "Steel Industry," *West Virginia Encyclopedia*, 681–82.
62. Eller, *Uneven Ground*, 30.
63. Thomas R. Ford, "The Passing of Provincialism," ed. Ford, *The Southern Appalachian Region*: 10–11.
64. J. Howard Myers, ed., *West Virginia Blue Book, 1957* (Charleston: Jarrett Printing, 1957), viii.
65. "Alex Schoenbaum," *Profiles: West Virginians Who Made a Difference* (Charleston: *Charleston Gazette*, 1999), 54.
66. By 2002, the number of drive in theaters had dwindled to ten: www.DriveinMovie.com.
67. "Dedication, WSAZ Television Station, Huntington, November 15, 1949," in Funk, *State Papers*, 105.
68. Myers, ed., *West Virginia Blue Book, 1957*, 425–31. The stations were WHIS, channel 6, Bluefield; WCHS, channel 8, Charleston; WBOY, channel 12, Clarksburg; WJPB, channel 35, Fairmont; WSAZ, channel 3, Huntington; WHTN, channel 13, Huntington; WOAY, channel 4, Oak Hill; WTAP, channel 15, Parkersburg; WTRF, channel 7, Wheeling.
69. "Carl Gainer," *Profiles*, 21; Ira Homer Ferrell, "Memoirs from Early History of Cable TV in the Tri-Towns," (written about 1957) with introductory note by Bryan F. Putnam: http://mysite.verizon.net/bfputnam/caty/catv1.html. The author remembers "running the line" to clear fallen branches and debris on a neighborhood system in Pineville in the mid-1950s.
70. Henry Louis Gates Jr., *Colored People: A Memoir* (New York: Alfred A. Knopf, 1994), 21.
71. Susan Chambers, "Recollections of Susan Chambers," in "History of WSAZ-TV, Huntington, WV," http://jeff560.tripos.com/wsaz2.html.
72. William Kelley interview by Gary Simmons, July 30, 2002, for West Virginia Documentary Consortium, Inc.
73. Ivan M. Tribe, *Mountaineer Jamboree: Country Music in West Virginia* (Lexington: University Press of Kentucky, 1984), 138–45. Tribe provides details of the performers and a discography.

74. Ibid., 146.
75. Shirley Love interview, by Gary Simmons, July 2, 2002, for West Virginia Documentary Consortium, Inc.
76. Tribe, *Mountaineer Jamboree*, 152.
77. Patterson, *Grand Expectations*, 351–55.
78. Jack E. Weller, *Yesterday's People: Life in Contemporary Appalachia* (Lexington: University of Kentucky Press, 1965), 57.
79. Cecil Underwood interview by Gary Simmons, Aug. 20, 2002, W.Va. Documentary Consortium, Inc. and chap. 2, below; Sherrill, "West Virginia Miracle," 529–35. Chapters 6 and 7 below provide further discussion of the "miners' revolt."
80. Migration and its impact on the homeland, on the area where the migrants arrive, and on the migrants themselves is a complicated story. We have much impressionistic evidence and a growing body of academic research by sociologists, demographers, historians, urban planners, and others. An excellent study that relies heavily on migrant testimony to debunk persistent stereotypes about the migrants is Berry, *Southern Migrants*. A summary and anthology of some the best work is Phillip J. Obermiller, Thomas E. Wagner, and E. Bruce Tucker, eds., *Appalachian Odyssey: Historical Perspectives on the Great Migration* (Westport, Conn.: Praeger, 2000), which see for the statistics cited, xii. Useful and succinct summaries may be found in Kirby, *Rural Worlds Lost*, 309–33; John Alexander Williams, *Appalachia: A History* (Chapel Hill: University of North Carolina Press, 2002), 312–24; and Ronald D Eller, *Uneven Ground: Appalachia Since 1945*, 20–28.
81. "West Virginia 1950–1960 Population Changes," map 1 in *An Economic Atlas for West Virginia*, 5. Chad Berry says over a half million people left West Virginia between 1950 and 1960. This seems to overstate the amount of migration, however, because the decline in population was only 145, 131. See Berry, *Southern Migrants*, 110.
82. James S. Brown and George A. Hillary Jr., "The Great Migration, 1940–1960," ed. Thomas R. Ford, *The Southern Appalachian Region: A Survey* (Lexington: University of Kentucky Press, 1962): 54–78; Berry, *Southern Migrants*, 116.
83. James S. Brown, "Population and Migration Changes in Appalachia," chap. 2, ed. John D. Photiadis and Harry Schwarzweller, *Change in Rural Appalachia: Implications for Action Programs* (Philadelphia: University of Pennsylvania Press, 1970), 23–49; Susan Johnson, "West

Virginia Rubber Workers in Akron," ed. Ken Fones-Wolf and Ronald L. Lewis, *Ethnic Communities and Economic Change, 1840–1940* (Morgantown: West Virginia University Press, 2002), 299–315; Eller, *Uneven Ground*, 20–22.

84. Quotes from Bynum "Junior" Gilbert, Raleigh County Coal Miners Collection, West Virginia State Archives.
85. Berry, *Southern Migrants*, 105.
86. An early study of migrants from West Virginia to Cleveland suggests that the main motivation for leaving the state was economic and, though family connections and sentimental attachments to their former homes remained important, the primary motivation for returning also was economic. John Photiadis, *West Virginians in Their Own State and in Cleveland, Ohio: Selected Social and Sociopsychological Characteristics* (Morgantown: Appalachian Center Report 3, 1962), 171–72. A highly readable impressionistic account of the Appalachian migration to Ashtabula County, Ohio, including many portraits of West Virginia families who left hard times in farming, mining, and lumbering from all parts of the state is Carl E. Feather's *Mountain People in a Flat Land: A Popular History of Appalachian Migration to Northern Ohio, 1940–1965* (Athens: Ohio University Press, 1998). See also Rebecca J. Bailey's account of her parents' exodus in 1955 from southern West Virginia to Chicago and later to northern Virginia: "I Never Thought of My Life as History: A Story of the 'Hillbilly' Exodus and the Price of Assimilation," ed. Obermiller et al., *Appalachian Oddyssey*, 27–37 and Shirley L. Stewart and Connie L. Rice, "The 'Birds of Passage' Phenomenon in West Virginia's Out Migration," ibid., 39–47.
87. Berry, *Southern Migrants*, quotes, 192, 194.
88. For a good summary of the revisionist scholarship, see ibid., 135, 172–205. See also Eller, *Uneven Ground*, 27.
89. Quotes from Willie Collins, interviewed by William Mares in 1973: Raleigh County Coal Miners Collection.
90. Feather, *Mountain People in a Flat Land*, 238.
91. Berry, *Southern Migrants*, 212–13.
92. Ralph Rinzler, liner notes, and Hazel Dickens, "West Virginia My Home," in *Hard Hitting Songs for Hard Hit People* (Rounder Records, 1994).
93. Ford, "Passing of Provincialism," 15–21.

2. American Paradox, Appalachian Stereotype

1. Alan Brinkley, *The End of Reform: New Deal Liberalism in Recession and War* (New York: Albert A. Knopf, 1995), see especially "Epilogue," 265–271; Nelson Lichtenstein, "From Corporatism to Collective Bargaining, Organized Labor and the Eclipse of Social Democracy in the Post War Era," in *The Rise and Fall of the New Deal Order, 1930–1980*, eds. Steve Frazier and Gary Gerstle (Princeton: Princeton University Press, 1989): 122–152; see John Gaventa, *Power and Powerlessness: Quiescence and Rebellion in an Appalachian Valley* (Urbana: University of Illinois Press, 1980).

2. Thomas R. Ford, ed., "The Changing Society," *The Southern Appalachian Region: A Survey* (Lexington: University of Kentucky Press, 1962): 149–50.

3. The term "American Paradox" appears in Roul Tunley, "The Strange Case of West Virginia," *Saturday Evening Post*, Feb. 6, 1960, 19. Tunley's article and similar literature are further discussed later in this chapter and in chapter 4.

4. Otis K. Rice, "The Alienation of the Land," chap. 6, *The Allegheny Frontier: West Virginia Beginnings, 1730–1830* (Lexington: University Press of Kentucky, 1970): 119–149. For similar conclusions see Barbara Rasmussen's thoughtful study of land ownership in five West Virginia counties—Randolph, Tucker, Pocahontas, Monroe, and Clay. This study finds that counties with less absentee ownership fared better: *Absentee Landowning and Exploitation in West Virginia, 1760–1920* (Lexington: University of Kentucky Press, 1994). A collection of insightful interdisciplinary articles on frontier Appalachia that sheds new light on the early roots of contemporary issues is Robert D. Mitchell, ed., *Appalachian Frontiers: Settlement, Society, and Development in the Preindustrial Era* (Lexington: University Press of Kentucky, 1991). Of special note in regard to West Virginia, see Van Beck Hall, "The Politics of Appalachian Virginia, 1790–1830," chap. 10, 166–186 and Paul Salstrom, "The Agricultural Origins of Economic Dependency, 1840–1880," chap. 15, 261–283.

5. Wilma A. Dunaway, *The First American Frontier: Transition to Capitalism in Southern Appalachia*, (Chapel Hill: University of North Carolina Press, 1996), 56–57.

6. Rice, *Allegheny Frontier*, quote, 149.

7. Ronald D Eller, *Uneven Ground: Appalachia since 1945* (Lexington: University Press of Kentucky, 2008), 199–200.

8. A distinction noted by Harry Caudill in his foreword to Jack Weller, *Yesterday's People: Life in Contemporary Appalachia* (Lexington: University of Kentucky Press, 1965), xii.
9. Charles H. Ambler and Festus P. Summers, *West Virginia: The Mountain State*, 2nd ed. (Englewood Cliffs: Prentice-Hall, 1958), 272–75.
10. Paul J. Kaufman, "Troubled State Crying for Drastic Revision," *Charleston Gazette*, Feb. 27, 1965. Kaufman cited information from a study by the Public Administration Service in an unusual speech given to Phi Beta Kappa and the Capitol District Kiwanis Club and reprinted by the *Gazette*. Kaufman was a member of the State Senate from Kanawha County, 1960–68. Hulett C. Smith (Commissioner of Commerce, 1961–65; Governor, 1965–69) also consistently advocated constitutional revision. In 1957 the legislature created the West Virginia Commission on Constitutional Revision, to consist of forty-eight members, with the governor to serve as honorary chair. This commission had little effect. Revision would prove to be difficult and would come slowly and piecemeal over the next decades. J. Howard Myers, ed., *West Virginia Blue Book, 1963* (Charleston, 1964), 278–79.
11. Paul W. Wager, "Local Government," in *Southern Appalachian Region*, ed. Ford, chap. 10: 151–68, quotes on 157.
12. Ibid., chap 10: 156–57.
13. Ronald D Eller, *Uneven Ground*, 33–35.
14. John Alexander Williams, *West Virginia and the Captains of Industry* (Morgantown: West Virginia University Library, 1976), 220–50.
15. Jerry Bruce Thomas, *An Appalachian New Deal, West Virginia in the Great Depression* (Lexington: University Press of Kentucky, 1998), 86–90.
16. Wager, "Local Government," in *Southern Appalachian Region*, ed. Ford, chap. 10: 161, quoting *Governor's Commission on State and Local Finance* (Charleston, 1954).
17. Quoted by K. W. Lee, "Fair Elections in West Virginia," in *Appalachia in the Sixties: A Decade of Reawakening*, ed. David S. Walls and John B. Stephenson, (Lexington: University Press of Kentucky, 1972), 165. The history of political corruption in West Virginia makes a fascinating but depressing story. A recent study that catalogs many transgressions is Allen Hayes Loughry II, "'Don't Buy Another Vote: I Won't Pay for a Landslide': The Sordid and Continuing History of Political Corruption in West Virginia," (doctoral diss., American University, Washington College of Law, 2003). A highly readable account of corruption in the 1950s and 1960s is: Thomas F. Stafford, *Afflicting the Comfortable:*

Journalism and Politics in West Virginia (Morgantown: West Virginia University Press, 2005).

18. Theodore H. White, *The Making of the President, 1960* (New York: Atheneum House, 1961), 116.
19. "Hard Test in West Virginia of Kennedy's Momentum—A Small State Takes the Limelight"; Donald Wilson, "In Logan County, the Half-Pint Vote, Slating and 'Lever Brothers'"; *Life* 48, no. 18 (May 9, 1960): 24–28.
20. Charles H. Ambler and Festus P. Summers, *West Virginia: The Mountain State*, 2nd ed. (Englewood Cliffs, 1958), 486–87; Rice and Brown, *West Virginia, A History*, 275.
21. John G. Morgan, "Okey Leonidas Patteson," in *West Virginia Governors*, 2nd ed. (Charleston Newspapers, 1980), 191–93.
22. Ray Cavendish, State Road Commissioner, "A Communication to the Forty-Ninth Legislature of West Virginia," in Papers of the Governors, b. 4, West Virginia and Regional History Collection, West Virginia University; Okey Patteson, "Message to the Fifty-First Legislature, January 14, 1954," in *State Papers and Public Addresses, Okey L. Patteson, Twenty-Third Governor of West Virginia, 1949–1953*, ed. Rosalind Funk (Charleston: Rose City Press, 1953), 621. In April 1953, *West Virginia State Magazine* devoted an issue to the roads problem with articles by Commissioner Cavendish and others in the State Road Commission: 3, no. 6.
23. Harry Radcliffe, "50 Million Program is Lifesaver," in *West Virginia State Magazine* 3, no. 6: 8, 32.
24. Jack Temple Kirby, *Rural Worlds Lost: The American South, 1920–1960* (Baton Rouge: Louisiana State University Press), 181.
25. "Magazine Calls State Turnpike 'Most Controversial' New Road," reprinted from *Business Week*, in *Charleston Gazette*, May 16, 1954.
26. Ibid.; George H. Waltz Jr., "Newest Super-Road Hops Daniel Boone's Mountains," *Popular Science Monthly* (August 1954): 65–69.
27. *West Virginia State Magazine* 3, no. 11 (September 1952): 10; Tom Lewis, *Divided Highways: Building The Interstate Highways, Transforming American Life* (New York: Viking Penguin, 1997), 111.
28. "Turnpike Thorn Growing Bigger" *Charleston Gazette*, July 3, 1965.
29. Okey Patteson, "Message to the Fiftieth Legislature"; "Message to the Fifty-First Legislature," in *State Papers*, ed. Funk, 305–07; 620.
30. Harry G. Hoffman, "Road Price Tag Nation's Highest," *Charleston Gazette*, May 23, 1954.

31. Ibid.; Wallace E. Knight, "How Do Our Roads Compare?" *Gazette Magazine*, April 18, 1954.
32. Kenneth T. Jackson, *Crabgrass Frontier: The Suburbanization of the United States* (New York: Oxford University Press), 269–271.
33. From statement by Charles Hodel, prepared for submission to a congressional committee, April 1, 1955, Harley Kilgore Papers, series 10, b. 4., West Virginia and Regional History Collection, West Virginia University Library.
34. Okey Patteson, "Message to the Fifty-First Legislature," in *State Papers*, ed. Funk, 617–18.
35. Okey Patteson, "Message to the Fiftieth Legislature," in *State Papers*, ed. Funk, 302–04.
36. Morgan, *West Virginia's Governors*, 196–99; Patteson, "Announcement of Site for West Virginia Medical School, June 30, 1951" and "West Virginia Medical School Decision," in *State Papers*, ed. Funk, 374–82.
37. Karen Kruse Thomas calls Hill-Burton "the last and most progressive expression of New Deal liberalism and the first legislative victory of the twentieth century civil rights movement," because it required racial parity—though not integrated wards—and it used an allocation formula that favored poor states and underserved rural communities. Thomas's point is that it benefited black southerners as a group more than any other New Deal era legislation. It can also be said that it helped all underserved rural populations move toward better health care: "The Hill-Burton Act and Civil Rights: Expanding Hospital Care for Black Southerners 1939–1960," *Journal of Southern History*, 62, no. 4 (Nov. 2006): 870.
38. John G. Morgan, "State Hospitals 'Better Off' for Program; $64,182,386 Spent in Past 11 Years," *Sunday Gazette-Mail*, Dec. 7, 1958.
39. Ivana Krajcinovic, *From Company Doctors to Managed Care: The United Mine Workers Noble Experiment*, (Ithaca: Cornell University Press, 1997), 107–130.
40. C. Horace Hamilton, "Health and Health Services," in *Southern Appalachian Region*, ed. Ford, chap. 14: 242.
41. Richard Fried, *Men Against McCarthy* (New York: Columbia University Press, 1976), 43–46, quote on 43; James T. Patterson, *Grand Expectations: The United States, 1945–1974* (New York: Oxford University Press, 1996), 196–205.
42. "Ernie Weir," *Profiles: West Virginians Who Made a Difference* (Charleston: *Charleston Gazette*, 1999), 59; Elizabeth Fones-Wolf and

Ken Fones-Wolf, "Cold War Americanism: Business, Pageantry, and Anti-Unionism in Weirton," *Business History Review* 77, no. 1 (Spring 2003): 66–68.
43. Fones-Wolf and Fones-Wolf, "Cold War Americanism," 62–73.
44. Ibid., 73–91.
45. Lou Athey, "Widen," *The West Virginia Encyclopedia*, ed. Ken Sullivan (Charleston: West Virginia Humanities Council, 2006), 793.
46. Robert Franklin Maddox, *The Senatorial Career of Harley Martin Kilgore* (East Rockaway: Cummings and Hathaway, 1997), 288–94; quote from Patterson, *Grand Expectations*, 240.
47. Charles H. McCormick, *This Nest of Vipers: McCarthyism and Higher Education in the Mundel Affair, 1951–52* (Urbana: University of Illinois Press, 1989). In 1983, ABC News did a television documentary on the Mundel Affair.
48. "Tom Cummings of the *Charleston Daily Mail* Reviews Governor Patteson's Administration Through the Eyes of the Republican Press," in *State Papers*, ed. Funk, 649.
49. Paul F. Lutz, *From Governor to Cabby: The Political Career and Tragic Death of West Virginia's William Casey Marland, 1950–1965* (Huntington: Marshall University Library Associates, 1996), 5–40; Maddox, *Kilgore*, 306–15; Syd Barksdale, "Marland Takes Office As State's Youngest Governor," *West Virginia State Magazine* (Jan., 1953): 13–14; 30–31; Rod Hoylman, "The Hard Road Home: Governor William Casey Marland," *Goldenseal: West Virginia Traditional Life*, vol. 24, no. 3 (Fall 1998): 12–19; Revercomb quotes from transcript of radio address, undated, but clearly from the 1952 election campaign in Chapman Revercomb Collection, West Virginia State Archives, Charleston. See also James H. Smith, "Red-Baiting Senator Harley Kilgore in the Election of 1952: The Limits of McCarthyism during the Red Scare," *West Virginia History: A Journal of Regional Studies*, New Series, I, no. 1 (Spring 2007): 55–74; and Fried, *Men Against McCarthy*, 248.
50. These conclusions are based primarily on Lutz, *From Governor to Cabby* and Lutz, "Governor Marland's Political Suicide: The Severance Tax," *West Virginia History* 50 (Fall 1978): 13–27. See also Stafford, *Afflicting the Comfortable*, chapter 5, "A Man for Another Season," 44–55; "William Casey Marland," in Morgan, *West Virginia Governors*, 208–27; Robert Eugene Lanham, "The West Virginia Statehouse Democratic Machine: Structure, Function and Process" (PhD diss., Claremont Graduate School and University Center, 1972"; and Otis K. Rice and Stephen W. Brown, *West Virginia: A History*, 2nd ed. (Lexington:

University Press of Kentucky, 1993), 275–78; Hoylman, "The Hard Road Home," 12–19, 22–23.

51. In oral history interview by Gary Simmons for WV Documentary Consortium, Aug. 20, 2002.
52. Lutz, *Marland*, 44–49.
53. Lutz, *Marland*, 44–57.
54. Quote in Hoylman, "The Hard Road Home,"16.
55. Ibid.
56. Lutz, *Marland*, 170–71.
57. Thomas, *Appalachian New Deal*, 90.
58. West Virginia Commission on State and Local Finance, *Tax Facts in West Virginia* (Charleston, 1956), no pagination, see in Marland Papers, b. 56, f. 277, Governors Papers, West Virginia and Regional History Collection.
59. Kilgore Papers, series 10, passim.
60. "Labor Market Information on Mingo County, West Virginia, January 15, 1954," Typescript copy, Kilgore Papers, series 10, b. 4.
61. Slab Fork District Forum to Harley M. Kilgore, March 8, 1954, Kilgore Papers. series 10, b. 7.
62. Hedrick quotes, G. C. Hedrick to Kilgore, March 12, 1954; Kilgore to Hedrick, March 17, 1954, Kilgore Papers, series 10, b. 7.
63. G. C. Hedrick to Kilgore, March 12, 1954, Kilgore Papers, series 10, b. 7.
64. Statement by Charles Hodel, prepared for submission to a congressional committee, April 1, 1955, Kilgore Papers, series 10, b. 4.
65. Elmer W. Prince to Harley M. Kilgore, Feb. 15, 1954, Kilgore Papers, series 10, b. 4.
66. Sam S. Politano to Kilgore, Jan. 8, 1954; "Causes of Unemployment in Huntington," Records of the Office of Economic Opportunity, Inspection Division Reports, 1964–67, b. 80, RG 381, National Archives, Washington, D.C.; John Alexander Williams, *West Virginia: A Bicentennial History* (New York: W. W. Norton, 1976), 179.
67. Neil Boggs, "Marland Suggests Highway Building to Employ Jobless," *Charleston Gazette*, April 20, 1954.
68. Wallace E. Knight, "Luring Industry Held Job of Cities," *Charleston Gazette*, May 24, 1954. In 1959, Congress passed a bill devised by economist and Democratic senator from Illinois, Paul Douglas, called the Area Redevelopment Bill, which called for public works, job retraining, and increased welfare benefits. President Eisenhower vetoed the

bill, calling it too costly and inflationary: John Patrick Diggins, *The Proud Decades: America in War and Peace, 1941–1960* (New York: W. W. Norton, 1988) 322.

69. Wallace E. Knight, "Diversification Is Not Easy: One Economy Pattern in W.Va. Cities No Longer Adequate to Insure Employment," *Charleston Gazette*, May 3, 1954.

70. I.V. Perry, Vice President of Crum Industrial Organization to Senator Chapman Revercomb, Feb. 11, 1957 in Governor Underwood papers, b. 59, file 299, Governors Papers, West Virginia and Regional History Collection, West Virginia University.

71. Bigart, "Depression Hit Town Is Buoyant"; West Virginia Department of Commerce, *West Virginia Economic Atlas*, Charleston, WV, n.d., map 1.

72. Wallace E. Knight, "Logan Hustling for Factories: Forming Local Industrial Promotion Group Is Easy," *Charleston Gazette*, May 5, 1954; "Natural Advantages Not Enough, New Industrial Development Groups Find Unknown Assets in Most Towns," *Charleston Gazette*, May 6, 1954.

73. Wallace E. Knight, "Hard Work, Good Publicity Are Keys to Luring Industry," *Charleston Gazette*, May 7, 1954.

74. Wallace E. Knight, "Massachusetts Firm Hired; Governor Baits Industrial Hook," *Charleston Gazette*, May 13, 1954.

75. Lutz, *Marland*, 179–80. For efforts of other states, see Numan V. Bartley, *The New South, 1945–1980: The Story of the South's Modernization* (A History of the South, v. 11, Baton Rogue, 1995), 18–19 and James C. Cobb, *The Selling of the South: The Southern Crusade for Industrial Development, 1936–1982* (Baton Rogue: Louisiana State University Press, 1982), 3–63. Economic historian Harold G. Vatter notes that many states engaged in such activities in the 1950s, some even sponsoring privately financed development credit corporations to encourage growth, but he says it is difficult to assess the growth impact, if any, of this kind of interstate competition. Vatter, *The U.S Economy in the 1950s* (New York: W. W. Norton, 1963), 25.

76. Lutz, *Marland*, 180.

77. *New York Times*, March 8, 1956: 43.

78. Ibid., April 10, 1956: 33; April 11, 1956: 35.

79. Ibid., April 19, 1956: 51.

80. Lutz, *Marland*, 182–88.

81. Ibid., 173.
82. Ibid., 202–07; Morgan, *West Virginia Governors*, Patteson quote, 201, 209–10; Charleston *Gazette*, April 11 and April 20, 1954.
83. Stafford, *Afflicting the Comfortable*, 47.
84. Tim Massey, "Never Late for Court: An Interview with Milton J. Ferguson," *Goldenseal: West Virginia Traditional Life* 9, no. 4 (Winter 1983): 38–40.
85. Cecil Underwood interview by Rod Hoylman, July 20, 1998, published as "Underwood on Marland," *Goldenseal: West Virginia Traditional Life*, vol. 24, no. 3 (Fall 1998): 20–21.
86. Hoylman, "The Hard Road Home," 16–17.
87. Lanham, "Democratic Machine," 215–16.
88. Hoylman, "The Hard Road Home," 12, 22–23; Lutz, *From Governor to Cabby*, 220–240; Stafford, *Afflicting the Comfortable*, 44–55; Morgan, *West Virginia Governors*, 208–27 and Rice and Brown, *West Virginia*, 275–77. Though political opponents exaggerated stories of Marland's drinking while he was governor, his younger sister Grace Marland Beck later confirmed that her brother had started drinking at an early age and confessed to her in 1960 that it had become a problem for him. Marland's wife Valery traced the beginning of his drinking to his despondency over the death of his mother in 1936. She said that Bill and his father drank together, but that in the hard-drinking culture of the coal camps, few saw it as unusual. When Marland became governor, he increased his drinking, although neither Mrs. Marland nor the governor thought he was an alcoholic at the time. After he accepted a job with the West Kentucky Coal Company in Chicago, drinking became, as he said "a twenty-four hour proposition." According to Mrs. Marland, after he spent a thirty-day period in an alcoholic ward of an Illinois hospital, he became sober and turned to cab driving as a way to remain anonymous and sober. Bud Perry and Karl C. Lilly, III, *Reopening Glen Rogers* (privately produced, n.d., n.p.), 89–105.
89. Lanham, "Democratic Machine," 218–19; Morgan, "Cecil Harland Underwood," in *West Virginia Governors*, 235–37.
90. Cecil Underwood interview by Gary Simmons for WV Documentary Consortium, Inc., Aug. 20, 2002.
91. Lanham, "Democratic Machine," 218–19; Morgan, "Underwood," Rice and Brown, *West Virginia*, 278–79; Lutz, *Marland*, 102; Brad Crouser, *Arch: The Life of Governor Arch Moore, Jr.* (Chapmanville: Woodland Press, LLC, 2008), 60–63.

92. Quotes in Morgan, "Underwood," 241–43; oral history interview by Gary Simmons for WV Documentary Consortium, Inc., Aug. 20, 2002.
93. Kenneth T. Jackson, *Crabgrass Frontier: The Suburbanization of the United States* (New York: Oxford University Press, 1985), 248–50; Owen D. Gutfreund, *20th Century Sprawl: Highways and the Reshaping of the American Landscape* (New York: Oxford University Press, 2004), 58–59; Lewis, *Divided Highways*, 121–23; Patterson, *Grand Expectations*, 274; Diggins, *Proud Decades*, 131.
94. Cecil Underwood to Ross B. Johnston, October 26, 1960. Cecil Underwood Papers in West Virginia Governors Papers, b. 68, file 355.
95. "Better Roads Are Cheaper in the End," editorial in *Charleston Sunday Gazette-Mail* October 25, 1958; Thomas F. Stafford, "Interstate Plans Outlined By Underwood," *Charleston Gazette*, November 2, 1968; George Lawless, "West Virginia's Top Ten Stories in 1958," *Charleston Sunday Gazette-Mail*, December 28, 1958.
96. *West Virginia School Journal*, 82 (Sept. 1953): 8; "When the Roof Falls in," 88 (December 1959): 3.
97. A. L. Hardman, "How Florida is Stealing Our Teachers," *Charleston Gazette-Mail, Sunday Magazine*, April 4, 1954.
98. Telephone interview with Jeanine Christian, June 1, 2009.
99. Phares Reeder, "Another Survey," *West Virginia School Journal* 86 (September 1957): 3.
100. Phares Reeder, "The Sputnik Era," 5; J. Martin Taylor, "The Finger Points," 7; "Our Science Teachers Give Voice on Sputnik," 7, 29, all in *West Virginia School Journal* 86 (Jan. 1958).
101. Homer H. Hickam Jr., *October Sky: A Memoir* (originally published as *Rocket Boys)* (New York: Dell Publishing, 1998), quotes on 38–39, 164. The book *October Sky* was made into a motion picture by Universal Pictures.
102. Lawless, "West Virginia's Top Ten Stories"; Robert C. Byrd, *Child of the Appalachian Coalfields* (Morgantown: West Virginia University Press, 2005), 104–13; Crouser, *Arch*, 77–79.
103. William H. Hardin, "Elizabeth Kee, 1899–1975," in West Virginia Women's Commission, *Missing Chapters II: West Virginia Women in History*: 61–70
104. Jo Boggess Phillips, "'I Greatly Appreciate Your Courage,' West Virginia's Women Legislators," *Goldenseal: West Virginia Traditional Life*, vol. 24, no. 3 (Fall 1998): 27–32; Thomas F. Stafford, "Mrs. Holt Trying to Break Male Grip," *Charleston Gazette*, Nov. 2, 1958; Harry Hoffman,

"Democrats Win in State, County," *Charleston Gazette*, November 5, 1958; J. Howard Myers, ed., *West Virginia Blue Book, 1957* (Charleston, Jarrett Printing, 1958), 585–90.

105. Morgan, "Underwood," 245; Lawless, "Top Ten Stories."
106. Diggins, *Proud Decades*, 322.
107. Charleston *Gazette*, October 12, 1958.
108. Truman Sayre to Governor Underwood, March 30, 1959 (et al.) in b. 59, f. 299, Governors Papers.
109. Morgan, "Underwood," 243–44.
110. Festus P. Summers to Charles Hodel, March 14, 1959 in West Virginia Centennial Commission, Correspondence, 1956–62, West Virginia and Regional History Collection, West Virginia University.
111. Roul Tunley, "The Strange Case of West Virginia," *Saturday Evening Post*, February 6, 1960: 19–20, 64–66.
112. *New York Times*, May 2, 1960.
113. A brief summary of this literature can be found in Jay Carlton Mullen, "West Virginia's Image: The 1960 Presidential Primary and the National Press," *West Virginia History*, vol. 32, no. 4 (July 1971): 215–23.
114. *New York Times*, April 30, 1960: 21; Mullen, "West Virginia's Image": 221. Underwood told interviewer Gary Simmons of Nixon's promise in Underwood Interview, WV Documentary Consortium. Of course the promised cabinet position depended on Nixon winning, and both Underwood and Nixon lost.
115. Robert C. Byrd, *Child of the Appalachian Coalfields* (Morgantown: West Virginia University Press, 2005), first quote, 122 (also from Tunley, "Strange Case": 20); second quote, 122–23; third quote, 124.
116. Theodore H. White, *The Making of the President, 1960* (New York: Athenaeum House, 1961), 116–19.
117. Mullen, "West Virginia's Image": 223.
118. See chap. 1, n. 45.
119. West Virginia Department of Commerce, *An Economic Atlas for West Virginia*, "West Virginia Income by Counties," map 2; Williams, *West Virginia*, 176–77.
120. Glen Edward Taul, "Poverty, Development, and Government in Appalachia: Origins of the Appalachian Regional Commission (unpublished doctoral dissertation, University of Kentucky, 2001), 150–65; Eller, *Uneven Ground*, 55–56.

121. Elizabeth Jill Wilson, "West Virginia University," *West Virginia Encyclopedia*, 776; Tara Curtis, "Defining Mountaineer Greatness," *West Virginia University Alumni Magazine* (Summer 2005): 26–28.

3. Civil Rights in the New Machine Age

1. A useful summary of the historiography of civil rights is Charles W. Eagles, "Toward New Histories of the Civil Rights Era," *Journal of Southern History* 66, no. 4 (November, 2000): 815–48.
2. See table 1.
3. John C. Belcher, "Population Growth and Characteristics," in *The Southern Appalachian Region: A Survey*, ed. Thomas R. Ford (Lexington: University of Kentucky Press, 1962), 37–53. Ronald L. Lewis, "Beyond Isolation and Homogeneity: Diversity and the History of Appalachia," in *Back Talk from Appalachia: Confronting Stereotypes*, ed. Dwight B. Billings, Gurney Norman, and Katherine Ledford (Lexington: University Press of Kentucky, 1999), 35–38.
4. Joe William Trotter, *Coal, Class, and Color: Blacks in Southern West Virginia, 1915–32* (Urbana and Chicago: University of Illinois Press, 1990), 1–31, 257; see also the following useful memoirs of African American life in the coalfields: Ancella R. Bickley and Lynda Ann Ewen, *Memphis Tennessee Garrison: The Remarkable Story of A Black Appalachian Woman* (Athens: Ohio University Press, 2001) about a teacher and community leader in McDowell County and Huntington; *Black Days, Black Dust: The Memories of an African American Coal Miner*, as told to S. L. Gardner (Knoxville: University of Tennessee Press, 2002), the recollections of Robert Armstead, whose family came from Alabama to Watson, near Fairmont, in 1925; and William M. Drennen Jr. and Kojo (William T.) Jones Jr., *Red, White, Black, and Blue: A Dual Memoir of Race and Class in Appalachia* (Athens: Ohio University Press, 2004). Of course not all African Americans in West Virginia lived in the coalfields. Henry Louis Gates Jr., a Mineral County native who received a PhD from Cambridge University and now is a noted writer and scholar of African American studies at Harvard University, provides a touching memoir of growing up "colored" in a small eastern West Virginia town: *Colored People* (New York: Alfred A. Knopf, 1994).
5. Table based on table and data in William P. Jackameit, "A Short History of Negro Public Higher Education in West Virginia, 1890–1965," *West Virginia History* 37 (1976): 318.

6. Jerry Bruce Thomas, *An Appalachian New Deal: West Virginia in the Great Depression* (Lexington: University Press of Kentucky, 1998), 200–07.
7. Gates, *Colored People*, 17.
8. C. Robert Barnett, "'The Finals': West Virginia's Black Basketball Tournament, 1925–1957," *Goldenseal: West Virginia Traditional Life* 9, no. 2 (Summer 1983): 30–36.
9. Personal recollection of the author. For a brief account of Glen Rogers, see Bud Perry and Karl C. Lilly III, *Reopening Glen Rogers* (Privately printed, n.p., n.d.).
10. *Annual Report of the West Virginia State Extension Program for Mining Education, 1947*, Ulysses Grant Carter Collection, West Virginia and Regional History Collection, West Virginia University, b. 1, f. 4. The material in this collection contains excellent drawings of the mining equipment of the day.
11. Ronald L. Lewis, *Black Coal Miners in America: Race, Class, and Community Conflict, 1790–1980* (Lexington: University Press of Kentucky, 1987), 170–179 and appendix, 191–193. Robert H. Woodrum notes similar circumstances in Alabama's coalfields: *"Everybody Was Black Down There": Race and Industrial Change in the Alabama Coalfields* (Athens: University of Georgia Press, 2007).
12. Interview of Willie Collins by William Mares, 1973, in "Raleigh County Coal Miners," Oral history collection in West Virginia State Archives.
13. C. F. Hopson, "Annual Report of the Bureau of Negro Welfare and Statistics, 1953," 1–6, manuscript text in William C. Marland Miscellaneous Papers, 1953, b. 534, West Virginia Governors Papers, West Virginia and Regional History Collection, West Virginia University. See table 1.
14. Otis K. Rice and Stephen W. Brown, *West Virginia: A History*, 2nd ed. (Lexington: University Press of Kentucky, 1993), 248; Douglas C. Smith says that school integration in West Virginia became a *fait accompli* in 1954 with the *Brown* decision, in: "In Quest of Equality: The West Virginia Experience," *West Virginia History* 37 (April 1976), 213.
15. Numan V. Bartley, *The New South, The Story of the South's Modernization, 1945–1980* (Baton Rouge: Louisiana State University Press, 1995), 1st quote, 164, 2nd quote, 198; Ira M. Lechner, "Massive Resistance: Virginia's Great Leap Backward," *Virginia Quarterly Review* (Autumn 1974), 631–40.
16. Bartley, *The New South*, quoting Stephen Channing, 163; Paul F. Lutz, *From Governor to Cabby: The Political Career and Tragic Death of*

West Virginia's William Casey Marland, 1950–1965 (Huntington: Marshall University Library Associates, 1996), 62–63; *Charleston Gazette*, May 18, 1954. On Byrd, see n. 94 below. Two recent summaries of West Virginia's response to *Brown* are Nelson Bickley, "*Brown v. Board of Education* in West Virginia," *West Virginia Law Review* 107 (Spring 2005): 1–10 and Sam F. Stack Jr., "Implementing *Brown v Board of Education* in West Virginia: The *Southern School News* Reports," *West Virginia History*, New Series 2, no. 1 (Spring 2008): 59–81.

17. Lutz, *From Governor to Cabby*, 62–64; John G. Morgan, "William Casey Marland, 1863-1980," in *West Virginia Governors*, 2nd ed. (Charleston: Charleston Newspapers), 208–09.

18. The historiography of these matters is extensive. Numan Bartley, *The Rise of Massive Resistance: Race and Politics in the South During the 1950s* (Baton Rouge: Louisiana State University Press, 1969), Bartley, *The New South*, and Taylor Branch, *Parting the Waters: America in the King Years, 1954–1963* (New York: Simon and Schuster, 1988) are good starting points.

19. Gates, *Colored People*, 91.

20. *Charleston Gazette*, May 18, 1954, 20.

21. Ancella Bickley, "Black Education in West Virginia, 1861–1971," lecture at Shepherd College, Shepherdstown West Virginia, April 8, 2003.

22. "Racial Integration in West Virginia: The Unfinished Task Ahead," Speech to Unitarian Fellowship of Charleston, author and date unclear, West Virginia Human Rights Commission Papers, b. 4, West Virginia and Regional History Collection, West Virginia University.

23. "Pooling the Assets"; "The WVSTA—A Resume," *The WVSTA Bulletin* 21, no. 4 (Oct. 1954): 46–48, 51–53, 59 in b. 1, Ancella Bickley Collection, West Virginia State Archives.

24. For statements by Marland and Trent, see *Charleston Gazette*, May 18, 1954, 1; *Huntington Herald-Dispatch*, Sept. 15, 1954; Sept. 24, 1954.

25. Tom Stimmel, "W.Va in Midst of Segregation Squabble," *Huntington Herald-Advertiser*, Sept. 19, 1954; *Huntington Herald-Dispatch*, Sept. 10, 15, 1954; "West Virginians Bar End of Segregation," Sept. 14, 1954; "Whites' 'Revolt,' End Desegregation," Sept. 15, 1954; "Strike Aids Bias in West Virginia," *New York Times*, Sept. 19, 1954.

26. *Charleston Gazette*, Sept. 11, 1955.

27. *Huntington Herald-Advertiser*, September 22, 1954.

28. Stimmel, "Segregation Squabble," *Huntington Herald-Dispatch*, Sept. 8, 1954, 1; Connie Rice, *OurMonongalia: A History of African*

Americans in Monongalia County, West Virginia (Terra Alta, WV: Headline Press, 1999): 6. See also Connie L. Rice, "The 'Separate But Equal Schools' of Monongalia County's Coal Mining Communities," *Journal of Appalachian Studies* 2 (Fall 1996).
29. Bickley, "Black Education"; Drennen and Jones, *Red, White, Black, and Blue*, 32; *Charleston Gazette*, Sept. 7, 8, 14, 1955: Clippings from "Mrs. Rayford's Scrapbook," in Bickley Collection.
30. Armstead, *Black Days*, 147–148.
31. Unident, newspaper clipping, 1955, "Rayford Scrapbook," Bickley Collection.
32. *Charleston Gazette*, Sept. 18 1955, in "Rayford Scrapbook," Bickley Collection.
33. *Charleston Gazette*, Oct. 15, 1955, in "Rayford Scrapbook," Bickley Collection.
34. Stack, "Implementing *Brown*," 68–69. For a compelling account of the Little Rock crisis see Elizabeth Jacoway, *Turn Away Thy Son: Little Rock, The Crisis that Rocked the Nation* (New York: Free Press, 2007).
35. *Huntington Herald-Dispatch*, September 14, 1958, 19.
36. James B. Dickson, "Charleston Leaders Believe South's School Problem Can Be Solved," Charleston *Gazette*, Sept. 28, 1958, 1.
37. *West Virginia Advisory Committee Report to the United States Civil Rights Commission* (March 31, 1959) in Cecil Underwood Papers, b. 64, f. 329, West Virginia Governors Papers, West Virginia and Regional History Collection, West Virginia University.
38. West Virginia Human Rights Commission, *Second Annual Report, 1963–63* (Charleston, 1963), 19–20.
39. Ibid. 19–22.
40. Based on a perusal of the *West Virginia School Journal* for the period, the most notable thing about integration that emerges is how little comment it occasioned.
41. *Charleston Gazette*, May 18, 1954.
42. Barnett, "'The Finals': West Virginia's Black Basketball Tournament," 30–36.
43. Bob Baker, "Things Never Dull With 'Gloomy Jim,'" *Charleston Gazette*, Dec. 14, 1958; "Poor Planning Creates Bad Coaching Situation," Dec. 6, 1958; Dec. 6, 1958.
44. Bickley, "Black Education"; Drennen and Jones, *Red, White, Black and Blue*, 66–70; *Annual Report of the West Virginia Human Rights*

Commission, 1966–67 (Charleston, 1967), 11–12. See also the comments on the toll of integration on African American educational leaders in McDowell County in Carter, "Segregation and Integration . . . ," 99–100. In some cases, persistent efforts from the black community led to the restoration of African American names. In Fairmont, Dunbar High School, named after the black poet Paul Lawrence Dunbar, closed in 1955 but later reopened as Fairmont Junior High. William Armstrong, a former principal of Dunbar, led a campaign that led to the restoration of the Dunbar name in 1971. Jefferson, the former black Page-Jackson High School became the administrative headquarters of the school system, but the name later reemerged as the name of a new elementary school. Douglass High School in Huntington became Fairfield School for special education and in 1981 became the administrative center for the school board. In 1985, at the urging of the black community, the board restored the Douglass name to the building. Armstead, *Black Days*, 148; Taylor, *Jefferson County*, 51; Platania, "Douglass High School," 28.

45. West Virginia Human Rights Commission, *Annual Report, 1965–66* in b. 2, West Virginia Human Rights Commission Papers, West Virginia and Regional History Collection, West Virginia University.
46. *Charleston Gazette*, March 5, 1965.
47. Glade Little, "Race Relations Issue Reviewed," *Charleston Gazette*, September 8, 1965.
48. Alice E. Carter, "Segregation and Integration in the Appalachian Coal Fields: McDowell County Responds to the *Brown* Decision," *West Virginia History* 54 (1995): 82.
49. Ibid., 84–85.
50. *Second Annual Report of the West Virginia Human Rights Commission, 1962–63* (Charleston, 1963), 21.
51. Ibid., 98–99; *Annual Report of the West Virginia Human Rights Commission, 1966–67* (Charleston, 1967), 11–12.
52. Hunter, Caldwell, and Campbell, *Survey Report of the Public Schools of Jefferson County, West Virginia* (n.p., March 1954), quotations 6, 41; passim, in West Virginia Collection, Scarborough Library, Shepherd University. The black high school dated to 1942, when the Jefferson County school board had erected an annex to the Charles Town District Colored Graded School and named it Page-Jackson, after two pioneer black educators in the county, Littleton L. Page and Philip Jackson. In 1951 the board moved the high school to a separate structure, and only then did Jefferson County African Americans have a complete high school program available to them: James L. Taylor, *A History of Black*

Education in Jefferson County, West Virginia, 1866–1966 (Jefferson County, n.p., 2000), 1–6, 51 in West Virginia Collection, Shepherd University.

53. Ibid., 51; Millard Kessler Bushong, *Historic Jefferson County* (Boyce, Va.: Carr Publishing, 1972), 385; "Federal Aid to Schools May be Lost in County Unless Full Integration," *Martinsburg Journal*, July 14, 1965 in Jefferson County NAACP Clipping file, West Virginia Collection, Shepherd University.

54. West Virginia Human Rights Commission, *Annual Report, 1964–65*, (Charleston, 1965), 28–29.

55. Lutz, *From Governor to Cabby*, 62–84; Morgan, "Marland," 208–209.

56. *Annual Report West Virginia Human Rights Commission,1968–69* (Charleston: 1969), 35; Stack, "Implementing *Brown*," n. 81, quoting Nelson Bickley, "*Brown v. Board of Education* in West Virginia," 7.

57. Ancella Bickley, "Black Education."

58. Joseph Platania, "Getting Ready for Life: The Douglass High School Story," *Goldenseal* 19, no. 3 (Fall 1993): 21–28, quotation, 28.

59. Gates, *Colored People*, quotes, 91–92.

60. Drennen and Jones, *Red, White, Black, and Blue*, 65–66. Jones' perspective is elaborated by Derrick Bell in *Silent Covenants: Brown v. Board of Education and the Unfulfilled Hopes for Racial Reform* (New York: Oxford University Press, 2004).

61. Dawn Raines Burke, *An American Phoenix: A History of Storer College from Slavery to Desegregation, 1865–1955* (Pittsburgh: Geyer Printing, [2007?]), 22–30. This book is based on Burke's dissertation "Storer College: A Hope for Redemption in the Shadow of Slavery, 1865–1955," (PhD diss., Virginia Polytechnic Institute and State University, 2004).

62. Jackameit, "Negro Public Higher Education," 309–18; see also C. Stuart McGehee and Frank Wilson, *Bluefield State College: A Centennial History, 1895–1995* (Bluefield: Bluefield State College, 1996) and Dolly Withrow, *West Virginia State College, 1891–1991: From the Grove to the Stars* (Institute: West Virginia State College Foundation, 1991).

63. David R. Goldfield, *Promised Land: The South since 1945* (Wheeling, Ill.: Harlan-Davidson, 1987), 45.

64. Charles H. Ambler, *A History of Education in West Virginia from Colonial Times to 1949* (Huntington: Standard Printing, 1951), quotation, 819.

65. W. E. "Ned" Chilton III, "Desegregation/Integration and the Media: Fallout from the Brown Decision in West Virginia" in *Brown v Board*

of Education of Topeka: An Assessment Thirty Years Later, Series of Lectures and Discussions (Institute: West Virginia State College, 1984), 43.
66. Jackameit, "Negro Public Higher Education," 319.
67. *Charleston Gazette*, November 11, 1955, "Rayford Scrapbook," Bickley Collection.
68. "Hal Greer," *Profiles: West Virginians Who Made a Difference* (Charleston: *Charleston Gazette*, 1999), 23.
69. Burke, *An American Phoenix*, 142; Bushong, *Historic Jefferson County*, 385.
70. Jackameit, "Negro Public Higher Education": 320–323; Withrow, *West Virginia State College*, 45; See addenda to Withrow: Harry W. Ernst and Andrew W. Galloway, "Reverse Integration: A Negro College in West Virginia Proves Desegregation is a Two-Way Street," *New York Times Magazine*, January 8, 1957.
71. William J. L. Wallace, "The Impact of *Brown v. Board of Education of Topeka, Kansas* on West Virginia State College," in *Brown v Board of Education of Topeka: An Assessment Thirty Years Later: A Series of Lectures and Discussions* (Institute, WV: West Virginia State College, 1984): 106–07. One of the other presenters at this forum presented a view quite different from Wallace's. Lawrence D. Reddick of Dillard University said West Virginia "state powers cultivated the myth that the coming of white students to the college was spontaneous, thus concealing the campaign to attract and bring them in." He said the catalog began to feature more pictures of whites than blacks and that the curriculum was transformed from black oriented liberal arts to a vocational and commercial program more suitable for the white business community of Charleston: "Wisdom and Courage Can Often Prevent Horrible Consequences," in *An Assessment Thirty Years Later*: 94–96. In 1967 *Gazette* columnist John Yago reported that many in the WVSC black community felt that desegregation of faculty and staff had been pushed too fast and that "much of the alumni would prefer to see West Virginia State remain the last Negro enclave of higher education in the state." John Yago, "Split Personality Harms College," *Charleston Gazette*, March 26, 1967.
72. Jackameit, "Negro Public Higher Education" 320–323; McGehee and Wilson, *Bluefield State College*, 126–27.
73. Miles C. Stanley, Chairman, "Report of the West Virginia Advisory Committee to the United States Civil Rights Commission, Conclusions

and Recommendations," March 31, 1959 in West Virginia Governors' Papers, (Governor Cecil Underwood), b. 64, f. 329, West Virginia and Appalachian Regional Collection, West Virginia University. For an account of Miles Stanley's role in supporting civil rights see: Colin Fones-Wolf, "A Union Voice for Racial Equality: Miles Stanley and Civil Rights in West Virginia, 1957–1968," *Journal of Appalachian Studies* 10 (Spring/Fall 2004): 111–28.

74. Gates, *Colored People*, 27–28.
75. Edward D. Hoffman, "U.S. Civil Rights Commission Community Survey, Charleston, West Virginia" (July 30, 1964), 19, typescript in WVHRC Papers, b. 4.
76. Ibid.
77. Thomas W. Gavett, Speech to Conference on Equal Employment Opportunity, West Virginia State College, June 21, 1963 in WVHRC Papers, b. 2.
78. J. Harvey Kerns, *A Summary Report of the Economic and Cultural Conditions of Charleston, West Virginia As They Relate to the Negro People* (National Urban League, April 15–May 15, 1948) in Elizabeth Gilmore Collection, West Virginia State Archives.
79. Handwritten tribute to Cynthia H. Burks by Elizabeth Gilmore in spiral bound notebook, CORE file, Gilmore Collection.
80. Patterson, *Grand Expectations*, 468–69.
81. "Charleston CORE Accomplishments," typed list in CORE folder, Gilmore Collection; James Farmer, *Lay Bare The Heart: An Autobiography of The Civil Rights Movement* (New York: Arbor House, 1965), 176–88.
82. Harry Ernst, "Segregation Faces Attack in Kanawha," *Charleston Gazette*, Sept. 7, 1958; Gilmore quote in Gladys Little, "Race Group Plans County Campaign," September 14, 1958; editorial quotation: "Education Key to Integration," *Charleston Gazette*, September 21, 1958.
83. Hoffman, "Rights Commission Community Survey," 19–20, WVHRC; *CORE-LATOR*, Fall 1958; Charleston CORE (Elizabeth Gilmore, Secretary) to James Peck, editor or CORE-LATOR, January 18, 1960 in CORE file, Gilmore Collection. Gilmore became a member of the West Virginia Board of Regents in 1969: "Elizabeth Harden Gilmore," in "Salute to Black Women," *Sunday Gazette-Mail*, May 4, 1986: 1D.
84. "Charleston CORE Accomplishments," typed list in CORE folder, Gilmore Collection.

85. "Baylor, NBA Star, Balks at Hotel Ban" *New York Times*, Jan. 17, 1959, 1, 7; Joseph C. Nichols, "Basketball Unit Will Discuss Bias," *New York Times*, January 18, 1959.
86. Gates, *Colored People*, 98–99.
87. WVHRC Annual Report, 1964–65, 7–8 in WVHRC Papers, b. 2.
88. News Release, Jan. 2, 1962 in WVHRC Papers, b. 1.
89. See comments of W. Paul Burig, news editor of the *Wheeling News-Register* in a speech to the Kanawha Valley Unitarian Fellowship, n.d. but early 1961 in WVHRC Papers, b. 1.
90. News release, Jan. 2, 1962, in WVHRC Papers, b. 1.
91. Douglas C. Smith, "Race Relations and Institutional Responses in West Virginia—A History" *West Virginia History* 39 (Fall 1977): 30–48.
92. "Charleston CORE Accomplishments."
93. Hoffman, "Rights Commission Survey," 20; *Charleston Daily Mail*, n.d., in clippings file, Gilmore Collection.
94. Taylor Branch, *Pillar of Fire: America in the King Years, 1963–65* (New York: Simon and Schuster, 1998), 335–36. In his memoir, Byrd admits that "due to immaturity and a lack of seasoned reasoning" he organized a Raleigh County chapter of the Ku Klux Klan in 1942 (when he was living in Crab Orchard and working as a meat cutter at the Carolina Market) and signed up 150 members. For his efforts the klavern elected him Exalted Cyclops. Emphasizing the patriotic and anticommunistic appeal of the Klan, Byrd nonetheless admits to the racism of the organization and that he "definitely reflected the fears and prejudices" of his boyhood. Byrd, *Child of the Appalachian Coalfields*, 51–55.
95. *Charleston Gazette*, March 17, 1965.
96. Bruce Thompson, "An Appeal for Racial Justice: The Civic Interest Progressives' Confrontation with Huntington, West Virginia and Marshall University," MA thesis, Marshall University, 1986, 4, 17. Quote in "Causes of Unemployment in Huntington," Records of the Office of Economic Opportunity, Inspection Division Reports, 1964–67, b. 80, RG 381, National Archives, Washington, D.C.
97. Thompson, "An Appeal for Racial Justice," 10.
98. Ibid., 21–24.
99. Ibid., 37–51.
100. Ibid., 55–80.
101. Trotter, *Coal, Class, and Color*, 145–46; Michael M. Meador, "Carving a

Niche: The Blacks of Bluefield," *Goldenseal, West Virginia Traditional Life* 13, no. 4 (Winter 1987): 26–27.

102. James A. Haught, "Chasm in Mercer: Bluefield, Target of Civil Rights Crusades, Scene of Racial Disharmony Since 1954," *Sunday Gazette-Mail*, February 14, 1965.

103. Ibid.

104. C. Stuart McGhee and Frank Wilson, *Bluefield State College: A Centennial History* (Bluefield: The College, 1996), 129–30.

105. Bluefield Human Relations Commission Report, Malcolm Fuller, Chairman, October 15, 1963 in WVHRC Papers, b. 2.

106. *Charleston Gazette*, Oct. 4, 1964.

107. *Charleston Gazette*, Nov. 22, Dec. 7, 13, 16, 1964.

108. *Charleston Gazette*, Dec. 22, 1964.

109. *Charleston Gazette*, Jan. 28, 1965.

110. Ibid., Feb. 9, 1965.

111. Ibid., February 11, 1965; Ibid., Feb. 10, 1965.

112. WVHRC Annual Report, 1964–65, 18–20, 24–25, in WVHRC papers, b. 2.

113. Michael M. Meador, "The Blacks of Bluefield," 19–27; *Charleston Gazette*, November 18, 1964.

114. *Charleston Gazette*, Feb. 28, 1965.

115. WVHRC, *Annual Report, 1964–65*, 8–9, in WVHRC Papers, Box 2; *WVHRC Annual Report, 1965–66* (Charleston, 1966), 5–6; "Charleston CORE Accomplishments," typed list in CORE folder, Gilmore Collection.

116. K. W. Lee, "UNION: Revolt of the Valley's 'New Negro,'" *Charleston Gazette* Aug. 8, 1965.

117. Ibid. Lee also profiled new generation leaders Albert Evans, Richard Payne, and Spencer Burton and noted others involved in UNION, including Rev. Paul Gilmer, Mrs. Ellen Christian, Miss Nellie Walker, Marco Nelson, Dr. Virgil Matthews, the Rev. Moses Newsome, Clarence Wanzer, Henry Hale, Henry Haynes, and Charles Booker. James A. Haught, "City's White Churches: Failing or Leading March to Equality?" *Charleston Gazette*, Jan. 24, 1965; *Charleston Gazette*, Aug. 1, 2, 4, 6, 7, 8, 10, 13, 1965.

118. James A. Haught, "City's White Churches: Failing or Leading March to Equality?" *Charleston Gazette*, Jan. 24, 1965, 1D.

119. Ibid.
120. *Charleston Gazette*, August 1, 2, 4, 6, 7, 8, 10, 13, 1965; James A. Haught, "Clergymen Will Seek Pledges of Churchgoers," *Charleston Gazette*, Oct. 16, 1965.
121. *Charleston Gazette*, Nov. 9, 1964; Dec. 14, 1964.
122. Joe W. Trotter, "Memphis Tennessee Garrison and the West Virginia African American Experience," historical afterward in *Garrison*, ed. Bickley and Ewen, 225.
123. These issues are addressed in chapter 6.

4. Good Intentions

1. Theodore White, *The Making of the President, 1960* (New York: Atheneum House, 1961), 95–137. For other aspects of the 1960 primary, see Ronald D Eller, *Uneven Ground: Appalachia Since 1945* (Lexington: University Press of Kentucky, 2008), 53–55 and Harry W. Ernst, The *Primary that Made a President: West Virginia, 1960* (New York: McGraw–Hill, 1962). The sleaziness of West Virginia politics haunts even this epochal election. Thomas C. Reeves (citing Judith Campbell's autobiography *My Story*) claims that Kennedy arranged through Campbell to secretly meet with Mafia boss Sam Giancana to raise money for the West Virginia campaign. Kennedy and Campbell had allegedly just begun an affair: Reeves, *A Question of Character: A Life of John F. Kennedy* (New York: The Free Press, 1991), 164–66. Dan B. Fleming Jr., *Kennedy versus Humphrey, West Virginia, 1960: The Pivotal Battle for the Democratic Presidential Nomination* (Jefferson, North Carolina: McFarland Publishing, 1992) discounts charges that Kennedy bought the election or that the Mafia had anything to do with it. Fleming says Kennedy won because of his personal appeal: 150–54. In his memoir, Thomas Stafford, political reporter for the Charleston *Gazette* and a Humphrey supporter, says votes were bought in Kennedy's name in Charleston and in the southern coal mining counties. In any case, it is clear that the Kennedy campaign vastly outspent the poorly funded Humphrey campaign. Thomas F. Stafford, *Afflicting the Comfortable: Journalism and Politics in West Virginia* (Morgantown: West Virginia University Press, 2005), 67–78; Huey Perry, who became the Mingo County Community Action director during the War on Poverty repeated local lore that Kennedy trailed in the primary until he made the appropriate payments to local politicians: Gibbs Kinderman interview

of Huey Perry, July 7, 1987, 015–001, in Voices of Sixties Oral History Collection, Hutchins Library Special Collections, Berea College, Berea, Kentucky. Topper Sherwood tells how Kennedy's forces spent what was needed but concludes that his popularity in West Virginia led to his primary victory: "Kennedy in West Virginia," *Goldenseal* 26, no. 3 (Fall 2000): 15–19, 21–23.

2. Allen J. Matusow, *The Unraveling of America: A History of Liberalism in the 1960s* (New York: Harper and Row, 1984), 100.
3. Irwin Unger, *The Best of Intentions: The Triumph and Failure of the Great Society Under Kennedy, Johnson, Nixon* (New York: Doubleday, 1996), 27–28.
4. Ibid., 28.
5. Allen J. Matusow, *The Unraveling of America: A History of Liberalism in the 1960s* (New York: Harper and Row, 1984), 103–04.
6. Unger, *Best of Intentions*, 28–30; Eller, *Uneven Ground*, 100–01.
7. Eller, *Uneven Ground*, 102.
8. *Charleston Gazette*, February 15, 1965.
9. Eller, *Uneven Ground*, 58.
10. David E. Whisnant, *Modernizing the Mountaineer: People, Power, and Planning in Appalachia* (Boone: Appalachian Consortium Press, 1980), 70–78.
11. *Charleston Gazette*, April 24; May 3; May 5; May 6; May 7, 1954. See chapter 2, above.
12. For a more detailed and highly critical assessment of the ARA see Whisnant, *Modernizing the Mountaineer*, 70–91. See also Eller, *Uneven Ground*, 60–61; Matusow, *Unraveling of America*, 100–102; Michael Bradshaw, *Appalachian Regional Commission, Twenty-Five Years of Government Policy* (Lexington: University Press of Kentucky), 30–33.
13. George Lawless, "Death of a Business—Who's to Blame?" *Charleston Gazette*, Jan. 3, 1965.
14. Ibid., see for the quotations and characterizations of media opinion in Lawless's report.
15. Ibid.
16. James Harless letter, "'Fault Not Management'—Harless," *Charleston Gazette*, Jan. 17, 1965.
17. Matusow, *Unraveling of America*, 101.
18. Eller, *Uneven Ground*, 64.

19. Michael Harrington, *The Other America: Poverty in the United States* (New York: Macmillan, 1962), 46.
20. James T. Patterson, *Grand Expectations: The United States, 1945–1974* (New York: Oxford University Press, 1996), 533.
21. Thomas R. Ford, ed., *The Southern Appalachian Region: A Survey* (Lexington: University Press of Kentucky, 1962); Harry M. Caudill, *Night Comes to the Cumberlands: A Biography of a Depressed Area* Boston: Little, Brown, and Company, 1963); Eller, *Uneven Ground*, quote, 66.
22. Russell Baker, "Observer," *New York Times*, Aug. 22, 1963: 26.
23. Margaret Ripley Wolfe, "Eastern Kentucky and the War on Poverty: Grass Roots Activism, Regional Politics, and Creative Federalism in the Appalachian South during the 1960s," *Ohio Valley History*, 3, no. 1 (Spring 2003): 34; Homer Bigart, "Promise of US Aid for Tourism Elates Hinton, W. Va.," *New York Times*, Oct. 29, 1963. See also Thomas J. Kiffmeyer, *Reformers to Radicals: The Appalachian Volunteers and the War on Poverty* (Lexington: University Press of Kentucky, 2008), 34–38 and Whisnant, "Appalachia and the War on Poverty: The Office of Economic Opportunity," in Modernizing *the Mountaineer*, 92–125; Eller, *Uneven Ground*, chap. 2.
24. John G. Morgan, "William Wallace Barron; The Legislative Magician" *Charleston Sunday Gazette-Mail, State Magazine*, January 16, 1965: 2m–8m; 17m–21m; Stafford, *Afflicting the Comfortable*, 9–90.
25. Morgan, "Barron"; *Charleston Gazette*, Jan. 16, 1965. Stafford, *Afflicting the Comfortable*, 90.
26. Thomas Stafford, "Barron's Successes as Chief Executive Surprise Friend, Foe," *Charleston Gazette*, Jan. 10, 1965.
27. *Charleston Gazette*, Oct. 21, 1964.
28. Andrew Rucker to Festus Summers, July 9, 1956 (calling Summers to the first meeting of the commission) b. 1; *Final Report of the West Virginia Centennial Commission*, 9–15, b. 4, West Virginia Centennial Commission, Correspondence, 1956–62, West Virginia and Regional History Collection, West Virginia University; Stafford, *Afflicting the Comfortable*, 80.
29. Quotes from "Yes Virginia, There Is a James Johnson Sweeney," *Time Magazine*, February 8, 1963; Larry Elveru, "The High-Tech Artistry of Joe Moss: Bending Light and Sculpting Sound," *University of Delaware Magazine*," I, no. 1 (Fall 1988): 16–23.
30. Lyndon Baines Johnson, *Vantage Point: Perspectives of the Presidency*,

1963–1969 (New York: Holt, Rinehart and Winston, 1971), 73–74; Eller, *Uneven Ground*, 75–76.

31. Matusow, *Unraveling of America*, 97–107; Patterson, *Grand Expectations*, 535.
32. Whisnant, *Modernizing the Mountaineer*, 95–98.
33. Johnson, *Vantage Point*, 79; Wolfe, "Eastern Kentucky," 35; Eller, *Uneven Ground*, 80–81.
34. Among several summaries and analyses of the War on Poverty and other programs of the 1960s are Matusow, *The Unraveling of America*; Irving Bernstein, *Guns or Butter: The Presidency of Lyndon Johnson* (New York: Oxford University Press, 1997); David Chalmers, *And the Crooked Places Made Straight: The Struggle for Social Change in the 1960s*, 2nd ed. (Baltimore: Johns Hopkins University Press, 1996); Michael B. Katz, *From the War on Poverty to the War on Welfare* (New York: Pantheon, Random House, 1989); and Irwin Unger, *The Best of Intentions: The Triumph and Failure of the Great Society Under Kennedy, Johnson, and Nixon* (New York: Doubleday, 1996). An early critical assessment by a Kennedy administration insider was Daniel Patrick Moynihan, *Maximum Feasible Misunderstanding: Community Action in the War on Poverty* (New York: The Free Press, 1969). A useful anthology is Sidney M. Milkus and Jerome M. Mileur, *The Great Society and the High Tide of Liberalism* (Amherst: University of Massachusetts Press, 2005).
35. Stafford, *Afflicting the Comfortable*, 203–04.
36. Marie Tyler-McGraw interview with Jefferson Monroe, 0010 (summer 1982), Appalachian Volunteers Oral History Collection, Hutchins Library Special Collections, Berea College, Berea, Kentucky.
37. John G. Morgan, "The Pursuit of Excellence," preface to Canfield, *State Papers*, xiii–xlvii; Otis K. Rice and Stephen B. Brown, *West Virginia, A History*, 2nd ed. (Lexington: University Press of Kentucky, 1993), 283.
38. Generalizations based on: Hulett C. Smith Collection in Governor's Papers, 1965–1969, West Virginia and Regional History Collection, West Virginia University Library, Morgantown, West Virginia; RG 381 Records of Office of Economic Opportunity, Inspection Division, Inspection Reports, 1964–1967, WV, b. 80; Daniel P. Moynihan, *Maximum Feasible Misunderstanding: Community Action in the War on Poverty* (New York: Free Press, 1969), 140.
39. Memorandum to Edgar May from Martha McKay and Tom Kelley, April 7, 1965, State-Wide Work Experience, Title V, West Virginia, March

13–18, 1966: 17 in RG 381 Office of Economic Opportunity Inspection Division, Inspection Reports, 1964–67, West Virginia, b. 80. This is a 34-page report of the status of the OEO Title V program in West Virginia.

40. Ibid.
41. Thomas F. Stafford, "$11,848,000 Poverty Grant to State Told by Celebrezze," *Charleston Gazette*, June 6, 1965; Harry Hoffman, "Jobless Fight Takes Meaning," *Charleston Gazette*, June 8, 1965.
42. Narrative of West Virginia Title V Work Experience and Training Project Application, in OEO Inspection Reports, WV, 1–6, b. 80.
43. Hoffman, "Jobless Fight."
44. Memorandum to the Director from Edgar May, "Title V, West Virginia," April 11, 1966, 1–5, in OEO Inspection Reports, WV, b. 80.
45. *Charleston Gazette*, April 24, 1965; J. Howard Myers, ed., *West Virginia Blue Book, 1965* (Charleston: Jarrett Printing, 1965), 167.
46. Memorandum to the Director, 8–11.
47. Ibid, 1.
48. Sandra Freed, "Welfare Agencies Revamp System," *Charleston Gazette*, March 18, 1965; Hulett C. Smith, "Congressional Testimony before the Subcommittee on Intergovernmental Relations of the U.S. Senate, February 2, 1967," in Canfield, ed., *State Papers and Public Addresses*, 491.
49. Handwritten comments by "Sarge" and "B.H.B.," Memorandum to the Director, 1.
50. Memorandum to the Director, 11.
51. Quotes in ibid., 12.
52. Numan V. Bartley, *The New South: The Story of the South's Modernization, 1945–1980* (Baton Rouge, 1995), 22; John C. Morgan, "Smith's Third Year, Achievement, Tragedy," *Charleston Gazette*, January 7, 1968, reprinted in State *Papers and Public Addresses*, 448.
53. Stafford, *Afflicting the Comfortable*, 203.
54. Jeff Monroe to Governor Hulett C. Smith, June 11, 1968 in Smith Papers, b. 241; John Barnes, "A Case Study of the Mingo County Economic Opportunity Commission: The Use of Title II of the Economic Opportunity Act of 1964 in a Rural County of West Virginia" (DSW diss., University of Pennsylvania, 1971), 593–597. See also Douglas Yarrow, "How to Improve Title V Programs: Union Organization vs. Community Action," in Appalachian Volunteer Records.

55. "Work Incentive Program," News Release, July 15, 1968, in State *Papers*, 751–53; Hulett C. Smith, "Message to the Legislature, September 11, 1968," in *State Papers*, 767.

56. R. Sargent Shriver to Hulett C. Smith, Dec. 9, 1965, Records of the Office of Economic Opportunity, Inspection Division, West Virginia, b. 80.

57. *Charleston Gazette*, March 31, 1965.

58. Smith to Shriver, January 3, 1966, Smith Papers, b. 145.

59. Ibid; John G. Morgan, "State Singled Out for Poverty Program," *Charleston Gazette*, July 29, 1965; Don Marsh, "Teachers, Officials, Praise Impact of Head Start Programs in State," *Charleston Sunday Gazette-Mail*, Sept. 5, 1965, 8B.

60. Unger, *Best of Intentions*, 90–91.

61. Douglas Carnes, *Third Quarterly Status of West Virginia in the Economic Opportunity Program under Public Law 88–452, October 1, 1965*, 1–3, OEO Inspection Reports, b. 80.

62. Unger, *Best of Intentions*, 176–77.

63. William C. Blizzard, "Jobs Corps Home Where Buffalo Roam," *Gazette-Mail State Magazine*, June 20 1965; Sandra Freed, "Dignitaries Speak in Rite for Job Center," *Charleston Gazette*, July 26, 1965; Nan Robertson, "Job Corps Center Struggling with Trouble," *New York Times News Service* reprinted in *Charleston Gazette*, January 6, 1967, clipping in Appalachian Volunteer Collection, Berea College, b. 1, f. 6.

64. Unger, *Best of Intentions*, 4–7.

65. Ibid., 13–14.

66. Edward Peeks, "Homegrown: State People Getting Training to Aid Mental Health Effort," *Sunday Gazette Mail*, Aug. 18, 1968, 4A.

67. See chapter 5.

68. Matusow, *Unraveling of America*, 107–122.

69. Johnson, *Vantage Point*, 73–74.

70. Moynihan, *Maximum Feasible Misunderstanding*, 128–50. A professor of urban affairs at Harvard when he wrote this book, Moynihan later served as an assistant to President Nixon on urban affairs and was elected as a Democrat to the United States Senate from New York. See also Kinderman Interview with David Hackett, Sept. 11, 1987, 034–001, in Voices of the Sixties.

71. Eller, *Uneven Ground*, 98–99.

72. Matusow, *The Unraveling of America*, 125.

73. Johnson, *Vantage Point*, 75.
74. Unger, *Best of Intentions*, 173.
75. Kinderman interview with Darrell V. McGraw, May 21, 1987, 012–001, Voices from the Sixties.
76. *New York Times*, Feb. 5, 1964, 33.
77. These matters are discussed in Chapter 5.
78. Harry Ernst, "No Magic: Much Work Remains Ahead for Poor of Hardy County," *Charleston Gazette*, May 2, 1965, 3B.
79. Ralph Fisher, "Community Action," *Moorefield Examiner*, November 10, 1965, clipping in Smith Collection, b. 146.
80. Ernst, "No Magic."
81. Marie Tyler-McGraw interview with Jefferson Monroe, summer 1982, 0010, 0011, Appalachian Oral History Collection; Gibbs Kinderman interview with Jefferson Monroe, Aug. 18, 1987, 023001, Voices of the Sixties; Roger Morris, "Poverty Assault—Vista Team Tackles Depressed Hollows of McDowell in Program," *Charleston Gazette*, May 16, 1965.
82. Tyler-McGraw interview with Monroe; Kinderman interview with Monroe.
83. Quotes from "Memorandum, Eastern Kentucky Report, Frank Prial to Bill Haddad (OEO), June 7, 1965" in Kiffmeyer, *Reformers to Radicals*, 129–31.
84. Ibid., 131–32, citing Jack Ciaccio to Sidney Woolner, June 21, 1965.
85. Ibid.
86. Fisher, "Community Action."
87. Material prepared for Governor Smith by Paul Crabtree, November 17, 1965, regarding poor relations with OEO officials, Smith Papers, b. 147.
88. Ray Collins to Theodore Berry, Highlight Memorandum for State Technical Assistance, November 9, 1965, Records of the Office of Economic Opportunity, West Virginia, b. 80.
89. Memorandum to the Director, from Edgar May, November 11, 1965, ibid.
90. Quotations in ibid.
91. Hulett C. Smith to Theodore M. Berry, November 3, 1965, ibid.
92. All quotations from material prepared for Governor by Crabtree, November 17 in Smith papers, b. 147.
93. Hulett C. Smith to Hubert Humphrey, November 18, 1965, in ibid.

94. Bob Mellace, "Antipoverty Program Progress Not Satisfactory, Smith Says," *Charleston Daily Mail*, Dec. 9, 1965, clipping in ibid.
95. Unger, *Best of Intentions*, 167.
96. Ibid., 168–69.
97. Ibid., 195–96.
98. Quote from Matusow, *Unraveling of America*, 251; Unger, *Best of Intentions*, chap. 5, "Guns and Butter," 198–238.
99. Tyler-McGraw interview with Jefferson Monroe, summer 1982, 0010, Appalachian Volunteer Oral History Collection; Kinderman interview with Jefferson Monroe, 023-001, Aug. 19, 1987, Voices of the Sixties.
100. Memorandum, Jack Gonzalez to Edgar May, March 19, 1966, in Records of the Office of Economic Opportunity, West Virginia, b. 80.
101. Tyler-McGraw interview with Monroe; Kinderman interview with Monroe. Monroe summarized his views in a letter to Governor Smith, June 11, 1968, Smith Papers, b. 241.
102. Confidential Memorandum, to Governor Smith, from John D. Frisk, September 27, 1967, in b. 167, Smith Collection. Frisk wrote to warn the governor as he prepared to go to Moorefield for a "Government to the People" meeting.
103. Memo from Jack Whiting to Eugene Thoenen, January 4, 1966, b. 146, Smith Papers.
104. The McDowell county site visit team included Faye Rattner and Richard Wenner of OEO, Milton Ogle of Appalachian Volunteers, John Frisk of the West Virginia Technical Assistance Office, Richard G. Schmitt of the Department of Agriculture. Memo to Richard G. Lewis, Administrator from Richard G. Schmitt, Jr., Oct. 28, 1966; Memo to Everett Crawford from D. Richard Wenner, November 8, 1966 in National Archives RG 381, Office of Economic Opportunity Inspection Division, Inspection Reports, 1964–67, CAP, WV, Compilation, b. 80.
105. Wenner to Crawford, Nov. 8, 1966, ibid.
106. Faye Rattner to Richard Wenner, October 31, 1966 in ibid.
107. Richard Wenner to Whom It May Concern, October 31, 1966 in ibid.
108. Edward Peeks, "AAY Given Anti-Poverty Role," *Charleston Gazette*, November 11, 1964; "AAY to Turn Full Attention to War on Poverty This Year," *Charleston Gazette*, July 31, 1965.
109. Memo to Ed May from Dick Parsons, "Charleston, West Virginia, Action for Appalachian Youth—Community Development (March 2–3,

1966)," March 16, 1966; Memo to Edgar May from Tom Kelley and Bill Sheehan, "Charleston, West Virginia, Action for Appalachian Youth—Community Development, April 11–13, 1966," April 27, 1966 in OEO Inspection Reports, West Virginia, Kanawha, b. 80. On Rockefeller at Emmons, see *Charleston Gazette*, June 27, 1965; August 13, 1965 and Richard Grimes, *Jay Rockefeller: Old Money, New Politics* (Parsons and Charleston, McClain Printing and Jalamap Publications, 1984), 50–57.

110. Eller, *Uneven Ground*, 180–81.
111. "Appalachia Bill Needs Changes," Charleston *Gazette*, Feb. 2, 1965.
112. Harry Ernst, "Smith Says State Can Match Funds," *Charleston Gazette*, Feb. 2, 1965; Hulett C. Smith, "Congressional Testimony, Appalachian Regional Development Act, Special Subcommittee on Appalachian Development, Senate Committee on Public Works, January 21, 1965 in John A. Canfield (ed.), *State Papers and Public Addresses of Hulett C. Smith, 1965–1969* (Charleston: 1969), 102–07.
113. Harry M. Caudill, "Misdeal in Appalachia," *The Atlantic* (June 1965).
114. Eller, *Uneven Ground*, 183–84.
115. "West Virginia State Plan, 1971:" "16 in Appalachian Regional Commission Archives, West Virginia, b. 347, Margaret I. King Library, Special Collections and Archives, University of Kentucky.
116. Ralph Widner to Angus E. Peyton, Commissioner, Department of Commerce, June 24, 1968, b. 344, in Appalachian Regional Commission Archives.
117. Kathleen Hamm to Bill Blumer, Subject: West Virginia Development Plan, 1970, b. 347, f. 5, Appalachian Regional Commission Archives.

5. Raising Hell in the Hills and Hollows

1. The story of the Mingo EOC is told with much passion and verve by its executive director: Huey Perry, *"They'll Cut Off Your Project": A Mingo County Chronicle* (New York: Praeger, 1972). Also useful is John Barnes, "A Case Study of the Mingo County Economic Opportunity Commission: The Use of Title II of the Economic Opportunity Act of 1964 in a Rural County of West Virginia" (Doctoral diss., University of Pennsylvania, 1971); Barnes spent three months in the county in 1967. See also Gibbs Kinderman's interview with Perry (July 7, 1987) in Voices from the Sixties Oral History Collection, 1985–1987, in Hutchins Library, Special Collections, Berea College, Berea, Kentucky.

2. Barnes, "A Case Study," 235–43; West Virginia Department of Commerce, *An Economic Atlas for West Virginia* (Charleston, n.p., n.d.), "Map 1, 1950–1960 Population Changes"; "Census Counts, Population of Counties, 1970 and 1960," in Howard W. Carson, ed., *West Virginia Blue Book, 1973* (Charleston: State Senate, 1973), 996–97.
3. Perry, *Mingo County Chronicle*, 13.
4. See above, chapter 4.
5. Perry, *Mingo County Chronicle*, 1–6.
6. Ibid., 6.
7. Ibid., 13. Of course, most of those to whom Perry ascribes "silicosis" likely had pneumoconiosis, "black lung" disease.
8. Ibid., quotations from 10, 11.
9. Ibid., 17–21, 30–35, 200–12.
10. Ibid., 20–21.
11. Marjorie Hunter, *New York Times News Service*, "West Virginia's Poor Solving Own Problems," in Louisville *Courier-Journal*, n.d., clipping in Appalachian Volunteers Collection, Berea College, b. 132, f. 3; Perry, *Mingo County Chronicle*, 38–42
12. William G. Phillips, Assistant Director for Congressional Relations to Robert C. Byrd, July 22, 1966, in OEO Inspection Reports, b. 80, WV, RG 381, Records of the Office of Economic Opportunity, National Archives.
13. Hunter, "West Virginia's Poor Solving Own Problems."
14. Perry, *Mingo County Chronicle*, 97–110; quotations on 103, 105, 109. See also for Byrd's comments, *Charleston Gazette*, "Cut Poverty War—Byrd," Dec. 24, 1966.
15. Perry, *Mingo County Chronicle*, 10.
16. Ibid., 134–35.
17. Ibid., 97–110; Dave Peyton, "Anti-Poverty Effort in Mingo Lets Poor Run Own Projects," undated clipping attached to memo, Jeff Monroe to Governor Smith, August 11, 1967, in Hulett C. Smith Papers, b. 147, West Virginia and Regional History Collection, West Virginia University.
18. "The Records of the Appalachian Volunteers, 1963–1970," Descriptive Account of Records of the Appalachian Volunteers, 1963–1970, in AV Records, Southern Appalachian Archives, Berea College; Thomas J. Kiffmeyer, *Reformers to Radicals: The Appalachian Volunteers and the War on Poverty* (Lexington: University Press of Kentucky, 2008), 1–92.

Kiffmeyer's account focuses on Kentucky, with some attention to West Virginia (see 255, n 53). On the Council of the Southern Mountains, see also David E. Whisnant, *Modernizing the Mountaineer: People, Power, and Planning in Appalachia* (Boone: Appalachian Consortium Press, 1980), 3–33.

19. Kiffmeyer, *Reformers to Radicals*, 93–116. Whisnant, *Modernizing the Mountaineer*, 187–91.

20. Gibbs Kinderman interview by Marie Tyler-McGraw, 1982, in Appalachian Volunteer Oral History Collection, Hutchins Library, Special Collections, Berea College, Berea, Kentucky.

21. See AV Oral History Collection and Voices from the Sixties. Two former AVs who read a draft of this chapter independently reaffirmed this point. Thomas Rodenbaugh, who served as an AV field man in Kentucky and on the AV staff in the Berea and Bristol offices, strongly emphasized the motivation AVs derived from the social issues of the day. Rodenbaugh to author, email, December 1, 2009. Joseph Mulloy, who also served in Berea and Bristol and as a Kentucky field man expressed a similar view in email to the author, December 6, 2009.

22. Kiffmeyer, *Reformers to Radicals*, 114–21.

23. Whisnant, *Modernizing the Mountaineer*, 190.

24. Sociologist and former AV David Walls notes "the uneasy relationship" between AVs and OEO staff who wanted to the use the AVs as their "shock troops" to push maximum feasible participation: "The Appalachian Volunteers in Perspective"; Thomas Kiffmeyer, "Reformers to Radicals: The Appalachian Volunteers and the War on Poverty," *Appalachian Journal* (Fall 2009/Winter 2010) 37: nos. 1–2: 100–05.

25. Kiffmeyer, *Reformers to Radicals*, 123–46, quoting correspondence in AV Records, b. 5.

26. Ibid., 148–49, and quoting Caudill to Ogle, May 5, 1966, AV Records, b. 21. See also *Charleston Gazette*, April 12, 1966 in AV Records, b. 131, f. 6.

27. Rhodenbaugh email to author, December 1, 2009. David Walls's paper "Travelin' Down That Coal Town Road—The Appalachian Volunteers in Perspective: Community Organizing Then and Now" at the March 2009 meeting of the Appalachian Studies Association addressed this issue. I am indebted to Professor Wall for providing me with a copy. His review article, "Appalachian Volunteers," is an abridged version of the paper. See also box 61, f. 1, AV Records and interviews of AVs in AV Oral History Collection and Voices from the Sixties.

28. Memorandum, Ken Schlossberg to Edgar May, "Raleigh County West Virginia—VISTA Program, February 27, 1967," in OEO Inspection Reports, West Virginia, Raleigh, CA, AV-VISTA, b. 80.
29. Ibid.
30. John G. Morgan, "Hulett Carlson Smith," in *West Virginia Governors, 1863–1980* (Charleston: Charleston Newspapers, 1980), 2nd ed., 342–45.
31. Byrd, *Child of the Appalachian Coalfields*, 1–2; 12–17; 37, 41–53; 108–13.
32. Schlossberg to May.
33. Ibid., 2–3.
34. Whisnant, *Modernizing the Mountaineer*, 193.
35. Marie Tyler-McGraw interview with Naomi Weintraub Cohen, summer 1984, 004, Appalachian Volunteers Oral History Collection.
36. Schlossberg to May, "Raleigh County," 4; see Kinderman interview with Kramer (July 15, 1987), Voices of the Sixties.
37. Milton Ogle to Sanford Kravitz and Padriac Kennedy, Dec. 17, 1965, re: "points of general agreement" in AV Records, b. 26, f 8.
38. Narrative, "Vista Associates in 1966," ibid., b. 57, f. 3.
39. Schlesinger to Shriver, August 9, 1966, OEO Inspections Reports, Raleigh County, CA, AV-VISTA, b. 80.
40. Ibid., Shriver to Schlesinger, Sept. 28, 1966.
41. Ibid., Schlossberg, "Raleigh County . . . VISTA Program," 4–6. The first issue of the *Raleigh Peoples Press* appeared on Oct. 15, 1966, and contains an account of Chester Workman's rise to the presidency of the Raleigh County Community Action Association: in AV Records, b. 130, f. 11.
42. Velma Shumate to Jennings Randolph, January 12, 1967, in OEO Inspection Reports, West Virginia, Raleigh County, CA, AV-VISTA, Box 80.
43. Okey Mills to Jennings Randolph, February 17, 1967, Smith Papers, b. 243. See also the 1987 interview with Mills in Voices of the Sixties, 025–001.
44. Schlossberg, "Raleigh County . . . ," quotes on 13, 14.
45. Ibid., 15.
46. Kiffmeyer, *Reformers to Radicals*, 160.
47. James A. Haught, "Carrying Ideas, 300 Poor Map Trip to Capital," *Charleston Gazette*, Aug. 2, 1966; in AV Records, b. 132, f 1.

48. Kiffmeyer, *Reformers to Radicals*, 162–63.
49. Quotes from Joseph Mulloy email to author, December 6, 2009.
50. Harry Ernst, VISTA, "Job Corps Rapped: Cut Poverty War—Byrd," *Charleston Gazette*, December 24, 1966, in AV Records, b. 132, f.2.
51. Dave Peyton, "Region's Poor Jab 'Politicians,' OEO," *Huntington Herald-Advertiser*, Jan. 29, 1967, in AV Records, b. 132, f. 3.
52. Ben Franklin, "Group Wants Appalachian Coal under Public Control," March 26, 1967; "Is Rural Revolution Near in Appalachia?" March 27, 1967, *Huntington Herald Dispatch*. David Whisnant devotes a chapter to CAD ("Power for the People: The Congress for Appalachian Development"), noting that it could never develop adequate political or financial support. Among West Virginians involved were state senator Paul Kaufman, Charleston newspaperman Bill Blizzard, Don West, Lloyd Davis of West Virginia University, and Richard Austin of the West Virginia Mountain Project: Whisnant, *Modernizing the Mountaineer*, 220–37. See also William Blizzard, "Dawn over Appalachia," *Charleston Gazette-Mail State Magazine*, November 6, 1966, and Paul Kaufman, "Wistfulginia: A Fable with a Sad Ending," *Appalachian South*, 2 (Spring, Summer 1967), 24–25.
53. Eric Metzner to Chester Workman, Chairman, and Milton Ogle, Director, "Year End Report, (Interem)[sic]," AV Records., b. 52, f. 5.
54. Ibid.; Kinderman interview with Hershel Shrewsberry, May 13, 1987, 007–001 and with Roscoe Plumley, county agent, May 12, 1987, 006–001 in Voices of the Sixties.
55. Whisnant, *Modernizing the Mountaineer*, 197–98; Kiffmeyer, *Reformers to Radicals*, 185–86.
56. Mulloy email to author, December 6, 2009. For more detailed and slightly different accounts of the events of 1967 in Eastern Kentucky, see Whisnant, *Modernizing the Mountaineer*, 199–205 and Kiffmeyer, *Reformers to Radicals*, 185–95.
57. Mulloy email to author. See also Kiffmeyer, *Reformers to Radicals*, 187–99; Whisnant, *Modernizing the Mountaineer*, 204–05.
58. Hulett C. Smith to R. Sargent Shriver, August 14, 1967 in Hulett C. Smith Papers, b. 241.
59. All quotes in ibid. Smith also forwarded to Shriver copies of letters he had received regarding the incidents, including: Clyde Crowley, Superintendent of Babcock State Park, to Kermit McKeever, Chief of Parks, DNR, July 23, 1967, and Carl E. Gainer, State Senate, to Smith, August 8, 1967, in Smith Papers, b. 241.

60. "Transcript of Governor Smith's Press Conference," August 18, 1967 in Smith Papers, b. 241.
61. Milton Ogle to Jeff Monroe, August 14, 1967, Smith Papers, b. 241.
62. William H. Crook, Director, VISTA to Hulett C. Smith (n.d.) but ca. late August, 1967 in Smith Papers, b. 241.
63. See Byrd's comments in *Congressional Record*, CXIII, October 3, 1967, 27620–276201, cited by Kiffmeyer, *Reformers to Radicals*, n. 53, 199; and Robert C. Byrd, *Robert C. Byrd: Child of the Appalachian Coalfields* (Morgantown: West Virginia University Press 2005), 220.
64. Robert C. Byrd to R. Sargent Shriver, March 15, 1968, copy in Smith Papers, b. 241.
65. Alan J. Matusow, The *Unraveling of America: A History of Liberalism in the 1960s* (New York: Harper and Row, 1984), 269–70; Irwin Unger, *The Best of Intentions: The Triumph and Failure of the Great Society under Kennedy, Johnson and Nixon* (New York: Doubleday, 1996), 261–64.
66. All quotes from Robert C. Byrd to R. Sargent Shriver, March 15, 1968, copy in Smith Papers, b. 241.
67. Quoted by Garry Baker, "Byrd Opposes VISTA, Job Corps," *Charleston Gazette*, Dec. 4, 1968.
68. Telegram, Richard Cartwright Austin to John Slack, Smith Papers, b. 241.
69. Manuel Arvon to Hulett C. Smith, April 3, 1968, Smith Papers, b. 241.
70. Edward S. Cogen, Acting Regional Director OEO, to Hulett C. Smith, April 1, 1968, Smith Papers, b. 241.
71. Memo, Jeff Monroe to Governor Hulett C. Smith, April 3, 1968, Smith Papers, b. 241.
72. K.W. Lee, "Lightning Rod for Controversy," *Charleston Sunday Gazette-Mail State Magazine*, December 8, 1968. See also Jack E. Weller, *Yesterday's People: Life in Contemporary Appalachia* (Lexington: University of Kentucky Press, 1965), dust jacket.
73. Smith to Manuel Arvon, July 9, 1968, Smith Papers, b. 241.
74. Smith to Dr. Mildred Bateman, July 17, 1968, Smith Papers, b. 242.
75. Memo, A. Lytle to The Governor, July 23, 1968; typescript of comments of Chester Wiseman, President of B-CAN, August 12, 1968 in Smith Papers, b. 241.
76. "History of Community Action in Webster County, West Virginia," n.d. but ca. June 1968 (a document prepared by original board members), in Smith Papers, b. 147. Mott remained in the good graces of OEO. He

became a CAP trainer for a time and then, in March, 1969, he became the senior program officer for VISTA in West Virginia: *West Virginia Activist*, I, no. 5, March 25, 1969: 2 in AV Records, b. 130, f. 13.

77. All quotes from Jeanne M. Rasmussen, "Don West Does His Thing at Pipestem," *West Virginia Hillbilly*, October 26, 1968 clipping in AV Records, b. 64, f. 2.
78. Matusow, *The Unraveling of America*, 270.
79. Memo, Paul Crabtree to the Governor, June 9, 1968, Smith Papers, b. 241.
80. *Charleston Gazette*, April 2, 1968.
81. Quotes in memo, Jeff Monroe to Governor Hulett C. Smith, June 11, 1968, Smith Papers, b. 241; See also *Charleston Sunday Gazette-Mail*, June 2, 1968, and Alan Derickson, *Black Lung: Anatomy of a Public Health Disaster* (Ithaca: Cornell University Press, 1998), 146.
82. Crabtree to the Governor, July 18, 1968, Smith Papers, b. 43.
83. Virginia Dingess to Whom it May Concern, September 4, 1968 (and other letters supporting control of the EOC by local officials), in Smith Papers, b. 28.
84. Perry, *Mingo County Chronicle*, 213, 222; Hulett C. Smith to W. Astor Kirk, Mid-Atlantic Director, OEO, Oct. 28, 1968, in Smith Papers, b. 26.
85. Perry, *Mingo County Chronicle*, 227–37.
86. Unger, *Best of Intentions*, 343–44.
87. Eric Metzner, Year End Report, December 15, 1967, in b. 52, f. 5, AV Records.
88. Kiffmeyer, *Reformers to Radicals*, 200–01.
89. Both quotes from James A. Haught, "State 'Clobbered Hell' Out of Vistas," *Charleston Gazette*, Oct. 1, 1968: 52.
90. Archie Green, *Only a Miner: Studies in Recorded Coal-Mining Songs* (Urbana: University of Illinois Press, 1972), 429; See also Appalachian Volunteers Oral History Collection, Mike Kline, 008. Some of Kline's songs were used in radio programs about the sixties done by Gibbs Kinderman: Voices from the Sixties, Radio Programs, 036–001, 037–001.
91. William Greider, "US Abandons Social Thrust in Appalachia," *Washington Post*, Sept. 29, 1969, clipping in AV Records, b. 133, f. 2.
92. Memo, Don Grooms to Edgar May, Robert Clampitt, Gary Lefkowitz, re: "Clay County Development Corp." December 3, 1965, in OEO Investigative Reports, b. 80.

93. The allegation is attributed to "an OEO official" by William Grieder in *Washington Post*, Sept. 29, 1969, clipping in AV Records, b. 133, f. 2.
94. All quotations from Biesemeyer interview by Marie Tyler-McGraw, summer 1982, Appalachian Volunteers, Oral History Collection.
95. Kinderman interview with Jaffe, Aug. 20, 1987 (019–002), Voices of the Sixties.
96. Kinderman interview with Shrewsberry, May 13, 1987 (007–001), Voices of the Sixties.
97. Coles, *Migrants, Sharecroppers, Mountaineers*, 571–77.
98. Don West, "Romantic Appalachia," ed. David S. Walls and John B. Stephenson, *Appalachia in the Sixties: A Decade of Reawakening* (Lexington: University Press of Kentucky, 1972), 210–16.
99. Kiffmeyer, *Reformers to Radicals*, 206.
100. Whisnant, *Modernizing the Mountaineer*, 212.
101. Tyler-McGraw interview with Cohen.
102. Some examples (whose activities are further discussed, either in this chapter or the following ones) of local men and women, black and white, who made important contributions to community activism include: James Washington, an African American former miner became president of the Mingo Fair Elections Committee; Robert Guerrant, a black miner, headed the Winding Gulf Community Association, one of the most active and independent groups in Raleigh County, and became a board member of the abortive West Virginia Fund; Chester Workman, a middle-aged white miner from Richmond district became an activist chairman of the Raleigh County Community Action Agency, chaired the Appalachia Speaks poor people's conference in Huntington and helped organize in Wyoming County; Margaret Workman, Chester's wife, also played an active roles in community organizing in Richmond district; Hettie Trent, an African American leader of East Beckley became secretary of the Raleigh County CAP board; Chester Wiseman led a Boone County poor people's group that managed to get funding for a school hot lunch program; in Mingo County, Leah Curry headed the independent Head Start program, which became one of the first in the state to establish a year-round program, using welfare mothers as teachers, and local school teacher Huey Perry became the director of the Mingo County CAP; Hershel Shrewsberry, a typesetter for area newspapers, became the director of the Wyoming County CAP after being encouraged by AV and VISTA organizers. Among others, Alan Dickerson has noted that the movements developed by AVs and VISTAs helped develop indigenous leadership: *Black Lung*, 146.

103. Walls, "Travelin' Down That Coal Town Road" and "Appalachian Volunteers in Perspective": 105.
104. Margaret Ripley Wolfe, "Eastern Kentucky and the War on Poverty: Grass Roots Activism, Regional Politics, and Creative Federalism in the Appalachian South during the 1960s," *Ohio Valley History* 3 (Spring 2003), 32–33.
105. Barbara Ellen Smith, *Digging Our Own Graves: Coal Miners and the Struggle over Black Lung Disease* (Philadelphia: Temple University Press, 1987), 90–93. Whisnant, *Modernizing the Mountaineer*, lists several former AV-VISTAs who remained in Appalachia and the organizations for which they worked: 211–12. In interviewing AVs and VISTAs for the Appalachian Volunteer Collection in 1982, Marie Tyler-McGraw identified thirty who remained in West Virginia after their period of service with OEO programs. See "Staying on: Poverty Warriors in West Virginia after Fifteen Years," in Box 1, "Correspondence Regarding the Appalachian Volunteers Oral History Collection," Appalachian Volunteers Oral History Collection and "Staying on: Poverty Warriors in West Virginia," *Journal of American Culture* 8, no. 4 (Winter 1985): 93–103.
106. Irwin Unger summarizes critiques of the 1960s programs in *Best of Intentions*, 348–66.
107. Matusow, *Unraveling of America*, quote, 270.
108. Ibid., 252.
109. Kinderman interview with Perry, July 7, 1987 (015–001), and with Monroe, August 18, 1987 (023–001), in Voices of the Sixties.
110. Whisnant, *Modernizing the Mountaineer*, 118–19.
111. Smith, *Digging Our Own Graves*, 86.
112. Kinderman interview with Marsh, May 21, 1987 (011–001), Voices of the Sixties.
113. Unger, *Best of Intentions*, 366.

6. From the Silver Bridge to Farmington

1. Sidney Blumenthal used the term *annus horribilis* in reviewing Jules Witcover's *The Year the Dream Died: Revisiting 1968 in America* (New York: Warner Books, 1997). Journalist David Shribman uses it in "Lyndon Johnson: Means and Ends, and What His Presidency Means in the End," in *The Great Society and the High Tide of Liberalism*,

ed. Sidney M. Milkis and Jerome M. Mileur (Amherst: University of Massachusetts Press, 2005), 235. A thoughtful evaluation of the impact of 1968 on American society is William H. Chafe, "1968," in *The Unfinished Journey: America since World War II*, 4th ed. (New York: Oxford University Press, 1999), 343–80. See also "The Most Turbulent Year: 1968," in James T. Patterson, *Grand Expectations: The United States 1945–1974* (New York: Oxford University Press, 1996), 678–709.

2. John G. Morgan, "Hulett Carlson Smith, Twenty-seventh Governor, 1965–69," *West Virginia Governors, 1863–1980*, 2nd ed. (Charleston: Charleston Newspapers, 1980), 353–55; Thomas F. Stafford, *Afflicting the Comfortable: Journalism and Politics in West Virginia* (Morgantown: West Virginia University Press, 2005), 201–204; Bob Mellace, "As to Politics . . .," in *State Papers and Public Addresses of Hulett C. Smith, Twenty-seventh Governor of West Virginia*, ed. John A. Canfield, (Charleston: 1969), 730.

3. James Phillips and Holger Jensen, "Bridge Disaster Toll May Reach 46; Shocked Point Pleasant Seeking Dead," *Charleston Daily Mail*, December 16, 1967; Richard B. Grimes, "Town's Mayor Warned SRC Officials of Weak Span," *Charleston Daily Mail*, December 16, 1967; George Steel, "Point Pleasant Span Collapses, 70 Vehicles Plunge into River;" John G. Morgan, "All Possible Help Pushed by Governor," *Charleston Gazette*, December 17, 1967. All of the above in Silver Bridge Clipping Files, West Virginia State Archives, Charleston. See also "Ohio River Span Collapses: Heavy Death Toll Feared," *New York Times*, December 16, 1967:1; Canfield, ed., "The Silver Bridge Tragedy at Point Pleasant," *State Papers;* Ed Tunstall, "Why Did Silver Bridge Collapse? Answer Missing Yr. Later," *Sunday Gazette-Mail*, December 15, 1968.

4. *New York Times*, December 18, 19, 1967.

5. National Transportation and Safety Board, *Highway Accident Report: Collapse of U.S. Highway Bridge, Point Pleasant West Virginia, December 15, 1967* (Washington, n.d.), 126–27.

6. Terry Wallace, "25 Years Later, Bridge Collapse Still Haunts W.Va. Town," *Sunday Gazette-Mail*, December 13, 1992; The 1968 Federal Aid Highway Act, however, applied only to bridges built with federal aid. Most bridges in the country did not fall under that category and included the oldest and most in need of repair. The NTSB report recommended that all bridges be brought under the act, which required stricter safety and inspection standards: NTSB, *Point Pleasant*, 126–27. Wallace noted that a 1992 national survey found West Virginia (along

with Massachusetts) had the worst bridges in the nation, with 55 percent judged to be substandard. The Federal Aid Highway Act of 1971 established for the first time uniform national standards for bridge inspections, provided some funds for replacement of defective bridges in the federal aid highway system, and established qualifications and training for bridge inspectors. See U.S. Department of Transportation, Federal Highway Administration, "Overview and Evaluation of Bridge Program," *Status of the Nation's Highways, Bridges, and Transit: 2002 Condition and Performance Report*: www.gov/policy/2002cpr/p3.htm.

7. Ronald D Eller, *Uneven Ground: Appalachia since 1945* (Lexington: University Press of Kentucky, 2008), 187.

8. "Silver Bridge Awards Made," *Charleston Gazette*, August 14, 1973; Terry Wallace, "25 Years Later, Bridge Collapse Still Haunts W.Va. Town," *Sunday Gazette-Mail*, December 13, 1992. Wallace noted that in 1992 a national survey of bridges found 55 percent of West Virginia and Massachusetts bridges substandard, the worst in the nation. All of the above in Silver Bridge Clipping File, West Virginia State Archives, Charleston. See also Canfield, ed., "The Silver Bridge, Tragedy at Pt. Pleasant," *State Papers*, 633–59.

9. Stafford, *Afflicting the Comfortable*, 206. All quotes from: "Graft Is Denied in West Virginia," *New York Times*, Dec. 17, 1967. See "100 Years of Progress," *Consol News*, 100th Anniversary Edition, 3, no. 11 (First Quarter, 1964): 3–17.

10. Morgan, "Smith," 354–55; Stafford, *Afflicting the Comfortable*, 201–03. For a brief summary of the many scandals of the Barron era see James A. Haught, "Barron Era Brought Chaos," in *Fascinating West Virginia: Wild, Memorable Episodes from the Longtime Editor of the Mountain State's Largest Newspaper*, the Charleston Gazette (Charleston: Charleston Gazette, 2008), 47–75.

11. Stafford's *Afflicting the Comfortable* relates his efforts to uncover the facts behind the Barron scandals. See also Tim Massey, "Never Late for Court: An Interview with Milton J. Ferguson," and "'It Wasn't Any Pleasure for Me', Ferguson's Most Celebrated Trial," *Goldenseal: West Virginia Traditional Life* 9 (Winter 1983): 35–40; Morgan, "William Wallace Baron," *West Virginia Governors*, 277–78; Otis Rice and Stephen W. Brown, *West Virginia: A History*, 2nd ed. (Lexington: University Press of Kentucky), 282–83.

12. Stafford, *Afflicting the Comfortable*, 236.

13. Gibbs Kinderman interview with Don Marsh, May 20, 1987, 011–001, in

Voices of the Sixties Oral History Collection, Hutchins Library Special Collections, Berea College, Berea, Kentucky.

14. James D. McAteer, *Coal Mine Health and Safety: The Case of West Virginia* (New York: Praeger, 1973), 185–89.

15. Huey Perry, *They'll Cut Off Your Project: A Mingo County Chronicle* (New York: Praeger, 1972), 137; K. W. Lee, "Fair Elections in West Virginia," in *Appalachia in the Sixties: Decade of Reawakening*, ed. David S. Walls and John B. Stephenson (Lexington: University Press of Kentucky, 1972), 167.

16. Perry, *Mingo County Chronicle*, 139; Lee, "Fair Elections," 167–68.

17. All quotes from Lee, "Fair Elections," 164–67.

18. Quotes in ibid., 168–69; Perry, *Mingo County Chronicle*, 142–46; see also oral history interviews by Gibbs Kinderman with Judy Trent, Aug. 20, 1987 (030–001); Claudia Schecter, Aug. 18, 1987 (022–001); and Huey Perry, July 7, 1987 (015–001); and radio program, "Fair Elections" in Voices of the Sixties, Oral History Collection, Hutchins Library Special Collections, Berea College, Berea, Kentucky.

19. James Washington Jr., and Okey Spence to Governor Hulett C. Smith, April 10, 1968; Washington and Spence to Smith, April 23, 1968; Hulett C. Smith to James Washington, President, Fair Elections Committee, May 2, 1968, all in Hulett C. Smith Papers, West Virginia and Regional History Collection, West Virginia University, b. 43; Lee, "Fair Elections," 170–71; Perry, *Mingo County Chronicle*, 172–74, quote on 174; "Honest People Not Angered By Election Probe in Mingo," *Sunday Gazette-Mail*, April 21, 1968, 2B.

20. Lee, "Fair Elections," 172–75 (Washington quote, 174).

21. Ibid., 174–76; Perry, *Mingo County Chronicle*, 239.

22. Perry, *Mingo County Chronicle*, 252–56, quote, 256. Noah Floyd lost his senate seat in the 1970 election but remained chairman of the Democratic executive committee in Mingo County.

23. Brad Crouser, *Arch: The Life of Governor Arch A. Moore, Jr.* (Chapmanville: Woodland Press, 2008), 253.

24. Don Marsh, "Smith Changes Mind, Endorses No Successor," *Charleston Gazette*, April 3, 1968.

25. Fanny Seiler, "Behind Scenes at Statehouse," *Martinsburg Journal*, April 8, 1968.

26. Canfield to author, August 16, 2007.

27. Boyer, *Promises to Keep*, 308–09.
28. K. W. Lee, "Shock, Grief, Anger Expressed in Area," *Charleston Gazette*, April 5, 1968; K. W. Lee, "State Mourns Slain Negro," *Charleston Gazette*, April 6, 1968; Don Marsh, "City Memorial for Dr. King," *Charleston Gazette*, April 8, 1968; K. W. Lee, "Calm, Restraint, Mark State Scene," *Charleston Gazette*, April 10, 1968; "'Positive' Reaction Noted in State on Death of King," *Martinsburg Journal*, April 11, 1968; "King Slaying Stirs W.VA," *Martinsburg Journal*, April 5, 1968; "King Services Set in Many W.Va. Cities," *Martinsburg Journal*, April 6, 1968.
29. *Sunday Gazette-Mail*, April 7, 1968.
30. *Charleston Gazette*, April 14, 1968; Richard Grimes, *Jay Rockefeller: Old Money, New Politics* (Parsons: McClain Printing, 1984), 71.
31. George Lawless, "Industrial Units Praised for Actions in Gas Escape," *Charleston Gazette*, Aug. 1, 1968.
32. Quotes from George Lawless, "Official Warns Valley of Disaster Potential," *Charleston Gazette*, August 9, 1968.
33. Allen J. Matusow, *The Unraveling of America: A History of Liberalism in the 1960s* (New York: Harper and Row, 1984), 362–63.
34. K. W. Lee, "Tension in State: Rights Unit Cites Racial 'Triggers,'" *Charleston Gazette*, Aug. 9, 1968.
35. Ibid.
36. K. W. Lee, "Can Rent From SRC: Triangle Evictions 'Out,'" *Charleston Gazette*, July 30, 1968, 13.
37. James A. Haught, "Mood of the Triangle: The Frustration Begins to Boil," 29.
38. K. W. Lee, "After Two Nights of Rumbling, Calm Returns With Sign of Pride," *Charleston Gazette*, August 8, 1968, 29; "City Can Avert Disorders by Facing Racial Facts," *Charleston Gazette*, Aug. 10, 1968, 4.
39. *Charleston Sunday Gazette-Mail*, Aug. 11, 1968; *Charleston Gazette*, Aug. 12, 13; *New York Times*, Aug. 11, 1968:1
40. Patterson, *Grand Expectations*, 695–97.
41. Canfield, "Recollections," 12. Ribicoff quote from Patterson, *Grand Expectations*, 696.
42. Stafford, *Afflicting the Comfortable*, 210–11. Stafford based his account of the back room dealing of the 1968 election on the investigative reporting of his former colleague at the *Charleston Gazette*, James Haught. A similar account appears in Morgan, "Arch Alfred Moore, Jr." *West Virginia Governors*, 404–05. On Kaufman, see "Kaufman Can Meet

Needs to Win as a Democrat," *Charleston Gazette*, April 1, 1968. See also Grimes, *Jay Rockefeller*, 71–72.

43. Crouser, *Arch*,154–60, quote, 161.
44. Sprouse later served as a member of the West Virginia Court of Appeals and as a member of the U.S. Court of Appeals, Fourth Circuit. The quotation came from Morgan, "Arch Alfred Moore, Jr.," *West Virginia Governors*, 375. See also Loughry, "Don't Buy Another Vote," 159–61; "The 1968 Campaign," in *State Papers*, ed. Canfield, 807–48; Crouser, *Arch*, 154–72.
45. Patterson, *Grand Expectations*, 686; Paul S. Boyer, *Promises to Keep: The United States Since World War II*, 2nd ed. (Boston: Houghton Mifflin, 1999), 306.
46. Jeffrey A. Drobney interview with Joseph Gluck, September 22, 1992, cited in Drobney, "A Generation in Revolt: Student Dissent and Political Repression at West Virginia University," *West Virginia History* 50, no. 9 (1995): 107, 120.
47. Ibid., 107.
48. *West Virginia Activist* 1, no. 2 (February 15, 1969), in Appalachian Volunteer Archives, b. 130, f. 13.
49. John Hennen, "A Struggle for Recognition: Marshall University Students for A Democratic Society and the Red Scare in Huntington, 1965–1969," *West Virginia History* 52 (1993): 127–47.
50. William J. L. Wallace, "The Impact of *Brown v. the Board of Education of Topeka, Kansas* on West Virginia State College," in *Brown v. Board of Education of Topeka, Kansas, Thirty Years Later: A Series of Lectures and Discussions* (Institute: West Virginia State College), 103–05.
51. C. Stuart McGehee and Frank Wilson, *A Centennial History of Bluefield State College, 1895–1995* (Bluefield: Bluefield State College, 1995), 129–32.
52. Ibid., 136. Some of the correspondence and documents relative to the Bluefield State crisis can be found in Canfield, ed., "Special Section: Bluefield State College," *State Papers*, 859–74. Other documents can be found in Smith Papers, b. 4. See especially West Virginia Human Rights Commission to Smith, "Report on Problems of Discrimination and Racial Tensions at Bluefield State College," December 14, 1967. Both the reports of the West Virginia Human Rights Commission and the State Board of Education are reprinted in the *Charleston Gazette*, December 10, 1968, and quotations from the documents are from this source.

53. *Charleston Gazette*, December 10, 1968.
54. K. W. Lee, "NAACP Demands Tragedy Be Corrected," *Charleston Gazette*, December 12, 1968.
55. *Charleston Gazette*, December 3, 1968; December 13, 1968.
56. Ibid., December 21, 1968.
57. McGehee and Wilson, *A Centennial History*, 138.
58. Nyden, "Struggle in the Coalfields," 473; Clark, *Miners' Fight*, 18; Finley, *Corrupt Kingdom*, 163–68; Hume, *Death and the Mines*, 174–75. Richard P. Mulcahy offers some defense of Lewis, whom he sees as responding pragmatically to the economic and political realities of the fifties: *A Social Contract for the Coal Fields: The Rise and Fall of the United Mine Workers of America Welfare and Retirement Fund* (Knoxville: University of Tennessee Press), 131–39.
59. Smith, *Digging Our Own Graves*, 79.
60. Richard P. Mulcahy argues that given the condition of the industry, higher payments might have been counterproductive: *A Social Contract for the Coal Fields*, 128–32. Ivana Krajcinovic is more critical of Lewis, suggesting that a royalty increase might have been sought after the recession of 1959–61, or alternatively, the union treasury could have been used to bail out the Fund: *From Company Doctors to Managed Care: The United Mine Workers Noble Experiment* (Ithaca: Cornell University Press), 158–61.
61. In 1960, with the fund continuing to bleed resources at a rate of more than $1 million per month, the trustees revoked the hospital and medical coverage of all miners unemployed for more than a year, denied coverage to members working for operators who had not signed the national wage agreement or those operating their own mines, and reduced pension payments from $100 to $75 per month. Some 17.7 percent of beneficiaries lost their health coverage, and most of the cuts came from the miners of central Appalachia among whom unemployment was highest and families in greatest distress. In 1962 (instead of supporting the membership against union–busting companies) the trustees canceled the health cards of miners whose employers made only token payments to the welfare funds. Krajcinovic, *From Company Doctors to Managed Care*, 148–56; Mulcahy, *A Social Contract for the Coal Fields*, 133–36; Nyden, "Struggle in the Coal Fields," 473; Melvyn Dubofsky and Warren Van Tine, *John L. Lewis: A Biography* (Urbana: University of Chicago Press, 1986), 370; Finley, *Corrupt Kingdom*, 184–98.
62. Finley, *Corrupt Kingdom*, 242. Clark, *Miners' Fight*, 20–21; Hume, *Death and the Mines*, 43–52.

63. Smith, *Digging Our Graves*, 79–82.
64. Ibid., 81–82.
65. Nyden, "Struggle in the Coal Fields," 474–77.
66. Roger W. Haynes, "Opportunities for the Young Man in the Coal Industry," presented April 21, 1967, at the West Virginia Coal Mining Institute, Morgantown, West Virginia, *1967 Proceedings of the West Virginia Coal Mining Institute* (Morgantown: Morgantown Printing, 1968), 77–81.
67. Bynum Junior Gilbert interviewed by William Mares, Stotesbury, 1973, in "Raleigh County Coal Miners," West Virginia State Archives.
68. Quote from Smith, *Digging Our Graves*, 75; Nyden, "Struggle in the Coal Fields," 475; Clark, *Miners' Fight*, 22–23.
69. Silas House and Jason Howard, *Something's Rising: Appalachians Fighting Mountaintop Removal* (Lexington: University Press of Kentucky, 2009), 39.
70. James A. Haught, "Heartbreak in the Coal Fields—Something to Sing About," *Charleston Gazette*, April 4, 1965; Jean Ritchie, *A Time for Singing* (Warner Brothers Records); Billy Edd Wheeler, *Little Brown Shack Out Back* (Kapp Records); Archie Green, *Only A Miner: Studies in Recorded Coal Mining Songs* (Urbana: University of Illinois Press, 1972), 424, 430.
71. Green, *Only a Miner*, 424.
72. John A. Canfield, "Miracle of Hominy Falls," in *State Papers*, ed. Canfield, 730–31.
73. William M. Kelley Jr. (WSAZ television technician), interview by Gary Simmons, July 30, 2002, for West Virginia Documentary Consortium, Inc.
74. Hume, *Death and the Mines*, 6–10.
75. Ibid., 16.
76. Quotes in *New York Times*, Nov. 22, 1968; Nyden, "Struggle in the Coal Fields," 476–77; Finley, *Corrupt Kingdom*, 213.
77. Franklin, "The Scandal of Death and Injury in the Mines," 26–27.
78. Clark, *Miners' Fight*, 24.
79. Sherrill, "West Virginia Miracle," 529–535.
80. "Statement by the Governor, December, 1968," in *State Papers*, ed. Canfield, 854.
81. Quotes from Hume, *Death and the Mines*, 75.
82. Ibid., 80.

83. Derickson, *Black Lung*, 78.
84. The idea of the benevolent consequences of inhaling coal dust came at least in part from U.S. Public Health Services studies conducted at Gulf Smokeless Coal Company's Wyco works in southern West Virginia between 1923 and 1927. Although the company doctor did the work and followed no scientific regimen, he reported he found no disabling lung impairment among 200 miners there, and PHS disseminated the finding. PHS also arranged for Leroy Gardner, one of its consultants, to test the hypothesis that coal dust could prevent tuberculosis. Though Gardner never visited the site, the cooperative company doctor at Wyco used guinea pigs supplied by Gardner. Guinea pigs placed in the dust-laden cleaning plant at Wyco and deliberately infected with tuberculosis did better than a group also injected but not exposed to the coal dust, leading Gardner to conclude (in a 1933 article in the *Journal of Industrial Hygiene*) that the bituminous coal dust might have some protective benefit. Ibid., 73.
85. Martin Cherniak, *The Hawks Nest Incident: America's Worst Industrial Disaster* (New Haven: Yale University Press, 1986), 69–75.
86. Smith, *Digging Our Own Graves*, 24–29; Mulcahy, *A Social Contract for the Coal Fields*, 144–45; Finley, *Corrupt Kingdom*, 224; Derickson, *Black Lung*, 130–34.
87. Hume, *Death and the Mines*, 102–03.
88. Derickson, *Black Lung*, 139; quotes from Mulcahy, *A Social Contract for the Coal Fields*, 141.
89. Mulcahy, *A Social Contract for the Coal Fields*, 144–48; Smith, *Digging Our Own Graves*, 108–09; Derickson, *Black Lung*, 140–42.
90. Smith, *Digging Our Own Graves*, 30. See also Sherrill, "West Virginia Miracle," 531–32; Franklin, "The Scandal of Death and Injury in the Mines," 25–27; Davitt McAteer, *Coal Mine Health and Safety: The Case of West Virginia*.
91. Hume, *Death and the Mines*, 102–04; Derickson, *Black Lung*, 147–48, quote on 147.
92. Donald L. Rasmussen, et al., "Pulmonary Impairment in Southern West Virginia Coal Miners," *American Review of Respiratory Disease* 98 (October 1968): 658–67, cited in Smith, *Digging Our Own Graves*, 29.
93. Hume, *Death and the Mines*, 105–06.
94. Ibid., 106–107.
95. K. W. Lee, "Catalyst of the Black Lung Movement" in *Appalachia in the Sixties*, ed. Walls and Stephenson, 201–09, quote, 208; Derickson, *Black Lung*, 144–46.
96. Hume, *Death and the Mines*, 104.

97. Ibid., 104–05.
98. Ibid., 108–09; Nyden, "Struggle in the Coalfields," 691–92.
99. *Charleston Gazette*, Dec. 23, 1968; Smith, *Digging Our Own Graves*, 110–12.
100. Boyer, *Promises to Keep*, 309; Patterson, *Grand Expectations*, 361.
101. The investigations of the Purchasing Practices and Procedures Commission set up by the special session in 1968 led to 107 indictments against thirty-two individuals and eleven corporations on charges involving state purchasing irregularities in the period 1961 to 1969, but the State Supreme Court of Appeals in a series of rulings held the indictments invalid because they were based on an unconstitutional law. Governor Moore called for a special session to pass new reform legislation, but Thomas Stafford maintained that the court rulings had effectively derailed the effort to clean house. The Justice Department took up the work and secured indictments that sent several of Barron's associates to prison. The PPPC evolved into the Commission on Special Investigations, and its existence and the threat of federal indictment created sufficient fear to bring about some progress in cleaning up purchasing procedures and practices. It did not, as it turned out, sufficiently inoculate the state against future malfeasance and scandal. Stafford, *Afflicting the Comfortable*, 234–44.
102. Drobney, "Generation in Revolt," 111–13.

7. An Appalachian Reawakening

1. Though no general account of West Virginia grassroots movements in the period exists, scholars and journalists have given attention to many of the issues of the time. An excellent anthology, which contains a bibliography of "Dissent in Appalachia," is Stephen L. Fisher, ed., *Fighting Back in Appalachia: Traditions of Resistance and Change* (Philadelphia: Temple University Press, 1993). Among the useful accounts are the following: Alan Derickson, *Black Lung: Anatomy of a Public Health Disaster* (Ithaca: Cornell University Press, 1998); Barbara Ellen Smith, *Digging Our Own Graves: Coal Miners and the Struggle over Black Lung Disease* (Philadelphia: Temple University Press, 1987); Chad Montrie, *To Save the Land and The People: A History of Opposition to Surface Coal Mining in Appalachia* (Chapel Hill: University of North Carolina Press, 2003); Paul F. Clark, *The Miners' Fight for Democracy: Arnold Miller and the Reform of the United Mine Workers* (Ithaca: New York State School of Industrial and Labor Relations, Cornell

University, 1981); Paul John Nyden, "Miners for Democracy: Struggle in the Coal Fields" (Ph.D. diss., Columbia University, 1974); Ronald L. Lewis, *Black Coal Miners in America: Race Class, and Community Conflict, 1780–1980* (Lexington: University Press of Kentucky, 1987); Ivana Krajcinovic, *From Company Doctors to Managed Care*; Richard P. Mulcahy, *A Social Contract for the Coal Fields The Rise and Fall of the United Mine Workers of America Welfare and Retirement Fund*; David S. Walls and John B. Stephenson, eds., *Appalachia in the Sixties: Decade of Reawakening* (Lexington: University Press of Kentucky, 1972); Brit Hume, *Death and the Mines: Rebellion and Murder in the UMW* (New York: Grossman, 1971); Joseph E. Findley, *The Corrupt Kingdom: The Rise and Fall of the United Mine Workers* (New York: Simon and Schuster, 1972). See also Catherine Moore, "'Let's Show Them What a Fight We Can Give Them': The Black Lung Movement in West Virginia," *Goldenseal* 32, no. 2 (Summer 2006): 6–13.

2. Huey Perry, *They'll Cut Off Your Project: Mingo County Chronicle* (New York: Praeger, 1972), 238. Although some categories of social spending actually increased in the Nixon administration, driven by continuing Democratic influence in Congress and growth through entitlements, OEO gradually shrank as the administration parceled its programs out to other agencies. Between 1969 and 1974, the OEO budget dropped from $1.9 billion to $328 million, and soon thereafter it closed shop. Irwin Unger, *The Best of Intentions: The Triumph and Failure of the Great Society Under Kennedy, Johnson, and Nixon* (New York: Doubleday, 1996), 331–32.

3. *West Virginia Activist* 1, no. 5 (March 25, 1969): 2, in Appalachian Volunteer Archives, Berea College, b. 130, f. 115.

4. Perry, *Mingo County Chronicle*, 238–39. "Tri-Cap Goals, 1969–70," b. 2, M.L. Sill Collection, Special Collections, Marshall University, Huntington.

5. *West Virginia Activist* 9, 10 (June 10, 1969): 2, in Appalachian Volunteer Archives, Berea College, b. 130, f. 13.

6. Ibid., 1, no. 5 (March 25, 1969).

7. James Thibault, interviewed by Marie Tyler-McGraw, Summer, 1982, 0014, Appalachian Volunteers Oral History Collection, Hutchins Library Special Collections, Berea College.

8. *West Virginia Activist* 9, 10 (June 10, 1969) in Appalachian Volunteer Archives, Berea College, b. 130, f. 13.

9. "Background, West Virginia Service Corps, 1969"; "West Virginia Service Corps Information Sheet," Appalachian Volunteers Archives, b. 64, f. 5.

Notes to Pages 262–267

10. "West Virginia Fund Proposal Draft for Final Change and Approval, OEO Planning and Development Grant," in Appalachian Volunteers Archives, b. 64, f.4; Marie Tyler-McGraw interview with Jefferson Monroe, 0010, Summer, 1982, Appalachian Volunteer Oral History Collection.
11. Smith, *Digging Our Own Graves*, 157–59; Marie Tyler McGraw interview with Gibbs Kinderman, Summer 1982, 007, Appalachian Volunteer Oral History Collection.
12. *Charleston Gazette*, Feb. 17, 1972.
13. Smith, *Digging Our Own Graves*, 162; "Paul J. Kaufman," *Profiles: West Virginias Who Made a Difference* (Charleston: *The Gazette*, 1999): 35.
14. Ibid., 110–11; Hume, *Death and the Mines*, 111–12.
15. Smith, *Digging Our Own Graves*, 111–12; Hume, *Death and the Mines*, 111–13; Nyden, "Miners for Democracy," 693–98.
16. Quote in *Washington Post*, Jan. 27, 1969: in Scrapbook, Kenneth Hechler Collection, Alderman Library, Marshall University, Huntington.
17. Quotes from Russ Lilly, "3500 Yell Demand for Black Lung Law," *Huntington Herald-Dispatch*, Jan. 27, 1969, Hechler Scrapbook.
18. Ben A. Franklin, "Miners Organize to Reduce Risks," Jan. 27, 1969, *New York Times*, Hechler Scrapbook.
19. For a good brief summary of revisionist thinking about the sources of "quiescence" among coal miners and other poor Appalachians and the rise of social activism, see Dwight B. Billings, "Introduction: Writing Appalachia: Old Ways, New Ways, and WVU Ways," in *Culture, Class and Politics in Modern Appalachia: Essays in Honor of Ronald L. Lewis*, eds. Jennifer Egolf, Ken Fones-Wolf, and Louis C. Martin (Morgantown: West Virginia University Press, 2009).
20. Nyden, "Miners for Democracy," 694; Hume, *Death and the Mines*, 123–24.
21. Niles Jackson, "Crusading Black Lung Physicians—Alarmists or Humanitarians?" *Charleston Gazette*, January 26, 1969, Hechler Scrapbook.
22. Quotes from "Coal Association Attacks Sideshow Tactics of Black Lung Legislation Advocate," *Morgantown Post*, February 13, 1969, Hechler Scrapbook.
23. Ibid.
24. *Kanawha Valley Leader*, February 13, 1969, Hechler Scrapbook.
25. Derickson, *Black Lung*, 156–58; Hume, *Death and the Mines*, 124–28.

26. Quotes from Hume, *Death and the Mines*, 130–31; Derickson, *Black Lung*, 156–58.
27. Hume, *Death and the Mines*, 131–33; Derickson, *Black Lung*, 158.
28. In "Faces of Coal," transcript of interviews by William Mares, 1972–73, in Raleigh County Coal Miners Collection, West Virginia State Archives, Charleston, WV.
29. "Protest Strike Sweeps Southern Coal Fields," *Huntington Herald-Advertiser*, Feb. 21, 1969 in Hechler Scrapbook; Smith, *Digging Our Own Graves*, 114–16; Hume, *Death and the Mines*, 134–35; Derickson, *Black Lung*, 158–59.
30. Hume, *Death and the Mines*, 134.
31. *Welch Daily News*, Feb. 22, 1969, in Hechler Scrapbook.
32. Hume, *Death and the Mines*, 136–39; Smith, *Digging Our Graves*, 116–17; Nyden, "Miners for Democracy," 696.
33. "Widows, Wives Carry Miners Safety Battle to Washington," *Charleston Gazette*, Feb. 25, 1969, Hechler Scrapbook; Barbara Smith, "Miners Widow: Sara Kaznoski, Fighter and Survivor," *Goldenseal: West Virginia Traditional Life* 14, no. 2 (Summer 1988): 52–57; Hume, *Death and the Mines*, 92–93; Derickson, *Black Lung*, 173.
34. Hume, *Death and the Mines*, 140–41; Edward Peeks, "Coal Miners Sound Call of 'No Law, No Work,'" *Charleston Gazette*, Feb. 27, 1969 Hechler Scrapbook.
35. Peeks, "Coal Miners"; Hank Burchard, "Who Speaks for U.S. Coal Miners?" *Washington Post*, March 2, 1969, Hechler Scrapbook; Derickson, *Black Lung*, 160; Hume, *Death and the Mines*, 140–42; Smith, *Digging Our Own Graves*, 121–22; Nyden, "Miners for Democracy," 694–96.
36. Derickson, *Black Lung*, 160–61.
37. All quotes from Hume, *Death and the Mines*, 143, 145. Hume gives a fascinating account of the intricate legislative maneuvering including the important roles of Democratic House Speaker Ivor Boiarsky and Republican Delegate Cleo Jones in arriving at an acceptable compromise between opposing House and Senate bills: 140–51.
38. The full definition reflected the earlier Alabama statute: "The term 'occupational pneumoconiosis' shall include, but shall not be limited to, such diseases as silicosis, anthracosilicosis, coal worker's pneumoconiosis, commonly known as black lung or miner's asthma, silicotuberculosis (silicosis accompanied by active tuberculosis of the lungs), coal worker's pneumoconiosis accompanied by active tuberculosis of

the lungs, tuberculo-silicosis, asbestosis, siderosis, anthrax, and any and all other dust diseases of the lungs and conditions and diseases caused by occupational pneumoconiosis which are not specifically designated herein." Quoted from the statute by Derickson, *Black Lung*, 161.

39. Quotes from ibid, 161–62; Hume, *Death and the Mines*, 151. Curtis Seltzer notes that the law did nothing to control dust in the mines, a needed preventative measure. He also says presumption did not go far enough. The applicant still had to prove his disability, which made determination an adversarial case-by-case task that generated much work for lawyers and established an unfortunate precedent for the federal legislation, which came later in 1969. Nevertheless, he concedes, continuation of the strike in the hope of producing stronger legislation probably would have failed and discredited the BLA and its methods: *Fire in the Hole*, 99–100.

40. Seltzer, *Fire in the Hole*, 101; Finley, *Corrupt Kingdom*, 206–07.

41. Ibid., 100–101; Derickson, *Black Lung*, 178–80.

42. Seltzer, *Fire in the* Hole, 102–03; Derickson, *Black Lung*, 178–81; Smith, *Digging Our Own Graves*, 130–44.

43. Derickson, *Black Lung*, 178–80; Seltzer, 102.

44. Smith, *Digging Our Own* Graves, 127–28; Seltzer, *Fire in the Hole*, 188–89.

45. Derickson, *Black Lung*, 180–81.

46. Ibid., 181.

47. Clark, *The Miners' Fight for Democracy*, 25–26; Hume, *Death and the Mines*, 170–71; Nyden, *Miners for Democracy*, 492–502; Seltzer, *Fire in the Hole*, 108–11.

48. Richard Harewood, "Yablonski, Two in Family Slain," *Washington Post*, Jan. 6, 1970; "Yablonski of UMW Slain With Wife and Daughter," *New York Times*, Jan. 6, 1970, Hechler clipping file; Hume, *Death and the Mines*, 240–41; Clark, *The Miners Fight for Democracy*, 26; Seltzer, *Fire in the Hole*, 112–13.

49. Seltzer, *Fire in the Hole*, 112–13; Hume, *Death and the Mines*, 240–59.

50. Ibid., 90–91; Smith, *Digging Our Own Graves*, 78–85; Jeanne M. Rasmussen, "On the Outside Looking In," in *Appalachia in the Sixties: Decade of Reawakening*, ed. David S. Walls and John B. Stephenson (Lexington: University Press of Kentucky, 1972): 176–83.

51. Nyden interview with Payne, Itmann, WV, Aug. 18, 1973, recording at WV and Appalachia Collection, WVU; Nyden, "Miners for Democracy," 709–13.

52. Nyden interview with Payne.
53. Ben A. Franklin, "Reform Miners Select Candidates to Run Against Boyle," *New York Times*, May 29, 1972; "Angry Insurgent, Arnold Ray Miller," *New York Times*, May 30, 1972; Clark, *Miners' Fight for Democracy*, 27. Paul J. Nyden, who traveled throughout the coal fields in this period interviewing rank-and-file miners and pensioners and wrote sympathetically of their organizations, wrote that the MFD in the Wheeling Convention turned its back on black miners, failing to nominate Charles Brooks, the first president of the BLA, or Robert Payne, organizer of the Disabled Miners and Widows of Southern West Virginia, or any other black for leadership positions. He also claims that MFD stifled all discussion of the special problems black miners faced. Nyden, "Miners for Democracy," 574–82.
54. Clark, *Miners' Fight for Democracy*, 28–31; *New York Times* quote, 31; Nyden, "Miners for Democracy," 583–91.
55. Perry, *Mingo County Chronicle*, 152–53.
56. "Salute to Black Women," *Charleston Gazette*, May 4, 1980.
57. Hume, *Death and the Mines*, 107–10.
58. See biographical sketch online at East Tennessee State University's Web site: Reecemus@etsu.edu. See there also Jeanne M. Rasmussen (1934–1992), "Coal Country in Black and White: Photographs, 1968–1973."
59. Testimony of Nora Noonkester, Secretary, Chapter 5, Association of Disabled Miners and Widows, n.d., b. 327, f. 62; Nora Noonkester to Hechler, August 6, 1969; Hechler to Noonkester, Aug. 14, 1969 in b. 328, f. 14, Hechler Collection.
60. Email correspondence to author from Douglas Yarrow and Gibbs Kinderman, January 12, 2010.
61. Barbara Smith, "Miner's Widow: Sara Kaznoski, Fighter and Survivor," *Goldenseal: West Virginia Traditional Life* 14, no. 2 (Summer 1988): 52–58.
62. Jo Boggess Phillips, "Lawmaker Jackie Withrow: A Rose Among the Thorns," *Goldenseal: West Virginia Traditional Life* 24, no. 3 (Fall 1998): 32–35; "Jackie Withrow," *Profiles: West Virginians Who Made a Difference* (Charleston: *Charleston Gazette*, 1999): 60–61.
63. Tom D. Miller, "Elizabeth V. Hallanan," in *West Virginia Encyclopedia*, ed. Ken Sullivan, 308.
64. Ancella R. Bickley, "Mildred Mitchell-Bateman," in ibid., 489.
65. Jo Boggess Phillips, "'I Greatly Appreciate Your Courage': West Virginia

Women Legislators," *Goldenseal: West Virginia Traditional Life* 24, no. 3 (Fall 1998): 27–32; Women in the House of Delegates in 1972 included Lucille Engle Gillespie (R-Kanawha), elected 1972; Judith Herndon (R-Ohio), appointed 1970, elected 1970, 72; Jean Holt (R-Kanawha), elected 1972; Jody Guthrie Smirl (R-Cabell), elected 1966, 68, 70, 72; Phyllis Given (D-Kanawha), elected 1972; Mary Martha Merritt (D-Raleigh), elected 1970, 72; Sarah Lee Neal (D-Greenbrier), elected 1972; G. Michele Prestera (D-Cabell), elected 1972; Phyllis J. Rutledge (D-Kanawha), elected 1968, 70, 72; Mrs. W.W. "Jackie" Withrow, elected 1960, 62, 64, 66, 68, 70, 72. Howard W. Carson, ed., *West Virginia Bluebook, 1973* (Charleston, 1973), Senate roster, 2; House of Delegates Roster, 26, Press Roster, 80–81.

66. Carson, ed., *Bluebook, 1973*, 801–03; 803–05.
67. Carol Mason, *Reading Appalachia from Left to Right: Conservatives and the 1974 Kanawha County Textbook Controversy* (Ithaca: Cornell University Press, 2009), see especially, chap. 3, "Sweet Alice and Secular Humanism."
68. Chris Weiss, "Appalachian Women Fight Back: Organizational Approaches to Non-Traditional Job Advocacy," in *Fighting Back*, ed. Fisher, 151–64; Sally Ward Maggard, "Coalfield Women Making History," in *Back Talk from Appalachia: Confronting Stereotypes*, ed. Dwight B. Billings, Gurney Norman, and Katherine Ledford (Lexington: University Press of Kentucky, 1999): 228–50.
69. Brad Crouser, *Arch: The Life of Governor Arch A. Moore, Jr.* (Chapmanville: Woodland Press, LLC, 2008), 210–60. Useful brief accounts are Thomas F. Stafford, *Afflicting the Comfortable: Journalism and Politics in West Virginia* (Morgantown: West Virginia University Press, 2005): 245–255; Otis K. Rice, Stephen W. Brown, *West Virginia: A History*, 2nd ed. (Lexington: University Press of Kentucky, 1993), 284–85; John G. Morgan, *West Virginia Governors, 1863–1980*, 2nd ed. (Charleston: Charleston Newspapers, 1980); "Arch Alfred Moore Jr.," chap. 28, quote, 367.
70. Crouser, *Arch*, 224–6; Morgan, "Arch Alfred Moore, Jr.," 365–408; *Charleston Gazette*, Feb. 18, 1972.
71. Stafford, *Afflicting the Comfortable*, 245–55, quote, 250; see also Morgan, "Moore," 371–74.
72. Stafford, *Afflicting the Comfortable*, 310.
73. Rumors of corrupt practices plagued Moore throughout his career, which included one term in the House of Delegates, six consecutive terms in Congress (1956–1969), and three terms as Governor (1969–1977;

1985–1989). During his second term as governor, he survived a trial in federal court based on charges going back to his first term. Eventually, on April 12, 1990, faced with evidence federal prosecutors had uncovered, Moore agreed to plead guilty to charges of extortion, tax evasion, and obstruction of justice related to his third term as governor. Though he later tried to retract his pleas, Moore received a sentence of five years and ten months and a fine of $170,000. He actually served thirty-three months. In the end the Moore era, instead of erasing the image of corruption, became another chapter in the long history of West Virginia as a rotten borough. Morgan, "Moore," 367, 423–33; Stafford, *Afflicting the Comfortable*, 310–17. Biographer Crouser devotes a chapter, "The Feds vs. Arch Moore," to a generally sympathetic account of Moore's legal dilemma which Crouser ascribes primarily to the governor's use of "the underground campaign," the accepting and distribution of unreported cash for political purposes. In doing this Moore simply followed West Virginia practice, Crouser maintains. Crouser, *Arch*, 542–78.

8. The Strip Mining Dilemma and a Climactic Debate

1. The best general account of strip mining and the opposition to it is Chad Montrie, *To Save the Land and the People: A History of the Opposition to Surface Coal Mining in Appalachia* (Chapel Hill: University of North Carolina Press, 2003). See also Ronald D Eller, *Uneven Ground: Appalachia Since 1945* (Lexington: University Press of Kentucky, 2008), 161–70. For a succinct summary of the development of strip mining and especially mountain top removal mining and its consequences in Southern West Virginia from its origins to recent times, see Shirley Stewart Burns, *Bringing Down the Mountains: The Impact of Mountaintop Removal on Southern West Virginia Communities* (Morgantown: West Virginia University Press, 2007). Other books that cover parts of the story and give testimony to the rising opposition to mountaintop removal mining include: Silas House and Jason Howard, eds., *Something's Rising: Appalachians Fighting Mountaintop Removal* (Lexington: University Press of Kentucky, 2009); Penny Loeb, *Moving Mountains* (Lexington: University Press of Kentucky, 2007); Michael Shnayerson, *Coal River* (New York: Farrar, Straus, and Giroux, 2008).

2. W. E. E. Kepler, "Contour Mining in the Pocahontas Field," in Pocahontas Operators Association Papers, microfilm reel 1, West Virginia and Regional History Collection, West Virginia University Library. Unfortunately, this document, apparently a speech manuscript, bears no date, but it is with other documents of the 1929 to 1930 era,

and the mechanical equipment mentioned would seem to be the type used well before World War II.

3. James Gay Jones, "West Virginia in World War II" (Doctoral diss., West Virginia University, 1952), 81.

4. *Business Week*, April 18, 1944: 29–32; Jones, "West Virginia in World War II," 91.

5. Montrie, *To Save the Land*, 22–23; C. L. Christenson, *Economic Redevelopment in Bituminous Coal*, 33–34; Dubofsky and Van Tine, *John L. Lewis*, 350; "Continuous Coal Mining," *Fortune*, June, 1950: 111–114; Jack Temple Kirby, *Rural Worlds Lost: The American South, 1920–1960* (Baton Rouge: Louisiana State University Press, 1987), 109; Robert F. Munn, "The Development of Strip Mining in Southern Appalachia," *Appalachian Journal*, III (Autumn 1975): 87–92; M. G. Zabetakis, L. D. Phillips, *Safety Manual No.1: Coal Mining* (Washington: Mining Enforcement and Safety Administration, Department of the Interior, 1972), 7–13; James A. Barlow, *Coal and Coal Mining in West Virginia, Coal Geology Bulletin, No. 2* (Morgantown: West Virginia Geological and Economic Survey, 1974), 31–38; Brit Hume, *Death and the Mines: Rebellion and Murder in the UMW* (New York: Grossman Publishers, 1971), 98–99.

6. Wilson to Underwood, b. 60, f. 307, Governors' Papers, WVRHC.

7. Thomas F. Stafford, "Mixed View Meets State Bid to Alter Mine Law," *Charleston Gazette*, July 28, 1965; Kenneth R. Bailey, "Development of Surface Mine Legislation, 1939–1967," *West Virginia History: A Quarterly Magazine* 30, no. 3 (April 1969): 525–29; Robert F. Munn, "The First Fifty Years of Strip Mining in West Virginia, 1916–1965," *West Virginia History* 35 (Oct. 1973): 66–74.

8. Thomas F. Stafford, "Strip Mine Law Too Feeble Now," *Charleston Gazette*, July 31, 1965.

9. "State Must Get Tough for Change With Plundering Coal Strippers," *Charleston Gazette*, Jan. 3, 1965.

10. "Statewide Organizations Back Strip Mining Measure," *Huntington Herald-Dispatch*, January 22, 1967.

11. Dave Peyton, "Region's Poor Jab 'Politicians,' OEO," *Huntington Herald-Dispatch*, Jan. 29, 1967 in Records of the Appalachian Volunteers, b. 132, f. 3, Southern Appalachian Archives, Hutchins Library, Berea College.

12. Montrie, *To Save the Land*, 112–13.

13. Elveru, "High Tech Artistry of Joe Moss," 20–23. In 1970, feeling

typecast by all the attention relating to *West Virginia Moon*, Moss moved to the University of Delaware.

14. Bailey, "Surface Mine Legislation," 529; John G. Morgan, "The Pursuit of Excellence" preface to *State Papers and Public Addresses of Hulett H. Smith*, ed. Canfield, xiii–xlvii; Rice and Brown, *West Virginia*, 283; quote from Montrie, *To Save the Land*, 114.
15. Montrie, *To Save the Land*, 107; Mary Beth Bingham, "Stopping the Bulldozers: What Difference Did It Make?" in *Fighting Back in Appalachia: Traditions of Resistance and Change*, ed. Stephen L. Fisher (Philadelphia: Temple University Press, 1993): 17–30.
16. Montrie, *To Save the Land*, 85–105.
17. "Strip Mining Industry Shot Through With Evil," *Charleston Gazette*, Aug. 24, 1965.
18. *Charleston Gazette*, February 2, 1967, cited by Montrie, *To Save the Land*.
19. *Charleston Gazette*, February 11, 27, 1971.
20. Howard W. Carson, ed., *West Virginia Blue Book, 1973* (Charleston: 1973), 1048.
21. Montrie, *To Save the Land*, 108–14.
22. Ibid., 115. The Si Galperin Collection, West Virginia State Archives, contains information on his efforts on behalf of the strip mine abolition movement, 1971–73.
23. J. Howard Myers, ed., *West Virginia Blue Book, 1963* (Charleston: 1963): 90.
24. Grimes, *Jay Rockefeller*, 99–100.
25. Montrie, *To Save the Land*, 115–16.
26. "Testimony of Richard Cartwright Austin," Subcommittee on Mines and Mining, Committee on Interior and Insular Affairs, US House of Representatives, November 29, 1971, typescript in b. 329, f. 1; Appalachia Strip Mining Information Service, "About the Service, b. 320, f. 12, Hechler Papers.
27. Montrie, *To Save the Land*, 115–16.
28. Ibid., 116–17; *Charleston Gazette*, March 9, 10, 1971.
29. Quoted in *Wheeling News- Register*, February 14, 1971, Hechler Papers, b. 329, f. 16.
30. Brad Crouser, *Arch: The Life of Governor Arch A. Moore, Jr.*, (Chapmanville: Woodland Press, LLC, 2008), 244.
31. Grimes, *Jay Rockefeller*, 101.

32. Montrie, *To Save the Land*, 109.
33. Ibid., 118–19.
34. Ibid., 120.
35. Grimes, *Jay Rockefeller*, 101.
36. Courage—Human Rights Fighters," *Charleston Gazette*, August 28, 2009, a *Gazette* editorial and review of Norman Williams' *Gandhi's American Ally: How an Education Missionary Joined Mahatma's Struggle Against Untouchability* (Lincoln: iUniverse.com, 2008). In 2009 Williams was living in retirement in Washington, D.C.
37. Quotes from "Strip Law Has Failed, Williams Charges," *Charleston Gazette*, February 26, 1971 (excerpts from testimony before the WV House Judiciary Committee), clipping in Hechler Papers, b. 329, f. 15.
38. "A Voice Cries—Will It Ring Over Scarred State?" *Charleston Gazette*, Feb. 26, 1971, Clipping in Hechler papers, b. 329, f. 15.
39. Quotes in ibid.
40. Robert Daoust, "Future Being Stripped Away," *Charleston Gazette*, Feb. 14, 1971, Hechler Papers, b. 329, f. 15.
41. Mary Walton, "State Conservation Districts Harbor Antistrip Sentiments," *Charleston Gazette*, March 3, 1971.
42. *Charleston Gazette*, March 2, 1972.
43. Ibid., March 5, 1971.
44. Harry Hoffman, "Moore with Strippers," *Charleston Gazette*, March 9, 1971.
45. Crouser, *Arch*, 248.
46. *Beckley Post-Herald and Register*, April 18, 1971, Hechler Papers, b. 329, f. 1.
47. *Charleston Gazette*, March 5, 1971.
48. Grimes, *Jay Rockefeller*, 102.
49. Ibid., March 10, 1971.
50. Ibid., March 14, 15, 1971.
51. Garry J. Moes, "All That's Left of Fight: New Strip Bill Praised, Chastised," *Charleston Gazette*, March 15, 1971.
52. *Beckley Post-Herald and Register*, April 18, 1971.
53. Crouser, *Arch*, 244.
54. Ward Sinclair, "House Bill Would Forbid All Strip-Mining in U.S.," *Louisville Courier-Journal*, Feb. 19, 1971, Hechler Papers, b. 329, f. 15.
55. Hechler to "Dear Colleague," Hechler Papers, b. 329, f. 15.

56. "Testimony of Richard Cartwright Austin."
57. *Charleston Gazette*, February 12, 18, 1972.
58. Montrie, *To Save the Land*, 124–25.
59. "Dispassionate Stripping Study Really Vital to State," editorial, *Charleston Gazette*, March 11, 1971.
60. Quotes from the report by Mary Walton, "Stanford Report: It Bores in on Facts," *Charleston Gazette*, February 20, 1972; Montrie, *To Save the Land*, 124–25.
61. Crouser, *Arch*, 288–314. Howard W. Carson, ed., *West Virginia Bluebook, 1973* (Charleston, 1974): 625–26, 1042.
62. William E. Leuchtenburg, *A Troubled Feast: America Since 1945* (Boston: Little, Brown, 1984), 253–63; James T. Patterson, *Grand Expectations: The United States, 1945–1974* (New York: Oxford University Press, 1997), 758–65.
63. Grimes, *Jay Rockefeller*, 99–100.
64. Ibid., 100–01; *Charleston Gazette*, November 3, 7, 1972.
65. Crouser, *Arch*, 248, 308.
66. George Steele, "All's Quiet Outside Mingo Polls," *Charleston Gazette*, November 9, 1972.
67. Grimes, *Jay Rockefeller*, 104–05.
68. Crouser, *Arch*, 302.
69. Grimes, *Jay Rockefeller*, 106–20.
70. Ibid., 102–03, 121.
71. Ibid., 121.
72. Ibid., 127.
73. Carson, ed., *Bluebook, 1973*, 627–28.
74. *Charleston Gazette*, Nov. 10, 1972.
75. Carson, ed., *Bluebook, 1973*, 632–33; Montrie, *To Save the Land*, 124–26.
76. Quotes from *If Elected . . .* by Wayne Ewing (TRT: 55:15), Wayne Ewing Films, Inc., 1973.
77. Tracy Hylton interview in Raleigh County Coal Miners, Oral History in West Virginia State Archives, Charleston.
78. Montrie, *To Save the Land*, 127–53.
79. The term "expedient" is Chad Montrie's in "Expedient Environmentalism: Opposition to Coal Surface Mining and the United Mine Workers of America, 1945–1977," *Environmental History* 5 (Jan. 2000): 75–98.

80. Montrie, *To Save the Land*, 126.
81. Eller, *Uneven Ground*, 165.

9. Buffalo Creek

1. The worst flood before Buffalo Creek had been in August 1916, along Paint Creek and Cabin Creek, near Charleston, when forty-six persons died. James A. Hill, "Buffalo Creek State's Most Murderous Flood," *Charleston Gazette*, February 1972.
2. Tom Nugent, *Death at Buffalo Creek: The 1972 West Virginia Flood Disaster* (New York: Norton, 1973), 20–27; Nyden, "Miners for Democracy," 226–27; Erikson, *Everything in Its Path*, 21–26. For Smith's comments see Harry Ernst, "Smith Says State Can Match Funds," *Charleston Gazette*, February 5, 1965. For a brief summary of the environmental impact of coal mining, see James A. Barlow, *Coal and Coal Mining in West Virginia* (Morgantown: West Virginia Geological and Economic Survey, Coal Geology Bulletin No. 2, February, 1974), 43–46.
3. James T. Patterson, *Grand Expectations: The United States, 1945–1971* (New York: Oxford University Press, 1996), 726.
4. John G. Morgan, "The Pursuit of Excellence," in *State Papers and Public Addresses of Hulett C. Smith*, ed. John A. Canfield (Beckley: Biggs, Johnston and Withrow, 1969), xxxix.
5. Quotes from the act by Gerald M. Stern, *The Buffalo Creek Disaster* (New York: Vintage Books, 1977), 166.
6. A paper presented at the spring 1967 meeting of the West Virginia Coal Mining Institute (about a year before the construction of the Buffalo Creek Dam No. 3) suggests that the whole process of disposing of acid runoff and sludge residue from mining remained highly experimental. The authors noted that despite much study by many people and agencies, "No one has come up with a really satisfactory . . . method of handling acid mine drainage." Charles T. Holland, James L. Corsaro, Charles W. McGlothlin, and Douglas J. Ladish, "Research on Acid Mine Drainage Control," *Proceedings of the West Virginia Coal Mining Institute* (Morgantown Printing, 1968), 115–48.
7. West Virginia Governor's Ad Hoc Commission of Inquiry, *The Buffalo Creek Flood and Disaster, Official Report* (Charleston: 1973); Erickson, *Everything in Its Path*, 21–26; Nugent, *Death at Buffalo Creek*, 23–24.
8. Nyden, "Miners for Democracy," 247. For 1950s see West Virginia

Department of Commerce, *An Economic Atlas for West Virginia*, Economic Statistical Series 1 (Charleston, n.d., ca. 1963), map 1, 1950–1960 Population Changes.

9. West Virginia Coal Association, *West Virginia Coal and 1972: A Report on the Current Status of the West Virginia Coal Industry* (Charleston, 1973), 9, in Pocahontas Coal Operators Association Papers, microfilm reel 5, West Virginia and Regional History Collection, West Virginia University.

10. Erikson, *Everything in Its Path*, 21–26; Nugent, *Death at Buffalo Creek*, 23–24. The other villages were Pardee, Lorado, Craneco, Lundale, Stowe, Crites, Latrobe, Robinette, Amherstdale, Becco, Fanco, Braeholm, Accoville, Crown, and Kistler.

11. Quote from Tom F. Waddington, "Report of the President," Southern Virginias Coal Association Annual Meeting, March 22, 1971, 2–3, Pocahontas Coal Operators Association Papers, microfilm reel 5. On the environmental legislation, see Patterson, *Grand Expectations*, 727–30.

12. Waddington, "Report of the President."

13. West Virginia Coal Association, *West Virginia and Coal in 1972*, 10–12; West Virginia *Bluebook*, 1974, 969.

14. U.S. Department of the Interior, *Preliminary Analysis of the Coal Refuse Dam Failure at Saunders, West Virginia, February 26, 1972* (Washington: Task Force to Study Waste Hazards, 1972), 4–5, in Buffalo Creek Disaster Collection, at West Virginia Archives and History, Division of Culture and History, Charleston, WV.

15. Stern, *Buffalo Creek Disaster*, 152–53.

16. Nyden, "Miners for Democracy," 226–40; West Virginia Division of Culture and History, "Buffalo Creek," online exhibit.

17. Ibid.; Nugent, *Death at Buffalo Creek*, 22–28; Erikson, *Everything in Its Path*, 24–27; Nyden, "Miners for Democracy," 225–28; *Buffalo Creek Flood*, directed by Mimi Pickering (Appalshop, 1975, videocassette). For the studies of the dams see William E. Davies, James F. Bailey, and Donavan B. Kelly, *West Virginia's Buffalo Creek Flood: A Study of the Hydrology and Engineering Geology* (Washington, GPO, 1972); U.S. Army Corps of Engineers, *Buffalo Creek WV Disaster, 1972*. Prepared for the Subcommittee on Labor for the Committee on Labor and Public Welfare, United States Senate, Washington, D.C., 1972); and U.S. Department of the Interior, *Preliminary Analysis of the Coal Refuse Dam Failure*, all to be found in Buffalo Creek Disaster Collection, WV Archives and History.

18. Davies, Bailey, and Kelly, *West Virginia's Buffalo Creek Flood*; Nugent,

Death at Buffalo Creek, 33; Nyden, "Miners for Democracy," 240; Harry Caudill, "Buffalo Creek Aftermath," *Saturday Review* (August 26, 1972): 16–17 in clipping file, "Buffalo Creek Disaster," State Archives.

19. Quote in Nyden, "Miners for Democracy," 239; Nugent, *Death at Buffalo Creek*, 32.
20. Ad Hoc Commission, *Official Report*, Section 2.2.
21. Both the Governor's Ad Hoc Commission and the Citizens Commission focused on the inadequacy of the several agencies with responsibility to enforce the environmental and safety laws. See Ad Hoc Commission, *Official Report*, Section 6 and Citizens' Commission, *Disaster on Buffalo Creek: A Citizens' Report on Criminal Negligence in a West Virginia Mining Community* (1972), 20–25, reprinted at http://wvgazette.com/static/series/buffalocreek/commission.html.
22. Gerald Stern quotes Inspector Joe Holley's testimony to this effect in *Buffalo Creek Disaster*, 162.
23. Nugent, *Death at Buffalo Creek*, 33–37.
24. Nyden, "Miners for Democracy," 229, 237–38.
25. Stern, *Buffalo Creek Disaster*, 160–64.
26. *Charleston Gazette*, February 12, 1972.
27. "Guard Helps Logan Families Flee Flooding," *Charleston Gazette*, February 25, 1972.
28. Nugent, *Death at Buffalo Creek*, 20–22; Nyden, "Miners for Democracy," 230.
29. Mannix Porterfield, "25 Years Later Survivors Remember Flood Tragedy," *Beckley Register-Herald*, February 16, 1997:38, in Clipping File, Buffalo Creek Disaster, State Archives; Nugent, *Death at Buffalo Creek*, 50–55.
30. Ad Hoc Commission, *Official Report*; Erikson, *Everything in Its Path*, 27–41; Nyden, "Miners for Democracy," 231–32.
31. *Charleston Gazette*, February 29, 1972, cited by Nyden, "Miners for Democracy," 236.
32. Brad Crouser, *Arch: The Life of Governor Arch A. Moore, Jr.* (Chapmanville, WV: Woodland Press, 2008), 282; Stern, *Buffalo Creek*, 12.
33. Quotes from George Vecsey, "Rival Units Study West Virginia Flood," *New York Times*, March 12, 1972, cited by Nyden, "Miners for Democracy," 237; Crouser, *Arch*, 282.
34. "After the Dam Broke, Cries for Controls," *Business Week*, March 11,

1972, in Clipping File, Buffalo Creek Disaster, State Archives.

35. Ad Hoc Commission, *Official Report,* Introduction. Commission members in addition to the chairman: John Ashcraft, Director, Department of Mines; Dr. Robert B. Erwin, WV State Geologist; Ira Latimer, Jr., Director, DNR; Elizabeth Hallanan, Chair, PSC; Dr . Dan Nealy, representative of the U.S. Bureau of Mines; William E. Davies, US Geological Survey; Charles D. Hylton, editor of *Logan Banner,* citizen representative, and Julian Murrin, citizen representative.

36. Citizens' Commission, *Disaster on Buffalo Creek,* 3–4; Stern, *Buffalo Creek Disaster,* 11–12.

37. Ad Hoc Commission, *Official Report,* Section 6.2.

38. Citizens' Commission, *Disaster on Buffalo Creek,* 32.

39. Stern, *Buffalo Creek Disaster,* 7.

40. Stern, *Buffalo Creek Disaster,* 72–75; *Charleston Gazette,* November 2, 16, 1972.

41. Nugent, *Death at Buffalo Creek,* 180.

42. Stern, *Buffalo Creek Disaster,* 301–03.

43. Crouser, *Arch,* 283.

44. For further details on this controversy, see Haught, *Fascinating West Virginia* (Charleston: *Charleston Gazette,* 2008), 82–85 and Crouser, *Arch,* 284–87.

45. Beth Spence, "Buffalo Creek Tragedy Continues," *Logan News,* February 21, 1975, in Buffalo Creek clipping file.

46. West Virginia Division of Culture and History, "Buffalo Creek," online exhibit; Beth Spence, e-mail to author, August 29, 2009.

47. Erikson, *Everything in Its Path,* 9–10.

48. Lynda Ann Ewen and Julia A. Lewis, "Buffalo Creek Revisited: Deconstructing Kai Erikson's Stereotypes," *Appalachian Journal: A Regional Studies Review* 27, no. 1(Fall 1999): quote, 22, 22–44. For a critical early review of Erikson's book, see Dwight Billings and Sally Maggard in *Social Forces* 57, no. 2 (Dec. 1978): 722–23.

49. Erikson, *Everything in Its Path,* 250–51.

50. Jack Weller, *Yesterday's People: Life in Contemporary Appalachia* (Lexington: University of Kentucky Press, 1965); Brit Hume, *Death and the Mines: Rebellion and Murder in the UMW* (New York: Grossman Publishers, 1971).

51. Beth Spence, e-mail to author, August 29, 2009. Spence reported for the

Logan News and did community work in Buffalo Creek in the aftermath of the flood. She later helped organize the Appalachian Alliance.
52. "After the Dam Broke," *Business Week*.
53. Ken Ward Jr., "Coal Dams Still Loom Over W.Va.," *Sunday Gazette-Mail*, March 2, 1997, 8A–9A, in WV State Archives, Buffalo Creek Clipping file. Ward's article was part of a series to mark the twenty-fifth anniversary of the disaster. The series included interviews with survivors, recollections of reporters, a chapter on the disaster from Paul Nyden's dissertation "Miners for Democracy," and the full text of the Citizen's Commission report: http://wvgazette.com/static/series/buffalocreek/BUF302B.html.
54. Ken Ward Jr., "Agencies Failed to Protect People," *Charleston Gazette*, Feb. 27, 1997.
55. See Shirley Stewart Burns, *Bringing Down the Mountains: The Impact of Mountaintop Removal on Southern West Virginia Communities* (Morgantown: West Virginia University Press, 2007), Appendix 3, 208–09, for a list of 30 impoundment spills in nine southern West Virginia counties, 1972–2003.
56. Ward, "Coal Dams," quoting DEP safety engineer Jim Pierce. Steve Dasovich, badly shaken by the disaster, left Buffalo Mining for other mining jobs. In 1977, seeking to take his ten-year-old son to Philadelphia for medical treatment, he arranged for a private flight out of a Logan airport. The plane slammed into a mountain and both Dasovich and his son were killed. "Steve Dasovich," *Profiles: West Virginians Who Made a Difference* (Charleston: *Charleston Gazette*, 1999), 16–17.
57. Eric Eyre, "Water 'too toxic to touch' in Boone County," *Charleston Gazette*, December 17, 2008. The West Virginia Department of Environmental Protection has issued permits for sludge injection to thirteen companies. Several lawsuits were pending in 2009 claiming that chemical and metal contaminants from the slurry had leaked into aquifers, contaminating well water and causing a range of serious health problems. After a long study of the issue, the DEP declared its findings inconclusive and ordered companies to install monitoring systems to determine if contaminants are reaching off-site locations. "Critics Question Safety of Storing Coal Slurry," March 22, 2009; "West Virginia to Require Coal companies to Monitor Coal Slurry," *Martinsburg Journal*, June 18, 2009.
58. Jack Spadaro, then heading the Mine Safety and Health Administration training facility in Beckley, joined a team sent to investigate the Martin County incident. With the change from the Clinton to Bush

administration, however, the new policy was to produce a less thorough report. Spadaro refused to sign it and went public with the information that both MSHA and Massey had known of a previous failure of the dam. He was eventually forced to resign. Spadaro discusses his career in mine safety work from the time of the Buffalo Creek flood to the Martin County incident in "Jack Spadaro: Appalachian Patriot," Silas House and Jason Howard, eds., *Something's Rising: Appalachians Fighting Mountaintop Removal* (Lexington: University Press of Kentucky, 2009), 179–200. See also Ronald D Eller, *Uneven Ground: Appalachia since 1945* (Lexington: University Press of Kentucky, 2008), 250–51.

59. The Corps of Engineer's inventory makes no distinction between coal slurry and other dams so the exact number of coal dams is unclear. "High Hazard" means that failure would likely lead to loss of human life and property damage. See the U.S. Army Corps of Engineers National Inventory of Dams at http://nid.usace.mil. The West Virginia Department of Environmental Protection also has dam information at www.wvdep.org. J. Davitt McAteer at Wheeling Jesuit University lists the dams that are coal impoundments by name at "Coal Impoundment Location and Information System" on the Wheeling Jesuit University Web site. "Hundreds of Dams Are Hazardous," *Martinsburg Journal*, April 17, 2007.

Epilogue

1. Brad Crouser, *Arch: The Life of Governor Arch A. Moore, Jr.* (Chapmanville, Woodland Press, 2008), 265–66.
2. Ronald D Eller, *Uneven Ground: Appalachia Since 1945* (Lexington: University Press of Kentucky), 203.
3. Allen G. Breed, "Forty Years Later, War on Poverty Still Being Waged in McDowell," *Charleston Gazette-Mail*, May 23, 2004.
4. Shirley Stewart Burns, *Bringing Down the Mountains: The Impact of Mountaintop Removal Mining on Southern West Virginia Communities* (Morgantown: West Virginia University Press, 2007), 68–69.
5. Breed, "Forty Years Later"; Deborah Thorne, Ann Tickmyer, and Mark Thorne, "Poverty and Income in Appalachia," *Journal of Appalachian Studies* 10 (2004).
6. J. Howard Myers, comp., *West Virginia Blue Book, 1957* (Charleston, 1958), 819–20.
7. Michael Tomasky, "Night Comes to the Appalachians," *New York Review of Books* (September 25, 2008): 81.

8. Eller, *Uneven Ground*, 203–04.
9. From a report of Workforce West Virginia in *Martinsburg Journal*, September 9, 2009.
10. Rory McIlmoil and Evan Hansen, *The Decline of Central Appalachian Coal and the Need for Economic Diversification* (Thinking Downstream, White Paper, No. 1, Morgantown: Downstream Strategies, 2010), 1.
11. Burns, *Bringing Down the Mountains*, 28–32.
12. Paul J. Nyden, "UMW Rally Speakers Call for Health Reform"; Davin White, "Part Concert, Part Political Rally," *Charleston Gazette*, September 7, 2009.
13. See "Occupational Respiratory Disease Surveillance; Enhanced Coal Workers Health Surveillance Program," October, 2008 (periodically updated), http://www.cdc.gov/NIOSH/. See also Alan Ducatman, MD, "Recurrence of Black Lung Saddens," Op-Ed Commentary, Charleston *Gazette*, October 26, 2008. Dr. Ducatman is Chair, Department of Community Medicine, West Virginia University. On the persistent flooding, see Eller, *Uneven Ground*, 200, 249–51.
14. Michael Hendryx and Melissa Ahern, "Mortality in Appalachian Coal Mining Regions: The Value of Statistical Life Lost," *Public Health Reports* 124 (July–Aug. 2009): 541–50. This article is available on Ken Ward Jr.'s blog at the *Charleston Gazette*, "Coal Tattoo."
15. M. A. Palmer, et al., "Mountaintop Mining Consequences," *Science* (8 January 2010) 327, no. 5962: 138–49; quotations from David A. Fahrenthold, *Washington Post*, January 8, 2010, A3.
16. Michael Shnayerson, *Coal River* (New York: Farrar, Straus, and Giroux), 63. Among the several other recent books dealing with mountaintop removal mining are: Burns, *Bringing Down the Mountains*; House and Howard, eds., *Something's Rising*; Penny Loeb, *Moving Mountains: How One Woman and Her Community Won Justice from Big Coal* (Lexington: University Press of Kentucky, 2007).
17. For Koepler's comments see chap. 8, above; Bill Estep, Linda J. Johnson, "Mountains of Potential? Reclaimed Surface Mines Offer Level Land, but Very Little of It Is Used for Development," October 18, 2009, at http://www.kentucky.com/reclaiming_mountains/v-print/story/981954.html.
18. Patrick Angel, "Returning Surface-Mined Land to Forests," lecture at Shepherd University, Nov. 6, 2007; U.S. Department of the Interior, Office of Surface Mining and Reclamation Enforcement, *Reforestation and Mine Land Reclamation: Establishment of Sustainable Ecosystems Through the Reclamation of Surface Coal Mines to Forests* (Washington, DC, 2006). Some worry that the loose grading recommended for forest

renewal compounds the problems of erosion and sedimentation filling the rivers: John McQuaid, "Mining the Mountains," *Smithsonian* (Jan. 2009): 82.

19. Union of Concerned Scientists, "Leveling a Mountain of Research on Mountaintop Removal Mining," in http://www.ucsusa.org/scientific_integrity/abuses_of_science/case_studies_and_evidence/.

20. E-mail to author from Logan county organizer Beth Spence, September 16, 2009; Stephen L. Fisher, "Introduction," in *Fighting Back in Appalachia: Traditions of Resistance and Change*, ed. Fisher (Philadelphia: Temple University Press, 1993): 1–13.

21. Alan Banks, Dwight Billings, Karen Tice, "Appalachian Studies, Resistance, and Postmodernism," chap. 14 in *Fighting Back*, ed. Fisher.

22. Tomasky, "Night Comes to the Appalachians," 81.

23. See House and Howard, eds., *Something's Rising* and Jeff Biggers, "The Coalfield Uprising," *The Nation* 289, no. 12 (Oct. 19, 2009): 16–21.

24. "Jack Spadaro, Appalachian Patriot," in *Something's Rising*, ed. House and Howard, 200. The House and Howard book offers sketches and interviews with eleven Appalachian activists opposed to MTM, including West Virginians Spadaro, Denise Giardina, Kathy Mattea, and Judy Bonds.

25. Kari Lydersen, "Miners Boycott Tenn. Over Alexander's Bill," *Washington Post*, July 26, 2009: 8A.

26. "WV Leaders Unified for Coal," *Bluefield Daily Telegraph*, November 11, 2009; David A. Fahrenthold, Frank Ahrens, Steve Mufson, "With W.Va. Politics, a New Edge," *Washington Post*, April 19, 2010.

27. Robert C. Byrd, "Coal Must Embrace the Future," December 3, 2009, archived at http://byrd.senate.gov/speeches/view. For a thoughtful and more detailed assessment of coal's future somewhat along the lines Byrd discusses, see McIlmoil and Hansen, "The Decline of Central Appalachian Coal." The authors advocate economic diversification in the coalfield counties.

28. At a public hearing in October 2009, on an Army Corps of Engineers proposal to halt streamlined review processes of strip mining that would result in valley fills that bury streams, an overflow crowd made up largely of miners and their supporters met in the Charleston Civic Center Auditorium. Environmentalists and coalfield residents who attempted to speak were shouted down as the meeting turned into a rally against the proposed changes. UMWA representatives joined coal industry spokesmen in denouncing the proposed changes. Surface miners

who spoke expressed fears that a slower approval process would cause them to lose good-paying jobs in the midst of a recession in a region where well-paying jobs are difficult to find. Ken Ward Jr., "Mining Protesters Shouted Down," *Charleston Gazette*, October 14, 2009 at: http://www.wvgazette.com/News/200910140016. (Accessed October 21, 2009.) Manchin issued his statement after a similar confrontation at the University of Charleston in January 2010: *Washington Post*, January 28, 2010.

Bibliography

Manuscript Collections

Alderman Library, Marshall University, Huntington, West Virginia (MU)
>Ken Hechler Papers.
>M. L. Sills Papers.

National Archives, Washington, DC (NA). RG 381, Records of the Office of Economic Opportunity, 1964–1970.

Southern Appalachian Archives, Hutchins Library, Berea College, Berea, Kentucky (BC).
>Archives of the Appalachian Volunteers, 1963–1970.
>Records of the Council of the Southern Mountains, 1960–1970.

Margaret I King Library, University of Kentucky, Lexington, Kentucky (UK), Special Collections.
>Archives of the Appalachian Regional Commission, 1964-1972.

West Virginia and Regional History Collection West Virginia University Libraries, Morgantown, (WVRHC)
>Ulysses Grant Carter Papers.
>Harley Martin Kilgore Papers, 1937–1956.
>Pocahontas Coal Operators Association Papers, 1939–1972.
>Hulett C. Smith Papers.
>West Virginia Centennial Commission Correspondence, 1956–1964.
>West Virginia Human Rights Commission, Archives, 1961–1966.
>West Virginia Labor Federation, AFL-CIO Papers.
>West Virginia Governors Papers, 1931–1964.
>West Virginia Centennial Commission Correspondence, 1956–1964.
>West Virginia War History Commission Records, 1928–1946.

West Virginia Collection, Scarborough Library, Shepherd University (SU).
>Jefferson County NAACP Clipping File.

West Virginia State Archives, Charleston (WVSA)
>Ancella Bickley Collection.
>Buffalo Creek, Clipping File.
>Elizabeth Gilmore Collection.
>John B. Long Manuscript.
>Chapman Revercomb Collection.

Raleigh County Coal Miners.
Silver Bridge, Clipping File.
West Virginia State University, Institute (WVSU). Special Collections.

Oral History

Appalachian Volunteers Oral History Collection. Interviews by Marie Tyler-McGraw. 1982. Tape recordings, Southern Appalachian Archives, Berea College.

Robert Payne, President of Disabled Miners and Widows of Southern West Virginia, at Itmann, WV, 24 June, 1972. Tape recording. West Virginia University.

Raleigh County Coal Miners, interviewed by William Mares at Stotesbury, WV, 1972–73, in West Virginia State Archives, Charleston. Transcribed typescript.

Interviews by Gary Simmons for West Virginia Documentary Consortium, Inc.
    William J. Kelley, July 30, 2002.
    Shirley Love, July 2, 2002.
    Hulett C. Smith, July 26, 2002.
    Cecil Underwood, August 20, 2002.

Voices from the Sixties: Interviews by Gibbs Kinderman of Kentucky and West Virginia activists, politicians, and scholars regarding government-funded anti-poverty programs in 1960s and 1970s. Tape Recordings, Southern Appalachian Archives, Berea College

Newspapers and Periodicals

Long runs of the *Charleston Gazette*, 1950–1972; *Huntington Herald Dispatch*, 1945, 1965–66; *Martinsburg Journal*, 1941–1961 were read. *New York Times* and other newspaper were consulted for particular episodes, and much of the archival material consulted contained periodical materials, as noted.

West Virginia School Journal, 1940–1960.
West Virginia State Magazine, 1950–1958.

Printed Documents, Government Publications

An Economic Atlas for West Virginia. Charleston: West Virginia Department of Commerce Planning and Research Division, n.d.

Barlow, James A. *Coal and Coal Mining in West Virginia, Coal Geology*

Bulletin, No. 2. Charleston: West Virginia Geological Survey, 1974.

Canfield, John A., ed. *State Papers and Public Addresses of Hulett C. Smith, 1965–1969.* Charleston, 1969.

Carson, Howard W., ed. *West Virginia Blue Book, 1973.* Charleston: West Virginia Senate, 1973.

Davies, William E, James F. Failey, and Donavan B. Kelly. *West Virginia's Buffalo Creek Flood: A Study of the Hydrology and Engineering Geology.* Washington, DC: GPO, 1972.

Funk, Rosalind Carroll, comp. *State Papers and Public Addresses, Okey L. Patteson, Governor of West Virginia, 1949–1953.* Charleston: Rose City Press, 1953.

Jefferson County Schools. *Survey Report of the Public Schools of Jefferson County, West Virginia.* March 1954.

Meyers, J. Howard, ed. *West Virginia Bluebook, 1957.* Charleston, 1957.

National Transportation and Safety Board. *Highway Accident Report, Collapse of U.S. Highway Bridge, Point Pleasant, West Virginia, December 15, 1967.* Washington, DC: n.d.

Pavlik, Anthony L. *Towards Solving the Low Income Problem of Small Farmers in the Appalachian Area.* West Virginia University Experiment Station, Bulletin 499T, June 1954.

Photiadis, John D. *West Virginians in Their State and in Cleveland, Ohio: Selected Social and Sociopsychological Characteristics.* Appalachian Center, West Virginia University, Research Report 3. 1970.

State Papers and Public Addresses, Clarence W. Meadows, Twenty-Second Governor of West Virginia, 1945–1949. Charleston: Jarrett Printing, 1950.

State Papers and Public Addresses, Matthew Mansfield Neely, Twenty-First Governor of West Virginia, January 13, 1941 to January 15, 1945. Charleston: Mathews Printing, 1945.

U.S. Army Corps of Engineers. *Buffalo Creek WV Disaster, 1972.* Prepared for Subcommittee on Labor for the Committee on Labor and Public Welfare, United States Senate. Washington, DC: 1972.

U.S. Department of Commerce, Bureau of the Census. *Historical Statistics of the United States: Colonial Times to 1790.* Bicentennial ed., pt. 1. Washington, DC: 1975

U.S. Department of the Interior. *A Medical Survey of the Bituminous Coal Industry: Report of the Coal Mines Administration.* Washington, DC: Government Printing Office, 1947.

———. *Preliminary Analysis of the Coal Refuse Dam Failure.* Washington, DC: 1972.

West Virginia Commission on State and Local Finance. *Tax Facts in West Virginia.* Charleston, WV: 1956.

West Virginia Department of Commerce. *An Economic Atlas for West Virginia.* Charleston: n.d. (ca. 1963)

West Virginia Governor's Ad Hoc Commission of Inquiry. *The Buffalo Creek Flood and Disaster, Official Report.* Charleston: 1973.

West Virginia Human Rights Commission. *Annual Reports.* Charleston: 1962–1970.

West Virginia State College. *Brown v. Board of Education of Topeka: An Assessment Thirty Years Later; A Series of Lectures and Discussions.* Institute: West Virginia State College, 1984.

West Virginia State Planning Board. *Report of the Coordinating Committee in the Field of Agriculture and Rural Life, July 1, 1946.* Charleston: 1946.

Zabetakis, M. G. and L. D. Philipps. *Safety Manual No.1: Coal Mining.* Washington: Mining Enforcement and Safety Administration, Department of the Interior, 1972.

Books

Ambler, Charles H. *A History of Education in West Virginia from Colonial Times to 1949.* Huntington: Standard Printing, 1951.

Ambler, Charles H., and Festus P. Summers. *West Virginia: The Mountain State*, 2nd ed. Englewood Cliffs, Prentice Hall, 1958.

Armstead, Robert. *Black Days, Black Dust: The Memories of an African American Coal Miner.* Knoxville: University of Tennessee Press, 2002.

Bartley, Numan V. *The New South, 1945–1980.* Baton Rouge, 1995.

———. *The Rise of Massive Resistance: Race and Politics in the South During the 1950s.* Baton Rogue: Louisiana State University Press, 1969.

Bell, Derrick. *Silent Covenants: Brown v. Board of Education and the Unfulfilled Hopes for Racial Reform.* New York: Oxford University Press, 2004.

Berry, Chad. *Southern Migrants, Northern Exiles.* Urbana: University of Illinois Press, 2000.

Bernstein, Irving. *Guns or Butter: The Presidency of Lyndon Johnson.* New York: Oxford University Press, 1997.

Bickley, Ancella R. and Lynda Ann Ewen. *Memphis Tennessee Garrison: The Remarkable Story of a Black Appalachian Woman.* Athens: University of Ohio Press, 2001.

Billings, Dwight B., and Kathleen M. Blee. *The Road to Poverty: The Making of Wealth and Hardship in Appalachia.* Cambridge: University of Cambridge Press, 1969.

Billings, Dwight B., Gurney Norman, and Katherine Ledford, eds. *Back Talk from Appalachia: Confronting Stereotypes.* Lexington: University Press of Kentucky, 1999.

Blumenthal, Sidney. *The Year the Dream Died: Revisiting 1968 in America.* New York: Warner Books, 1997.

Borman, Kathyrn, and Phillip J. Obermiller, eds. *From Mountains to*

Metropolis: Appalachian Migrants in American Cities. Westport, Conn.: Bergin and Garvey, 1994.

Boyer, Paul S. *Promises to Keep: The United States Since World War II.* 2nd ed. Boston: Houghton Mifflin, 1999.

Bradshaw, Michael. *The Appalachian Regional Commission: Twenty-Five Years of Government Policy.* Lexington: University Press of Kentucky, 1992.

Branch, Taylor. *Parting the Waters: America in the King Years, 1954-1963.* New York: Simon and Schuster, 1988.

———. *Pillar of Fire: America in the King Years, 1963-65.* New York: Simon and Schuster, 1998.

Burke, Dawn Raines. *An American Phoenix: A History of Storer College from Slavery to Desegregation, 1865-1955.* Pittsburgh: Geyer Printing, ca. 2007.

Burns, Shirley Stewart. *Bringing Down the Mountains: The Impact of Mountaintop Removal Mining on Southern West Virginia Communities.* Morgantown: West Virginia University Press, 2007.

Bushong, Millard K. *Historic Jefferson County.* Boyce, Va.: Carr Publishing, 1972.

Byrd, Robert C. *Child of the Appalachian Coalfields.* Morgantown: West Virginia University Press, 2005.

Caudill, Harry M. *Night Comes to the Cumberland: A Biography of a Depressed Area.* Boston: Little, Brown, 1972.

Chafe, William H. *The Unfinished Journey: America Since World War II*, 6th ed. New York. Oxford University Press, 2004.

Chalmers, David. *And the Crooked Places Made Straight: The Struggle for Social Change in the 1960s.* 2nd ed. Baltimore: Johns Hopkins University Press, 1996.

Cherniak, Martin. *The Hawks Nest Incident. America's Worst Industrial Disaster.* New Haven: Yale University Press, 1986.

Christenson, C. L. *Economic Redevelopment in Bituminous Coal: The Special Case of Technological Advance in United States Coal Mines, 1930-1960.* Cambridge: Harvard University Press, 1962.

Citizens Commission. *Disaster on Buffalo Creek: A Citizens' Report on Criminal Negligence in a West Virginia Mining Community.* 1972.

Clark, Paul F. *The Miners' Fight for Democracy: Arnold Miller and the Reform of the United Mine Workers.* Ithaca, NY: New York School of Industrial and Labor Relations, 1981.

Clarkson, Roy B. *Tumult on the Mountains: Lumbering in West Virginia, 1770-1920.* Parsons, WV: McClain, 1964.

Cobb, James C. *The Selling of the South: The Southern Crusade for Economic Development, 1936-1982.* Baton Rogue: Louisiana State University Press, 1982.

Coles, Robert. *Migrants, Sharecroppers, and Mountaineers.* Vol. 2, *Children of Crisis.* Boston: Little, Brown, 1971.
Couto, Richard A. *An American Challenge: A Report on Economic Trends and Social Issues in Appalachia.* Dubuque: Kendall-Hunt, 1994.
Crouser, Brad. *Arch: The Life of Governor Arch A. Moore, Jr.* Chapmanville, WV: Woodland Press, 2008.
Derickson, Alan. *Black Lung: Anatomy of a Public Health Disaster.* Ithaca, N.Y.: Cornell University Press, 1998.
Diggins, John Patrick. *The Proud Decades: America in War and Peace, 1941–1960.* New York: W. W. Norton, 1988.
Dix, Keith. *"What's a Coal Miner to Do?" The Mechanization of Coal Mining.* Pittsburgh: University of Pittsburgh Press, l988.
Drake, Richard B. *A History of Appalachia.* Lexington: University Press of Kentucky, 2001.
Drennen, William M. Jr., and Kojo (William T.) Jones Jr. *Red, White, Black, and Blue: A Dual Memoir of Race and Class in Appalachia.* Athens: Ohio University Press, 2004.
Dubofsky, Melvyn, and Warren Van Tine. *John L. Lewis: A Biography.* New York: Quadrangle, 1977.
Dunaway, Wilma A. *The First American Frontier: Transition to Capitalism in Southern Appalachia.* Chapel Hill: University of North Carolina Press, 1996.
Egolf, Jennifer L., Ken Fones-Wolf, and Louis C. Martin, eds. *Culture, Class, and Politics in Modern Appalachia: Essays in honor of Ronald L. Lewis.* Morgantown: West Virginia University Press, 2009.
Eller, Ronald D. *Miners, Millhands, and Mountaineers: Industrialization of the Appalachian South.* Knoxville: University of Tennessee Press, 1982.
———. *Uneven Ground: Appalachia Since 1945.* Lexington: University Press of Kentucky, 2008.
Erikson, Kai T. *Everything in Its Path: Destruction of Community in the Buffalo Creek Flood.* New York: Simon and Schuster, 1976.
Ernst, Harry W. *The Primary That Made a President: West Virginia, 1960.* New York: McGraw-Hill, 1962.
Farmer, James. *Lay Bare the Heart: An Autobiography of the Civil Rights Movement.* Arbor House: 1965.
Feaster, E. K. (Survey Director). *A Survey of Education Programs of the West Virginia Public Schools: A Summary of the Report.* Charleston, 1957.
Feather, Carl E. *Mountain People in a Flat Land: A Popular History of Appalachian Migration to Northeast Ohio, 1940–1965.* Athens: Ohio University Press, 1998.
Finley, Joseph E. *The Corrupt Kingdom: The Rise and Fall of the United Mine Workers.* New York: Simon and Schuster, 1972.

Fisher, Stephen, ed. *Fighting Back in Appalachia: Traditions of Resistance and Change.* Philadelphia: Temple University Press, 1993.

Fleming, Dan B. Jr. *Kennedy versus Humphrey, West Virginia, 1960: The Pivotal Battle for the Democratic Presidential Nomination.* Jefferson, N.C.: McFarland Publishing, 1992.

Ford, Thomas R., ed. *The Southern Appalachian Region: A Survey.* Lexington: University of Kentucky Press, 1962.

Frazier, Steve, and Gary Gerstle, eds. *The Rise and Fall of the New Deal Order, 1930–1980.* Princeton: Princeton University Press, 1989.

Fried, Richard. *Men Against McCarthy.* New York: Columbia University Press, 1976.

Gates, Henry Louis Jr. *Colored People: A Memoir.* New York: Alfred A Knopf, 1994.

Gaventa, John. *Power and Powerlessness: Quiescence and Rebellion in an Appalachian Valley.* Urbana: University of Illinois Press, 1980.

Gaventa, John, Barbara Ellen Smith, and Alex Willingham, eds. *Communities in Economic Crisis: Appalachia and the South.* Philadelphia: Temple University Press, l990.

Goldfield, David R. *Promised Land: The South Since 1945.* Wheeling, Ill.: Harlan-Davidson, 1987.

Green, Archie. *Only a Miner: Studies in Recorded Coal Mining Songs.* Urbana: University of Illinois Press, 1972.

Grimes, Richard, *Jay Rockefeller: Old Money, New Politics.* Parsons, WV: McClain, l984.

Gutfreund, Owen D. *Twentieth-Century Sprawl: Highways and the Reshaping of the American Landscape.* New York: Oxford University Press, 2004.

Harrington, Michael. *The Other America: Poverty in the United States.* New York: Macmillan, 1962.

Halberstam, David. *The Fifties.* New York: Villard Books, 1993.

Harris, Evelyn L. K., and Frank J. Krebs. *From Humble Beginnings: West Virginia Federation of Labor, 1903–1957.* Charleston: West Virginia Labor History Publishing Fund, 1960.

Haught, James A. *Fascinating West Virginia: Wild, Memorable Episodes from the Longtime Editor of the Mountain State's Largest Newspaper, the Charleston Gazette.* Charleston: Charleston Gazette, 2008.

Hensley, Francis, ed. *Missing Chapters II: West Virginia Women in History.* Charleston: West Virginia Women's Commission, 1986.

Hickam, Homer, Jr. *October Sky* (originally published as *Rocket Boys*). New York: Dell, 1998.

Holland, Charles T., James L. Corsaro, Charles W. McGlothlin, and Douglas J. Ladish. "Research on Acid Mine Drainage Control." *Proceedings of the*

West Virginia Coal Mining Institute. Morgantown: Morgantown Printing, 1968.
House, Silas, and Jason Howard. *Something's Rising: Appalachians Fighting Mountaintop Removal.* Lexington: University Press of Kentucky, 2009.
Hume, Brit. *Death and the Mines: Rebellion and Murder in the UMW.* New York: Grossman Publishers, 1971.
Jacoway, Elizabeth. *Turn Away Thy Son: Little Rock, the Crisis that Rocked the Nation.* New York: Free Press, 2007.
Jackson, Kenneth T. *Crabgrass Frontier: The Suburbanization of the United States.* New York: Oxford University Press, 1985.
Johnson, Lyndon Baines. *The Vantage Point: Perspectives of the Presidency, 1963–1969.* New York: Holt, Rinehart, and Winston, 1971.
Katz, Michael. *From the War on Poverty to the War on Welfare.* New York: Pantheon, Random House, 1989.
Kennedy, David M. *Freedom From Fear: The American People in Depression and War, 1929–1945.* New York: Oxford University Press, 1999.
Kiffmyer, Thomas. *Reformers to Radicals: The Appalachian Volunteers and the War on Poverty.* Lexington: University Press of Kentucky, 2008.
Kilty, Keith M., and Elizabeth A. Segal, eds. *Rediscovering the Other America: The Continuing Crisis of Poverty and Inequality in the United States.* New York: Haworth Press, 2003.
Kirby, Jack Temple. *Mockingbird Song: Ecological Landscapes of the South.* Chapel Hill: University of North Carolina Press, 2006.
———. *Rural Worlds Lost: The American South, 1920–1969.* Baton Rouge and London: Louisiana State University Press, 1987.
Kunstler, James Howard. *The Geography of Nowhere: The Rise and Decline of America's Manmade Landscape.* New York: Simon and Schuster, 1993.
Krajcinovic, Ivana. *From Company Doctors to Managed Care: The United Mine Workers' Noble Experiment.* Ithaca, N.Y.: Cornell University Press, 1997.
Laslett, John H. M. *The United Mineworkers of America: A Model of Industrial Solidarity?* University Park: The Pennsylvania State University Press, 1996.
Lewis, Ronald L. *Black Coal Miners in America: Race, Class, and Community Conflict, 1780–1980.* Lexington: University Press of Kentucky, 1987.
———. *Transforming the Appalachian Countryside: Railroads, Deforestation, and Social Change in West Virginia, 1880–1920.* Chapel Hill: University of North Carolina Press, 1998.
Lewis, Tom. *Divided Highways: Building the Interstate Highways, Transforming American Life.* New York: Viking Penguin, 1996.
Loeb, Penny. *Moving Mountains: How One Woman and Her Community Won Justice from Big Coal.* Lexington: University Press of Kentucky, 2007.

Lutz, Paul F. *From Governor to Cabby: The Political Career and Tragic Death of West Virginia's William Casey Marland, 1950–1965*. Huntington, WV: Marshall University Library Associates, 1996.

MacMaster, Richard K. *A History of Hardy County, 1786–1986*. Moorefield: Hardy County Centennial Commission and Hardy County Public Library Commission, 1986.

Maddox, Robert Franklin. *The Senatorial Career of Harley Martin Kilgore*. East Rockaway, NY: Cummings and Hathaway, 1996.

Mason, Carol. *Reading Appalachia from Left to Right: Conservatives and the 1974 Kanawha County Textbook Controversy*. Ithaca, NY: Cornell University Press, 2009.

Marx, Leo. *The Machine in the Garden: Technology and the Pastoral Idea in America*. New York: Oxford University Press, 1974.

Matusow, Allen J. *The Unraveling of America: A History of Liberalism in the 1960s*. New York: Harper and Row, 1984.

McAteer, Davitt. *Monongah: The Tragic Story of the 1907 Monongah Mine Disaster, the Worst Industrial Accident in U.S. History*. Morgantown: West Virginia University Press, 2007.

McAteer, James D. *Coal Mine Health and Safety: The Case of West Virginia*. New York: Praeger, 1973.

McCormick, Charles H. *This Nest of Vipers: McCarthyism and Higher Education in the Mundel Affair, 1951–2*. Urbana: University of Illinois Press, 1989.

McGehee, C. Stuart and Frank Wilson. *Bluefield State College: A Centennial History, 1885–1995*. Bluefield, WV: Bluefield State College, 1996.

McIlmoil, Rory and Evan Hansen. *The Decline of Central Appalachian Coal and the Need for Economic Diversification*. Thinking Downstream, White Paper, No. 1. Morgantown, WV: Downstream Strategies, 2010.

Milkis, Sidney M. and Mileur, Jerome, eds. *The Great Society and the High Tide of Liberalism*. Amherst: University of Massachusetts Press, 2005.

Mitchell, Robert D., ed. *Appalachian Frontiers: Settlement, Society, and Development in the Preindustrial Era*. Lexington: University Press of Kentucky, 1991.

Montrie, Chad. *To Save the Land and the People: A History of Opposition to Surface Coal Mining in Appalachia*. Chapel Hill: University of North Carolina Press, 2003.

Morgan, John G. *West Virginia Governors, 1863–1980*, 2nd ed. Charleston: Charleston Newspapers, 1980.

Moynihan, Daniel P. *Maximum Feasible Misunderstanding: Community Action in the War on Poverty*. New York: Free Press, 1969.

Mulcahy, Richard P. *The Rise and Fall of the United Mine Workers of America Welfare and Retirement Fund*. Knoxville: The University of Tennessee Press, 2000.

Bibliography

Nash, Gerald D. *The Crucial Era: The Great Depression and World War II*, 2d ed. New York: St. Martins, 1992.

Nugent, Tom. *Death at Buffalo Creek: The 1972 West Virginia Flood Disaster.* New York: Norton, 1973.

Obermiller, Phillip J., Thomas E. Wagner, and E. Bruce Tucker, eds. *Appalachian Odyssey: Historical Perspectives on the Great Migration.* Westport, Conn: Praeger, 2000.

Patterson, James T. *Grand Expectations, The United States, 1945–1971.* New York: Oxford University Press, 1996.

Patteson, Okey L. *State Papers and Public Addresses.* Ed. Rosalind Carroll Funk. Charleston, n.d.

Perry, Bud and Karl C. Lilly. *Reopening Glen Rogers.* n.p., n.d.

Perry, Huey. *They'll Cut Off Your Project: A Mingo County Chronicle.* New York: Praeger, 1972.

Photiadis, John D. *West Virginians in Their Own State and in Cleveland, Ohio: Select Social and Sociopsychological Characteristics.* Morgantown: Appalachian Center Report 3, 1962.

Photiadis, John D., and Harry K. Schwarzweller, eds. *Change in Rural Appalachia: Implications for Action Programs.* Philadelphia: University of Pennsylvania Press, 1970.

Pierce, Neal R. *The Border South States: People, Politics and Power in the Five Border South States.* New York: W. W. Norton and Company, 1975.

Profiles: West Virginians Who Made a Difference. Charleston: Charleston Gazette, 1999.

Rasmussen, Barbara. *Absentee Landowning and Exploitation in West Virginia, 1760–1920.* Lexington: University Press of Kentucky, 1994.

Rayback, John G. *A History of Labor in the United States.* New York: Free Press, 1966.

Reeves, Thomas C. *A Question of Character: A Life of John Kennedy.* New York: Free Press, 1991.

Rice, Connie. *Our Monongalia: A History of African Americans in Monongalia County, West Virginia.* Terra Alta, WV.: Headline Press, 1999.

Rice, Otis K. *The Allegheny Frontier: West Virginia Beginnings, 1730–1830.* Lexington: University Press of Kentucky, 1970.

Rice, Otis K., and Stephen W. Brown. *West Virginia: A History.* 2nd ed. Lexington: University Press of Kentucky, 1993.

Ross, Malcolm Harrison. *Machine Age in the Hills.* New York: Macmillan, 1933.

Seltzer, Curtis. *Fire in the Hole: Miners and Managers in the American Coal Industry.* Lexington: University Press of Kentucky, 1985.

Shapiro, Henry D. *Appalachia on Our Mind: The Southern Mountains and Mountaineers in the American Consciousness.* Chapel Hill: University of North Carolina Press, 1978.

Shifflet, Crandall A. *Coal Towns: Life, Work and Culture in the Company Towns of Southern Appalachia, 1880–1960.* Knoxville: University of Tennessee Press, 1991.

Slonaker, Arthur Gordon. *A History of Shepherd College.* Parsons, WV: McClain Printing, 1967.

Smith, Barbara Ellen. *Digging Our Own Graves: Coal Miners and the Struggle over Black Lung Disease.* Philadelphia: Temple University Press, 1987.

Shnayerson, Michael. *Coal River.* New York: Farrar, Strauss, and Giroux, 2008.

Stafford, Thomas F. *Afflicting the Comfortable: Journalism and Politics in West Virginia.* Morgantown: West Virginia University Press, 2005.

Stern, Gerald M. *The Buffalo Creek Disaster.* New York: Vintage Books, 1977.

Straw, Richard A., and H. Tyler Blethen. *High Mountains Rising: Appalachia in Time and Place.* Urbana and Chicago: University of Illinois Press, 2004.

Strayer, George D. (Survey Director). *A Report on a Survey of Public Education in the State of West Virginia.* Charleston, l945.

Stricker, Frank. *Why America Lost the War on Poverty—and How to Win It.* Chapel Hill: University of North Carolina Press, 2007.

Sullivan, Ken, ed. *The West Virginia Encyclopedia.* Charleston: West Virginia Humanities Council, 2006.

Taylor, James L. *A History of Black Education in Jefferson County, West Virginia, 1866–1966.* Privately printed, n.d.

Thomas, Jerry Bruce. *An Appalachian New Deal: West Virginia in the Great Depression.* Lexington, University of Kentucky Press, 1998.

Thurmond, Walter R. *The Logan Coalfield of West Virginia: A Brief History.* Morgantown: West Virginia University Library, 1964.

Tindall, George B. *The Emergence of the New South, 1913–1945.* Baton Rogue: Louisiana State University Press, 1967.

Tribe, Ivan M. *Mountaineer Jamboree: Country Music in West Virginia.* Lexington: University Press of Kentucky, 1984.

Trotter, Joe William. *Coal, Class and Color: Blacks in Southern West Virginia, 1915–32.* Urbana: University of Illinois Press, 1990.

Unger, Irwin. *The Best of Intentions: The Triumph and Failure of the Great Society Under Kennedy, Johnson, and Nixon.* New York: Doubleday, 1996.

Vatter, Harold, G. *The U.S. Economy in the 1950s.* New York: W. W. Norton, 1963.

———. *The U.S. Economy in World War II.* New York: Columbia University Press, 1985.

Walls, David S. and John B. Stephenson, eds. *Appalachia in the Sixties: A Decade of Reawakening.* Lexington: University Press of Kentucky, 1972.

Weller, Jack. *Yesterday's People: Life in Contemporary Appalachia.* Lexington: University of Kentucky Press, 1965.
Whisnant, David E. *Modernizing the Mountaineer: People, Power, and Planning in Appalachia.* Boone: Appalachian Consortium Press, 1980.
White, Theodore H. *The Making of the President, 1960.* New York: Athenaeum, 1961.
Willams, John Alexander. *Appalachia: A History.* Chapel Hill: University of North Carolina Press, 2002.
———. *West Virginia: A Bicentennial History.* New York: W. W. Norton: 1976.
———. *West Virginia and the Captains of Industry.* Morgantown: West Virginia University Library, 1976.
Witcover, Jules. *The Year the Dream Died: Revisiting 1968 in America.* New York: Warner Books, 1997.
Withrow, Dolly. *West Virginia State College, 1891–1991: From the Grove to the Stars.* Institute: West Virginia State College Foundation, 1991.
Woodrum, Robert H. *"Everybody Was Black Down There": Race and Industrial Change in the Alabama Coalfields.* Athens: University of Georgia Press, 2007.

Articles, Lectures

"Alex Schoenbaum." *Profiles: West Virginians Who Made a Difference.* Charleston: *Charleston Gazette*, 1999.
Angel, Patrick. "Returning Stripped Land to Forests." Lecture at Shepherd University, Nov. 6, 2007.
Athey, Lou. "Widen." *West Virginia Encyclopedia.* Ed. Ken Sullivan. Charleston: West Virginia Humanities Council, 2006: 793.
Banks, Allen, Dwight Billings, Karen Tice. "Appalachian Studies, Resistance, and Postmodernism." Chap. 14 in *Fighting Back: Traditions of Resistance and Change.* Ed. Stephen Fisher. Philadelphia: Temple University Press, 1993.
Barksdale, A. S. "Bluefield Coal Show, Gala Event." *West Virginia State Magazine* 3, no. 7 (May 1954): 17–18, 21, 24.
Barksdale, Syd. "Marland Takes Office As State's Youngest Governor." *West Virginia State Magazine* (Jan. 1953): 13–14.
Bailey, Kenneth R. "Development of Surface Mine Legislation, 1939–1967." *West Virginia History: A Quarterly Magazine* 30, no. 3 (April 1969): 525–29.
Bailey, Rebecca J. "I Never Thought of My Life as History: A Story of the 'Hillbilly' Exodus and the Price of Assimilation." Chap. 2 in *Appalachian Odyssey*, eds. Phillip J. Obermiller, Thomas E. Wagner, and E. Bruce

Tucker. *Appalachian Odyssey: Historical Perspectives on the Great Migration*. Westport, Conn: Praeger, 2000.

Barnett, C. Robert. "'The Finals': West Virginia's Black Basketball Tournament, 1925-1957." *Goldenseal: West Virginia Traditional Life* 9, no. 2 (Summer 1983): 30-36.

Belcher, John C. "Population Growth and Characteristics." Chap. 3 in *The Southern Appalachian Region: A Survey*. Ed. Thomas R. Ford. Lexington: University of Kentucky Press, 1962.

Bickley, Ancella. "Black Education in West Virginia, 1861-1971." Lecture at Shepherd College, April 8, 2003.

Bickley, Ancella. "Mildred Mitchell-Bateman." *West Virginia Encyclopedia*. Ed. Ken Sullivan. Charleston: West Virginia Humanities Council, 2006: 489.

Bickley, Nelson. "*Brown v Board of Education* in West Virginia." *West Virginia Law Review* 107 (Spring 2005): 1-10.

Bingham, Mary Beth. "Stopping the Bulldozers: What Difference Did It Make?" *Fighting Back in Appalachia: Traditions of Resistance and Change*. Ed. Stephen L. Fisher. Philadelphia: Temple University Press, 1993, 17-30.

Brown, James, and George A Hillary, Jr. "The Great Migration, 1940-1960." Chap. 4 in *The Southern Appalachian Region: A Survey*. Ed. Thomas R. Ford. Lexington: University of Kentucky Press, 1962.

Brown, James S. "Population and Migration Changes in Appalachia." Chap. 2 *Change in Rural Appalachia: Implications for Action Programs*. Eds. John D. Photiadis and Harry Schwarzweller. Philadelphia: University of Pennsylvania Press, 1970.

Byrd, Robert C. "Coal Must Embrace the Future." http://byrd.senate.gov/speeches/view.

Canfield, John A. "Recollections of 1968." Address, West Virginia Chapter, Public Relations Society of America, Charleston, WV, March 16, 2005.

Caudill, Harry. "Buffalo Creek Aftermath." *Saturday Review* 72 (Aug. 26, 1972): 16-17.

"Carl Gainer." *Profiles: West Virginians Who Made a Difference*. Charleston: *Charleston Gazette*, 1999.

Carter, Alice E. "Segregation and Integration in the Appalachian Coal Fields: McDowell County Responds to the *Brown* Decision." *West Virginia History* 54 (1995): 79-104.

Casdorpf, Paul D. "Clarence W. Meadows, W. W. Trent and Educational Reform in West Virginia." *West Virginia History* 41 (1980): 126-141.

Chilton, W. E. "Ned" III. "Desegregation/Integration and the Media: Fallout from the Brown Decision in West Virginia." *Brown v. Board of Education of Topeka: An Assessment Thirty Years Later, a Series of Lectures and*

Discussions. Institute: West Virginia State College, 1984.
"Continuous Coal Mining." *Fortune* (June 1950), 111–114.
Curtis, Tara. "Defining Mountaineer Greatness." *West Virginia University Alumni Magazine.* Summer 2005: 26–28.
Daniel, Pete. "Going Among Strangers: Southern Reactions to World War II." *Journal of American History* 77 (December 1990): 886–911.
Drobney, Jeffrey A. "A Generation in Revolt: Student Dissent and Political Repression at West Virginia University." *West Virginia History* 50 (1995): 105–25.
Eagles, Charles W. "Toward New Histories of the Civil Rights Era." *Journal of Southern History* 66, no. 4 (Nov. 2000): 815–48.
Ducatman, Allan, MD. "Recurrence of Black Lung Saddens." Op-Ed Commentary, *Charleston Gazette,* Oct. 28, 2008.
Elveru, Larry. "The High-Tech Artistry of Joe Moss: Bending Light and Sculpting Sound." *University of Delaware Magazine* 1, no. 1 (Fall 1988): 16–23.
Ewen, Lynda Ann and Julia A. Lewis. "Buffalo Creek Revisited: Deconstructing Kai Erikson's Stereotypes." *Appalachian Journal: A Regional Studies Review* 27, no. 1 (Fall 1999): 22–45.
Ferrell, Ira Homer. "Memoirs from Early History of Cable TV in the Tri-Towns." With introductory note by Bryan F. Putnam. http://mysite.verizon.net/bfputnam/caty/catv1.html.
Fones-Wolf, Colin. "A Union Voice for Racial Equality: Miles Stanley and Civil Rights in West Virginia, 1957–1968." *Journal of Appalachian Studies* 10 (Spring/Fall 2004): 111–28.
Fones-Wolf, Elizabeth, and Ken Fones-Wolf. "Cold War Americanism: Business, Pageantry, and Anti-unionism in Weirton." *Business History Review* 77, no. 1 (Spring 2003): 66–91.
Franklin, Ben. "The Scandal of Death and Injury in the Mines." *New York Times Magazine,* March 30, 1969: 26–27.
Goldstein, George. "The Rise and Decline of the UMWA Health and Retirement Funds Program, 1946–1995." Chap. 10 in *The United Mineworkers of America: A Model of Industrial Solidarity?* Ed. John M. Laslett. University Park: The Pennsylvania State University Press, 1996.
"Hal Greer." *Profiles: West Virginians Who Made a Difference.* Charleston: *Charleston Gazette,* 1999.
Hamilton, C. Horace. "Health and Health Services." Chap. 14 of *The Southern Appalachian Region: A Survey*. Ed. Thomas Ford. Lexington: University of Kentucky Press, 1962.
Hardin, William H. "Elizabeth Kee, 1899–1975." West Virginia Women's Commission, *Missing Chapters II: West Virginia Women in History.* Charleston, 1986.

Holland, Charles, James L. Corsaro, Charles W. McGlothlin, and Charles Leach. "Research on Acid Mine Drainage Control." *roceedings of the West Virginia Coal Mining Institute.* Morgantown Printing, 1968. 115–148.

Haynes, Roger W. "Opportunities for the Young Man in the Coal Industry." Presented April 21, 1967, in *Proceedings of the West Virginia Coal Mining Institute.* Morgantown: Morgantown Printing, 1968.

Hendyrx, Michael, and Melissa Ahern. "Mortality in Appalachian Coal Mining Regions: The Value of Statistical Life Lost." *Public Health Reports* 124 (July–Aug 2009): 541–550.

Hennen, John. "A Struggle for Recognition: Marshall University Students for a Democratic Society and the Red Scare in Huntington, 1965–1969." *West Virginia History* 52 (1993): 127–147.

Hensley, Frances S. "Women in the Industrial Work Force in West Virginia, 1880–1945." *West Virginia History* 49 (1990): 115–124.

Hyatt, R. E., A. D. Kristin, and T. K. Mahan. "Respiratory Disease in Southern West Virginia Miners." *American Review of Respiratory Disease* 89, no. 3: 387–401.

Holland, Charles T, James L. Corsaro, Charles W. McGlothlin, and Douglas J. Ladish. "Research on Acid Mine Drainage Control." *Proceedings of the West Virginia Coal Mining Institute* (1968): 115–148.

Houston, Craig. "'A Little Pregnant': The *Charleston Gazette's* Editorial Response to the Vietnam War, 1963–1965." *West Virginia History* 51 (1992): 15–26.

Hoylman, Rod. "The Hard Road Home: Governor William Casey Marland." *Goldenseal: West Virginia Traditional Life* 24 (Fall 1998): 12–19, 22–23.

———. "Underwood on Marland." Interview. *Goldenseal: West Virginia Traditional Life* 24 (Fall 1998): 20–21.

Jackameit, William P. "A Short History of Negro Public Higher Education in West Virginia, 1890–1965." *West Virginia History* 37 (1976): 309–324.

Johnson, Susan. "West Virginia Rubber Workers in Akron." *Transnational West Virginia: Ethnic Communities and Economic Change, 1840–1940.* Eds. Ken Fones-Wolf, and Ronald L. Lewis. Morgantown: West Virginia University Press, 2002.

Kaufman, Paul J. "Wistfulginia: A Fable with a Sad Ending." *Appalachian South* 2 (Spring, Summer 1967): 24–25.

Lechner, Ira M. "Massive Resistance: Virginia's Great Leap Backward." *Virginia Quarterly Review* (Autumn 1974): 631–640.

Lee, K. W. "Fair Elections in West Virginia" and "Catalyst of the Black Lung Movement." *Appalachia in the Sixties: Decade of Reawakening.* Eds. David S. Walls and John B. Stephenson. Lexington: University Press of Kentucky, 1972: 154–176, 201–209.

Lichtenstein, Nelson. "From Corporatism to Collective Bargaining: Organized

Labor and Eclipse of Social Democracy in the Post War Era." Chap 5 in *The Rise and Fall of the New Deal Order, 1930–1980*. Eds. Steve Frazier and Gary Gerstle, 122–43. Princeton: Princeton University Press, 1989.

"Long Super Car Co. is Nationally Known Firm." *West Virginia State Magazine* 2, no. 8 (June 1951): 19.

Lutz, Paul. "Governor Marland's Political Suicide: The Severance Tax." *West Virginia History* 50 (Fall 1978): 13–27.

Martin, Lou. "Steel Industry," in *West Virginia Encyclopedia*. Edited by Ken Sullivan. Charleston:
West Virginia Humanities Council, 2006: 681–682.

Massey, Tim. "Never Late for Court: An Interview with Milton J. Ferguson." and "It Wasn't Any Pleasure for Me: Ferguson's Most Celebrated Trial." *Goldenseal: West Virginia Traditional Life* 9, no. 4 (Winter 1983): 35–40.

McQuaid, John. "Mining the Mountains." *Smithsonian* (Jan. 2009): 74–85.

Meador, Michael M. "Carving a Niche: The Blacks of Bluefield." *Goldenseal: West Virginia Traditional Life* 13, no. 4 (Winter 1987): 19–26.

Montrie, Chad. "Expedient Environmentalism: Opposition to Coal Surface Mining and the United Mine Workers of America, 1945–1977." *Environmental History* 5: (Jan. 2000) 75–98.

Moore, Catherine. "'Let's Show Them What a Fight We Can Give Them': The Black Lung Movement in West Virginia." *Goldenseal, West Virginia Traditional Life* 52, no. 2 (Summer 2006): 6–13.

Morgan, John G. "William Wallace Barron, The Legislative Magician." *Charleston Sunday Gazette-Mail*. January 16, 1965: 2m–8m, 17m–21m.

Mullen, Jay Carlton. "West Virginia's Image: The 1960 Presidential Primary and the National Press." *West Virginia History* 32 (July 1971): 215–223.

Munn, Robert F. "The Development of Strip Mining in Southern Appalachia." *Appalachian Journal* III (Autumn 1975): 87–92.

Munn, Robert F. "The Latest Rediscovery of Appalachia." *Appalachian Decade of the Sixties*. Eds. David S. Walls and John B. Stephenson. Lexington: University Press of Kentucky, 1972: 25–30.

"100 Years of Progress." *Consol News*. 100th Anniversary Edition. Vol. 3, no. 1 (1st quarter, 1964).

Palmer, M. A. et al. "Mountaintop Mining Consequences." *Science* 327, no. 596: (8 January 2010): 148–49.

Phillips, Jo Boggess. "'I Greatly Appreciate Your Courage': West Virginia's Women Legislators." *Goldenseal: West Virginia Traditional Life* 24, no. 3 (Fall 1998): 27–31.

———. "Lawmaker Jackie Withrow: A Rose Among the Thorns." *Goldenseal: West Virginia Traditional life* 24, no. 3 (Fall 1998): 32–35.

Platania, Joseph. "Getting Ready for Life: The Douglass High School Story." *Goldenseal: West Virginia Traditional Life* 19, No. 3 (Fall 1993): 21–28.

Proctor, Roy E., and T. Kelley White. "Agriculture: A Reassessment." Chap. 6 in *The Southern Appalachian Region: A Survey*. Ed. Thomas R. Ford. Lexington: University of Kentucky Press, 1962.

Radcliffe, Harry. "50 Million Program is Lifesaver." *West Virginia State Magazine* 3, no. 6 (1952): 8, 32.

Rakes, Paul H. "Casualties on the Home Front: Scott's Run Mining Disasters During World War II." *West Virginia History* 53 (1994): 95–118.

———. "West Virginia Coal Mine Fatalities: The Subculture of Danger and a Statistical Overview of the Pre-enforcement Era." *West Virginia History: A Journal of Regional Studies*. New Series, Vol. 2, no. 1 (Spring, 2008): 1–26.

Rasmussen, Donald L. et al. "Pulmonary Impairment in Southern West Virginia Coal Miners." *American Review of Pulmonary Disease* 98 (Oct. 1968): 658–67.

Rasmussen, Jeanne. "On the Outside Looking In." *Appalachia in the Sixties: Decade of Reawakening.* Eds. David S. Walls and John B. Stephenson. Lexington: University Press of Kentucky, 1972: 176–83.

Reddick, Lawrence D. "Wisdom and Courage Can Often Prevent Horrible Consequences." *Brown v. Board of Education of Topeka Kansas: An Assessment Thirty Years Later.* Institute: West Virginia State College, 1984.

Rice, Connie L. "The 'Separate But Equal Schools' of Monongalia County's Coal Mining Communities." *Journal of Appalachian Studies* 2 (Fall 1996).

Schribman, David. "Lyndon Johnson: Means, Ends, and What His Presidency Means in the End." *The Great Society and the High Tide of Liberalism*. Eds. Sidney M. Milkus and Jerome M. Mileur. Amherst: University of Massachusetts Press, 2005.

Sherrill, Robert G. "West Virginia Miracle: The Black Lung Rebellion." *The Nation* (April 28, 1969): 529–35.

Sherwood, Topper. "Kennedy in West Virginia." *Goldenseal: West Virginia Traditional Life* 26, no. 3 (Fall 2000): 15–19, 21–23.

Smith, Barbara. "Miner's Widow: Sara Kaznoski, Fighter and Survivor." *Goldenseal: West Virginia Traditional Life* 14, no. 2 (Summer 1998): 52–58.

Smith, Douglas C. "In Quest of Equality: The West Virginia Experience." *West Virginia History* 37 (1976): 211–220.

———. "Race Relations and Institutional Responses in West Virginia—A History." *West Virginia History* 39 (1977): 30–48.

Smith, James H. "Red-Baiting Senator Harley Kilgore in the Election of 1952: The Limits of McCarthyism during the Second Red Scare." *West Virginia History: A Journal of Regional Studies*, New Series, I, no. 1 (Spring 2007): 55–74.

Stack, Sam, Jr. "Implementing *Brown v Board of Education* in West Virginia: The *Southern School News* Reports." *West Virginia History: A Journal of Regional Studies*, New Series, vol. 2, no. 1 (Spring 2008): 59–81.

Stewart, Shirley L. and Connie L. Rice. "The Birds of Passage Phenomenon in West Virginia's Out Migration." Chap. 3 in *Appalachian Odyssey*. Eds. Obermiller et al, 2000.

Thomas, Jerry Bruce. "Some Common Appalachian Themes in Hardy County, 1890–1940." Keynote Address, Symposium on "Good Times and Hard Times, 1890–1940." August 5, 2006, Lost River State Park, Mathias, West Virginia.

Thomas, Karen Kruse. "The Hill-Burton Act and Civil Rights: Expanding Hospital Care for Black Southerners, 1939–1960." *Journal of Southern History*, 62, no. 4 (Nov. 2006): 823–870.

Tomasky, Michael. "Night Comes to the Appalachians." *New York Review of Books* (September 25, 2008): 81–83.

Thorne, Deborah, Ann Tickmyer, and Mark Thorne. "Poverty and Income in Appalachia." *Journal of Appalachian Studies* 10: 2004.

Tunley, Roul. "The Strange Case of West Virginia." *Saturday Evening Post* (Feb 6, 1960): 19–20, 64–66.

Tyler-McGraw, Marie. "Staying on: Poverty Warriors in West Virginia." *Journal of American Culture* 8, no. 4 (Winter 1985): 93–103.

Wallace, William J. L. "The Impact of *Brown v. Board of Education of Topeka, Kansas* on West Virginia State College." *Brown v Board of Education of Topeka, Kansas: An Assessment Thirty Years Later, a Series of Lectures and Discussions*. Institute: West Virginia State College, 1984.

Walls, David. "The Appalachian Volunteers in Perspective: Thomas Kiffmeyer, *Reformers to Radicals: The Appalachian Volunteers and the War on Poverty. Appalachian Journal 37*, Nos. 1–2 (Fall 2009/Winter 2010): 100–105.

Walls, David. "Travelin Down that Coal Town Road-The Appalachian Volunteers in Perspective: Community Organizing Then and Now." Paper presented at March 2009 meeting of Appalachian Studies Association.

Waltz, George H. Jr. "Newest Super Road Hops Daniel Boone's Mountains." *Popular Science Monthly* (Aug. 1954): 65–69.

"Ernie Weir." In *Profiles: West Virginians Who Made a Difference*. Charleston: *Charleston Gazette*, 1999.

Weiss, Chris. "Appalachian Women Fight Back: Organizational Approaches to Nontraditional Job Advocacy." Chap. 8 in *Fighting Back in Appalachia: Traditions of Resistance and Change*. Ed. Stephen L. Fisher, 151–164.

West, Don. "Romantic Appalachia." *Appalachia in the Sixties: A Decade of Reawakening*. Eds. David S. Walls and John B. Stephenson. Lexington: University of Kentucky Press, 1972.

Wilson, Donald. "In Logan County, the Half-Pint Vote, Slating and 'Lever Brothers'"; "Hard Test in West Virginia of Kennedy's Momentum—A Small State Takes the Limelight," *Life* 48, no. 18 (May 9, 1960): 24–28.

Wilson, Elizabeth Jill. "West Virginia University." *West Virginia Encyclopedia.* Ed. by Ken Sullivan Charleston: West Virginia Humanities Council, 2006: 775–76.

Wolfe, Margaret Ripley. "Eastern Kentucky and the War on Poverty: Grass Roots Activism, Regional Politics, and Creative Federalism in the Appalachian South during the 1960s." *Ohio Valley History* 3 (Spring 2003): 31–44.

"Yes, West Virginia, There is a James Johnson Sweeney." *Time Magazine* (February 8, 1963).

Unpublished Dissertations and Theses

Barnes, John. "A Case Study of the Mingo County Economic Opportunity Commission: The Use of Title II of the Economic Opportunity Act of 1964 in a Rural County of West Virginia." DSW diss., University of Pennsylvania, 1971.

Burke, Dawn Raines. "Storer College: A Hope for Redemption in the Shadow of Slavery, 1865–1955." PhD diss., Virginia Polytechnic Institute and State University, 2004.

Burns, Shirley Stewart. "Bringing Down the Mountains: The Impact of Mountaintop Removal Surface Coal Mining on Southern West Virginia Communities, 1970–2004." PhD diss., West Virginia University, 2005.

Jenrette, Jerra. "'There's No Damn Reason For It—It's Just Our Policy': Labor-Management Conflict in Martinsburg, West Virginia's Textile and Garment Industries." PhD diss., West Virginia University, 1996.

Jones, James Gay. "West Virginia in World War II." PhD diss., West Virginia University, 1952.

Kiffmeyer, Thomas J. "From Self-Help to Sedition: The Appalachian Volunteers and the War on Poverty in Eastern Kentucky, 1964–1970." PhD diss., University of Kentucky, 1998.

Lanham, Robert Eugene. "The West Virginia Statehouse Democratic Machine: Structure, Function, and Process." PhD diss., Claremont Graduate School and University Center, 1971.

Loughry, Allen Hayes II. "'Don't Buy Another Vote. I Won't Pay for a Landslide': The Sordid and Continuing History of Political Corruption in West Virginia." JDS diss., Washington College of Law, American University, 2003.

Nyden, Paul John. "Miners for Democracy: Struggle in the Coal Fields." PhD diss., Columbia University, 1974.

Rakes, Paul H. "Acceptable Casualties: Power, Culture, and History in the West Virginia Coalfields, 1900–1945." PhD diss., West Virginia University, 2002.
Seltzer, Curtis. "The United Mine Workers of America and the Coal Operators: The Political Economy of Coal in Appalachia, 1950–1973." PhD diss., Columbia University, 1977.
Taul, Glen Edward. "Poverty, Development, and Government in Appalachia: Origins of the Appalachian Regional Commission." PhD diss., University of Kentucky, 2001.
Thompson, Bruce. "An Appeal for Racial Justice: The Civic Interest Progressives' Confrontation with Huntington, West Virginia, and Marshall University." MA thesis, Marshall University, 1986.

Electronic Sources

"Long Airdox Company." *Occupational Respiratory Disease Surveillance: Coal Workers Health Surveillance Program.* National Institute for Occupational Safety and Health http://www.marmon.com/Publications/Interchange/95febp2.htm.
U.S. Department of Transportation, Federal Highway Administration. "Overview and Evolution of Bridge Program." *Status of the Nation's Highways, Bridges, and Transit: 2002 Condition and Performance Report.* http://www.fhwa.dot.gov/policy/2002cpr/ch11.htm#11a
Union of Concerned Scientists. "Leveling a Mountain of Research on Mountaintop Removal Mining." http://www.ucsusa.org/scientific_integrity/abuses_of_science/mountaintop-removal-mining.html
Wheeling Jesuit University. "Coal Impoundment Location and Information System."
W.V Department of Environmental Protection. WV Dam Inventory. www.wvdep.org.

Sound Recordings

Hazel Dickens, *Hard Hitting Songs for Hard Hit People.* Rounder Records, 1994. Liner notes by Ralph Rinzler.
Rich Kirby and Michael Kline. *They Can't Put it Back . . . .* Dillon Run Records, nd.
Jean Ritchie. *A Time for Singing.* Warner Brothers Records, 1966.
Billy Edd Wheeler. *Ode to the Little Brown Shack Out Back.* Kapp Records, 1964.

Video Recordings

Buffalo Creek Flood. Directed by Mimi Pickering. Appalshop, 1975.

If Elected. Produced by Wayne Ewing. Wayne Ewing Films, Inc., 1973. (A video account of the 1972 election in West Virginia, based on the campaign of Warren McGraw, an anti-strip mining candidate for the state senate).

Modern Marvels, Engineering Disasters, 5. A&E Television Networks, 2000/2001. (Contains approx. 8 min. on Buffalo Creek).

UMWA 1970: A House Divided. Directed by Ben Zickafoose. Appalshop, 1971.

Index

A

Aberfan, Wales, gob pile collapse in, 321
Action for Appalachian Youth, 152–53
Action for Appalachian Youth--Community Development (AAY-CD), 164–65, 233
Activism. *See* Community action; specific issues
Ad Hoc Commission, on Buffalo Creek disaster, Governor's, 328–29, 415n35
Ad Hoc Committee for the Poor, Unemployed, and Disadvantaged Citizens of West Virginia, 203
African Americans, 359n37. *See also* Civil rights movement; Congress of Racial Equality (CORE); NAACP; Race relations; Segregation
  communities of, 103–4, 109–10, 118, 122–25
  education for, 89–90, 93–94, 103–8
  effects of migration of, 238, 241–42
  effects of school integration on, 98–101, 103–4, 241, 369n44
  housing for, 109, 232
  jobs for, 88, 91–92, 101–2
  migrations of, 37, 86, 92–93, 123–24
  militancy of, 237–42
  Miners for Democracy and, 125, 406n53
  political influence of, 77, 86–88, 124
  sense of community among, 86, 88
  unemployment of, 85–86, 90–91, 232–33
  urban life of, 109–10
Agriculture, 35, 84, 189
  decline of, 7, 24–26, 52, 153–54
  desire for regional self-sufficiency in, 52, 64
  jobs lost in, 11, 27–28, 82, 352n57
  proposal to get farming land for unemployed miners, 63–64
  proposals to maintain, 25, 260
  strip mining destroying, 287–88
  subsistence, 25–26

Ahern, Melissa, 339
Aid to Dependent Children of the Unemployed (ADCU), 135, 144–47, 189
Aid to Families with Dependent Children (AFDC), 147
Air pollution, from burning slag piles, 15–16
Airports, 167, 234, 284, 340
Alexander, Lamar, 342
Alinsky, Saul, 151, 180
Allen, Leroy, 239
Alliance for Appalachia, 342
Ambler, Charles Henry, 105
American Revolution, land speculation after, 41
Anderson, Jack, 284
Andrews, Carl, 60
Anti-labor regulations, 21
Antiwar movement, 211, 236–37
Appalachia, 126, 134
  definition of region, 82, 333n2
  pessimism about future of, 132–33
  unique problems of, 82, 156
Appalachia on Our Mind: The Southern Mountains and Mountaineers in the American Consciousness (Shapiro), 4
Appalachia Speaks conference (Huntington), 188–89, 291, 391n102
Appalachian Alliance, 42, 341
Appalachian Center for the Economy and Environment, 342
Appalachian Coalition, 314
Appalachian Community Meeting, 187
Appalachian Group to Save the Land and People (AGSLP), 192–93, 292
Appalachian Land Ownership Study, 341
Appalachian Regional Commission (ARC), 42, 135
  achievements of, 219, 337
  formation of, 82–83
  funding public works projects, 165–67
Appalachian Regional Development Act, 166–68

Appalachian Research and Defense Fund (Appalred), 262
Appalachian South Folklife Center, 201
Appalachian Strip Mining Information Service, 296
Appalachian Studies Association, 341
Appalachian Voices, 342
Appalachian Volunteers, 7, 176–89
   achievements of, 8, 189–90, 191, 223, 227
   activism by former members of, 259, 262, 285
   administration of, 156, 178–80, 192, 205, 386n21
   assessing effectiveness of War on Poverty, 188–89
   characteristics of volunteers, 177–79, 186, 207–9, 211, 386n21
   cooperation with other organizations, 182, 291–92
   Council of Southern Mountains and, 156, 178–80
   criticisms of, 193–96
   criticisms of morality of, 179, 204
   criticized as outsiders, 203, 209–11
   demise of, 205, 261
   disillusionment among, 205–6
   evolution of, 177–79, 186–87, 192
   Fair Elections Committee and, 224, 227
   funding cut for, 206–7
   goals of, 179–80
   grassroots organizing by, 153, 182–84, 191, 199, 291, 391n102
   opposition to, 185, 202, 206
   radicalization of, 178–79, 191–92, 202–3, 205
   relations with local people, 207–9
   support for, 193–95, 203
   training and, 183, 186, 201
   VISTA and, 183, 186
Appalachian Youth, 170
Appalshop, 341
Aptheker, Herbert, 237
Area Redevelopment Administration (ARA), 129–32, 153, 172, 177
Area Redevelopment bill, Eisenhower vetoing, 78, 83, 126, 361n68
Army Corps of Engineers, 219, 420n28
   cleaning up after Buffalo Creek disaster, 326, 330
   in combined survey of coal dams, 333–35
Artis, Harry, 228
Arts and crafts cooperatives, 260–61
Arvon, Manuel, 198, 199, 260
Association of Disabled Miners and Widows, 275, 278–79
Auger mining, 15, 288–90
Austin, Richard Cartwright, 197, 199, 296, 304, 310, 387n52
Automobiles, 11, 29–30, 48
Auvil, Ken, 300
Ayer, Perley F., 179

B

Babcock State Park, 194
Bailey, Ellis, 291
Bailey, Larrie, 145
Baker, Russell, 3–4, 133
Bank, Richard, 254–55, 263, 273
Banks, influence on Turnpike Commission, 48–49
Barbour County, 96
Barron, Mrs. William, 221–22
Barron, William Wallace "Wally," 114, 129–30, 136
   appointees of, 141–42, 281
   on centennial art, 138–39
   corruption of, 220–22
   corruption under, 134–37, 220–21, 401n101
   initiatives under, 135–36
   Moore and, 235–36
   political career of, 134, 137
Basso, Nick, 32, 72
Bateman, Mildred, 150, 199–200, 281
Batt, William L., 131
Baylor, Elgin, 112–13
Beauty, West Virginia's, 80, 287, 291, 301
Beck, Grace Marland, 363n88
Beckley, 54, 181, 185, 337
   Area Redevelopment Administration launched in, 129–30
   in black lung movement, 253–55
   efforts to attract new industries by, 66–67
Beckley Area Rural Development Program, 64
Berea College, 177
Berkeley County, 29
Berry, Chad, 36–37, 38, 354n81
Berry, Theodore, 158
Bias, Dallas, 233
Bickel, Gary, 192

Bickley, Ancella, 104
Biesemeyer, David, 184–85, 206, 208
Bigart, Homer, 133
Bishop mine explosion, 15
Black lung. *See also* Black lung movement
   compensation for, 19, 262, 266–72
   debate over theories on, 265–67, 399n84
   definitions of, 271, 404n38
   incidence of, 15, 338–39
   legislation on, 125, 266–72, 280, 283, 405n39
   prevention of, 272, 405n39
   research on, 249–51, 253–54, 267
Black Lung Association (BLA), 8, 263–64, 405n39
   on black lung compensation bill, 271
   at rally, 268
   rejecting black lung compensation bill, 270–71
   supporting MFD, 276
   UMW trying to squelch, 265
Black lung movement, 125, 252–53, 286, 319
   fight for compensation, 254, 256, 262–64, 274
   participants in, 211, 254, 262, 273, 278
"Black Lungs" (Wyatt), 264
Blankenship v. Boyle, 275, 277–79, 285
Blizzard, William, 65–66, 387n52
Bluefield, race relations in, 99, 118–22
Bluefield Coal Show, 16
Bluefield Human Rights Commission, 119
Bluefield State College, 105, 121
   race at, 107–8, 238–42
   student activism at, 231, 237–38
Boiarsky, Ivor, 404n37
Boone, Joel T., 21
Boone, Richard, 151, 177
Boone County, 96, 197–200, 318
Boone County Association for the Needy (B-CAN), 200, 260
Boone County Community Association, 260
Boone Report, 21
Boreman, Herbert S., 47
Borrelli, Richard, 296
Boyle, William Anthony "Tony," 243, 252, 274–75
   election voided, 276–77
   miners' discontent with, 248, 264, 270, 276
   relations with coal companies, 244, 248

Bradley, Joseph Gardner "J. G.", 57
Breathitt, Edward, 193
Bridges, 218, 393n6, 394n8
Brinkley, David, 81
Brooks, Charles, 263, 406n53
Brooks, Rufus, 323–24
Brotherton, William T., 302
Brown, Bonn, 221
Brown, Willard A., 96, 123–24
Brown v. Board of Education of Topeka, Kansas
   compliance with, 92–104
   effects on colleges, 106–8
   resistance to, 92–93, 95–104
Brownie Benson's Combo, 31
Browning, Chauncey, 330
Buff, Isadore Erwin, 252–55, 264–66, 273
Buffalo Creek, 318, 324, 325
Buffalo Creek disaster, 5, 8, 16, 23, 166, 284, 310, 315, 327
   as "act of God," 326, 328
   Army Corps of Engineers cleaning up, 326, 330
   blame for, 326, 332
   commissions studying, 328–29, 415n35
   deaths and damage in, 325–26
   effects of, 333, 338
   efforts to prevent recurrence, 332–33
   lawsuits following, 323, 326, 330
   lessons not learned from, 333–35
   predictions of, 322, 323–24
   successful activism following, 341–42
   victims of, 326, 329–30, 331, 332
Buffalo Hollow, 320
   evacuation of, 324, 328–29
Buffalo Mining Company, 320, 322–23, 329–30, 417n56
Bureau of Mines, in survey of coal dams, 333
Burks, Cynthia H., 110
Burnette, George, 255
Burns, Rowland, 265, 267
Burton Mine explosion, 15
Bush, George W., 341
Business, 46, 60, 130, 209, 238, 326–27, 352n57
   community action groups and, 174, 190, 198
   efforts to attract new, 65–66
   race and, 111–12, 118
   with Weirton Steel *vs.* unionization, 56–57
Byrd, Harry Flood, 92

Byrd, Robert C., 81, 160, *188*, 227, 253
  calls for coal to "embrace the future," 343
  community action groups and, 174, 203
  complaints about AV-VISTA volunteers, 195, 197
  Democratic comeback under, 76–77
  KKK and, 115, 181–82, 374n94
  opposition to Civil Rights Act, 93, 115
  organizing conference on economic development, 65–66
  picketing of speech by, 114–15
  War on Poverty and, 140, 187–88, 203
Byrd Amendment, to OEO funding, 196–97

C

Cabin Creek Quilts, 261
Caldwell, Albert S., 29
Califano, Joseph, 161
Callebs, John, 223, 225–26
Camicia, Nicholas, 320
Campbell, Judith, 376n1
Canaan Valley, 301
Cander, Leon, 266–67
Canfield, Jack, 229, 234, 308
Cardin, Benjamin L., 342
Carter, Jimmy, 314
Carter, Phil, 116, 118
Caudill, Harry, 4–5, 10, 133, 156, 177, 180, 190
  at "Appalachia Speaks" conference, 188–89
  on Appalachian Regional Development Act, 166–67
Celebrezze, Anthony J., 144
Centennial celebration, 136–39
Centennial Commission, 80, 137–38
Chafin, Gerald, 171
Chafin, Lafe, 329
Chamber of Commerce, West Virginia, 66–67, 137
Chambers, Sue, 31
Channing, Steven, 92
Charleston, 28, 80, 231
  African Americans in, 109–10, 125
  civil rights movement in, 97, 99, 114–16, 122–24, 232–33
  CORE chapter of, 110–12
  growth of, 65, 232
  juvenile delinquency program in, 150–53, 168
  march for black lung compensation bill through, *269*, 270
  Piedmont Airlines crash, 234
  turnpike and, 48, 50
Charleston Gazette. See also Media
  on causes of economic problems, 78–79
  on civil rights movement, 98, 111
Cheat River, 301
Chemical industry, 11, 107, 231, 317
Cheney, Richard, 260
Chesapeake and Ohio Railroad, 65, 66
Chicago, 36, 234–35
The Children of Sanchez (Lewis), 5, 128, 346n13
Chilton, Ned, 262
Christian, Jack Buford and Jeanine, 75
Ciaccio, Jack, 156
Citizens against Strip Mining, 314
Citizens' Commission, to study Buffalo Creek disaster, 328–29
Citizen's task force, 184–85
Citizens' Task Force on Surface Mining (CTFSM), 291, 297
Citizens to Abolish Strip Mining (CASM), 296, 304–5, 310–12, 324
Civic Interest Progressives (CIP), at Marshall University, 115–18
Civil rights, 57, 230
  support for, 135–36, 140
  violations of, 227, 231–32 (*See also* Race, discrimination on; Segregation)
Civil Rights Act of 1964, 114
  effects of, 118, 121–22, 281
  enforcing school desegregation, 98, 101–3
  resistance to, 93, 115
Civil rights movement, 336–37. *See also* NAACP
  actions against segregation, 111–13
  Charleston CORE chapter in, 110–12
  demonstrations, 232
  demonstrations in, 6, 108, 114–18
  effects of, 85, 123–24, 178
  role of churches in, 122–23
  spread of skills learned in, 178, 211
  student activism in, 119–21, 236
  tactics in, 116–19, 125, 211
  women in, 277–78
Civil service system, 146, 159, 283
Civilian Conservation Corps, 148
Class, in Appalachia, 30, 156
Clean Air Act (1963), 317

Index

Clean Air Act (1970), 319
Clean Water Act (1965), 317
Cleckley, Gus, 116
Climate change, impact on coal industry, 343
Clinchfield Coal Company, 57
Cloward, Richard, 150
Coal
  demand for, 65, 294, 314, 343
  low *vs.* high sulfur, 319–20
Coal company towns, 1–2, 57, 89
  companies abandoning, 23–24
  housing in, 91, 318
Coal industry, 278. *See also* Coal mining
  abandoning less productive mines and towns, 23–24
  African Americans in, 86, 90–91, 101–2
  agreeing with limited federal regulations, 290, 313
  avoiding enforcement of regulations, 249, 299, 322–23
  on benefits of strip mining, 288–89, 293, 339
  big companies taking over smaller, 18–19, 320
  black lung compensation and, 264, 270–72
  black lung prevention in, 250, 272, 339
  on black lung research, 265–67
  bought out by oil companies, 273
  Buffalo Creek disaster and, 328–29
  changes in, 273, 343
  competition to, 12, 60
  decline of, 11, 306–7, 319, 348n15
  declining production in, 64, 319
  Democratic ties to, 46, 58
  economic influence of, 28, 84, 308, 318–19, 338, 343
  effects of decline of, 28, 64, 82, 118, 123–24, 171
  efforts to reduce dependence on, 64–66, 131
  efforts to revive, 66
  as exploitative, 44, 60–61
  flourishing, 63, 337
  ignoring regulations, 248–49, 292
  increasing mortality, 14–15, 339
  increasingly competitive, 19–20, 68
  job losses from mechanization in, 91, 93, 337–38
  jobs lost in, 11, 20, 37, 352n57
  labor needs in, 68, 101–2, 244
  layoffs in, 23, 68, 90–91, 243, 337–38
  on legislation about strip mining, 292, 293–94, 302–3, 420n28
  legislature representing interests of, 222–23, 297, 299
  loss of jobs in, 12–13, 36, 63–64, 79, 82
  media as watchdog of, 342
  new regulations on, 327, 333
  pensions and health plans in, 21, 23
  people blamed for problems caused by, 4
  political influence of, 60, 71, 156, 192–93, 220, 283, 305, 308–9, 311, 342–43
  production in, 19–20, 305, 343
  production put above health and safety in, 21, 222–23, 251, 272, 315, 320
  regulations and, 17, 298, 319
  relation of underground *vs.* surface mining in, 286
  small operations in, 16–18, 21, 327
  strikes against, 270, 284
  strip mining and, 290, 299, 305
  structural unemployment and, 127
  technological advances in, 13–14, 18–20, 79, 220, 339–40
  UMWA no longer balancing influence of, 243, 338
  union acceptance of mechanization in, 21, 242
  union cooperating with, 21, 244, 252, 272
Coal Mine Safety Act (1952), 272, 320
Coal miners, 328
  activism on black lung, 252–57, 262–64, 267–68, 273
  benefits for, 242–43, 275–76
  black, 89–91, 107
  black lung compensation for, 271, 273
  in Buffalo Hollow, 319–20
  disabled and widows of, 243, 267–68, 275–76
  discontent with Boyle, 270, 276
  discontent with UMW, 248, 256–57
  diseases of, 15, 249–54
  effects of experience with UMW on, 182
  efforts to help, 63–64, 262
  failed by Boyle and union, 264
  fear of defying union, 263
  fear of losing jobs, 343, 420n28
  increasing rebelliousness among, 34, 244–45
  injuries and diseases of, 36–37, 250–54

misconceptions about, 265
not supporting ban on strip mining, 286–87
other jobs for, 127, 243
retirement of, 242–44, 271
shortage of, 244, 288
striking for black lung compensation bill, 268–70, *269*
in strip mines, 293, 308–9, 420n28
told to accept dangers of job, 266
training for unemployed, 89–90, 131–32, 172
underground *vs.* surface, 286, 289–90, 294, 296–97, 300–301
unemployed, 68, 91–92, 131–32, 242, 288
wives and widows of, 269–70, 273, 278–79, 284–85
Coal mines
dominating coal company towns, 1–2
slurry injected into, 334, 417n57
Coal mining. *See also* Coal industry; Mining machines; mountaintop removal mining; Strip mining
auger, 15, 288–90
dangers of, 7, 10, 14–15, 247–50, 266, 320, 349n19
disposal of wastes from, 316–18, 333–34, 413n6, 417n57
effects of mechanization of, 39, 259, 316
effects of mechanization on health and safety, 10, 14–15, 23, 246–47, 251–52
effects of mechanization on working conditions in, 15, 21, 350n38
environmental effects of, 15–16, 27, 305–6
explosions in, 14–15
fatalism in, 249–50
health and safety regulations, 14, 249, 269–70
longwall, 16
mechanization, 12–13, 22–23, 89–90, 259, 272
methods of haulage in, 14, 16, 18–20
rescues in, 15, 246
underground *vs.* strip, 305–6
waste products of, 23, 166, 316–18 (*See also* Gob piles)
Coal Refuse Act (1973, West Virginia), 332–33

Coal River basin, 306
Coal River Mountain Watch, 342
Coalfield region
Appalachian Regional Development Act not focusing on, 167
Appalachian Volunteers in, 180, 186
McDowell County Community Action Plan as model program in, 154–55
media coverage of, 245
Coffindaffer, Billy L., 168
Cohen, Mrs. Wilbur, 201
Cold War, 40, 54–56, 63, 76
Coleman, Howard, 174
Coleman, Lewis "Pops," 268
Coles, Robert, 192, 209
Collins, Ray, 157–58
Collins, Willie, 37, 91
Colored People (Gates), 104
Combs, Bert, 82–83
Commerce, Department of (West Virginia), 131, 135, 141, 144, 167–68
Communism
accusations of, 59, 193–94, 201
fear of, 55–57, 237
Community action, 8, 179, 196, 202, 391n102. *See also* Demonstrations; Maximum feasible participation; specific issues
by community action agencies, 150–53
continued hope for, 212, 342
local governments challenged by, 151–52
models for, 211, 258–59
organizing theories, 180–81, 187, 190–91, 205, 386n27
programs' inadequacy in, 164–65
range of topics addressed, 259
student, 236–42, 261 (*See also under* Education, higher)
successes of, 182, 186, 341
by VISTA and Appalachian Volunteers, 180, 182, 186
VISTA and Appalachian Volunteers really believing in, 186, 210
women in, 6–7, 277–79
working with, not for, poor people, 39, 156, 199, 259
Community action agencies (CAAs), 150–54, 157, 212
Green Amendment on, 196, 201–2
local governments allowed to take over, 196, 201–2, 204–5

promoting cooperatives, 260–61
Community action plans, McDowell County's, 153–56
Community action programs (CAPs), 150–53, 160, 291
  changing organization theories for, 171–75, 180–81, 187, 190–91, 205, 259–60, 386n27
  county courts seeking takeovers of, 202–4, 224–25
  criticisms of, 158, 160, 187–88
  declining support for, 160, 202, 259
  levels of participation in, 170, 189, 260
  Monroe defending, 162–63, 203
  multi-county, 156, 212
  obstacles to, 157–58, 201–2
  Smith on, 160, 202–4
  sources of information on, 7–8
  taken over by poor people, 190–91, 191–92, 200–201
  usefulness of, 160, 191, 208
Community associations, formation of encouraged, 183–84
Community centers/facilities, 154–55, 164–65, 175, 331
Community groups, 328
  diversity within, 210–11
  OEO recognition for, 213–14
  roles of, 175, 211, 230
Congress for Appalachian Development, 190, 387n52
Congress of Racial Equality (CORE), 114
  Charleston chapter of, 110–12, 115
  Gilmore and, 122, 278
  national, 110–11
Conservation, 190, 280, 290– 291, 300. *See also* Environment
Consolidation Coal Company, 273, 305
  Farmington disaster at, 246–49, *247*
  union and, *22*, 248
Constitution, West Virginia
  amendments to, 142, 283–84
  need for revision of, 43, 142, 357n10
  segregation requirement in, 92, 106
  tax limitations in, 45, 62
Construction, 11, 82, 352n57
Cooper, John Sherman, 196
Cooper, Samuel, 241
Cooperatives, 174, 260
Copenhaver, John, 113
Copley, Sidney, 174
Corporations, non-resident, 39, 84, 263

control of resources by, 44–45, 214
as exploitative, 6, 44–45, 133
relation to Appalachian poverty, 133, 167, 214
resistance to tax increases, 44–45, 62
Corruption, 81, 84, 93, 143
  in Barron's administration, 134–37, 220–21
  in county governments, 228, 329
  Democrats accused of, 71–72
  effects of indictments on Democratic Party, 235–36
  in political campaigns, 227, 235–36, 376n1
  in purchasing practices, 221, 401n101
  revolt against, 125, 175, 223–25
  rumors of Moore's, 284, 330, 407n73
  in Smith administration, 141–42, 220, 229
  in state government, 43, 45–47, 59, 222, 256
  in State Road Commission, 61, 69
  in United Mine Workers, 8, 277
  voting fraud as, 223, 225, 227
Council of the Southern Mountains, 170
  Appalachian Volunteers and, 177–80
  McDowell County Community Action Plans and, 155–56
  on strip mining ban, 309–10, 341
Crabtree, Paul
  opposition to community action, 158, 173–74, 202, 203
  state OEO and, 159–60, 162
"Crash program," 135, 143–47
Creative federalism, failures of, 143, 168
Crime, 149
  juvenile delinquency, 109, 150, 152–53, 168
Crouser, Brad, 330, 407n73
Crozet Super Highway Commission, 50
Crum Industrial Organization, efforts to revive coal mines, 66
Culture, Appalachian, 198–99
  effects of beliefs about, 4–5, 200–201
  fatalism attributed to, 4–5, 30, 34, 39, 259, 265
  growing militancy in, 189–90
  influences on, 6, 33
  mountain character and, 81, 159
  poverty blamed on, 128–29, 132–33
  stereotypes of, 3–4, 37, 39, 210, 331–32
Culture, national, 11, 29–30, 33, 40

Culture of poverty theory, 4–5, 128–29
  efforts to eradicate, 6, 147–48
  Head Start based on, 147–48, 212
  influence of, 140–41, 151, 210
Cumberland Valley Economic Opportunity Council, 190
Curry, Leah, 277, 391n102

D

Dahill, Dan, 46
Daley, Richard, 234–35
Dam Control Act (1973, West Virginia), 332–33
Dams, on Buffalo Creek, *325*
  collapse of, 324–25
  creation of, 320–21
  current dams bigger than, 333–35
  problems with, 321–23
Dams, slag pile, 190, 327
  continued danger from, 333–35, 418n59
  new regulations on, 332–33
Daniel Boone Hotel, 112–15
Daoust, Robert, 300
Dasovich, Steve, 322–24, 333, 417n56
Davies, William E., 321–22
Davis, C. Anderson, 122
Davis, Homer, 122, 124
Davis, Lloyd, 387n52
Deforestation, 27
Democratic Party, in West Virginia, 306
  African Americans and, 87–88
  comeback of, 76–77, 134
  corruption and, 46, 71–72, 220, 235–36
  disunity of, 79–80, 235
  dominance in government, 33–34, 47, 58, 72, 311
  effects of national politics on, 307, 310–11
  election reform movement and, 228–29
  in fight over severance tax proposal, 60–61
  loss of control by, 71–72
  opposition to community action programs in, 143, 185, 203
  patronage politics of, 46, 175
  ties to coal industry, 46, 58–59
Democratic Party, national, 160, 234–35, 307
Demonstrations, 203
  about strip mining, 192–93, 292, 298
  for black lung compensation bill, 268–70, *269*
  in civil rights movement, 95–97, 110–11, 114–20, 232–33
  by community action programs, 202–3
  against county court taking over community action program, *224*, 224–25
  effects of, 113, 211, 260
  outside 1968 Convention, 234–35
  in student activism, 236–42, 256
Denver, John, 336
DePaulo, Elizabeth, 148
Depression, 9, 35
  militancy of unions in, 10, 20–21, 211, 265
  tax limitations placed during, 45, 62
Derickson, Alan, 251, 270, 273
Designs for Rural Action, 262, 276
Detroit, workers traveling to, 65
Dewey, Thomas E., 47
Diamond, integration of, 111–12
Dickens, Hazel, 38
Dickerson, Alan, 391n102
Dieffenbach, Henry, 65–66
Disabled Miners and Widows of Southern West Virginia, 275–76
Diseases. *See also* Black lung
  of miners, 36, 250–54, 266–67, 404n38
  mining-related, 15, 339
Dodson, Elmer, 233
"Dog holes," unemployed miners working, 17–18, 23
Douglas, Paul, 361n68
Drewry, Elizabeth Simpson, 77, 280
Duiguid, John P., 222
Dunaway, Wilma A., 41–42
Dunbar, shooting in, 230, 238
Duscha, Julius, 132

E

Eastern West Virginia Community Action Program, 163
Eastern West Virginia Planning and Development Association, Inc., 157
Eccles mine explosion, 14
Economic development funds, 167–68. *See also* OEO; War on Poverty
Economic growth, War on Poverty trying to stimulate, 166
Economic Opportunity Act, 140
  bureaucratic issues of, 157–58, 214
  Green Amendment to, 201–2

Index

Economic opportunity commissions, counties required to form, 152–53
Economy, Appalachian, 10, 23
  causes of problems in, 6, 28, 84, 338
  low incomes in, 25, 27, 171
  problems in, 7, 40, 84, 126
Economy, national, 68, 135
  Appalachia as paradox in prosperity of, 2, 4, 6, 10, 127
  postwar prosperity, 9, 37, 40, 133
Economy, West Virginia's, 29–30, 67, 93, 182, 355n86
  causes of problems in, 51–52, 64–65, 78–79, 82
  coal industry's importance in, 64–65, 82, 338, 343
  crisis in, 62–63, 80–81, 127
  deterioration of, 78, 82
  effects of strip mining ban on, 305–6
  efforts to diversify, 65–66, 130–32, 138, 172, 362n75
  highway system and, 51–52, 64
  improvements in, 11, 64, 136, 283, 306–7
Education, 45. *See also* Head Start programs; Job training
  for African Americans, 87–90, 93–94, 109, 241
  call to add Appalachian history to, 189
  consolidation of schools, 48
  desegregation of, 92–104, 121
  discrimination in, 99–101, 109, 119, 121, 241
  funding for, 60–62, 73, 135, 142, 212
  improvements in, 76, 154, 167, 177
  integration of, 95–98, 98–101, 98–104, 114, 191, 369n44
  in Job Corps, 140
  migrations and, 35, 74–75, 104
  percentage pursuing college, 3
  poor quality of, 41, 67, 74–76, 167, 173–74
  poverty of, 74–76, 154
  problems of, 7, 80
  reform of, 191
  school construction push, 52–53
  school lunches, 192, 197–98, 200
  segregation in, 86, 88, 119, 370n52
  teachers' organizations in, 94–95
Education, adult, 144–45
Education, higher, 284
  integration of, 105–8, 372n71
  student activism and, 114–15, 119–21, 236–42, 256, 261

students wanting to confront injustice, 177–78
  work-study jobs in, 149–50
Eisenhower, Dwight D., 58–59, 71, 73, 98
  vetoing Area Redevelopment bill, 78, 83, 126, 361n68
Election reform, 8, 191, 223–29, 256
Electricity generation, 12, 68, 190, 319
Elk River Coal and Lumber Company, 57
Elkins, 50
Eller, Ronald D, 133, 334n2
Ellis, Peter Steven, 206
Elmore, Clarence, 141, 220, 235
England, J. Paul, 290
England Committee, on strip mining, 290, 292
Environment, 135, 252
  abandoned company towns in, 24
  damage from strip mining, 8, 289, 294–95, 299, 324
  damage to, 7, 84, 316
  danger of slurry injected into old mines to, 334, 417n57
  effects of lumbering on, 27–28
  effects of mining on, 15–16, 23, 318
  effects of mountaintop removal mining on, 341
  effects of strip *vs.* underground mining on, 305–6, 316
  exploitation of, 27–28
  in land reclamation after strip mining, 167, 296, 341
  movement against strip mining for, 286–87, 304
  new legislation about, 317, 319
  responsibility for protection abdicated, 301
Environmental groups, 211, 313
  working for strip mining ban, 291, 296–97, 301
Environmental Protection, Department of (West Virginia), 417n57
Environmental Protection Agency (federal), 319, 333
Environmental Protection Agency (West Virginia), 333
Environmental regulations, blamed for Buffalo Creek disaster, 326
Equal Opportunity Act (EOC)
  commissioners wanting patronage funds from, 225
  requirement for maximum feasible participation, 175

Erikson, Kai, 5, 331–32
Ernst, Harry, 154
Everything in Its Path: Destruction of Community in the Buffalo Creek Flood (Erikson), 331–32
Ewen, Lynda Ann, 332
Ewing, Wayne, 312–13

F

Fair Elections Committee (FEC), Mingo County, 8, *224*, 224–29, 256, 277, 391n102
Fairmont, 67, 97
Families, 147, 154
Farmington disaster, 8, 23, 246–49, *247*, 264, 272, 274
 activism following, 269–70, 341–42
 effects of, 269, 317, 338
 widows of miners killed in, 269–70, 279
Farmington No. 9 Widow's Mine Disaster Committee, 279
Fatalism, attributed to Appalachian culture, 4–5, 30, 34
 in mining, 249–50, 265
 rejection of, 39, 189–90, 259, 265
Fayette County, resisting school desegregation, 103
FBI, and Fair Elections Committee, 227
Feaster, Eston K., 75
Feaster Report, on schools, 75–76
Feather, Carl E., 37–38
Federal Aid Highway Acts (1968/1971), 393n6
Federal Coal Mine Health and Safety Act, 272, 283
Federal Coal Mine Health and Safety Act of 1969, 272
Federalism, bringing new coal mine regulations, 273
Federation of Labor (AFL-CIO), West Virginia, 296
Feminism, 211, 277, 279–81
Ferguson, Milton J., 69, 221
Ferrell, Ira Homer, 31
Ferris, Frances, 269
Finance, Department of (West Virginia), 73
Fire departments, blacks in, 109, 121
Fisher, Ralph, 153, 157–58, 157–60
Flatt, Lester, 32
Flinn, Virgil, 97
Flooding, 324, 338, 413n1
 in Buffalo Creek disaster, 315, 325–26
 strip mining causing, 289, 300, 306, 324
Florida, exodus of teachers to, 74–75
Flower Fund, 69, 71–72
Floyd, George, 260
Floyd, Noah, 174, 203–4, 308
 corruption of, 175, 228
 influence of, 228, 259–60
FMC Corporation, 231
Food stamps, 129, 155
Ford Foundation, 40, 54, 177
 survey of Appalachian households by, 29–30, 84, 133
Forests, destroyed by mountaintop removal mining, 341
Forman, James, 114–15
Forum of the Future, 138
Fox, Daniel, 179
Fox, John G., 106
Franklin, Ben, 189–90, 265
Frederick, Gil, 303
Free University, at West Virginia University, 237

G

Gainer, Carl, 31, 194
Galperin, Simon Hersh, Jr., 295–98, 303, 310
 bills for strip-mining ban by, 302, 304–5
 on jobs in strip mining *vs.* underground, 300–301
Gans, Herbert, 4–5
Gardner, Leroy, 399n84
Garrison, Memphis Tennessee, 116
Gates, Henry Louis, Jr., 31, 88, 93, 104, 108, 113
Gates, Rocky, 113
Gaujot, Phillip, 330
Gavett, Thomas W., 113–14
Gay, Marian T. "Bunche," 116
Gender, 148
 male domination in West Virginia, 77–78, 277, 279–81
 women's growing activism, 6–7, 277–79, 285, 406n65
 women's increasing involvement in politics, 277–81
Gender relations/roles, of AV-VISTA volunteers, 210
Gesell, Gerhard, 275
Gilbert, Bynum "Junior," 35–36, 244

Gilbert Creek community action group, 174
Gilmore, Elizabeth Harden, 110, 114, 122–23, 278
Gipson, Charles, 116
Gish, Tom, 156
Glass, Richard, 191
Glass industry, decline of, 29, 78
Glatt, Carl W., 230
Gluck, Joseph, 237
Gob piles, 2, 15–16, 166, 331
   as construction material for dams, 315–17, 320, 333–34
   growing size of, 305, 320, 340
   role in disasters, 320–21, 325
Goldwater, Barry, 141
Gore, Truman, 141, 221
Gough, Jethro, 266–67
Government
   benefits from, 19, 23
   failures of oversight by, 315–16, 328, 333–34
   regulations on slag piles and dams, 332–34
   role in helping the poor, 128–29, 211
   state *vs.* federal, 143–44, 158, 161–62, 167–68, 214
   survey of coal dams, 333–35
   taking over mines during strikes, 20–21
Government, county, 180
   challenges to corruption in, 175, 179, 223–25
   corruption in, 46, 329
   lack of adequate funding for, 43–44
   OEO programs and, 152–53, 154
   taking over community action agencies/programs, 202–5, 224–25
   women serving in, 77–78
Government, federal, 56, 129, 212, 227, 273, 341. *See also* Office of Economic Opportunity (OEO); War on Poverty
   addressing problems of Appalachia, 78, 82–83, 126, 137
   on bridge and highway construction, 73–74, 218, 393n6
   call for strip mining ban by, 292–93
   denying black lung, 252–53
   new regulations on slag piles, 332–33
   subsidizing rural hospital construction, 53–54
Government, local, 41, 66
   in civil rights movement, 117–18, 121, 232–33
   influences on, 44, 156
   lack of funding for, 45, 166
   taking over community action agencies, 196, 201–2
   threatened by community activism, 151–52, 160, 170, 180
Government, state, 41, 330. *See also* Legislature, West Virginia
   on civil rights, 113–14
   community action groups challenging, 170, 173, 180, 227
   cooperating on regional redevelopment, 82–83
   corruption in, 45–47, 59, 84, 134–37, 222, 256, 401n101
   Democratic domination of, 33–34, 47, 58
   denying black lung, 252–53
   effects of divided executive in, 43–44, 61–62, 72, 79–80, 135
   efforts to address economic crisis, 79–80, 145
   governors' initiatives in, 142, 283–84, 306
   jobs in as political spoils, 146–47
   reform of, 84, 336–37
   regulations on coal industry, 289–90, 332–33
   revenue for, 45, 62, 135, 283
   unwillingness to enforce regulations on coal companies, 322–23, 329
   women in, 6–7, 77
Governor's Ad Hoc Commission, to study Buffalo Creek disaster, 328–29
Governor's Commission on State and Local Finance, 62
Governor's Task Force on Strip Mining, 142
Grafton, decline of, 78–79
Grant County, 157
Great Appalachian Migration, 3, 7, 23, 78. *See also* Migrations
   destinations of, 35–36
   hope for reversal of, 36–39
   population loss in, 34–35, 66
   race and, 37, 86
Great Society, environmental concern in, 317
Green, Edith, 148, 196
Green Amendment, to OEO, 196, 201–2, 204, *224*
Greenbrier County, school desegregation in, 96–98

Greenbrier resort, contrasted with state's poverty, 80
Greer, Hal, 106
Gregg, Hugh, 68
Grieder, William, 206–7
Grimes, Richard, 297–98, 308–9
Growth center concept, 166–67, 337
Guerrant, Robert, 391n102
Guyandotte River, Buffalo Creek flowing into, 318

H

Hackett, David, 151
Hall, Gus, 185
Hallanan, Elizabeth, 77, 280–81
Hamilton, Chris, 339
Hampshire County, 157
Happy Pappies program, 135, 143
Hardman, A. L., 74–75
Hardway, Wendell, 107, 238–39, 241
Hardy County, 26–28, 153–54
Hardy County Rural Area Development Committee, 153–54
Harlan County, USA, 279
Harless, James H. "Buck," 130–32
Harrah, Delvin D., 96
Harrington, Michael, 132–33
Harris, Jerry, 233
Hatch Act, 159, 180
Haught, James A., 330
Hawks Nest tragedy, 250
Head Start programs, 141, 158, 173, 192
  adaptation of, 159, 189
  as benefit of War on Poverty, 147–48, 212, 337
  Byrd wanting to maintain, 187–88
  Mingo County's as model, 277, 391n102
Health and safety, in mining, 14, 310, 338. *See also* Black lung; Mining disasters
  focus on mining production *vs.*, 223
  miners demanding improvements, 244, 264
  mining machines' effects on, 20
  production put above, 21, 222–23, 251, 272, 315, 320
  proximity to coal industry increasing disease, 339
  strip mining, 288–89
Health and safety regulations, in mining, 17, 250, 285, 327, 338

activism for stricter, 279, 336
coal industry and, 223, 243, 248–49
coal industry avoiding enforcement of, 249, 269, 272, 299, 322–23
federal, 269–70, 272, 283, 285, 317
rock dusting requirement, 246–48
Health care
  efforts to upgrade, 53–54, 73
  federal aid for, 167, 359n37
  inadequacies in, 53, 167
  medical schools and, 53, *282*, 284
  for miners, 20–21, 54, 242–43, 275–76, 398n60
  programs providing, 144–45, 148, 154, 192
  race and, 114, 119, 359n37
Hechler, Ken, 77, 249, 264, 275, 322
  activism for black lung compensation, 252, 268
  reelection of, 311, 313
  working for strip mining ban, 303–4, 314
  working on mine health and safety regulations, 269–70, 272
Hedrick, E. H., 59, 63
Hedrick, G. C., 63–64
Henderson, Herbert H., 116, 230, 241
Hendryx, Michael, 339
Hereford, John W., 117
Hickam, Homer, Jr., 76
Hickel, Walter J., 269
Higginbotham, P. R., 118
Highway system. *See* Roads; West Virginia Turnpike
  deficiencies of, 49–51
  interstate, 50, 52
  intra- *vs.* interstate, 64, 73
Highway systems
  interstate construction causing displacement of families in Triangle, 232–33
Hill-Burton Hospital Survey and Construction Act (1946), 53–54, 359n37
Hinton, 12, 66
Hoblitzell, John D., 76–77
Hodel, Charles, 64
Hodel, Emil, 185
Hodel, John, 185
Hodges, Luther, 129–30
Hoffmann, Harry, 144–45
Holcomb, Robert, 193
Holland, Charles, 185

Holly, Joseph C., 322
Holt, Helen, 77
Holt, Homer, *136*
Holt, Rush Dew, 59, 77
Homes, 11–12, 192
  for blacks, 109, 232–33
  in coal company towns, 1–2, 23–24, 91, 318
  destroyed in Buffalo Creek disaster, 318, 326, 331
  need for improvements in, 109, 154, 171, 232
  race and, 108, 123–24
Hominy Falls disaster, 8, 246, 264
Housing and Urban Development, Department of (US), 232–33
Huge, Harry, 275
Human Rights Commission, West Virginia, 109, 113–14, 117, 135–36, 238
  on Bluefield's lack of progress, 118–19
  on effects of Civil Rights Act, 121–22
  on race relations, 231–32, 239–42
  on school desegregation, 98–99, 101
Hume, Brit, 278, 404n37
Humphrey, Hubert H., 80, 127, 160–61, 234, 236, 376n1
Humphreys, R. R., 265
Hundley, Rodney "Hot Rod," 83
Hunter, Marjorie, 174
Hunter, Murray, 266
Huntington, 284
  economy of, 28, 65, 82
  race relations in, 96–97, 99, 106, 115–18
Huntington Human Rights Commission, 117–18
Huntington State Hospital, 279, 281
Hylton, Tracy W., 312–13

I

Illegitimacy, West Virginia's rate of, 80
Income, 109, 337
  from coal mining, 288, 319–20, 338
  from coal mining *vs.* other jobs, 64–65, 288
  in West Virginia *vs.* national, 80, 82
Industry, 78
  Appalachian economy moving to service-based, 338
  decline of, 11, 65, 78
  efforts to attract new, 62, 65–68, 66–67, 71, 362n75
  growth of, 29, 63, 68
  of mining equipment, 19–20
  need for, 64, 127
  obstacles to, 67, 84, 362n75
Infrastructure, 42, 337
International Ladies Garment Workers Union, 29
Interstate Highways Act of 1956, 73–74
Island Creek Coal Company, explosion in no. 22 mine, 15
Isolation, of Appalachia, 2–3, 48–50

J

Jackameit, William P., 108
Jackson, Kenneth T., 52
Jackson, Lloyd, 228
Jaffe, Ronnie Sue, 208–9
Jardin, Charles, 231
Jarret, James R., 88, 100
Jarret, Ruth, 88
Jefferson County, 86, 101–3
Job Corps, 140–41, 148–49, 158
  as benefit of War on Poverty, 212, 337
  Byrd's complaints about, 187, 197
Job creation, 352n57
  efforts for, 130, 138, 166
  need for, 154, 203
  in War on Poverty, 154, 161
Job placement
  for strip miners, 304
Job training
  in Action for Appalachian Youth-- Community Development, 165
  federal grant to "fill in gaps" in state program, 144
  in Job Corps, 140
  moved to state department of employment security, 147
  need for new, 127–28
  in New Frontier program, 129
  for new jobs, 127–28, 172
  retraining for unemployed miners, 131–32
  for unemployed fathers, 144
  in West Virginia Work and Training program, 144–47
Jobs. *See also* Work relief programs
  for African Americans, 88, 104, 109, 113, 121
  in coal industry, 15, 68, 127, 243, 244

discrimination in, 108–9, 114, 118, 122
effects of losses in coal industry, 23, 64–65, 175
increasing competition for, 91–92, 109
itinerant, 25, 27, 36, 65
lack of, 3, 171
limited options for, 37, 127, 277
loss of, 11, 28–29, 352n57
lost by mechanization in coal industry, 12–13, 18–23, 89–91, 288–89
lost in agriculture, 27–28
lost in coal industry, 36–37, 63–64, 107, 337–38, 343
lost in railroads, 12, 65
miners' fear of losing, 243, 420n28
need for full employment, 63, 128
as political spoils, 146–47
programs providing, 88, 149–50, 175
racial hierarchy in, 89, 107, 124
in recreation and tourism, 301
in strip mining, 288–89, 296, 300, 420n28
in strip mining vs. underground, 288, 289–90, 294, 300–301
teaching, 100, 104
traditionally black, 91–92, 109
for women, 277, 281
Johnkoski, Vincent J., 221
Johnson, Bos, 32
Johnson, Lyndon B., 115, 137–38, 141, *188*, 212, 229
   on community action programs, 161, 213
   Economic Opportunity Act under, 140, 214
   War on Poverty under, 133–34, 139–40, 151–54, 166–67
Jones, Cleo, 226, 404n37
Jones, Kojo, 104, 124
Justice, Alma Jean, 225, 277
Justice Department, US, 227, 256, 401n101

K

Kanawha County, 97, 99, 152, 231
Kanawha County community action program, 164–65, 170
Kanawha Valley, 122–23, 262–64
Kanawha Valley Council on Human Relations, 113, 124
Kanawha Valley Industrial Emergency Planning Council, 231
Kaufman, Paul, 235, 263, 268, 357n10

in black lung movement, 264–65, 270–71
organizations of, 226, 262, 387n52
Kaymoor, 23–24
Kaznoski, Sara Lee, 269–70, 279, *280*
Keats, John, 52
Kee, Elizabeth, 77
Kee, James, 174, 311
Kee, John, 77
Keeper of the Mountains Foundation, 342
Kelley, Jay Hilary, 328
Kennedy, John F., 128, 133, 138–39, 150, 256, 272, 376n1
   election of, 126–27
   initiatives for Appalachia, 127, 133–34, 137, 166–67, 176–77
   media focus on West Virginia during campaign of, 82, 126
   social programs of, 129–30, 139–40
   volunteers inspired by, 177–78
   West Virginia's importance in election of, 3, 80, 135
Kennedy, Robert
   assassination of, 216, 230, 234
   on juvenile delinquency, 150, 152
Kentuckians for the Commonwealth, 342
Kentucky, 41, 82, 92, 135, 177, 182, 211
   strip mining in, 292, 340
Kerr, Loren E., 250–52
Kiffmeyer, Thomas J., 178, 209–10
Kilgore, Harley M., 57, 59
   death of, 69, 72
   on economic crisis, 63–65
Kinderman, Gibbs, 178, 183–84, 187, 262
King, Frank B., 14
King, Martin Luther, 122, 216, 229–30, 238
Kline, Michael, 206
Knight, Wallace, 66
Koepler, W. E. E., 287, 340
Koontz, Arthur Burke, 137–38
Korean War, 40, 54–55, 59
Krajcinovic, Ivana, 398n59
Kramer, Steve, 183, 191
Ku Klux Klan, Byrd in, 115, 182
Kump, Cyrus, 59
Kump, Guy, 62
Kuralt, Charles, 177

L

La Vida (Lewis), 128
Labor-capital accord, after WWII, 21–22

Index

Labor Department, US, 175, 274–77
Labor relations, 21, 40, 56, 283–84, 319
Land ownership
   absentee, 39, 66
   benefiting from limited property taxes, 45
   effects of, 41, 356n4
   local politicians' ties to, 44, 46
   ambiguities of titles and, 42
   residents needing to regain, 189
Land speculation, 41–42
Land uses, limitations of, 66
Landslides, as danger of strip mining, 300, 306, 324
Latimer, Ira S., Jr., 299, 303
Lawless, George, 131–32
Lawyers, and Appalachian Research and Defense Fund, 262
Lazenby, J. H., 120
Lease, Antoinette, 116
Lee, K. W., 225, 254
Leeber, James, 254–55, 276
Legal assistance, 173, 189, 262
Legislation, federal
   to ban mountaintop removal mining, 342
   on black lung, 405n39
   on climate change, 343
   on mine health and safety, 269, 285
Legislation, state
   under Barron, 135
   on black lung compensation, 254, 256, 263–72, 280, 283, 405n39
   blocking constitutional convention, 142
   extending unemployment benefits, 78
   ineffectiveness of strip mining, 295, 297, 303
   for mine health and safety, 285
   on reclamation of land after strip mining, 294–95
   resisting election reform, 228
   on strip mining, 289–92, 298, 301–3, 305
Legislature, state, 8, 73, 317, 357n10
   anti-strip mining candidates elected to, 311–12
   black lung compensation bill in, 270–71
   Citizens' Task Force on Surface Mining lobbying, 291, 297
   coal industry's interests represented in, 222–23, 297, 299
   debating strip mining, 293, 297–98, 301–4

   Democratic dominance in, 33–34, 47, 58, 72, 311
   forming Human Rights Commission, 113–14
   hearings on black lung, 266–67
   Marland vs., 60–62, 68–70
   Moore vs., 283–84, 306
   regulation of strip mining by, 290, 292
   urged to act on economic crisis, 79, 203
   voting against interests of constituents, 222
   women in, 279–81
Leonard, Louise, 281
Lewis, John L., 59, 127
   coal company officials and, 21, *22*
   on effects of mining machines, 20, 89
   ignoring mechanization's effects, 10, 251–52, 350n38
   leadership of, 242–44, 274
   management of welfare and retirement funds, 242–43
   on mechanization, 20–23
Lewis, Julia A., 332
Lewis, Oscar, 5, 128
Liberalism, waning of, 256, 258
Linde, O. V., 295–96
Little, Herb, 71
Little Kanawha Regional Council, 67
The Logan Coal Field of West Virginia (Thurmond), 18–19
Logan County, 129, 191, 228, 318–19, 324, 329
Long, Armistead Rosser, 19
Long, John B. "Jack," 19– 20, 22–23, 83, 127
Long-Airdox Company, 19–20
Longwall mining, subsidence from, 16
Lorado Coal Mining Company, 320
Lorenson, Willard, 329
Love, Shirley, 32–33
Lumber industry, 44, 287
   decline of, 28, 35, 352n57
   environmental damage from, 27–28
Lynch, Wallace J., 154

M

MacDonald, Dwight, 133
The Making of the President (White), 81
Malay, Joe, 254–55
Man, 54
Manchin, Joe, 342–43

Manufacturing. *See* Industry
Marland, Joseph Wesley, 58, 69
Marland, Valery, 363n88
Marland, William Casey, 58, 65, 70, 134, 137
　bold proposals of, 59–60
　complying with school desegregation, 92–93, 95
　efforts to attract new industry, 67–68, 71
　failings of, 69–71, 363n88
　legislature *vs.*, 61–62, 68–70, 135
　political career of, 69, 71, 93
　taxes and, 45, 60–62, 68–69
Marriage, 80, 88
Marsh, Don, 214–15, 222
Marshall, Molly, 254
Marshall University, 106, 237
　airline crash with football team, 284
　Civic Interest Progressives at, 115–18
　Medical School, 281, *282*, 284
Martin, John, 206
Martin, Joseph E., 250
Martin, Laura, 269
Martin County, Kentucky, 334, 417n58
Martinsburg, textile industry in, 28–29
Mason, Carol, 281
Massey Energy, on Martin County incident, 417n58
Matewan, 289
Mathews, Virgil, 124
Matusow, Allen J., 7, 151–52, 196, 212
"Maximum feasible participation," 151, 170–71, 179, 213–15, 260
McAteer, J. Davitt, 14
McCarran Internal Security Act, 57
McCarthy, Eugene, 234
McCarthy, Joseph, 55, 57, 59
McCarthyism, 40, 54–55, 57, 59
McCormick, Charles H., 57
McDonough, Robert P., 230, 308
McDowell County, 101–2, 129, 171, 337
McDowell County Community Action Agency, 163–64, 170
McDowell County Community Action Plan, 154–56
McGovern, George, 234–35, 279, 307, 310–11
McGraw, Darrell, 152, 186, 312–13
McGraw, Warren, 264–65, 298, 312–13
McHugh, Thomas, 330
McKee, Bruce, 254
McKinney, Howard W., 114
McLuan, Marshall, 33
McSurely, Alan, 192, 193

McSurely, Margaret, 193
McWilliams, Carey, 46
Meadows, Clarence, 47
Mechanization. *See* Technology
Media, 2–3, 55, 201, 281
　on Barron's administration, 135, 137
　on black lung movement, 266
　on Buffalo Creek disaster, 326, 333
　on community action groups, 154, 170, 174
　on corruption in government, 81, 284
　coverage of Appalachian issues, 34, 126, 245, 278
　coverage of *Blankenship v. Boyle*, 278–79
　focus on West Virginia in presidential campaign, 80–82, 126
　on mining disasters, 246, 248–49
　Moore *vs.*, 284, 306
　portrayals of Appalachia in, 137–39
　on poverty in Appalachia, 2–4, 80–81, 132–33, 177
　on racial issues, 112–13, 240
　on severance tax proposal, 60, 69
　on strip mining, 290–93, 299, 303–4
　as watchdog on coal industry, 269–70, 342
Medicaid and Medicare as benefit of War on Poverty, 212
Medicare, as benefit of War on Poverty, 212
Mellace, Bob, 61, 71
Mental health, 150, 279–80
Mental Health, Department of (West Virginia), 73, 150
Mercer County, 103, 118–19, 121, 203
Mercer County Council on Human Relations, 113
Mercer County Equal Opportunity Commission, 191
Metzner, Eric, 191, 205–6
Michael, Mrs. Guy H., 281
Michaels, Sam, 149
Middle class, 156, 206
Migrations, 65, 171, 355n86. *See also* Great Appalachian Migration
　of African Americans, 92–93, 104, 107, 123–24, 238, 241–42
　effects of, 93, 107, 126, 238, 241–42, 354n80
　encouragement to leave rural areas, 167, 169
　population loss from, 68, 80, 354n81
　of teachers, 74–75

Index

Miller, Arnold Ray, 263, 276, 297, 313–14, 337
Mills, Oakley, 185
Millsop, Thomas, 56
Mine Health and Safety Act of 1969, 317, 320, 323, 327
Mine Health and Safety Administration, inspectors with, 333
Mine health and safety regulations, 14, 272
   agitation for, 269–70, 284–86
   health and safety regulations, 249, 269–70
Mine Rescue Training Station, 90
Mineral County Rural Area Development Committee, 153–54
Mineral-Hardy County Rural Area Development, 154, 157, 170
Miners for Democracy (MFD), 211, 276–77
   black miners and, 125, 406n53
   leadership of, 125, 276
   on strip mining ban, 313–14
Miners Memorial Hospital Association, 54
Mingo County, 63, 103, 308. *See also* Fair Elections Committee (FEC), Mingo County
   Area Redevelopment Administration project in, 130–32
   corruption in, 175, 223, 227–28
   election reform movement in, 223–24
   War on Poverty programs in, 129, 277
Mingo County Equal Opportunity Commission, 180, 224, 391n102
   challenging old order, 173–74, 204
   county court attempts takeover, 203–5
   demise of, 259
   successes of, 171, 175, 277
Mining disasters, 327. *See also* Farmington
   deaths in, 264, 345n3
   at Hominy Falls, 8, 246, 264
   media coverage of, 248–49
   Sago Creek, 338
Mining machines, 13. *See also* Technology
   effects on health and safety, 14–15, 20–21, 23, 246–47, 251–52
   jobs lost to, 4, 12–13, 20, 89–91, 288–89
   manufacture and sale of, 16, 18–20, 304
   open-pit, 339–40
   for strip mining, 288–89, 292, 304
Missouri ex rel. Gaines, 105
Mitchell, John, 228
Mitchell-Bateman, Mildred, 150, 199–200, 281
Modern Budget Amendment, to West Virginia constitution, 142, 283

Modernization, 6
   effects of, 22–23, 38–39
   responses to, 27, 40
Modernization theory, 5
Modernizing the Mountaineer (Whisnant), 179, 214
Mollohan, Robert H., 72, 77, 141
Monongah mine explosion, 14
Monroe, Jefferson, 142, 155, 161, 203, 262
   AV-VISTA volunteers and, 194–95, 198, 206
   support for community action programs, 162–63, 186, 199
   Webster County Program Development Council *vs.*, 200–201
Montgomery, 263
Montrie, Chad, 292, 297
Moore, Alice, 281
Moore, Arch Alfred, 72, 168, 256, 261, 278, 282
   achievements under, 283–84, 311
   on black lung compensation bill, 270–71
   Buffalo Creek disaster and, 324, 326, 328, 330–31, 415n35
   on community action agencies, 204–5
   corruption and, 284, 401n101, 407n73
   election of, 77, 258
   governorship under, 283–85, 306
   ordering draining of water impoundments, 332–33
   politics of, 235–36, 308–9, 407n73
   strip mining and, 298–99, 301–2, 307–11
Moore, Ben, 48, 98
Morality, criticisms of Appalachian Volunteers' and VISTA, 179, 194–96, 199, 204, 210
Morgan, John G., 221–22, 283, 284
Morgan, Keith, 253–54, 265, 267
Morgantown, 64–66, 82
Morton, James "Tiger," 308, 311
Morton, Quinn, 270–71
Moss, Joe, 138–39, 291, 409n13
Mott, Millard, 200–201
Mountain Justice, 342
Mountain Project, West Virginia, 198–200
Mountaineer Freedom Party, 237
Mountaintop removal mining, 303, 339–43
Movies, 29–30
Moynihan, Daniel Patrick, 151, 381n70
Mulcahy, Richard P., 251–52, 398n59
Mullins, Woodrow, 255–56, 262–63

Mulloy, Joseph, 187, 192–93, 205
Mumford, Lewis, 52
Mundel, Luella Raab, 57–58
Munn, Robert F., 3
Munson, Charles, 145
Murphy, Lerly, 225, 277
Music, 29, 32–33
Mutters, Otto, 324

N

NAACP, 110, 116, 119, 230
  in Bluefield, 118, 120, 239
  Charleston chapter, 115, 123–24
  in school desegregation, 95–98, 102
Nader, Ralph, 264, 274, 275
National Bank of Washington (UMWA-owned), 275
National Seating and Dimension, Inc., 130–32
National Service Corps, 177
National Youth Corps, 158
Natural Resources, Department of (US), 292, 298–300, 303, 306
Natural Resources, Department of (West Virginia), 295, 301
  inspection of coal dams, 322, 333
  outclassed by coal industry, 300, 322–23
Neal, Will E., 72, 77
Neely, Harold E., 134
Neely, Matthew Mansfield, 57–59, 76–77, 290
Neighborhood Youth Corps (NYC), 149–50, 173, 187–88
Nelson, Roland H., 237
Nettles, John, 120
New Deal, 140, 143
  liberalism of, 55–57
  reformism and activism in, 21–22, 40, 56
  work relief programs in, 63, 88
New Frontier programs, 7, 129, 134–35, 143, 168, 317
New settlements, in Congress for Appalachian Development plans, 190
Newsome, Moses, 230
Nicholas County, 194–95, 203
"Night Comes to the Appalachians" (Tomasky), 342
Night Comes to the Cumberlands (Caudill), 4–5, 10, 133, 177, 182

Nixon, Richard, 81, 127, 270, 309, 319
  anti-poverty spending under, 205, 402n2
  election of, 236, 258, 307
  mining health and safety legislation under, 269, 272, 283
Noonkester, Nora, 278–79
Noran, George "Nub," 18
Nuckols, Jack, 141
Nunn, Louie, 206–7
Nyden, Paul J., 406n53

O

Oaklund, Harvey, 329
Occupational Health and Safety Administration (OSHA), 319
Office of Economic Opportunity (OEO), 140, 158
  Appalachian Volunteers and, 177, 179, 185, 191, 206–7
  assessing programs under, 145–46, 163–64, 190
  bureaucratic issues of, 156–58, 214
  changing focus of, 156–57, 191, 205, 213, 260
  complaints about programs to, 185, 187–88, 194, 197–98
  conflicts with local organizations, 157–58, 163, 189, 191, 200–201
  effectiveness of, 187–88
  funding for cut, 161, 196, 402n2
  lack of technical assistance from, 164, 172
  on maximum feasible participation, 169–70, 172–73, 202, 205, 213, 260
  organizations' difficulty getting recognition from, 213–14
  programs funded by, 147–49, 154, 171, 261
  regional agents of, 156–57, 157–58, 161–62
  relations with staff of, 157–58, 386n21
  support for grassroots organizing, 154–55, 174, 179–80
  technical assistance by, 201, 214
Office of Economic Opportunity (OEO), West Virginia agency of, 142, 157–58, 202–3
  Crabtree's proposal to abolish, 159–60
  governor's influence on, 159, 162
Office of Federal-State Relations (West

Virginia), 168
Office of Surface Mining, 340–41
Ogle, Milton, 179–80, 190, 192–93, 207
  Appalachian Volunteers and, 177, 194–95
Ohio, migration destinations in, 35, 37–38
Ohio Valley Environmental Coalition, 342
Ohlin, Lloyd, 150
Oil industry, 12, 308
O'Leary, John F., 269–70
Opportunity theory, 150, 152, 161
The Other America (Harrington), 132–33

P

Palmer, Margaret, 339
Parker, Rex and Eleanor, 32
Patrick, Harry, 276
Patronage politics, 175
  African Americans in, 86–87
  in community action programs, 160, 209
  in state government, 43, 46
  with War on Poverty funds, 144, 146–47, 152, 225
Patteson, Okey, 47, *136*
  improvements under, 48, 51–53
  Marland *vs.*, 60, 69–70
  ties to coal industry, 58–59
Payne, Mrs. E. Wyatt, 237
Payne, Robert, 275–76, 406n53
Pearson, Drew, 185
Pendergrass, Eugene, 266–67
Pendleton County, 157
Pennsylvania, turnpike linking to, 50
Perry, Huey, 175
  on corrupt elections, 227, 376n1
  Mingo County EOC project under, 171–73, 259, 391n102
  organizing community action groups, 172–73, 204–5
Peyton, Angus, 167
Physicians for Miners' Health and Safety, 255, 264–66, 278
Pierce, Jim, 334
Pike County, Kentucky, 192–93, 205
Pipestem, 201
Pittston Coal Company
  practices of, 320, 323–24
  responsibility for Buffalo Creek disaster and, 326, 328–30
  victims of Buffalo Creek disaster and, 329–30

Pnakovich, L. J., 297
Podoloff, Maurice, 112
Police, 185, 230
  blacks as, 109, 121
  at demonstrations, 111–12, 119–20, 232–35, 256
  political intimidation and, 225, 309
Political Action League, of Fair Elections Committee, 226
Politics, in West Virginia, 44, 181, 191. *See also* Corruption; Legislation, state; Legislature, state; specific politicians
  Barron's career in, 134, 137
  blacks' influence in, 86–87, 124
  coal industry dominating, 297, 299, 342–43
  community action agencies supposed to stay out of, 159, 174
  community action groups and, 180–81, 194–95, 209
  community activism challenging, 143, 151–52, 173–74, 209
  Democratic strength in, 76–77, 306
  elections of 1948, 47
  elections of 1952, 58–59
  elections of 1954, 69
  elections of 1956, 69, 72
  elections of 1958, 76–77
  elections of 1960, 81–82, 126–27, 336n1
  elections of 1964, 141
  elections of 1968, 220, 234–36
  elections of 1972, 306–13
  influences on, 33–34, 46, 59, 72, 209
  jobs as spoils in, 146–47
  male domination of, 77–78, 277, 279–81
  Marland's career in, 60, 69, 71, 93
  over community action programs, 146–47, 162–63
  over severance tax proposal, 60–61, 68–69
  public employees barred from, 159, 180
  sleaziness of, 46, 136–37, 228–29, 235–36, 376n1, 407n73
  on strip mining, 290, 295–96, 301–3, 307–13
  Underwood's career in, 72–73, 81
  waning liberalism in, 256, 258
  women in, 259, 277–81, 406n65
Politics, national, 140, 230, 307
  media focus on West Virginia in presidential campaign, 82, 126
  West Virginia's importance in Kennedy's election, 3, 80, 135

Politics of consensus, 7, 40, 85
Poor peoples conference (Huntington), 188–89, 291, 391n102
"Poor Peoples Congress" (Athens), 223
Poor people's march on Washington, 203
Population, 42. *See also* Great Appalachian Migration; Migrations
   of African Americans, 86, 87, 88, 118
   decline of black, 92, 107, 124
   diversity of West Virginia's, 86
   loss of, 135, 181, 337, 354n81
Postal service, blacks not hired by, 109
Poverty. *See also* War on Poverty
Poverty, in Appalachia, 2–3. *See also* Culture of poverty theory
   causes of increasing, 10, 23, 35
   as chronic problem, 82–83, 156, 337–38
   efforts to address causes of, 173, 175, 179, 187
   explanations for, 4–6, 133, 140
   extent of, 126, 132–33, 177, 337–38
   Kennedy mobilizing help, 133–34
   media focus on, 3–4, 82, 132–33
   migration and, 35, 169
   of mountain farms, 25, 27
   need for help, 126, 132–33
   OEO not addressing specifics of, 156, 214
   regional conference of governors to address, 82–83
   solutions proposed for, 5–6, 156, 169
   tactics used in fight against, 125, 156
Poverty, in Mingo County, 171
Poverty, in West Virginia, 78
   effects of, 82, 172
   good intentions about, 166–67
   as media image, 138
   as paradox, 80–81
Poverty, national
   explanations for, 5, 127
   proposals for eradicating, 9–10, 212
   urban *vs.* rural, 140, 214
Preiser, Stanley, 330
Presbyterian Church, West Virginia Mountain Project of, 198–99
President's Appalachian Regional Commission, 134
Prial, Frank, 156
Pride Inc. (Logan County CAP), 191
Prince, Elmer, 64–65
Protests. *See* Demonstrations
Public accommodations
   integration of, 111–12, 114, 117–19, 121–22
   segregation and discrimination in, 108, 115, 118–20, 232
Public assistance. *See* Welfare
Public Health Service, U.S., 253
Public Service Commission, US, 322
Public utility districts (PUDs), 190
Public works projects, 65, 165–67
Purchasing Practices and Procedures Commission, 222, 256, 401n101

Q

Queen, Irwin, 191
Quesenberry, Roba, 117–18

R

Race, discrimination based on, 91, 107–8, 125. *See also* Segregation
Race relations, 89, 109, 231
   in Appalachian Volunteers and VISTA, 185, 194–95, 204, 210
   in Bluefield, 118–19
   at Bluefield State College, 121, 238–42
   cooperation in, 114–15, 184
   efforts to improve, 113–14, 122
   lack of effort to improve, 99, 109
   violating civil rights laws, 231–32
   in West Virginia *vs.* states of former Confederacy, 92–93, 99, 105, 108–9, 115
Railroads, 44, 63, 138
   jobs lost in, 12, 79, 352n57
   switch to diesel locomotives, 12, 65
Raleigh County, 97, 181, 263, 331, 337
   response to community action programs in, 182, 185, 194, 203
Raleigh County Community Action Agency, 204, 391n102
Raleigh County Community Action Program, 180, 182, 183–84, 190
Raleigh County Memorial Airport, 64
Randolph, Jennings, 76, 79, 129–30, 140, 160, 185, 311
Rasmussen, Barbara, 356n4
Rasmussen, Donald, 252–55, 264–66, 273
Rasmussen, Jeanne, 255, 278
Rauh, Joseph, 274
Ray, James Earl, 229
Ray, Jink, 193

Reagan, Ronald, 281
Reconstruction, West Virginia constitution from, 43
Recreation
 jobs in, 301
 use of strip-mined land for, 190, 304, 340
Reddick, Lawrence D., 372n71
Reeb, James, 115
Reeder, Phares, 75–76
Reeves, Thomas C., 376n1
Reforms, 10, 40, 175, 338.
 See also Election reform
 education, 191
 legislators voting against interests of constituents on, 222
 miners and wives supporting movements for, 284–85
 in New Deal, 21–22, 56
 range of, 336–37
 resistance to, 259
 tax, 62, 191
 of UMWA, 262, 274–76, 278
 welfare, 147, 191
 women in movements for, 277–79, 285
Relief, 129, 203
Religion, 109
 civil rights movement and, 116–17, 122–23
 election of Kennedy as Catholic, 126–27
Republican Party, 46, 59–60
 black vote for, 86–87
 changes in War on Poverty under, 205, 260
 divisiveness in, 235–36
 resurgence of, 71–72
Resources, 80, 295
 exportation of, 44–45, 66, 189
 ownership of, 41–42, 190, 214
 severance tax on, 60
Retirement, pensions for miners after, 21, 23, 125, 276, 398n60
Retirement Fund Board, UMWA, 275, 278
Revercomb, Chapman, 59, 66, 72, 76
Rhodenbaugh, Thomas, 180
Rhodes, James A., 217
Rhododendron (showboat), 138
Ribicoff, Abraham, 67–68, 235
Rice, Otis, 42
Riddle, Ernest, 263
Ritchie, Jean, 245
Road Bond Amendment, to West Virginia constitution, 142

Road Branch community action group, 173–74
Roads
 construction of, 47–51, 65, 73–74, 166, 186, 337
 damaged in Buffalo Creek disaster, 330–31
 deficiencies in, 51, 67, 154, 173
 funding for, 45, 60–62, 73, 135, 142, 283
 relation to economy, 64, 67, 166
 upgrades of, 30, 52, 64, 167, 191
Roberts, Dennis J., 68
Roberts, John, 248
Robertson, C. Donald, 229, 235
Robinson, Craig, 254–55, 263, 273
Robinson, Marvin, 122–23
Robinson, Nancy Smith, 104
Rockefeller, John D., IV "Jay," 165, 261–62
 becoming supporter of strip mining, 314, 343
 campaign against Moore, 307–12, 308
 defeat of, 311–13
 effects of McGovern's campaign on, 310–11
 election reform and, 226, 228
 on strip mining ban, 295–96, 298, 302, 307–11, 336–37
Rodenbaugh, Thomas, 386n21
Rogers, Lawrence H. "Bud," 72, 79
Rogers, Mary Kay, 269, 279
Rohrbaugh, R. Virgil, 72
Roosevelt, Franklin Delano, 140
Roosevelt, James, 128
Ross, Malcolm Harrison, 4
Rumsfeld, Donald, 207, 260
Rupert, 96

S

Safety regulations. *See* Health and safety regulations, in mining
Sago, mine explosion at, 338
Salisbury, Harrison, 80
Sanchez, Leveo, 188–89
Saunders, 325
Save Our Cumberland Mountains, 342
Save Our Kentucky, 292, 314
Sawyers, Burl, 141, 221, 235
Schlesinger, Arthur, Jr., 183–84
Schlesinger, Kathy, 183
Schoenbaum, Alex, 30
Scruggs, Earl, 32

Sedition, activists arrested for, 193–95
Segregation and integration, 2, 86, 123, 214. *See also* Civil rights movement
    in Bluefield, 118–22, 238, 240
    Charleston CORE chapter and, 110–12
    de facto *vs.* de jure, 88, 115
    effects of Civil Rights Act on, 121–22
    integration of higher education, 105–8, 238, 240
    persistence of segregation, 117–18
    racial tension during integration, 108–9
    school integration, 92–104, 114, 121, 191, 241, 370n52
    of teachers' organizations, 94–95
Seiler, Fanny, 281
Seltzer, Curtis, 21, 348n15, 405n39
Service industry, 338, 352n57
Settlers, *vs.* land speculation, 41–42
Shanklin, John, 149
Shapiro, Henry, 4
Sheriffs, influence of, 43–44
Sherrill, Robert G., 34, 248–49
Sherwood, Topper, 376n1
Shoney's, starting in Charleston, 30
Short, Robert, 112–13
Shott, John, 120
Shrewsberry, Hershel, 192, 209, 391n102
Shriver, R. Sargent, 140, 161, 183–84
    complaints about volunteers to, 193–94, 197
    efforts to save OEO, 196, 213
    wanting to spend anti-poverty funds, 153–54
    West Virginia programs and, 146–48, 159
Shroath, Alfred, 221
Silver Bridge
    collapse of, 8, 216–18, *219*, 220
    construction of, 217–18, 220
Silver Memorial Bridge, construction, 219–20
Sims, Franklin, 190
Sinclair, Ward, 304
Sirhan Sirhan, 230
Sizemore, Gerald, 310, 324
Skeen, Orel, 136–37
Slack, John M., 79, 197
Slag piles. *See* Gob piles
Sludge, 321
    from black water impoundments, 317–18, 326, 334, 417n58
Sly, John F., 62
Small Business Administration, 131
Smith, Barbara Ellen, 214
Smith, Charles, 116, 122, 241
Smith, Hulett C., 7–8, 115, 181
    allowing county courts to take over community action programs, 202–4
    coal industry and, 299, 316, 322
    community action programs and, 155, 158–60, 162–63, 173, 202
    complaints about community action programs and, 201, 203
    corruption and, 141–42, 146, 220–22, 229
    at disasters, 217, 247–48
    federal OEO and, 147, 194
    political career of, 141, 220–21, 229, 234
    political reform and, 227, 357n10
    on race relations at Bluefield State College, 239–42
    social programs under, 144, 146–48, 166
    state OEO and, 159, 161–62, 162–63
    strip mining and, 185, 189, 290–92, 299
    on VISTA and Appalachian Volunteers, 185–86, 193–200
Smith, Joe L., 141, 181
Smith, John, 185
Smith, Lewis G., 190
Smith, Mrs. Hulett (Mary Alice), 148, 155, 159, 163
Smith, Smitty, 32
Smith, Stewart H., 117
Smith, W. Bernard, 141
Snuffer, Nora, 269
Snyder, Harold, 322
Social infrastructure, 42
Social Security Administration, 144, 272–73
Social services, programs providing, 144–48, 161
Social workers, inadequate number of, 144–46
Soil Conservation Service, 333
Somerville, James, 199
South
    improving economy of, 9–10
    resistance to school desegregation in, 92–93, 95–104
South Charleston, gas leak at FMC plant in, 231
The Southern Appalachian Region: A Survey, 133
Southern Conference Educational Fund (SCEF), 120

Southern Governors' Conference, 98
Southern Regional Cooperative Business Development Corporation (SRCC), 260–61
Southern Virginias Coal Association, 319
Spadaro, Jack, 333, 342, 417n57
Spence, Beth, 416n51
Spence, Okey Ray, 223–24
Spoil
  from mountaintop removal, 303
  from strip mining, 289
Sports, 284
  race and, 99–100, 239, 241
  segregation in, 88, 100–101, 106, 112–13, 117
  support for collegiate, 83–84
Sprouse, James M., 204–5, 230, 235–36, 284
Stafford, Thomas F., 69, 141–42, 284, 376n1, 401n101
Standard of living. *See also* Poverty
  in eastern Kentucky *vs.* southern West Virginia, 182–83
  national postwar rise in, 9, 29–30
Stanford Research Institute, studying effects of strip mining, 304–6, 313
Stanley, Miles, 296, 308
Starcher, Buddy, 32
Starr, Arnold, 228
State Board of Education, 121
  on race relations at Bluefield State College, 239–42
  on school desegregation, 95, 101, 114
State Road Commission, 186, 219
  accusations of corruption in, 61, 69
  causing displacement of families in Triangle, 232–33
  engineering delays of, 73–74
  unemployed parents working for, 143–45
State Water Board, 317
Steel industry, 11–12, 29, 55–57
Steptoe, Robert, 298
Stereotypes, of Appalachia, 3–4, 37, 39, 210, 331–32
Stern, Gerald, 330
Stevenson, Adlai, 58, 71
Stewart, F. H., 293
Storer College, 105–6
Strange, Mrs. William, 297–98
"The Strange Case of West Virginia" (Tunley), 3, 80
Streams, destruction of, 340–41

Strikes, 276, 283
  for black lung compensation bill, 268, 269, 270, 405n39
  government taking over mines during, 20–21
Strip mining, 17, 167, 286, *294, 301*
  AV initiative against, 191–93
  effects of, 8, 294–95, 300, 304–6, 324
  effects on nearby residents, 289, 291, 295, 299–300, 324
  history of, 287–88
  ineffectiveness of land restoration after, 294–95, 296, 300, 304, 340–41
  jobs in, 294, 300–301, 420n28
  lax enforcement of regulations on, 289–90, 292, 296–97
  legislation as victory for industry, 286, 302–3
  machines for, 16, 288–89, 292, 304
  miners' difference from underground, 296–97
  moratoriums on, 302–3
  mountaintop removal in, 303, 339–43
  participants in movement against, 278–80, 291, 296–97
  permits for, 341, 420n28
  profitability of, 15, 290, 305
  purported benefits of, 287–88, 293, 300
  reclamation/restoration of land after, 290–92, 298, 314
  regulation as unenforceable, 295, 298–300, 299–300
  regulation of, 291–92, 313
  Rockefeller becoming supporter of, 314, 343
  role in state elections, 311–13
  Smith trying to regulate, 142, 185, 189
  state regulation of, 289–90, 291–92, 298
  uses of land afterwards, 340, 343
Strip mining ban, 190, 283, 341
  allies abandoning, 336–37
  calls for, 292–303, *310*
  effects of, 296, 298, 305–6
  election as referendum on, 311–12
  federal, 303–4, 314
  opposition to, 293–94, 297–98
  Rockefeller running against Moore on, 307–11
  supporters of, 298–302, 309–10, 313
  UMWA on, 286–87, 296–97
The Strip Mining Information of America (Austin and Borrelli), 296
Stroud, Ozzie, 36–37

Student Nonviolent Coordinating
  Committee (SNCC), 114–16, 178
Students for a Democratic Society, 237
Students Now for Action and Progress
  (SNAP), 121
Sturm, Dean, 31
Summers, Festus P., 80
Surface Miner Auxiliary of West Virginia,
  297–98
Surface Mining Act (1967), 292, 297, 300
Surface Mining Control and Reclamation
  Act (1977, US), 340
Surface Mining Control and Reclamation
  Act (US), 314
Surface Mining Reclamation Act (1967),
  298–99
Surratt, Cecil, 32
Sweeney, James Johnson, 138

T

Taft-Hartley Act (1947), 21, 40
"Take Me Home, Country Roads"
  (Denver), 336
Tanner, Bob, 191
Tanneries, 27
Task Force on Strip Mining, under Smith,
  291–92
Tax Limitation Amendment, 45, 62
Taxes
  corporate, 189
  efforts to increase, 72–73, 189
  efforts to reform, 60, 62, 191
  inadequate to provide services, 44–45,
    62, 72–73
  income, 135
  increasing to upgrade education, 74–76
  limitations placed during Depression,
    45, 62
  negative income, 161
  nonresidents' resistance to increases,
    42, 44–45
  property, 61–62
  sales, 60–61, 135
  severance, 44–45, 60–61, 68–69, 71,
    189, 338
  structured for out-of-state investors,
    167
Taylor, J. Martin, 75–76
Technology, 10, 29, 40
  effects on coal industry from, 13–15,
    18–19, 68, 339–40

increasing unemployment from, 11–12,
  65, 79, 84
machines replacing labor, 127–28
in mechanization in agriculture, 25, 27
in mechanization of coal industry,
  16–18, 21–23, 68, 89–90
structural unemployment and, 127–28
Television, 29–31
  influence of, 2, 11, 33–34, 72
  West Virginia programming on, 31–34
Textile industry, 28–29, 352n57
Thaw, Pete, 296, 307–8
They'll Cut Off Your Project (Perry), 172
Thibault, James, 261
Thoenen, Eugene, 162
Thomas, Ed, 155, 161–62
Thomas, Karen Kruse, 359n37
Thompson, William J., 165
Thurmond, Walter R., 18–19
Titler, George, 17
Tomasky, Michael, 342
Tomblin, Earl Ray, 228
Topography, effects of, 84
Tourism, 130, 301
Toynbee, Arnold, 4
Trbovich, Mike, 276
Trent, Curtis B., 228
Trent, Hettie, 184, 391n102
Trent, Judy, 225, 277
Trent, William Woodson, 72, 92–93, 95
TRI-CAP, 212, 260
Triangle, displacement of families in,
  232–33
Triangle Improvement Association, 165
Tribe, Ivan, 33
Triumphalism, post-war, 133
Trotter, Joe William, 86, 124
Truman, Harry S., 47, 57, 138
Tudor, Ben, 326
Tug Fork River, 66
Tunley, Roul, 3, 80

U

Udall, Stuart, 249, 321
Underwood, Cecil Harland, 33–34, 70, 77,
  98, *136*, 226, 262, 289
  appointments by, 280–81
  criticizing media focus on state's
    poverty, 79, 81
  efforts to improve services and roads,
    73–74

Moore vs., 235, 284
political career of, 72–73, 81, 135, 141, 235
at regional conference of governors, 82–83
resurgence of Republicans under, 71–72
urged to act on economic crisis, 29, 79
Unemployment, 29, 181
benefits for, 78, 91, 203
as chronic problem of Appalachia, 82–83, 214
effects of, 28, 65, 93, 398n60
efforts to address, 65–66
fear of increasing, 296, 305
need for help, 126, 203
racial differences in, 85–86, 90–91, 109, 233
rate declining, 68, 135, 169
rate rising, 65, 78, 82, 307
social services for families in, 144–45
structural, 127–28
technology increasing, 4, 7, 79, 84
in West Virginia vs. national, 11, 80
Unger, Irwin, 152
Unionism, 211, 283, 338
dual, 255, 263, 265
Unionization
focus on wage increases, 22–23
resistance to, 17, 28–29, 55–57
Unions, 60, 72, 265, 319
United Appalachian Communities, 190
United Mine Workers of America (UMWA), 17, 277, 420n28. *See also* Welfare and Retirement Fund, UMWA
acquiescence of membership, 10–11
activism of, 10, 20–21, 211, 265
benefits from, 20–21, 23, 54, 125, 242–43, 275–76
black lung compensation and, 263, 268
black lung movement and, 251–52, 254–56, 265, 270, 273
blamed for Area Redevelopment Administration fiasco, 131–32
corruption in, 8, 274–76
declining influence of, 23, 175, 182, 243, 338, 343
dual unionism as taboo in, 255, 263
elections in, 274–76
focus on production, not safety, 10, 272
management of, 242–44, 263
miners' discontent with, 243–44, 248, 256–57, 270
political influence of, 58–59, 182

race relations in, 89–91, 110
reform of, 262, 274–76, 278, 285, 336
relations with coal companies, 20–22, 57, 252, 272
responses to mining disasters, 248–49
Retirement Fund Board of, 275, 278
on strip mining ban, 286–87, 296–97, 313–14, 341
supporting severance tax, 60–61
United Mountain Defense, 342
United Neighborhood Interest Organization Network (UNION), 122–23
United States Civil Rights Commission, 99, 108–9
United Steel Workers, vs. Weirton Steel, 56–57
The Unraveling of America: A History of Liberalism in the 1960s (Matusow), 7
Upper Big Branch mine, explosion in, 338
Urban League, survey of Charleston by, 109–10
Urban Villagers (Gans), 4–5
Urbanization, 167

V

Vance, Rupert, 5, 129
Vantage Point (Johnson), 151–52
Varney, T. I., 204, 228
Vatter, Harold, 9, 362n75
Vietnam War, 216, 229
protests against, 194–95, 256
taking funding from War on Poverty, 161, 169
Vincent, Lontz, 145
Virginia, land speculation in, 41–42
VISTA, 155, 183
accused of leading rebellions, 197–98, 203, 268
activities of, 8, 150, 224, 227, 292
at "Appalachia Speaks" conference, 188–89
Appalachian Volunteers training, 176, 178, 186
assessing effectiveness of war on Poverty, 188–89
as benefit of War on Poverty, 212, 337
in black lung movement, 252, 254–55, 263, 268, 273
Byrd's continuing complaints about, 187–88, 196–97

characteristics of, 196–97, 207–9, 211
community action programs and, 153, 182, 291
continuation of, 259, 261, 337
criticisms of activities of, 197–98, 203
criticisms of clothing and hygiene, 172, 198, 207
criticisms of increasing, 193–96, 194–96
criticisms of morality of, 199, 204
criticized as outsiders, 197–98, 203, 211
disillusionment among, 205–6
encouraging indigenous leadership, 191, 391n102
former volunteers staying in area, 259, 285
grassroots organizing by, 170, 185–86, 191
Presbyterian Mountain Project sponsoring, 198–99
in Raleigh County, 182, 185
relations with local people, 202, 206–9
Smith rethinking support for, 193–94
successes of, 189–90
training for, 182–83, 201
Volunteers in Service to America (VISTA), 140–41
Voting registration
cleanup of lists, 228, 256
fraudulent, 223, 225
Voting rights, 86–88, 115, *116*

W

Waddington, Tom, 319
Wagner Act, 56
Wallace, William J. L., 106–7, 238, 393n6, 394n8
Wallerstein, Immanuel, 6
Walls, David, 207, 386n21
Walmart, as biggest employer, 338
War on Poverty, 135, 277
Byrd's opposition to, 187–88, 196
community action programs in, 150–53, 155, 160–61
criticisms of, 154, 193, 203
demise of, 161, 204–5, 337
evaluation of, 187–88, 211–15
failings of, 167, 214
funding for, 161, 196, 259, 261–62
Hardy County as model for projects, 153–54
Head Start as favored program of, 147–49
Job Corps arising from, 148–49
Johnson taking over, 133–34, 139–40
maximum feasible participation requirement in, 151, 160–61, 170, 205
models for activism from, 211, 260–62
sources of information on programs, 7–8
state *vs.* federal government in, 143–44
tactics in, 161, 172–73
theories underlying, 151, 166
Vietnam War competing with, 161, 169
West Virginia as priority for, 160, 168
West Virginia conference during, 5–6
Ward, Ken, Jr., 333–34, 342, 417n53
Washington, George, 41
Washington, James, 223–24, *226*, 227, 262, 308, 391n102
Water impoundments, 2, 16, 320
accidents with, 333–34, 417n58
building, 316–17, 321, 327
Moore ordering draining of, 332–33
regulations about, 317, 323, 326
supposed to clarifying water, 317–18
Water pollution
efforts to clarify waste water, 317–18
other sources of, 16, 27–28
from slurry injected into old mines, 334, 417n57
from strip mining, 289, 306
Water Pollution Control Act (1972), 319
Watershed, effects of strip mining on, 287
Watson, J. E. "Ned," 268
WE (World Equality), 111–12
Webster County, community action programs in, 200–201, 203–4
Webster County Program Development Council, 200–201
Weeks, Sinclair, 74
Weintraub Cohen, Naomi, 182–85, 210
Weir, Ernest, 55–56
Weirton Steel Company, 55–57
Welfare, 23, 41, 129, 262, 284
administration of, 44, 45, 88
dependence on, 39, 171
reform of, 147, 191
Welfare and Retirement Fund, UMWA, 23, 242, 398n59, 398n60
black lung and, 250–52
Lewis's management of, 242–43
Welfare capitalism, 57
Welfare Department, 144–47
Weller, Jack E., 4–6, 33, 129, 159, 198–99

Index

Wells, Hawey, Jr. "Sonny," 252–53, 255, 264–65, 273
Welty, T. A., 230
Wenner, Richard, 164
West, Don, 201, 209, 387n52
West, Jerry, 83
West Virginia. *See also* Government, state
  all counties Appalachian, 134
  analyses of economic problems in, 78–79
  Appalachian Volunteers spreading into, 180
  bad image of, 336
  complying with school desegregation, 92–104
  construction of highways to link, 48–49, 52
  economy, 29–30
  effects of mining decline throughout economy, 28
  especially difficult road construction in, 48–51
  excessive small counties in, 43
  industry in, 11
  land speculation in, 41–42
  media coverage of called unbalanced, 81–82
  migrants' hope of return to, 36–37
  migration destinations from, 35
  need for help, 126
  as paradox of prosperity and poverty, 41, 80–81
  positive signs for economy in, 11
  residents' affection for, 83, 336
  road improvements by, 30, 47–48
"West Virginia, My Home," 38
West Virginia Coal Association, 319, 339
West Virginia Environmental Coalition, 342
West Virginia Fund, 262, 391n102
West Virginia Governors (Morgan), 221–22
West Virginia Highlands Conservancy, 342
West Virginia Industrial and Publicity Commission, 67–68
West Virginia Moon (Moss), 138–39, *139*
West Virginia Service Corps, 261
West Virginia State College, 89–90, 105, 114, 150
  integration of, 106–7, 242, 372n71
  student activism at, 111–12, 115, 231, 237–38
West Virginia Surface Mining Association (WVSMA), 295, 303
West Virginia Turnpike, 2, 48–51, *49*, 331
West Virginia Turnpike Commission, 48–49
West Virginia University, 237
  Appalachian Center's Extension Service, 153–54
  black lung research at, 253–54, 265
  schools of medicine, nursing, and dentistry added to, 53
  sports teams of, 83–84
  student activism at, 237, 256
West Virginia Work and Training program, 144–47
Wetherby, Lawrence, 92
Wheeler, Billy Edd, 245
Wheeling, 229–30
Whisnant, David, 179, 192, 209–10, 214, 387n52
White, Ivan, 255, 297, 311–13
White, Theodore H., 46, 81
White Sulphur Springs, 96
Whittle, Randolph G., Jr., 120
Widen, as company town, 57
Widner, Ralph, 167–68
Williams, Norman, 298–300, 322
Williamson, 54, 63
Wilson, Crawford, 17, 289
Wilson, Pat, 191
Winding Gulf Community Association, 391n102
Winner, Tom, 307–8
Wiseman, Chester, 200, 391n102
Withrow, Jackie, 279–80, 312–13
Wofford, Jimmy, 172
Wolfe, Margaret Ripley, 211
Women's movement, 336–37
Woodrum, Pearl, 322
Work Incentive Program (WIN), 147, 260
Work-relief programs, 63, 129, 135, 143–47, 158
Workman, Chester, 184, 188–89, 279, *301*, 391n102
Workman, Margaret, 279, 391n102
Workman, Nimrod, 225
Works Progress Administration, 88
World systems concept, 6
World War II, 88, 133
  coal industry in, 20–21, 63
  labor relations and, 20–22
  migration in, 35, 37
  mining boom in, 63, 288
Wren, Ethel, *176*
Wyatt, James E., 264

Wyoming County, 103, 194–95, 203, 318
Wyoming County Community Action
 Program, 191–92, 391n102
Wyoming County United Communities,
 191–92

Y
Yablonski, Joseph A. "Jock"
 campaign of, 274–75, 278–79
 murder of family and, 274–75, 276
Yago, John, 372n71
Yesterday's People (Weller), 4–6, 33, 129
YMCA-YWCA, in Bluefield, 119–21